D1824834

CODIFYING CHOICE OF LAW AROUND THE WORLD

Codifying Choice of Law Around the World

AN INTERNATIONAL COMPARATIVE ANALYSIS

Symeon C. Symeonides

Foreword by Lord Collins of Mapesbury

OXFORD
UNIVERSITY PRESS

Oxford University Press is a department of the University of Oxford. It furthers the University's objective of excellence in research, scholarship, and education by publishing worldwide.

Oxford   New York

Auckland   Cape Town   Dar es Salaam   Hong Kong   Karachi   Kuala Lumpur   Madrid   Melbourne
Mexico City   Nairobi   New Delhi   Shanghai   Taipei   Toronto

With offices in

Argentina   Austria   Brazil   Chile   Czech Republic   France   Greece   Guatemala   Hungary
Italy   Japan   Poland   Portugal   Singapore   South Korea   Switzerland   Thailand
Turkey   Ukraine   Vietnam

Oxford is a registered trademark of Oxford University Press in the UK and certain other countries.

Published in the United States of America by
Oxford University Press
198 Madison Avenue, New York, NY 10016

Library of Congress Cataloging-in-Publication Data

Symeonides, Symeon, 1949- author.
    Codifying choice of law around the world : an international comparative analysis / Symeon C. Symeonides ;
Foreword by Lord Collins of Mapesbury.
        pages cm
    Includes bibliographical references and index.
    ISBN 978-0-19-936084-0 ((hardback) : alk. paper)
1. Comparative law. 2. Conflict of laws. I. Title.
    K583.S96 2014
    340.9—dc23

                                                                                                2013040833

9 8 7 6 5 4 3 2 1

Printed in the United States of America on acid-free paper

Note to Readers

This publication is designed to provide accurate and authoritative information in regard to the subject matter covered. It is based upon sources believed to be accurate and reliable and is intended to be current as of the time it was written. It is sold with the understanding that the publisher is not engaged in rendering legal, accounting, or other professional services. If legal advice or other expert assistance is required, the services of a competent professional person should be sought. Also, to confirm that the information has not been affected or changed by recent developments, traditional legal research techniques should be used, including checking primary sources where appropriate.

*(Based on the Declaration of Principles jointly adopted by a Committee of the
American Bar Association and a Committee of Publishers and Associations.)*

**You may order this or any other Oxford University Press publication
by visiting the Oxford University Press website at www.oup.com.**

To Lythrodontas,
my humble village

Summary Table of Contents

Detailed Table of Contents

List of Charts

List of Figures

List of Maps

List of Tables

Foreword

IT IS AN honor to be asked to write the foreword to Professor Symeon Symeonides's new book. I have known his work for more than 20 years, and he is one of the foremost scholars in the world in the field of the conflict of laws. His work has been cited by federal and state courts in the United States and by the House of Lords and the Supreme Court in the United Kingdom.

This is a truly monumental contribution to the study of codification in the conflict of laws. When I first came to the subject of the conflict of laws in the 1960s, codification was in a state of arrested development. There had been the civil law codes of the nineteenth century, which had dealt with some aspects of choice of law, such as the French Civil Code in 1804, and its successors later in the century, especially in Spain and Germany. There was also the Bustamante Code in Latin America.

The attempts by the Hague Conference at unification by international convention had met with only limited success, and the enormously distinguished authors of the American Law Institute Restatements of the Conflict of Laws, the first by Professor Beale and the second by Professor Reese, failed to achieve unqualified acceptance.

As Professor Symeonides shows, there was an explosion of codification by states in the latter part of the twentieth century, amounting to almost 100 new codifications. But it has been the unending quest for harmonization and unification by what is now the European Union that has resulted in what Professor Symeonides rightly describes as a virtual revolution, starting with the jurisdictional efforts in the Brussels Convention of 1968 and choice of law in contract in the Rome Convention of 1980, and eventually accelerating to the widespread enactment of Regulations in the fields of jurisdiction and choice of law, in commercial law, and in family law. Whether this has been a success is a matter of some controversy, but what is not in doubt is that Professor Symeonides has made an outstanding contribution to the science of law in this comprehensive treatment of codification in choice of law.

Lawrence Collins
(Lord Collins of Mapesbury, LLD, FBA)
Former Justice, UK Supreme Court
October, 2013

Preface

THIS BOOK IS the last of an unplanned trilogy on Choice of Law. The first book, written 33 years ago, was a neophyte's doctrinal début, comparing the American and European academic approaches to choice of law.[1]

The second book, written 25 years later, took a more practical direction. Descending into the trenches of litigation, the book examined the choice-of-law decisions of American courts in the previous 50 years.[2] Its principal aim was to understand and transmit the lessons doctrinal writers could derive from the "real world" of judicial decisions. In reviewing that book, a distinguished author found it to be grounded "on the principle that what courts do, and their measure of agreement in what they do, are phenomena to be taken very seriously indeed," and on "the strong conviction that to glean truth from reality one has to handle a great deal of reality, and to do so with utmost care."[3]

This book is based on the same conviction. Ascending to the galleries of legislative chambers, somewhat familiar from the author's previous drafting experience, the book attempts to "glean truth" from the official and plentiful reality of legislation around the world. The book is a comparative study of the choice-of-law codifications and conventions adopted in each of the inhabited continents in the last 50 years. Its main purpose is to document and inform rather than to critique. Although I do not always hide my

---

[1] *See* S. Symeonides, *An Outsider's View of the American Approach to Choice of Law: Comparative Observations on Current American and Continental Conflicts Doctrine* (Doctoral Dissertation, Harvard Law School, 1980).

[2] *See* S. Symeonides, *The American Choice-of-Law Revolution: Past, Present, and Future* (Hague Academy of International Law Monographs, 2006).

[3] L. Weinberg, Theory Wars in the Conflict of Laws, 103 *Mich. L. Rev.* 1631, 1648 (2005) (*reviewing* S. Symeonides, The American Choice-of-Law Revolution in the Courts: Today and Tomorrow, 298 *Recueil des Cours* 1 (2003)).

opinion, I continue to act on the conviction that what we can learn from legislators is far more important than what they can learn from us.[4]

As I look at the calendar, I realize that today is Labor Day, and that the two previous books were also completed on Labor Day; and this reminds me of the dual meaning of the word *labor* in denoting toil but also connoting the pain and exhilaration of childbirth.

Labor Day, 2013
Salem, Oregon, USA
S.C.S.

---

[4] In keeping with this conviction, the book avoids the use of the first person, except in this Preface.

Abbreviations

The following works are used in abbreviated form as shown in *italics*

Audit & d'Avout, *DIP*: B. Audit & L. d'Avout, Droit international privé (6th ed. 2010).

Bělohlávek, *Rome I*: A.J. Bělohlávek, Rome Convention, Rome I Regulation (2010).

Babič, D., *Croatian Report* on PIL to the 18th Int'l Congress of Comparative Law (2010).

Bazinas, S., *Uncitral Report* on PIL to the 18th Int'l Congress of Comparative Law (2010).

Beale, *Treatise*: J. Beale, *Treatise on the Conflicts of Laws* (1935).

Boele-Woelki, K. & van Iterson D., *Dutch Report* on PIL to the 18th Int'l Congress of Comparative Law (2010).

Bonomi, A., *Swiss Report* on PIL to the 18th Int'l Congress of Comparative Law (2010).

Bonomi, *Overriding Mandatory Provisions*: A. Bonomi, Overriding Mandatory Provisions in the Rome I Regulation on the Law Applicable to Contracts, 10 Ybk. Priv. Int'l L. 285 (2008).

Borchers, *Categorical Exceptions*: P. Borchers, Categorical Exceptions to Party Autonomy in Private International Law, 82 Tul. L. Rev. 1645 (2008).

Briggs, *Agreements on Choice of Law*: A. Briggs, Agreements on Jurisdiction and Choice of Law (2008).

Calliess, *Rome Regulations*: C-P. Calliess (ed.), Rome Regulations (2011).

Carruthers, J. & Crawford, E., *Scottish Report* on PIL to the 18th Int'l Congress of Comparative Law (2010).

Cavers, *Choice of Law Process*: D. Cavers, The Choice of Law Process (1965).

Cavers, *Critique*: D. Cavers, A Critique of the Choice-of-Law Problem, 47 Harv. L. Rev. 173 (1933).

Chen, R-C., *Taiwanese Report* on PIL to the 18th Int'l Congress of Comparative Law (2010).

Chen, W., *Chinese Report* on PIL to the 18th Int'l Congress of Comparative Law (2010).

Codif.: Refers to any choice-of-law statute, regardless of its formal designation as an act, statute, decree, ordinance, or code, or as a part of another code, such as a civil code.

Cordero Moss, G., *Norwegian Report* on PIL to the 18th Int'l Congress of Comparative Law (2010).

Currie, *Selected Essays*: B. Currie, Selected Essays on the Conflict of Laws (1963).

de Boer, *Facultative Choice of Law*: T.M. de Boer, Facultative Choice of Law: The Procedural Status of Choice-of-Law Rules and Foreign Law, 257 Recueil des cours 223 (1996).

de Boer, *Living Apart Together*: T.M. de Boer, Living Apart Together: The Relationship between Public and Private International Law, 57 Neth. Int'l L. Rev. 183 (2010).

de Boer, *Party Autonomy*: T.M. de Boer, Party Autonomy and its Limitations in the Rome II Regulation, 9 Ybk. Priv. Int'l L. 19 (2008).

De Jonge, A., *Australian Report* on PIL to the 18th Int'l Congress of Comparative Law (2010).

de Lima Pinheiro, L., *Portuguese Report* on PIL to the 18th Int'l Congress of Comparative Law (2010).

Dicey, Morris & Collins: L. Collins et al., *Dicey, Morris & Collins on the Conflict of Laws* (15th ed. 2012).

Einhorn, T., *Israel Report* on PIL to the 18th Int'l Congress of Comparative Law (2010).

Erauw, J. & Fallon, M., *Belgian Report* on PIL to the 18th Int'l Congress of Comparative Law (2010).

Esplugues Mota, C. & Azcárraga Monzonís, C., *Spanish Report* on PIL to the 18th Int'l Congress of Comparative Law (2010).

Fresnedo de Aguirre, C., *Uruguayan Report* on PIL to the 18th Int'l Congress of Comparative Law (2010).

Giuliano & Lagarde Report: M. Giuliano & P. Lagarde, Report on the Convention on the Law Applicable to Contractual Obligations, OJ C 282, pp. 1, 30 (31 Oct. 1980).

Hay, Borchers & Symeonides, *Conflict of Laws*: P. Hay, P. Borchers & S. Symeonides, Conflict of Laws (5th ed. 2012).

Hellner, *Third Country Overriding Mandatory Rules:* M. Hellner, Third Country Overriding Mandatory Rules in the Rome I Regulation: Old Wine in New Bottles? 5(3) J. Priv. Int'l L. 447 (2009).

Hernández-Bretón, E., Venezuelan Report on PIL to the 18th Int'l Congress of Comparative Law (2010).

Jayme, *The American Conflicts Revolution:* E. Jayme, The American Conflicts Revolution and Its Impact on European Private International Law, in Univ. van Amsterdam Centrum voor Buitenlands Recht en IPR (eds.), Forty Years On: The Evolution of Postwar Private International Law in Europe, 15 (1992).

Juenger, *Multistate Justice*: F.K. Juenger, Choice of Law and Multistate Justice (1993).

Kanzaki, T., *Japanese Report* on PIL to the 18th Int'l Congress of Comparative Law (2010).

Kegel & Schurig, *IPR*: G. Kegel & K. Schurig, Internationales Privatrecht (9th ed. 2004).

Kropholler, et al., *Aussereuropäische IPR-Gesetze*: J. Kropholler, H. Krüger, W. Riering, J. Samtleben & K. Siehr, Aussereuropäische IPR-Gesetze (1999).

Liukkunen, U., *Finnish Report* on PIL to the 18th Int'l Congress of Comparative Law (2010).

Lookofsky, J., *Danish Report* on PIL to the 18th Int'l Congress of Comparative Law (2010).

Maintenance Regulation: Council Regulation (EC) No 4/2009 of 18 December 2008 on Jurisdiction, Applicable Law, Recognition and Enforcement of Decisions and Cooperation in Matters Relating to Maintenance Obligations L 7/1 [2009] O.J. 10.1.2009.

Mankowski, P., *German Report* on PIL to the 18th Int'l Congress of Comparative Law (2010).

Martinek, *Seven Pillars of Wisdom*: M. Martinek, The Seven Pillars of Wisdom in Private International Law—The German and the Swiss Experience with the Codification of Conflicts Law Rules, Chinese Ybk. Priv. Int'l L. & Comp. L. 15 (2001), *available at* http://www.jura.uni sb.de/projekte/Bibliothek.

Mexico City Convention: Inter-American Convention on the Law Applicable to International Contracts, Signed at Mexico, D.F., Mexico, on 17 March 1994, at the Fifth Inter-American Specialized Conference on Private International Law (CIDIP-V).

Nafziger, J., *United States Report* on PIL to the 18th Int'l Congress of Comparative Law (2010).

Najurieta M.S. & Noodt Taquela, M.B., *Argentinean Report* on PIL to the 18th Int'l Congress of Comparative Law (2010).

Nishitani, *Party Autonomy*: Y. Nishitani, Party Autonomy and Its Restrictions by Mandatory Rules in Japanese Private International Law: Contractual Conflicts Rules, in J. Basedow, H. Baum & Y. Nishitani (eds.), Japanese and European Private International Law in Comparative Perspective, 77 (2008).

Nygh, *Autonomy*: P.E. Nygh, Autonomy in International Contracts (1999).

Nygh, *Reasonable Expectations*: P. E. Nygh, The Reasonable Expectations of the Parties as a Guide to the Choice of Law in Contract and Tort, 251 Recueil des cours 269 (1995).

Pauknerová, M., *Czech Report* on PIL to the 18th Int'l Congress of Comparative Law (2010).

Pazdan, M., *Polish Report* on PIL to the 18th Int'l Congress of Comparative Law (2010).

Raffai, K. & Szabó, S., *Hungarian Report* on PIL to the 18th Int'l Congress of Comparative Law (2010).

Remy, B., *French Report* on PIL to the 18th Int'l Congress of Comparative Law (2010).

Restatement (Second): American Law Institute, Restatement (Second) of Conflict of Laws (1971).

Restatement: American Law Institute, Restatement of the Law, Conflict of Laws (1934).

Rome Convention: Convention 80/934/ECC on the law applicable to contractual obligations opened for signature in Rome on 19 June 1980, OJ L 266, 9.10.1980, pp. 1–19.

Rome I: Regulation (EC) No. 593/2008 of the European Parliament and of the Council of 17 June 2008 on the Law Applicable to Contractual Obligations (Rome I), [2008] OJ L 177/6.

Rome II: Regulation (EC) No. 864/2007 of the European Parliament and of the Council of 11 July 2007 on the Law Applicable to Non-contractual Obligations (Rome II), [2007] OJ L 199/40.

Rome III: Council Regulation (EU) No 1259/2010 of 20 December 2010 implementing enhanced cooperation in the area of the law applicable to divorce and legal separation (OJ L 343, p. 10 ff.) (2010).

Roodt, C., *English Report* on PIL to the 18th Int'l Congress of Comparative Law (2010).

Rühl, *Unilateralism*: G. Rühl, Unilateralism, in J. Basedow, K. Hopt & R. Zimmermann (eds.), Max Planck Encyclopedia of European Private Law (2013).

Sabourin, F., *Quebec Report* on PIL to the 18th Int'l Congress of Comparative Law (2010).

Savigny, *System*: F.C. von Savigny, System des heutigen Römischen Rechts (1849).

Story, *Commentaries*: J. Story, Commentaries on the Conflict of Laws (1834).

Successions Regulation: Regulation (EU) No 650/2012 of the European Parliament and of the Council of 4 July 2012 on jurisdiction, applicable law, recognition and enforcement of decisions and acceptance and enforcement of authentic instruments in matters of succession and on the creation of a European Certificate of Succession (OJ n. L 201, p. 107 ff.)

Suk, K.H., *South Korean Report* on PIL to the 18th Int'l Congress of Comparative Law (2010).

Symeonides, *A New Conflicts Restatement*: S. Symeonides, A New Conflicts Restatement: Why Not?, 5 J. Priv. Int'l L. 383 (2009).

Symeonides, *Accommodative Unilateralism*: S. Symeonides, Accommodative Unilateralism as a Starting Premise in Choice of Law, in H. Rasmussen-Bonne, R. Freer, W. Lüke & W. Weitnauer (eds.), Balancing of Interests: Liber Amicorum Peter Hay 417 (2005).

Symeonides, *American PIL*: S. Symeonides, American Private International Law (2008).

Symeonides, *At the Dawn of the 21st Century*: S. Symeonides, American Conflicts Law at the Dawn of the 21st Century, 37 Willamette L. Rev. (2000).

Symeonides, *Choice of Law in 2012*: S. Symeonides, Choice of Law in the American Courts in 2012: Twenty-Sixth Annual Survey, 61 Am. J. Comp. L. 217 (2013).

Symeonides, *Cross-Border Torts*: S. Symeonides, Choice of Law in Cross-Border Torts: Why Plaintiffs Win, and Should, 61 Hastings L.J. 337 (2009).

Symeonides, *Les grands problèmes*: S. Symeonides, Les grands problèmes de droit international privé et la nouvelle codification de Louisiane, 81 Rev. critique DIP 223 (1992).

Symeonides, *Louisiana Exegesis*: S. Symeonides, Louisiana's New Law of Choice of Law for Tort Conflicts: An Exegesis, 66 Tul. L. Rev. 677 (1992).

Symeonides, *Mixed Jurisdiction*: S. Symeonides, Private International Law Codification in a Mixed Jurisdiction: The Louisiana Experience, 57 RabelsZ 460 (1993).

Symeonides, *Oregon Contracts Exegesis*: S. Symeonides, Oregon's Choice-of-Law Codification for Contract Conflicts: An Exegesis, 44 Willamette L. Rev. 205 (2007).

Symeonides, *Oregon Torts Exegesis*: S. Symeonides, Oregon's New Choice-of-Law Codification for Tort Conflicts: An Exegesis, 88 Or. L. Rev. 963 (2010).

Symeonides, *Party Autonomy*: S. Symeonides, Party Autonomy in Rome I and II from a Comparative Perspective, 28(2) Ned. IPR 191 (2010).

Symeonides, *Private Law-Making*: S. Symeonides, Party Autonomy and Private Law-Making in Private International Law: The *Lex Mercatoria* That Isn't, in Festschrift für Konstantinos D. Kerameus 1397 (2009).

Symeonides, *Progress or Regress?*: S. Symeonides, Private International Law at the End of the 20th Century: Progress or Regress? (2000).

Symeonides, *Reciprocal Lessons*: S. Symeonides, The American Revolution and the European Evolution in Choice of Law: Reciprocal Lessons, 82 Tul. L. Rev. 1741 (2008).

Symeonides, *Revising Puerto Rico's Conflicts Law*: S. Symeonides, Revising Puerto Rico's Conflicts Law: A Preview, 28 Colum. J. Transn'l L. 601 (1990).

Symeonides, *Revolution*: S. Symeonides, The American Choice-of-Law Revolution: Past, Present and Future (2006).

Symeonides, *Rome II*: S. Symeonides, Rome II and Tort Conflicts: A Missed Opportunity, 56 Am. J. Comp. L. 173 (2008).

Symeonides, *Territoriality and Personality*: S. Symeonides, Territoriality and Personality in Tort Conflicts, in T. Einhorn & K. Siehr (eds.), Intercontinental Cooperation through Private International Law: Essays in Memory of Peter Nygh 401 (2004).

Symeonides, *The "Dismal Swamp"*: S. Symeonides, Exploring the "Dismal Swamp": Revising Louisiana's Conflicts Law on Successions, 47 La. L. Rev. 1029 (1987).

Symeonides, *The Conflicts Book*: S. Symeonides, The Conflicts Book of the Louisiana Civil Code: Civilian, American, or Original?, 83 Tul. L. Rev. 1041 (2009).

Symeonides, *The First Conflicts Restatement*: S. Symeonides, The First Conflicts Restatement through the Eyes of Old: As Bad as Its Reputation?, 32 So. Ill. U. L.J. 39 (2007).

Symeonides, *The Hague Principles*: S. Symeonides, The Hague Principles on Choice of Law for International Contracts: Some Preliminary Comments, 61 Am. J. Comp. L. 873 (2013).

Symeonides, *The Need for a Third Conflicts Restatement*: S. Symeonides, The Need for a Third Conflicts Restatement (And a Proposal for Tort Conflicts), 75 Ind. L.J. 437 (2000).

Symeonides, *The Puerto Rico Projet*: S. Symeonides, Codifying Choice of Law for Contracts: The Puerto Rico Projet, in J. Nafziger & S. Symeonides (eds.), Law and Justice in a Multistate World: Essays in Honor of Arthur T. von Mehren 419 (2002).

Symeonides, *Two Surprises*: S. Symeonides, Louisiana Conflicts Law: Two "Surprises," 54 La. L. Rev. 497(1994).

Tarman, Z.D., *Turkish Report* on PIL to the 18th Int'l Congress of Comparative Law (2010).

Tu, G., *Macau Report* on PIL to the 18th Int'l Congress of Comparative Law (2010).

Vassilakakis, E., *Greek Report* on PIL to the 18th Int'l Congress of Comparative Law (2010).

Wendehorst, C., *Austrian Report* on PIL to the 18th Int'l Congress of Comparative Law (2010).

List of Choice-of-Law Codifications

AFGHANISTAN: Civil Code of the Republic of Afghanistan, arts. 3–35 (1977).

ALBANIA: Law No. 10428 of 2 July 2011 on Private International Law.

ALGERIA: Algerian Civil Code, arts. 9-24, as amended by Ordinance No. 75-58 of 26 Sept. 1975.

ANGOLA: Civil Code of Angola, arts. 14–63, Law-Decree 496 of 25 Nov. 1977.

ARGENTINA: Anteproyecto de Código Civil y Commercial de la Nación (2012) by Commisión de Reformas decreto presidencial 191/2011, arts. 2594–2671.

ARMENIA: Civil Code of Armenia as adopted in 1998, Division 12, arts. 1253–1293.

AUSTRIA: Bundesgesetz vom 15. 6. 1978 über das internationale Privatrecht, as subsequently amended.

AZERBAIJAN: Law of 6 June 2000 on Private International Law.

BELARUS: Civil Code of Belarus (Law of 7 December 1998, as amended on 28 Dec. 28 2009), arts. 1093–1136.

BELGIUM: Code de droit international privé (Loi du 16 juillet 2004).

BOSNIA-HERZEGOVINA: [Former Yugoslav] Act of 15 July 1982 on the Resolution of Conflicts of Laws with Laws and Regulations of Other Countries in Certain Matters.

BULGARIA: Bulgarian Private International Law Code (Law No. 42 of 2005 as amended by Law No. 59 of 2007).

BURKINA FASO: Code of Persons and Family, arts. 988–1050 (Law VII 0013 of 19 Nov. 1989).

BURUNDI: Code of Persons and Family, arts. 1–10, 94 (Decree-Law No. 1/1 of 15 Jan. 1980 as revised by Decree-Law No. 1/024 of 28 April 1993).

CAPE VERDE: Civil Code of Cape Verde, arts. 14–63, re-enacted by Legislative Decree No. 12-C/97 of 30 June 1997.

CENTRAL AFRICAN REPUBLIC: Law No. 65-71 of 3 June 1965 regarding the obligatory force of laws and the conflict of laws in time and space, arts. 38–45.

CHAD: Ordinance No. 6 of 21 March 1967 for the Reform of Judicial Organization, arts. 70–72.

CHINA: Statute of Application of Law to Foreign Civil Relations, adopted at the 17th session of the Standing Committee of the 11th National People's Congress on 28 October 2010.

CONGO-BRAZZAVILLE: Family Code, arts. 38–39, 155, 819–832 (Law No. 073/1984 of 17.10.1984).

COSTA RICA: Civil Code of Costa Rica arts. 23–30, as revised by Law No. 7020 of 6 Jan. 1986.

CROATIA: [Former Yugoslav] Act of 15 July 1982 on the Resolution of Conflicts of Laws with Laws and Regulations of Other Countries in Certain Matters.

CUBA: Civil Code of 1987, arts. 11–21, adopted by Law No. 59 of 16 July 1987.

CZECH REPUBLIC: Law No. 91 of 25 January 2012 on Private International Law, effective 1 Jan. 2014.

CZECHOSLOVAKIA: Act 97 of 1963 on Private International law and Procedure.

EAST TIMOR: Civil Code of East Timor, arts. 13–62, re-enacted by Law No. 10/2011 of 14 Sept. 2011.

ECUADOR: Ecuador Civil Code as revised by Law of 10 May 2005, arts. 13–17, 43, 91–93, 103, 129, 137, 139, 1019, 1057–1058, 1087–1089, and 2337.

EL SALVADOR: Civil Code of El Salvador, arts. 14–18, 53–55, 617, 740, 966, 994–995, 1021, 1333, and 2160, as revised by Law-Decree No. 724, 30/09/1999.

ESTONIA: Private International Law Act of 27 March 2002.

FINLAND: Act on Law Applicable to Sale of Goods of International Character of 1964; Marriage Act (Act 234/1929, as amended); Code of Inheritance (Act 40/1965 as amended).

FYROM: (Former Yugoslav Republic of Macedonia): Private International Law Act of 4 July 2007.

GABON: Civil Code arts. 25–77 (Law No. 15/1972 of 29.7.1972 adopting Part I of Civil Code).

GEORGIA: Act No. 1362 of 29 April 1998 on Private International Law.

GERMANY: Gesetz zur Neuregelung des IPR vom 25.7.1986; Gesetz zum IPR für außervertragliche Schuldverhältnisse und das Sachenrecht vom 21.5.1999.

GUATEMALA: Ley del Organism Judicial, arts. 21–35 (Decreto 2-89, of 18.3.1989).

GUINEA-BISSAU: Civil Code of Guinea-Bissau, arts. 14–65, re-enacted by Guinea-Bissau Law No. 1/73 of 27 Sept. 1973.

HUNGARY: Law-Decree No. 13 of 1979 on Private International Law.

ITALY: Act No. 218 of 31 May 1995 (Riforma del sistema italiano di diritto internazionale privato).

JAPAN: Law No. 10 of 1898 as Newly Titled and Amended on 21 June 2006, effective 1 Jan. 2007, on the General Rules of Application of Laws.

JORDAN: Jordanian Civil Code of 1 August 1976, arts. 1–3, 11–29.

KAZAKHSTAN: Civil Code of the Republic of Kazakhstan, arts. 1158–1124, enacted by Law No. 409-1 ZRK of 1 July 1999.

KOREA (NORTH): The Law of the Democratic People's Republic of Korea on External Civil Relations, adopted by Resolution No. 62 of the Standing Committee of the Supreme People's Assembly on 6 Sept. 1995, and amended by Decree No. 251 of the Presidium of the Supreme People's Assembly on 10 Dec. 1998.

KOREA (SOUTH): Law 6465 of 7 April 2001, Amending the Conflict of Laws Act of the Republic of Korea.

KYRGYZSTAN: Law of 5 Jan. 1998 revising Civil Code arts. 1167–1208.

LATVIA: Latvian Civil Code (1993), arts. 8–25.

LIECHTENSTEIN: Private International Law Act of 1996.

LITHUANIA: Civil Code of the Republic of Lithuania of 2000, arts. 1.10–1.62.

LOUISIANA: Book IV of the Louisiana Civil Code, enacted by La. Act No. 923 of 1991.

MACAU: Civil Code of Macau, arts. 13–62, Approved by Law-Decree No. 39/99 of 3 Aug. 1999.

MADAGASCAR: Arts. 20–35, Ordonnance No. 62-041 du 19 sept. 1962 relative aux dispositions générales de droit interne et de droit international privé, complétée par la loi no. 98-019 du 2 déc. 1998.

MAURITANIA: Code des Obligations et des Contrats, arts 6–11 (Ordonnance no. 89-126 du 14 sept. 1989).

MEXICO: Arts. 12–15, 29–34, 2736–2738 of Civil Code for the Federal District in Ordinary Matters and for the Entire Republic in Federal Matters, as amended by Decree of 11 Dec. 1987.

MOLDOVA: Moldova Civil Code (Law 1107 of 6 June 2002), arts. 1578–1625.

MONGOLIA: Mongolian Civil Code, arts. 539–552, enacted 2 Jan. 2, 2002.

MONTENEGRO: [Former Yugoslav] Act of 15 July 1982 on the Resolution of Conflicts of Laws with Laws and Regulations of Other Countries in Certain Matters.

MOZAMBIQUE: Mozambique Civil Code, arts. 14–65, enacted by Portuguese Ordinance No. 22,869 of 4 Sept. 1967.

NETHERLANDS: Act of 19 May 2011 adopting and implementing Book 10 (Private International Law) of the Dutch Civil Code.

OREGON: Or. Rev. Stat. §§ 15.300–15.380 (2001); Or. Rev. Stat. §§ 15.400B15.460 (2009).

PANAMA: Panama Civil Code, arts. 1, 5–8, 631–632, 765–770, as revised by Law No. 18 of 1992.

PARAGUAY: Civil Code of Paraguay as revised by Law No. 1183 of 18 December 1985, arts. 11–26, 101, 132–136, 163–167, 177–178, 297, 699, 1196, 1199, 2184, 2447–2448, 2609, and 2626.

PERU: Peruvian Civil Code of 1984, Book X, arts. 2046–2111.

POLAND: Act of Private International Law of 4 Feb. 2011.

PORTUGAL: Portuguese Civil Code, arts. 14–65, as revised in 1966 and subsequently.

PUERTO RICO: Proyecto de Ley para la Revisión y Reforma del Código Civil De Puerto Rico, Libro Séptimo (Derecho Internacional Privado), 25 de mayo 2002.

QATAR: Arts. 10–38 of the Civil Code of Qatar, as amended by law 22/2004 of 8 August 2004.

QUEBEC: L.Q. 1991, ch. 64, composing Book Ten of the Quebec Civil Code (arts. 3076–3168).

ROMANIA: Law No. 105 of 22 Sept. 1992 on the Settlement of Private International Law Relations.

RUSSIA: Civil Code of the Russian Federation, Part III, arts. 1186–1224, enacted by Federal law no. 146 of 26 Nov. 2001.

RWANDA: Law no. 42/1988 (Preliminary Title and First Book of the Civil Code) in force since 1 May 1992.

SENEGAL: Family Code of Senegal, arts. 840–854, Law No. 76-61 of June 1972.

SERBIA: Serbian Ministry of Justice Draft of 20 July 2012 on Private International Law Code.

SLOVAKIA: Czechoslovakian Act 97 of 1963 on Private International law and Procedure, as subsequently amended

SLOVENIA: Private International Law and Procedure Act of 30 June 1999.

SOMALIA: Civil Code of Somalia, arts. 10–28, Law no. 37 of 2 July 1973.

SPAIN: Spanish Civil Code, arts. 8–16, as revised in 1974 and subsequently.

SUDAN: Civil Code of Sudan, arts. 10–16, 655, 684, Law of 24 May 1971 as amended by Law of 14 Feb. 1984.

SWITZERLAND: Bundesgesetz über das Internationale Privatrecht (IPRG) vom 18. Dez. 1987—Loi féderale sur le droit international privé (LDIP) du 18 déc. 1987.

TAIWAN: Act Governing the Application of Laws in Civil Matters Involving Foreign Elements, promulgated on 26 May 2010.

TAJIKISTAN: Civil Code of the Republic of Tajikistan, arts. 1191–1234, enacted by Law No. 3 of 1 March 2005.

TUNISIA: Code of Private International Law (Law No. 98-97 of 27 Nov. 1998).

TURKEY: Law No. 5718 of 27 Nov. 2007 adopting the Turkish Code of Private International Law and International Civil Procedure.

U.A.E. (United Arab Emirates): Code of Civil Transactions of the United Arab Emirates, arts. 1–3, 10–18.

UKRAINE: Law of 23 June 2005 No. 2709-IV on Private International Law, as subsequently amended.

UNITED KINGDOM: Private International Law (Miscellaneous Provisions) Act of 8 Nov. 1995 (c 42).

URUGUAY: Proyecto de Ley General de Derecho Internacional Privado, 19.1.2009

UZBEKISTAN: Civil Code of the Republic of Uzbekistan, arts. 1158–1199, enacted by Law 257-I of 29.08.1996.

VENEZUELA: Act of 6 Aug. 1998 on Private International Law.

VIETNAM: Civil Code of the Socialist Republic of Vietnam of 1995, Arts. 826–838.

YEMEN: Law of 29 March 1992 on Private International Law.

YUGOSLAVIA: Act of 15 July 1982 on the Resolution of Conflicts of Laws with Laws and Regulations of Other Countries in Certain Matters.

List of EU Regulations (and Conventions)

BRUSSELS CONVENTION: Brussels Convention of 27 September 1968 on jurisdiction and the enforcement of judgments in civil and commercial matters.

LUGANO CONVENTION: Convention on Jurisdiction and the Enforcement of Judgments in Civil and Commercial Matters, Done at Lugano on 16 September 1988.

BRUSSELS I REGULATION: European Community Council Regulation (EC) No. 44/2001 of 22 December 200 on Jurisdiction and the Recognition of Judgments in Civil and Commercial Matters.

BRUSSELS IIBIS (IIA) REGULATION: Council Regulation (EC) No 2201/2003 of 27 November 2003 concerning jurisdiction and the recognition and enforcement of judgments in matrimonial matters and the matters of parental responsibility.

INSOLVENCY REGULATION: Council Regulation (EC) No 1346/2000 of 29 May 2000 on Insolvency Proceedings.

MAINTENANCE REGULATION: Council Regulation (EC) No 4/2009 of 18 December 2008 on Jurisdiction, Applicable Law, Recognition and Enforcement of Decisions and Cooperation in Matters Relating to Maintenance Obligations.

ROME I REGULATION: Regulation (EC) No. 593/2008 of the European Parliament and of the Council of 17 June 2008 on the Law Applicable to Contractual Obligations (Rome I).

ROME II REGULATION: Regulation (EC) No. 864/2007 of the European Parliament and of the Council of 11 July 2007 on the Law Applicable to Non-contractual Obligations (Rome II).

ROME III REGULATION: Council Regulation (EU) No 1259/2010 of 20 December 2010 implementing enhanced cooperation in the area of the law applicable to divorce and legal separation.

SUCCESSIONS REGULATION: Regulation (EU) No 650/2012 of the European Parliament and of the Council of 4 July 2012 on jurisdiction, applicable law, recognition and enforcement of decisions and acceptance and enforcement of authentic instruments in matters of succession and on the creation of a European Certificate of Succession.

List of International Conventions

I. HAGUE CONVENTIONS

ACCESS TO JUSTICE: Hague Convention of 25 October 1980 on International Access to Justice.

ADMINISTRATION OF ESTATES: Hague Convention of 2 October 1973 Concerning the International Administration of the Estates of Deceased Persons.

ADOPTION: Hague Convention of 15 November 1965 on Jurisdiction, Applicable Law and Recognition of Decrees Relating to Adoptions.

ADOPTION: Hague Convention of 29 May 1993 on Protection of Children and Co-operation in Respect of Intercountry Adoption.

AGENCY: Hague Convention of 14 March 1978 on the Law Applicable to Agency.

CHILD ABDUCTION: Hague Convention of 25 October 1980 on the Civil Aspects of International Child Abduction.

CHILD SUPPORT: Hague Convention of 23 November 2007 on the International Recovery of Child Support and Other Forms of Family Maintenance.

CHOICE OF COURT: Hague Convention of 30 June 2005 on Choice of Court Agreements.

CONTRACTS: Hague Choice of Law Principles for International Contracts, Approved by the Special Commission on 12–16 November 2012.

DIVORCE: Hague Convention of 1 June 1970 on the Recognition of Divorces and Legal Separations.

EVIDENCE: Hague Convention of 18 March 1970 on the Taking of Evidence Abroad in Civil or Commercial Matters.

FOREIGN JUDGMENTS: Hague Convention of 1 February 1971 on the Recognition and Enforcement of Foreign Judgments in Civil and Commercial Matters.

LEGALIZATION: Hague Convention of 5 October 1961 Abolishing the Requirement of Legalisation for Foreign Public Documents.

MAINTENANCE: Hague Convention of 2 October 1973 on the Law Applicable to Maintenance Obligations.

MAINTENANCE PROTOCOL: Hague Protocol of 23 November 2007 on the Law Applicable to Maintenance Obligations.

MATRIMONIAL PROPERTY: Hague Convention of 14 March 1978 on the Law Applicable to Matrimonial Property Regimes.

MARRIAGE: Hague Convention of 14 March 1978 on Celebration and Recognition of the Validity of Marriages.

PARENTAL RESPONSIBILITY: Hague Convention of 19 October 1996 on Jurisdiction, Applicable Law, Recognition, Enforcement and Co-operation in Respect of Parental Responsibility and Measures for the Protection of Children.

PRODUCTS LIABILITY: Hague Convention of 2 October 1973 on the Law Applicable to Products Liability.

SALES: Hague Convention of 22 December 1986 on the Law Applicable to Contracts for the International Sale of Goods.

PROTECTION OF ADULTS: Hague Convention of 13 January 2000 on the International Protection of Adults.

PROTECTION OF INFANTS: Hague Convention of 5 October 1961 Concerning the Powers of Authorities and the Law Applicable in Respect of the Protection of Infants.

SECURITIES: Hague Convention of 5 July 2006 on the Law Applicable to Certain Rights in Respect of Securities held with an Intermediary.

SERVICE OF DOCUMENTS: Hague Convention of 15 November 1965 on the Service Abroad of Judicial and Extrajudicial Documents in Civil or Commercial Matters.

SUCCESSIONS: Hague Convention of 1 August 1989 on the Law Applicable to Succession to the Estates of Deceased Persons.

TESTAMENTARY FORM: Hague Convention of 5 October 1961 on the Conflicts of Laws Relating to the Form of Testamentary Dispositions.

TRAFFIC ACCIDENTS: Hague Convention of 4 May 1971 on the Law Applicable to Traffic Accidents.

TRUSTS: Hague Convention of 1 July 1985 on the Law Applicable to Trusts and on their Recognition.

II. INTER-AMERICAN CONVENTIONS

ADOPTION: Inter-American Convention on Conflict of Laws Concerning the Adoption of Minors (1984).

ARBITRATION: Inter-American Convention on International Commercial Arbitration (1975).

BILLS OF EXCHANGE: Inter-American Convention on Conflict of Laws Concerning Bills of Exchange, Promissory Notes, and Invoices (1975).

CAPACITY: Inter-American Convention on Personality and Capacity of Juridical Persons in Private International Law (1984).

CARRIAGE OF GOODS: Inter-American Convention on Contracts for the International Carriage of Goods by Road (1989).

CARRIAGE OF GOODS: Negotiable Inter-American Uniform Through Bill of Lading for the International Carriage of Good by Road (2002).

CARRIAGE OF GOODS: Non-Negotiable Inter-American Uniform Through Bill of Lading for the International Carriage of Good by the Road (2002).

CHECKS: Inter-American Convention on Conflict of Laws Concerning Checks (1975).

CHECKS: Inter-American Convention on Conflicts of Laws Concerning Checks (1979).

CONTRACTS: *See* "Mexico City Convention."

COMPANIES: Inter-American Convention on Conflicts of Laws Concerning Commercial Companies (1979).

DOMICILE: Inter-American Convention on the Domicile of Natural Persons in Private International Law (1979).

EVIDENCE: Inter-American Convention on the Taking of Evidence Abroad (1975).

EVIDENCE PROTOCOL: Additional Protocol to the Inter-American Convention on the Taking of Evidence Abroad (1984).

FOREIGN LAW PROOF: Inter-American Convention on Proof and Information on Foreign Law (1979).

GENERAL RULES OF PIL: Inter-American Convention on General Rules of Private International Law, Done at Montevideo, Uruguay, on 8 May 1979.

JUDGMENTS AND ARBITRAL AWARDS: Inter-American Convention on Extraterritorial Validity of Foreign Judgments and Arbitral Awards (1979).

JURISDICTION AND JUDGMENTS: Inter-American Convention on Jurisdiction in the International Sphere for the Extraterritorial Validity of Foreign Judgments (1984).

LETTERS ROGATORY: Inter-American Convention on Letters Rogatory (1975).

LETTERS ROGATORY PROTOCOL: Additional Protocol to the Inter-American Convention on Letters Rogatory (1979).

"MEXICO CITY" CONVENTION: Inter-American Convention on the Law Applicable to International Contracts, Signed at Mexico, D.F., Mexico, on 17 March 1994.

POWERS OF ATTORNEY: Inter-American Convention on the Legal Regime of Powers of Attorney to Be Used Abroad (1975).

PREVENTIVE MEASURES: Inter-American Convention on Execution of Preventive Measures (1979).

RETURN OF CHILDREN: Inter-American Convention on International Return of Children (1989).

SECURED TRANSACTIONS: Model Inter-American Law on Secured Transactions (2002).

SUPPORT: Inter-American Convention on Support Obligations (1989).

TRAFFIC IN MINORS: Inter-American Convention on International Traffic in Minors (1994).

1 Introduction

I. Introduction

This book chronicles and celebrates an extraordinary development in the history of Private International Law (PIL) or Conflict of Laws[1]—a massive codification movement around the globe in the last 50 years (1962–2012). During this period, we have witnessed

---

[1] This book uses the terms "Private International Law" (PIL) and "Conflict of Laws" interchangeably, as that branch of domestic law that covers jurisdiction, choice of law, and recognition of foreign judgments in multi-state or transnational cases. The book covers only the choice-of-law part. Chapter 7 discusses the origin of the

the adoption of more choice-of-law codifications and international conventions than in all previous years since the inception of PIL.

This book provides a horizontal discussion and comparison of these codifications and conventions. After comparing the way they resolve tort and contract conflicts, the discussion compares the answers of these to some of the fundamental philosophical and methodological dilemmas of PIL. In the process, the book re-examines certain widely held assumptions about choice of law and the art and science of codification in general.

II. National or Sub-national Choice-of-Law Codifications

A. THE FIRST GENERATION

The first choice-of-law codifications in modern times were part and parcel of the substantive-law codification movement of the nineteenth century. The French Civil Code of 1804,[2] the Austrian Civil Code of 1811,[3] the Italian Civil Code of 1865,[4] the Spanish Civil Code of 1889,[5] and the German Civil Code of 1896/1900[6] each contained a modest number of broad choice-of-law rules, which later became the models for similar rules in other countries.[7] The 1928 "Code of Private International Law," better known as the "Bustamante Code,"[8] was far more comprehensive, and its adoption by 15 Latin American states[9] appeared at the time to generate a momentum in favor of choice-of-law codification.

---

quoted terms, their usage in different parts of the world, and the different assumptions underlying them. See Chapter 7, at I.A., *infra*.

[2] *See* French Civil Code, arts. 3, 14–15, 309, 311.

[3] *See* Austrian Civil Code, arts. 4, 33–38, 300.

[4] Originally drafted by Pasquale Mancini, the choice-of-law articles of the Italian Civil Code of 1865 were reproduced as Articles 17–31 of the Italian Civil Code of 1942.

[5] *See* Spanish Civil Code, arts. 8–11.

[6] *See* Introductory Law of the Civil Code (EGBGB) of 15 August 1896, arts. 3–38. *See also* the Civil Code of the Canton of Zurich 1854–1856, arts. 1–7.

[7] *See, e.g.,* the Japanese Horei (Act No. 10) of 1898, which was primarily based on the Introductory Law to the German Civil Code (EGBGB) (*see* T. Kanzaki, *Japanese Report,* at I.1); Chinese Statute on the Application of Laws of 1918, which was based on the Japanese Horei of 1898 and the EGBGB (*see* W. Chen, *Chinese Report,* at I.A.); Greek Civil Code of 1940, arts. 4–33; Italian Civil Code of 1942, arts. 17–31.

[8] *See* Convention on Private International Law (Bustamante Code), adopted in Havana, Cuba, on 20 February 1928, ava*ilable at* http://www.oas.org/juridico/spanish/firmas/a-31.html; A.S. de Bustamante y Sirvén, *El código de derecho internacional privado y la sexta conferencia panamericana* (1929). For an English translation, *see* J. Romanach, *Bustamante Code—Código Bustamante* (1996).

[9] The Bustamante Code was adopted without reservations by Cuba, Guatemala, Honduras, Nicaragua, Panama, and Peru, and with reservations by Bolivia, Brazil, Chile, Costa Rica, Dominican Republic, Ecuador, El Salvador, Haiti, and Venezuela. For discussion, *see* J. Samtleben, *Derecho Internacional Privado en América Latina, Teoría y práctica del Código Bustamante* (1983).

This momentum was short-lived, however. During the ensuing decades, the prevailing view in many countries was that choice of law was insusceptible to codification. This sentiment seemed to prevail not only in common-law countries such as the United States, where the dismal failure of the First Conflicts Restatement led many to reject both statutory rules and Restatement-type non-state rules,[10] but also in European countries, where many scholars expressed serious misgivings about the need or desirability of codifying or re-codifying choice of law.[11]

In the 1960s, those misgivings began to dissipate, paving the way for a new codification movement. Slow at the beginning, the movement gradually gained momentum, mushrooming around the turn of the twentieth century. As a knowledgeable author observed, "from China to Germany, from Turkey, Yemen to Burkina Faso, everybody—that is, the whole world or just about—has codified its private international law."[12] Indeed, the codification movement may have begun in continental Europe, but it has since spread to other continents and to countries from all legal families and traditions. By the end of the century, another author could accurately observe that "a most striking feature of the development of private international law over the [twentieth] century has been that statute law has been the primary instrument of change."[13] This change continues into the twenty-first century.

Even England, the epicenter of the common law, has joined the codification movement, at least in part. In 1982, Sir Peter North, then Law Commissioner for England and Wales, thought it necessary to assure his readers that "[c]odes are not monsters...[and that], [e]ven if they are, they can be trained."[14] North predicted a "major transformation of English private international law from case law to reformed statute law" leading toward a "continental style of code."[15] This transformation began with the enactment of a statute for tort conflicts in 1995.[16] Although this statute was not "in the style" of a continental code, the United Kingdom's subsequent decision to adopt the European Union's Rome I and Rome II Regulations on contract and tort conflicts, respectively,[17] significantly advanced the transformation.

---

[10] *See infra* Chapter 4, at VIII.A.

[11] *See, e.g.,* P.H. Neuhaus, Empfiehlt sich eine Kodifizierung des internationalen Privatrechts?, 37 *RabelsZ* 453 (1973); O. Kahn-Freund, *General Problems of Private International Law* 80–84 (1976); F. Schwind, Problems of Codification of Private International Law, 17 *Int'l & Comp. L.Q.* 428, 431 (1968).

[12] H. Muir Watt, La codification en droit international privé, 27 *Droits: Rev. Franc. de Théorie Jurid.* 149, at 150 (1998).

[13] P. North, Private International Law: Change or Decay?, 50 *Int'l & Comp. L.Q.* 477, 496 (2001).

[14] P. North, Problems of Codification in a Common Law System, 46 *RabelsZ* 490, at 500 (1982).

[15] *Id.* at 501.

[16] *See* Private International Law (Miscellaneous Provisions) Act of 8 November 1995 (c 42) (choice-of-law rules for torts conflicts other than defamation).

[17] *See infra* at III, this chapter.

B. THE SECOND GENERATION

The 50-year period covered by this book begins in 1962 and ends in 2012. The first codification of the period was that of Madagascar in 1962,[18] followed by that of the former Czechoslovakia, which was adopted in 1963 and went into effect in 1964.[19]

The decade of the 1960s produced only five other codifications[20] for a total of seven. They were followed by 17 codifications in the 1970s, 19 in the 1980s, 26 in the 1990s, and 25 since the turn of the century. (See chart 1.1).

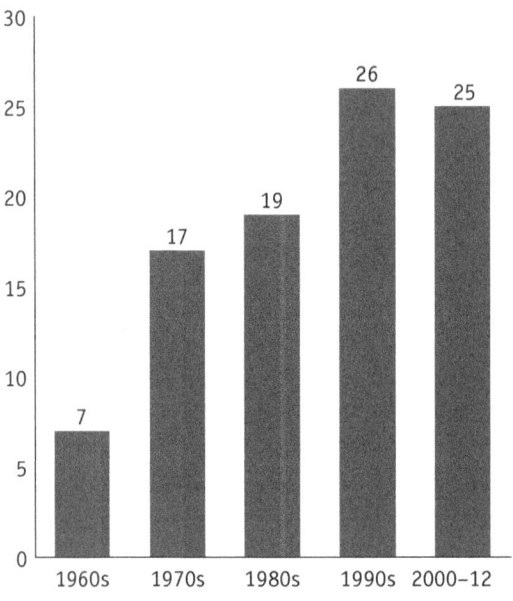

CHART 1.1. Choice-of-Law Codifications by Decade

---

[18] *See* arts. 20–35 of Ordinance No. 62-041 of 19 September 1962 on General Provisions of Internal Law and Private International Law (J.O No. 244 of 28.9.1962, p. 1989), completed by Law No. 98-019 of 2 December 1998 (J.O. No. 2549 du 15.12.98, pp. 3642 and 3654).

[19] *See* Act 97 of 1963 (effective April 1964) on Private International law and Procedure. This Act remains in force in Slovakia, as amended by Acts Nos. 158/1969, 234/1992, 264/1992, 48/1996, 510/2002, 589/2003, 382/2004, 36/2005, 336/05, 273/07, 384/2008, 388/2011 Coll. It also remained in effect in the Czech Republic until 1 January 2014 (as amended by Acts Nos. 158/1969, 234/1992, 264/1992, 125/2002, 37/2004, 257/2004, 361/2004, 377/2005, 57/2006, 70/2006, 233/2006, 296/2007, 123/2008, 7/2009 and 409/2010 Coll.). For the new Czech codification of 2012, *see* note 116, *infra*.

[20] *See* the codifications of Albania (1964), Central African Republic (1965), Poland (1965), Chad (1967), and Portugal (1967), cited *infra*.

1. Chronological List

These codifications are listed below in chronological order, followed by the year of enactment,[21] and accompanied by basic citations to sources.[22] Appendix I, at the end of this book, provides an alphabetical list of these codifications, accompanied by a bibliography for each.

(1) Madagascar (1962);[23]
(2) Czechoslovakia (1964);[24]
(3) Albania (1964*);[25]
(4) Poland (1965*);[26]
(5) Central African Republic (1965);[27]
(6) Chad (1967);[28]
(7) Portugal (1967);[29]
(8) Ecuador (1970);[30]

---

[21] The asterisk following some of these years indicates that the codification of that year was supplemented by a subsequent partial codification or replaced by a subsequent comprehensive codification.

[22] For collections or discussions of conflicts codifications from several countries, *see* Asser Instituut, *Les legislations de droit international privé* (1971); D. Fernández Arroyo, *La codificación del derecho internacional privado en América Latina* (1994); J. Kropholler, H. Krüger, W. Riering, J. Samtleben & K. Siehr, *Aussereuropäische IPR-Gesetze* (1999); G. Parra-Aranguren, *Codificación del derecho internacional privado en America* (1998); W. Riering, *IPR-Gesetze in Europa* (1997); E. Vassilakakis, *Orientations méthodologiques dans les codifications récentes du droit international privé en Europe* (1987); D.F. Cavers, Legislative Choice of Law: Some European Examples, 44 *So. Calif. L. Rev.* 340 (1971); A. Ferrer-Correia, Les problèmes de codification en droit international privé, 145 *Recueil des Cours* (1975); E. Jayme, Considerations historique et actuelles sur la codification du droit international privé, 177 *Recueil des Cours* 9, 51–85 (1982-IV); C. Kessedjian, Codification du droit commercial international et droit international privé, 300 *Recueil des Cours* 79 (2004); F. Rigaux, La méthode des conflits de lois dans les codifications et projets de codification de la dernière décennie, 74 *Rev. critique DIP* 1 (1985); F. Rigaux, Codification of Private International Law: Pros and Cons, 60 *La. L. Rev.* 1321 (2000); A.E. von Overbeck, Les questions générales du droit international privé à la lumiere des codifications et projets récents, 176 *Recueil des Cours* 9 (1982–III); A.E. von Overbeck, De quelques règles générales de conflit de lois dans les codifications récentes, in (J. Basedow et al., eds.), *Private Law in the International Arena: Liber Amicorum Kurt Siehr* 545 (2000).

[23] *See* note 18, *supra.*

[24] *See* note 19, *supra.*

[25] *See* Law No. 3920 of 21 November 1964 on the Enjoyment of Civil Rights by Aliens. This codification was repealed by the new codification of 2011 cited at note 112, *infra.*

[26] *See* Act of 12 November 1965, effective 1 July 1966, on Private International Law. This codification was repealed by the new codification of 2011, cited *infra* at note 115.

[27] *See* Articles 38–45 of Law No. 65-71 of 3 June 1965 Regarding the Obligatory Force of Laws and the Conflict of Laws in Time and Space, effective on 1 July 1965.

[28] *See* arts. 70–72 of Ordinance No. 6 of 21 March 1967 for the Reform of Judicial Organization.

[29] *See* Portuguese Civil Code, arts. 14–65, as enacted by Decree-Law No. 47,344 of 25 November 1966. This code was also introduced in the then Portuguese colonies of Angola, Cape Verde, East Timor, Guinea-Bissau, and Mozambique. In 1977, the provisions of the Portuguese Civil Code were revised by Law No. 496/77 to conform to Portugal's new constitution.

[30] *See* Ecuador Civil Code as amended by Law No. 000.RO/Sup 104, of 29 September 1970, arts. 13–17, 43, 91–93, 103, 129, 137, 139, 1019, 1057–1058, 1087–1089, and 2337.

(9) Sudan (1971);[31]

(10) Gabon (1972);[32]

(11) Senegal (1972);[33]

(12) Guinea-Bissau (1973);[34]

(13) Somalia (1973);[35]

(14) Spain (1974);[36]

(15) Algeria (1975);[37]

(16) German Democratic Republic (the former East Germany) (1975);[38]

(17) Mozambique (1975);[39]

(18) Afghanistan (1977);[40]

(19) Angola (1977);[41]

(20) Jordan (1977);[42]

(21) The former Yugoslavia (1978–1982);[43]

---

[31] See Civil Code of Sudan, arts. 10–16, 655, 684, of 24 May 1971 as amended by Law of 14 February 1984, Off. J. Democratic Republic of Sudan No. 1340 of 16 February 1984.

[32] See Civil Code of Gabon, arts. 25–77, Law No. 15/1972 of 29.7.1972 adopting Part I of Civil Code, Official J. Rep. Gabon of 20.12.1972 p.1.

[33] See Family Code of Senegal, arts. 840–54, Law No. 76-61 of June 1972, J.O. Rep. of Senegal No. 4243 of 12.8.1972, 1295.

[34] See Civil Code of Guinea-Bissau, arts. 14–65. This code was a copy of the Portuguese Civil Code of 1966, which was introduced to the then Portuguese colonies by Portuguese Ordinance No. 22,869, of 4 September 1967. Upon declaring its independence in 1973 (recognized in 1974), Guinea-Bissau renewed the force of this code by Law No. 1/73 of 27 September 1973, published in Boletim Oficial No. 1, of 4 January 1975.

[35] See Civil Code of Somalia, arts. 10–28, Law no. 37 of 2 July 1973, Off. Bul. of Democratic Republic of Somalia, 2 July 1973, n.6.

[36] See Spanish Civil Code arts. 8–16, as revised in 1974.

[37] See Ordinance No. 75-58 of 26 September 1975, amending articles 9 through 24 of the Algerian Civil Code.

[38] See Act of 5 December 1975 on Private International Law, DDR GBL I 748 (1975), translated into English and discussed in F. Juenger, The Conflicts Statute of the German Democratic Republic: An Introduction and Translation, 25 Am. J. Comp. L. 332 (1977). This codification is not discussed in this book.

[39] See Mozambique Civil Code, arts. 14–65, initially enacted by Portuguese Ordinance No. 22,869, of 4 September 1967, which extended to the then Portuguese colonies the force of the Portuguese Civil Code adopted by Decree-Law No. 47,344 of 25 November 1966. This code remained in effect after Mozambique gained its independence from Portugal on 6 June 1975.

[40] See Civil Code of the Republic of Afghanistan, arts. 3–35, Official Gazette No. 353, published 1977/01/05 (1355/10/15 A.P.)

[41] See arts. 14–65 of the Civil Code of Angola. This code was initially enacted by Portuguese Decree-Law No. 47,344 of 25 November 1966 and extended to the then Portuguese colonies by Ordinance No. 22,869, of 4 September 1967. Angola renewed the force of this code by Law-Decree 496 of 25 November 1977.

[42] See arts. 1–3, 11-29 of Jordanian Civil Code of 1 August 1976 (effective 1 Jan. 1977), J.O. No. 2645 of 1 Aug. 1976.

[43] The Yugoslav codification was enacted in three installments in 1978, 1979, and 1982. For the specifics, see bibliography in Appendix I, infra, under Yugoslavia. This codification remains in force with occasional slight amendments in Bosnia-Herzegovina, Croatia, Montenegro, and Serbia. This book treats these versions as one codification and cites only to the Croatian version. For the codifications of the other former Yugoslav republics (Slovenia and FYROM), and the Serbian draft codification, see infra.

(22) Austria (1979);[44]

(23) Hungary (1979);[45]

(24) Arab Republic of Yemen (the former North Yemen) (1979*);[46]

(25) Burundi (1980);[47]

(26) Togo (1980);[48]

(27) Turkey (1982*);[49]

(28) Congo-Brazzaville (1984);[50]

(29) Peru (1984);[51]

(30) China (1985*);[52]

(31) Paraguay (1985);[53]

(32) United Arab Emirates (1985);[54]

(33) Costa Rica (1986);[55]

---

[44] *See* Bundesgesetz vom 15. 6. 1978 über das internationale Privatrecht (IPR-Gesetz), BGBl I 1978/304. For subsequent amendments, *see* BGBl I No. 119/1998, I No. 18/1999, I No. 135/2000, I No. 117/2003, I No. 58/2004, I No. 109/2009, I No. 135/2009.

[45] *See* Law No. 13 of 1979 on Private International Law. For amendments adopted after Hungary's membership in the EU, see Appendix I, *infra*.

[46] *See* arts. 1–11, 20, 23–35 of the Civil Code of the Arab Republic of Yemen, promulgated by Law 10 of 21 April 1979 in J.O. of 30 April 1979. This codification is not discussed here. In 1990, this country merged with the People's Democratic Republic of Yemen to form the Republic of Yemen, the present-day Yemen. For Yemen's new codification of 1992, *see* note 70, *infra*.

[47] *See* arts. 1–10, and 94 of the Code of Persons and Family, Law-Decree No. 1/1 of 15 January 1980 as revised by Law-Decree No. 1/024 of 28 April 1993.

[48] *See* Code of Persons and Family, arts. 707–734 (Law 80-16 of 31 January 1980 as revised by Law of 29 June 2012).

[49] *See* Law No. 2675 of 22 November 1982, on Private International Law and Procedure. This law was repealed by the codification of 2007, cited at note 107, *infra*.

[50] *See* Family Code, arts. 38–39, 155, and 819–832, Law No. 073/1984 of 17.10.1984.

[51] *See* Book X of the Peruvian Civil Code of 1984 (arts. 2046–2111).

[52] *See* Law of the People's Republic of China on Economic Contracts Involving Foreign Interest of 21 March 1985, and effective 1 July 1985, *available at* http://www.lawinfochina.com/. For an authoritative quasi-legislative interpretation of this Act by China's Supreme Court, *see* "Responses of the Supreme Court to Questions Arising Out of the Application of the Foreign Economic Contract Law" of 19 October 1987. For discussion of this and other Acts, *see* W. Chen, Private International Law of the People's Republic of China: An Overview, 35 *Am. J. Comp. L.* 445 (1987); L. Junming, Choice of Law for Contracts in China: A Proposal for the Objectivization of Standards and Their Use in Conflicts of Law, 6 *Ind. Int'l & Comp. L. Rev.* 439 (1996); H.R. Zheng, Private International Law in the People's Republic of China: Principles and Procedures, 22 *Tex. Int'l L.J.* 231 (1987); G. Xu, Contract in Chinese Private International Law, *Int'l & Comp. L.Q.* 648 (1989); Y. Zhang & J.S. McLean, China's Foreign Economic Contract Law: Its Significance and Analysis, 8 *N.W. J. Int'l L.& Bus.* 120 (1987). For subsequent partial codifications in 1987 and 1999, *see* notes 57 and 86, *infra*. For the comprehensive codification of 2010, *see* note 111, *infra*.

[53] *See* arts. 11–26, 101, 132–136, 163–167, 177–178, 297, 699, 1196, 1199, 2184, 2447–2448, 2609, and 2626 of the Civil Code of Paraguay as revised by Law No. 1183 of 18 December 1985.

[54] *See* arts. 1–3, and 10–28 of Code of Civil Transactions of the United Arab Emirates (J.O. of U.A.E, No. 185, December 1985, p. 11).

[55] *See* arts. 23–30 of Civil Code of Costa Rica as revised by Law No. 7020 of 6 January 1986.

(34) Germany (1986*);[56]

(35) China (1987*);[57]

(36) Cuba (1987);[58]

(37) Switzerland (1987);[59]

(38) Finland (1988);[60]

(39) Mexico (1988);[61]

(40) Rwanda (1988);[62]

(41) Guatemala (1989);[63]

(42) Mauritania (1989);[64]

(43) Burkina Faso (1990);[65]

(44) Louisiana (1991);[66]

(45) Quebec (1991);[67]

(46) Soviet Union (1991*);[68]

(47) Romania (1992);[69]

---

[56] See Gesetz zur Neuregelung des IPR vom 25.7.1986, Bundesgesetzblatt I/1986, 810. This is the first installment of a revision of the Introductory Law of the German Civil Code (EGBGB) of 1900. For the second installment, enacted in 1999, see note 88, infra.

[57] See chapter 8 of General Principles of the Civil Law, Order No. 37 of the President of the People's Republic of China of 12 April 1986, effective 1 January 1987. For an authoritative quasi-legislative interpretation of this chapter, see Part 7 of "Opinions of the Supreme Court on Several Issues concerning the Implementation of the General Principles on Civil Law" of 26 January 1988. For a subsequent partial codification in 1999, see note 86, infra. For the comprehensive codification of 2010, see note 111, infra.

[58] See Civil Code of 1987, arts. 11–21, Law No. 59 of 16 July 1987, Gaceta Oficial Extraordinaria of 15 October 1987, effective 12 April 1988.

[59] Bundesgesetz über das Internationale Privatrecht (IPRG) vom 18. Dezember 1987–Loi féderale sur le droit international privé (LDIP) du 18 décembre 1987, 1988 BB I 5 (German, French. and Italian text).

[60] See Hallituksen esitys Eduskunnalle kansainvälisluonteisiin sopimuksiin sovellettavaa lakia koskevaksi lainsäädännöksi, HE 44/1987 vp, p. 25. See also the 1964 Act on Law Applicable to Sale of Goods of International Character; the Marriage Act (Act 234/1929, with amendments up to Act 1226/2001); and Code of Inheritance (Act 40/1965 with amendments up to Act 1228/2001).

[61] See arts. 12–15, 29–34, 2736–2738 of the Civil Code for the Federal District in Ordinary Matters and for the Entire Republic in Federal Matters, as amended by Decree of 11 December 1987 (effective 8 January 1988), Diario official, 7 January 1988, p.2.

[62] See Law No. 42/1988 (Preliminary Title and First Book of the Civil Code) in force since 1 May 1992.

[63] See Law of Judicial Organization, arts. 21–35, Decree No. 2-89, of 18.3.1989.

[64] See Code of Obligations and Contracts, arts. 6–11, Ordinance no 89-126 of 14 September 1989, Off. J Islamic Republic of Mauritania no. 739 of 25 October 1989.

[65] See arts. 988–1050 of the Code of Persons and Family (Law VII 0013 of 19 November 1989, effective 4 August 1990).

[66] See Book IV of the Louisiana Civil Code, enacted into law by La. Act No. 923 of 1991, effective 1 January 1992.

[67] See L.Q. 1991, ch. 64 (adopted in 1991, effective 1994) and composing Book Ten of the Quebec Civil Code (arts. 3076–3168).

[68] See Fundamentals of Civil Legislation of the U.S.S.R. and Union Republics, Bulletin of the Congress of People's Deputies of the S.S.S.R. and the Supreme Council of S.S.S.R. (1991) No. 26, item 733, effective 3 August 1992. This statute was replaced by the 2002 Russian codification cited in note 97, infra.

[69] See Law No. 105 of 22 September 1992, effective 26 October 1993, on the Settlement of Private International Law Relations, Official Gazette of Romania No. 245 of 1 October 1992.

(48) Yemen (1992);[70]

(49) Panama (1992, 1994);[71]

(50) Latvia (1993);[72]

(51) United Kingdom (1995);[73]

(52) Italy (1995);[74]

(53) North Korea (1995);[75]

(54) Vietnam (1995);[76]

(55) Liechtenstein (1996);[77]

(56) Cape Verde (1997);[78]

(57) Uzbekistan (1997);[79]

(58) Armenia (1998);[80]

(59) Belarus (1998);[81]

(60) Georgia (1998);[82]

(61) Kyrgyzstan (1998);[83]

(62) Tunisia (1998);[84]

(63) Venezuela (1998);[85]

(64) China (1999*);[86]

---

[70] *See* Law of 29 March 1992 on Private International Law.

[71] *See* Panama Civil Code arts. 1, 5–8, 631–632, 765–770, as revised by Law No. 18 of 1992; Panama Family Code, arts. 6–11, as revised by Law No. 3 of 17 May 1994.

[72] *See* Latvian Civil Code of 1993, arts. 8–25.

[73] *See* Private International Law (Miscellaneous Provisions) Act of 8 November 1995 (c 42) (choice-of-law rules for torts conflicts other than defamation).

[74] *See* Act No. 218 of 31 May 1995 (Riforma del sistema italiano di diritto internazionale privato).

[75] *See* minju-juui innin konghwaguk tae'oe minsa kwan'gye bop (The Law of the Democratic People's Republic of Korea on External Civil Relations) adopted by Resolution No. 62 of the Standing Committee of the Supreme People's Assembly on 6 September 1995, and amended by Decree No. 251 of the Presidium of the Supreme People's Assembly on 10 December 1998.

[76] *See* Civil Code of the Socialist Republic of Vietnam of 1995, arts. 826–838.

[77] *See* Private International Law Act of 1996, in *Liechensteinisches Landesgesetzblatt* 1996 No. 194.

[78] *See* arts. 14–63 of Civil Code of Cape Verde, Legislative Decree No. 12-C/97 of 30 June 1997, renewing the force of the Portuguese Civil Code, initially adopted by [Portuguese] Decree-Law No. 47,344 of 25 November 1966 and extended to then Overseas Provinces by Ordinance No. 22,869, of 4 September 1967.

[79] *See* arts. 1158–1199 of Civil Code of the Republic of Uzbekistan, enacted by Law 257-I of 29.08.1996, effective 1 March 1997.

[80] *See* Division 12, arts. 1253–1293 of the Civil Code of Armenia of 1998.

[81] *See* arts. 1093 *et seq.* of Civil Code of Belarus (Law of 7 December 1998), as amended as of 28 December 2009.

[82] *See* Act No. 1362 of 29 April 1998 on Private International Law, effective 1 October 1998.

[83] *See* Law of 5 January 1998 revising Civil Code arts. 1167–1208.

[84] *See* Code of Private International Law (Law No. 98-97 of 27 November 1998), Official Journal of the Republic of Tunisia, 1 December 1998, p. 2332.

[85] *See* Act of 6 August 1998 on Private International Law (Official Gazette No. 36.511), effective 6 February 1999.

[86] *See* Contract Law of the People's Republic of China of 15 March 1999, effective 1 October 1999. For discussion of the choice-of-law provisions, *see* M. Zhang, Choice of Law in Contracts: A Chinese Approach, 26 *N.W. J. Int'l L. & Bus.*, 289 (2006). For an authoritative quasi-legislative interpretation, *see* "Rules of the Supreme People's Court on Related Issues concerning the Application of Law in Hearing Foreign-Related Contractual

(65) El Salvador (1999);[87]

(66) Germany (1999);[88]

(67) Kazakhstan (1999);[89]

(68) Macau (1999);[90]

(69) Slovenia (1999);[91]

(70) Azerbaijan (2000);[92]

(71) Lithuania (2000);[93]

(72) South Korea (2001);[94]

(73) The Netherlands (2001*);[95]

(74) Oregon (2001*);[96]

(75) Russia (2002);[97]

(76) Estonia (2002);[98]

(77) Moldova (2002);[99]

(78) Mongolia (2002);[100]

Dispute Cases Related to Civil and Commercial Matters" of 8 August 2007. For China's comprehensive codification of 2010, *see* note 111, *infra*.

[87] *See* arts. 14–18, 53–55, 617, 740, 966, 994–995, 1021, 1333, and 2160 of Civil Code of El Salvador, as revised by Decreto Ley No 724, 30/09/1999, published in Diario Oficial No. 198, T. 345, 23/10/1999.

[88] *See* Gesetz zum IPR für außervertragliche Schuldverhältnisse und das Sachenrecht vom 21.5.1999, Bundesgesetzblatt 1999, I, 1026 (amending the provisions of the Introductory Law of the German Civil Code (EGBGB) on non-contractual obligations and property).

[89] *See* arts. 1158–1124 of the Civil Code of the Republic of Kazakhstan, enacted by Law No. 409-1 ZRK of 1 July 1999.

[90] *See* arts. 13–62 of the Civil Code of Macau, as amended in 1999.

[91] *See* Private International Law and Procedure Act of 30 June 1999 (Zakon o mednarodnem zasebnem pravu in postopku—ZMSPP) Ur.l. RS, no. 56/1999, in Official Gazette of the Republic of Slovenia 1999/56.

[92] *See* Law of 6 June 2000 on Private International Law.

[93] *See* arts. 1.10 through 1.62 of the Civil Code of the Republic of Lithuania of 2000.

[94] *See* Law 6465 of 7 April 2001, effective 1 July 2001, amending the Conflict of Laws Act of the Republic of Korea.

[95] *See* Act of 11 April 2001 (effective 1 June 2001) Regarding Conflict of Laws on Torts, Staatsblad 2001, 190. For an English translation with an introductory note by P. Vlas, *see* Netherlands Int'l L. Rev. 221 (2003.2). For the new comprehensive codification of 2011, *see* note 114, *infra*.

[96] *See* Or. Rev. Stat. §§ 15.300–15.380 (2001) (codifying choice of law for contract conflicts). For the 2009 codification of choice-of-law rules for tort conflicts, *see* note 109, *infra*.

[97] *See* federal law no. 146 of 26 November 2001, enacting Part III of the Civil Code of the Russian Federation, Rossyiskaya Gazeta, n. 49 item 4553, 28/11/2001, effective 1 March 2002. The conflicts provisions comprise Title VI of Part Three, arts. 1186–1224. For conflicts rules in other statutes, *see* Family Code of the Russian Federation, Collection of Laws R.E. (1996) No. 1, item 16, effective 1 March 1996; Federal Law on International Commercial Arbitration, Bulletin of the Congress of People's Deputies R.E. and the Supreme Soviet R.E (1993) No. 32, item 1240, effective 1 July 1995.

[98] *See* Private International Law Act of 22 March 2002, effective 1 July 2002, The State Gazette, "Riigi Teataja" I 2002, 35, 217.

[99] *See* Moldova Civil Code (Law 1107 of 6 June 2002), Book V, arts. 1578–1625.

[100] *See* arts. 539–552 of Mongolian Civil Code, adopted on 2 January 2002, effective 1 September 2002 (initially enacted in 1994). *See also* Family Code of Mongolia of 1.10.1973, arts. 107–113.

(79) Belgium (2004);[101]

(80) Qatar (2004);[102]

(81) Bulgaria (2005);[103]

(82) Tajikistan (2005);[104]

(83) Ukraine (2005);[105]

(84) Japan (2007);[106]

(85) Turkey (2007);[107]

(86) Former Yugoslav Republic of Macedonia (FYROM) (2007);[108]

(87) Oregon (2009);[109]

(88) Taiwan (2010);[110]

(89) China (2010);[111]

(90) Albania (2011);[112]

(91) East Timor (2011);[113]

(92) Netherlands (2011);[114]

(93) Poland (2011);[115] and

(94) Czech Republic (2012).[116]

---

[101] *See* Code de droit international privé (Loi du 16 juillet 2004), Moniteur Belge 27 Juillet 2004.

[102] *See* arts. 10–38 of the Civil Code of Qatar, as amended by law 22/2004 of 8 August 2004.

[103] *See* Bulgarian Private International Law Code (Law No. 42 of 2005 as amended by Law No. 59 of 2007).

[104] *See* Section VII of the Civil Code of the Republic of Tajikistan, comprising articles 1191–1234, enacted by Law No. 3 of 1 March 2005.

[105] *See* Law of 23 June 2005 No. 2709-IV on Private International Law, as amended by Law of 21 January 2010, No. 1837-VI, and Law of 19 May 2011, No. 3390-VI.

[106] *See* Law No. 10 of 1898 as Newly Titled and Amended on 21 June 2006, effective 1 January 2007, on the General Rules of Application of Laws [Hô no tekiyô ni kan suru tsûsoku-hô].

[107] *See* Law No. 5718 of 27 November 2007 adopting the Turkish Code of Private International Law and International Civil Procedure. For the previous codification of 1982, *see* Law No. 2675 of Nov. 22, 1982, on Private International Law and Procedure.

[108] *See* Private International Law Act of 4 July 2007, effective on 19 July 2008, of the Former Yugoslav Republic of Macedonia.

[109] *See* Or. Rev. Stat. §§ 15.400–15.460, effective 1 January 2010 (codifying choice of law for tort conflicts). For the 2001 codification for contract conflicts, *see* note 96, *supra*.

[110] *See* Act Governing the Application of Laws in Civil Matters Involving Foreign Elements, promulgated on 26 May 2010, effective on 26 May 2011.

[111] *See* Statute of Application of Law to Foreign Civil Relations, adopted at the 17th session of the Standing Committee of the 11th National People's Congress on 28 October 2010, effective 1 April 2011.

[112] *See* Law No. 10428 of 2 July 2011 on Private International Law.

[113] *See* arts. 13-62 of the Civil Code of East Timor, enacted by Law No. 10/2011 of 14 September 2011 approving the Civil Code.

[114] *See* Act of 19 May 2011 adopting and implementing Book 10 (Private International Law) of the Dutch Civil Code, Bulletin of Acts and Decrees 2011, 272; Decree of 28 June 2011 fixing the time of entry into force of the Adoption and Implementation Act of Book 10, Bulletin of Acts and Decrees 2011, 340.

[115] *See* Act of Private International Law of 4 February 2011, Ustawa z dnia 4 lutego 2011 r. Prawo prywatne międzynarodowe, Dz U. z dnia 15 kwiethnia 2011 r. nr 80, poz. 432.

[116] *See* Law No. 91 of 25 January 2012 on Private International Law, effective 1 January 2014.

At the time of this writing in 2013, codification or re-codification projects were under-way in other countries, including Argentina,[117] Puerto Rico,[118] Serbia,[119] Uruguay,[120] Israel,[121] Mexico,[122] and Montenegro.[123] The drafts of the first four jurisdictions are suf-ficiently final and are discussed in this book.

2. The Numbers

Altogether—and without counting the EU Regulations that are listed later—the last 50 years have produced 94 national (or in some instances, sub-national) codifications or re-codifications (Charts 1.2 and 1.3). This averages to a rate of almost two codifications per year (1.88).

The 94 codifications or recodifications were adopted in 84 states. The two counts do not match because the first count includes:

(1) Four codifications that were replaced by subsequent re-codifications in Albania (1964 and 2011), Poland (1965 and 2011), Turkey (1982 and 2007), and the Soviet Union/Russia (1991 and 2002).[124]

---

[117] *See* Anteproyecto de Código Civil y Commercial de la Nación (2012) by Commicion de Reformas decreto presidencial 191/2011, arts. 2594–2671.

[118] *See* Academia Puertorriqueña de Jurisprudencia y Legislacion, *Proyecto para la Codificación del Derecho inter-nacional privado de Puerto Rico* (S. Symeonides & A. von Mehren, Rapporteurs, 1991). For a revised ver-sion pending before the Puerto Rico legislature as Book VII of the proposed new Puerto Rico Civil Code, *see* Proyecto de Ley para la Revisión y Reforma del Código Civil De Puerto Rico, Libro Séptimo (Derecho Internacional Privado), por Symeon Symeonides, 25 de mayo 2002, *available at* http://www.codigocivilpr. net/. Hereinafter, all references are to the revised version.

[119] *See* Serbian Ministry of Justice Draft of 20 July 2012 on Private International Law Code, *available at* http:// arhiva.mpravde.gov.rs/cr/news/vesti/zakon-o-medjunarodnom-privatnom-pravu-radna-verzija.html. For discussion, *see* Council of Europe (C. Jessel-Holst & R. Farrugia), Opinion on the Draft Private International Law Code of the Republic of Serbia (22 October 2012) *available at* http://arhiva.mpravde.gov.rs/cr/news/ vesti/zakon-o-medjunarodnom- privatnom-pravu-radna-verzija.html; M. Stanivuković & M. Zivković, *International Encyclopaedia of Laws: Private International Law - Serbia* (2008).

[120] *See* Proyecto de Ley General de Derecho Internacional Privado, 19.1.2009 (Draft General Law of Private International Law of 19 January 2009), *available at* http://www.parlamento. gub.uy/indexdb/Repartidos/ ListarRepartido.asp?Id=6052.

[121] *See* Einhorn, *Israeli Report*; T. Einhorn, *Private International Law in Israel* (2009); A. Levontin, *Choice of Law: A Model Statute and Detailed Commentary* (2nd ed.1998) (in Hebrew); C. Fassberg, Problems in the Codification of Private International Law in Israel, in A. Rabello (ed.), *European Legal Traditions and Israel: Essays on Legal History, Civil Law and Codification, European Law, Israeli Law* 531 (1994); R. Schuz, Choice of Law in Relation to Matrimonial Property: The Existing Law and Proposals for Reform, 16 *Bar-Ilan Law Studies* 425 (2001) (in Hebrew); R. Schuz, On the "Closest Connection" Approach in Israeli Private International Law, in A. Barak et al. (eds.), *Moznei Mishpat: Essays in Honor of Avner H. Shaki* 349 (2005) (in Hebrew); K. Siehr, A Statute on Private International Law for Israel, in A. Kellermann, et al. (eds.), *Israel among the Nations: International and Comparative Law Perspectives on Israel's 50th Anniversary* 353 (1998).

[122] *See* D. Fernández Arroyo, What's New in Latin American Private International Law? 7 *Ybk. Priv. Int'l L.* 85, 100–104 (2005). For existing and proposed codifications in Latin America in general, *see* D. Fernández Arroyo, *La codificación del derecho internacional privado en América Latina* (1994).

[123] *See* M. Kostič-Mandič, M. Stanivuković & M. Živković, *International Encyclopaedia of Laws: Private International Law –Montenegro* (2010).

[124] This book discusses only the four re-codifications.

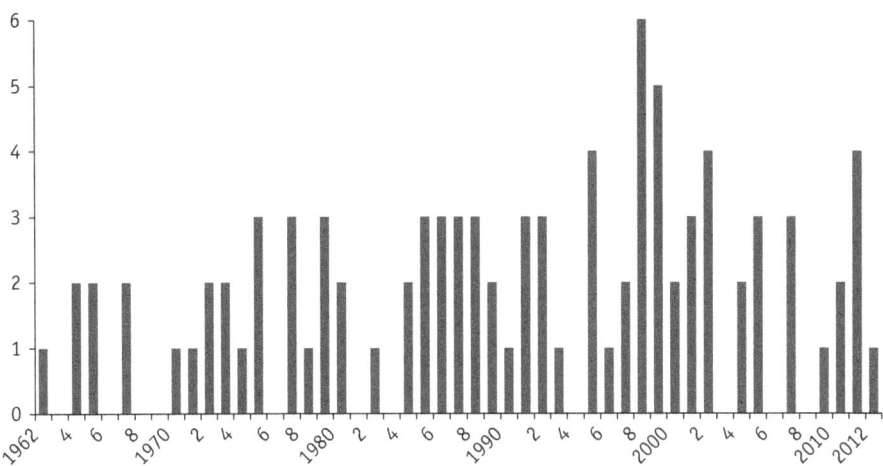

CHART I.2. Choice-of-Law Codifications 1962–2012—Chronology

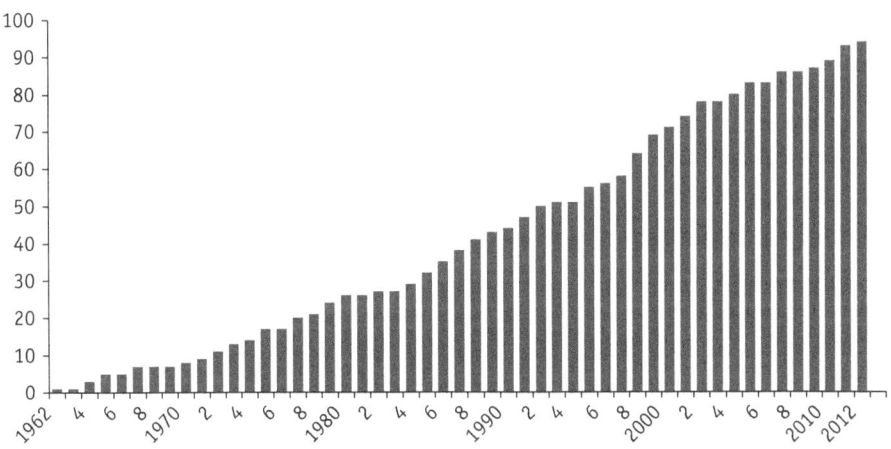

CHART I.3. Choice-of-Law Codifications, 1962–2012—Cumulative

(2) One partial codification in the Netherlands (the 2001 statute for torts), which was followed by a comprehensive codification in 2011;[125]

(3) Three partial codifications in China (1985, 1987, and 1999), which were followed by a comprehensive codification in 2010;[126] and

(4) Two complementary partial codifications in Germany (1986 and 1999) and two in Oregon (2001 and 2009).[127]

---

[125] This book discusses the 2011 codification (referred to as the "Dutch codif."), and occasionally the 2001 torts statute (referred to as "the 2001 torts statute").

[126] This book discusses only the 2010 codification and refers to it as the "Chinese codif."

[127] This book treats the two partial codifications as one and refers to them as the "German codif." and the "Oregon codif.," respectively.

In 1990, two of the above 84 states ceased to exist: (a) the former German Democratic Republic (East Germany) was absorbed by the Federal Republic of Germany; and (b) the former Arab Republic of Yemen (North Yemen) merged with the People's Democratic Republic of Yemen (South Yemen) to form the Republic of Yemen, the present-day Yemen. This book does not discuss the codifications of the former East Germany and North Yemen.

The 1990s brought other rearrangements of the Eurasian map, which however, do not alter the list of the remaining codifications. Specifically:

(1) In 1991, the Soviet Union was dissolved and replaced by 15 new states, all but one of which (Turkmenistan) have since enacted new choice-of-law codifications.[128] This book discusses all 14 codifications, including the 2002 Russian codification, but not the 1991 Soviet codification.

(4) Beginning in 1991, Yugoslavia was divided into its six former constituent republics. Since then, Slovenia and FYROM have enacted their own codifications, and Serbia is in the final stages of doing likewise. This book discusses these two codifications, as well as the Serbian draft. Today, the old Yugoslav codification of 1978–1982 remains in force in Bosnia-Herzegovina, Croatia, Montenegro, and Serbia. To avoid over-counting, this book treats the four versions as one and cites only to the Croatian version.

(5) With the 1993 split of the former Czechoslovakia, the 1964 codification remained in force in both the Czech Republic and in Slovakia, subject to different amendments in the two countries. In 2012, the Czech Republic enacted a new codification, effective on January 1, 2014. This book discusses the Slovak continuation of the 1964 codification and the new Czech codification.

Altogether, this book discusses the codifications of 82 extant states, as well as four draft codifications that are in final form—those of Argentina, Puerto Rico, Serbia, and Uruguay.

3. Geographical Distribution

Map 1.1 shows the geographical distribution of the 82 codifications and the four drafts adopted during the period 1962–2012.

As one would expect, virtually all of these codifications come from countries that belong, or aspire to belong, to the civil law tradition, a mixed tradition, or at least a tradition of statutory law. This is certainly true of the European codifications (including those from the former soviet republics and the formerly communist-controlled countries of Eastern Europe), and the codifications of Latin America, Quebec, and Louisiana. It is also true of the Asian codifications, and even the African codifications, virtually all of which

---

[128] The 15 new states are: Armenia, Azerbaijan, Belarus, Estonia, Georgia, Kazakhstan, Kyrgyzstan, Latvia, Lithuania, Moldova, Russia, Tajikistan, Turkmenistan, Ukraine, and Uzbekistan.

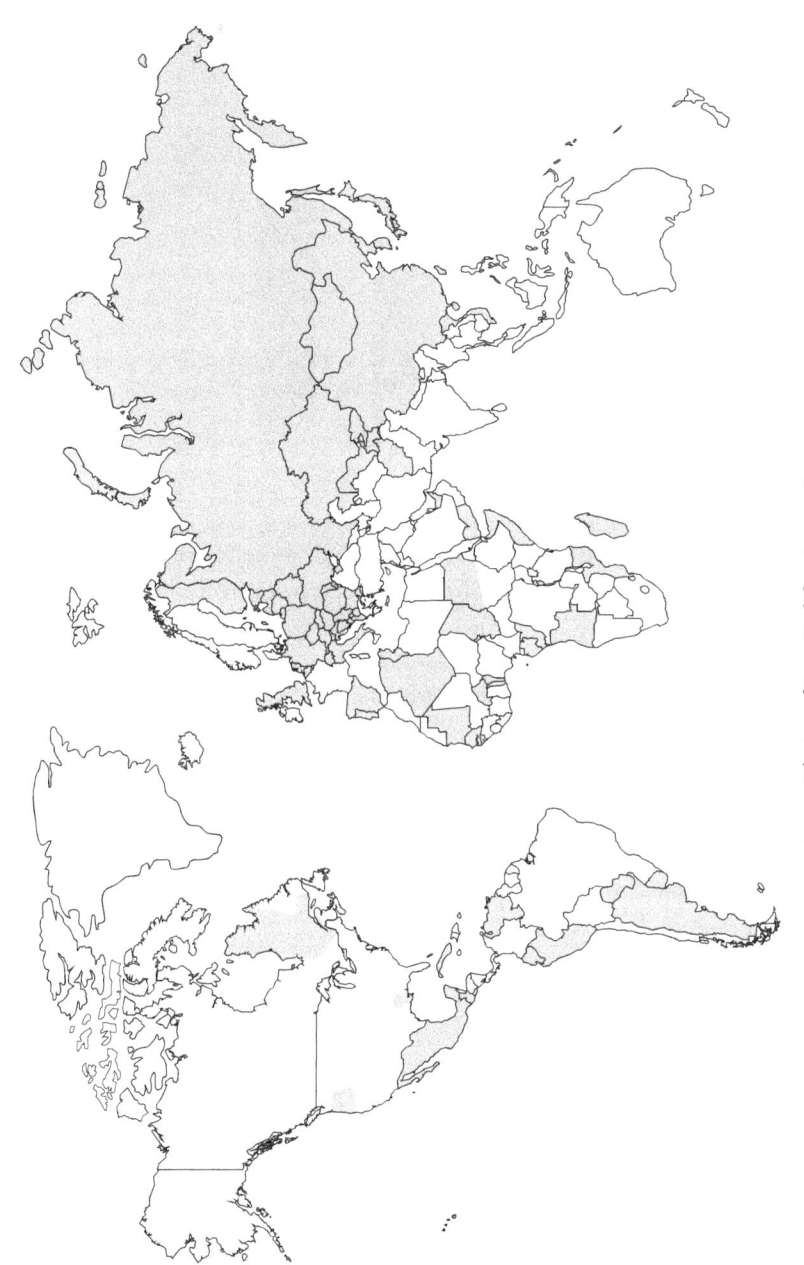

MAP 1.1. Choice-of-Law Codifications, 1962–2012

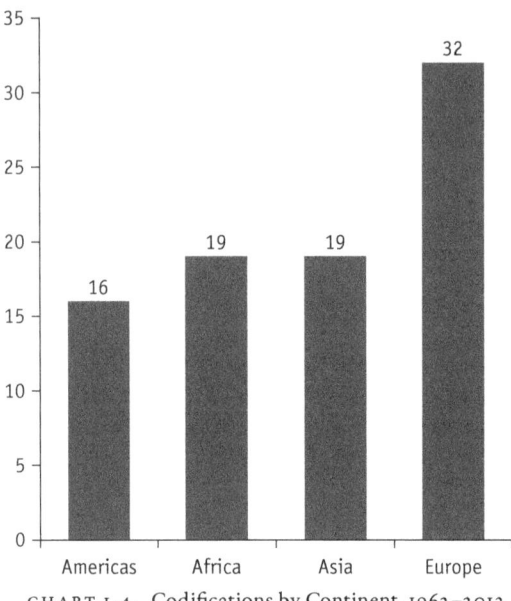

CHART 1.4. Codifications by Continent, 1962–2012

come from former colonies of civil-law countries.[129] The only exceptions are: (a) the 1995 English statute, which covers only tort conflicts and is superseded by Rome II;[130] (b) the Finnish statutes, which cover marriage, matrimonial property, and succession matters;[131] and (c) the Oregon codification, which covers tort and contract conflicts.[132]

Perhaps unsurprisingly, Europe has produced the highest number of codifications, a total of 31, plus one draft,[133] followed by Asia and Africa with 19,[134] and the Americas with 13 codifications and three drafts (Chart 1.4) (Table 1.1).

A perusal of the European map (Map 1.2) shows how deeply rooted the codification movement is in that continent, even without including countries such as France and Greece, which enacted their codifications before the period covered in this book. Of the 32 European codifications discussed here:

- Ten come from former Soviet republics (Armenia, Azerbaijan, Belarus, Estonia, Georgia, Latvia, Lithuania, Moldova, Russia, and Ukraine);
- Four come from former Yugoslav republics (Croatia, FYROM, Serbia, and Slovenia);[135]

---

[129] The only exception is Sudan, which was under British control from 1899 to 1956.

[130] See supra notes 16–17.

[131] See supra note 60.

[132] See supra notes 96, 109.

[133] This count does not include the 1975 East German codification, and the numerous EU Regulations.

[134] The Asian count does not include the 1979 codification of the former North Yemen.

[135] This book does not discuss the Bosnian and Montenegrin versions of the old Yugoslav codification because they are essentially identical to the Croatian version.

TABLE I.I. CODIFICATIONS BY CONTINENT

Africa	Asia	Europe	Americas
Madagascar-1962	Afghanistan-1977	Albania-1964 & 2011	Ecuador-1970
Centr. Afric.	Jordan-1977	Czechoslovakia-1964	Peru-1984
Rep.-1965	U. Arab Emir.-1985	Poland-1965 & 2011	Paraguay-1985
Chad-1967	Yemen-1992	Portugal-1967	Costa Rica-1986
Sudan-1971	North Korea-1995	Spain-1974	El Salvador-1986
Gabon-1972	Vietnam-1995	Hungary-1979	Cuba-1987
Senegal-1972	Uzbekistan-1997	Yugoslavia-1978-83	Mexico-1988
Guinea-Bissau-1973	Kyrgyzstan-1998	Austria-1979	Guatemala-1989
Somalia-1973	Kazakhstan-1999	Germany-1986 & 1999	Louisiana-1991
Algeria-1975	Macau-1999	Switzerland-1987	Quebec-1991
Mozambique-1975	South Korea-2001	Finland-1988	Panama-1992–94
Angola-1977	Mongolia-2002	USSR-1991, Russia-2002	Venezuela-1998
Burundi-1980	Qatar-2004	Romania-1992	Oregon-2001 &
Togo-1980	Tajikistan-2005	Latvia-1993	2009
Congo-Braz. 1984	Japan-2007	United Kingdom-1995	- - - - - - - - - - - -
Rwanda-1988	Turkey-1982 & 2007	Italy-1995	Drafts
Mauritania-1989	Taiwan-2010	Liechtenstein-1996	Puerto Rico-1991,
Burkina Faso-1990	China-1985, 1987	Armenia-1998	2002
Cape Verde-1997	1999 & 2010	Belarus-1998	Uruguay-2009
Tunisia-1998	East Timor-2011	Georgia-1998	Argentina-2011
		Slovenia-1999	
		Azerbaijan-2000	
		Lithuania-2000	
		Estonia-2002	
		Moldova-2002	
		Belgium-2004	
		Bulgaria-2005	
		Ukraine-2005	
		FYROM-2007	
		Netherlands-2001 &	
		2011	
		Czech Republic-2012	
		- - - - - - - - - - - - - - -	
		Drafts	
		Serbia-2012	
19	19	31+1draft	13+3 drafts

- Two come from the split of the former Czechoslovakia (Czech Republic and Slovakia); and
- Five come from other countries of the former communist bloc (Albania, Bulgaria, Hungary, Poland, and Romania).

MAP 1.2. European Codifications, 1962–2012

Thus, 21 of the 32 European codifications come from countries of the former communist bloc, an area that previously had only seven choice-of-law codifications, those of Albania (1964), Czechoslovakia (1964), East Germany (1975), Hungary (1987), Poland (1965), the Soviet Union (1991), and Yugoslavia (1978–1982)(Table 1.2).

Twenty of the 32 European codifications belong to countries that now are members of the European Union.[136] Fourteen of the 20 countries had adopted their codifications

---

[136] The 20 countries and the years they became members are: Austria (1995), Belgium (1952), Bulgaria (2007), Croatia (2013), Czech Republic (2004), Estonia (2004), Finland (1995), Germany (1952), Hungary (2004), Italy (1952), Latvia (2004), Lithuania (2004), Netherlands (1952), Portugal (1987), Poland (2004), Romania (2007), Slovakia (2004), Slovenia (2004), Spain (1987), and the United Kingdom (1973).

TABLE 1.2. EUROPEAN CODIFICATIONS

European Union Member States (20)		Non-EU Countries (12)	
	Former Soviet Sphere		
Austria	Bulgaria	Albania	Switzerland
Belgium	Croatia	Armenia	Liechtenstein
Finland	Czech Republic	Azerbaijan	
Germany	Estonia	Belarus	
Italy	Hungary	FYROM	
Netherlands	Latvia	Georgia	
Portugal	Lithuania	Moldova	
Spain	Poland	Russia	
United Kingdom	Romania	Serbia	
	Slovakia	Ukraine	
	Slovenia		
9	11	10	2

before,[137] and six after,[138] joining the EU or its predecessor entities. All 20 codifications are preempted with respect to certain conflicts that are covered by EU Regulations, such as tort, contract, and succession conflicts.[139] Nevertheless, because of their historical and methodological significance, these codifications are part of the raw material for this book.

Of the 19 Asian codifications, five belong to former soviet republics (Georgia, Kazakhstan, Kyrgyzstan, Tajikistan, and Uzbekistan), and one to a previously soviet-controlled country (Mongolia), but all of them were enacted after the respective countries gained their independence (Map 1.3). In contrast, the codifications of the former Portuguese colonies of East Timor and Macau were copies of the Portuguese codification of 1967, although their force was renewed by acts passed shortly before the transfer of sovereignty to China in the case of Macau,[140] and after independence in the case of East Timor.

---

[137] These are the codifications of: Austria (1979), Bulgaria (2005), Croatia (1982), Czech Republic (1964), Estonia (2002), Finland (1988), Hungary (1979), Latvia (1993), Lithuania (2000), Portugal (1967), Romania (1992), Slovakia (1964), Slovenia (1999), and Spain (1974).

[138] These are the codifications of Belgium (2004), Germany (1986 & 1999), Italy (1995), Netherlands (2011), Poland (2011), and the United Kingdom. (1995).

[139] *See infra* III, this chapter.

[140] *See* G. Tu, *Macau Report,* at I.

MAP 1.3. Asian Codifications, 1962–2012

All of the 19 African countries that have adopted choice-of-law codifications during the last 50-year period were former European colonies. Fifteen of those countries adopted their codifications after gaining independence.[141] In contrast, the codifications of Angola, Cape Verde, Guinea-Bissau, and Mozambique were copies of the Portuguese codification of 1967, which was introduced in the then Portuguese colonies. However, all four of these former Portuguese colonies renewed the force of this codification in their territories after gaining their independence (Map 1.4).

---

[141] Ten of those countries gained their independence in 1960 and enacted their codifications in the years shown in parentheses: Madagascar (1962), Central African Republic (1965), Chad (1967), Gabon (1972), Senegal (1972), Somalia (1973), and Togo (1980). Three of those countries gained independence in 1962 and adopted their codifications in the year shown in parentheses: Algeria (1975), Burundi (1980), and Rwanda (1980). Sudan and Tunisia gained their independence in 1956 and enacted their choice-of-law codifications in 1972 and 1998, respectively. Interestingly, Tunisia was one of the first countries to gain independence, yet it was the last to enact such a codification. However, the Tunisian codification is the most complete of the African codifications.

MAP 1.4. African Codifications, 1962–2012

The Americas map (Map 1.5) shows fewer codifications than the continents depicted in the previous three maps. The reasons are obvious. Much of the territory of North America belongs to the United States and Canada, where, with few exceptions, the codification movement has never taken root. As for Latin America, the map can be misleading unless the viewer remembers that it only covers the period *after* 1962, whereas most Latin American countries had adopted their codifications before that year. In fact, with the exception of the Peruvian and to a lesser extent the Paraguayan codifications, the other Latin American codifications adopted after 1962 consist of rather minor revisions of traditional Civil Code provisions derived from the Bustamante Code. In contrast, the two new draft codifications of Argentina and Uruguay are both comprehensive and modern.

4. Placement, Length, and Scope

Almost all of the choice-of-law codifications of the previous generation were part of a Civil Code, and were usually placed in the code's introductory part. In contrast, as Table 1.3 below indicates, this tradition is changing. Of the 86 codifications (including four final drafts) produced in the last 50 years:[142]

- A slight plurality of 42 form part of a civil code, and many of them are placed at the end rather than the beginning of the code;

---

[142] This count includes three draft codifications that are designed as parts of a civil code—those of Argentina, Puerto Rico, and Uruguay—and one draft (Serbia), which will be a freestanding statute. It does not include the codifications of the former East Germany and the former North Yemen, both of which were freestanding statutes.

MAP 1.5. Codifications in the Americas, 1962–2012

- Eight codifications form part of another code, such as a Family Code, which inter alia means that their choice-of-law rules are limited to the subject matter of that code; and
- The remaining 36 codifications are freestanding statutes.

Most of the latter codifications are quite comprehensive, covering not only choice of law but also jurisdiction and recognition of foreign judgments. In contrast, the codifications that form part of a civil code—several of which are also comprehensive—usually do not include rules on jurisdiction and recognition of judgments, because these rules usually are contained in civil procedure codes or other statutes.

TABLE 1.3. PLACEMENT OF CHOICE-OF-LAW CODIFICATIONS

Codification	In Civil Code	In Other Code	Free standing
Afghanistan (1977)	X		
Albania (1964 & 2011)			X
Algeria (1975)			X
Angola (1977)	X		
Argentina (draft 2012)	X		
Armenia (1998)	X		
Austria (1979)			X
Azerbaijan (2000)			X
Belarus (1998)	X		
Belgium (2004)			X
Bulgaria (2005)			X
Burkina Faso (1990)		Family Code	
Burundi (1980)		Persons Code	
Cape Verde (1997)	X		
Central African Republic (1965)			X
Chad (1967)		Judicial Org.	
China (1987, 85, 99, 2010)			X
Costa Rica (1986)	X		
Congo-Brazzaville (1984)		Family Code	
Croatia (former Yugoslav codif.)			X
Cuba (1987)	X		
Czech Republic (2012)			X
East Timor (2011)	X		
Ecuador (1970)	X		
El Salvador (1986)	X		
Estonia (2002)			X
Finland (1988)			X
FYROM (2007)			X
Gabon (1972)	X		
Georgia (1998)			X
Germany (1986 & 1999)	X		
Guatemala (1989)		Judicial Org.	
Guinea-Bissau (1973)	X		
Hungary (1979)			X
Italy (1995)			X

Codification	In Civil Code	In Other Code	Free standing
Japan (2007)			X
Jordan (1977)	X		
Kazakhstan (1999)	X		
Korea, North (1995)			X
Korea, South (2001)			X
Kyrgyzstan (1998)	X		
Latvia (1993)	X		
Liechtenstein (1996)			X
Lithuania (2000)	X		
Louisiana (1991)	X		
Macau (1999)	X		
Madagascar (1962)			X
Mauritania (1989)		Oblig.& Contr.	
Mexico (1988)	X		
Moldova (2002)	X		
Mongolia (2002)	X		
Mozambique (1975)	X		
Netherlands (2011)	X		
Oregon (2001 & 2009)			X
Panama (1992-94)	X		
Paraguay (1985)	X		
Peru (1984)	X		
Poland (1965 & 2011)			X
Portugal (1967)	X		
Puerto Rico (draft 1991, 2002)	X		
Qatar (2004)	X		
Quebec (1991)	X		
Romania (1992)			X
Russia (2002)	X		
Rwanda (1988)	X		
Senegal (1972)		Family Code	
Serbia (draft 2012)			X
Slovakia (Czechoslov. 1964)			X
Slovenia (1999)			X
Somalia (1973)	X		
Spain (1974)	X		
Sudan (1971)	X		

Codification	In Civil Code	In Other Code	Free standing
Switzerland (1987)			X
Taiwan (2010)			X
Tajikistan (2005)	X		
Togo (1980)		Family Code	
Tunisia (1998)			X
Turkey (1982 & 2007)			X
Ukraine (2005)			X
United Arab Emirates (1985)	X		
United Kingdom (1995)			X
Uruguay (draft 2009)			X
Uzbekistan (1997)	X		
Venezuela (1998)			X
Vietnam (1995)	X		
Yemen (1992)			X
Totals (86)	42	8	36

In this book, all of these codifications are referred to as "codifications" regardless of their formal designation, such as a PIL Act, statute, decree, ordinance, etc.,[143] and regardless of whether:

(a) they are freestanding "codes" or statutes or whether they form part of another code, such as a civil code;

(b) they cover only choice of law,[144] or also jurisdiction and judgment recognition; or

(c) they cover choice of law for only certain subjects.[145]

Some of these codifications (especially in Africa and Latin America) are quite brief, consisting of fewer than 20 articles, while others are quite long, consisting of nearly 200 articles. To be sure, the number of articles is not always a reliable measure of a codification's length, if only because some articles are long while others are short. Nevertheless, the number of articles is roughly indicative of a codification's comprehensiveness.

Be that as it may, the codification with the highest number of articles is that of Switzerland, which consists of 200 articles, while the codification with the fewest articles is that of Mauritania, which consists of six articles. Table 1.4 below shows the 15 codifications with the highest and the lowest number of articles (indicated in parentheses).

---

[143] Hereinafter, these codifications are referred to with the country of origin and the abbreviation "codif."

[144] The codifications that are placed in a civil code usually cover only choice of law.

[145] For example, the UK codification covers only torts other than defamation; the Oregon codification covers only torts and contracts; the Finish codification covers only marriage, marital property, and succession; and the codifications of Burkina Faso, Burundi, Congo-Brazzaville, Senegal, and Togo cover only family law and personal status.

TABLE 1.4. CODIFICATIONS WITH THE HIGHEST AND LOWEST NUMBER OF ARTICLES

Highest				Lowest
Switzerland (200)				Somalia (19)
Serbia draft (196)				U.A.E (17)
Romania (182)				Ecuador (17)
Netherlands (165)				Panama (11+6)
Belgium (140)				Rwanda (16)
Bulgaria (124)				El Salvador (16)
Czech Rep. (124)				Madagascar (15)
FYROM (124)				Chad (13)
Slovenia (119)				Guatemala (12)
Croatia (108)				Mexico (12)
Quebec (93)				Sudan (12 equiv.)
Albania (89)				Burundi (11)
Ukraine (82)				Cuba (11)
Poland (81)				Costa Rica (8)
Argentina draft (78)				Mauritania (6)

III. European Union Conventions and Regulations

The period covered by this book coincides with the period during which what is now known as the European Union (EU) grew from a loose association of six states to a tight union of 28 Member States. Although technically the EU is not a federation, it has been acting like one, producing an avalanche of Regulations and Directives on PIL matters. Several authors have described this phenomenon as a federalization,[146] Europeanization,[147] or communitarization[148] of PIL amounting to a virtual

---

[146] See J. Heymann, *Le droit international privé à l'épreuve du fédéralisme européen* (2010); H. Muir-Watt, European Federalism and the "New Unilateralism," 82 *Tul. L. Rev.* 1983 (2008); A. Mills, Federalism in the European Union and the United States: Subsidiarity, Private Law, and the Conflict of Laws, 32 *U. Pa. J. Int'l L.* 369 (2010). *Cf.* J. Basedow, Federal Choice of Law in Europe and the United States: A Comparative Account of Interstate Conflicts, 82 *Tul. L. Rev.* 2119 (2008).

[147] See P. Lagarde & B. von Hoffmann (eds.), *L'européisation du droit international privé—Die Europäisierung des internationalen Privatrechts—The Europeanisation of International Private Law* (1996); K. Boele-Woelki, For Better or for Worse: The Europeanization of International Divorce Law, 12 *Ybk. Priv. Int'l L.* 1 (2010); A. Dutta, Succession and Wills in the Conflict of Laws on the Eve of Europeanisation, 73 *RabelsZ* 547 (2009); A. Fiorini, The Codification of Private International Law in Europe: Could the Community Learn from the Experience of Mixed Jurisdictions? 23 *Tul. Eur. Civ. L.F.* 89 (2008); J. Harris, Understanding the English Response to the Europeanisation of Private International Law, 43 *J. Priv. Int'l L.* 347 (2008); H. Muir Watt & G. Canivet, Européanisation du droit privé et justice sociale, 13 *Zeitschrift für Europäisches Privatrecht* 517 (2005); S. Nott, For Better or Worse? The Europeanisation of the Conflict of Laws, 24 *Liverpool L. Rev.* 3 (2002).

[148] See K. Boele-Woelki, The Communitarization of Private International Law, 4 *Ybk. Priv. Int'l L.* 1 (2002); K. Boele-Woelki, Unification and Harmonization of Private International Law in Europe, in J. Basedow et al. (eds.), *Private Law in the International Arena: Liber Amicorum Kurt Siehr* 61 (2000); R. Fentiman, Choice of Law in Europe: Uniformity and Integration, 82 *Tul. L. Rev.* 2021 (2008); M. Harding, The Harmonisation

revolution.[149] To be sure, the term "revolution" is always hyperbolic when used for any field of law, especially one as esoteric as choice of law is reputed to be. Even so, one may question whether the increasing federalization of European PIL possesses some of the essential attributes of a revolution, if only because it is a top-down movement, methodically planned and gradually implemented by the EU's lawmaking institutions.[150] What is beyond question, however, is that this movement is massive and as permanent as the Union hopes to be.[151] What is now known as "EU PIL" was virtually nonexistent three decades ago. Now it is the fastest-growing body of PIL in history.[152]

---

of Private International Law in Europe: Taking the Character Out of Family Law?, 7 *J. Priv. Int'l L.* 203 (2011); C. Kessedjian, Le passé et l'avenir du droit international privé européen dans le cadre de l'intégration de l'Union européene, 4 *Rev. des affaires européennes* 411 (2001–2002). *See also* H-P. Mansel, K. Thorn & R. Wagner, European Conflict of Laws: Progressing Process of Codification—Patchwork of Uniform Law, *IPRax* 1 (2013); H. Sonnenberger, Europarecht und Internationales Privatrecht, 95 *Zeitschrift für Vergleichende Rechtswissenschaften* 3 (1996); A.V.M. Struycken, Les consequences de l'intégration européenne sur le développement du droit international privé, 232 *Recueil des cours* 257 (1992-I).

[149] R. Michaels, The New European Choice-of-Law Revolution, 82 *Tul. L. Rev.* 1607 (2008); J. Meeusen, Instrumentalisation of Private International Law in the European Union: Towards a European Conflicts Revolution?, 9 *Eur. J. Migr. & L.* 287 (2007); Symposium, The New European Choice-of-Law Revolution: Lessons for the United States, 82 *Tul. L. Rev.* 1607 (2008); F. Pocar, The Communitarization of Private International Law: A "European Conflict of Laws Revolution"? 26 *Riv. dir. Int'l priv. e proc.* 873 (2000).

[150] *See* Symeonides, *Reciprocal Lessons*, 1742–1743. In contrast, the phenomenon known as the American choice-of-law revolution was a grassroots scholastic, and then judicial, rebellion intent on abruptly and completely demolishing rather than reforming the traditional system. *See* Symeonides, *Revolution*.

[151] The author can speak from some firsthand experience, after spending six months in Brussels chairing five PIL working groups of the EU Council.

[152] One small indication of the growth rate of this body of law is the number of *general books* published in the last few years on this subject. The following is an illustrative list. It does not include books dealing specifically with the Brussels I, Rome I, or Rome II regulations (*see infra*); nor does it include *articles*, which are simply too numerous to list. *See* S. Bariatti, *Cases and Materials on EU Private International Law* (2011); M. Bogdan, *Concise Introduction to EU Private International Law* (2012); M. Bogdan & U. Maunsbach, *EU Private International Law: An ECJ Casebook* (2012); B. Campuzano Diaz, M. Czepelak, A. Rodriguez Benot & A. Rodriguez Vazquez (eds.), *Latest Developments in EU Private International Law* (2011); P. De Cesari, *Diritto internazionale privato dell'unione europea* (2011); M. Fallon, P. Kinsch & C. Kohler (eds.), *Building European Private International Law: Twenty Years' Work by GEDIP* (2011); R. Fentiman, et al. (eds.), *L'espace judiciaire européen en matière civile et commerciale—The European Judicial Area in Civil and Commercial Matters* (1999); I.F. Fletcher, *Conflict of Laws and European Community Law* (1982); A. Fuchs et al. (eds.), *Les conflits de lois et le système juridique communautaire* (2004); P. Hommelhoff et al. (eds.), *Europäisches Binnenmarkt, IPR und Rechtsangleichung* (1995); E. Jayme, *Ein Internationales Privatrecht für Europa* (1991); E. Jayme, *Ein Internationales Privatrecht für Europa* (1991); S. Klauer, *Das europäische Kollisionsrecht der Verbrauchervetäge zwischen Römer EVÜ und EG-Richtlinien* (2002); J-J. Kuipers, *EU Law and Private International Law: The Interrelationship in Contractual Obligations* (2011); J. Lookofsky & K. Hertz, *EU-PIL: European Union Private International Law in Contract and Tort* (2009); U. Magnus, *European Commentaries on Private International Law* (2007); A. Malatesta, S. Bariatti & F. Pocar, *The External Dimension of EC Private International Law in Family and Succession Matters* (2008); J. Meeusen et al. (eds.), *Enforcement of International Contracts in the European Union: Convergence and Divergence between Brussels I and Rome I* (2004); J. Meeusen, M. Pertegás, G. Straetmans & F. Swennen (eds.), *International Family Law for the European Union* (2007); R. Nickel,

This movement accelerated when, following the revisions of the relevant treaties, the EU acquired competence directly to legislate on PIL matters and to act through "Regulations" rather than conventions.[153] Thus, the 1968 Brussels Convention,[154] later supplemented by the parallel Lugano Convention in 1988,[155] was replaced by the Brussels I Regulation in 2001,[156] which in turn was "recast" again in 2012.[157]

In the meantime, Brussels I acquired two siblings: (a) Brussels II (2003), which covers jurisdiction and judgment recognition in matrimonial matters and matters of parental responsibility;[158] and (b) the Maintenance Regulation (2008), which covers jurisdiction, choice of law, and judgment recognition in maintenance matters.[159]

Conflict of Laws and Laws of Conflict in Europe and Beyond: Patterns of Supranational and Transnational Juridification (2010); A. Philip, *EU-IP. Europæisk international privat- og procesret* (2nd ed. 1994); P. Picone, *Diritto internazionale privato e diritto comunitario* (2004); P. Plender & M. Wilderspin, *The European Private International Law of Obligations* (3d ed. 2009); G. Reichelt (ed.), *Das Herkunftslandprinzip im europäischen Gemeinschaftsrecht* (2006); P. Stone, *EU Private International Law* (2d ed. 2012); G. van Calster, *European Private International Law* (2013); B. von Hoffmann (ed.), *European Private International Law* (1998); C. Von Bar (ed.), *Europäisches Gemeinschaftsrecht und Internationales Privatrecht* (1991). *See also* G. Badiali, Le droit international privé des Communautés européennes, 191 *Recueil des cours* 9 (1985).

[153] *See* Articles K1 and K3 of the Maastricht Treaty (Treaty on European Union or TEU) of February 1992; Article 65 of the Treaty of Amsterdam amending the Treaty of the European Union, signed on 2 October 1997, effective 1 May 1999; Article 81 of the Treaty of Lisbon (Treaty on the Functioning of the European Union, or TFEU), signed on 13 December 2007, effective on 1 December 2009. For discussion, *see* R. Baratta, Réflexions sur la coopération judiciaire civile suite au traité de Lisbonne, in *Nuovi strumenti del diritto internazionale privata: Liber Fausto Pocar*, 3 (2009); I. Barrière Brousse, Le traité de Lisbonne et le droit international privé, *Clunet* 1 (2010); P.E. Partsch, *Le droit international privé européenCDe Rome à Nice* (2003); G.R. Groot & J-J. Kuipers, The New Provisions on Private International Law in the Treaty of Lisbon, 15 *Maastricht J. Eur. & Comp. L.* 109 (2008). For the EU's external competence, *see* M. Wilderspin & A. Rouchaud-Joët, La compétence externe de la Communauté européenne en droit international privé, *Rev. critique DIP* 1 (2004).

[154] *See* Brussels Convention of 27 September 1968 on Jurisdiction and the Enforcement of Judgments in Civil and Commercial Matters, OJ [1990] C 189.

[155] *See* Convention on Jurisdiction and the Enforcement of Judgments in Civil and Commercial Matters, Done at Lugano on 16 September 1988, OJ [1988] L 319/9. In 2007, this Convention was replaced by the Lugano Convention of 30 October 2007 on Jurisdiction and the Recognition and Enforcement of Judgments in Civil and Commercial Matters, [2007] O.J. L 393/3. This convention, which essentially duplicates the provisions of the Brussels I Regulation, is in force in the EU on the one hand, and in Denmark, Iceland, Norway, and Switzerland, on the other hand.

[156] *See* European Community Council Regulation (EC) No. 44/2001 on Jurisdiction and the Recognition of Judgments in Civil and Commercial Matters, [2001] OJ L.12/1, effective 1 March 2002.

[157] *See* Regulation (EU) No 1215/2012 of the European Parliament and of the Council of 12 December 2012 on jurisdiction and the recognition and enforcement of judgments in civil and commercial matters (recast) OJ 20 December 2012, L 351/1, effective on 10 January 2015.

[158] *See* Council Regulation (EC) No 2201/2003 of 27 November 2003 concerning jurisdiction and the recognition and enforcement of judgments in matrimonial matters and the matters of parental responsibility, [2003] OJ L 338/1 (also known as "Brussels IIa" or "Brussels IIbis").

[159] *See* Council Regulation (EC) No 4/2009 of 18 December 2008 on Jurisdiction, Applicable Law, Recognition and Enforcement of Decisions and Cooperation in Matters Relating to Maintenance Obligations L 7/1 [2009] O.J. 10.1.2009, effective on 18 June 2011.

The 1980 EEC Convention on the Law Applicable to Contractual Obligations (Rome Convention)[160] entered into force in 1991; in 2008, it was converted into a Regulation known as "Rome I."[161] The Convention exercised widespread influence on the codifications of many countries outside the EU.[162]

In 2007, the much-anticipated (if not much-acclaimed) Regulation on the Law Applicable to Non-Contractual Application, known as Rome II, was promulgated.[163]

In 2010, we saw the enactment of Rome III, on the law applicable to divorce and legal separation[164] and, in 2012, the enactment of a Regulation on Successions, which will take effect on August 17, 2015, and will apply to the succession of persons who die on or after that date.[165]

In the intervening years, other Regulations have been enacted on subjects such as insolvency,[166] taking of evidence,[167] service of documents,[168] the European payment order,[169] small claims procedure,[170] and enforcement of uncontested claims.[171]

---

[160] Convention 80/934/ECC on the law applicable to contractual obligations opened for signature in Rome on 19 June 1980, OJ L 266, 9.10.1980, pp. 1–19. 23; Giuliano & Lagarde, Report to the Council, *id.* No. C 282/1 (1980).

[161] *See* Regulation (EC) No. 593/2008 of the European Parliament and of the Council of 17 June 2008 on the Law Applicable to Contractual Obligations (Rome I), [2008] OJ L 177/6.

[162] *See* Chapter 3, *infra*.

[163] *See* Regulation (EC) No. 864/2007 of the European Parliament and of the Council of 11 July 2007 on the Law Applicable to Non-Contractual Obligations (Rome II), [2007] OJ L 199/40.

[164] *See* Council Regulation (EU) No 1259/2010 of 20 December 2010 implementing enhanced cooperation in the area of the law applicable to divorce and legal separation (OJ L 343, p. 10 ff.) (2010). This regulation applies in the 15 Member States participating in "enhanced cooperation" (Belgium, Bulgaria, Germany, Spain, France, Italy, Latvia, Lithuania, Luxembourg, Hungary, Malta, Austria, Portugal, Romania and Slovenia).

[165] *See* Regulation (EU) No 650/2012 of the European Parliament and of the Council of 4 July 2012 on jurisdiction, applicable law, recognition and enforcement of decisions and acceptance and enforcement of authentic instruments in matters of succession, and on the creation of a European Certificate of Succession (OJ n. L 201, p. 107 ff.). This Regulation will go into effect on 17 August 2015, in all EU Member States, except Denmark, Ireland, and the United Kingdom.

[166] *See* Council Regulation (EC) No 1346/2000 of 29 May 2000 on Insolvency Proceedings, OJ L 160/1, 30.6.2000. On 12 December 2012, the EU Commission released a proposal for amending this regulation. *See* Proposal for a Regulation of the European Parliament and of the Council amending Council Regulation (EC) No 1346/2000 on insolvency proceedings, COM(2012) 744 final, 2012/0360 (COD).

[167] *See* Council Regulation (EC) No 1206/2001 of 28 May 2001 on Cooperation Between the Courts of the Member States in the Taking of Evidence in Civil or Commercial Matters, OJ L 174, 27.6.2001.

[168] *See* Regulation (EC) No 1393/2007 of the European Parliament and of the Council of 13 November 2007 on the Service in the Member States of Judicial and Extrajudicial Documents in Civil or Commercial Matters (Service of Documents), and Repealing Council Regulation (EC) No 1348/2000, OJ L 324/79, 10.12.2007.

[169] *See* Regulation (EC) No 1896/2006 of the European Parliament and of the Council of 12 December 2006 creating a European order for payment procedure, OJ L 399, 30.12.2006, pp. 1–32.

[170] *See* Regulation (EC) No 861/2007 of the European Parliament and of the Council of 11 July 2007 Establishing a European Small Claims Procedure, OJ L 199/1, 31.7.2007.

[171] *See* Regulation (EC) No 805/2004 of the European Parliament and of the Council of 21 April 2004 Creating a European Enforcement Order for Uncontested Claims, OJ L 143/15, 30.4.2004.

At the time of this writing in 2013, three new Regulations are in the drafting and negotiation stage. They cover cross-border freezing of bank accounts;[172] and jurisdiction, choice of law, and judgment recognition in Matrimonial Regimes and Registered Partnerships.[173] Moreover, discussion is underway about codifying the "general part" of European PIL.[174]

This book focuses only on the six Regulations that include choice-of-law provisions, namely: Rome I, II, and III, and the Regulations on Successions, Maintenance, and Insolvency. These regulations have displaced the corresponding provisions of several European national codifications on the same subjects. Nevertheless, for the purposes of this book—which is written from an educational and comparative perspective, rather than from a practitioner's perspective—the superseded provisions remain relevant and are therefore included.

IV. International Choice-of-Law Conventions

At the international level, the period since 1960 has been marked by the proliferation of international and regional PIL conventions, protocols, and other international instruments.[175] The period began slowly in the 1960s, with only seven conventions, including the Brussels Convention. They were followed by 27 conventions in the 1970s, 18 in the 1980s (including the Rome and Lugano conventions), 18 in the 1990s, and 19 since then (Chart 1.5).[176]

Since 1961, the Hague Conference of Private International Law has produced 28 PIL conventions and protocols. Twenty-two of those conventions are now in force.[177]

---

[172] See Proposal for a Regulation of the European Parliament and of the Council Creating a European Account Preservation Order to facilitate cross-border debt recovery in civil and commercial matters, COM/2011/0445 final - 2011/0204 (COD).

[173] See European Commission Proposal for a Council Regulation, on jurisdiction, applicable law and the recognition and enforcement of decisions in matters of matrimonial property regimes, Brussels, 16.3.2011, COM/2011/0126 final - CNS 2011/0059, available at http://eur lex. europa.eu/Result.do?T1=V5&T2=20 11&T3=126&RechType=RECH_naturel&Submit=Search; European Commission Proposal for a Council Regulation on jurisdiction, applicable law and the recognition and enforcement of decisions regarding the property consequences of registered partnerships, Brussels, 16.3.2011, COM/2011/0127 final - CNS 2011/0060, available at http://eur-lex.europa.eu/Result.do?T1=V5&T2=2011&T3=127&RechType=R ECH_naturel&Submit=Search.

[174] See S. Leible & M. Müller, A General Part for European Private International Law? The Idea of a "Rome 0 Regulation," 14 Ybk. Priv. Int'l L. 137 (2012–2013); L. De Lima Pinheiro, The Methodology and the General Part of the Portuguese Private International Law Codification: A Possible Source of Inspiration for the European Legislator?, 14 Ybk. Priv. Int'l L. 153 (2012–2013);. Muir Watt, A Semiotics of Private International Legal Argument, 14 Ybk. Priv. Int'l L. 51 (2012–2013).

[175] For a recent comprehensive report on this phenomenon, see I. M. Weiberg de Roca, Conflict of Laws Conventions and Their Reception, in G. Berman & J. Sanchez Cordero (eds.), The Impact of Uniform Law on National Law: Limits and Possibilities 273 (2010).

[176] This count does not include the EU Regulations adopted during the same period.

[177] The following is a chronological list of the 28 conventions. An asterisk (*) indicates that the convention is not in force: Convention of: 5 October 1961 Concerning the Powers of Authorities and the Law Applicable in Respect of the Protection of Infants; 5 October 1961 on the Conflicts of Laws Relating to the Form of Testamentary Dispositions; 5 October 1961 Abolishing the Requirement of Legalisation for Foreign Public

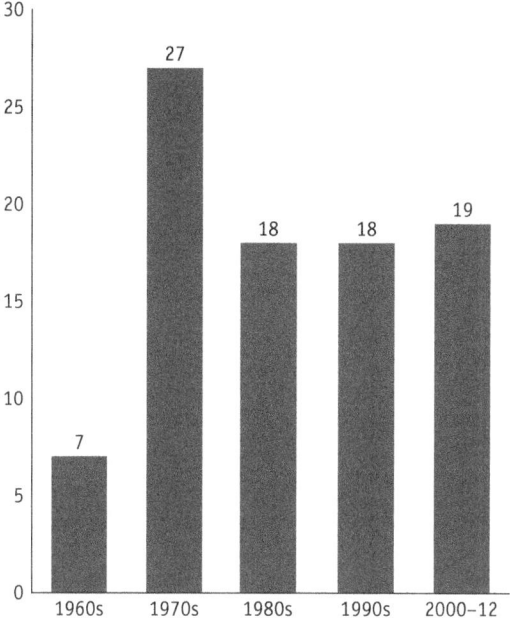

CHART 1.5. PIL Codifications and Protocols, 1962–2012

In addition, in November 2012, the Hague Conference has adopted a soft instrument, the Hague Principles on Choice of Law for International Contracts.[178]

Documents; 15 November 1965 on Jurisdiction, Applicable Law and Recognition of Decrees Relating to Adoptions; 15 November 1965 on the Service Abroad of Judicial and Extrajudicial Documents in Civil or Commercial Matters; 25 November 1965 on the Choice of Court (*); 1 February 1971 on the Recognition and Enforcement of Foreign Judgments in Civil and Commercial Matters; 1 June 1970 on the Recognition of Divorces and Legal Separations; 4 May 1971 on the Law Applicable to Traffic Accidents; 18 March 1970 on the Taking of Evidence Abroad in Civil or Commercial Matters; 2 October 1973 Concerning the International Administration of the Estates of Deceased Persons; 2 October 1973 on the Law Applicable to Products Liability; 2 October 1973 on the Recognition and Enforcement of Decisions Relating to Maintenance Obligations; 2 October 1973 on the Law Applicable to Maintenance Obligations; 14 March 1978 on the Law Applicable to Matrimonial Property Regimes; 14 March 1978 on Celebration and Recognition of the Validity of Marriages; 14 March 1978 on the Law Applicable to Agency; 25 October 1980 on the Civil Aspects of International Child Abduction; 25 October 1980 on International Access to Justice; 1 July 1985 on the Law Applicable to Trusts and on Their Recognition; 22 December 1986 on the Law Applicable to Contracts for the International Sale of Goods (*); 1 August 1989 on the Law Applicable to Succession to the Estates of Deceased Persons (*); 29 May 1993 on Protection of Children and Co-operation in Respect of Intercountry Adoption; 19 October 1996 on Jurisdiction, Applicable Law, Recognition, Enforcement and Co-operation in Respect of Parental Responsibility and Measures for the Protection of Children; 13 January 2000 on the International Protection of Adults; 5 July 2006 on the Law Applicable to Certain Rights in Respect of Securities held with an Intermediary (*); 30 June 2005 on Choice of Court Agreements (*); 23 November 2007 on the International Recovery of Child Support and Other Forms of Family Maintenance (*). For the texts of these conventions and the list of party-States, *see* the Conference's official website at http://www. hcch.net/index_en.php?act=conventions.listing.

178 *Available at* http://www.hcch.net/upload/wop/contracts2012principles_e.pdf; discussed in S. Symeonides, *The Hague Principles*.

During the same 50-year period, the Inter-American Specialized Conferences on Private International Law (known by its Spanish acronym, CIDIP[179]) has produced 26 Inter-American PIL conventions, protocols, and other instruments.[180]

Other international regional organizations have also produced conventions, protocols, and other international instruments bearing on choice of law. For example, the MERCOSUR countries (Mercado Común del Sur)[181] of Argentina, Brazil, Paraguay, Uruguay, and Venezuela[182] have produced several such instruments on jurisdiction,

---

[179] The full Spanish name is Conferencia Interamericana sobre Derecho Internacional Privado. The Conference is an arm of the General Assembly of the Organization of American States. For discussion, *see* D. Fernández Arroyo, *Derecho internacional privado interamericano: evolución y perspectivas* (2nd ed. 2003); D. Fernández Arroyo, *La codificación del Derecho internacional privado en América Latina* (1994); D. Fernández Arroyo, What's New in Latin American Private International Law?, 7 *Ybk. Priv. In'l L.* 85 (2005); D. Fernández Arroyo. & N. González Martín, *Tendencias y Relaciones Derecho Internacional Privado Americano Actual* (2010); D. Operetta Baden, The Relationships between Latin America and the Hague Conference regarding the Recent Developments of Private International Law, in *A Commitment to Private International Law: Essays in Honor of Hans Van Loon* 421 (2013); T. de Maekelt, La Codificación Interamericana en Material de Derecho Internacional Privado en el Contexto Universal y Regional, in *Libro Homenaje a Haroldo Valladao* 157 (1997); G. Parra-Aranguren, *Codificación del derecho internacional privado en America* (1998); A.M. Villela, L'unification du droit international privé en Amérique Latin, *Rev. critique DIP* 233 (1984).

[180] The Conference convenes approximately every four to six years under the auspices of the Organization of American States. In chronological order, the instruments adopted by the Conference are: (1) 1975: Inter-American Convention on Conflict of Laws concerning Bills of Exchange, Promissory Notes, and Invoices; Inter-American Convention on Conflict of Laws Concerning Checks; Inter-American Convention on International Commercial Arbitration; Inter-American Convention on Letters Rogatory; the Inter-American Convention on the Taking of Evidence Abroad; Inter-American Convention on the Legal Regime of Powers of Attorney to Be Used Abroad; (2) 1979: Inter-American Convention on Conflicts of Laws Concerning Checks; Inter-American Convention on Conflicts of Laws Concerning Commercial Companies; Inter-American Convention on Extraterritorial Validity of Foreign Judgments and Arbitral Awards; Inter-American Convention on Execution of Preventive Measures; Inter-American Convention on Proof and Information on Foreign Law; Inter-American Convention on the Domicile of Natural Persons in Private International Law; Inter-American Convention on General Rules of Private International Law; the Additional Protocol to the Inter-American Convention on Letters Rogatory; (3) 1984: Inter-American Convention on Conflict of Laws Concerning the Adoption of Minors; Inter-American Convention on Personality and Capacity of Juridical Persons in Private International Law; Inter-American Convention on Jurisdiction in the International Sphere for the Extraterritorial Validity of Foreign Judgments; Additional Protocol to the Inter-American Convention on the Taking of Evidence Abroad; (4) 1989: Inter-American Convention on International Return of Children; Inter-American Convention on Support Obligations; Inter-American Convention on Contracts for the International Carriage of Goods by Road; (5) 1994: Inter-American Convention on Law Applicable to International Contracts; Inter-American Convention on International Traffic in Minors; (6) 2002: Model Inter-American Law on Secured Transactions; Negotiable Inter-American Uniform Through Bill of Lading for the International Carriage of Good by the Road; Non-Negotiable Inter-American Uniform Through Bill of Lading for the International Carriage of Good by the Road. For the texts of these instruments, *see* http://www.oas.org/dil/CIDIPVI_home.htm. and http://www.oas.org/en/topics/treaties_agreements.asp.

[181] *See* generally, A. Dreyzin de Klor, *El Mercosur. Generador de una nueva fuente de derecho internacional privado* (1997); D. Fernández Arroyo (ed.), *Derecho internacional privado de los Estados del Mercosur* (2003); M.T. Franca Filho, L. Lixinski & M.B. Olmos Giupponi. *The Law of Mercosur* (2010).

[182] Bolivia, Chile, Colombia, Ecuador, and Peru are associate members of Mercosur.

judicial assistance, arbitration,[183] consumer contracts,[184] transportation and traffic accidents,[185] and intellectual property,[186] among other subjects.[187]

The United Nations Commission on International Trade Law (UNCITRAL) has also been very productive during the same period. Although much of UNCITRAL's work is on substantive-law unification or harmonization, it nevertheless affects choice of law to the extent that it eliminates many conflicts previously resolved through choice of law. For example, much of UNCITRAL's work on international commercial arbitration,[188] international sale of goods (CISG),[189] security interests,[190] insolvency,[191] international payments,[192] international transport of goods,[193] and electronic commerce[194] has a more direct and significant bearing on choice of law.[195]

---

[183] *See, e.g.,* Protocolo sobre Jurisdicción en Material Contractual (done in Buenos Aires, 6 April 1994); Protocolo de Cooperación y Asistencia Juridical en Material Civil, Commercial, Laboral y Adminstrativa (Las Leñas) (done in Mendoza, 27 June 1992); Protocolo de Medidas Cautelares (done in Ouro Preto, 7 December 1994); Acuerdo sobre Arbitraje Comercial Internacional del Mercosur (done in Buenos Aires, 23 July 1998); Acuerdo sobre el Beneficio de Litigar sin Gastos y Asistencia Jurídica Gratuita entre los Estados Partes del Mercosur (done in Florianópolis, 15 December 2000).

[184] *See* Protocolo de Santa María sobre Jurisdicción Internacional en Materia de Relaciones de Consumo (done in Santa María, 20 November 1996). Mercosur/CMC/Dec. No 10/96.

[185] *See* Acuerdo sobre Transporte de Mercancías Peligrosas en el Mercosur. Mercosur/GMC/Dec. No 2/94; Protocolo de San Luis en Materia de Responsabilidad Civil Emergentes de Accidentes de Tránsito entre los Estados Partes del Mercosur (done in San Luis, 25 June 1996); Documentos de cada Estado Parte que Habilitan el Tránsito de Personas en el Mercosur. Mercosur/GMC/Res. No 75/96.

[186] *See* Protocolo de Armonización de Normas en Materia de Diseños Industriales (done in Río de Janeiro, 10 December 1998), Mercosur/CMC/Dec. No 16/98; Protocolo de Armonización de Normas sobre Propiedad Intelectual en el Mercosur en Materia de Marcas, Indicaciones de Procedencia y Denominaciones de Origen. Mercosur/CMC/Dec. No 8/95.

[187] All of the above instruments can be found at Mercosur's official website at http://www.mercosur.int/t_generic.jsp?contentid=2639&site=1&channel=secretaria.

[188] *See, e.g.,* UNCITRAL Arbitration Rules (1976, revised in 2010); UNCITRAL Model Law on International Commercial Conciliation (2001); UNCITRAL Model Law on International Commercial Arbitration (1985, amended in 2006); UNCITRAL Conciliation Rules (1980).

[189] *See* United Nations Convention on Contracts for the International Sale of Goods (CISG) (1980); Convention on the Limitation Period in the International Sale of Goods (1974).

[190] *See* UNCITRAL Legislative Guide on Secured Transactions, Supplement on Security Rights in Intellectual Property (2010), discussed in S. Bazinas, *UNCITRAL Report, infra*; United Nations Convention on the Assignment of Receivables in International Trade (2001).

[191] *See* UNCITRAL Practice Guide on Cross-Border Insolvency Cooperation (2009); UNCITRAL Model Law on Cross-Border Insolvency (1997).

[192] *See* United Nations Convention on Independent Guarantees and Stand-by Letters of Credit (1995); UNCITRAL Model Law on International Credit Transfers (1992); United Nations Convention on International Bills of Exchange and International Promissory Notes (1988).

[193] *See* United Nations Convention on Contracts for the International Carriage of Goods Wholly or Partly by Sea ("Rotterdam Rules" 2008); United Nations Convention on the Liability of Operators of Transport Terminals in International Trade (1991); United Nations Convention on the Carriage of Goods by Sea ("Hamburg Rules" 1978).

[194] *See* United Nations Convention on the Use of Electronic Communications in International Contracts (2005); UNCITRAL Model Law on Electronic Signatures with Guide to Enactment (2001).

[195] All of the above documents can be found on UNCITRAL's official website at http://www.uncitral.org/uncitral/en/uncitral_texts.html. For a recent thoughtful discussion on UNCITRAL's work on choice of law, *see* S. V. Bazinas, Towards Global Harmonization of Conflict-of-Laws Rules in the Area of Secured Financing: The

Finally, mention should be made of the International Institute for the Unification of Private Law known as UNIDROIT, an independent intergovernmental organization based in Rome.[196] As with UNCITRAL, most of the conventions, model laws, and other instruments produced by UNIDROIT deal with the modernization, harmonization, and unification of private *substantive* law. However, some of these instruments have a significant bearing on choice of law. For example, a decision to adopt the 1995 UNIDROIT Convention on Stolen or Illegally Exported Cultural Objects[197] means that the adopting country will resolve conflict of laws involving stolen cultural objects through means other than (and in some instances in addition to) choice-of-law means. In a different way, the UNIDROIT Principles of International Commercial Contracts of 2004[198] may affect the law applicable to arbitration and, in the long run, the law applicable in the adjudication of certain international contracts.

V. Sorting the Data

In conclusion, the last 50-year period has been an extraordinarily productive period for choice of law. During this period, we have witnessed the adoption of:

(a) Ninety four choice-of-law codifications and four drafts,[199] in 88 states;[200]

(b) At least 15 EU Regulations directly involving choice of law, in addition to the Brussels, Lugano, and Rome conventions; and

(c) Eighty-seven international or regional conventions, regulations, protocols, model laws, and other instruments on choice of law (Chart 1.6).

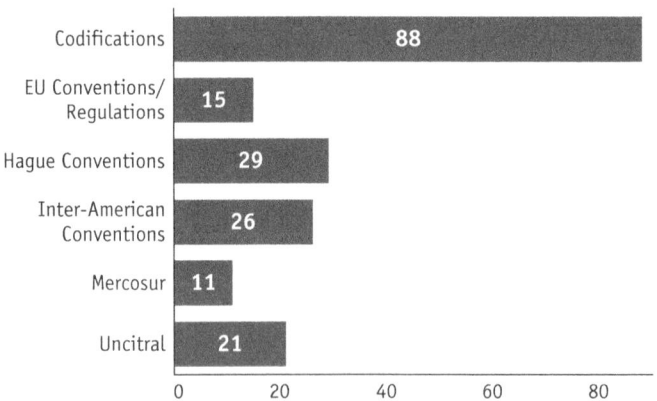

CHART 1.6. Codifications, Regulations, Conventions, Protocols and Other Instruments, 1962–2012

Conflict-of-Laws Recommendations of the UNCITRAL Legislative Guide on Secured Transactions, in *A Commitment to Private International Law: Essays in Honour of Hans Van Loon* 1 (2013).

[196] For the mission and work of UNIDROIT, *see* its official website at http://www.unidroit.org/.

[197] For the text of this convention, and a list of the countries that have ratified it, *see* http://www.unidroit.org/english/conventions/1995culturalproperty/main.htm.

[198] For the text, *see* http://www.unidroit.org/english/principles/main.htm.

[199] This count includes partial codifications and re-codifications.

[200] This count includes the two non-extant states of East Germany and North Yemen.

VI. This Book

A. NATIONAL REPORTS

This book began as a "general report" on the topic "Recent Private International Law Codifications" for the 18th International Congress of Comparative Law.[201] Thirty-three national reports were submitted from the countries or jurisdictions listed below, along with the names and affiliations of the national reporters.[202]

- Argentina: María Susana Najurieta & María Blanca Noodt Taquela (University of Buenos Aires);
- Australia: Alice De Jonge (Monash University);
- Austria: Christiane Wendehorst (University of Vienna);
- Belgium: Marc Fallon (Louvain-la-Neuve) & Johan Ugent Erauw (Gent);
- China: Weizuo Chen (Tsinghua University School of Law, Beijing);
- Croatia: Davor Babić (University of Zagreb);
- Czech Republic: Monika Pauknerová (Charles University, Prague);
- Denmark: Joseph Lookofsky (University of Copenhagen);
- England: Christa Roodt (University of Aberdeen);
- Finland: Ulla Liukkunen (University of Helsinki);
- France: Benjamin Remy (University of Poitiers);
- Germany: Peter Mankowski (University of Hamburg);
- Greece: Evangelos Vassilakakis (University of Thessaloniki);
- Hungary: Katalin Raffai & Sarolta Szabó (Pázmány Péter Catholic University);
- Israel: Talia Einhorn (Ariel University);
- Japan: Tadashi Kanzaki (Gakushuin University);
- Macau: Guangjian Tu (University of Macau);
- Netherlands: Katharina Boele-Woelki & Dorothea Van Iterson (Utrecht University);
- New Zealand: Tony Angelo (Victoria University of Wellington);
- Norway: Giuditta Cordero Moss (University of Oslo);
- Poland: Maksymilian Pazdan (University of Śląski);
- Portugal: Luís De Lima Pinheiro (University of Lisbon);
- Quebec: Frédérique Sabourin (Quebec Ministry of Justice);
- Scotland: Janeen M. Carruthers & Elizabeth B. Crawford (University of Glasgow);
- South Korea: Kwang Hyun Suk (Seoul National University);

---

[201] The International Academy of Comparative Law organizes this congress every four years. The 18th congress was held on 25 July to 1 August 2010, in Washington, DC.

[202] One report was submitted from UNCITRAL by Dr. Spiros Bazinas, Senior Legal Officer, UNCITRAL.

- Spain: Carlos Esplugues Mota & Carmen Azcárraga Monzonís (University of Valencia);
- Switzerland: Andrea Bonomi (Swiss Institute of Comparative Law);
- Taiwan: Rong-chwan Chen (National Taipei University);
- Turkey: Zeynep Derya Tarman (Koç University);
- United States: James A.R. Nafziger (Willamette University);
- Uruguay: Cecilia Fresnedo de Aguirre (Catholic University of Uruguay); and
- Venezuela: Eugenio Hernández-Bretón (Universidad Monteávila, Caracas).

These reports have been extremely helpful to this author,[203] although this book covers much more ground. Twenty-three of the 33 reports come from countries that have enacted a choice-of-law codification in the last 50 years, whereas the book covers codifications from 86 countries, as well as numerous EU Regulations and international conventions.

B. A ROAD MAP

As noted at the beginning of this chapter, this book is confined to the choice-of-law part of PIL codifications and conventions. It offers a horizontal comparison and discussion of the answers these codifications provide to some of the fundamental philosophical and methodological questions that the choice-of- law process has encountered throughout its history. In identifying these answers, the book looks at all fields of law covered by a codification, but does not attempt to cover in any depth fields other than torts and contracts.

Chapter 2 focuses on choice of law in tort conflicts. The chapter documents that, although all codifications retain the old rule of *lex loci delicti* (applying the law of the place of the tort), virtually all of them have introduced exceptions to it. The chapter compares these exceptions and the results they produce with the results reached by American courts since the choice-of-law revolution, which coincidentally also began 50 years ago.

Chapter 3 focuses on the role of party autonomy in contract conflicts. The principle that contracting parties should retain the power to agree in advance on the law that will govern their future contractual dispute has gained more ground during this 50-year period than in all previous years. It is now the dominant principle for contract conflicts, endorsed by all but four codifications enacted during this period. However, these codifications differ in delineating the "horizontal" scope of this principle (i.e., which contracts and issues it may encompass), as well as its "vertical" limitations (i.e., which level of public policy can defeat the parties' choice). The chapter compares and evaluates the various horizontal and vertical combinations.

---

[203] These reports are on file with the author. They are referred to hereinafter by the author's name, the country of origin, and the pertinent section and subdivision of each report. Some of the reports have been published elsewhere.

Chapter 4 discusses the responses of the new codifications to the competing systemic needs for legal certainty on the one hand and flexibility on the other. The discussion reveals that these codifications differ significantly from those of the previous generation in recognizing the need for flexibility. This is evident in the introduction of several new tools and techniques, such as the use of soft connecting factors and multiple escape clauses, which provide controlled dosages of flexibility. This development suggests that, despite contrary assumptions in the common-law world, a codification need not petrify the law, nor render it unduly inflexible for unanticipated or exceptional cases.

Chapter 5 focuses on a relatively new question of choice-of-law methodology: Whether the choice of the applicable law should always lead to the law of a single state for the entire case, or whether it is permissible, in appropriate cases, to apply the laws of different states to different aspects of the case—a process known as "issue-by-issue analysis" and *dépeçage*. Outside the United States, the prevailing academic doctrine is hostile to *dépeçage* and most codifications are supposed to prohibit or at least avoid it. However, the chapter reveals that, despite this hostile climate, *dépeçage* is a far more frequent occurrence than commonly assumed.

Chapter 6 discusses the positions of modern codifications on two conflicting views regarding the goal of the choice-of-law process. The first is the traditional view, according to which the choice-of-law process should aim for the law of the *state* that has the "proper" connection(s) to the case, without being concerned with the quality of the solution that law provides ("conflicts justice"). In contrast, the second view subscribes to the notion that the choice-of-law process should aim directly for the law that will produce the "right" *result* ("material justice"). The discussion reveals that the "material justice" view, which was considered heretical until a couple of decades ago, has gained significant ground at the expense of the "conflicts justice" view, which remains the official goal of most codifications.

Chapter 7 discusses the extent to which choice-of-law codifications continue to serve the supreme goal of classic PIL—international uniformity. The discussion shows that, although uniformity remains the official desideratum, it is often subordinated to the need to protect the interests of the enacting state. The discussion identifies several mostly overt mechanisms for such protection, and suggests that choice of law is no longer—and perhaps never was—as "innocent" or ideologically neutral as it is claimed to be.

Chapter 8 summarizes the conclusions flowing from the previous seven chapters.

2   Law Governing Tort Conflicts

I. Introduction

Private international law intersects with the law of torts whenever the particular tort or the involved parties have significant contacts with more than one state. Examples of such "multistate" torts include cases in which the tortious conduct occurs in one state and the resulting injury in another (cross-border torts), or those in which the conduct and the injury both occur in one state (intra-state torts) but either the tortfeasor, the victim, or both, are domiciled in, or have another significant connection with, another state. This chapter explores the question of how the codifications enacted in the last 50 years choose the law that governs tort conflicts.

At least since the emergence of modern nation-states and Jean Bodin's (1530–1596) sixteenth century seminal works on territorial sovereignty,[1] the operating principle for resolving

---

[1] *See* J. Bodin, *Les Six Livres de la République* (1576).

tort conflicts has been the principle of territoriality, a principle that attributes decisive importance to the location of events rather than to the affiliation or allegiance of the parties. In the seventeenth century, the Dutch commentator Ulrich Huber (1636–1694) imported this principle from public international law into private international law. According to his later famous axioms: (1) the laws of each state have force within its territory, but not beyond; and (2) these laws bind all persons found within the territory, whether permanently or temporarily.[2] Following Huber, the American scholar and Supreme Court Justice Joseph Story (1779–1845) gave his own strong endorsement of territoriality in the nineteenth century,[3] and Professor Joseph Beale (1861–1943) elevated it to a commanding position in the twentieth century. Beale believed that "by its very nature law must apply to everything and must exclusively apply to everything within the boundary of its jurisdiction."[4] Thus, under Beale's scheme, a state's law should govern all torts occurring, contracts made, and property located within its territory. This view was "codified" in the first conflicts Restatement of 1933,[5] which commanded the allegiance of American courts for at least one generation.

The principle of territoriality also took hold in the rest of the world, more so in the field of torts than in other areas of PIL. One of the first codifications of the modern era, the French *Code Civil* of 1804, followed this principle when it provided in Article 3 that "[t]he laws of police and safety are binding on all those inhabiting the territory."[6] This was the unilateral version of a rule that was later bilateralized in the rest of the world and came to be known as the rule of *lex loci delicti*, namely applying the law of the place of the delict or tort. This was the dominant rule throughout the nineteenth century and the first part of the twentieth century.

This chapter examines the status of this rule in the codifications of the last 50 years. Before doing so, however, it summarizes the experience of American courts in deciding tort conflicts during the same 50-year period. It may appear odd to begin a book on codifications with a country that (with the exception of Louisiana and, recently, Oregon) has consciously stirred away from codification. Nevertheless, a review of the American experience belongs to this book for at least two reasons.

---

[2] U. Huber, De conflictu legum diversarum in diversis imperiis, in *Praelectiones Juris Romani et hodierni* § 2 (1689) ("*Leges cujusque imperii vim habent intra terminus ejusdem Reipublicae omnesque ei subjectos obligant, nec ultra; Pro subjectis imperio habendi sunt omnes, qui intra terminus ejusdem reperiuntur, sive in perpetuum, sive ad tempus ibi commorentur.*").

[3] *See* Story, *Commentaries*, 19, 21 ("Every nation possesses an exclusive sovereignty and jurisdiction within its territory ... [and its laws] ... bind directly all property, whether real or personal, within its territory, and all persons who are residents within it, and also all contracts made, and acts done within it. ... [N]o state or nation can by its laws directly affect or bind property out of its own territory, or bind persons not resident therein.").

[4] Beale, *Treatise*, 46 (v. 1).

[5] *See* American Law Institute, *Restatement of the Law, Conflict of Laws* § 1 (1934) hereinafter *Restatement* ("No state can make a law which by its own force is operative in another state; the only law in force in the sovereign state is its own law, but by the law of each state rights or other interests in that state may, in certain cases, depend upon the law in force in some other state or states").

[6] *Code Civil* art. 3(1) ("Les lois de police et de sureté obligent toux ceu qui habitent le territoire.").

The first is that, since the 1930s and continuing to the beginning of the 50-year period under review here (i.e., 1962), the United States had something quite similar to, and some might say worse than, a codification: Joseph Beale's Restatement, which he drafted with the absolutism of an imperial code, and whose black-letter rules were not dissimilar to those of the continental codes of its time.[7]

The second reason is that, although during the last 50-year period the Restatement was overthrown and replaced by a multitude of malleable and decidedly anti-rule "approaches," the courts following these approaches have reached solutions that are similar, and in some cases identical, to the solutions adopted in countries that have codified or recodified their PIL during the same period. This chapter examines the similarities as well as the differences between these two sets of solutions.

II. The American Experience in Tort Conflicts

A. THE AMERICAN CHOICE-OF-LAW REVOLUTION

Like many of the codifications of the early twentieth century, the Restatement adopted the *lex loci delicti* rule. If there was a difference, it was that unlike some other codifications that either did not define the *locus delicti* or defined it as the place of the wrongful conduct, the Restatement categorically defined the *locus delicti* as the place of the resulting *injury* (i.e., *lex loci damni*).[8] At the beginning, American courts faithfully followed this rule and the Restatement's rigid territorialist-rule system.[9] However, over time, this system proved completely inadequate to rationally resolve the more frequent and complex conflicts brought about by increased cross-border activity and mobility. Courts gradually began searching for oblique ways to avoid the often arbitrary and artificial results dictated by the traditional system. By the 1960s, judicial dissension against that system acquired the dimensions and intensity of an open "revolution," as many courts began abandoning the *lex loci delicti* rule.[10]

The first court to raise the revolutionary banner was New York's highest court, the Court of Appeals, in the 1963 landmark case *Babcock v. Jackson*.[11] *Babcock* involved an intra-state tort, a single-car accident, which occurred in the Canadian province of Ontario, but in which both the defendant driver and his injured passenger were domiciled in New York. Ontario had a "guest statute" that would bar the passenger's action merely because of her status as a gratuitous guest in the defendant's car. The court refused

---

[7] *See* Symeonides, *The First Conflicts Restatement* 53–54, 72–76.

[8] *See Restatement* § 377 (defining the *locus delicti* as the place where "the last event necessary to make an actor liable for an alleged tort takes place.").

[9] For a discussion of the traditional choice-of-law system, *see* Hay, Borchers & Symeonides, 18–24, 145–175, 794–807, 1159–1162.

[10] For documentation and discussion of this movement, *see* Symeonides, *Revolution*.

[11] 191 N.E.2d 279 (N.Y. 1963).

to apply that statute and instead applied New York law, which allowed the action. The court reasoned, inter alia, that:

(a) The only "issue" with regard to which the laws of the two states conflicted was the defendant's immunity from suit because of Ontario's guest statute;

(b) The purpose of that statute was *not* to regulate conduct on Ontario roads but rather to protect insurers from collusive suits;

(c) This purpose would not be served by applying the statute in this case because the insurer was not an Ontario insurer, or one that had insured an Ontario car, and consequently Ontario had no "interest" in applying the statute; and

(d) Conversely, New York had a strong interest in applying its plaintiff-protecting rule because the plaintiff, the driver, and the insurer responsible for her compensation were all domiciled there.

Babcock was a watershed development in American conflicts law. It did not simply begin the erosion of the *lex loci delicti* rule; it introduced a new way of thinking about conflict of laws in general—it began what has since come to be known as the choice-of-law revolution.

Courts in other states moved in the same direction, and by 1977, half of the states had abandoned the *lex loci delicti* rule. By the time of this writing in 2013, a total of 42 jurisdictions (including the District of Columbia and the Commonwealth of Puerto Rico) had done likewise. Chart 2.1, below, shows the chronology of this movement.[12]

The revolution did not replace the *lex loci* rule with another rule or rules. Rather it generated a multitude of competing choice-of-law methodologies or "approaches,"[13] such as those of the Restatement (Second) of 1971,[14] Brainerd Currie's "governmental interest analysis,"[15] or Professor Leflar's "better law" approach.[16] Indeed, the revolution attacked not only the *lex loci* rule as such, but also the very premises and goals of the established choice-of-law system. The very concept of rules was denounced,[17] issue-by-issue analysis and *dépeçage* became the new terms du jour,[18] "material justice" or "justice in the individual case" became an overt goal,[19] unilateralism was resurrected,[20] and the principle of territoriality lost significant ground to the principle of personality, especially in contract conflicts.[21]

---

[12] For documentation, *see* Symeonides, *Revolution* §§ 41–42.

[13] For a succinct discussion of these approaches and their differences, *see* S. Symeonides, *American Private International Law* 92–117 (2008). For their following in the various states, *see* S. Symeonides, *Revolution* 63–116.

[14] *See* American Law Institute, *Restatement (Second) of Conflict of Laws* (1971) [hereinafter *Restatement (Second)*].

[15] *See* B. Currie, *Selected Essays on the Conflict of Laws* (1963).

[16] *See* R. Leflar, Choice-Influencing Considerations in Conflicts Law, 41 *N.Y.U. L. Rev.* 367 (1966); R. Leflar, Conflicts of Law: More on Choice Influencing Considerations, 54 *Cal. L. Rev.* 1584 (1966).

[17] *See* Chapter 4, at VIII.A, *infra*; Symeonides, *Revolution*, at 426–429.

[18] For the definition of issue-by-issue analysis and *dépeçage*, *see* Chapter 5, at I.C.1, *infra*.

[19] For the tension between "material justice" and "conflicts justice," *see* Chapter 6, *infra*.

[20] For discussion of unilateralism and multilateralism, *see* Chapter 7, *infra*.

[21] *See infra* this chapter, at X.

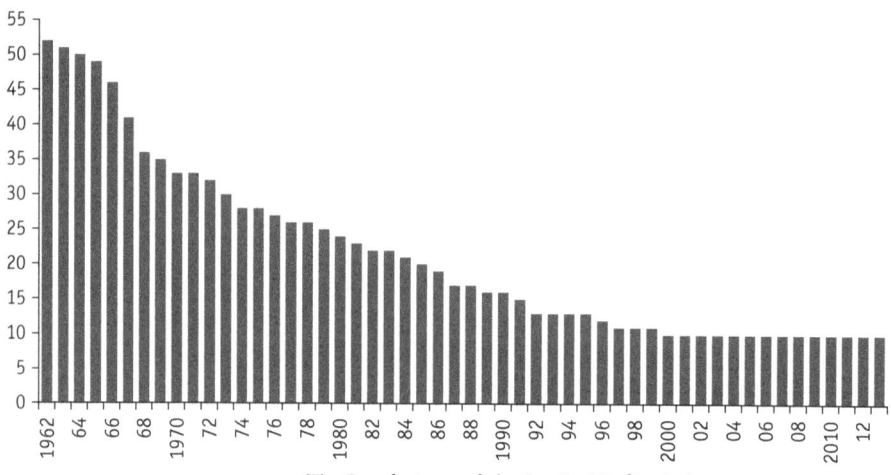

CHART 2.1 The Revolution and the *Lex Loci Delicti* Rule

From the perspective of methodology, general philosophy, and even terminology, the choice-of-law revolution instigated significant, and, in many respects, beneficial, changes. Three of these changes exemplify the difference between the single-mindedness of Beale's system and the post-revolutionary state of affairs.

The first is that the choice of the applicable law is no longer based on a single contact, such as the place of the conduct or injury. Instead, the choice is based on multiple contacts, including the parties' domiciles or other affiliations with a particular state, or the place of their preexisting relationship, if any.

The second change was the acceptance of the notion that, prior to choosing between the laws of the contact states, the court should consider the content of these laws and their underlying policies, as well as other policies and considerations, such as the needs of the interstate and international systems. Thus, the choice of law moved from "jurisdiction-selection" to a content-dependent law selection, that is, from the selection of a *state* without regard to the content of its substantive law[22] to the selection of a state's *law* based in part on that law's content.[23]

The third change was the emergence of a distinction, first articulated in *Babcock v. Jackson,* between torts rules whose primary purpose is to deter injurious conduct (hereinafter referred to as "conduct-regulating rules") and those whose primary purpose is to allocate the economic and social losses resulting from the tort (hereinafter referred to as "loss-allocating" or "loss-distributing" rules). The next section discusses this distinction.

---

[22] The term "jurisdiction-selection" was first coined by Professor Cavers. *See* D. Cavers, A Critique of the Choice-of-Law Problem, 47 *Harv. L. Rev.* 173 (1933).

[23] For a full discussion of these concepts, *see* Symeonides, *At the Dawn of the 21st Century,* 46–60.

B. DIFFERENTIATING BETWEEN CONDUCT-REGULATION
AND LOSS-DISTRIBUTION

In the United States, the substantive law of torts is viewed as having two general objectives: deterrence and reparation/compensation. Although each rule of tort law serves both objectives to some extent, it is possible to classify some rules as serving one objective primarily and the other only secondarily. Thus, a rule of tort law may be primarily conduct-regulating[24] or primarily loss-distributing.[25]

Conduct-regulating rules resemble, but do not coincide with, what some PIL codifications call "rules of conduct and safety," which are discussed later in this chapter.[26] Examples include not only "rules of the road," such as speed limits and traffic-light rules, but also: rules prescribing the civil sanctions for violating rules of the road, including presumptions and inferences attached to the violation;[27] rules prescribing safety standards for worksites, buildings, and other premises; rules imposing punitive damages; and rules defining as tortious certain anticompetitive conduct, or conduct amounting to "interference with contract," "interference with marriage," or "alienation of affections."

Examples of loss-distributing rules include not only guest statutes, such as the one involved in *Babcock*, which are now virtually extinct, but also rules that prescribe the amount of compensatory damages, as well as rules of interspousal immunity, parent-child immunity, worker's compensation immunity, and loss of consortium.

Although many academic authors dispute the clarity or usefulness of this distinction, most courts have adopted it, albeit without always using the same terminology and without a consensus on its precise contours.[28] Admittedly, the line between the two categories is not always bright. While some tort rules are clearly conduct-regulating and some are clearly loss-distributing, there are many tort rules that do not easily fit in either category, and there are some rules that appear to fit in *both* categories in that they both regulate conduct and effect or affect loss distribution.

Nevertheless, despite the difficulties in its application in some cases, this distinction provides a useful starting point for analyzing many tort conflicts, although the distinction will not make a difference in many other conflicts. The starting point is a presumption that conduct-regulating rules are territorially oriented, whereas loss-distribution rules are not *necessarily* territorially oriented. Consequently, territorial contacts (namely, the places of conduct and injury) remain relevant in conduct-regulation conflicts, whereas both territorial and personal contacts (i.e., the parties' domiciles) are relevant in loss-distribution conflicts.

---

[24] In the words of the New York Court of Appeals, conduct-regulating rules are those that "have the prophylactic effect of governing conduct to prevent injuries from occurring." Padula v. Lilarn Props. Corp., 644 N.E.2d 1001, 1002 (N.Y. 1994).

[25] Loss-distributing rules are those that "prohibit, assign, or limit liability after the tort occurs." *Id.*

[26] *See infra* at V.

[27] Examples of such presumptions include rules providing that: (1) a person involved in a collision while driving in excess of the speed limit, or while intoxicated, is presumed to be negligent; and (2) in a rear-end vehicular collision, the driver of the rear car is presumed to be at fault.

[28] *See* Symeonides, *Revolution*, 123–129, and authorities cited therein.

C. SUMMARIZING THE RESULTS OF THE CASE LAW

Although all three of the above methodological changes have been both necessary and beneficial, they have also dramatically increased the complexity of choice-of-law analysis. Fortunately, when one looks beyond methodology and language and focuses on substantive outcomes in tort conflicts, the picture becomes clearer. At least in the three patterns of tort conflicts described below, courts have produced fairly uniform results.

1. Common-Domicile Cases

The first pattern encompasses cases in which the tortfeasor and the victim are domiciled in (or have a similar affiliation with) one state and are involved in a tort occurring entirely in another state. If, in such a case, the conflict is confined to loss-distribution (rather than conduct-regulation) issues, then most American courts would apply the law of the parties' common domicile. As documented elsewhere,[29] the vast majority (33 out of 42) of cases in which a state supreme court decided to abandon the *lex loci delicti* rule involved such loss-distribution common-domicile conflicts. All but one of these cases applied the law of the common domicile. Subsequently, an additional 18 common-domicile cases have reached the highest courts of the states that had previously abandoned the *lex loci* rule, thus increasing the total number of common-domicile cases that have reached state supreme courts in the post-*lex loci* era to 60. Of these 60 cases, 51 cases (85 percent) have applied the law of the common domicile, *regardless* of the particular choice-of-law methodology the court followed.

The majority of these cases (34 out of 60) involved the *Babcock v. Jackson* pattern, in which the law of the parties' common domicile favors recovery more than the law of the state of conduct and injury. These cases present the classic false conflict paradigm in which only the state of the common domicile has an interest in applying its law. All but one of these cases applied the law of the common domicile.

The remaining 26 cases involved the converse-*Babcock* pattern, in which the law of the common-domicile prohibits or limits recovery more than the law of the state of conduct and injury. These cases are not such clear false conflicts as *Babcock* was because the accident state arguably has an interest in applying its law to compensate those injured in its territory and to facilitate recovery of local medical costs. On balance, however, the application of the law of the common domicile in both the *Babcock* pattern and its converse is entirely justified. Eighteen of the 26 cases (69 percent) applied the law of the common domicile, thus supporting the emergence of a common-domicile rule that does not depend on the content of the law of the common domicile (i.e., a "jurisdiction-selecting" rule).[30]

It is important to stress that *all* of the above American cases that applied the law of the parties' common domicile involved conflicts between loss-distribution rules (as opposed to conduct-regulation rules). In contrast, the common-domicile rule featured in Rome

---

[29] For citations and discussion, *see id.* at 145–159; Hay, Borchers & Symeonides, 884–892.
[30] *See* Symeonides, *Revolution*, 150–157.

II and other codifications that are discussed later is much broader in that it encompasses not only loss-distribution issues, but also conduct-regulation ones.[31]

The two American codifications, the Louisiana codification of 1991[32] and the Oregon codification of 2009,[33] as well as the Puerto Rico draft codification,[34] have adopted a common-domicile rule. In all three codifications, this rule: (1) is confined to loss-distribution (as opposed to conduct-regulation) issues; (2) is confined to disputes between the victim and the tortfeasor and does not encompass disputes between third parties or joint tortfeasors;[35] (3) is extended to encompass cases in which the tortfeasor and the victim are domiciled in different states whose laws would produce the same outcome;[36] and (4) is subject to an escape, which can prove useful, at least in *converse-Babcock* cases.[37]

2. Split-Domicile Intra-state Torts

The second pattern of cases in which American courts, regardless of methodology, have produced fairly uniform results are tort cases in which the tortfeasor and the victim are domiciled in different states but in which both the conduct and the injury occur in one of those states, namely, in the domicile of either the tortfeasor or the victim.

---

[31] *See infra* IV.C2.d and VI.

[32] The Louisiana rule is contained in La. Civ. Code art. 3544(1), which provides that the law of the common-domicile applies to "[i]ssues pertaining to loss distribution and financial protection…as between a person injured by an offense or quasi-offense and the person who caused the injury…" For a discussion of this article by its drafter, *see* Symeonides, *Louisiana Exegesis*, 715–723.

[33] The Oregon rule is contained in Or. Rev. Stat. § 15.440(2)(a), which provides that the law of the common domicile of the tortfeasor and the victim applies (as between those parties) to issues other than determining the standard of care by which the injurious conduct is judged. For a discussion of this provision by its drafter, *see* Symeonides, *Oregon Torts Exegesis*, 1000–1012.

[34] The Puerto Rico rule is contained in Article 41, which provides that "[i]ssues pertaining to loss distribution and financial protection are governed, as between the injured person and the person who caused the injury…by the law of the state in which both of them were domiciled at the time of the injury." For a discussion by the rule's drafter regarding its origin in Puerto Rico jurisprudence, *see* Symeonides, *Revising Puerto Rico's Conflicts Law*, 421–426.

[35] Disputes between joint tortfeasors, or between a tortfeasor and a person vicariously liable for his acts, are relegated to the flexible choice-of-law approach of Article 3542 of the Louisiana codification, Sections 15.450, 15.445 of the Oregon codification, and Article 39 of the Puerto Rico draft codification.

[36] *See* La. codif. art. 3544(1); Or. Rev. Stat. § 15.440(2)(b); Puerto Rico draft codif. art. 41. This legal fiction, which is particularly useful in cases with multiple victims or defendants, enables a court to resolve these *false conflicts* by applying the law of the domicile of either party, unless the general escape of the codification dictates a different result.

[37] The Louisiana escape is contained in Article 3547, which authorizes a judicial deviation from the common-domicile rule if such deviation is appropriate under the codification's general article. The Oregon escape authorizes deviation from the common-domicile rule upon a showing that the application of another law would be "substantially more appropriate" under the codification's general approach. Or. Rev. Stat. § 15.440(4). The Puerto Rico escape authorizes a deviation from the common-domicile rule if its application "would produce a result that is clearly contrary to the objectives" of Article 39, which enunciates the codification's general approach. Puerto Rico draft codif. art. 39.3.

In these cases, courts tend to apply the law of the state with the three contacts, regardless of whether that law favors the tortfeasor or the victim, and regardless of whether the conflict involves conduct-regulation or loss-distribution issues.[38]

The Louisiana and Puerto Rico codifications authorize the same result.[39] The Oregon codification does likewise,[40] but also takes a further step by providing that, if both the injurious conduct and the resulting injury occurred in a state *other than* the state in which either the victim or the tortfeasor were domiciled, the law of the state of conduct and injury still governs.[41] However, this rule is subject to an escape that depends on showing that the application of that law to a disputed issue under the circumstances of the particular case will "not serve the objectives of that law," in which case that issue will be governed by the law selected under the codification's general approach.[42] In contrast, the Louisiana and Puerto Rico codifications do not provide a dispositive rule for these conflicts, relegating them instead to the codification's general residual approach.[43]

3. Split-Domicile Cross-Border Torts

The third pattern of tort conflicts in which American courts have reached uniform results encompasses cross-border torts (other than products liability),[44] namely cases in which the parties are domiciled in different states with different laws, and the conduct occurs in one state (often, but not always, the tortfeasor's home state) and the injury occurs in another state (often, but not always, the victim's home state). In these cases, American courts are almost evenly split between applying the law of the place of conduct and the law of the place of injury. However, in the vast majority of cases (86 percent), courts have applied whichever of the two laws favored the *plaintiff*.[45] Thus, American courts have reached the same results as those codifications that allow plaintiffs to choose the applicable law or authorize the court to choose whichever of the two laws favors the plaintiff.[46]

---

[38] *See* Symeonides, *Revolution,* at 163–191 for loss-distribution conflicts, and 213–220 for conduct-regulation conflicts. Courts also tend to apply the same law even in the less common cases in which the state of conduct and injury does not coincide with the domicile of either party, although exceptions are possible if the conflict involves only loss-distribution issues and that state's contacts are transient or otherwise fortuitous.

[39] *See* La. codif. art. 3544(2)(a) (applicable to issues of loss-distribution and providing that "when both the injury and the conduct that caused it" occurred in the domicile of one party, the law of that state applies); and art. 3543 (providing that, regardless of the parties' domiciles, the law of the state of conduct and injury governs issues of conduct regulation). For the corresponding Puerto Rico provisions, *see* Puerto Rico draft codif. arts. 41 and 40.

[40] *See* Or. Rev. Stat. § 15.440(3)(a).

[41] Or. Rev. Stat § 15.440(3)(b).

[42] *Id.*

[43] *See* La. codif. art. 3542; Puerto Rico draft codif. art. 39.3.

[44] For product liability conflicts, *see infra* II.C.4.

[45] For documentation and discussion, *see* Symeonides, *Cross-Border Torts,* 379–381.

[46] *See infra* III.C.

The Louisiana and Puerto Rico codification provide for the same result in conduct-regulation conflicts. They provide for the application of the law of the state of conduct, unless the state of injury has a higher standard of conduct and the occurrence of the injury in that state was objectively foreseeable, in which case the law of the state of injury governs.[47]

For loss-distribution conflicts, these two codifications take a cautious position by providing a dispositive rule only for cases in which the state of injury has a higher standard of financial protection for the victim. They provide that, when the parties are domiciled in different states with different laws, and the conduct and injury occur in different states, the law of the state of injury governs, provided that (1) the injured person was domiciled in that state, (2) the tortfeasor's actual or intended course of conduct was such as to make foreseeable the occurrence of the injury in that state, and (3) the law of that state provided for a higher standard of financial protection for the injured person than did the law of the state in which the injurious conduct occurred.[48] Clause (1) makes this rule narrower than some of the American cases referred to earlier because it limits the rule to those cases in which the victim is domiciled in the state of injury. Clause (3) makes the rule inapplicable in the converse situation, namely, cases in which the victim is injured (and domiciled) in a state that has a pro-defendant law. These cases are relegated to the general flexible approach of the two codifications.[49]

In contrast, the Oregon codification provides dispositive rules for all categories of cross-border torts. Section 15.440(c) of the codification provides in pertinent part that, in cross-border torts (other than products liability), the law of the state of conduct governs. However, this provision also allows the application of the law of the state of injury if: (1) the activities of the tortfeasor were "such as to make foreseeable the occurrence of injury in that state," and (2) the victim "formally requests the application of that state's law by a pleading or amended pleading."[50] Presumably, the victim will likely make this request only when the conduct in question does not violate the standards of the state of conduct but does violate the standards of the state of injury.

---

[47] *See* La. codif. art. 3543; Puerto Rico draft codif. art. 40. The Louisiana article also contains an exception (not present in the Puerto Rico article) that requires the application of the law of the forum state in cases in which the conduct had been undertaken in that state "by a person who was domiciled in, or had another significant connection with, th[at] state." This "home-town justice" exception is criticized in R. Weintraub, The Contributions of Symeonides and Kozyris to Making Choice of Law Predictable and Just: An Appreciation and Critique, 38 *Am. J. Comp. L.* 511, 515–516 (1990). For a muted response, *see* Symeonides, *Louisiana Exegesis*, 713–714.

[48] La. codif. art. 3544(2)(b); Puerto Rico draft codif. art. 41(b)(2).

[49] *See* La. codif. art. 3542(1) (calling for the application of the law of "the state whose policies would be most seriously impaired if its law were not applied to [the particular] issue"); Puerto Rico draft codif. art. 39 (calling for the application of the law of the state that, "with regard to the particular issues, has the most significant connection to the parties and the dispute.").

[50] Or. Rev. Stat. § 15.440(c). In such a case, the request "shall be deemed to encompass all claims and issues against the particular defendant." *Id.* This provision is subject to an exception if a party demonstrates that the application to a disputed issue of the law of another state is "substantially more appropriate under the principles of [Or. Rev. Stat. § 15.445]" (which articulates the codification's residual choice-of-law approach), in which case the law of the other state applies to that issue.

4. Other Tort Conflicts and Products Liability

In tort conflicts involving different alignments of contacts and laws than those described above, American case law does not reveal decisional patterns that are uniform enough to be expressed in the form of descriptive rule. This is particularly true of product liability conflicts. A comprehensive review of American product-liability conflicts cases failed to reveal uniform results other than to support the rather intuitive conclusion that the more contacts a state has with a case, the more likely it is that its law will be applied. For example:

(a) In 42 percent of the cases, the victim's domicile and injury, and the product's acquisition were in the same state. The majority of those cases (79 percent) applied that state's law, but in the majority of those cases (76 percent) that law favored the defendant; and

(b) 77 percent of all cases applied the law of a state that had only plaintiff-affiliating contacts, but in 56 percent of those cases, that state had a pro-defendant law.[51]

The study also produced some surprising negative findings, which dispel certain widely held assumptions about the current state of American conflicts law. Specifically, the study found that American courts did *not* unduly favor plaintiffs, local litigants (plaintiffs or defendants), or the law of the forum as such. Only 52 percent of the cases applied a pro-plaintiff law, only 41 percent of the cases applied a law that favored a local litigant, and only 55 percent of the cases applied the law of the forum.[52]

5. Summary

This brief description of the American choice-of-law experience suggests that the initial (and arguably continuing) appearance of chaos and anarchy created by the multiplicity of diverse and malleable approaches employed by the courts that joined the American choice-of-law revolution no longer translates into an unusual degree of dis-uniformity of results. Indeed, although the revolution brought major methodological changes, it brought significantly fewer changes in terms of the final choice of the law governing tort conflicts.

Table 2.1 below depicts the results reached in tort conflicts (other than products liability) by American courts that have joined the choice-of-law revolution. In this table, the letters *A* and *B* represent states. The use of uppercase letters represents a state with a pro-plaintiff law and the use of lowercase letter represents a state with a pro-defendant law. The dash (—) means that the content of that state's law is immaterial. The shaded cells represent the state of the applicable law.

---

[51] For documentation and discussion, *see* Symeonides, *Revolution*, 320–337.

[52] *See id.* at 332–337.

TABLE 2.1. AMERICAN SOLUTIONS IN TORT CONFLICTS

	#	Plaintiff's domicile	Injury	Conduct	Defendant's Domicile
Common domicile intra-state	1	A	b	b	A
	2	a	B	B	a
Split-domicile intra-state	3	A	A	A	b
	4	a	a	a	B
	5	a	B	B	B
	6	A	b	b	b
Cross-border	7	—	A	b	—
	8	—	a	B	—

As the table indicates, American courts that have joined the revolution continue to apply the law of the *locus delicti* in several patterns (and a significant number) of tort conflicts, despite using different rationales from each other and from the traditional theory. Specifically:

(1) Courts continue to apply the law of the state in which both the conduct and the injury occurred, if that state is also the domicile of either the tortfeasor (cases 5–6 in Table 2.1) or the victim (cases 3–4) (the intrastate split-domicile cases described above), regardless of which party that law favors and regardless of whether the conflict involves conduct-regulation or loss-distribution issues. Thus, these cases are compatible with the old *lex loci delicti* rule, even if they base the choice of law on additional contacts and factors.

(2) In cross-border torts in which the parties are not domiciled in the same state or states with identical laws (cases 7–8), courts apply the law of either the state of conduct or the state of injury, whichever favors the plaintiff.
   (a) When courts apply the law of the state of injury (case 7), they reach the same result as that dictated by the American version of the *lex loci* rule, even when invoking a different rationale.
   (b) When courts apply the law of the state of conduct (case 8), they deviate from the *American* version of the *lex loci* rule, which mandated the application of the law of the state of *injury*. However, because the place of conduct is a territorial contact rather than a personal one, these cases are consistent with the principle of territoriality, which is the foundation of the *lex loci* rule. Thus, if these cases represent a change, it is an "intra-territorial" and less than dramatic change, especially from the perspective of foreign systems, which did not subscribe to the Restatement's notion of always applying the law of the place of injury in cross-border torts.

(3) The only major departure from both the philosophy and the results of the traditional system has occurred in one pattern of tort conflicts, namely,

common-domicile cases (cases 1–2 in Table 2.1). In these conflicts, the distinction between conduct regulation and loss distribution makes a difference:

(a) In loss-distribution conflicts, all the American courts that joined the revolution have almost unanimously applied the law of the common domicile, thus switching from territoriality to personality.

(b) In contrast, in conduct-regulation conflicts, American courts continue to apply the law of the state of conduct and injury (*See* the cells with the horizontal lines in Table 2.1).

In *Babcock v. Jackson*,[53] the seminal case that launched the revolution, the New York Court of Appeals thought that the basic question was whether "the place of the tort [should] *invariably* govern the availability of relief for the tort."[54] More than four decades later, 42 state supreme courts, including the *Babcock* court, have answered the question in the negative. However, although none of the 42 courts profess categorical adherence to the *lex loci* rule *as such*, the only categorical exception from it is the application of the law of the common domicile in loss-distribution conflicts.[55] One wonders whether a revolution was necessary for such a relatively minor change.

III. The *Lex Loci Delicti* Rule in the Codifications of the Last 50 Years

A. GENERAL INVENTORY

Outside the United States, virtually all codifications enacted in the last 50 years, continue to follow the *lex loci delicti* rule as the basic rule for tort conflicts. The difference from the previous generation of codifications is that now the *lex loci* rule is subject to express exceptions. Table 2.2 below presents a panoramic picture of the status of the *lex loci* rule and its exceptions, in the codifications of the last 50 years. In perusing this table (as well as subsequent tables in this chapter), the reader should keep in mind that:

- The table does not include 16 codifications that, because of their limited scope, do not contain rules for tort conflicts.[56] The table does include four draft codifications: Argentina, Puerto Rico, Serbia, and Uruguay.
- The table includes the 19 European Union countries that have enacted a choice-of-law codification in the last 50 years,[57] although the Rome II Regulation (which is

---

[53] 191 N.E.2d 279 (N.Y. 1963).

[54] *Id.* at 280–281 (emphasis in original).

[55] Less categorical exceptions are the application of the law of the state of conduct in certain cross-border torts (*see supra*) and the availability of general escapes for atypical cases.

[56] The omitted codifications are those of: Burkina Faso, Chad, Congo-Brazzaville, Costa Rica, Ecuador, El Salvador, Finland, Guatemala, Mexico, Panama, Paraguay, Panama, Paraguay, Rwanda, Senegal, and Togo.

[57] Sixteen of those codifications were adopted before Rome II, whereas the Czech, Dutch, and Polish codifications were enacted after Rome II and incorporate its provisions by reference.

also included in the table) preempts these codifications with regard to most tort conflicts.[58] The table does not include the remaining nine EU countries, which (except for Denmark) are bound by Rome II, but which have not enacted a codification in the last 50 years.[59]

- The table depicts only the rules that apply to torts in general, rather than to specific torts, such as defamation, products liability, etc. Many codifications contain separate rules (or exceptions) for these and other specific torts.[60]

B. THE *LEX LOCI* STILL RULES

As Table 2.2 graphically shows, the *lex loci* rule is very much alive and well; indeed it continues to be the dominant rule in the codifications of the last 50 years.

The only codifications in which the *lex loci* is not the *basic* rule—although it is one of the rules—are those of Louisiana and Oregon, which were described earlier, and those of Belgium, Puerto Rico, Serbia, and Switzerland, which are discussed later.

- The only codification in which the *lex loci* is neither the basic rule nor one of the rules is the Yemeni codification, which has unequivocally adopted the *lex fori* without any exceptions.[61]
- The only codifications in which the *lex loci* rule is *not* subject to any express exceptions, other than the *ordre public* exception, are those of Burundi, the Central African Republic, Cuba, Gabon, Latvia, Madagascar, Mauritania, and Spain.[62]
- Thirty codifications have an intentionally flexible definition of the *locus delicti*, which affects the outcome in cross-border torts because it authorizes the application of the law of either the state of conduct or the state of injury, whichever favors the victim (*favor laesi*).[63]

---

[58] The second-to-last row ("Total I") counts Rome II as simply one codification, and also includes the 19 EU countries that have enacted choice-of-law codifications in the last 50 years. The last row ("Total II") shows how the totals would change if one were to exclude the 19 codifications and give 28 "votes" to Rome II (i.e., one for each country in which it is in force).

[59] Besides Denmark (which is not bound by Rome II and many other EU Regulations), these countries are: Cyprus, Finland, France, Greece, Ireland, Luxembourg, Malta, and Sweden. The book covers Finland only with regard to subjects, such as family law, matrimonial property, and successions, for which it enacted detailed statutes.

[60] *See infra* VII–VIII.

[61] *See* Yemeni codif. art. 32 (providing that torts occurring outside Yemen are governed by Yemeni law). The former Arab Republic of Yemen (North Yemen) had adopted the same rule (*see* North Yemen codif. art. 31), whereas the People's Republic of Yemen (South Yemen) allowed the tort victim to choose between the law of the place of conduct and the law of the forum state.

[62] *See* Burundi codif. art. 9; Central African Republic codif. art. 42.2; Cuban codif. art. 16; Gabon codif. art. 41; Latvian codif. art. 20; Madagascar codif. art. 30.2; Mauritania codif. art. 11; and Spanish codif. art. 10.9. The Spanish codification is superseded by Rome II, which contains several exceptions to the *lex loci* rule.

[63] For documentation and discussion, *see infra* at III.C.

TABLE 2.2. THE *LEX LOCI DELICTI* RULE AND ITS EXCEPTIONS

	Lex Loci rule	Favor laesi	Bilateral Exceptions				Lex fori Exceptions		
			Common domicile	Preexisting relationship	Closer connection	"Conduct & safety"	Double actionability	Damages	Forum domic.
Afghanistan	x						x		
Albania	x		x	x	x	x			
Algeria	x						x		
Angola	x	x	x			x			
Argentina	x		x		x				
Armenia	x								
Azerbaijan	x		x*						
Belarus	x		x*				x		
Burundi	x								
Centr. Afric. Rep.	x								
Cape Verde	x	x	x			x			
China	x	x	x						
Cuba	x								
East Timor	x	x	x			x			
FYROM	x	x			x				
Gabon	x								
Georgia	x	x	x						
Guinea-Bissau	x	x	x			x			

	Lex Loci rule	Favor laesi	Bilateral Exceptions				Lex fori Exceptions		
			Common domicile	Preexisting relationship	Closer connection	"Conduct & safety"	Double actionability	Damages	Forum domic.
Japan	x	x	x	x	x		x	x	
Jordan	x						x		
Kazakhstan	x		x*				x		
Korea, North	x						x	x	
Korea, South	x	x	x	x				x	
Kyrgyzstan	x		x*				x		
Liechtenstein	x				x				
Louisiana	x		x		x	x			
Macau	x	x	x			x			
Madagascar	x								
Mauritania	x								
Moldova	x								
Mongolia	x								x
Mozambique	x	x	x			x			
Oregon	x	x	x		x	x			
Peru	x	x							
Puerto Rico	x		x		x	x			
Qatar	x						x		
Quebec	x	x	x		x				
Russia	x	x	x*						

	Lex Loci rule	Favor laesi	Bilateral Exceptions				Lex fori Exceptions		
			Common domicile	Preexisting relationship	Closer connection	"Conduct & safety"	Double actionability	Damages	Forum domic.
Serbia	x		x	x	x	x			
Somalia	x						x		
Sudan	x						x		
Switzerland	x	x	x	x	x	x			
Taiwan	x				x				
Tajikistan	x		x*				x		
Tunisia	x	x	x			x			
Turkey	x				x				
Ukraine	x		x*				x		
U. Arab Emirates	x						x		
Uruguay	x	x	x						
Uzbekistan	x		x*				x		
Venezuela	x	x							
Vietnam	x	x	x*						x
Yemen									
Subtotal non-EU 53	52	20	30	5	13	13	15	3	2
EUROPEAN UNION									
Rome II	x		x	x	x	x			
Austria	x		x	x	x	x			
Belgium	x		x	x	x	x			

	Lex Loci rule	Favor laesi	Bilateral Exceptions				Lex fori Exceptions		
			Common domicile	Preexisting relationship	Closer connection	"Conduct & safety"	Double actionability	Damages	Forum domic.
Bulgaria	x		x		x	x			
Croatia	x	x							
Czech Rep.	x	x							
Estonia	x	x	x	x	x			x	
Germany	x	x	x	x	x			x	
Hungary	x	x	x			x		x	
Italy	x	x	x						
Latvia	x								
Lithuania	x	x	x		x				
Netherlands	x		x	x	x	x			
Poland	x		x	x	x	x			
Portugal	x	x	x			x			
Romania	x					x			
Slovakia	x	x							
Slovenia	x	x			x				
Spain	x				x				
United Kingdom	x				x				
Total I 73	**72**	**30**	**41**	**12**	**24**	**22**	**15**	**6**	**2**
Total II 80	79	20	57	29	40	40	15	3	2

- The most common of the *lex loci* exceptions is the common-domicile exception, which is present in 41 codifications. It provides that, if the tortfeasor and the victim affiliate with the same state (through nationality, domicile, or residence), the law of that state displaces the *lex loci delicti*.[64] In nine of those codifications, marked with an asterisk, the common domicile exception applies only to foreign torts.[65]

- Twenty-four codifications provide for a "closer connection" exception. This means that if the case has a closer connection with a state other than that of the presumptively applicable law, the law of the state with the closer connection applies. This exception operates primarily against the *lex loci delicti*, but in some codifications, it also operates against the laws of other states, such as the state of the common domicile or the state of the preexisting relationship.[66]

- Twelve codifications contain a preexisting relationship exception, usually phrased as an example of the closer-relation concept. This exception means that, if the tortfeasor and the victim are parties to a preexisting factual or legal relationship, such as a contract, the law that governs that relationship will also govern a related tort.[67]

- Twenty-two codifications provide that, if a state other than the state of conduct (e.g., the state of injury or the state of the common domicile) governs the tort, the court should nevertheless "take into account," or apply, the rules of "conduct and safety" of the state of conduct.[68]

- Fifteen codifications subject foreign torts to the "double actionability" requirement, according to which a tort governed by a foreign law does not entitle the victim to recovery unless the tortfeasor's conduct is actionable under both the foreign law and the law of the forum qua forum.[69]

- Six codifications impose a unilateral *lex fori* exception affecting the level or type of recoverable damages. These codifications provide that, for torts governed by foreign law, the plaintiff may not recover higher or different damages than those available under the *lex fori*.[70]

- Finally, in addition to Yemen, which applies the *lex fori* to all torts, foreign and domestic, the codifications of Mongolia and Vietnam apply the *lex fori* to foreign torts involving domestic defendants.[71]

---

[64] This exception is discussed at IV.C, *infra*.

[65] The codifications comprising this group are those of: Azerbaijan, Belarus, Kazakhstan, Kyrgyzstan, Russia, Tajikistan, Ukraine, Uzbekistan, and Vietnam. For citations and discussion, *see infra* at IV.C.2.c.

[66] In the Lithuanian codification, this exception applies only if it is impossible to determine the place of conduct or the place of injury. *See* Lithuanian codif. art. 1.43(2).

[67] For documentation and discussion, *see infra* at IV.E.

[68] For documentation and discussion, *see infra* at V.

[69] For documentation and discussion, *see infra* at IV.F. One of those codifications, the Mongolian, imposes this requirement only in favor of Mongolian defendants. *See id.*

[70] For documentation and discussion, *see infra* at IV.G.

[71] *See id.*

C. DEFINING THE *LOCUS DELICTI* IN CROSS-BORDER
TORTS: THE *FAVOR LAESI* PRINCIPLE

Before discussing the exceptions to the *lex loci delicti* rule, it would be helpful to examine how recent codifications define the *locus delicti*. This definition affects the outcome in cases in which (1) the two constituent elements of a tort, the injurious conduct and the resulting injury, are located in different states—namely, in *cross-border* (as opposed to intra-state) torts; and (2) the way those states' laws differ in result. Obviously, cross-border torts have become far more frequent in the last 50 years than before.[72]

Unlike the first American Restatement, which categorically defined the *locus delicti* as the place of injury (*lex loci damni*),[73] many recent codifications either refrain from defining it[74] or opt for constructive ambiguity, which in turn provides flexibility. For example, at least a dozen codifications use phrases such as "the fact that gives rise" to the obligation,[75] which arguably can be *either* the injurious conduct or the resulting injury. About a dozen codifications define the *locus delicti* as the place of conduct,[76] and an equal number as the place of injury,[77] although in many of those codifications the definitions leave room for contrary arguments.

However, a plurality of codifications avoids potentially interminable localization arguments by providing a direct *substantive* solution to this dilemma. Following a principle known as *favor laesi*,[78] they directly authorize the application of the law of *either* the place of conduct or the place of injury, whichever favors the victim.[79] They do so by either choosing the more favorable of the two laws or allowing the tort victim to choose between them. Table 2.3 below lists these codifications, and the following text provides the necessary explanations.

---

[72] *See* Symeonides, *Cross-Border Torts*, 339–341.

[73] *See supra* note 8.

[74] *See, e.g.,* Burundi codif. art. 6; Central African Republic codif. art. 42.2; Madagascar codif. art. 30; Puerto Rico codif. art. 40.

[75] *See* Afghanistan codif. art. 29.1; Algerian codif. art. 20(1); Cuban codif. art 16; Jordanian codif. art. 22; Latvia codif. art. 20; Somalian codif. art. 21.1; Spanish codif. art. 10.9; Sudanese codif. art. 11.14a; U.A.E. codif. art. 20(1); Ukrainian codif. art. 49.1; Uzbekistan codif. art. 1194.

[76] *See, e.g.,* Austrian codif. art. 48(2); Armenian codif. art. 1289; Azerbaijan codif. art. 26.1; Belarus codif. art. 1129(1); Chinese codif. art. 44; Kazakhstan codif. art. 117.1; North Korean codif. art. 31; South Korean codif. art. 31; Kyrgyzstan codif. art. 1203(1); Qatar codif. art. 30.

[77] *See, e.g.,* Rome II art. 4(1); Albanian codif. art. 56.1; Argentinean draft codif. art. 2657; Belgium art. 99.2.1; Bulgarian codif. art. 105(1); Gabon codif. art. 41; Italian codif. art. 62; Liechtenstein codif. art. 52(1); Mongolian codif. art.551.1; Netherlands art. 157; Polish codif. art. 33; United Kingdom Codif. § 11. The codifications of Moldova (art. 1615.3), Romania (arts. 107–108), and Turkey (art. 34.2) provide that the law of the state of injury governs cross-border torts.

[78] For a discussion of this principle in comparative conflicts law, *see* Symeonides, *Progress or Regress?* 57–59. *See also* Nygh, *Reasonable Expectations* 292–293 (1995); F. Vischer, General Course on Private International Law, 232 *Recueil des cours* 9, 119 (1992).

[79] *See* Angolan codif. art. 45.2; Cape Verde codif. art. 45.2; Croatian codif. art. 28.1; Estonian codif. art. 50; FYROM codif. art. 33; German codif. art. 40; Hungarian codif. art. 32; Italian codif. art. 62; Japanese codif. art. 17; Lithuanian codif. art. 1.43.1; Macau codif. art. 44.1; Mozambique codif. art. 45.2; Peruvian codif. art. 2097; Portuguese codif. art. 45.2; Quebec codif. art. 3126; Russian codif. art. 1219; Slovenian codif. art. 30.1; Swiss codif. art. 133.2; Taiwanese codif. art. 25; Tunisian codif. art. 70; Uruguay codif. art. 52.1; Venezuelan codif. art. 32; Vietnam codif. art. 773.1.

TABLE 2.3. THE *FAVOR LAESI* PRINCIPLE IN CROSS-BORDER TORTS

For all cross-border torts (29)	Express (21)	**(a) Victim's choice:** Estonia, FYROM, Germany, Italy, Lithuania, Oregon, Tunisia, Uruguay, Venezuela (9).
		(b) Court's choice: Angola, Cape Verde, Croatia, East Timor, Georgia, Guinea-Bissau, Hungary, Macau, Mozambique, Peru, Portugal, Slovenia (12).
	Implied (6)	China, Japan, South Korea, Quebec, Russia, Switzerland (6).
	Discretionary (2)	Slovakia, Vietnam.
Express for some cross-border torts (23)	Albania, Austria, Azerbaijan, Belarus, Belgium, Bulgaria, Czech Republic, Kazakhstan, Kyrgyzstan, Louisiana, Moldova, Poland, Puerto Rico, Romania, Rome II, Russia, Serbia, Switzerland, Taiwan, Tajikistan, Turkey, Ukraine, Uzbekistan.	

1. Express *Favor Laesi* Rule

Twenty-one codifications contain an express rule applicable to all cross-border torts; it allows the court or the victim to choose between the laws of the state of conduct and the state of injury.[80] Specifically:

  (a) Nine codifications directly authorize the victim to choose the applicable law. For example, the German codification provides that, although torts are generally governed by the law of the state of conduct, "[t]he injured party can demand that instead of this law, the law of the country in which the injury occurred is to be applied."[81] The codifications of Estonia,[82] Italy,[83] Lithuania,[84] Tunisia,[85] Uruguay,[86]

---

[80] In addition, the idea of allowing the tort victim to choose between the laws of the place of conduct and the place of injury has also been adopted in draft legislation pending in Mexico (2006 Draft). *See* C. Fresnedo de Aguirre & D. Fernández Arroyo, A Quick Latin American Look at the Rome II Regulation, 9 *Ybk. Priv. Int'l L.* 193, 197–198 (2007).

[81] German codif. art. 40.1. This principle, known as *Gunstigkeitsprinzip*, is traceable to an 1888 decision of the German Reichsgericht. *See* the decision of 20 November 1888, 23 Entscheidungen des Reichsgerichts in Zivilsachen [RGZ] 305 (1888).

[82] *See* Estonian codif. art. 50 (providing for the application of the law of the state of conduct, unless the victim requests the application of the law of the state of injury).

[83] *See* Italian codif. art. 62 (providing that torts are governed by the law of the state of injury, but "the person suffering damage may request the application of the law of the State in which the event causing the injury took place.")

[84] Lithuanian codif. art. 1.43(1). *See also id.* art. 1.45 (defamation by mass media: victim's choice from among the laws of the victim's domicile, the tortfeasor's domicile or place of business, or the state of injury).

[85] *See* Tunisian codif. art. 70 (providing for the application of the law of the state of conduct, unless the victim requests the application of the law of the state of injury).

[86] *See* Uruguayan draft codif. art. 52(1) (providing that torts are governed by the law of the state of conduct or the state of injury "at the option of the injured.").

and Venezuela[87] give the tort victim the same choice. The Oregon codification gives the same choice but only if the activities of the tortfeasor were "such as to make foreseeable the occurrence of injury in that state."[88] The FYROM codification also subjects the victim's choice to a similar foreseeability proviso.[89]

(b) Twelve codifications authorize the court to choose the law that is more favorable to the victim. For example, the Croatian codification provides that the law of the place of conduct or the law of place of injury governs torts, "depending on which is most favorable for the injured party."[90] Again, there is no foreseeability proviso for the defendant. The same is true of the corresponding provisions of the codifications of Georgia,[91] Hungary,[92] and Slovenia.[93] In contrast, the Peruvian codification provides that if the tortfeasor is not liable under the law of the state of conduct but is liable under the law of the state of injury, the law of the latter state governs, provided that the tortfeasor should have foreseen the occurrence of the injury in that state as a result of his conduct.[94] The Portuguese codification, as well as the codifications of Angola, Cape Verde, East Timor, Guinea-Bissau, Macau, and Mozambique that are based on it, contain a substantially identical provision.[95]

---

[87] *See* Venezuelan codif. art. 32 (providing for the application of the law of the state of injury, unless the victim requests the application of the law of the state of conduct).

[88] Or. Rev. Stat. 15.440(3)(c). In order to avoid an inappropriate dépeçage, this provision states that the victim's request for the application of the law of the state of "shall be deemed to encompass all claims and issues" against the particular defendant. *Id.* This provision is subject to an exception if a party demonstrates that the application of the law of another state to a disputed issue is "substantially more appropriate under the principles of [Or. Rev. Stat. 15.445]" (which articulates the codification's residual choice-of-law approach), in which case the law of the other state applies to that issue. For a discussion of this provision by its drafter and its differences from the corresponding provisions of other codifications, *see* S. Symeonides, *Oregon Torts Exegesis*, 1022–1032.

[89] *See* FYROM codif. art. 33 (providing for the application of the law of the state of conduct, but also providing that the injured party may request the application of the law of the state of injury if the tortfeasor could and should have foreseen the occurrence of the injury in that state).

[90] Croatian codif. art. 28.1. Serbia has the same rule (*see* art. 28.1 of the (Yugoslav) Law of 15 July 1982 Concerning Conflicts with Foreign Laws, which is still in force in Serbia), but the 2012 Serbian draft adopted the *favor laesi* principle only with regard to environmental torts, restrictions to competition, and defamation.

[91] *See* Georgian codif. art. 42.1.

[92] *See* Hungarian codif. art. 33(2) (choice between the laws of the place of conduct and the place of injury). *See also id.* art. 32(4) (choice between the laws of the place of conduct and the tortfeasor's personal law for issues of culpability); *id.* art. 10(3) (choice between the *lex loci* and the *lex fori* for damages in cases of violation of personal rights). Article 32 was deleted by Act IX of 2009 as inconsistent with Rome II but it remains applicable for torts occurring before that year/

[93] *See* Slovenian codif. art. 30(1).

[94] Peruvian codif. art 2097(2).

[95] *See* Portuguese codif. art. 45.2 (providing for the application of the law of the place of conduct, but "[i]f the law of the state of injury holds the actor liable but the law of the state of conduct does not, the law of the former state shall apply, provided the actor could foresee the occurrence of damage in that country as a consequence of his act or omission."); Angola codif. art. 45.2; Cape Verde codif. art. 45.2; East Timor codif. art. 44.2, Guinea-Bissau codif. art. 45.2; Macau codif. art. 44.2; Mozambique codif. art. 45.2.

2. Implied *Favor Laesi*

In China[96] and South Korea,[97] the courts have interpreted the applicable statutory provisions as authorizing the application of the law most favorable to the victim.

The codifications of Japan, Quebec, Russia, and Switzerland contain a rule, also applicable to all cross-border torts, which provides that the law of the state of injury displaces the law of the state conduct, if the occurrence of the injury in the former state was objectively foreseeable.[98] Obviously, the foreseeability proviso is meaningful only if the law of the state of injury is more favorable to the victim than the law of the state of conduct.

3. Discretionary *Favor Laesi*

The Slovakian and Vietnamese codifications allow the court to choose between the laws of the state of conduct and the state of injury without specifying whether the choice must favor the victim.[99] It would not be surprising if this factor proves determinative in most cases.

4. Partial *Favor Laesi*

Twenty-three codifications, including Rome II, which is applicable to 27 EU countries, contain an express *favor laesi* rule applicable only to the cross-border torts shown in parentheses:

- Albania (environmental torts, infringement of rights of personality, and certain cases involving anticompetitive restrictions);[100]
- Austria (nuclear damage);[101]

---

[96] Article 187 of the Opinions of the Supreme People's Court on Several Questions Regarding the Implementation of the General Principles of Civil Law (1988) provides that the *lex loci delicti* includes the law of the place of conduct and the law of the place of injury, and that in cross-border torts, a court may choose either law. For discussion, *see* W. Chen, *Chinese Report*; Q. He, Recent Developments with Regard to Choice of Law in China, 11 *Ybk. Priv. Int'l L.* 211 (2009); Xu Donggen, Chronique de jurisprudence chinoise, *J. dr. int'l* 191 (1994). Article 44 of the Chinese codification of 2010 provides that the applicable law is the law of the state in which the "tortious act" occurred. It remains to be seen whether the quoted phrase will be interpreted to mean either the place of conduct or the place of injury.

[97] *See* K. Hyun Suk, The New Conflict of Laws Act of the Republic of Korea, 5 *Ybk. Priv. Int'l L.* 99, 127 n.45 (2003) (describing supreme court cases allowing choice of law most favorable to victim).

[98] *See* Japanese codif. art. 17; Quebec codif. art. 3126; Russian codif. art. 1219.1; Swiss codif. art. 133.2.

[99] *See* Slovak codif. art. 15; Vietnam codif. art. 773(1).

[100] *See* Albanian codif. art. 66.2 (environmental torts; applying the law of the state of injury, unless the plaintiff opts for the law of the place of conduct), art. 67 (infringement of rights of personality; the victim may choose from among the laws of the place of injury, or the victim's or the defendant's domicile), art. 64.5–6 (allowing the plaintiff to choose between the otherwise applicable law and the law of the forum in certain cases involving anticompetitive restrictions).

[101] *See* Liability for Nuclear Damage Act § 231(1), discussed in C. Wendehorst, *Austrian Report* at III. *See also id.* describing judicial decisions allowing such a choice in other cases under the stronger connection escape of codif. art. 48(2).

- Azerbaijan (products liability);[102]
- Belarus (products liability);[103]
- Belgium (defamation and direct actions against insurers);[104]
- Bulgaria (defamation, environmental torts, and direct action against insurer);[105]
- Czech Republic (violation of privacy and defamation);[106]
- Kazakhstan (products liability);[107]
- Kyrgyzstan (products liability);[108]
- Louisiana (conduct-regulation issues other than punitive damages);[109]
- Moldova (injury to rights of personality and products liability);[110]
- Poland (injury to rights of personality);[111]
- Puerto Rico (conduct regulation issues);[112]
- Romania (defamation, unfair competition, and products liability);[113]

---

[102] *See* Azerbaijan codif. art. 27 (victim may choose from among the laws of the victim's or the defendant's domicile, or the place of the product's acquisition).

[103] *See* Belarus codif. art. 1130 (victim may choose from among the laws of the victim's or the defendant's domicile, or the place of the product's acquisition).

[104] *See* Belgian codif. art. 99(2) (1) (applicable to defamation; allowing plaintiff to choose between the laws of the state of conduct and, subject to a foreseeability proviso, the state of injury); art. 106 (applicable to direct actions against the tortfeasor's insurer, providing that the action will be allowed if it is allowed by either the law governing the tort or the law governing the insurance contract).

[105] *See* Bulgarian codif. art. 108 (defamation: victim's choice among laws of victim's or tortfeasor's habitual residence or place of injury); art. 109 (environmental torts: victim's choice between laws of place of conduct or place of injury); and 116 (direct action against insurer: victim's choice between the law that governs the tort and the law that governs the insurance contract).

[106] See Czech codif. art. 101 (victim may choose the law of her or the defendant's habitual residence or registered office or of the place of foreseeable injury).

[107] *See* Kazakhstan codif. art. 1118 (victim may choose from among the laws of the victim's or the defendant's domicile, or the place of the product's acquisition).

[108] *See* Kyrgyzstan codif. art. 1204 (victim may choose from among the laws of the victim's or the defendant's domicile, or the place of the product's acquisition).

[109] *See* Louisiana codif. art. 3543 (law of state of conduct applies unless injury occurred in another state imposing a higher standard of conduct and the occurrence of the injury in that state was objectively foreseeable).

[110] *See* Moldova codif. art. 1617 (injury to rights of personality; victim may choose from among the laws of the victim's or the defendant's domicile, or the place of injury), art. 1618 (products liability; victim may choose between the law of the victim's domicile or, subject to a foreseeability proviso, the law of the place of the product's acquisition).

[111] *See* Polish codif. art. 16 (victim may choose between the law of the place of conduct and the law of the place of injury).

[112] *See* Puerto Rico draft codif. art. 40 (law of state of conduct applies unless injury occurred in another state imposing a higher standard of conduct and the occurrence of the injury in that state was objectively foreseeable).

[113] *See* Romanian codif. art. 112 (applicable to defamation; allowing victim to choose between the laws of the defendant's domicile or residence and, subject to a foreseeability proviso, the plaintiff's domicile or residence, or the state of injury); arts. 117–118 (applicable to unfair competition; applying the law of the state of injury but also allowing the victim to choose another law in certain cases); art. 114 (products liability).

- Rome II (environmental torts, direct actions against insurers, and certain cases involving anticompetitive restrictions);[114]
- Russia (products liability);[115]
- Serbia (environmental torts and defamation);[116]
- Switzerland (injuries from emissions, injury to rights of personality, and products liability);[117]
- Taiwan (products liability, unfair competition, and direct actions against tortfeasor's insurer);[118]
- Tajikistan (products liability);[119]
- Turkey (defamation, direct actions against insurer, and products liability);[120]
- Ukraine (products liability);[121] and
- Uzbekistan (products liability).[122]

---

[114] *See* Rome II art. 7 (environmental torts; applying the law of the state of injury, unless the plaintiff opts for the law of the place of conduct); art. 6(3)(b) (allowing the plaintiff to choose between the otherwise applicable law and the law of the forum in certain cases involving anticompetitive restrictions); art.18 (authorizing a direct action against the insurer if such action is allowed by either the law applicable to the tort or the law applicable to the insurance contract).

[115] *See* Russian codif. art. 1221 (victim may choose from among the laws of the victim's or the defendant's domicile, or the place of the product's acquisition).

[116] *See* Serbian draft codif. art. 165 (applicable to environmental torts: allowing victim to choose between the laws of the state of conduct and the state of injury), and art. 170 (applicable to defamation: allowing plaintiff to choose between the laws of the defendant's habitual residence and, subject to a foreseeability proviso, the states of the victim's domicile or injury). *See also id*. art. 164 (applicable to cases involving anticompetitive restrictions: allowing choice of forum law if the forum's market is one of the affected markets).

[117] *See* Swiss codif. art. 138 (applicable to emissions: allowing victim to choose between the laws of the state of conduct and the state of injury); art. 139 (injury to rights of personality: giving victims a choice from among the laws of the tortfeasor's habitual residence or place of business, and, subject to a foreseeability defense, the victim's habitual residence or the place of the injury); art. 135 (products liability).

[118] *See* Taiwanese codif. art. 26 (products liability: choice from among the laws of the manufacturer's or the victim's nationality, the place of injury, or the place of the product's acquisition), art. 27 (unfair competition: choice between the law governing the tort or the contract, if any), art. 29 (choice between the law governing the tort and the law governing the insurance contract).

[119] *See* Tajikistan codif. art. 1227 (victim may choose from among the laws of the victim's or the defendant's domicile, or the place of the product's acquisition).

[120] *See* Turkish codif. art. 35 (applicable to defamation: allowing plaintiff to choose between the laws of the defendant's habitual residence or place of business and, subject to a foreseeability proviso, the states of the victim's domicile or injury); art. 34(4) (applicable to direct actions against the tortfeasor's insurer, providing that the action will be allowed if it is allowed by either the law governing the tort or the law governing the insurance contract); art. 36 (products liability).

[121] *See* Ukrainian codif. art. 50 (victim may choose from among the laws of the victim's or the defendant's domicile, or the place of the product's acquisition).

[122] *See* Uzbekistan codif. art. 1195 (victim may choose from among the laws of the victim's or the defendant's domicile, or the place of the product's acquisition).

5. Summary and Comparison

To summarize, of the 73 choice-of-law codifications surveyed in this chapter:

- 29 codifications follow the *favor laesi* principle for all cross-border torts; and
- 23 codifications, including Rome II, which is in force in 27 EU countries, follow the same principle in some categories of cross-border torts.
- In sum, 52 out of 73 codifications (or 71 percent) follow the *favor laesi* principle and apply whichever of the two laws favors the tort victim (Chart 2.2).

As noted earlier in this chapter, in 86 percent of the cases involving cross-border torts other than products liability, American courts have applied the law of either the state of conduct or the state of injury, whichever favored the tort victim.[123] Although a handful of these cases were decided under the "better-law" approach, which can be analogized to the *favor laesi* principle,[124] most other cases were decided under approaches that considered the policies and interests of the involved states in deterring wrongful conduct and preventing injuries from occurring, as well as other factors. In other words, the courts applied a pro-plaintiff law not necessarily because they subscribed to the pursuit of "material justice," but rather in order to achieve what they considered to be "conflicts justice." Although plaintiffs as a class have been the beneficiaries of these choice-of-law decisions, the individual plaintiffs were not the *stated* reason for these choices.[125] Nevertheless, the results were quite similar to the results reached in 71 percent of codifications of the last 50 years.

Admittedly, the comparison between codifications on the one hand and individual judicial decisions on the other hand is, in many respects, a comparison of apples and oranges. It is also an incomplete comparison in that: (1) the American side of the comparison does not include product liability conflicts in which American courts applied a pro-plaintiff law in only 52 percent of the cases;[126] and (2) the codification side of the comparison does not take account of escape clauses and other available exceptions.

Nevertheless, there is something intriguing and perhaps instructive in seeing that comparable percentages of legislative decision-makers in diverse countries and judicial decision-makers in a plurilegal country have arrived at the same results. Although it is true that there is a significant degree of mutual influence among the decision-makers of the first group, there is no evidence of any influence between the two groups, namely between American judges on the one hand and foreign codifiers on the other.

---

[123] *See supra* II.C.3.

[124] *See* J. von Hein, Something Old and Something Borrowed, but Nothing New? Rome II and the European Choice-of-Law Evolution, 82 *Tul. L. Rev.* 1663, 1682 (2008) (characterizing the *favor laesi* principle as a "cousin of the better law approach.").

[125] *See* Symeonides, *Cross-Border Torts*, 391.

[126] *See supra* II.C.4.

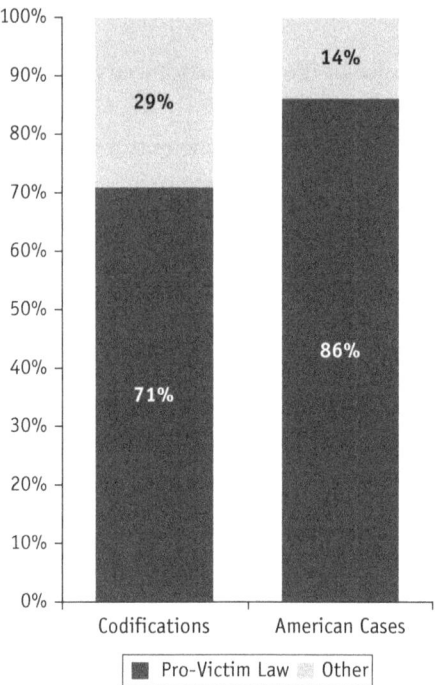

CHART 2.2. Applicable Law in Cross-Border Tort Conflicts

All of this suggests the intrinsic soundness of applying pro-victim law in cross-border torts. By definition, these torts involve conflicting value judgments of at least two societies as to who should bear the social and economic losses caused by injurious conduct that at least one state considers tortious. In another publication, this author has explained why the application of pro-victim law is appropriate from the perspective of policy analysis.[127] This result is equally defensible from the perspective of fairness to the parties involved. In the final analysis, of the two parties involved in the conflict, the tortfeasor is the one who is in a better position to avert the injury. All other factors being equal, it is not unfair to place the resulting loss on the tortfeasor.

If the application of the pro-victim law by the court is appropriate, does the same hold true for giving that choice directly to the plaintiff, as many codifications do? Substantively, the answer is no. From the defendant's perspective, it makes no difference because the outcome would be the same. The same is true from the plaintiff's perspective. The only difference, then, is from the court's perspective. When the choice is given to the court, the court has to determine and explain why one state's law is more favorable than the other state's law. Surprisingly, perhaps, this is not always easy, and an erroneous determination would be a ground for appeal.

---

[127] See Symeonides, *Cross-Border Torts*, 391, 405–411.

On the other hand, if the choice is given to the plaintiff, this would obviate the need for a judicial answer to the question of whether a given law indeed favors the victim. This is particularly helpful, not only in cases in which that answer is unclear, but also in cases in which one state's law favors the plaintiff on some issues and the defendant on other issues. The plaintiff will have to carefully weigh all of the pros and cons of exercising or not exercising the right to choose. If the plaintiff exercises that right, the choice must be—as the Oregon codification expressly mandates—for "all claims and issues against the defendant,"[128] so as to avoid the possibility of an inappropriate *dépeçage* or "picking and choosing."[129] If the choice proves ill-advised, it will not be appealable, and the plaintiff will have only himself or herself to blame. In conclusion, therefore, one can say that the idea of giving the choice to one party is a smart, efficient, and cost-saving tool that helps conserve judicial resources.

IV. Exceptions to the *Lex Loci Delicti* Rule

A. PRECURSORS

The need for exceptions to *the lex loci delicti* rule was recognized in the first European effort to codify choice of law for torts at a multinational level, the Benelux Uniform Law on Private International Law of 1969, which was based on work that began as early as 1951.[130] The escape was elegantly simple and wisely flexible. It provided that "if the *consequences* of a wrongful act belong to the legal sphere of a country other than the one where the act took place, the obligations which result therefrom shall be determined by the law of that other country."[131] This phrasing would cover, and properly resolve, not only cross-border torts in which the consequences of conduct in one country are felt in another country, but also many other cases, such as those involving common-domicile intra-state torts. Although the Benelux Law never entered into force, it represented a real breakthrough in drafting technique and philosophy. Not only did it break the continental taboo against escape clauses, but it also set an example of how the escapes should be drafted.

Subsequent codification efforts got the general message, but not the nuances. For example, the next attempt at a multinational codification, the EEC Draft Convention on Contractual and Noncontractual Obligations of 1972,[132] also provided an escape from

---

[128] Or. Rev. Stat. § 15.440(3)(c)(A).

[129] *See* Chapter 5 at I.C.2, *infra*.

[130] *See* K. Nadelmann, The Benelux Uniform Law on Private International Law, 18 *Am. J. Comp. L.* 406 (1970).

[131] Traité Benelux portant loi uniforme relative au droit international privé, art. 14 (1969), (emphasis added).

[132] For an English translation of the Draft Convention, *see* 21 *Am. J. Comp. L.* 587 (1973). For discussion, *see* K. Nadelmann, Impressionism and Unification of Law: The EEC Draft Convention on the Law Applicable to Contractual and Non-contractual Obligations, 24 *Am. J. Comp. L.* 1 (1976).

the *lex loci* rule, but one that was perceptibly tighter than the Benelux escape. Article 10(2) of the EEC draft provided:

> [I]f, on the one hand, no significant link exists between the situation resulting from the event which caused the damage and the State in which the event occurred and if, on the other hand, such situation has a predominant connection (*connexion prépondérante*) with another State, the law of that State shall apply.[133]

The article continued with a common-domicile presumption, stating that "[s]uch a connection must normally be based on a connecting factor common to the victim and the author of the damage."[134] Although the Draft Convention was eventually abandoned,[135] the substance of this article survived and was later recast in even tighter language in Rome II and other codifications.

B. THE CLOSER-CONNECTION EXCEPTION

Since 1972, the *connexion prépondérante* exception has morphed into the "closer connection" exception, which is the most ubiquitous exception in the codifications and conventions adopted since that time.[136] In the area of torts, 24 codifications employ this exception. The exception appears in different formulations, including the following:

(1) Codifications that use the "closer connection" phraseology, without providing examples of what the closer connection may be;

(2) Codifications that use the "closer connection" phraseology and also contain language suggesting that the parties' common affiliation with the same state (through domicile, habitual residence, or nationality) or the parties' preexisting relationship, or both, are examples of such a closer connection;

(3) Codifications that provide separate exceptions based, respectively, on (a) the closer connection, (b) common party affiliation, and (c) any preexisting relationship; and

(4) Codifications stating directly that either such an affiliation or a preexisting relationship (or both) are a basis for an exception from the otherwise applicable law, but without using the closer connection terminology.

---

[133] EEC Draft Convention on Contractual and Noncontractual Obligations, art. 10(2).

[134] *Id.* art. 10(3).

[135] The expansion of the EEC to nine Member States in 1973, following the accession of the United Kingdom, Ireland, and Denmark, slowed down the codification effort and led to a decision to abandon the tort provisions of the Draft Convention and instead to concentrate on contract conflicts. This bifurcation produced, in a relatively short time, the 1980 Rome Convention on Contractual Obligations, which included a "closer connection" escape. A tort codification proved much more elusive. It only materialized 27 years later, by which time the EU had 27 Member States with all the attendant difficulties in attaining consensus.

[136] For a discussion of this exception in areas other than torts, *see* Chapter 4 at V.A and VI.B.1, *infra*.

1. Closer Connection without Specific Examples

Five codifications provide that the *lex loci* shall be displaced by the law of the state that has a closer connection with the tort, but without providing explicit examples of such a closer connection. The Turkish codification simply provides that if "the obligational relationship arising from the tort is more closely connected with another country, the law of that country shall apply."[137] The codifications of FYROM, Slovenia, and Taiwan are equally brief and similar in substance.[138] The Austrian codification uses the same exception but provides more direction, stating that "if the persons involved have a stronger connection to the law of one and the same state, that law shall be determinative."[139] The Liechtenstein codification also provides that the closest connection must be sought in the parties' common affiliation with the same state.[140]

The 1995 United Kingdom statute for tort conflicts does not actually use the phrase "closer connection" but uses the comparable one "substantially more appropriate." The statute provides for the displacement of the normally applicable law if it is "substantially more appropriate" to apply the law of another country to a disputed issue or issues. Such appropriateness is determined through a comparison of: "(a) the significance of the factors which connect a tort or delict with the country whose law would be the applicable law under the general rule; and (b) the significance of any factors connecting the tort or delict with another country."[141] These factors include "factors relating to the parties, to any of the events which constitute the tort or delict in question or to any of the circumstances or consequences of those events."[142]

2. Closer Connection with Examples

Like the Austrian and Liechtenstein codifications—which, as noted earlier, tie the closer connection exception to the parties' common affiliation with the same state—the Estonian and Japanese codifications also provide similar examples of the exception's intended meaning. The Estonian codification provides that a closer connection "may arise, above all: (1) from a legal relationship or factual connection between the parties; [or] (2)...from the fact that at the [pertinent] time...the residence of the parties is in the same state."[143] The Japanese codification provides that the law of the place that is "manifestly more closely connected with the tort" is determined by "considering that the parties had their habitual residence in the same jurisdiction at the time when the tort

---

[137] Turkish codif. art 34(3).
[138] *See* FYROM codif. art. 33(2); Slovenian codif. art. 30(2); Taiwanese codif. art. 25.
[139] Austrian codif. art. 48(2).
[140] Liechtenstein codif. art. 52(1).
[141] U.K. Codif. § 12(1).
[142] *Id.* at § 12(2).
[143] Estonian Codif. § 53(2)

occurs, the tort constitutes a breach of obligations under a contract between the parties, or other circumstances of the case."[144]

The Chinese Model Law states the closer connection exception in Article 113,[145] and then provides for common affiliation[146] and preexisting relationship[147] situations in two subsequent articles in a way that suggests that such situations are examples of a closer connection. However, the Chinese codification makes the parties' common habitual residence in the same state a categorical exception to the *lex loci* rule, without using the phrase "closer connection."[148]

3. Closer Connection as an Exception from Both the *Lex Loci* and the Parties' Common Law

Rome II, as well as the codifications of Albania, Bulgaria, Germany, the Netherlands, Serbia, and Switzerland, provide that: (1) a common affiliation between the tortfeasor and the victim with the same state displaces the *lex loci*, (2) the law of a state that has a closer connection displaces both the normally applicable law and the law of the state with the common affiliation, and (3) a preexisting relationship between the parties is an example of a closer connection.

Paragraph 2, Article 4 of Rome II provides that when both the tortfeasor and the victim maintain their habitual residence in the same country, the law of that country displaces the *lex loci damni* designated as applicable by paragraph 1. However, paragraph 3 of the same article provides that, if the tort is "manifestly more closely connected" with a country other than that indicated in paragraphs 1 or 2, the law of that other country shall apply. It further provides that a manifestly closer connection with another country "might be based in particular on a preexisting relationship between the parties, such as a contract, that is closely connected with the tort/delict in question."[149]

Likewise, the German codification provides that, if the parties have their habitual residence in the same country, the law of that country governs,[150] but if there is a "substantially

---

[144] Japanese codif. art 20. For discussion, *see* T. Kanzaki, *Japanese Report*, at XII.5.

[145] *See* Chinese Model Law art. 113. ("Where the whole process of a tort shows that the domicile, habitual residence, nationality, seat of business of the parties or the place in which other connecting points are centered has a closer connection with the tortious incident, the law of the place which has the closest connection shall apply.")

[146] *See* Chinese Model Law art. 114 ("Where the injuring party and the injured party have the same nationality or have domicile or habitual residence in the same country or district, the law of the same nationality, or that of the domicile or habitual residence in the same country or district may also apply.").

[147] *See* Chinese Model Law art. 115. ("The law governing the civil and commercial relationship previously existed between the injuring party and the injured party may also apply, *if the application of the law is more favorable to the injured party*.") (emphasis added).

[148] *See* Chinese codif. art. 46 ("Tortious liability shall be governed by the *lex loci damni* or the *lex loci delicti* commissi, but it shall be governed by the law of common habitual residence if the parties have common habitual residence.").

[149] Rome II, art. 4(2) and (3).

[150] German codif. art. 40(2).

closer connection" with another country, then the law of that other country shall apply.[151] The Albanian,[152] Bulgarian,[153] Dutch,[154] and Serbian[155] codifications provide rules to the same effect. The South Korean codification is similar in that the law of the parties' common habitual residence displaces the *lex loci,* and the law that governs a preexisting relationship displaces both laws, but the codification does not use the closer-connection phraseology.

The Swiss and Belgian codifications are slightly different. The Swiss codification provides that: (1) the law of the state in which both parties have their habitual residence is the primarily applicable law to the exclusion of the *lex loci delicti,* and (2) a preexisting relationship between the parties displaces both laws.[156] The codification does not provide a closer-connection exception specifically for torts. However, the general escape of Article 15, which qualifies all of the codification's provisions,[157] is applicable to torts as well.

The Belgian codification provides that: (1) the law of the state of the parties' common habitual residence is the primarily applicable law; (2) the *lex loci* applies only if there is no common habitual residence, and only if both the conduct and the injury occurred in the same *locus*; (3) in all other cases, the law of the state with the closer connection applies;[158] and (4) a close connection with an existing legal relationship between the parties displaces all of the above laws.[159]

---

[151] *Id.* Art 41(1). This article also provides that a substantially closer connection "may be based in particular…on a special legal or factual relationship between the persons involved in connection with the obligation."

[152] *See* Albanian codif. art. 56 para. 2 (common habitual residence), para. 3 (closer connection), para. 4 (preexisting relationship as an example of a closer connection).

[153] *See* Bulgarian codif. art. 105, paragraph (2) ("Where the author of the tort or delict and the person sustaining damage both have their habitual residence or a place of business in the same State at the time when the damage occurs, the law of that State shall apply.") and paragraph (3) ("Notwithstanding the provisions of Paragraphs (1) and (2), if it appears from the circumstances as a whole that the tort or delict is manifestly more closely connected with another State, the law of that other State shall apply. A manifestly closer connection may be based on a pre-existing relationship between the parties, such as a contract that is closely connected with the tort or delict in question.").

[154] *See* the 2001 Dutch Act for Torts § 1(3) ("Where the perpetrator and the injured party are habitually resident, or have their seat, in the same State, the law of that State shall apply by way of derogation from the preceding subsections.") and § 3 ("Where a tort…is closely connected with an existing legal relationship between the parties, any matter relating to such tort…may, by way of derogation from the preceding Sections, be subject to the law governing that other relationship."). The 2011 Dutch codification has repealed this act and replaced it with a cross-reference to Rome II, which leads to the same result. *See* Dutch codif. art. 159.

[155] *See* Serbian draft codif. art. 159 (common domicile is the primary rule), art. 160 (*lex loci* applies in the absence of common domicile), art. 161.1 (exception from both arts. 159 and 160, if another state has a manifestly closer connection with another state), and art. 161.2 (a closer connection "might be based in particular on a pre-existing relationship between the parties, such as a contract, that is closely connected with the tort/delict or the facts in question.").

[156] *See* Swiss codif. art. 133 (1) ("When the tortfeasor and the injured party have their habitual residence in the same state, delictual liability is governed by the law of that state"), and art. 133(3) ("Notwithstanding the above paragraphs, when the tortious act constitutes a violation of a pre-existing legal relationship between the tortfeasor and the injured party, claims founded on this act are governed by the law applicable to that legal relationship.")

[157] *See infra* Chapter 4 at VI.A.

[158] *See* Belgian codif. art. 99. However, the *lex loci delicti* governs certain specified torts, subject to conditions and exceptions stated in Articles 99 *et seq.*

[159] *See id.* art. 100.

4. Common Party Affiliation as the Sole Exception

Finally, 24 codifications provide that a common affiliation with the same state between the tortfeasor and the victim displaces the *lex loci delicti*, but do not phrase this exception in closer- connection terminology.[160] These codifications are discussed below, along with codifications that use this exception together with other exceptions.

C. THE COMMON DOMICILE EXCEPTION OR RULE

As Table 2.2 above indicates, 39 codifications adopted in the last 50 years, plus Rome II, which is in force in 27 countries, have adopted the notion that, when the tortfeasor and the victim are affiliated with the same state, the law of that state should displace the otherwise applicable law.[161] In addition, six other codifications have adopted the "closer connection" exception to the *lex loci* rule, an exception that is likely to lead to the same result as the common domicile exception,[162] thus raising the total number of codifications that have adopted this notion to 45.[163] Table 2.4 below lists those codifications. Indeed, it is easier to count the codifications that have *not* adopted this notion (or a similar exception that would produce the same result) than those that have.[164]

1. The Common Affiliation

The various codifications differ slightly in describing the parties' common affiliation. With regard to juridical persons, the affiliation can be the person's seat, central administration, principal place of business, or simply place of business. With regard to natural persons, the most commonly used affiliation is habitual residence, but some codifications use domicile or nationality, singly, alternatively, or (in some cases) cumulatively. For example, the common affiliation consists of:

(a) domicile in the Argentinian, Hungarian, Lithuanian, and Uruguayan codifications;[165]

---

[160] This group consists of the codifications of: Angola, Argentina, Azerbaijan, Belarus, Cape Verde, China, East Timor, Estonia, Georgia, Guinea-Bissau, Hungary, Italy, Japan, Kazakhstan, Kyrgyzstan, Lithuania, Macau, Mozambique, Portugal, Russia, Tunisia, Uruguay, Uzbekistan, and Vietnam.

[161] *See* Table 2.2, *supra* at III.A.

[162] *See id.*

[163] The Hague Convention on Products Liability also provides a common party affiliation exception (together with other exceptions) from the otherwise applicable law. Article 5 provides in part that the law of the state of the victim's habitual residence displaces the otherwise applicable law if that state is also the manufacturer's principal place of business. *See* Hague Convention on the Law Applicable to Products Liability, art. 5 (1972).

[164] The following 24 codifications do *not* contain a common-domicile rule or an equivalent (e.g., closer connection): Afghanistan, Algeria, Armenia, Burundi, Central African Republic, Croatia, Gabon, Jordan, North Korea, Latvia, Madagascar, Mauritania, Moldova, Mongolia, Peru, Qatar, Romania, Slovakia Somalia, Spain, Sudan, U.A.E., Venezuela, and Yemen. Four of these codifications (the Croatian, Romanian, Slovak, and Spanish) are superseded by Rome II, which provides such an exception.

[165] *See* Argentinian draft codif. art. 2657; Hungarian codif. art. 32(3); Lithuanian codif. art 1.43(4); Uruguayan draft codif. art. 52(2).

(b) habitual residence in the Chinese, Tunisian Serbian, and Ukrainian codifications;[166]

(c) domicile *or* residence in the Quebec codification;[167]

(d) nationality in the codifications of Azerbaijan, Belarus, Kazakhstan, Kyrgyzstan, and Uzbekistan;[168]

(e) nationality *and* residence in the Italian codification;[169]

(f) nationality *or* residence in the Russian codification;[170]

(g) nationality *or* habitual residence in the Portuguese codification and the five other codifications based on it (Angola, Cape Verde, East Timor, Macau, Mozambique);[171] and

(h) forum state nationality in the Vietnam codification.[172]

For the sake of brevity, this chapter refers to this affiliation as "domicile," and to the notion of applying the law of the parties' common affiliation as the "common-domicile rule."

2. The Various Versions of the Common-Domicile Rule

Table 2.4 below lists the codifications that have adopted a common-domicile rule, either explicitly, or implicitly as part of the "closer-connection" concept. The table also shows the three versions of this rule and the exceptions to which it is subject.

As Table 2.4 indicates, the common-domicile rule appears as an express bilateral rule in 32 codifications, as an implied bilateral rule in six codifications, and as an express unilateral rule in nine codifications.

a. Express Bilateral Rule

The common domicile rule is stated as the primary rule in some codifications, as the sole exception to the *lex loci* rule in other codifications, and as part of the closer-connection package (together with other exceptions) in other codifications.

---

[166] *See* Chinese codif. art. 46; Tunisian codif. art. 70(3); Serbian draft codif. art. 159; Ukrainian codif. art. 49(2). In the Ukrainian codification, the common-domicile rule is subject to a double-actionability requirement (discussed *infra*) that restricts both the *lex loci* rule and the common-domicile rule.

[167] *See* Quebec codif. art. 3126. ("If the parties have their domiciles or residences in the same country, the law of that country applies.").

[168] *See* Azerbaijan codif. art. 26.2; Belarus codif. art. 1129(2); Kazakhstan codif. art. 1117.2; Kyrgyzstan codif. art. 1203(2); Uzbekistan codif. art. 1194. In these countries, the common-domicile rule: (1) is phrased as a unilateral rule applicable only to torts committed abroad, and (2) is subject to a double-actionability exception. Both of these points are discussed *infra* at IV.C.2.c and IV.F.

[169] *See* Italian codif. art 62(2).

[170] *See* Russian codif. art. 1219(2). However, this exception applies only for torts "causing harm *abroad*." (emphasis added.) *See infra* at IV.C.2.c.

[171] *See* Portuguese codif. art. 45(3); Angolan codif. art. 45.3; Cape Verde codif. art. 45.3; East Timor codif. art. 44.3; Guinea-Bissau codif. art. 45.3; Macau codif. art. 44(3); Mozambique codif. art. 45.3.

[172] *See* Vietnamese codif. art 773(3) (providing that Vietnamese law applies when the tortfeasor and the victim are Vietnamese nationals and the injurious conduct occurs outside Vietnam).

TABLE 2.4. THE COMMON-DOMICILE RULE AND ITS EXCEPTIONS

	Common-domicile rule		Exceptions				
			Closer connection	Preexisting relationship	"Conduct & safety"	Double actionability	Damages
			(a) Express Bilateral Common-Domicile Rule (32 codifications)				
1	Rome II	Y	x	x	x		
2	Albania	Y	x	x	x		
3	Angola	Y			x		
4	Argentina	Y					
5	Austria	Y	x				
6	Belgium	Y	x	x	x		
7	Bulgaria	Y	x	x	x		
8	Cape Verde	Y			x		
9	China	Y					
10	East Timor	Y			x		
11	Estonia	Y	x	x			x
12	Germany	Y	x	x			x
13	Georgia	Y					
14	Guinea-Bissau	Y			x		
15	Hungary	Y			x	x	x
16	Italy	Y					
17	Japan	Y	x	x		x	x

	Common-domicile rule	Exceptions				
		Closer connection	Preexisting relationship	"Conduct & safety"	Double actionability	Damages
18	South Korea	Y	x	x			x
19	Lithuania	Y					
20	Louisiana	Y	x		x		
21	Macau	Y			x		
22	Mozambique	Y			x		
23	Netherlands	Y	x	x	x		
24	Oregon	Y	x		x		
25	Poland	Y	x	x	x		
26	Portugal	Y			x		
27	Puerto Rico	Y	x		x		
28	Quebec	Y	x				
29	Serbia	Y	x	x	x		
30	Switzerland	Y	x	x	x		x
31	Tunisia	Y			x		
32	Uruguay	Y					
	(b) Bilateral rule inferred from "close connection" exception (six codifications)					
33	FYROM	Y					
34	Liechtenstein	Y					
35	Slovenia	Y					
36	Taiwan	Y					

	Common-domicile rule		**Exceptions**			
			Closer connection	Preexisting relationship	"Conduct & safety"	Double actionability	Damages
37	Turkey	Y					x
38	U.K.	Y					

(c) Express unilateral common-domicile rule (nine codifications)

			Closer connection	Preexisting relationship	"Conduct & safety"	Double actionability	Damages
39	Azerbaijan	Y					
40	Belarus	Y				x	
41	Kazakhstan	Y				x	
42	Kyrgyzstan	Y				x	
43	Russia	Y					
44	Tajikistan	Y				x	
45	Ukraine	Y	x			x	
46	Uzbekistan	Y				x	
47	Vietnam	Y					
48		Y	18	12	20	9	7

The Belgian,[173] Serbian,[174] and Swiss[175] codifications belong to the first category because they have adopted the common-domicile rule as the primary rule, although they subject it to the preexisting relationship exception, as well as other exceptions for particular torts. In the codifications of Louisiana, Oregon, and Puerto Rico, the common-domicile rule also occupies a prominent position, but it is confined to loss-distribution, as opposed to conduct-regulation issues.[176]

In the codifications of Azerbaijan, China, Georgia, Italy, Lithuania, Russia, Uruguay, and Vietnam, the parties' common domicile in, or similar affiliation with, the same state is the sole exception from the *lex loci*.[177]

As noted earlier, Rome II[178] and the codifications of Albania,[179] Belgium,[180] Bulgaria,[181] Estonia,[182] Germany,[183] Japan,[184] South Korea,[185] and Switzerland[186] use

---

[173] Article 99 of the Belgian codification provides that torts are governed by the law of the parties' common habitual residence, or, in the absence thereof, by the law of the state of conduct, and in all other cases by the law of the state of the closest connection. Article 100 provides an exception in favor of the law that governs an existing legal relationship between the parties for cases in which the obligation has a close connection with that relationship.

[174] *See* Serbian draft codif. arts. 159–161, described at note 155, *supra*.

[175] *See* Swiss codif. art. 133, *supra* note 156.

[176] For citations and explanations, *see supra* II.C.2.

[177] *See* Azerbaijan codif. art. 26; Chinese codif. art. 44, Georgian codif. art. 42; Italian codif. art. 62; Lithuanian codif. art. 1.43; Russian codif. art. 1219; Uruguay draft. codif. art. 52; and Vietnamese codif. art. 773.

[178] *See* Rome II, Arts. 4(2), 5(1), 6(2), and 9 (law of parties' common habitual residence applies to the exclusion of the *lex loci,* unless the case is "manifestly more closely connected" with another country in which case the law of that other country governs).

[179] *See* Albanian codif. arts. 56.2, 64.2, 69.2 (law of parties' common habitual residence applies to the exclusion of the *lex loci*, unless the case is manifestly more closely connected with another country in which case the law of that other country governs).

[180] *See* Belgian codif. arts. 99–100, providing that torts are governed by the law of the parties' common habitual residence and, in the absence thereof by the *lex loci*, but if the obligation has a "close connection with an existing legal relationship between parties" the tort is governed by the law that is applicable to that relationship.

[181] *See* Bulgarian codif. art. 105.3 (law of parties' common habitual residence applies to the exclusion of the lex loci, unless the case is manifestly more closely connected with another country, in which case the law of that other country governs).

[182] *See* Estonian codif. art. 53.2(2) (providing that, if there is a "closer connection" with a state other than the one whose law is otherwise applicable under that codification, the law of the other state applies, and that a "closer connection may arise…from the fact that…the residence of the parties is in the same state").

[183] *See* German codif. 40(2) ("If the person liable to provide compensation and the injured person had their habitual residence in the same state at the time the act took place, the law of that state shall be applied.") This is an exception to the *lex loci* rule of art. 40(1), *id.*

[184] *See* Japanese codif. art. 20 (providing that the law of a state that has a manifestly closer connection displaces the otherwise applicable law and that, in determining whether such closer connection exists, one must consider whether the parties had their habitual residence in the same jurisdiction or whether the tort constitutes a breach of obligations under a contract between the parties).

[185] *See* South Korean codif. arts. 32, and 8 (providing that the *lex loci delicti* is displaced by the law of the common domicile, which is displaced by the law of the preexisting relationship, which is displaced by the law of the state that has a closer connection).

[186] *See* Swiss codif. arts. 133 and 15 (providing that the applicable law is (1) the law of the common domicile; and (2) in the absence thereof, the law of the state of conduct or injury, but both laws are displaced by the law of the preexisting relationship, if any, which in turn is displaced by the law of the state of the closest connection).

the common-domicile exception—together with other exceptions—as part of the closer-connection package.[187]

b. Implied Common-Domicile Rule

The codifications of FYROM, Liechtenstein, Slovenia, Taiwan, Turkey, and the United Kingdom provide a closer-connection exception to the *lex loci*, but not a common-domicile exception.[188] However, it is reasonable to expect that if in a given case the parties are affiliated with the same state, the law of that state is likely to apply under the closer-connection exception.[189]

c. Unilateral Common-Domicile Rule

The Russian codification provides that, if the tortfeasor and the victim are nationals or residents of the same country and cause harm "abroad," then the tort is governed by the law of the parties' common nationality or residence.[190] The word "abroad" is arguably ambiguous. It could mean (1) harm occurring outside Russia, or (2) harm occurring in a country other than the country of the parties' common nationality or residence. The first meaning is more logical because the second meaning would render the word "abroad" superfluous.[191] Indeed, according to Russian authors, the drafters of the Russian codification intended the former meaning, that is, harm occurring outside Russia.[192] This means that:

(1)   A tort committed outside Russia and involving a tortfeasor and a victim who are nationals of a third state will be governed by the law of the third state;

---

[187]   The same is true of the Dutch (art. 157) and Polish (art. 33) codifications, which incorporate by reference the provisions of Rome II.

[188]   *See supra* IV.B.1.

[189]   The same will likely be true under the 1971 Hague Convention on the Law Applicable to Traffic Accidents. Articles 4–6 of the Convention provide various exceptions to the *lex loci delicti* rule in favor of the law of the place of the car's registration, which usually coincides with the domicile of the owner. The first exception applies to single-car accidents and provides that the law of the state of registration displaces the *lex loci delicti* (1) with regard to a victim who is a passenger if he habitually resides in a state other than the *locus delicti*, and (2) with regard to a victim who is not a passenger if she habitually resides in the state of registration. The second exception applies to accidents involving two or more vehicles, and provides that the law of the state of registration displaces the *lex loci delicti* only if all the vehicles are registered in the same state. For the text of the convention, *see* http://www.hcch.net/index_en.php?act=conventions.text&cid=81. The convention is in force in 20 countries: Austria, Belarus, Belgium, Bosnia, Croatia, Czech Republic, France, FYROM, Latvia, Lithuania, Luxemburg, Montenegro, Morocco, Netherlands, Poland, Serbia, Slovakia, Slovenia, Spain, and Switzerland.

[190]   Russian codif. art. 1219.2.

[191]   Because the common-domicile rule is an exception from the principal rule of *lex loci delicti,* a tort occurring *within* the country of the parties' common domicile is governed by the law of that country, which is both the *locus delicti* and the parties' common domicile.

[192]   *See* S. Lebedev, A. Muranov, R. Khodykin & E. Kabatova, New Russian Legislation on Private International Law, 4 *Ybk. Priv. Int'l L.* 117, 142 (2002) (stating that "the rule applies only to torts committed abroad, i.e. outside the Russian Federation."); A.L. Makovskii & E.A. Sukhanov (eds.), *Kommentarii k chasti tret'ei Grazhdanskogo kodeska Rossiiskoi Federatsi*i 467–468 (2002); O. Vorobieva, *International Encyclopedia of Laws: Private International Law—Russia* § 270 (2011).

(2) A tort committed outside Russia and involving two Russians will be governed by Russian law; *but*

(3) A tort committed in Russia and involving two nationals of the same foreign country will also be governed by Russian law.

Seven other codifications in the former soviet republics of Azerbaijan, Belarus, Kazakhstan, Kyrgyzstan, Tajikistan, Ukraine, and Uzbekistan contain a rule phrased in identical language.[193] For this reason, and also because of the influence of the Russian codification on these other codifications, it is safe to assume that they too would follow the same interpretation, although the literature from those countries is silent on this point.[194]

The Vietnamese codification is more direct and also narrower in that it captures only the last two of the above three possibilities. It provides that if the tortfeasor and the victim are Vietnamese nationals and the tort occurs outside Vietnam, Vietnamese law will govern the tort,[195] in derogation from the *lex loci* rule, which applies in all other circumstances.

d. Summary and Comparison

In summary, 47 of the 73 codifications discussed in this chapter (including Rome II) apply the law of the parties' common domicile in lieu of the *lex loci delicti*. This amounts to 64 percent (Chart 2.3).[196]

As noted earlier, 85 percent of the American cases decided during the same 50-year period *and involving loss-distribution* (as opposed to conduct-regulation) conflicts have applied the law of the parties' common domicile in lieu of the law of the place of the tort.[197]

The italicized phrase signifies an important difference between the American cases and the common-domicile rules of the above codifications. In all but four of the 47 codifications, the common-domicile rules applies in principle to both loss-distribution *and* conduct-regulation issues.[198] In this sense, the rule is overbroad

---

[193] *See* Azerbaijan codif. art. 26.2; Belarus codif. art. 1129.2; Kazakhstan codif. art. 1117.2; Kyrgyzstan codif. art. 1203.2; Tajikistan codif. art. 1225.2; Ukraine codif. art. 49.2; Uzbekistan codif. art. 1194.2.

[194] *See, e.g.,* A. Danilevich, *International Encyclopedia of Laws: Private International Law—Belarus* § 248 (2012); D. Solenik, Attempting a "Judicial Restatement" of Private International Law in Belarus, 10 *Ybk Priv. Int'l L.* 505 (2008); A. Dovgert, Codification of Private International Law in Ukraine, 7 *Ybk Priv. Int'l L.* 131, 154 (2005).

[195] *See* Vietnamese codif. art. 773.3.

[196] If one were to include in this count the 27 EU countries that are bound by Rome II and exclude the 19 EU countries that have enacted a choice-of-law codification in the last 50 years, the total number of countries that follow the common-domicile rule would rise to 57 (out of 80) and the percentage would rise to 71 percent.

[197] *See supra* II.C.1.

[198] The three clear exceptions are the codifications of Louisiana, Oregon, and Puerto Rico. A fourth possible exception is the Lithuanian codification in which the common-domicile rule applies to "the reparation of damage" (art. 1.43.4), thus seemingly excluding conduct-regulation issues, such as liability.

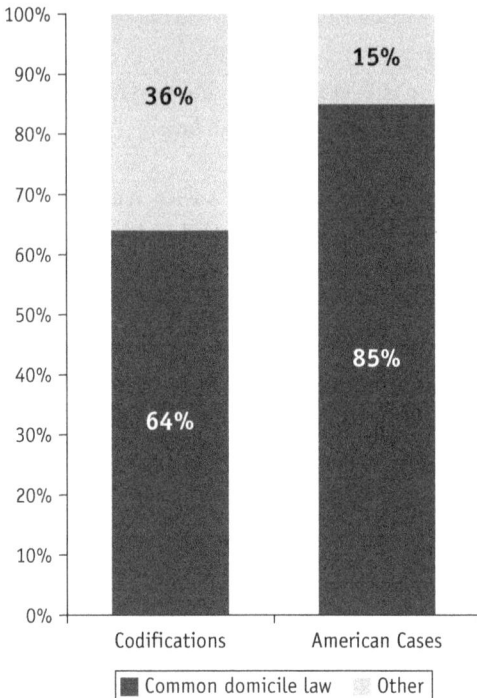

CHART 2.3. Applicable Law in Common-Domicile Cases

and, for reasons explained later, this can prove to be a serious handicap in certain cases.[199] This problem is only partly ameliorated in Rome II and the few codifications that contain a special provision for issues of "conduct and safety,"[200] which can function as a weak exception from the common-domicile rule. This provision is also discussed later.[201]

D. PARTIES DOMICILED IN STATES WITH THE SAME LAW

At the same time, the common-domicile rule is also too narrow in that it applies only when the parties are domiciled in the *same country* but not when they are domiciled in different countries that have the *same laws*. The better view is that the latter cases are functionally analogous to common-residence cases and should be treated accordingly.

Suppose, for example, that while hunting in Kenya, a French hunter injures a Belgian hunter with whom he has no preexisting relationship. Suppose that French and Belgian

---

[199] *See infra* VI.
[200] *See* the "conduct and safety" column in Table 2.4, *supra.*
[201] *See infra* V.

law provide the same amount of compensation, which is much higher than that provided by Kenya. In such a case, there is no reason to apply Kenyan law and every good reason to apply either Belgian or French law. This is the classic *false conflict* because: (1) Kenya has no interest in applying its low recovery law to a dispute between foreigners, (2) Belgium has every interest in applying its high recovery law for the protection of the Belgian victim, and (3) France has no countervailing interest because its law also provides the same high recovery as Belgium. Yet, because of the aversion by the drafters of many codifications to the concept of false conflict, this conflict will be resolved under Kenyan law. For example, Article 4(1) of Rome II mandates the application of Kenyan law, and—as explained elsewhere[202]—none of Rome II's exceptions to the *lex loci* rule would be operable in this case.

In contrast, the codifications of Louisiana, Puerto Rico, and Oregon treat this case as analogous to a common-domicile case, without using the term "false conflict." For example, the Oregon codification provides that "persons domiciled in different states shall be treated as if domiciled in the same state to the extent that the laws of those states on the disputed issues would produce the same outcome."[203]

E. THE PREEXISTING RELATIONSHIP EXCEPTION

As noted earlier, in many recent codifications, the parties' preexisting relationship (even if not accompanied by a common domicile or other common affiliation) provides a basis for an exception from the *lex loci delicti* or the normally applicable law.[204] The parties' relationship must be a contract in one codification,[205] and "may" be based on a contract in Rome II and three other codifications.[206] Other codifications refer to the relationship as "legal,"[207] "legal or factual,"[208] or simply as "pre-existing" relationship.[209]

---

[202] *See* Symeonides, *Rome II*, 196–206.

[203] Or. Rev. Stat. § 15.440(2)(b). *See also* La. Codif. Ann. art. 3544(1) ("[p]ersons domiciled in states whose law on the particular issue is substantially identical shall be treated as if domiciled in the same state."); Puerto Rico draft art. 41; American Law Institute, *Complex Litigation: Statutory Recommendations and Analysis* § 6.01(c) (2) & (3) (1994).

[204] In the United States, neither the literature nor the case law has sufficiently explored this notion. However, the place in which the parties' relationship, if any, is centered is one of the contacts that courts consider under the Restatement (Second), or other modern approaches, in selecting the applicable law. *See, e.g., Restatement (Second)* § 145(2)(d).

[205] *See* Japanese codification art. 20.

[206] *See* Rome II art. 4.3; Albanian codif. art. 56.4; Bulgarian codif. art. 105.3; Serbian draft. codif. art. 161.2.

[207] *See* Belgian codif. art. 100; Dutch Torts Act of 2001, codif. art. 5; South Korean codif. art. 32.3; Swiss codif. art. 133.3.

[208] *See* Estonian codif. art. 35.2; German codif. art. 41(2) (1).

[209] *See* Rome II art. 4(3); Bulgarian codif. art. 105(3).

This exception is phrased either: (1) as a particular example of the closer-connection exception, as in Rome II[210] and the Albanian,[211] Bulgarian,[212] Estonian,[213] German,[214] Japanese,[215] and Serbian[216] codifications; or (2) as an independent exception, as in the Belgian,[217] Dutch,[218] South Korean,[219] and Swiss[220] codifications.[221]

The codifications of the second group expressly state that, when the court finds the preexisting relationship exception applicable, the law that governs the relationship will also govern the tort. In Rome II and the codifications of the first group, this exception is more ambiguous. It may lead to the application of either (1) the same law as that which governs the preexisting relationship, or (2) the law of the same state in which the preexisting relationship is primarily *centered* and which is presumptively the state of the closest connection.

To be sure, in some cases, the two directions will lead to the same destination. For example, if the preexisting relationship is a family relationship centered in state X, then the law of that state will govern that relationship in general and, under the above exception, the court may apply the same law to a related delictual obligation.[222] If, however, the

---

[210] *See* Article 4(3) of Rome II (providing that the otherwise applicable law is displaced by the law of a state that has a "manifestly closer connection" and that such a connection "might be based…on a pre-existing relationship between the parties, such as a contract that is closely connected with the tort/delict in question").

[211] *See* Albanian codif. art. 56.4 (providing that a manifestly closer connection may be based on a preexisting relationship between the parties, such as a contract that is closely connected with the tort).

[212] *See* Bulgarian codif. art. 105(3) (providing that a manifestly closer connection "may be based on a pre-existing relationship between the parties, such as a contract that is closely connected with the tort or delict in question").

[213] *See* Estonian codif. art. 53(2) (providing that a closer connection "may arise" from a "legal relationship or factual connection" between the parties).

[214] *See* German codif. art. 41(2)(1) (providing that "a special legal or factual relationship between the parties in connection with the obligation" may indicate a "substantially closer connection" to a state other than the one whose law is designated as applicable by Articles 38–40, and that in such a case, the law of the state of the closer connection applies.)

[215] *See* Japanese codif. art. 20 (providing for the application of "the law of the place which is manifestly more closely connected with the tort…considering that…the tort constitutes a breach of obligations under a contract between the parties").

[216] *See* Serbian draft codif. art. 161.3, quoted at note 155, *supra*.

[217] *See* Belgian codif. art. 100 ("an obligation resulting from an injurious event having a close connection with a pre-existing legal relationship between the parties is governed by the law applicable to that relationship").

[218] *See* art. 5 of Dutch Act of 11 April 2001 Regarding Conflict of Laws on Torts (providing that when the tort "is closely connected with an existing legal relationship[,]" the law that governs that relationship displaces the otherwise applicable law).

[219] *See* Korean codif. art. 32(3) ("if the tort violates an existing legal relationship between the tortfeasor and the injured party, the tort shall be governed by the law applicable to the legal relationship").

[220] *See* Swiss codif. art. 133(3) ("when the tortious act constitutes a violation of a pre-existing legal relationship between the tortfeasor and the injured party, claims founded on this act are governed by the law applicable to that legal relationship").

[221] The Chinese Model Law (art. 115) provided that the law that governs the preexisting relationship would govern the tort only if that law was more favorable to the tort victim than the otherwise applicable law. The Chinese codification did not adopt the preexisting relationship exception.

[222] The common-domicile rule can obtain the result more directly. This means that this exception is superfluous in most cases in which the parties to the relationship are residents of the same state.

relationship is contractual,[223] then there is no guarantee that the state in which the relationship is centered will also be the state whose law will govern the contract. For example, the contract may contain a choice-of-law clause stipulating the application of the law of state Z, even if that state has a relatively tenuous but otherwise sufficient connection with the relationship. In such a case, the question is which (if either) of the two states, X or Z, will be the candidate for the closer- connection exception. State Z cannot be the candidate because, in this scenario, it does not have a close enough factual connection. On the other hand, state X has a factual connection, but the application of its law will defeat the apparent purpose of this exception, which is to apply the same law to both the tort and contract aspects of the case.

F. THE DOUBLE ACTIONABILITY RULE

A surprising number of codifications (15) continue to follow the old double-actionability rule for torts that otherwise would be governed by foreign law. This rule provides that, if the conduct is actionable under the normally applicable foreign law, the defendant will nevertheless not be held liable unless the conduct is also actionable under the law of the forum. This group consists of the codifications of: Afghanistan, Algeria, Belarus, Japan, Jordan, Kazakhstan, North Korea, Kyrgyzstan, Qatar, Somalia, Sudan, Tajikistan, Ukraine, the United Arab Emirates, and Uzbekistan.[224] In addition, the double actionability rule survives in the United Kingdom for defamation cases.[225] In contrast, the new codifications of China,[226] Russia,[227] and Taiwan,[228] as well as a revision of the Hungarian codification,[229] have abandoned the double-actionability rule.

---

[223] If the relationship is merely social rather than legal, as in *Babcock v. Jackson*, in which the parties were neighbors who drove together from New York to Ontario, it makes little sense to say that the tort will be governed by the same law that governs the relationship because the social relationship may not, as such, be governed by any law. However, it does make sense to say that the tort will be governed by the law of the state in which the relationship was centered.

[224] *See* Afghanistan codif. art.29.2; Algerian codif. art 20(2); Belarus codif. art. 1129(3); Japanese codif. art. 22; Jordanian codif. art. 22(2); Kazakhstan codif. art. 1117.3; North Korean codif. art. 31(2); Kyrgyzstan codif. art. 1203(3); Qatar codif. art. 30(2); Somali codif. art. 21.2; Sudanese codif. art. 11(14) (b); Tajikistan codif. art. 1225.4; U.A.E codif. art. 20(2); Ukrainian codif. art. 49.3; Uzbekistan codif. art. 1194.4.

[225] *See* C. Roodt, *English Report,* at C.I.(a), (c).

[226] Article 146(2) of the General Principles of Civil Law of 12 April 1986 provided that an act committed outside China shall not be treated as tortious if it was not tortious under Chinese law. The new Chinese codification of 2010 does not contain a similar provision. *See* Chinese codif. art. 46.

[227] *See* Russian codif. art. 1219; S. Lebedev, A. Muranov, R. Khodykin & E. Kabatova, New Russian Legislation on Private International Law, 4 *Ybk. Priv. Int'l L.* 117, 142–143 (2002).

[228] *See* Taiwanese codif. art. 25 (abolishing the double actionability rule of Article 9 of the codification of 1953); Rong-chwan Chen, *Taiwanese Report,* at XI.1.

[229] Until 2009, Article 34.1 of the Hungarian codification provided that a Hungarian court "shall not determine [impose?] liability for…conduct which is not unlawful under Hungarian law" and "shall not determine [impose?] legal consequences for infliction of tortious damages, which are not known under Hungarian law." This provision was deleted by Act IX of 2009 as inconsistent with Rome II, although it remains applicable for torts occurring before that year.

The latest and strictest expression of the double-actionability rule is found in the Japanese codification, which interposes a double hurdle in the plaintiff's recovery, with regard to both liability and damages. Paragraph 1 of Article 22 addresses the issue of liability. It provides that, when a foreign law governs a tort, the defendant cannot be held liable "if the actions causing the tort are not unlawful under Japanese law."[230] Paragraph 2 of the same article addresses the issue of damages or other remedies. It provides that "even if the actions causing the tort are unlawful both under that foreign law and Japanese law, the victim may not claim any greater recovery of damages or any other remedies than those available under Japanese law."[231]

Article 31 of the North Korean codification is also a double-hurdle rule. It precludes liability for conduct outside North Korea that is not tortious under North Korean law, and also provides that if the foreign conduct is tortious under both foreign law and North Korean law, the defendant "shall be liable within the scope prescribed by the law of [North Korea]."[232]

In 12 other codifications described below, the double-actionability rule does not carry this second hurdle regarding damages. For example, the Belarus codification provides that a foreign law that would otherwise governs a tort "shall not be applied" if the conduct is "not illegal" under the law of Belarus.[233]

The common feature of this and all other versions of the double-actionability rule is that they all function as an exception to the application of *foreign* law. Beyond that, the precise function of this rule depends on what the principal rule for tort conflicts is in the particular codification and what, if any, are its exceptions. In this context, the 13 codifications can be divided into two groups.

The first group consists of codifications that follow the *lex loci delicti* rule without exceptions other than the double-actionability requirement. The codifications of Afghanistan, Algeria, Jordan, Qatar, Somalia, Sudan, and the United Arab Emirates belong to this group.[234] They provide that the *lex loci delicti* does not apply to conduct that occurred in another state and that is not wrongful under forum law, even though it is wrongful under the law of the foreign state. Thus, in these codifications, the double-actionability rule functions as a *lex fori* exception to the *foreign lex loci delicti* for torts that occur abroad, regardless of whether they involve domestic or foreign parties and regardless of whether they are domiciled in the same or different states. In practice, domestic defendants are the most likely beneficiaries of the double-actionability requirement because they are always subject to jurisdiction in the forum state and are more likely to be sued there.

---

[230] Japanese codif. art. 22(1).

[231] *Id.* art. 22(2).

[232] North Korean codif. art. 31(2).

[233] Belarus codif. art. 1129(3).

[234] *See* Afghanistan codif. art.29.2; Algerian codif. art 20(2); Jordanian codif. art. 22(2); Qatar codif. art. 30(2); Somali codif. art. 21.2; Sudanese codif. art. 11(14)(b); U.A.E. codif. art. 20(2).

The second group consists of the codifications of Belarus, Kazakhstan, Kyrgyzstan, Tajikistan, Ukraine, and Uzbekistan, which have adopted the common-domicile exception to the *lex loci delicti* rule.[235] These codifications provide that the normally applicable "foreign law" "shall not apply" if the foreign conduct is not actionable under forum law, even though it is actionable under the foreign law.[236] Thus, here again, the double-actionability requirement functions as a *lex fori* exception to foreign law.

The difference from the previous group is that here the exception applies not only when the foreign law applies by virtue of the *lex loci delicti* rule but also when it applies by virtue of the common-domicile rule. For example, for a tort occurring in the non-forum state X, the applicable law will be: (1) the law of state X if the parties are not domiciled in the same state; (2) the law of state Y, if both parties are domiciled in state Y; and (3) the law of the forum state, for example, Belarus, if both parties are domiciled in Belarus. However, if the conduct is not actionable in Belarus (although it is actionable in state X), then the double-actionability requirement will prevent the application of the laws of states X and Y in cases (1) and (2), respectively. In case (3), the double-actionability requirement would be inapplicable because forum law, not foreign law, would govern that case. Thus, this scheme protects all foreign defendants involved in foreign torts and all forum defendants involved in foreign torts in which the victims are foreigners, but not forum defendants involved in foreign torts in which the victims are also forum domiciliaries.

G. OTHER UNILATERAL EXCEPTIONS IN FAVOR OF THE *LEX FORI*

As the discussion in the preceding section indicates, there are two versions of the double-actionability rule. The first and most common version addresses only the issue of liability (or actionability). The second and stricter version followed in Japan and North Korea addresses both the issue of liability and the issue of recoverable damages. Although these rules do not differentiate between foreign and domestic defendants, in actuality the latter defendants are the primary beneficiaries of this rule. This is because domestic defendants are more likely than foreign defendants to be subject to jurisdiction in the forum state for torts committed abroad.

Two codifications take a more direct route to protecting domestic defendants through the application of forum law.[237] The Mongolian codification provides that if the injury occurred outside Mongolia and the tortfeasor is a Mongolian natural or legal person,

---

[235] As noted at IV.C.2.c, *supra*, in these codifications, the common-domicile rule is phrased in unilateral terms covering only situations where the tort occurs *outside* the forum state and not torts occurring in the forum state.

[236] *See* Belarus codif. art. art. 1129(3); Kazakhstan codif. art. 1117.3; Kyrgyzstan codif. art. 1203(3); Tajikistan codif. art. 1225.4; Ukrainian codif. art. 49.3; Uzbekistan codif. art. 1194.4.

[237] This reference to "protection" assumes that the *lex fori* is more protective of defendants than foreign law, although this assumption may not be accurate in all cases.

then Mongolian law governs both liability and damages.[238] The Vietnamese codification has a similar but narrower rule, which provides that Vietnamese law applies to foreign torts if both the tortfeasor and the victim are Vietnamese nationals.[239]

Four other codifications have adopted a softer rule that does not address the issue of liability (and thus it is not an "actionability" rule) but which limits recovery to the standards of the *lex fori*. One of them, the Estonian codification, provides that, when a tort is governed by foreign law, "compensation ordered in Estonia shall not be significantly greater than the compensation prescribed for similar damage by Estonian law."[240]

The Swiss, Romanian, and Turkish codifications contain similar rules, but only for certain torts. The Swiss codification provides that, in products liability and obstruction-to-competition cases governed by foreign law, "no damages may be awarded in Switzerland *other than* those that would be awarded…under Swiss law."[241] The italicized words are from the French text of the codification. In the German text, the corresponding words are "no damages…*beyond that*." Thus, the two texts can be interpreted to mean different things. While the German text addresses the amount of damages, the French text addresses not only the amount but also the type of damages and thus would exclude, for example, punitive damages, which are not available under Swiss law. The Romanian codification provides that, in product liability and unfair competition cases, Romanian courts may award damages under the applicable foreign law, but "only within the limits fixed by Romanian law."[242] The Turkish codification has a similar provision regarding the amount of damages in cases of obstruction to competition.[243]

Before its 2009 revision, the Hungarian codification favored plaintiffs by allowing them to choose between the laws of the state of conduct and the state of injury in cross-border torts,[244] and between the laws of the forum and the state of injury in torts involving the "infringement of personal rights."[245] It also provided that: (1) if under the law governing the "tortious act" liability is conditioned on a finding of culpability, "the existence of culpability can be determined by either the personal law of the tortfeasor or the law of the place of injury";[246] and that (2) even in cases otherwise governed by foreign law, Hungarian courts "shall not impose liability for…conduct that is not unlawful under

---

[238] Mongolian codif. art. 551.2.

[239] Vietnamese codif. art. 773.3.

[240] Estonian codif. art. 52.

[241] Swiss codif. arts. 135(2) and 137(2) (emphasis added).

[242] Romanian codif. arts. 116, 119.

[243] Turkish codif. art 38(2).

[244] *See* Hungarian codif. art. 32(2), in force until 4 April 2009.

[245] *Id.* art. 10(2) (providing that "[c]laims arising from the infringement of personal rights shall be determined by the law of the place and time of the injury; if, however, the Hungarian law provides preferable compensation for the injured person, the claim shall be adjudicated according to Hungarian law."). This provision was retained by the 2009 revision and renumbered as art. 10(3).

[246] *Id.* art. 32(4). This provision was deleted in 2009 (see Act IX of 2009) but remains applicable to torts committed before that year.

Hungarian law…[nor] impose legal consequences not known to Hungarian law."[247] The 2009 revision deleted the above provisions as inconsistent with Rome II[248] but retained the provision regarding infringement of personal rights, a subject that is not covered by Rome II.[249]

The German and South Korean damages-limiting rules are more subtle. The German rule provides that damages claims for a tort governed by foreign law "cannot be raised insofar as they (1) go substantially beyond what is necessary for an adequate compensation of the injured party, [or] (2) obviously serve purposes other than an adequate compensation of the injured party[.]"[250] The South Korean rule provides that damages for a tort governed by foreign law "shall not be awarded if the nature of the damages is clearly not appropriate to merit compensation to the injured party or if the extent of the damages substantially exceeds appropriate compensation to the injured party."[251]

From a methodological perspective, these provisions differ in some respects from the Swiss provisions and those of the other countries described above. For example, strictly speaking, the German and South Korean provisions are not unilateral choice-of-law rules (or for that matter choice-of-law rules); they do not mandate the automatic application of forum law to the exclusion of foreign law. Rather they are substantivist provisions authorizing the judge to scrutinize foreign law through the lenses of the forum's substantive law and to reject claims considered excessive or punitive under that law. In this sense, these provisions may be characterized as specialized *ordre public* exception clauses.[252] At the same time, however, these provisions dramatically lower the threshold for interjecting the forum's public policy and are likely to produce the same pro-forum results as the Swiss, Romanian, and Turkish provisions.

V. Rules of "Conduct and Safety"

The 1966 Portuguese codification—which was among the first codifications to introduce the common-party–affiliation exception to the *lex loci delicti*—provided that the application of the law of the parties' common nationality or habitual residence shall be "without prejudice" to those provisions of the *lex loci delicti* that "must be applied to all persons

---

[247] Hungarian codif. art 34. For a critique, *see* L. Burián, *Hungarian Report*, in S. Symeonides, *Progress or Regress*, 267 (characterizing this provision as "[p]erhaps the most shocking example of promoting national interests.").

[248] *See* Hungarian codif. art. 32 as revised by Act IX of 2009. The old article remains applicable to torts committed before 2009.

[249] *See* Hungarian codif. art. 10(3) as revised by Act IX of 2009.

[250] German codif. art 40(3).

[251] South Korean codif art. 32(4).

[252] A draft of what later became Rome II provided specifically that the application of a foreign law that imposed exemplary or punitive damages was contrary to Community public policy. This provision was dropped in the final text on the assumption that the generic *ordre public* reservation would likely produce the same result in most cases without mandating it in all cases.

without differentiation."²⁵³ Thus, this codification differentiated between two categories of tort rules: (1) those that must be applied to all conduct within the *locus* state, and (2) those that need not be so applied. In time, the rules of the first category came to be known as rules of "conduct and safety," and, in the United States, as conduct-regulating rules (as opposed to loss-allocation rules).²⁵⁴ Obviously, this differentiation becomes important in all cases in which the applicable law is that of a state other than the state of conduct, such as: (1) cases governed by the law of the parties' common affiliation or preexisting relationship, or (2) cross-border torts in countries that apply the law of the state of injury.

A few years later, the 1972 Hague Products Convention used the term "rules of conduct and safety,"²⁵⁵ whereas the 1971 Hague Traffic Accidents Convention understandably referred to rules relating to the "control and safety of traffic." The latter convention provided that "[w]hatever may be the applicable law" on other issues, "in determining liability account shall be taken of rules relating to the control and safety of traffic which were in force at the place and time of the accident."²⁵⁶ The 1979 Hungarian codification provided that the law of the state of conduct "shall determine" whether the conduct was "realized by the violation of traffic or other security regulations."²⁵⁷

At least 16 other codifications have since adopted the same notion, albeit using slightly different phraseology. Among them are the following formulations, some of the nuances of which may be lost in translation:

- The 1987 Swiss codification provides that rules of "safety and conduct" in force at the place of the act "are taken into consideration,"²⁵⁸ regardless of the law applicable to the rest of the case;
- The 1992 Romanian codification provides that the "security and conduct" regulations of the conduct state "must be observed in all cases."²⁵⁹
- The 1998 Tunisian codification authorizes the "taking into consideration" of the rules "de sécurité et de comportement" of the conduct state;²⁶⁰

---

²⁵³ Portuguese codif. art. 45(3). The codifications of Angola, Cape Verde, East Timor, Guinea-Bissau, Macau, and Mozambique, which are identical to the Portuguese codification, contain an identical provision.

²⁵⁴ For this distinction in American conflicts law, *see supra* II.B.

²⁵⁵ Hague Convention on the Law Applicable to Products Liability of 1972, art. 9 ("The application of [another law] shall not preclude consideration being given to the rules of conduct and safety prevailing in the State where the product was introduced into the market.").

²⁵⁶ Hague Convention on the Law Applicable to Traffic Accidents, art. 7.

²⁵⁷ Hungarian codif. art. 33.1 (providing that the law of the state of conduct "shall determine" whether the conduct was "realized by the violation of traffic or other security regulations."). This provision is retained by the 2009 and renumbered as art. 34.1.

²⁵⁸ Swiss codif. art. 142(2) (providing that "[r]ules of safety and conduct in force at the place of the act are to be taken into consideration.")

²⁵⁹ Romanian codif. art. 110.110 (providing that the security and conduct rules of the conduct state "must be observed in all cases.").

²⁶⁰ Tunisian codif. art. 75 ("Les règles de sécurité et de comportement en vigueur au lieu où s'est produit le fait dommageable sont prises en considération.").

- The 2001 Dutch Torts Act authorized the "taking into account" of the "traffic and safety regulations and other comparable regulations for the protection of persons or property" in force at the place of the tort;[261]
- The 2004 Belgian codification provides that "consideration must be given" to the "safety and conduct" rules of the conduct state;[262]
- The 2005 Bulgarian codification provides that "regard must be had" to the rules of "safety and conduct" of the conduct state;[263] and
- The 2007 Rome II Regulation provides that "[i]n assessing the conduct" of the person claimed to be liable, "account shall be taken, as a matter of fact and in so far as is appropriate," of the rules of "safety and conduct" of the conduct state.[264]

It is possible that the precise scope of rules of conduct and/or safety varies from codification to codification,[265] although it appears similar to (albeit narrower than) the American concept of conduct-regulating rules, a variation of which is also used in the Louisiana and Puerto Rico codifications.[266] For example, the phrase "rules of safety and conduct," which is used in some of the above codifications, is arguably broader than other phrases, such as "rules of conduct *and safety*" (which is used in the Swiss codification), or "rules relating to the control and safety of traffic" (which is used in other codifications).[267] Another difference, discussed later, is between the Portuguese, Hungarian, and Romanian codifications, which require the application of the conduct and safety rules of the conduct state, and all the other codifications that only contain mild admonitions to the courts to "consider" or "take account" of those rules.

VI. Summary and Critique of the Exceptions

By way of summary, Figure 2.1 below depicts the various exceptions to the *lex loci delicti* rule.

---

[261] *See* art. 6 of Act of 11 April 2001 Regarding Conflict of Laws on Torts (authorizing the "taking into account" of the "traffic and safety regulations and other comparable regulations for the protection of persons or property" in force at the "place of the tort.").

[262] Belgian codif. art. 102 (providing that "consideration must be given to the safety and conduct rules" of the conduct state.).

[263] Bulgarian codif. art. 115 (providing that "regard must be had to the rules of safety and conduct" of the conduct state).

[264] Rome II art. 17. For a comprehensive discussion of this article, *see* J. von Hein, Die Behandlung von Sicherheits- und Verhaltensregeln nach Art. 17 der Rom II-Verordnung, in H. Kronke & K. Thorn (eds.), *Grenzen über- winden, Prinzipien bewahren: Festschrift für Bernd von Hoffmann* 139 (2012). Identical provisions are found in the codifications of Albania (art. 59); Austria (art. 48.1, incorporating Rome II), Poland (art. 33, incorporating Rome II), and Serbia (draft art. 176).

[265] It is also possible that some of these differences are the result of different translations of identical terms.

[266] *See* La. codif. art. 3543; Puerto Rico draft codif. art. 40.

[267] The phrase "traffic and safety regulations and other comparable regulations for the *protection of persons or property*," used in the Dutch Torts Act of 2001, occupies the enigmatic middle.

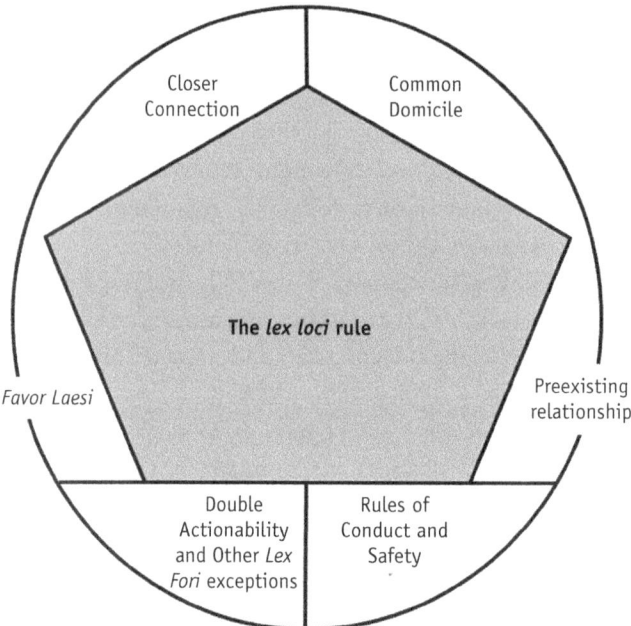

FIGURE 2.1. The *Lex Loci Delicti* Rule and Its Exceptions

It is first important to note that not all of the codifications that fall within the coverage of this chapter have all of these exceptions. Second, these exceptions operate differently. Some of them overlap, and some of them operate against the *lex loci* rule while others operate against each other and *in favor* of that rule. For example:

- In some codifications, the common domicile and preexisting relationship exceptions are particular, stated or unstated, examples of the closer-connection exception, while in other codifications the closer connection functions as an exception from the common domicile and preexisting relationship exceptions.
- The *favor laesi* exception operates only in cross-border torts. When it does operate, it leads to the application of either the law of the state of conduct (i.e., the *lex loci commissi*) or the law of the state of injury (i.e., the *lex loci damni*), depending on which of the two favors the victim. Strictly speaking, therefore, whether the *favor laesi* principle is an exception to the *lex loci delicti* rule depends on how the particular codification defines the *locus delicti*. In any event, like the *lex loci* rule itself, the *favor laesi* is a *territorial* exception because it leads from one territorially connected law to another.
- The double-actionability exception operates against the *lex loci* rule (in either cross-border or intra-state torts), but only when that rule points to a foreign law. It operates in the same fashion against exceptions to the *lex loci* rule (such as the common-domicile exception) when they point to a foreign law, and, in some of those cases, the result will be a return to the *lex loci*.

- Finally, the exception regarding rules of conduct and safety operates only when the applicable choice-of-law rule points to the law of a state *other than* the state of conduct.

Overall, the adoption of these exceptions is a sign of progress because they introduce a degree of flexibility that is necessary for a rational resolution of tort conflicts. However, some of these exceptions are overbroad, others are too narrow or timid, and with the exception of the "conduct and safety" exception, which is deficient in other respects, they are phrased in holistic, all-or-nothing terms, rather than on an issue-by-issue basis.

Let us take the common-domicile exception. As noted earlier, the exception is too narrow because it is limited to situations in which the parties are domiciled in the same *state* and does not encompass the functionally equivalent cases in which the parties are domiciled in states that have identical *laws*.[268]

At the same time, the common-domicile exception is too broad to the extent that it encompasses not only issues of loss-distribution but also ones of conduct regulation. This is a serious defect. As a general proposition, a state has an interest in enforcing its conduct-regulating rules even if neither the violator nor the victim is domiciled in that state, and even if both parties are domiciled in the same foreign state.

For example, an Austrian motorist involved in a French accident may not claim exemption from French traffic rules, and if injured by conduct that violates these rules, France may not deny her the benefit of their protection. Even if both parties are domiciled in Austria, France has the exclusive claim to apply its law to the conduct-regulating aspects of the case. These aspects are *not* limited to rules of public law or pure traffic rules, such as speed limits and red lights; they also extend to rules that impose civil liability for violations of traffic rules or attach presumptions and inferences of fault that arise from certain violations, such as not maintaining sufficient distance from the preceding car. Yet, a common-domicile rule that is phrased in global terms (as the rules of the codifications discussed earlier) would mandate the application of Austrian law to all aspects of the case.

This problem is exacerbated in codifications that do not subject the common-domicile rule to any escapes, especially the "conduct and safety" exception. Several codifications fall into this category, including those of Azerbaijan, China, Georgia, Italy, Kazakhstan, South Korea, Kyrgyzstan, Russia, Tajikistan, Ukraine, Uruguay, Uzbekistan, and Vietnam.[269] The problem could be resolved under Rome II and those other codifications that subject the common-domicile rule to a closer-connection exception. However, as

---

[268] *See supra* IV.C.2.d.

[269] *See* Azerbaijan codif. art. 26; Chinese codif. art. 44; Georgian codif. art. 42; Italian codif. art. 62(2); Kazakhstan codif. art. 1117; South Korean codif. art. 32.2; Kyrgyzstan codif. art. 1203; Russian codif. art. 1219.2; Tajikistan codif. art. 1225.2; Ukrainian codif. art. 49; Uruguay draft codif. art. 52; Uzbekistan codif. art. 1194; Vietnam codif. art. 773.

explained in detail elsewhere in discussing Rome II, this exception is not easily employ-able, at least as formulated in Rome II.[270]

What is left, therefore, is the "conduct and safety" exception. Unfortunately, even that exception can ameliorate the problem only partially, if at all. For example, Article 17 of Rome II authorizes the consideration—but not necessarily the *application*—of the rules of conduct and safety, and only "as a matter of fact and in so far as is appropriate" in "assessing the conduct" of the alleged tortfeasor. The equivocal wording of this article, along with its legislative history, suggests that it is intended as a mere evidentiary instruction about which facts to consider in assessing the defendant's culpability, rather than as a true choice-of-law rule calling for the *application* of the conduct and safety rules of the state of conduct.[271]

This restrictive phraseology contradicts the general proposition that conduct-regulating rules operate territorially. Travelers do not carry with them the conduct-regulating rules of their home state, even when they travel with their fellow citizens. Conversely, a state has an interest in enforcing its conduct-regulating rules, even if neither the viola-tor nor the victim is domiciled in that state and even if both parties are domiciled in the same foreign state.[272] For example, an Algerian worker injured in France at a work-site operated by an Algerian employer may not be denied the protection of the French conduct-regulating rules, nor may the employer claim exemption from those rules. Even if both parties are domiciled in Algeria, France has the exclusive claim to apply its law to the conduct-regulating aspects of the case. Yet, because of the broad and unqualified phrasing of the common-domicile rule of Rome II, Algerian law must apply to all aspects of the case, including conduct regulation. The timidity of Article 17 (and its tilt toward defendants) becomes problematic if the employer would be liable under French law but not under Algerian law. In such a case, any "taking into account" of French law that stops short of *applying* it would do little to protect France's interests in promoting work safety within its borders, or, for that matter, protecting a worker injured and hospitalized in France.[273]

It is rather ironic that American conflicts law, which embraced the principle of ter-ritoriality wholesale during Joseph Beale's time,[274] partially retreated from this principle fairly early by adopting an exception to it for common-domicile cases, but only for those involving loss-distribution conflicts. In contrast, many foreign systems, which in areas other than torts have been far less hospitable to the principle of territoriality,[275] clung to this principle much longer and then moved quite far in the opposite direction, toward the principle of personality, by adopting an overbroad common-domicile rule. This may

---

[270] *See* Symeonides, *Rome II*, 197–203.
[271] For extensive discussion and critique, *see id.* at 211–215.
[272] *See* Symeonides, *Reciprocal Lessons*, 1755–1762.
[273] *Id.*
[274] *See supra* at I; Symeonides, *The First Conflicts Restatement*, 57–59.
[275] *See id.*

be one of very few instances in which foreign conflicts law has been less cautious than its American counterpart.[276]

VII. Products Liability

Twenty-six codifications, including Rome II, contain special choice-of-law rules for product liability conflicts, as distinguished from generic tort conflicts. In alphabetical order, these codifications are those of: Albania, Azerbaijan, Belarus, Belgium, Bulgaria, China, Italy, Japan, Kazakhstan, Kyrgyzstan, Lithuania, Louisiana, Moldova, Oregon, Puerto Rico, Quebec, Romania, Rome II, Russia, Switzerland, Taiwan, Tajikistan, Tunisia, Turkey, Ukraine, and Uzbekistan.[277]

A. CONTACTS-BASED RULES

The first set of choice-of-law rules especially designed for products liability was adopted in 1973 with the Hague Convention on the Law Applicable to Products Liability,[278] which is now in force in 11 European countries.[279] This convention provides that the law of the state of the victim's habitual residence applies, as long as that state is also: (1) the defendant's principal place of business, or (2) the place where the victim acquired the product.[280] If these conditions are not met, then the law of the state of injury applies, as long as that state is also: (1) the victim's habitual residence, or (2) the defendant's principal place of business, or (3) the place where the victim acquired the product.[281] When none of the above conditions is met, the victim is given a choice between the law of the state of injury and the law of state of the defendant's principal place of business.[282] The Convention also protects the defendant by providing a defense that is now found in many other codifications, albeit in slightly different formulations. This defense provides

---

[276] For the movement of the pendulum between territoriality and personality, *see* Symeonides, *Territoriality and Personality*, 401, *et seq.*

[277] For citations, *see infra* VII.A-B.

[278] *See* Convention of 2 October 1973 on the Law Applicable to Products Liability at http://www.hcch.net/index_en.php?act= conventions.status&cid=84.

[279] These countries are Croatia, Finland, France, FYROM, Luxembourg, Netherlands, Montenegro, Norway, Serbia, Slovenia, and Spain. *See* http://www.hcch.net/index_en.php?act=conventions.status&cid=84

[280] *See* Convention art. 5 (providing that the applicable law shall be the internal law of the state of the habitual residence of the person directly suffering damage, if that state is also: (1) the principal place of business of the person claimed to be liable, or (2) the place where the product was acquired by the person directly suffering damage).

[281] *Id.* art. 4 ("…the applicable law shall be the internal law of the State of the place of injury, if that State is also: (a) the place of the habitual residence of the person directly suffering damage, or (b) the principal place of business of the person claimed to be liable, or (c) the place where the product was acquired by the person directly suffering damage").

[282] *Id.* art. 6 ("Where neither of the laws designated in Articles 4 and 5 applies, the applicable law shall be the internal law of the State of the principal place of business of the person claimed to be liable, unless the claimant bases his claim upon the internal law of the State of the place of injury.").

that the defendant may prevent the application of the law of the place of injury or of the victim's habitual residence by showing that he could not reasonably have foreseen that the product that caused the injury, or his products of the same type, would be made available in those states through commercial channels.[283]

The Lithuanian codification follows an identical combination of contacts as the Hague Convention.[284] The Louisiana, Oregon, and Puerto Rico codifications follow a similar combination of contacts but also combine unilateral rules with bilateral ones. The Louisiana rule provides that, subject to a foreseeability/commercial unavailability proviso, the law of the forum state governs cases in which: (1) the injury was sustained in that state by a domiciliary or resident of that state; or (2) the product was manufactured, produced, or acquired in that state, and the victim was a domiciliary of that state or the injury occurred there.[285] Cases in which the forum state lacks the above combinations of contacts are relegated to other rules that require an issue-by-issue analysis that, more likely than not, will lead to the application of non-forum law. The Oregon and Puerto Rico rules are substantially identical.[286]

The Belgian, Bulgarian, and Japanese codifications follow a simpler formula. The Belgian codification calls for the application of the law of the victim's habitual residence, subject to the preexisting relationship exception.[287] The Bulgarian codification calls for the application of the law of the victim's habitual residence, subject to a foreseeability proviso and subject to the common habitual residence and closer-connection exceptions.[288] The Japanese codification calls for the application of law of the state of the product's delivery, subject to a foreseeability proviso and the closer-connection exception, but also limits damages and other remedies to those provided by Japanese law.[289]

Article 5, paragraph 1 of the Rome II Regulation designates, in successive order, three countries whose law may govern: (1) the country of the victim's habitual residence, (2) the country in which the product was acquired, and (3) the country in which the injury

---

[283] *Id.* art. 7 ("Neither the law of the State of the place of injury nor the law of the State of the habitual residence of the person directly suffering damage shall be applicable…if the person claimed to be liable establishes that he could not reasonably have foreseen that the product or his own products of the same type would be made available in that State through commercial channels.").

[284] Article 1.43.5 of the Lithuanian codification provides for the application of the law of (1) the state of injury, if that state is also the victim's domicile or the defendant's place of business or the place of the product's acquisition; or (2) the victim's domicile, if that state is also the defendant's place of business or the place of the product's acquisition; and (3) if the above combinations are not present, the law of the defendant's place of business, unless the victim opts for the law of the state of injury.

[285] *See* La. codif. art. 3545. For an explanation of the rationale of this article by its drafter, including the reasons for using a unilateralist technique, *see* Symeonides, *Louisiana Exegesis*, 749–759. For a critique, *see* P.J. Kozyris, Values and Methods in Choice of Law for Products Liability: A Comparative Comment on Statutory Solutions, 38 *Am. J. Comp. L.* 475 (1990); R. Weintraub, The Contributions of Symeonides and Kozyris to Making Choice of Law Predictable and Just: An Appreciation and Critique, 38 *Am. J. Comp. L.* 511 (1990).

[286] *See* Or. Rev. Stat. § 15.435, discussed in Symeonides, *Oregon Torts Exegesis*, 986–993 (2010); Puerto Rico draft codif. art. 42.

[287] *See* Belgian codif. art. 99 § 2.4, and art. 100.

[288] *See* Bulgarian codif. art. 106.

[289] *See* Japanese codif. arts 18, 20, and 22(2).

occurred. The application of each country's law depends on whether the product was "marketed in that country."[290] For example, if a German plaintiff is injured in India by a product acquired in Egypt, the applicable law will be that of Germany if the product was marketed there; if not, Egypt, if the product was marketed there; if not, India, if the product was marketed there. It appears that the burden of proving that the product was marketed in the particular country would rest with the plaintiff, although the defendant may also have an incentive, and should be allowed to either disprove or prove that fact.

Moreover, the last sentence of paragraph 1 expressly gives defendants a defense whereby they can avoid the application of the law of each of the above three countries by demonstrating that they "could not reasonably foresee the marketing of the product, or a product of the same type" in that country.[291] If taken literally, this could mean that, even if the plaintiff proves (and the defendant does not disprove) that the product was actually marketed in the particular country, the defendant can still assert a second line of defense by showing that, despite actual marketing, "he or she could not reasonably foresee the marketing."

In any event, if either defense succeeds, the applicable law will not be that of the country next in line under paragraph 1 (e.g., Egypt after Germany, or India after Egypt), but rather the law of the defendant's habitual residence.[292] Thus, if a Japanese defendant manufactured the product, Japanese law will govern the case, unless, of course, Japanese law is more favorable to the plaintiff than Egyptian or Indian law, in which case the defendant would not likely invoke this defense to begin with.

Paragraph 1 of Article 5 applies "[w]ithout prejudice to Article 4(2)," which contains the common-residence rule. This means that, if the parties have their habitual residence in the same country, its law applies to the exclusion of all others, even if the product was not marketed in that country. Thus, if a German defendant manufactured the product in the above scenario, German law would govern, even if the product was not marketed in Germany.

Finally, all of paragraph 1 (including the cross reference to the common-residence rule) is subject to the "manifestly closer connection" escape contained in paragraph 2 of Article 5.[293] This escape authorizes a court to either: (1) deviate from the order established in paragraph 1 and apply the law of one of the countries listed there; or (2) apply the law of a country not listed in paragraph 1, such as the country of the product's manufacture,

---

[290] Rome II art. 5(1).

[291] *Id.*

[292] If the defendant is a juridical person, the place of its central administration is deemed to be its habitual residence. *See* Rome II art. 23(1). Even so, the defendant's "residence" (at least when the defendant is the manufacturer rather than the local importer or distributor) would seem to be the least relevant contact in today's world of corporate mobility. In most cases, the manufacturer is likely to be a corporate entity whose "residence," or central administration, may be located in a country that has little relationship with the case, the product, or its manufacture.

[293] Rome II, art. 5(2). The escape also repeats the "pre-existing relationship" exception, which means, inter alia, that in all cases in which the victim was also the acquirer of the product, either side can claim a "pre-existing relationship" between the victim and the defendant manufacturer, distributor, or retail seller. Article 63 of the Albanian codification is substantively identical with Article 5 of Rome II, except that the Albanian article contains only the closer-connection exception and not the common-domicile exception or the preexisting relationship example.

upon showing that this country has a manifestly closer connection than the country whose law would normally govern under paragraph 1.[294]

B. *FAVOR LAESI* RULES

A significant number of recent national codifications have adopted a more direct pro-plaintiff rule by allowing the victim to choose from among the laws of states that have certain specified contacts. Table 2.5 lists these countries and the victim's choices:[295]

TABLE 2.5. VICTIM'S CHOICES IN PRODUCT LIABILITY CONFLICTS

	V's dom. or similar affiliation	State of Injury	State of product's acquisition	D's PPB or similar affiliation
Moldova	X		X*	
Romania	X		X*	
Italy			X*	X
Switzerland			X*	X
Quebec			X	X
Turkey			X	X
Russia	X*		X*	X
Azerbaijan	X		X	X
Belarus	X		X	X
Kazakhstan	X		X	X
Kyrgyzstan	X		X	X
Tajikistan	X		X	X
Ukraine	X		X	X
Uzbekistan	X		X	X
China	X*	X		X
Tunisia	X	X	X	X
Taiwan	X	X	X	X

---

[294] For an assessment of this article from an American perspective, *see* Symeonides, *Rome II*, 206–209.

[295] In some codifications, the victim's choice is subject to a pro-manufacturer proviso that negates the plaintiff's choice of a particular state's law if the manufacturer could not have reasonably foreseen the presence of the product or similar products in that state. In Table 2.5, the presence of such a proviso is denoted by an asterisk.

As Table 2.5 indicates:

- The Moldovan and Romanian codifications allow the victim to choose between the laws of (1) the victim's domicile, and (2) the state of the product's acquisition (the latter subject to a foreseeability proviso).[296]
- The Italian and Swiss codifications allow the victim to choose between laws of (1) the defendant's principal place of business or, in the absence thereof, his habitual residence; and (2) the law of the state of the product's acquisition, "unless the defendant proves that the product has been marketed in that state without his consent."[297]
- The Turkish and Quebec codifications allow the same choices, but without the above-quoted proviso.[298]
- The Russian codification adds to these choices the law of the victim's habitual residence or principal place of activity, but subjects that choice and the choice of the law of the state of the product's acquisition to a pro-manufacturer proviso.[299]
- The codifications of Azerbaijan, Belarus, Kazakhstan, Kyrgyzstan, Tajikistan, Ukraine, and Uzbekistan provide the victim with the same three choices as the Russian codification, but without the pro-manufacturer proviso.[300]
- The Tunisian codification adds a fourth choice, the place of injury (without the proviso).[301]
- The Taiwanese codification provides for the application of the defendant's national law, but also allows the victim to choose her national law, the law of the state of injury, or the law of the state of the product's acquisition.[302]
- The Chinese codification provides for the application of the law of the state of the victim's habitual residence, unless the defendant has not conducted related business in that state, in which case the victim may choose between the laws of the state of injury, or the defendant's principal place of business.[303]

---

[296] *See* Moldova codif. art. 1618; Romanian codif. art. 114. *But see also id.* art. 116 (limiting damages to those provided by Romanian law).

[297] Article 135 of the Swiss codification provides in part: "(1) Claims based on a defect in, or a defective description of, a product are governed, at the choice of the injured party: (a) By the law of the state in which the tortfeasor has his principal place of business or, in absence thereof, his habitual residence; or (b) By the law of the state in which the product was acquired unless, the tortfeasor proves that the product has been marketed in that state without his consent." Article 63 of the Italian codification is substantially identical to the above, except that it speaks of the state in which the manufacturer has its "domicile or its head-office."

[298] *See* Turkish codif. art. 36; Quebec codif. art. 3128.

[299] *See* Russian codif. art. 1221. This article also provides that, if the victim does not take advantage of these choices, the applicable law shall be determined under the general article for tort conflicts.

[300] *See* Azerbaijan codif. art. 27; Belarus codif. art. 1130; Kazakhstan codif. art. 1118; Kyrgyzstan codif. art. 1203; Tajikistan codif. art. 1227; Ukrainian codif. art. 50; Uzbekistan codif. art. 1195.

[301] *See* Tunisian codif. art. 72.

[302] *See* Taiwanese codif. art. 26.

[303] *See* Chinese codif. art. 48. Article 121 of the Chinese Model Law calls for the application of (1) the law of the place where the tortious act is committed, if that is also (a) the place of the defendant's domicile, habitual

Similar rules have been proposed in the United States.[304]

VIII. Special Rules for Other Torts

In addition to (or aside from) products liability, many recent codifications provide separate choice-of-law rules for other categories of torts. Unfortunately, those rules cannot be discussed here due to space limitations. The following partial list of codifications provides a general idea regarding the torts that tend to be provided in this fashion:[305]

- Albania (arts. 64–67: unfair competition and restraints to competition, environmental torts, and infringement of intellectual property rights and rights of personality);
- Belgium (art. 99 § 2: defamation, unfair competition, environmental torts, and traffic accidents);
- Bulgaria (arts. 107–110: unfair competition and restraints to competition, violations of intellectual property and rights of personality, environmental torts, intellectual property);
- China (art. 46: infringement on rights of personality);
- Czech Republic (art. 101: violations of privacy and rights of personality and defamation);
- Georgia (art. 42.2: unfair competition);
- Japan (art. 19: defamation);
- North Korea (art. 32: collision on the high seas);
- Lithuania (arts. 1.44–46: traffic accidents, infringement of rights of personality, and unfair competition);
- Louisiana (art. 3546: punitive damages);
- Moldova (arts. 1617, 1619: injury to rights of personality, unfair competition);
- Quebec (art. 3129: injury outside Quebec caused by raw materials originating in Quebec);
- Romania (arts. 112–13, 117–19: injury to rights of personality, unfair competition);

---

residence, principal establishment or seat of business, or (b) the place where the product was acquired by the victim; or (c) the law of the victim's domicile or habitual residence, if that place is also (a) the place of the defendant's principal establishment or seat of business, or (b) the place where the product was acquired by the victim.

[304] *See* D. Cavers, The Proper Law of Producer's Liability, 26 *Int'l & Comp. L.Q.* 703, 728–729 (1977) (permitting the plaintiff to choose from among the laws of: (1) the place of manufacture; (2) the place of the plaintiff's habitual residence, if that place coincides with either the place of injury or the place of the product's acquisition; or (3) the place of acquisition, if that place is also the place of injury); R. Weintraub, Methods for Resolving Conflict-of-Laws Problems in Mass Tort Litigation, 1989 *U. Ill. L. Rev.* 129, 148 (1989) (giving both the victim and the tortfeasor a choice under certain circumstances); Symeonides, *The Need for a Third Conflicts Restatement*, 450–451, 472–474 (same notion but different choices).

[305] The list does not include unjust enrichment, *negotiorum gestio*, and *culpa in contrahendo*.

- Rome II (arts. 6–9: unfair competition and restraints to competition, environmental torts, infringement of intellectual property rights, and industrial action);
- Russia (art. 1222: unfair competition);
- Serbia (arts. 163–70: unfair competition, environmental torts, infringement on intellectual property rights, industrial action, traffic accidents, defamation, injuries on ships or aircraft);
- Switzerland (arts. 134, 136–39: traffic accidents, obstruction to competition, emissions, injury to rights of personality);
- Taiwan (arts. 27–28: unfair competition and torts committed through the media);
- Tunisia (art. 73: traffic accidents);
- Turkey (arts. 35, 37–38: injury to rights of personality, unfair competition, and restraints to competition);
- Ukraine (art. 51: misappropriation of property); and
- Vietnam (art. 774: copyright infringement).

IX. Party Autonomy

One question that recent codifications address is whether the tortfeasor and the victim can agree on the law applicable to the tort.[306] This question arises in two different scenarios: post-dispute and pre-dispute agreements.

A. POST-DISPUTE AGREEMENTS

The first, and not so common, scenario is when the tortfeasor and the victim, *after* each had knowledge of the events giving rise to the dispute, agree on the law that will govern the dispute (hereinafter "post-dispute agreements"). Such agreements present no problems whatsoever. After all, they differ little from agreements encompassing only contractual claims, and indeed they help facilitate settlement.

A common variation of this scenario is when neither litigant raises the applicability of foreign law. In such a case, most American courts will apply the law of the forum under a variety of rationales, one of which is that the parties have tacitly acquiesced (i.e., agreed) to the application of the *lex fori*.[307] Although express post-dispute agreements to apply non-forum law are slightly different, the need for predictability, efficiency, judicial economy, and respect for party autonomy are good reasons to enforce, indeed, encourage, these agreements.

---

[306] For a recent extensive discussion of this issue, *see* A. Vogeler, *Die freie Rechtswahl im Kollisionsrecht der außervertraglichen Schuldverhältnisse* (2013). *See also* K. Kroll-Ludwigs, *Die Rolle der Parteiautonomie im europäischen Kollisionsrecht* (2013) (covering both contractual and non-contractual obligations).

[307] *See* S. Symeonides, *American PIL*, at 90–91.

These solutions encounter conceptual difficulties in those countries in which courts are *required* to apply the forum's choice-of-law rules (even when the parties do not invoke them) and to ascertain ex officio the content of the applicable law.[308] Nevertheless, one suspects that in actual practice courts overcome these conceptual difficulties and apply the law that the parties agree upon, at least when that law is the law of the forum. The Chinese Supreme Court has taken exactly this position with regard to contractual disputes. The Court's instructions to the lower courts provide that they should permit the parties "to choose a law or alter a choice of law...prior to the end of court debate of the first instance," and that when the parties "both invoke the law of a same country or region and neither has raised any objection to the choice of law," the parties "shall be deemed as having made the choice of a law applicable."[309]

B. PRE-DISPUTE AGREEMENTS

The second (and increasingly more common) scenario involves pre-dispute agreements in which the eventual tortfeasor and the victim agree *in advance* on the law that will govern their rights and obligations arising from the tort. Clearly, this scenario can only occur when: (1) the eventual tortfeasor and the victim are parties to a preexisting contract, such as a contract of employment, carriage, or sale; and (2) the contract contains a choice-of-law clause that is phrased in a way that purports to include not only contractual claims but also non-contractual claims that may arise from, or which are connected to, the contractual relationship. If both of the foregoing elements are satisfied, then the next question is whether the legal system should enforce the clause.

The parties' position in pre-dispute agreements is qualitatively and significantly different than in post-dispute agreements. Before the dispute arises, the parties usually do not (or should not) contemplate a future tort, and the parties do not know (1) who will injure whom, or (2) the nature or severity of the injury. An unsophisticated party (or a party in a weak bargaining position) may sign uncritically or unwittingly a choice-of-law agreement, even when the odds of that party becoming the victim are much higher than the odds of that party becoming the tortfeasor. Thus, pre-dispute agreements may facilitate the exploitation of weak parties. In contrast, this danger is less pronounced in post-dispute agreements because, after the dispute arises, the parties are in a position to

---

[308] *See, e.g.,* the codifications of the following countries and the pertinent articles shown in parentheses: Albania (art. 5), Argentina (art. 2595), Austria (arts. 3–4), Belarus (art. 1095), Croatia (art. 13), Estonia (art. 4), FYROM (art. 13), Georgia 3), Italy (art. 14), Kazakhstan (art. 1086), South Korea (art. 5), Lithuania (art. 1.12.1), Netherlands (art. 2), Peru (art. 2051), Russia (art. 1191), Serbia (art. 37), Slovenia (art. 12), Switzerland (art. 16), Turkey (art. 2), Ukraine (art. 8), Uruguay (art. 3), Venezuela (art. 60).

[309] Article 4 of the Chinese Supreme People's Court's "Rules of the Supreme People's Court on Related Issues concerning the Application of Law in Hearing Foreign-Related Contractual Dispute Cases Related to Civil and Commercial Matters" (23 July 2007).

know their rights and obligations and have the opportunity to weigh the pros and cons of a choice-of-law agreement.

Until recently, the prevailing view internationally was to enforce *only post-dispute* agreements. The codifications of Belgium, Bulgaria, China, FYROM, Germany, Japan, and Turkey expressly provide to that effect.[310] The codifications of Estonia, South Korea, Lithuania, Russia, Switzerland, Taiwan, Tajikistan, Tunisia, and Ukraine also do likewise but limit such agreements to the law of the forum.[311] The codifications of Armenia, Austria, Belarus, Kyrgyzstan, and the Dutch Torts Act of 2001 authorize such agreements, but without any express limitation as to their timing and without limiting them to the law of the forum.[312]

In the United States, the question of the enforceability of pre-dispute choice-of-law agreements encompassing non-contractual claims has not been uniformly answered. The pertinent section of the Restatement (Second) speaks of the law of the state chosen by the parties to govern their "*contractual* rights and duties."[313] The Restatement is silent on whether the parties may agree *in advance* on the law that will govern the parties' non-contractual rights, especially those arising from a future tort between them. The most logical inference is that the Restatement does not sanction such agreements. At the time of the Restatement's drafting, the principle of party autonomy, which had been born in the contracts arena, had not migrated outside that arena. The case law on this issue in the United States remains unsettled.[314]

---

[310] *See* Belgian codif. art. 101 ("Parties may, after the dispute has arisen, choose which law will be applicable to the obligations resulting from the tort…."); Chinese codif. art. 47 ("The parties may agree to choose the applicable law after the occurrence of a tortious act."); German codif. art. 42 ("After the event giving rise to a non-contractual obligation has occurred, the parties may choose the law that shall apply to the obligation."); Turkish codif. art. 34(5) ("The parties may explicitly choose the applicable law after the tort occurs."); Bulgarian codif. art. 113(1); Japanese codif. art. 21; FYROM codif. art. 33(3).

[311] *See* Estonian Codif. § 54 ("The parties may agree on application of Estonian law after occurrence of the event or performance of the act from which a noncontractual obligation arose."); Swiss codif. art. 132 ("The parties may, at any time after the occurrence of the injurious event, agree on the application of the law of the forum."); South Korean codif. art. 33; Lithuanian codif. art. 1.43.3; Russian codif. art. 1219.3; Taiwanese codif. art. 31; Tajikistan codif. art. 1225.3; Tunisian codif. art. 71; Ukrainian codif. art. 49.4.

[312] *See* Armenian codif. art. 1289; Austrian codif. art. 48(1); Belarus codif. art. 1093(2); Kyrgyzstan codif. art. 1167(2); Dutch Torts Act of 2001, art. § 6.

[313] *Restatement (Second)* § 187(2) (emphasis added).

[314] The majority of cases have held that the choice-of-law clause did *not* encompass tort claims or other non-contractual claims arising from, or related to, the same contractual relationship. However, a sizeable number of cases have held that the clause *did* encompass tort claims, claims for attorney fees, and other non-contractual claims. Most courts tend to view this question as a matter of contractual *intent* (rather than contractual *power*), which in turn depends largely, but not exclusively, on the wording of the choice-of-law clause. Under this logic, a clause that uses the words "the agreement" or "the contract" does not encompass non-contractual claims, whereas a clause referring to the "relationship" resulting from the contract or to "any and all disputes" between the parties is deemed to include non-contractual claims. For citations and extensive discussion, *see* Hay, Borchers, & Symeonides, *Conflict of Laws*, 1141–1146.

The two American codifications have had the opportunity to address this issue. The 1991 Louisiana codification explicitly confines pre-dispute choice-of-law agreements to *contractual* issues.[315] Similarly, Oregon's contracts codification of 2001 does not allow pre-dispute choice-of-law agreements for non-contractual issues.[316] Oregon's torts codification of 2009 continues this policy. It differentiates between pre-dispute agreements (which are unenforceable) and post-dispute agreements, which it subdivides into those choosing Oregon law and those choosing the law of another state. Post-dispute agreements that choose Oregon law, if otherwise valid, are enforceable without any limitation.[317] Post-dispute agreements choosing the law of another state are enforceable, provided they conform to the statute that prescribes the requirements for enforcing choice-of-law agreements regarding contractual claims, including the public policy limitations of the otherwise applicable law.[318]

A draft of what later became the Rome II Regulation proposed abolishing the distinction between post-dispute and pre-dispute agreements and allowing enforcement of both. This author criticized that proposal at that time, as well as the compromise that later found its way into the final text of Rome II.[319] The compromise is now found in Article 14 of Rome II, which continues the differentiation between pre-dispute and post-dispute choice-of-law agreements for non-contractual claims and allows enforcement of both, but subject to different restrictions.[320] Post-dispute agreements are enforced regardless of the identity of the parties,[321] but pre-dispute agreements are enforced only if: (1) the parties are "pursuing a commercial activity,"[322] (2) the agreement is "freely negotiated,"[323] and (3) the choice of law is "expressed or demonstrated with reasonable certainty by the circumstances of the case."[324]

---

[315] *See* La. codif. art. 3540 ("conventional obligations"), and Reporter's comments thereunder.

[316] *See* Or. Rev. Stat. § 15.350 ("contractual rights and duties"). For discussion, *see* S. Symeonides, Codifying Choice of Law for Contracts: The Oregon Experience, 67 *RabelsZ* 726, 737 (2003).

[317] *See* Or. Rev. Stat. § 15.430(1). For discussion, *see* Symeonides, *Oregon Tort Exegesis*, 993–997.

[318] *See* Or. Rev. Stat. § 15.455, cross-referencing to the contracts codification.

[319] *See* S. Symeonides, Tort Conflicts and Rome II: Impromptu Notes on the Rapporteur's Draft (Remarks delivered at seminar hosted by European Parliament rapporteur MEP Diana Wallis in Brussels on 14 March 2005), *available at* http://www.dianawallismep.org.uk/resources/sites/82.165.40.25-416d2c46d399e8.07328850/Seminar%2014%20March/S.C.+Symeonides%2C+%27Tort+conflicts+and+Rome+II%3A+impromptu+notes+on+the+Rapporteur%27s+draft%27.pdf. *See also* S. Symeonides, Tort Conflicts and Rome II: A View from Across, in *Festschrift für Erik Jayme* 935 (2004).

[320] Article 14 applies to all non-contractual claims other than those arising from unfair competition, restrictions to competition, and infringement of intellectual property rights. *See* Rome II, arts. 6(4) and 8(3). These exclusions mean that choice-of-law agreements on these two subjects are unenforceable, regardless of whether they are entered into before *or* after the dispute. For discussions of Article 14, *see* T.M. de Boer, Party Autonomy and Its Limitations in the Rome II Regulation, 9 *Ybk. Priv. Int'l L.* 19 (2008); M. Zhang, Party Autonomy in Non-contractual Obligations: Rome II and Its Impacts on Choice of Law, 39 *Seton Hall L. Rev.* 861 (2009).

[321] Rome II, art. 14(1)(a).

[322] Rome II, art. 14(1)(b).

[323] *Id.*

[324] *Id.* Another requirement is that the agreement "shall not prejudice the rights of third parties." *Id.* Article 57 of the Albanian codification and Article 158 of the Serbian draft codification are virtually identical with Rome II, art. 14.

The requirement for free negotiation should be understood as being applicable even to post-dispute agreements. Despite a possible *a contrario* argument, the quoted phrase should be understood as evidence of the drafters' intent to ensure higher judicial scrutiny of pre-dispute agreements, rather than as a license to enforce coercive or not "freely negotiated" post-dispute agreements. The same argument could be made regarding the requirement for an express or clearly demonstrated choice of law. After all, Rome I contains a similar requirement for all choice-of-law agreements regarding contractual issues.[325] However, it is also possible that the drafters of Rome II intended to allow enforcement of merely implied post-dispute agreements, such as when both litigants tacitly acquiesce to the application of the *lex fori*.[326]

Be that as it may, the most crucial difference between pre-dispute and post-dispute agreements under Rome II is that pre-dispute agreements are enforceable only if the parties are engaging in "commercial activity." In all other respects, the two agreements are subject to the same restrictions, which are delineated by (1) the mandatory rules of a state in which "*all* the elements relevant to the situation…are located" in fully domestic cases;[327] (2) the mandatory rules of Community law, in multistate intra-EU cases;[328] and (3) the "overriding" mandatory rules[329] and the *ordre public* of the forum state in all cases.[330]

Compared to the uncertainty that characterizes American case law on this issue,[331] there is a certain attraction to the decision of the drafters of Rome II to adopt a clear-cut rule on this subject. However, the critical question is whether this rule provides sufficient safeguards to ensure that this newly granted freedom will not be abused by strong contracting parties. By limiting pre-dispute choice-of-law agreements to situations in which all the parties are "pursuing a commercial activity," Rome II seeks to protect certain presumptively weak parties, such as consumers, employees, and certain (but not all) individual insureds. This limitation, however, leaves a whole host of small commercial actors exposed, such as small businesses.

---

[325] *See* Rome I, art. 3(1).

[326] This argument runs contrary to current practice in several continental countries where courts are expected to ex officio apply foreign law. However, Rome II contemplates a reconsideration of this practice. *See* Commission Statement on the treatment of foreign law, accompanying Rome II.

[327] Rome II art. 14(2) (emphasis added) ("Where all the elements relevant to the situation […] are located in a country other than the country whose law has been chosen, the choice of the parties shall not prejudice the application of provisions of the law of that other country which cannot be derogated from by agreement.").

[328] *See* Rome II art. 14(3) ("Where all the elements relevant to the situation […] are located in one or more of the Member States, the parties' choice of the law applicable other than that of a Member State shall not prejudice the application of provisions of Community law […] which cannot be derogated from by agreement.").

[329] *See* Rome II art. 16 ("Nothing in this Regulation shall restrict the application of the provisions of the law of the forum in a situation where they are mandatory irrespective of the law otherwise applicable to the non-contractual obligation.").

[330] *See* Rome II art. 26 (providing that the application of a provision of the otherwise applicable law "may be refused only if such application is manifestly incompatible with the public policy (*ordre public*) of the forum").

[331] *See supra* note 314.

For example, suppose that a franchise contract between Starbucks, a corporation head-quartered in the State of Washington, and a French franchisee for a Starbucks franchise in France contains a "freely negotiated" choice-of-law clause selecting the law of the friendly Kingdom of Tonga, and the clause is broadly phrased to include non-contractual obligations. Suppose further that Starbucks commits a tort against the French franchisee and that, unlike French or Washington law, Tongan law favors Starbucks. This clause would meet the initial requirements of Article 14, thus shifting the burden on the franchisee to prove that the clause would be unenforceable under paragraphs 2 and 3 of Article 14, or Articles 16 or 26 of Rome II.

Paragraphs 2 and 3 of Article 14 use identical language to that of paragraphs 3 and 4, respectively, of Article 3 of Rome I, except for one difference on the issue of the pertinent time. Whereas the Rome I provisions speak of "all other elements relevant to the situation *at the time of the [contractual] choice*,"[332] the provisions of Rome II speak of "all the elements relevant to the situation *at the time when the event giving rise to the damage occurs*."[333] One could make a semi-plausible argument that the "relevant elements" contemplated by the Rome II provisions are the elements of the tort, rather than of the contractual relationship. If accepted, this argument could affect the outcome in a case in which "all" the elements of the tort are located in one country (here, France), even if the contractual relationship has contacts with another country. In any event, this argument would be unavailable in this case because the identity of the tortfeasor as a Washington corporation is a "relevant element" in both the contractual and the delictual relationship. The fact that this element is located outside France and outside the EU means that the contractual choice of Tongan law will satisfy the tests of paragraphs 2 and 3 of Article 14 of Rome II. Thus, the chosen law must be applied even if it "prejudices" the application of French mandatory rules (para. 2) or the mandatory rules of Community law (para. 3). The geographical contacts of the franchisor-franchisee relationship prevent the franchisee from invoking these provisions.

On the other hand, if this case is litigated in France, geography is not an obstacle to invoking Articles 16 and 26 of Rome II. If the franchisee is able to prove that the application of Tongan law violates the "overriding" mandatory rules of France[334] or is "manifestly incompatible" with the French *ordre public,*[335] the franchisee will be able to avoid the application of Tongan law. However, because the threshold for applying either of these two articles is considerably high, the franchisee, or similarly situated small commercial actors, will remain unprotected in all cases that do not meet this threshold. Moreover, a cagily drafted choice-of-forum clause can easily avoid litigation in France.

---

[332] Rome I art. 3(3) and (4) (emphasis added).
[333] Rome II art. 14(2) and (3) (emphasis added).
[334] *See* Rome II art. 16, *supra* note 133.
[335] *See* Rome II art. 26, *supra* note 134.

One reason many European commentators may find this result unobjectionable is because they have grown accustomed to the idea of applying the same law to the torts aspects of a case as the one that governs the underlying contract between the same parties. Rome II preserves this idea. In stating the "manifestly closer connection" exception to the *lex loci damni* rule, Article 4(3) of Rome II provides that "[a] manifestly closer connection […] might be based in particular on a pre-existing relationship between the parties, such as a contract, that is closely connected with the tort/delict in question."[336] One commentator has stated that "[e]ven if [the parties'] agreement would be invalid under Article 14(1), an action sounding in tort would still be governed by the law of their choice, as there is likely to be a closer connection between their contractual relationship and the tort at issue."[337]

This statement would be true only if the agreement chooses the law of a state that in fact has the "manifestly closest connection" with the case. However, Article 14 does not impose such a requirement. Indeed, Article 14 does not require *any* connection to the chosen state. Second, there is a difference between, on the one hand, applying the law of a given state because *a court* determines (after considering all the circumstances and exercising all proper discretion) that a state has a "manifestly closer connection," and, on the other hand, applying a law *solely* because of a choice-of-law clause, which is not negotiated at all in many cases. Rome II seems to recognize this difference, as well as the risk inherent in allowing pre-dispute choice-of-law clauses for non-contractual claims, by stating in Recital 32 that "[p]rotection should be given to weaker parties by imposing certain conditions on the choice."[338] As the franchise example illustrates, Rome II does not always live up to this principle. As with some other freedom-laden ideas, Article 14 may well become the vehicle for taking advantage of weak parties, many of whom are parties to "commercial" relationships.

Finally, it is not a consolation to assume that "in the area of non-contractual obligations parties seldom exercise their freedom of choice."[339] Even if this assumption were true today, it will not remain true for long. In a relatively short time after the effective date of Rome II, choice-of-law agreements encompassing tort claims will become routine. For example, one should not be surprised if product manufacturers begin inserting clauses selecting a pro-manufacturer law (the law of Nepal might be a good choice) in all contracts by which they sell their products to business entities. Because Article 14 does not require any particular connection with the chosen state, and because both parties would be pursuing a commercial activity, the clause would pass the initial test of Article 14, thus shifting to the injured party the rather heavy burden of proving the clause unenforceable

---

[336] Rome II art. 4(3).
[337] de Boer, *Party Autonomy*, at 27.
[338] Rome II Recital (31).
[339] de Boer, *Party Autonomy*, at 23.

under one of the grounds discussed above. If Rome II were really concerned with protecting the "weaker parties,"[340] it should not have imposed such a burden on them.

X. Interim Conclusions

Let us now return to basic principles. From the beginning of its history, PIL approached the task of delineating the operation of state and national laws by posing questions such as: (1) whether laws attach to a territory, or to the citizens or domiciliaries of that territory; (2) whether a law operates only within the enacting state's territory or beyond it as well; and (3) whether the application of a state's law within its territory necessarily excludes the application of the laws of other states. These questions usually are compressed into two competing basic principles, territoriality and personality of the laws, although it would be more accurate to speak of territoriality versus non-territoriality. Either way, the core question is when should the application of a state's law depend on territorial factors, and when should it depend on other, including personal, factors?[341]

The answers to this question vary over time from country to country and from one field to another. Fifty year ago, the answer that prevailed in the field of tort conflicts was single-mindedly and overwhelmingly in favor of territoriality: The *lex loci delicti* was a universal and all-encompassing rule subject to no exception. Today, the picture is quite different. The *lex loci* rule continues to be the basic rule in all but one of the 73 codifications that have addressed tort conflicts in this 50-year period. However, the *lex loci* rule is also subject to exceptions in all but eight of the 73 codifications. See Chart 2.4, below. The single-mindedness of PIL has come to an end.

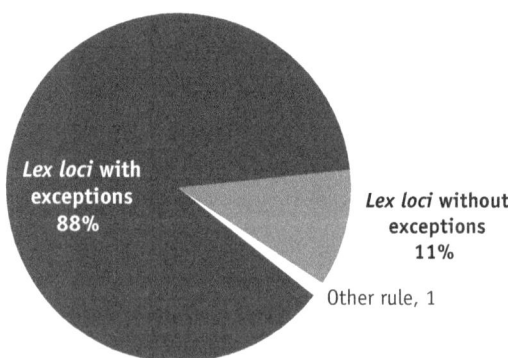

CHART 2.4. The *Lex Loci Delicti* Rule in the Codifications of the Last 50 Years

---

[340] *See* Rome II Recital (31).

[341] For an in-depth discussion of these questions, *see* Symeonides, *Territoriality and Personality in Tort Conflicts*, 405, *et seq.*

One of these exceptions—the common-domicile exception—is present in 64 percent of the codifications adopted during this period. This represents a significant gain of the personality principle at the expense of territoriality. It is important to stress, however, that this gain is limited to only one pattern of conflicts—those in which both the tortfeasor and the victim are domiciled or have significant affiliations with the same state and are involved in a tort that occurred in another state or states. As Table 2.6 below illustrates, in all other patterns of tort conflicts, territoriality continues to be the operating principle. Given the previous history of total war between these two principles, the fact that they can now coexist within the confines of the same codification is a new phenomenon. It exemplifies the maturity of PIL in rejecting simplistic "either-or" choices.

TABLE 2.6. TERRITORIALITY AND PERSONALITY IN TORT CONFLICTS

Parties' Domiciles	Common domicile	Split-domicile	
Conduct & Injury	Irrelevant	Same state	Cross-Border
Applicable Law	Common domicile.	Conduct *&* Injury	Conduct *or* Injury
Principle	**Personality**	**Territoriality**	

The other exceptions to the *lex loci* rule are not necessarily exceptions to the territoriality principle. However, they are encroachments against other previously dominant principles of PIL. For example, the *favor laesi* exception in cross-border torts does not operate against territoriality because it simply leads to the law of a state with a different territorial contact. But the exception operates against the heretofore-dominant principle of "conflicts justice," which was one of the reasons for which the *lex loci* rule was not subject to exceptions. Chapter 6 discusses the tension between "conflicts justice" and "material justice."

Likewise, the "closer connection" exception is not necessarily antithetical to territoriality because in many cases (though not all), the exception will point to a state because of its territorial contacts, albeit contacts other than the *locus delicti*.[342] The reason for, and goal of, this exception was not necessarily be to reduce the operating range of territoriality, but rather to inject a degree of flexibility in handling atypical tort conflicts. Chapter 4 discusses the tension between the need for legal certainty, which was another reason for the *lex loci* rule, and the need for flexibility.

The same can be said about the double-actionability requirement and other unilateral *lex fori* exceptions. The reason behind them is not hostility toward territoriality but rather a desire to protect the values or interests of the forum state, or certain defendants,

---

[342] The same is true of the preexisting relationship exception. Although this exception is similar to the common-domicile exception and in many cases points to the state of the parties' relationship, in other cases it will point to a state based on its territorial contacts, for example, the place of the contract.

from the application of a *foreign lex loci delicti* when it is too plaintiff-friendly. Chapter 7 discusses the tension between the desideratum of international uniformity, which can be served by a universal adherence to the *lex loci* rule, and the desire or need to protect the values or interests of the forum state.

Fifty years ago, choice of law in tort conflicts was a simple exercise, simple enough to be entrusted to a single and simple rule—the *lex loci* rule. Fifty year later, the world has become far more complex, if only because of a virtual explosion of cross-border mobility and cross-border activity. PIL had to respond to this increased complexity. The numerous exceptions to the *lex loci* rule reviewed in this chapter are the response to that complexity. But these exceptions represent more than a confirmation of the inadequacy of the *lex loci* rule. They represent a maturation of the legal mind, at least the PIL mind, which no longer looks at conflicts problems through the lenses of a single principle or value to the exclusion of all others, and no longer accepts "either-or" choices for complex problems. We shall return to this theme at the end of this book.

3   Party Autonomy in Contract Conflicts

I. Party Autonomy: Ancient Origins and Modern Triumph

This chapter discusses the role of party autonomy in the provisions of recent choice-of-law codifications and conventions dealing with contract conflicts. "Party autonomy" is a shorthand expression for the principle that parties to a multistate contract should be allowed, within certain parameters and limitations, to agree in advance on which state's law will govern the contract.[1]

---

[1] The literature on party autonomy is vast and growing exponentially. In addition to writings cited later in this chapter, *see* the following recent publications: M.M. Albornoz, *Choice of Law in International Contracts in Latin American Legal Systems* (2009); G. Cordero-Moss (ed.), *Boilerplate Clauses, International Commercial Contracts and the Applicable Law* (2011); T. Drygala, B. Heiderhoff, M. Staake & G. Zmijet (eds.), *Private Autonomy in Germany and Poland and in the Common European Sales Law* (2012); J. Fu, *Modern European and Chinese Contract Law—A Comparative Study of Party Autonomy* (2011); K. Kroll-Ludwigs, *Die Rolle der*

Thus defined, this principle is simply the "external" side of a domestic law principle, usually referred to as "freedom of contract," which allows contracting parties to derogate from all the waivable rules (*jus dispositivum*), as opposed to the non-waivable or mandatory rules (*jus cogens*), of that law.[2] This principle "extends to the freedom of parties to choose the law to govern their contract."[3]

However, neither the internal nor the external iterations of this freedom are boundless. For example, in contracts involving presumptively weak parties, such as consumers or employees, "an unfettered freedom to choose a law may be a freedom to exploit a dominant position."[4] Consequently, most domestic laws "curtail th[is] freedom,"[5] and this curtailment extends to the multistate arena: "The frameworks of private international

---

Parteiautonomie im europäischen Kollisionsrecht (2013); R. Plender & M. Wilderspin, *The European Private International Law of Obligations* (3d ed. 2009); A. Vogeler, *Die freie Rechtswahl im Kollisionsrecht der außervertraglichen Schuldverhältnisse* (2013); M.M. Albornoz, Choice of Law in International Contracts in Latin American Legal Systems, 6 *J. Priv. Int'l L.* 23 (2010); G. Alpa, Party Autonomy and Freedom of Contract Today, *Eur. Bus. L. Rev.* 119 (2010); P. Borchers, Categorical Exceptions to Party Autonomy in Private International Law, 82 *Tul. L. Rev.* 1645 (2008); P. Cross & H. Oxford, Floating Forum Selection and Choice of Law Clauses, 48 *S. Tex. L. Rev.* 125 (2006); T. Eisenberg & G. Miller, The Flight to New York: An Empirical Study of Choice of Law of Forum Clauses in Publicly-Held Companies' Contracts, 30 *Cardozo L. Rev.* 1475 (2009); J. Graves, Party Autonomy in Choice of Commercial Law: The Failure of Revised U.C.C. § 1-301 and a Proposal for Broader Reform, 36 *Seton Hall L. Rev.* 59 (2005); M. Gruson, Choice of Law Not Reasonably Related to the Transaction B Section 5-1401 of the General Obligations Law of New York, in *Festschrift Peter Hay* 191 (2005); J. Harris, Opting Out of Admiralty Law? Uniformity vs. Freedom of Contract in the Selection of State Choice of Law, 34 *Tul. Mar. L. J.* 167 (2009); F. Johns, Performing Party Autonomy, 71 *L. & Contemp. Probs.* 243 (2008); J. Kuipers, Cartesio and Grunkin Paul: Mutual Recognition as a Vested Rights Theory Based on Party Autonomy in Private Law, 2 *Eur. J. Leg. Stud.* 66 (2009); S. Leible, La importancia de la autonomía conflictual para el futuro del Derecho de los contratos internacionales, *Cuad. de Der. Transn'l* 214 (2011); F. Maultzsch, Choice of Law and *Jus Cogens* in Conflict of Laws for Contractual Obligations, 75 *RabelsZ* 60 (2011); A. Shapira, Territorialism, National Parochialism, Universalism, and Party Autonomy: How Does One Square the Choice of Law Circle?, 26 *Brooklyn J. Int'l L.* 199 (2000); D. Solomon, The Private International Law of Contracts in Europe: Advances and Retreats, 82 *Tul. L. Rev.* 1709 (2008); C. Walsh, The Uses and Abuses of Party Autonomy in International Contracts, 60 *U. N. Br. L. J.* 12 (2010); M. Wethmar-Lemmer, Party Autonomy and International Sales Contracts, 3 *J. So. Afr. L.* 431 (2011); A.J. Woodhouse, The Importance of Jurisdiction and Choice of Law Clauses: A European Perspective, 42 *Tort Trial & Ins. Prac. L. J.* 1027 (2007); W. Woodward, Constraining Opt-Outs: Shielding Local Law and Those It Protects from Adhesive Choice of Law Clauses, 40 *Loy. L.A. L. Rev.* 9 (2006); D. Wu, Timing the Choice of Law by Contract, 9 *Nw. J. Tech. & Intell. Prop.* 401 (2011); T. Yeo, Breach of Agreements on Choice of Law, 2010 *Lloyd's Marit. & Comm. L. Q.* 194 (2010); M. Zhang, Contractual Choice of Law in Contracts of Adhesion and Party Autonomy, 41 *Akron L. Rev.* 123 (2008); M. Zhang, Party Autonomy and Beyond: An International Perspective of Contractual Choice of Law, 20 *Emory Int'l L. Rev.* 511 (2006).

[2] *See* A. Briggs, *Agreements on Jurisdiction and Choice of Law*, 12 (2008):
> One characteristic of a mature legal system is that persons who have legal capacity should be able to make agreements in such terms as they consider to serve their interests…In principle, the degree to which the law should intrude on or override these private agreements should be no more than is necessary to serve and secure a broader public interest. So, for example, contracting parties should be able to make, and to expect the courts to enforce, agreements on jurisdiction and choice of law.

[3] *Id.* at 37.

[4] *Id.*

[5] *Id.*

law...are not subordinated to the private agreement of parties to litigation."[6] Moreover, the fact that the restrictions to freedom of contract, or the line separating *jus cogens* and *jus dispositivum,* vary from state to state is one of the many conflicts encountered when contracting parties assert their autonomy at the multistate level.

Historically, the first confirmed statutory rule sanctioning party autonomy at the multistate level appears in a decree issued in Hellenistic Egypt circa 120–118 B.C. The decree provided that contracts written in the Egyptian language were subject to the jurisdiction of the Egyptian courts, which applied Egyptian law, whereas contracts written in Greek were subject to the jurisdiction of the Greek courts, which applied Greek law.[7] Thus, by choosing the language of their contract, parties could directly choose the forum and indirectly the applicable law.

For centuries, the principle of party autonomy remained, as far as Western literature knows, unexploited and unexplored until it reappeared first in the writings of Charles Dumoulin (1500–1566) and then Ulrich Huber (1636–1694). These authors, and later Robert Pothier (1699–1772) and Joseph Story (1779–1845), used the *presumed* intent of the parties as the rationale for arguing against the rule of *lex loci contractus* and in favor of the *lex loci solutionis.*[8] In the late eighteenth and early nineteenth centuries, judicial decisions in England and the United States also relied on the parties' presumed intention to the same end.[9] Obviously, if the presumed intent of the parties deserves some deference, then, a fortiori, their actual intention *expressed* in a choice-of-law clause also deserves deference. Even so, express clauses were rare at the time, and when Pasquale Mancini (1817–1888) first proposed an autonomous choice-of-law rule calling for the application of the law expressly chosen by the parties, he did not have much of an appeal.[10] Ironically, until the end of the nineteenth century, European authors were more resistant to this idea than courts.[11]

In the United States, Joseph Beale (1861–1943), the drafter of the first Conflicts Restatement, personified this resistance well into the twentieth century. Although both Joseph Story and American transactional and judicial practice had previously recognized party autonomy,[12] Beale chose to ignore this reality because it did not fit into his

---

[6] *Id.* at 13.

[7] *See* Juenger, *Multistate Justice,* 7–8, and authorities cited therein.

[8] *See* Nygh, *Autonomy,* 4–7; B. Ancel & H. Muir Watt, Annotations sur la Consultation 53 de Du Moulin traduite en français, in *Le monde du droit, Mélanges Jacques Foyer* 1 (2008).

[9] *See* Robinson v. Bland, (1760) 2 Burr. 1077; Wayman v. Southard, 23 U.S. (10 Wheat.) 1, 48 (1825).

[10] *See* Y. Nishitani, *Mancini und die Parteiautonomie im Internationalen Privatrecht* (2000).

[11] *See* M. Caleb, *Essai sur le principe de l'autonomie de la volonté en droit international privé* (1927); J-P. Niboyet, La théorie de l'autonomie de la volonté, 16 *Recueil des cours* 53 (1927-I); Y. Nishitani, Party Autonomy and Its Restrictions by Mandatory Rules in Japanese Private International Law: Contractual Conflicts Rules, in J. Basedow, H. Baum & Y. Nishitani (eds.), *Japanese and European Private International Law in Comparative Perspective,* 77, 81–82 (2008).

[12] *See* Wayman v. Southard, 23 U.S. (10 Wheat.) 1, 48 (1825); Pritchard v. Norton, 106 U.S. 124 (1882). *See also* Thompson v. Ketcham, 8 Johns. 189, 193, 5 Am. Dec. 332 (N.Y. 1811); Andrews v. Pond, 38 U.S. (13 Pet.) 65, 78 (1839); J. Story, *Commentaries on the Conflicts of Laws* § 293(b) (2d ed. 1841).

territorialist scheme. In his view, giving contracting parties the freedom to agree on the applicable law would be tantamount to giving them a license to legislate.[13] Instead, Beale proposed an absolute and unqualified *lex loci contractus* rule for the Restatement, which mandated the application of the law of the state in which the contract was made to *all* aspects of the contract.[14]

During the discussion of this subject at the 1928 meeting of the American Law Institute,[15] Beale had to admit that party autonomy (which was then known as the doctrine of the parties' intention) had been accepted by "a majority of the cases,"[16] but argued that its restatement would lead to uncertainty because it would often be difficult to ascertain the parties' intent. When asked about situations in which the parties clearly expressed their intent in the contract, he replied with answers that assumed that the parties were attempting to evade a fundamental policy of the *locus contractus*. When asked about situations in which no fundamental policy was involved, he replied that "the man is not yet born who is wise enough"[17] to inventory all gradations of public policy. The discussion was obviously hopeless.[18] Judge Edward R. Finch, an ALI member, presciently warned Beale:

[Y]ou will never be able to hold your courts to that sort of a rule [*i.e.*, the *lex loci contractus*]. You can lay it down, but human nature is not so constituted that you can make a court adopt a general rule which will do injustice in a majority of the cases coming with it.[19]

History proved Judge Finch right and Beale terribly wrong. Even before the American choice-of-law revolution, which demolished Beale's Restatement, most courts chose to ignore his proscription of party autonomy.[20] Recognizing this reality, the Restatement (Second) formally sanctioned party autonomy in the all-important Section 187, which

---

[13] Beale, *Treatise*, 1080 ("at their will…[parties] can free themselves from the power of the law which would otherwise apply to their acts."). In fairness to Beale, other American writers of that period, including Lorenzen and Judge Learned Hand, took the same position against party autonomy. *See* E. Lorenzen, Validity and Effect of Contracts in the Conflict of Laws, 30 *Yale L. J.* 655, 658 (1921); R. Minor, *Conflict of Laws or Private International Law* 401–402 (1901); Judge Learned Hand in Gerli & Co. v. Cunard S. S. Co., 48 F.2d 115, 117 (2d Cir. 1931). One exception was W.W. Cook, *The Logical and Legal Bases of the Conflict of Laws* 389–432 (1942).

[14] *See Restatement* § 332.

[15] For a documentation of these discussions, *see* Symeonides, *The First Conflicts Restatement*, 68–74.

[16] 6 *American Law Institute Proceedings*, 454, 458 (1927–1928).

[17] *Id.* at 462 ("the man is not yet born who is wise enough to say as to a foreign law whether the foreign law really is to be obeyed…, whether [its] provisions are matters of such interest to the state that passed them that they would be enforced or are not.").

[18] For the reasons, *see* Symeonides, *The First Conflicts Restatement*, 70–74.

[19] 6 *American Law Institute Proceedings*, 454, at 466 (1927–1928).

[20] *See* Hay, Borchers & Symeonides, *Conflict of Laws*, 1086–1087.

is followed today by the vast majority of American courts, including some courts that otherwise do not follow the Restatement (Second).[21]

Meanwhile, in the rest of the world, party autonomy was steadily gaining ground and—with the notable exception of the Bustamante Code—it was eventually recognized in most choice-of-law codifications enacted in the twentieth century. The last 50 years in particular have been a triumphant period for party autonomy. It has been characterized as "perhaps the most widely accepted private international rule of our time,"[22] a "fundamental right,"[23] and an "irresistible" principle[24] that belongs to "the common core of the legal systems."[25] The vast majority of codifications and conventions adopted during this period have assigned a prominent role to this principle. In fact, as far can it can be ascertained, only three codifications enacted during this period have *not* adopted this principle for contract conflicts—those of Ecuador, Paraguay, and Guinea-Conakry.[26] However, none of these codifications is comprehensive, and the first two are from Latin America, a region that is still under the influence of the Bustamante Code and its negative position on this subject.[27]

By contrast, on the other side of the South Atlantic, virtually all the new African codifications have embraced the principle of party autonomy,[28] and, as this chapter later documents, so have virtually all other codifications and conventions adopted during this 50-year period. Indeed, many of them have also extended this principle beyond its

---

[21] *See* Symeonides, *Party Autonomy*, 192.

[22] R. Weintraub, Functional Developments in Choice of Law for Contracts, 187 *Recueil des Cours* 239, 271 (1984). *See also* de Boer, *Party Autonomy*, 19 ("Party autonomy is one of the leading principles of contemporary choice of law.").

[23] E. Jayme, Identité culturelle et intégration: Le droit international privé postmoderne, 251 *Recueil des Cours* 147 (1995) (characterizing party autonomy as a fundamental right).

[24] A.E. von Overbeck, L'irrésistible extension de l'autonomie de la volonté en droit international privé, in *Nouveaux itinéraires en droit: Hommage à François Rigaux*, 619 (1993).

[25] O. Lando, The EEC Convention on the Law Applicable to Contractual Obligations, 24 *Com. Mrkt. L. Rev.* 159, 169 (1987).

[26] *See* Ecuador Civ. Code arts. 15–17; Paraguayan Civ. Code arts. 23–24; Guinea-Conakry codif. art. 9. Article 3 of the Panamanian codification allows party autonomy, but the article is limited to the "forms and solemnities" of juridical acts. At the time of this writing (summer of 2013), the Paraguay Parliament was considering the adoption of the Hague Principles on Choice of Law for International Contracts, which strongly endorse party autonomy. These Principles are discussed *infra*.

[27] *See* M.M. Albornoz, Choice of Law in International Contracts in Latin American Legal Systems, 6 *J. Priv. Int'l L.* 23 (2010) (describing the negative position of Latin American codifications on party autonomy, but also noting its recognition by judicial practice). *See also* J. Basedow, Theorie der Rechtswahl odder Parteiautonomie also Groundage des Internationalen Privatrecht, 75 *RabelsZ* 34 (2011).

[28] See Angola codif. art. 41; Burundi codif. art. 5; Cape Verde codif. art. 41; Central African Rep. codif. art 42.1; Chad codif. art. 70.6; Gabon codif. art. 55; Guinea-Bissau codif. art. 41; Madagascar codif. art. 30; Mauritania codif. art. 10; Mozambique codif. art. 41; Rwanda codif. art. 14; Somalia codif. art. 19; Sudan codif. art. 11(14) (a). The codifications of Burkina Faso, Congo-Brazzaville, Senegal, and Togo are limited to matters of status, family law, and successions and do not provide for contracts in general. However, these codifications allow party autonomy in testaments and donations. See Burkina Faso codif. art. 1047–1048; Congo-Brazzaville codif. art. 826; Senegalese codif. art. 848; Togo codif. arts. 722, 724.

birthplace, the field of contracts, to areas such as succession,[29] trusts,[30] matrimonial property,[31] property,[32] and even family law[33] and torts.[34]

II. The Parameters of Party Autonomy

Although virtually all modern codifications and conventions espouse the principle of party autonomy, they also subject it to certain parameters and limitations. As the

---

[29] *See, e.g.,* Art. 5 of the Hague Convention of 1 August 1989 on the Law Applicable to Succession to the Estates of Deceased Persons; Art. 22 of Regulation (EU) No. 650/2012 of the European Parliament and of the Council of 4 July 2012 on jurisdiction, applicable law, recognition and enforcement of decisions and acceptance and enforcement of authentic instruments in matters of succession and on the creation of a European Certificate of Succession; Albanian codif. art. 33.3; Azerbaijan codif. art. 29; Armenian codif. art. 1292; Belarus codif. arts. 1133, 1135; Belgian codif. art. 79; Bulgarian codif. art. 89; Burkina Faso codif. art. 1044; Czech codif. art. 77.4; Estonian codif. art. 25; Italian codif. art. 46; Kazakhstan codif. art. 1121; South Korean codif. art. 49; Kyrgyzstan codif. art. 1206; Liechtenstein codif. art. 29.3; Moldovan codif. art. 1624; Dutch codif. art. 145; Polish codif. art. 64.1; Puerto Rico draft codif. art. 48; Quebec codif. arts. 3098–3099; Romanian codif. art. 68(1); Serbian draft codif. art. 104; Swiss codif. arts. 90(2), 91(2), 87(2), 95(2)(3); Tajikistan codif. arts. 1231–1232; Ukrainian codif. art. 70; Uzbekistan codif. art. 1197. *See also* A. Bonomi, Testamentary Freedom or Forced Heirship? Balancing Party Autonomy and the Protection of Family Members, 2010 *Neder. Int'l Priv.* 605 (2010); C.I. Nagy, What Functions May Party Autonomy Have in International Family and Succession Law? An EU Perspective, *Ned. IPR* 576 (2012); C. Roodt, Party Autonomy in International Law of Succession: A Starting Point for a Global Consensus, 2 *J. So. African L.* 241 (2009).

[30] *See* Art. 6 of Hague Convention of 1 July 1985 on the Law Applicable to Trusts and on their Recognition; D. Hayton, The Hague Convention on the Law Applicable to Trusts and on their Recognition, 36 *Int'l & Comp. L.Q.* 260 (1987).

[31] *See, e.g.,* Art. 3 of the Hague Convention of 14 March 1978 on the Law Applicable to Matrimonial Property Regimes; J. Scherpe (ed.), *Marital Agreements and Private Autonomy in Comparative Perspective* (2011); T. Frantzen, Party Autonomy in Norwegian International Matrimonial Property Law and Succession Law, 12 *Y.B. Priv. Int'l L.* 483 (2010); J.H. McLaughlin, Premarital Agreements and Choice of Law: "One, Two, Three, Baby, You and Me," 72 *Mo. L. Rev.* 793 (2007); A. Sanders, Private Autonomy and Marital Property Agreements, 59 *Int'l & Comp. L.Q.* 571 (2010).

[32] *See* R. Westrik & J. van der Weide (eds.), *Party Autonomy in International Property Law* (2011).

[33] *See, e.g.,* Art. 5 of Council Regulation (EU) No. 1259/2010 of 20 December 2010 implementing enhanced cooperation in the area of the law applicable to divorce and legal separation; Arts. 7–8 of the Hague Protocol of 23 November 2007 on the Law Applicable to Maintenance Obligations; Art. 15 of Council Regulation (EC) No. 4/2009 of 18 December 2008 on jurisdiction, applicable law, recognition and enforcement of decisions and cooperation in matters relating to maintenance obligations (incorporating the Hague Protocol); J. Carruthers, Party Autonomy in the Legal Regulation of Adult Relationships: What Place for Party Choice in Private International Law?, 61 *Int'l & Comp. L. Q.* 881 (2012); E. Jayme, Party Autonomy in International Family and Succession Law: New Tendencies, 11 *Y.B. Priv. Int'l L.* 1 (2009); Nagy, *supra* note 29; M. Torga, Party Autonomy of the Spouses under the Rome III Regulation in Estonia—Can Private International Law Change Substantive Law?, *Ned IPR* 547 (2012); I. Viarengo, The Role of Party Autonomy in Cross-Border Divorces, *Ned. IPR* 555 (2012).

[34] *See* Chapter 2 at IX, *supra*; Art. 14 of Regulation (EC) No. 864/2007 of the European Parliament and of the Council of 11 July 2007 on the law applicable to non-contractual obligations (Rome II); de Boer, *Party Autonomy*; F. Maultzsch, Choice of Law and *Jus Cogens* in Conflict of Laws for Contractual Obligations, 75 *RabelsZ* 60 (2011); Symeonides, *Party Autonomy,* 201–205; M. Zhang, Party Autonomy in Non-contractual Obligations: Rome II and Its Impacts on Choice of Law, 39 *Seton Hall L. Rev.* 861 (2009).

discussion below illustrates, many of those parameters are the same in all systems, while others vary significantly from one system to another.

A. INTERNATIONALITY

The most common of these parameters is the "internationality" of the contract. This means that: (1) party autonomy is allowed only in international or multistate contracts, namely contracts that have relevant contacts with more than one state; and (2) internationality cannot be created solely by the choice-of-law agreement.

At least the first of these requirements is implicit in the fact that, by definition, choice-of-law codifications and conventions apply only to international rather than domestic cases.[35] Even so, some conventions state both the first and the second requirement explicitly. For example, the 1986 Hague Sales Convention provides that it applies to contracts of sales of goods "between parties having their places of business in different States" or "involving a choice between the laws of different States, unless such a choice arises solely from a stipulation by the parties as to the applicable law...."[36] The Mexico City Convention provides that it applies to "international contracts," which it defines as those in which the parties "have their habitual residence or establishments in different States Parties" to the Convention, or which have "objective ties with more than one State Party."[37] Finally, the 2012 Hague Principles on Choice of Law for International Contracts (hereinafter "Hague Contracts Principles") define "international contracts" negatively by excluding contracts in which "the parties have their establishments in the same State and the relationship of the parties and all other relevant elements, regardless of the chosen law, are connected only with that State."[38]

Most national codifications do not find it necessary to restate the internationality requirement *among their contracts articles*, but some of them do. For example, the Ukrainian codification provides that a contractual choice of law is not allowed if the relationship has "no foreign element."[39] The Vietnamese codification allows contracting

---

[35] For example, the Ukrainian codification provides that it applies to "private-law relations with a foreign element" (art. 2), and that a foreign element is present when: (1) one of the participants in the relation is a foreign natural or juridical person, a stateless person, or a Ukrainian living abroad; (2) the object of the relationship is in the territory of the foreign state; or (3) the legal act or fact that creates, changes, or terminates the relationship occurred in the territory of the foreign state (art. 1).

[36] Hague Convention on the Law Applicable to Contracts for the International Sale of Goods of 22 December 1986, Art. 1.

[37] Mexico City Convention, Art. 1. The codifications of Afghanistan (art. 27), Jordan (art. 20), Mauritania (art. 10), Qatar (art. 27), Somalia (art. 19), Sudan (art. 11.13), U.A.E. (art. 19), and Yemen (art. 30) allow party autonomy only if the parties are not domiciled in the same state.

[38] Hague Contracts Principles, Art. 1(2). For an in-depth discussion of these principles, *see* S. Symeonides, The Hague Principles on Choice of Law for International Contracts: Some Preliminary Comments, 61 *Am. J. Comp. L.* 873 (2013).

[39] Ukrainian codif. art. 5(6), art. 43.

parties to choose the applicable law, but also provides that a contract "entered into and performed entirely in Vietnam must comply with the law of the Socialist Republic of Vietnam."[40] The Uruguayan draft codification provides that the parties to an "international" contract may choose the applicable law[41] and defines such a contract as one in which the parties have their habitual residences or establishments in different states or which has "objective links" with more than one state.[42] It goes on to say that a "contract cannot be internationalized through the sheer will of the parties."[43] Although other codifications do not contain an explicit statement such as the one last quoted, most of them would reach the same result through their provisions on *fraude à la loi*.[44]

A similar idea, but stated in more lenient terms, is found in the Rome Convention. Article 3(3) of the Convention provides that "[t]he fact that the parties have chosen a foreign law … shall not, where all the other elements relevant to the situation at the time of the choice are connected with one country only, prejudice the application of rules of the law of that country which cannot be derogated from by contract, hereinafter called 'mandatory rules.' "[45] Similar provisions are found in the codifications of Albania (art. 45.4), Bulgaria (art. 93.5), Estonia (art. 32.3), Germany (art. 27.3), South Korea (art. 25.4), Quebec (art. 3111), Serbia (draft art. 136.6), and Russia (art. 1210.5). Rome I rephrased this provision only slightly, as follows:

> Where all other elements relevant to the situation at the time of the choice are located in a country other than the country whose law has been chosen, the choice of the parties shall not prejudice the application of provisions of the law of that other country which cannot be derogated from by agreement.[46]

This provision, as well as that of the Rome Convention and the codifications influenced by it, is more lenient than, for example the Ukrainian or Uruguayan provisions quoted earlier because, rather than altogether prohibiting the particular choice of law in "non-international" contracts, it simply subordinates it to the mandatory rules of the state that has "all" the relevant contacts.

---

[40] Vietnamese codif. art. 769.

[41] Uruguayan Draft codif. art. 48.

[42] *Id*. at art. 44.

[43] *Id*. For discussion, *see* C. Fresnedo de Aguirre, *Uruguay Report*, at I.1.

[44] *See, e.g.,* Angolan codif. art. 21; Azerbaijan codif. art 8; Belarus codif. art 1097; Cape Verde codif. art. 21; Croatian codif. art. 5; East Timor codif. art. 20; Guinea-Bissau codif. art. 21; Hungarian codif. art. 8; Kazakhstan codif. art. 1088; Kyrgyzstan codif. art. 1171; Macau codif. art 19; Mexican codif. art. 15.1; Mozambique codif. art. 21; Portuguese codif. art. 21; Romanian codif. art. 8; Tunisian codif. art. 30; Ukrainian codif. art. 10; Uzbekistan codif. art. 1162.

[45] Rome Convention, art. 3(3).

[46] Rome I, art. 3(3).

B. CONNECTION WITH CHOSEN STATE

Internationality is a "geographic" requirement in the sense that it requires that the parties or the contract have pertinent contacts with more than one state. This requirement is different from a more specific geographic requirement imposed by some systems, which requires a specified connection with the state whose law is chosen by the parties.

1. Required for All Contracts

For example, Section 187 of the Restatement (Second) provides that, for issues that are beyond the parties' contractual power, the state of the chosen law must have a "substantial relationship" to the parties or the transaction,[47] or that there must be another "reasonable basis" for the parties' choice.[48] Similarly, the Uniform Commercial Code provides that the chosen state must bear a "reasonable relation" to the transaction.[49] The Spanish codification, now superseded by Rome I, provided that the chosen law must have "some connection" with the contract.[50] The Portuguese codification, also superseded by Rome I, provided that the parties' choice must fulfill a "serious interest" of the parties, or it must relate to an element of the contract that is relevant under PIL.[51] The codifications of the former Portuguese colonies also contain an identical article.[52] The Hague Securities

---

[47] *Restatement (Second)* § 187(2). The Restatement differentiates between: (1) issues that the parties "could have resolved by an explicit provision in their agreement directed to that issue," *id.* § 187(1), such as those "relating to construction, to conditions precedent and subsequent, to sufficiency of performance and to excuse for non-performance, [...] frustration and impossibility;" *id.* cmt c; and (2) issues that are beyond the parties' contractual power, such as those involving "capacity, formalities and substantial validity." *Id.* cmt d. For issues of the first category, the parties' choice of law is not subject to any geographical or substantive limitations.

[48] *Id.* Another "reasonable basis" can be, and usually is, not geographically based, such as the completeness of the chosen law or its expertise on the particular subject.

[49] U.C.C. § 1-301 provides that "when a transaction bears a reasonable relation to [the forum] state and also to another state or nation the parties may agree that the law of either [the forum] state or of such other state or nation shall govern their rights and duties." U.C.C. § 1-301(a). If literally applied, this provision would require a reasonable relation with *both* the chosen state *and* the forum state. Thus, a reasonable relation with one or more states *other* than the forum state would not suffice. Obviously, such a literal reading is nonsensical, if only because it contradicts the UCC's otherwise very liberal stance toward party autonomy. The forum's lack of a reasonable relation may be a factor in jurisdiction or *forum non conveniens* analysis, but it is not a good reason to preclude parties from choosing the law of another state that has such a relationship. This sloppy wording, which has survived nine amendments of this provision over the last four decades, has not caused much difficulty, but only because the courts have ignored it.

[50] Spanish codif. art. 10(5).

[51] Portuguese codif. art. 41(2). Professor L. de Lima Pinheiro, *Portuguese Report,* at XII, explains that the "serious interest" requirement is satisfied, for example, by "the nexus between the transaction and other transactions governed by the chosen law; the choice of the law of the forum of the agreed jurisdiction and the choice of a law which provides for a detailed regulation of the type of transaction at stake." The author concludes that "only in extreme cases will the choice be invalid for 'lack of a serious interest,' namely, those cases in which its motives are purely arbitrary or capricious."

[52] See Angola codif. art. 41.2; Cape Verde codif. art. 41.2; East Timor codif. art. 40.2; Guinea-Bissau codif. art. 41.2; Macau codif. art. 40.2; Mozambique codif. art. 41.2.

Convention requires that the relevant "intermediary" must have a "qualifying office" in the chosen state.[53]

2. Required for Some Contracts

The Rome I Regulation requires a specified geographic relation with the contractually chosen state in only two types of contracts: contracts for the carriage of passengers, and certain insurance contracts covering "small risks" situated in an EU Member State.[54] In contracts for the carriage of passengers, the parties may choose only the law of the country of: (1) the passenger's habitual residence, (2) the carrier's habitual residence or place of central administration, or (3) the place of departure or destination.[55] In "small risk" insurance contracts, the parties may choose only the law of: (1) a Member State in which the insured risk is situated; (2) the state in which the insured has his habitual residence; or (3) in the case of life insurance, the law of the Member State of which the insured is a national.[56]

For all other contracts, Rome I does not require a particular connection with the chosen country. As noted earlier, Rome I provides that when "*all* other elements relevant to the situation" are located in a country other than that of the contractually chosen law, Rome I mandates that the choice "shall not prejudice" the application of the mandatory rules of that other country.[57] Thus, as long as a contract has contacts with more than one country, the parties may choose the law of any other country, including one that lacks *any* connection.[58]

---

[53] *See* Hague Convention on the Law Applicable to Certain Rights in Respect of Securities Held with an Intermediary of 5 July 2006, art. 4(1).

[54] Article 7 of Rome I differentiates between contracts covering "large risks," wherever situated, and contracts covering other risks (i.e., "small risks") situated within the territory of an EU Member State. "Large risks" are defined through a cross reference to Article 5(d) of the First Council Directive 73/239/EEC of 24 July 1973. One of the differences between the two categories is that, in the absence of a choice-of-law agreement, the *lex causae* is the insurer's habitual residence in the large-risk contracts, *see* Rome I, art. 7(2), and the law of the member state in which the risk is located in the small-risk contracts. *See id.* art. 7(3).

[55] *See* Rome I, Art. 5(2). The parties' choice is also subject to the substantive limitations of party autonomy discussed *infra*. For an identical rule, *see* Albanian codif. art. 50; Serbian codif. art. 140.

[56] *See* Rome I, Art. 7(3), which also allows two additional choices in other types of insurance contracts. If the laws of the country in which the insured risk is located or the law of the insured's habitual residence allow more choices or have more liberal limits to party autonomy, the parties may choose a law within those limits. *Id.* For discussions of insurance contracts under Rome I, *see* F. Seatzu, *Insurance in Private International Law. A European Perspective,* (2003); H. Heiss, Insurance Contracts in Rome I: Another Recent Failure of the European Legislature, 10 *Ybk. Priv. Int'l L.* 261 (2008); L. Merrett, Choice of Law in Insurance Contracts under the Rome I Regulation, 5 *J. Priv. Int'l L.* 40 (2009); R. Merkin, The Rome I Regulation and Reinsurance, 5 *J. Priv. Int'l L.* 69 (2009).

[57] Rome I, Art. 3(3). Article 3(4) provides a similar rule for situations in which "all other elements relevant to the situation" are located in one or more EU Member States.

[58] According to an authoritative treatise, Rome I "permits a choice of law which involves the application of (a) a law which has the closest connection with the contract [...]; (b) a law which does not have the closest connection, but which has some apparent connection with the transaction (such as the place of performance or the residence of one of the parties); (c) a law which has no apparent connection with the contract, but which has

The Swiss codification requires a geographic nexus only in employment contracts. The parties may choose only the law of the state in which "the employee has his habitual residence or ... the employer has his place of business, his domicile or his habitual residence."[59]

3. Not Required

In contrast to the above, most other modern codifications, including more than 40 outside the EU,[60] and the two American codifications,[61] as well as five international conventions,[62] have eliminated the requirement for a geographic nexus to the chosen state. Among them, the Hague Principles took the next step of stating affirmatively that "[n]o connection is required between the law chosen and the parties or their transaction."[63]

III. The Modalities of the Choice-of-Law Agreement

A. MODE OF EXPRESSION

In recent transactional practice, choice-of-law agreements appear as express clauses usually contained in the same contract they purport to subject to the designated law. However, most recent codifications and conventions provide that the choice-of-law agreement need not be express but may also be implied. An implied choice is distinguished from a hypothetical choice, which most codifications do not recognize.[64]

---

some underlying connection, such as insurance, or connection with string contracts; (d) a law which has no apparent or actual connection with the transaction, but which is chosen as a neutral in an international contract [...]; (e) a law which has no apparent or actual connection with a transaction, all of whose elements are connected with one other country (an inevitably rare occurrence)." L. Collins et al., *Dicey, Morris & Collins on the Conflict of Laws* 1801 (15th ed. 2012).

[59] Swiss codif. art. 121.

[60] See the codifications of Afghanistan (art. 27); Albania (art. 45); Algeria (art. 18); Argentina (draft art. 2651); Armenia (art. 1284); Azerbaijan (art. 24); Belarus (art. 1124); Burundi (art. 5); Central African Repub. (art. 42); Chad (art. 70.6); China (art. 3, 41); Cuba (art. 17); FYROM (art. 21); Gabon (art. 55); Guatemala (art. 31); Japan (art. 7); Jordan (art. 20); Kazakhstan (art. 112); North Korea (art. 24); South Korea (art. 25); Kyrgyzstan (art. 1198); Liechtenstein (art. 39); Madagascar (art. 30); Mauritania (art. 10); Mexico (art. 13.V); Moldova (art. 1611); Mongolia (art. 549); Peru (art. 2095); Qatar (art. 27); Quebec (art. 3111); Russia (art. 1215); Rwanda (art. 14); Serbia (art. 140); Somalia (art. 19); Sudan (art. 11.13); Switzerland (art. 116); Taiwan (art. 20.1); Tajikistan (art. 1218); Tunisia (art. 62); Turkey (art. 24); Ukraine (art. 5); United Arab Emirates (art. 19); Uruguay (arts. 44, 48); Uzbekistan (art. 1189); Venezuela (art. 29); Vietnam (art. 769); and Yemen (art. 30).

[61] *See* La. Civ. Code Art. 3540; Or. Rev. Stat. § 15.350. *See also* art. 28 of the Puerto Rico draft codification.

[62] *See, e.g.,* Mexico City Convention, art. 7; Hague Convention of 15 June 1955 on the Law Applicable to International Sales of Goods, art. 5; Hague Convention of 14 March 1978 on the Law Applicable to Agency, art. 5; Hague Convention of 22 December 1986 on the Law Applicable to Contracts for the International Sale of Goods, art. 7(1).

[63] Hague Principles, art. 2(4).

[64] *See, e.g., Restatement (Second)* § 187, cmt a (stating that it "does not suffice to demonstrate that the parties, if they had thought about the matter, would have wished to have the law of a particular state applied.").

Although some codifications leave it to the court to determine how to infer a choice-of-law agreement,[65] other codifications contain more specific, as well as slightly different, requirements. They provide that an agreement may be inferred from: (1) the contract's terms alone,[66] (2) the surrounding circumstances alone,[67] (3) both the terms of the contract *and* the surrounding circumstances,[68] or (4) *either* the terms of the contract *or* the surrounding circumstances.[69]

It is likely that other codifications that do not explicitly require the choice-of-law agreement to be express would also recognize an implied choice of law. For example, a provision such as Article 29 of the Venezuela codification, which provides that conventional obligations are governed by the law "agreed to" by the parties, would recognize an implied choice because, under general contract principles, an agreement may be express or implied.[70] In contrast, a provision such as Article 2095 of the Peruvian codification, which provides that contractual obligations are governed by the law "expressly chosen" by the parties, would not allow an implied choice.

---

[65] For example, the Louisiana codification (art. 3540) allows the application of the law expressly chosen or "clearly relied upon" by the parties, the Macau codification (art. 40.1) provides for the law designated "or contemplated" by the parties, and the Taiwanese codification (art. 20.1) provides for the law "intended" by the parties. The Restatement (Second) probably belongs to this group, although the example given by a comment under Section 187 states that a court can infer a choice of law "from the [contract's] provisions." *Restatement (Second)*, §187 cmt a.

[66] *See, e.g.,* Armenian codif. art. 1284.5 (providing that the choice must be clearly expressed or "directly follow from the conditions of the contract."); Quebec codif. art. 3111 ("inferred with certainty from the terms of the act."); Uruguay draft codif. art. 48.3. The Oregon codification provides that the choice must be "clearly demonstrated from the terms of the contract," but also requires that, in standard-form contracts drafted primarily by one party, the choice must be "express and conspicuous." Or. Rev. Stat. § 15.350(2).

[67] *See, e.g.,* Slovak codif. art 9.1. (providing that a choice of law may be inferred from the circumstances); Liechtenstein codif. art. 39.1.

[68] *See, e.g.,* Mexico City Convention art. 7 (providing that the choice of law "must be evident from the parties' behavior and from the clauses of the contract, considered as a whole."); Hague Sales Convention art. 7.1 (the choice must be "clearly demonstrated by the terms of the contract and the conduct of the parties, viewed in their entirety."); Hague Agency Convention art. 5 (the choice must be express or "must be such that it may be inferred with reasonable certainty from the terms of the agreement between the parties and the circumstances of the case."); Belarus codif. art. 1124.2 (the choice must "directly follow from the conditions of the contract and circumstances of the case, being considered as a whole."); Kazakhstan codif. art. 112.2.

[69] *See* Rome I art. 3(1) (the choice must be "clearly demonstrated by the terms of the contract or the circumstances of the case."); Hague Contracts Principles art. 4 (the choice must "appear clearly from the provisions of the contract or the circumstances."). For codifications outside the EU, *see, e.g.,* the codifications of Albania (art. 45.2); Argentina (draft art. 2651); FYROM (art. 21.2); South Korea (art. 25.1); Moldova (art. 1611); Puerto Rico (art. 28); Qatar (art. 27); Russia (art. 1210.2); Serbia (art. 136.2); Switzerland (art. 116.2); Turkey (art. 24.1); U.A.E (art. 19.1); Ukraine (art. 5.2); and Yemen (art. 30).

[70] The same can be said about similar provisions in other codifications, such as those of China (art. 41), Croatia (art. 19), Japan (art. 7), Jordan (art. 20), North Korea (art. 24), and Kyrgyzstan (art. 1198.1).

B. MULTIPLE OR PARTIAL CHOICE

It is now accepted that the parties may choose the law of more than one state to govern different parts or issues of the contract. For example, in a contract to be performed in more than one state, the parties may subject questions of performance to the laws of the states of the respective performances. Similarly, the parties may choose a law to govern only part of their contract. In that case, the rest of the contract will be governed by the otherwise applicable, objectively chosen law, which is referred to hereinafter as the *lex causae*.[71] This partial choice of law, as well as the choice of more than one law, may result in *dépeçage*.

The Rome Convention was the first instrument to expressly recognize this possibility when it provided that the parties "can select the law applicable to the whole or to part only of the contract."[72] Since then, other international instruments have followed, such as the Mexico City Convention, the Hague Sales Convention,[73] and the Hague Contracts Principles, the last of which provides expressly for the choice of "different laws for different parts of the contract."[74] A partial or multiple choice of law is now recognized by the Restatement (Second), by the 27 EU countries that are bound by Rome I, and more than 20 codifications in countries outside the EU.[75] It is also accepted by judicial practice in other countries, such as China, Israel, and Switzerland.[76]

C. TIMING OF THE CHOICE OR CHANGE

Although the choice-of-law clause is usually contained in the same contract that the clause purports to regulate, recent codifications and conventions expressly allow the parties to choose the applicable law at a later time, or to modify a choice they had made earlier, as long as they do not prejudice the rights of third parties. For example, Rome I provides that the parties may "at any time agree to subject the contract to a law other than that which previously governed it," and that any such change "shall not prejudice" the formal validity of the contract or "adversely affect the rights of third parties."[77] Similar

---

[71] Some authors use the term *lex causae* to refer to the law that governs the contract, even if that law was contractually chosen. To avoid confusion, this chapter uses the term *lex causae* to refer to the law that is applicable in the absence of an effective choice of law by the parties and that is chosen through objective connecting factors.

[72] Rome Convention, art. 3(1). This provision is reproduced without change in Rome I, art. 3(1).

[73] *See* Mexico City Convention, art. 7; Hague Sales Convention, art. 7(1).

[74] Hague Contracts Principles art. 2.2.

[75] *See Restatement (Second),* § 187 cmt i, as revised in 1988; Albanian codif. art. 45.1; Argentine draft codif. art. 2651; Armenian codif. art. 1284(2); Azerbaijan codif. art. 24.1; Belarus codif. art. 1124(4); FYROM codif. art. 15(3); Kazakhstan codif. art. 112.3; South Korean codif. art. 25(2); Kyrgyzstan codif. art. 1198 (2); La. codif. art. 3540, cmt. (e); Moldova codif. art. 1611; Or. Rev. Stat. § 15.350(1); Puerto Rico draft, art. 28; Quebec codif. art. 3111(3); Russian codif. art. 1210(4); Tajikistan codif. art. 1218.3; Turkish codif. art. 24(2); Ukrainian codif. art. 5.3; Uruguayan Draft, art.48.3; Uzbekistan codif. art. 1189.2.

[76] *See* W. Chen, *Chinese Report,* at III; T. Einhorn, *Israeli Report,* at III.3; A. Bonomi, *Swiss Report,* at III.3.

[77] Rome I, art. 3(2).

provisions are found in many other conventions[78] and codifications outside the EU.[79] The Restatement (Second) does not address these issues, but general contract principles should lead to the same result.

A different question arises in cases in which, after the choice-of-law agreement, the chosen law *itself* changes because of legislative or judicial action. The question then is whether the contract should be governed by the chosen law as it was at the time of the agreement or, instead, by the *changed* law. None of the codifications discussed here address this question, leaving it instead to the courts or academic authors.

In searching for an answer, the parties' intention, if it can be proven, should be the starting point and perhaps the controlling factor. For example, some contracts contain "stabilization clauses" specifically designed to guard against subsequent changes in the chosen law.[80] However, in the vast majority of cases, the contract does not address this issue. Even assuming that the solution in such cases is to be found by inferring the parties' intent (a debatable assumption), one can think of good arguments for either inference. The parties could have chosen the law of state X, either (1) because of the specific substantive content of that law, as it then was; or (2) because of their preference for the general solutions of state X, whatever they may be at the time of the dispute. In English law, as well as under Rome I, a distinction is made between choice of law, on the one hand, and incorporation by reference, on the other hand. In the case of the former, the chosen law applies as it is at the time of the dispute (i.e., with the intervening changes in that law). In the case of incorporation by reference, the incorporated law applies as it was at the time of the incorporation (i.e., without any intervening changes).[81]

D. CHOICE OF AN INVALIDATING LAW

Last, another question that is not addressed by recent codifications and not uniformly answered by judicial practice is what to do when the chosen law invalidates (1) the whole contract, or (2) a part of the contract.

The first situation presents a clash between two general policies: the policy of giving effect to the parties' intent to have a binding contract, on the one hand, and the general policy of contract validation on the other hand. In some countries, particularly in Europe, the conflict

---

[78] *See* Mexico City Convention art. 8; Hague Sales Convention art. 7(2); Hague Contracts Principles art. 2.3.

[79] *See, e.g.,* Albanian codif. art. 45.3; Argentinean draft codif. art. 2651(a); Armenian codif. art. 1284.3–4; Belarus codif. art. 1124.3; Georgian codif. art. 35.2; Kazakhstan codif. art 112.3; South Korean codif. art. 25(3); Kyrgyzstan codif. art. 1198 (3); La. codif. art. 3540, cmt e; Moldova codif. art. 1611; Or. Rev. Stat. § 15.350(3)–(4); Puerto Rico draft, art. 28; Quebec codif. art. 3111(3); Russian codif. art. 1210(3); Serbian codif. art. 136.4; Swiss codif. art. 116(3); Tajikistan codif. art. 1218.3; Turkish codif. art. 24(3).

[80] These clauses are often found in contracts between a private party and a state entity and are usually designed to protect the private party from changes caused by the state entity. For the validity of such clauses under English law, *see* Collins et al. *supra* note 58, at 1803–1805.

[81] *See id.* at 1807–1809.

is resolved by applying the chosen law even if it invalidates the contract.[82] The rationale is that "grounds for invalidity often protect one of the parties and he, who chooses a law, chooses its protection."[83] Invalidity of the contract effectuates the parties' choice and serves to uphold party autonomy.

However, assuming that the parties bargained deliberately and in good faith, this result hardly comports with the parties' intention to create a contract and their expectation that it will be valid. For this reason, the Restatement (Second) suggests that the choice of an invalidating law be treated as a mutual mistake and therefore disregarded because the application of the chosen law would "defeat the expectations of the parties which it is the purpose of [Section 187] to protect."[84] The contract is then governed by the objectively chosen law, for example through the factors of Section 188. In a similar vein, the Quebec codification provides that, if the chosen law invalidates the contract, the court must apply the law of the country with which the contract is "most closely connected."[85] However, a number of American decisions have taken the opposite position and have invalidated the contract.[86]

When the law chosen by the parties invalidates *only a part* of the contract, such as a non-compete covenant, the parties' general expectation of having a binding contract is satisfied. Consequently, in the absence of special circumstances, there is little reason to allow one party to pick the favorable and discard the unfavorable provisions of the chosen law. The Restatement (Second) seems to recognize the difference between the two situations because it speaks only of situations in which the chosen law invalidates "the contract"[87] rather than part thereof.[88] Most American cases have taken the position asserted here, namely, that when an otherwise valid choice-of-law clause chooses a law that invalidates only a part of the contract, the clause should be upheld.[89]

---

[82] For France, *see* Cass. in 1967 Revue critique DIP 334; for Germany, BGH in 1969 *Neue Juristische Wochenschrift* 1760, 1761; OLG München in 1990 *IPrax* 320.

[83] G. Kegel & K. Schurig, *Internationales Privatrecht* 657 (9th ed. 2004).

[84] *Restatement (Second)* § 187, cmt e and Reporter's Note (1971).

[85] Quebec codif. art. 3112.

[86] *See* Hay, Borchers & Symeonides, *Conflict of Laws*, 1034.

[87] *Restatement (Second)* § 187, cmt e.

[88] However, the Reporter's Note cites cases in which the chosen law invalidates "the contract or a provision thereof." *See id.* Reporter's Note.

[89] *See, e.g.*, CS-Lakeview at Gwinnett, Inc. v. Simon Prop. Grp., Inc., 283 Ga. 426, 659 S.E.2d 359 (2008) (citing this author); Boatland, Inc. v. Brunswick Corp., 558 F.2d 818 (6th Cir. 1977) (invalidating under the chosen law a clause dealing with the termination of a dealership agreement); Hardy v. Monsanto Enviro-Chem Sys., Inc., 414 Mich. 29, 323 N.W.2d 270 (1982) (applying the chosen law to invalidate an indemnity clause); Stoot v. Fluor Drilling Servs., Inc., 851 F.2d 1514 (5th Cir. 1988) (accord); General Elec. Credit Corp. v. Beyerlein, 55 Misc. 2d 724, 286 N.Y.S.2d 351 (1967), *aff'd*, 30 A.D.2d 762, 292 N.Y.S.2d 32 (1968) (applying the chosen law to invalidate a clause that cut off defenses against an assignee). *But see* Kipin Indus. v. Van Deilen Int'l, Inc., 182 F.3d 490 (6th Cir. 1999) (disregarding the chosen law "to the extent" it invalidated a part of the contract).

IV. The Scope of Party Autonomy

A. INTRODUCTION

The requirement for a geographic nexus to the chosen state is only one of several tools—indeed the least precise or effective—for policing party autonomy. Other more effective techniques involve narrowing the scope of party autonomy by:

(1) Excluding from it certain contracts;

(2) Excluding certain contractual issues;

(3) Limiting party autonomy to contractual, as opposed to non-contractual, issues; or

(4) Otherwise limiting what "law" the parties can choose, that is:
  (a) Substantive, as opposed to procedural law,
  (b) Substantive or internal, as opposed to conflicts law, and
  (c) State law, as opposed to nonstate norms.

As the following discussion illustrates, the various codifications and conventions employ some or all of these techniques, thus leading to the conclusion that the scope of party autonomy differs widely from one system to the other.

B. EXEMPTED CONTRACTS

1. Total Exemptions

Many choice-of-law codifications contain rules that subject certain contracts to the law designated in the rule and explicitly or implicitly preclude the contractual choice of another law. One common example is contracts involving real rights, or in some instances, all rights, in immovable property. The exemption of these contracts from party autonomy appears either as a unilateral rule limited to immovables situated in the forum state[90] or, more commonly, as a bilateral rule applicable to both domestic and foreign immovables.[91]

Consumer contracts are an equally common example of contracts that are either completely exempted from the scope of party autonomy, or, as we shall see later, are subjected to special limitations designed to protect the consumer.[92] The Swiss codification is one

---

[90] *See, e.g.,* Uruguayan draft codif. art. 50.1 (subjecting to Uruguayan law and excluding party autonomy "contracts that constitute, modify or transfer real rights and leases" on immovable property situated in Uruguay); Vietnam codif. art. 769.2 ("Civil contracts relating to immovables in Vietnam must comply with the law of the Socialist Republic of Vietnam.").

[91] *See, e.g.,* Turkish codif. art. 25 ("Contracts relating to immovable property or their use shall be governed by the law of the country where such an immovable property is situated.") *See also* the codifications of Afghanistan (art. 27(3)); Algeria (art. 18); Belarus (art. 1125.2); Croatia (art. 21); FYROM (art. 23); Gabon (art. 55(2)); Jordan (art. 20.2); Qatar (art. 27); Somalia (art. 19.2); Sudan (art. 11.13b); U.A.E. (art. 19.2); and Yemen (art. 30).

[92] See *infra* at V.A.3 and VII.B. The literature on choice of law in consumer contracts is quite extensive. The following are some of the most recent writings on the subject: D. Fernández Arroyo (ed.), *Consumer Protection*

of those falling within the first category.[93] It subjects contracts involving a "passive" consumer[94] to the law of her habitual residence and specifically precludes the contractual choice of another law.[95] The 1986 Hague Sales Convention also exempts from its scope, and thus from the scope of party autonomy, consumer sales, which it defines as sales of "goods bought for personal, family or household use."[96]

---

in *International Private Relationships* (2010); L.E. Gillies, *Electronic Commerce and International Private Law: A Study of Electronic Consumer Contracts* (2008); J. Hill, *Cross-Border Consumer Contracts* (2008); S. Klauer, *Das europäische Kollisionsrecht der Verbraucherverträge zwischen Römer EVÜ und EG-Richtlinien* (2002); C. Lima Marques, *O novo direito privado e a proteção dos vulneráveis* (2012); C. Lima Marques, *Contratos no Código de Defesa do Consumidor* (6th ed. 2011); C. Lima Marques, A. Herman Benjamin & L. Bessa, *Manual de Direito do consumidor* (3d ed. 2011); Z. Tang, P. Beaumont & J. Harris, *Electronic Consumer Contracts in the Conflict of Laws* (2009); P.A. Brand, Cross-Border Consumer Protection within the EU—Inconsistencies and Contradictions in the European System of Conflict of Law Rules and Procedural Law, *IPRax* 126 (2013); P. Cachia, Consumer Contracts in European Private International Law: The Sphere of Operation of the Consumer Contract Rules in the Brussels I and Rome I Regulations, 34 *Eur. L. Rev.* 476 (2009); J. De Lisle & E. Trujillo, Consumer Protection in Transnational Contexts, 58 *Am. J. Comp. L.* 135 (2010 Supp.); P. Deumier, La protection des consommateurs dans les relations internationales, *Rev. int'l dr. comp.* 273 (2010); D. Fernández Arroyo, Current Approaches towards Harmonization of Consumer Private International Law in the Americas, 58 *Int'l & Comp. L.Q.* 411 (2009); F. Garcimartín Alférez, The Rome I Regulation: Exceptions to the Rule on Consumer Contracts and Financial Instruments, 5 *J. Priv. Int'l L.* 85 (2009); L.E. Gillies, Choice-of-Law Rules for Electronic Consumer Contracts: Replacement of the Rome Convention by the Rome I Regulation, 3 *J. Priv. Int'l L.* 89 (2007); L.E. Gillies, Addressing the "Cyberspace Fallacy": Targeting the Jurisdiction of an Electronic Consumer Contract, 16 *Int'l J.L. & Info. Tech.* 242 (2008); J.J. Healy, Consumer Protection Choice of Law: European Lessons for the United States, 19 *Duke J. Comp. & Int'l L.* 535 (2009); J. Hill, Article 6 of the Rome I Regulation: Much Ado about Nothing, 2009 *Nederl. IPR.* 437 (2009); S. Leible, Consumer Protection in International Relations, in J. Basedow, U. Kischel & U. Sieber (eds.), *German National Reports to the 18th International Congress of Comparative Law* 109 (2010); E.A. O'Hara, Choice of Law for Internet Transactions: The Uneasy Case for Online Consumer Protection, 153 *U. Pa. L. Rev.* 1883 (2005); Z. Papassiopi-Passia, Consumer Protection in Greek Private International Law, 63 *Rev. Hellénique Dr. Int'l* 79 (2010); G. Rühl, Consumer Protection in Choice of Law, 44 *Cornell Int'l L.J.* 569 (2011); P. Schlosser, Death-Blow to the So-Called "Supplementary Interpretation" of Contracts ("ergänzende Vertragsauslegung") in the Case of Invalid Terms in Consumer Contracts?, 2012/6 *IPRax* 507 (2012); Z. Tang, Private International Law in Consumer Contracts: A European Perspective, 6 *J. Priv. Int'l L.* 225 (2010); Z. Tang, Consumer Collective Redress in European Private International Law, 7 *J. Priv. Int'l L.* 101 (2011); Z. Tang, Parties' Choice of Law in E-Consumer Contracts, 3 *J. Priv. Int'l L.* 113 (2007); V. Trstenjak & E. Beysen, European Consumer Protection Law: *Curia Semper Dabit Remedium?*, 48 *Com. Mrkt. L. Rev.* 95 (2011).

[93] For other examples, *see* Argentinean draft codif. art. 2655; Chinese codif. art. 42; Uruguayan draft codif. art. 50.5. The Oregon codification exempts from the scope of party autonomy consumer contracts in which the consumer is an Oregon resident and "the consumer's assent to the contract is obtained in Oregon, or the consumer is induced to enter into the contract in substantial measure by an invitation or advertisement in Oregon." Or. Rev. Stat. § 15.320(4). For discussion, *see* S. Symeonides, Oregon's Choice-of-Law Codification for Contract Conflicts: An Exegesis, 44 *Willamette L. Rev.* 205 (2007); S. Symeonides, Codifying Choice of Law for Contracts: The Oregon Experience, 67 *RabelsZ* 726 (2003).

[94] A "passive" consumer is one whose assent to the contract is obtained in either her home state or in another state, but as a result of solicitation or other enticement taking place in the home state.

[95] *See* Swiss codif. art. 120.

[96] Hague Sales Convention, art. 2(c). However, the exemption does not apply if the seller "neither knew nor ought to have known that the goods were bought for any such use." *Id.*

The 2012 Hague Contracts Principles confine their scope to "commercial" contracts, which are defined as those in which "each party is acting in the exercise of its trade or profession,"[97] namely, B2B contracts.[98] To avoid any doubt, the Principles single out two noncommercial contracts, namely consumer contracts and employment contracts, and expressly exclude them from the scope of the Principles.[99] The Hague Choice of Court Convention also contains a similar exclusion.[100]

Other codifications also preclude party autonomy in employment contracts.[101] For example, the Ukrainian codification subjects to Ukrainian law contracts for employment to be performed in Ukraine, or contracts between Ukrainian employers and employees for employment outside Ukraine.[102] The Uruguayan draft codification allows the employee, but not the employer, to choose from among the laws of the place of employment, or the employee's or the employer's domicile.[103]

Insurance contracts are often among the excluded contracts.[104] For example, Article 3119 of the Quebec codification provides that "[n]otwithstanding any agreement to the

---

[97] Hague Contracts Principles, art. 1.

[98] This express bilaterality of commerciality is important because in some countries a contract is considered commercial even if only one of the contracting parties is acting in the exercise of its trade or profession.

[99] *See* Hague Contracts Principles, art. 1.

[100] *See* Hague Convention of 30 June 2005 on Choice of Court Agreements, art. 2(1).

[101] *See* Chinese codif. art. 43; Tunisian codif. art. 67. The Oregon codification exempts from the scope of party autonomy contracts of employment "for services to be rendered primarily in Oregon by a resident of Oregon." Or. Rev. Stat. § 15.320(3). For discussions of choice of law in employment contracts, *see, e.g.,* L. Ferret, *Employment Contracts in Private International Law* (2012); U. Liukkunen, *The Role of Mandatory Rules in International Labour Law* (2004); B. Cooper et al., Economic Globalization and Convergence in Labor Market Regulation: An Empirical Assessment, 60 *Am. J. Comp. L.* 703 (2012); D. Doorey, In Defense of Transnational Domestic Labor Regulation, 43 *Vand. J. Transn'l L.* 953 (2010); P. Goulding & M. Vinall, The English Approach to Jurisdiction and Choice of Law in Employment Covenants Not to Compete, 31 *Comp. Lab. L. & Pol'y* 375 (2010); U. Grušic, Jurisdiction in Employment Matters under Brussels I: A Reassessment, 61 *Int'l & Comp. L.Q.* 91 (2012); U. Grušic, The Territorial Scope of Employment Legislation and Choice of Law, 75 *Mod. L. Rev.* 722 (2012); S. Krebber, Qualifikationsrechtlicher Rechtsformzwang—Der Arbeitsvertrags- und Arbeitnehmerbegriff im Europäischen Kollisions- und Verfahrensrecht, in H. Kronke & K. Thorn (eds.), *Grenzen überwinden, Prinzipien bewahren: Festschrift für Bernd von Hoffmann* 218 (2012); G. Lester & E. Ryan, Choice of Law and Employee Restrictive Covenants: An American Perspective, 31 *Comp. Lab. L. & Pol'y J.* 389 (2010); T. Mahnhold, Choice of Law Provisions in Contractual Covenants Not to Compete: The German Approach, 31 *Comp. Lab. L. & Pol'y J.* 331 (2010); E. Menegatti, The Choice of Law in Employment Contracts: Covenants Not to Compete under the Italian Legislation, 31 *Comp. Lab. L. & Pol'y J.* 799 (2010); K. Roberts, Correcting Culture: Extraterritoriality and U.S. Employment Discrimination Law, 24 *Hofstra Labor & Empl. L.J.* 295 (2007); C. Smith & E. Moyé, Outsourcing American Civil Justice: Mandatory Arbitration Clauses in Consumer and Employment Contracts, 44 *Tex. Tech L. Rev.* 281 (2012); A. Stewart & J. Greene, Choice of Law and the Enforcement of Post-Employment Restraints in Australia, 31 *Comp. Lab. L. & Pol'y J.* 305 (2010); R. Yamakawa, Transnational Dimension of Japanese Labor and Employment Laws: New Choice of Law Rules and Determination of Geographical Reach, 31 *Comp. Lab. L. & Pol'y J.* 347 (2010).

[102] *See* Ukrainian codif. arts. 52–55.

[103] *See* Uruguayan draft codif. art. 50.6.

[104] *See, e.g.,* Puerto Rico codif. art. 37 (applicable to contracts with specified Puerto Rico connections); Uruguayan draft codif. art. 50.7–8.

contrary," insurance contracts with certain enumerated connections with Quebec are governed by Quebec law.[105]

Finally, the list of contracts exempted from the scope of party autonomy, or of the countries where such exemptions exist, grows significantly longer than the above examples indicate if one looks beyond choice-of-law codifications into the realm of substantive law. As documented in Capter 7, many substantive statutes contain "localizing" provisions mandating the application of the law of the enacting state to certain contracts with enumerated contacts with that state and excluding both the judicial and the contractual choice of another state's laws. Such "localizing substantive rules" are common, not only for the contracts listed above (e.g., consumer, employment, and insurance contracts), but also for construction contracts, carriage contracts, charter contracts, and franchise or distributorship contracts.[106] Under the principle of *lex specialis derogat legi generali*, these rules prevail over the rules of choice-of-law codifications that authorize party autonomy.

2. Partial Exemptions

Other codifications, including the Rome Convention and later the Rome I Regulation, have adopted a more nuanced approach to consumer and employment contracts, which is designed to protect the consumer or employee from the consequences of an adverse choice of law.[107] Rome I provides that a choice-of-law agreement may not deprive a "passive" consumer or an employee of the protection of the mandatory rules of the state whose law would have been applicable in the absence of the agreement—the *lex causae*.[108]

In consumer contracts, the state of the *lex causae* is the state in which the consumer has her habitual residence, if the other party pursues commercial or professional activities in that state or directs such activities to that state or to several states including that state.[109] In employment contracts, the state of the *lex causae* is ordinarily the state in which (or from which) the employee habitually works, unless the contract is more closely connected with another state.[110]

Similar provisions are found in many codifications outside the EU, for consumer contracts only,[111] or for both consumer and employment contracts.[112] However, the Japanese

---

[105] Quebec codif. art. 3119. The article applies to non-marine insurance contracts "respecting property or an interest situated in Québec or subscribed in Québec by a person resident in Québec...if the policyholder applies therefore in Québec or the insurer signs or delivers the policy in Québec" and contracts of "group insurance of persons...where the participant has his residence in Québec at the time he becomes a participant."

[106] *See* Chapter 7 at II.A *infra*.

[107] *See* Rome Convention, arts. 5–6.

[108] *See* Rome I, arts. 6(2), 8(1).

[109] Rome I, art. 6(1).

[110] Rome I, art. 8(2–4).

[111] *See* Albanian codif. art. 52; Argentinean draft codif. art. 2655; Russian codif. art. 1212; Ukrainian codif. art. 45.

[112] See FYROM codif. arts. 24–25; Japanese codif. arts. 11–12; South Korean codif. arts. 27–28; Liechtenstein codif. arts. 45, 48; Puerto Rico codif. arts. 35–36; Quebec codif. arts. 3117–3118; Serbian draft codif. arts.

codification is somewhat peculiar in that it makes the application of the mandatory rules dependent on the consumer or the employee "express[ing] his/her will to the business operator [or the employer, respectively,] to the effect that such mandatory rules should apply."[113] The stated reason for this requirement is to relieve the court from the burden of having to know and ex officio apply these rules.[114]

Apparently, it is unnecessary for the business operator or employer to agree to this "expression of will," but the available English translations of the Japanese articles leave doubts on whether this expression must be voiced at the time of the contract or later. If it is the former, then, particularly in the case of employees, this requirement will emasculate the protection the codification purports to provide. However, Japanese commentators confirm that the consumer or employee may invoke this protection "at any time" until the conclusion of the oral argument in the trial court,[115] as well as in "extrajudicial" proceedings.[116] Thus, this is another example of a post-dispute choice of law by one party,[117] which makes the Japanese codification both more practical and more protective of that party (here the consumer or employee) than Rome I and other codifications.[118]

C. EXEMPTED CONTRACTUAL ISSUES

A choice-of-law clause is itself an agreement that is usually contained in the contract that the clause purports to submit to the chosen law. Before one can properly speak of such an "agreement," however, one must verify that it actually came into existence. Thus, at least theoretically, there is always a preliminary question of which law will determine the existence and validity of the choice-of-law agreement itself, with regard to at least three categories of issues:

(a) Whether the parties have capacity to contract;
(b) Whether the parties have expressed their consent to the choice-of-law agreement, and whether that consent was free of defects, such as duress or error; and

---

141–142; Turkish codif. arts. 26–27. The Puerto Rico codification (art. 37) extends this protective treatment to insurance contracts with specified Puerto Rico connections.

[113] Japanese codif. arts. 11, 12.

[114] *See* T. Kanzaki, *Japanese Report*, at XIII.2; Nishitani, *Party Autonomy*, at 95–96; Y. Okuda, Reform of Japan's Private International Law: Act on the General Rules of the Application of Laws, 8 *Ybk Priv. Int'l L*. 145, 153 (2006).

[115] Y. Okuda, A Short Look at Rome I on Contract Conflicts from a Japanese Perspective, 10 *Ybk. Priv. Int'l L*. 301, 308 (2008).

[116] Y. Okuda, *Reform of Japan's Private International Law, supra* note 114, at 153 (quoting a government statement in Parliament).

[117] Rules allowing one party to choose the applicable law after the dispute arises are discussed in Chapter 6 at V.C.2, *infra*.

[118] *But see* Okuda, *A Short Look, supra* note 115, at 308–309 (stating that this rule "overly protect[s]" the consumer or employee and is "unfair to the other party").

(c) Whether the agreement, or the contract containing it, was clothed with the required form.

There are several possible answers to this question but, for purposes of this discussion, they can be grouped into two solutions.

(1) The first solution is to *exempt* these preliminary issues from the scope of party autonomy and to decide them under either: (a) the substantive law of the forum qua forum, or (b) the law that would be applicable under the forum's choice-of-law rules in the absence of a choice-of-law agreement, that is, the *lex causae.*

(2) The second solution is to *not* exempt these issues from the scope of party autonomy and thus decide them under the law "chosen" in the "agreement."

Obviously, the second solution involves a certain degree of "bootstrapping."[119] It "evoke[s] the unavoidable imagery of the chicken and the egg test."[120] As one commentator noted, "if the choice of law is contractual, but the parties do not agree that they made a binding contract" (or lacked contractual capacity), "it is hard to see how the law which would have governed that both-alleged-and-denied contract can have a legitimate role in resolving the dispute about formation."[121]

1. Capacity

The bootstrapping problem is most serious with regard to issues of contractual capacity. "[T]he ability of individuals to confer upon themselves a contractual capacity which they would otherwise lack ought not to be a matter of party choice."[122]

Most international conventions under discussion avoid this problem because they exempt contractual capacity from their scope and thus from the scope of party autonomy. For example, Article 5 of the 1986 Hague Sales Convention provides that the Convention "does not determine the law applicable to…the capacity of the parties or the consequences of nullity or invalidity of the contract resulting from the incapacity of a party."[123] Similar provisions are found in the 1955 Hague Sales Convention, the Hague Agency Convention, the Hague Contracts Principles, and the Mexico City Convention.[124]

---

[119] The word "bootstrapping" is a shorthand expression for the colloquialism that "one cannot pull oneself over an obstacle by one's own bootstraps."

[120] C-P. Calliess (ed.), *Rome Regulations* 68 (2011).

[121] *Id.* at 68–69.

[122] Briggs, *Agreements on Choice of Law,* 395–396.

[123] Hague Sales Convention of 1986, art. 5.

[124] *See* Hague Sales Convention of 1955, art. 5; Hague Agency Convention, art. 2; Hague Principles, art. 1(3)(a); Mexico City Convention, art. 5.

Rome I also exempts capacity from the scope of party autonomy, albeit through a circuitous route.[125] Virtually all national codifications also exempt contractual capacity from the scope of party autonomy and subject it instead to autonomous choice-of-law rules that typically refer this issue to the person's personal law.[126]

However, at least one codification does not avoid the bootstrapping problem. The Venezuela codification provides that: (1) contracts are governed "by the law agreed to by the parties" (Art. 29), and (2) "[a] person being incapable under the [law of his domicile] acts validly if deemed capable by the law governing the [contract's] contents" (Art. 18).[127] The combination of these two articles means that a party who lacks contractual capacity under the law of her domicile can somehow vest herself with capacity by "agreeing" to the choice of the law of a state that would consider her capable. The only way to avoid this problem is by applying the public policy exception of Article 8.[128] However, this exception: (1) has a very high threshold, and (2) operates only against a *foreign* law and in favor of the law of the forum.

The Restatement (Second) also falls into the bootstrapping trap because it provides that capacity is determined by "the law chosen by the parties, if they have made an effective choice."[129] However, this trap is not irreversible because: (1) as discussed later, the Restatement's public policy exception has a lower threshold; and (2) the exception operates in favor of the otherwise applicable law (the *lex causae*), whether that law is that of the forum *or* of another state.[130]

---

[125] Rome I Article 1(2)(a) exempts capacity from the scope of Rome I, but "without prejudice to Article 13." Article 13 provides that, in contracts concluded between persons who are in the same country, a natural person who would have capacity under the law of that country may invoke his incapacity under the law of another country only if the other party knew or should have known of that incapacity. In any event, the combined result of these two provisions is that contractual capacity is *not* governed by the contractually chosen law.

[126] *See* the following codifications and the pertinent articles shown in parentheses: Afghanistan (art. 17); Albania (art. 11); Algeria (art. 10); Angola (arts. 25, 28); Argentina (draft art. 2616); Armenia (art. 1265); Austria (art. 12); Azerbaijan (art. 10); Belarus (art. 1104); Belgium (art. 34); Bulgaria (art. 50); Burundi (art. 2); Cape Verde (arts. 25, 28); Central African Repub. (art. 40); China (art. 12); Croatia (art. 14); East Timor (arts. 24, 27); Estonia (art. 12); FYROM (art. 15); Gabon (art. 32); Germany (art. 7); Guinea-Bissau (arts. 25, 28); Hungary (art. 10); Italy (art. 23); Japan (art. 4); Jordan (art. 12); Kazakhstan (art. 1095); North Korea (art. 17); South Korea (arts. 13, 15); Kyrgyzstan (art. 1178); Latvia (art. 8); Liechtenstein (art. 12); Lithuania (art. 1.16); Louisiana (art. 3539); Macau (art. 27); Madagascar (art. 28); Mauritania (art. 7); Mexico (art. 13.II); Moldova (art. 1589–1590, 1592); Mongolia (arts. 543–544); Mozambique (arts. 25, 28); Netherlands (art. 11); Oregon (§ 15.330); Peru (art. 2070); Poland (arts. 11–13); Portugal (arts. 25, 28); Puerto Rico (art. 33); Qatar (art. 11); Quebec (arts. 3083, 3085–3087); Romania (arts. 11, 17); Russia (art. 1197); Serbia (draft art. 147); Slovakia (art. 3); Slovenia (art. 13); Somalia (art. 11); Sudan (art. 11.1); Switzerland (art. 36); Taiwan (art. 10); Tajikistan (art. 1201); Tunisia (art. 40); Turkey (art. 9); Ukraine (art. 18); U.A.E. (art. 11); Uruguay (art. 20); Uzbekistan (art. 1169); Vietnam (arts. 761–763, 765); and Yemen (art. 25).

[127] Venezuelan codif. arts. 18, 29.

[128] *See id.* at art. 8 (providing that a foreign law may be excluded only when it would "produce results being clearly incompatible with the essential principles of Venezuelan public policy.").

[129] *Restatement (Second)* § 198 cmt a.

[130] *See id.* at § 187(2)(b).

2. Consent and Contract Formation

The bootstrapping phenomenon can also occur if one applies the "chosen" law for determining whether the parties have actually expressed their consent to the choice-of-law agreement (or the contract containing it), for example, whether there was a "meeting of the minds," and whether that consent was free of defects, such as duress or error. As Professor Briggs noted,

> Problems of contractual formation are notorious for throwing up puzzles which test logic to destruction: if the parties do not agree that they made a binding contract, it is hard to see how the law which governs or would have governed that both-alleged-and-denied contract can have any legitimate role in resolving the dispute about formation.[131]

The search for a proper answer to this difficult question should distinguish among three possible situations, depending on whether the parties dispute: (1) the existence of a contract only on matters other than the choice of law, (2) only the existence of the choice-of-law agreement, or (3) both the existence of the choice-of-law agreement and the contract. Table 3.1 depicts these three situations.

It is suggested that the only situation in which it is appropriate to apply the chosen law for determining the existence and validity of a choice-of-law agreement, or of the contract, is the first situation. In contrast, in the second and third situations, the application of the allegedly chosen law to determine the existence of the *choice-of-law* agreement puts the cart before the horse. To avoid the bootstrapping phenomenon, the court must first determine whether the agreement came into existence, and can only do so on the basis of a law whose application does *not* depend on the will of the parties. This law can be the substantive law of the forum,[132] or arguably, in appropriate circumstances, an objectively

TABLE 3.1. FORMATION OF CHOICE-OF-LAW AGREEMENT

	Choice-of-law agreement	Contract	Applicable law	
			Agreement	Contract
1	Not disputed	Disputed		Chosen law
2	Disputed	Not disputed	*Lex fori* or *lex causae*	—
3	Disputed	Disputed	*Lex fori*	—

---

[131] Briggs, *Agreements on Choice of Law* 94–95.

[132] *See id.* at 396 ("As to the question of how a court should approach the task of deciding for this purpose whether there was an agreement on choice of law, … it is hard to see how it can do so by reference to anything

chosen law (*lex causae*). If, and only if, the court determines that a choice-of-law agreement does exist, then and only then may the court apply the chosen law to the contract itself.

The Restatement (Second) avoids the bootstrapping problem by assigning the validity of the choice-of-law agreement to the substantive law of the forum. It provides that

> a choice-of-law provision, like any other contractual provision, will not be given effect if the consent of one of the parties to its inclusion in the contract was obtained by improper means, such as…duress, or undue influence, or by mistake. Whether such consent was in fact obtained by improper means…will be determined by the forum in accordance with its own legal principles.[133]

The Louisiana codification also avoids the problem by providing that "[t]he existence, validity, and effectiveness of a choice-of-law agreement is decided according to the law applicable to the particular issue under Articles 3537–39," that is, *not* under Article 3540, which provides for party autonomy.[134] The Oregon and Puerto Rico codifications also exempt from the scope of party autonomy the issue of consent to, and formation of, the contract (and thus of the choice-of-law clause as well), and instead refer it to the *lex causae*.[135]

Rome I follows a middle solution. It assigns this issue to the chosen law, but also allows an exception in favor of the law of a party's habitual residence. Article 3(5) provides that "[t]he existence and validity of the consent of the parties as to the choice of the applicable law shall be determined in accordance with the provisions of Articles 10, 11 and 13."[136] Paragraph 1 of Article 10 provides that the "existence and validity" of a contract, or of "any term of a contract" (such as a choice-of-law clause) is determined by "the law which would govern it" under Rome I "if the contract or term were valid."[137] Thus, if the contract contains a choice-of-law clause, its validity is governed by the chosen law, thus leading to bootstrapping.

According to the authoritative Giuliano-Lagarde Report, which accompanied the initial convention, this solution was chosen in order "to avoid the circular argument that where there is a choice of the applicable law no law can be said to be applicable until the contract is found to be valid."[138] However, as other authors have noted, this leads to another circularity: "[Q]uestions of formation cannot be governed by the applicable law,

---

other than its own conception of what amounts to an agreement.… It is usually accepted that questions which need to be answered before a court has identified the *lex causae* have to be governed by the *lex fori*, for no applicable choice of law rule yet points to the application of some other law.").

[133] *Restatement (Second)* § 187, cmt b.

[134] La. Codif. art. 3537 cmt a.

[135] *See* Or. Rev. Stat. § 15.335; Puerto Rico draft codif. art. 34.

[136] Rome I, art. 3(5).

[137] Rome I, art. 10(1).

[138] M. Giuliano & P. Lagarde, Report on the Convention on the Law Applicable to Contractual Obligations, *Official Journal C 282*, p. 1, 30 (31 Oct. 1980).

for until such questions have been decided it is not a clear that there is a contract at all."[139] Stated differently, the "chosen law" is not *chosen* until it is established that the parties have agreed to choose it.

Fortunately, an agreement under paragraph 1 of Article 10 is subject to the limitations of Article 3 and other provisions of Rome I. One of those provisions is paragraph 2 of Article 10, which provides an exception that ameliorates the bootstrapping problem with regard to the existence of consent, though not its validity.[140] It provides that a party who claims lack of consent to the contract or one of its terms (such as a choice-of-law clause) "may rely upon the law of the country in which he has his habitual residence if it appears from the circumstances that it would not be reasonable to determine the effect of his conduct in accordance with the [chosen] law."[141]

Outside the EU, the codifications of South Korea, Serbia, and Turkey follow a similar solution,[142] as do the Hague Principles. Paragraph 1 of Article 6 of the Principles provides that, "[s]ubject to paragraph 2,...whether the parties have agreed to a choice of law is determined by the law that was purportedly agreed to." Paragraph 2 provides that "the law of the State in which a party has its establishment determines whether that party has consented to the choice of law if, under the circumstances, it would not be reasonable to make that determination under the law specified in paragraph 1."[143]

The 1986 Hague Sales Convention follows the same solution with regard to the contract as a whole,[144] but also provides specifically for the validity of the choice-of-law agreement. Article 10 of the Convention provides that "[i]ssues concerning the existence and material validity of the consent of the parties as to the choice of the applicable law...are determined by the law chosen." If under the chosen law the choice is invalid, then the contract is governed by the law chosen under the objective factors of Article 8.[145]

The remaining codifications do not contain a specific provision on the issue of consent to the contract or to the choice-of-law agreement. This silence can lead to one of two possibilities. The first is that the issue will be governed by the chosen law with all the attendant bootstrapping consequences noted above. The second is that the issue will be governed either by the law of the forum qua forum, or by the *lex causae*.

---

[139] C. Clarkson & J. Hill, *The Conflict of Laws* 207 (2011).

[140] *See* Giuliano & Lagarde Report, at 28 (noting that "paragraph 2 provides a special rule which relates only to the existence and not to the validity of consent.").

[141] Rome I, art. 10(2).

[142] *See* South Korean codif. art. 29; Serbian draft codif. art. 145; Turkish codif. art. 32.

[143] *Hague Principles,* Art. 6.

[144] *See* Hague 1986 Sales Convention, arts. 10(2)–(3).

[145] *Id.* at art. 10(1). Article 12 of the Mexico City Convention provides that "[t]he existence and the validity of the contract or of any of its provisions, and the substantive validity of the consent of the parties concerning the selection of the applicable law, shall be governed by the appropriate rules in accordance with Chapter 2 of this Convention." This article does not seem to resolve the issue because chapter 2 contains the rules for both situations in which the contract contains a choice-of-law clause and situations in which there is no such clause.

3. Form

Here, a distinction is, or should be, made between (1) the form of the choice-of-law agreement, and (2) the form of the contract that the agreement subjects to the chosen law. Some codifications and conventions provide separate rules for the two issues, while other codifications provide only one rule applicable to the form of both the contract and any of its terms, including the choice-of-law agreement.

The codifications of the first group provide an autonomous *substantive* (as opposed to conflicts) rule for determining the formal sufficiency of the choice-of-law agreement: the agreement may be express or it may be inferred from either the terms of the contract or, in the words of Rome I, from "the circumstances of the case,"[146] such as the conduct of the parties. More than a dozen codifications outside the EU,[147] and several conventions,[148] have a similar rule allowing the choice-of-law agreement to be inferred from the circumstances. Obviously, an agreement inferred "from the circumstances" need not be clothed with any particular form. Reflecting this logic, the Hague Contracts Principles state that "[a] choice of law is not subject to any requirement of form."[149]

With regard to the form of the contract as a whole, at least a dozen codifications contain a choice-of-law rule exempting this issue from the scope of party autonomy and referring it to a law or laws other than the law chosen by the parties.[150] Most other codifications,[151]

---

[146] Rome I art. 3(1).

[147] *See, e.g.*, the codifications of Albania (art. 45.2); Argentina (draft art. 2651); Belarus (art. 1124.2); FYROM (art. 21.2); Kazakhstan (art. 112.2); South Korea (art. 25.1); Liechtenstein (art. 39.1); Madagascar (33); Moldova (art. 1611); Qatar (art. 27); Russia (art. 1210.2); Serbia (art. 136.2); Switzerland (art. 116.2); Taiwan (art. 20.1); Tajikistan (art. 1218.2); Turkey (art. 24.1); U.A.E (art. 19.1); Ukraine (art. 5.2); Yemen (art. 30).

[148] *See, e.g.*, Hague Sales Convention art. 7.1; Hague Agency Convention art. 5; Mexico City Convention art. 7.

[149] Hague Contracts Principles art. 5. The article allows the parties to "agree otherwise," for example, that a future choice of law or a modification of it must be in a particular form.

[150] *See* the following codifications and the pertinent articles indicated in parentheses: Afghanistan (art. 28); Albania (art. 18); Algeria (art.19); Argentina (art. 2649); Armenia (art. 1281); Azerbaijan (art. 12); Belarus (art. 1116); Burundi (art. 5(1)); Guatemala (arts. 28–29); Kazakhstan (art. 1095); Kyrgyzstan (art. 1190); Mexico (art. 13.IV); Mongolia (art. 548.2–8); Russia (art. 1209); Tajikistan (art. 1210); Uzbekistan (art. 1181); Vietnam (art. 770); and Yemen (art. 31). *See also* 1955 Hague Convention, art. 5; Hague Agency Convention, art. 2.

[151] *See* the following codifications and the pertinent articles indicated in parentheses: Angola (art. 36); Austria (art. 8); Bulgaria (art. 61); Cape Verde (art. 35); Croatia (art. 7); Czech Republic (art. 42); East Timor (art. 34); Estonia (art. 8); FYROM (art. 7); Germany (art. 11); Guinea-Bissau (art. 36); Hungary (art. 30.1, 30.3); Italy (art. 23); Japan (art. 10); Jordan (art. 21); North Korea (art. 24); South Korea (art. 17); Liechtenstein (art. 8); Lithuania (art. 1.38); Louisiana (art. 3538); Macau (art. 35); Moldova (art. 1610); Mongolia (art. 548.2–8); Mozambique (art. 36); Netherlands (art. 12); Oregon (§ 15.325); Peru (art. 2094); Poland (art. 25); Portugal (art. 36); Puerto Rico (art. 32); Qatar (art. 29); Quebec (art. 3109); Romania (art. 71); Slovakia (art. 4); Slovenia (art. 8); Somalia (art. 20); Sudan (art. 11.13c); Switzerland (art. 124); Taiwan (art. 16); Tunisia (art. 68); Turkey (art. 7); Ukraine (art. 31); Uruguay (draft art. 43); Venezuela (art. 37). For a rule referring formalities exclusively to the law governing the substance of the contract, *see* Gabon codif. art. 57.

including Rome I,[152] and recent conventions,[153] provide an alternative-validation-reference rule that includes a reference to the law that governs the *substance* of the contract.

In its simplest form, the difference between the two groups is illustrated by the otherwise similar rules of the Algerian and Jordanian codifications. The Algerian codification provides that contracts are governed by the law of the place of making or the law of the parties' common nationality.[154] The Jordanian rule is identical, except that it adds a reference to the law that governs the substance of the contract.[155] The reference to the law that governs the substance of the contract means that: (1) if the parties have chosen the applicable law, as allowed by the Jordanian codification, the chosen law can also govern the formal validity of the contract; and (2) if the chosen law would uphold the contract but the other two laws would not, the contract will be upheld as to form.

Obviously, this last scenario presents the bootstrapping phenomenon. However, this phenomenon is far less objectionable with regard to formal validity than with regard to capacity or other substantive issues. In fact, it is a small price to pay in return for the desideratum of contract validation (*favor negotii*) that permeates most codifications on the issue of formal validity. As we shall see in Chapter 6, this desideratum is reflected in the fact that most choice-of-law rules on formal validity consist of alternative references authorizing the application of whichever of the enumerated laws would uphold the contract.[156] The justification for these result-oriented rules rests on the premise that, more often than not, the various state laws on contractual formalities differ only in minor detail, rather than fundamental policy. For this reason, failure to meet the technical requirements of one state should not, without more, defeat the intent of the parties in having a binding contract, if such a contract complies with the form requirements of another state reasonably related to the parties and the transaction.

D. LIMITATION TO CONTRACTUAL ISSUES

One important question regarding the scope of party autonomy is whether contracting parties should be allowed to choose a law for their non-contractual rights and duties, such as those arising from a past or future tort between them. This question is discussed

---

[152] *See* Rome Convention art. 9; Rome I art. 11. However, the alternative-validation-rule of paragraphs 1–3 of article 9 does not apply to contracts with passive consumers. The form of those contracts is governed by the law of the consumer's habitual residence. The Japanese also allows bootstrapping with regard to contracts in general (*see* art. 10, which provides an alternative-validation-rule) but avoids it in consumer contracts by requiring, under certain conditions, the application of the mandatory rules of the passive consumer's habitual residence to issues of formal validity, even if the contract is otherwise governed by another law. *See* Japanese codif. arts. 11(3)–(5).

[153] *See* Hague Sales Convention of 1955, art. 11, Mexico City Convention, art. 5.

[154] Algerian codif. art. 19.

[155] *See* Jordanian codif. art. 21 (providing that inter vivos juridical acts are governed by the law of the place of making or the law of the parties' common nationality, *or* the law that governs the substance of the act).

[156] *See infra*, Chapter 6, at V.A.2.

in detail in Chapter 2.[157] As that chapter documents, most codifications are silent on this issue. With the exception of Rome II, the codifications that do address this question allow *post-dispute* choice-of-law agreements and, *a contrario,* prohibit *pre-dispute* agreements. Rome II allows pre-dispute agreements if both parties are "pursuing a commercial activity."[158]

E. SUBSTANTIVE VERSUS PROCEDURAL LAW

All choice-of-law codifications and conventions under discussion here limit the scope of party autonomy to the chosen state's substantive law and exclude its procedural law. This is consistent with the principle that the law of the forum governs matters of procedure, a principle that prevails over the principle of party autonomy. Indeed, it would not be sensible or practical to allow the parties to impose on a court the burden of complying with the rules of conducting a trial or other purely procedural rules of another state. Consistent with these principles, Rome I exempts from its scope—and thus from the scope of choice-of-law clauses—the rules of evidence and procedure.[159]

However, the line between substance and procedure is not drawn in the same way in all systems, nor is the line always clear in each system. For example, in the civil law world, statutes of limitation (liberative prescription) are generally considered substantive.[160] Consistent with this characterization, Rome I includes within the scope of the applicable law, which may be chosen contractually or judicially, "the various ways of extinguishing obligations, and prescription and limitation of actions."[161] The Hague Sales Convention, the Mexico City Convention, and the Hague Contracts Principles, as well as several codifications, contain similar provisions.[162]

In contrast, many states of the United States continue to characterize statutes of limitation as procedural, even after having abandoned the traditional theory in other

---

[157] *See supra* Chapter 2, at IX.

[158] Rome II, Art. 14(1)(b). For identical provisions, *see* Albanian codif. art. 57; Serbian draft codif. art. 158.

[159] *See* Rome I, Art. 1(3). This provision contains an exception (through a cross reference to Article 18) regarding the burden of proof.

[160] *See, e.g.,* Swiss codif. art. 148 ("The law applicable to a claim governs its prescription and extinction."); Peruvian codif. art. 2099 ("The limitation of personal actions as a result of inaction for a period of time (prescripcion extintiva) is governed by the law of the underlying obligation."); Croatian codif. art. 8; Czech codif. art. 46; Lithuanian codif. art. 1.59; Moldovan codif. art. 1625; Polish codif. art. 26; Quebec codif. art. 3131; Romanian codif. art. 147; Taiwan codif. art. 36; Uruguay codif. art. 55. Since 1984, England follows the same position. *See* Collins et al., *supra* note 58, at 229–233, 1861.

[161] Rome I, art. 12(1)(d). For identical provisions, *see* Albanian codif. art. 47.1(d); Serbian draft codif. art. 143.1.(d).

[162] *See* Hague Sales Convention art. 12 ("The law applicable to a contract of sale...governs in particular...the various ways of extinguishing obligations, as well as prescription and limitation of actions."); Mexico City Convention art. 14 ("The law applicable to the contract...shall govern principally...prescription and lapsing of actions."); Hague Contract Principles, art. 9.1; Bulgarian codif. art. 102; German codif. art. 32; Romanian codif. art. 91; Tunisian codif. art. 64.

respects.[163] Perhaps for this reason, most American cases that have considered this issue have concluded that the choice-of-law clause did not include the chosen state's statute of limitation.[164] Recently, however, a handful of cases decided in the few states that have abandoned the traditional procedural characterization of statutes of limitation (such as California) have held that a choice-of-law clause included the chosen state's statute of limitations.[165] The particular facts of some of these cases, coupled with the questionable quality of their reasoning, suggest that they are of limited persuasive value, at least compared to the more numerous cases that have reached the opposite result.

Nevertheless, these cases illustrate, or at least suggest, that prescription or statute-of-limitations conflicts are sui generis conflicts that do not easily fit within the existing formulas for conflicts resolution. For reasons explained in detail elsewhere,[166] a prescription rule may be motivated by both procedural and substantive policies, or primarily by the one rather than the other. Thus, the uncritical assumption that, for choice-of-law purposes, prescription is always substantive or always procedural can be problematic. The traditional American characterization of statutes of limitation as procedural necessarily excludes them from the scope of a choice-of-law clause. Although this exclusion may unduly restrict party autonomy, the opposite solution of characterizing these statutes as substantive presents its own problems as well.

A substantive characterization automatically subjects prescription to the chosen law, even if the choice-of-law clause is silent on the particular issue. If the chosen law has a much shorter prescriptive period than the *lex fori*, the creditor's only hope will hinge on the mandatory rules or public policy of the *lex fori*. If the chosen law has an exceedingly long prescriptive period, the forum state will be deprived of the ability to protect its courts from the burdens and dangers of adjudicating claims that have long prescribed under its own law.

On balance, it would be preferable to adopt a middle solution that recognizes the sui generis character of prescription. Under such a solution, prescription would not be automatically governed by the chosen law unless the choice-of-law clause expressly so provides. This would give contracting parties the opportunity to consider the pros and cons of including prescription in the chosen law and to reach an informed decision on the matter. However, no codification has adopted such a solution.

F. SUBSTANTIVE VERSUS CONFLICTS LAW

When the parties choose the "law" of a certain state to govern their contract, there is a question, at least in theory, as to whether their choice is limited to the internal or substantive law of the chosen state or whether it encompasses its conflicts law, with the attendant

---

[163] *See* Symeonides, *American PIL,* 272–294.

[164] For citations, *see* Hay, Borchers & Symeonides, *Conflict of Laws,* 1137–1138.

[165.] For citations and discussion, *see id.* 1138–1141.

[166] *See* Symeonides, *Two Surprises,* 537–539.

possibility of renvoi. The further question is whether this should be a question of contractual *power* or rather contractual *intent*. These questions are explored below.

Few codifications explicitly address the renvoi question in provisions specifically applicable to *contract conflicts*. The majority of codifications contain, among their general provisions, articles that either preclude renvoi altogether or allow it in narrowly defined cases other than contracts.[167] The codifications of Albania, Argentina, Bulgaria, Estonia, FYROM, Germany, Italy, South Korea, Lithuania, Romania, Slovakia, and Uruguay are among those that specifically preclude renvoi in contract conflicts.[168] Multilateral instruments applicable to contracts, such as the Hague Sales Convention, the Hague Securities Convention, the Mexico City Convention, and the Hague Contracts Principles, also contain anti-renvoi provisions,[169] as does Rome I. Article 20 of Rome I provides that the application of the "law of any country specified by this Regulation" excludes the conflict rules of that country "unless provided otherwise in this Regulation."[170] Article 20 applies not only to a judicial choice of law, but also to a contractual choice of law because the latter law, no less than the former law, is a law whose application is authorized or "specified in this Regulation."

Under the above provisions, there is no question that a generic choice-of-law clause choosing the "law" of state X will be *interpreted* as a choice of only the internal or substantive law of state X, and not its conflicts law. This is a perfectly logical position because it conforms to the most likely intent of the parties. Indeed, the most logical assumption is that parties who had the foresight to address the choice-of-law issue in advance in hopes of thereby preventing litigation also intended to avoid the complexities of renvoi.

The remaining question is whether a codification's general anti-renvoi provision, or a provision precluding renvoi in contract conflicts, should be read as an absolute prohibition or instead as a presumption for interpreting the parties' intent. In other words, do the parties have the *power* to include in their choice the conflicts rules of the chosen state if they do so *expressly*? The answer to this question varies from system to system. Some codifications answer affirmatively by phrasing their provisions as presumptions. For example, the Slovakian codification provides that "[u]*nless the manifested will of the contracting parties indicates otherwise*, the provisions of the chosen law relating to conflict of laws shall be ignored."[171] The 2012 Czech codification reproduces the substance of this sensible

---

[167] *See, e.g.*, Belgian codif. art. 16; Dutch codif. art. 5; Kyrgyzstan codif. 1170(1); Peruvian codif. art. 2048; Quebec codif. art. 3080; Russian codif. art. 1190; Ukrainian codif. art. 9; Uzbekistan codif. art. 1161.

[168] *See* Albanian codif. art. 3.2(e); Argentinean draft codif. art. 2651(b); Bulgarian codif. art. 40(2)3; Estonian codif. art. 6(3); FYROM codif. art. 6(3); German codif. arts. 4(2), 35(1); Italian codif. art. 13(2); South Korean codif. art. 9(2); Lithuanian codif. art. 1.14(4); Romanian codif. art. 85; Slovakian codif. art. 9.2; Uruguayan draft codif. art. 48(2).

[169] *See* Hague Sales Convention, art. 15 (defining "law" as meaning "the law in force in a State other than its choice of law rules."); Hague Securities Convention art. 10; Mexico City Convention art. 17; Hague Contracts Principles art. 8.

[170] Rome I, Art. 20. For example, Rome I "provides otherwise" in Article 7(3)(e), second paragraph, regarding small-risk insurance contracts.

[171] Slovak codif. art. 9(2) (emphasis added).

provision.[172] The Argentinean draft provides that a contractual choice of law "shall be inter-preted" as not including the conflicts law of the chosen state "unless otherwise agreed."[173] Likewise, the Uruguayan draft provides that the parties' choice of law "should be under-stood" as a choice of the chosen state's rules "other than its rules on conflict of laws."[174] In the United States, the Restatement (Second) and the Louisiana and Oregon codifications take the same position, namely that a contractual choice of law is confined to the substan-tive law of the chosen state, but the parties are allowed to agree to the contrary.[175]

Allowing the parties to choose the conflicts law of the chosen country, if they so wish, is entirely consistent with, and may in fact be dictated by, the very principle of party autonomy. Nevertheless, a contrary opinion seems to prevail in many countries and is the prevailing opinion under Rome I.[176] In fact, the Giuliano-Lagarde Report is unequivocal:

> It is clear that there is no place for renvoi in the law of contract if the parties have cho-sen the law to be applied to their contract. If they have made such a choice, it is clearly *with the intention* that the provisions of substance in the chosen law shall be appli-cable; their choice accordingly excludes any possibility of renvoi to another law.[177]

Interestingly, the Report cites nothing other than the parties' *assumed* intention for this conclusion. To be sure, a legislator has all the power, and plenty of practical and other reasons, to limit the parties' choice to the substantive law of the chosen state. However, when the only justification provided is the parties' assumed intention, one is left to won-der about those cases where the assumption proves inaccurate because the parties have actually *expressed* a contrary intention.

G. STATE LAW VERSUS NONSTATE NORMS

The final question regarding the scope of party autonomy is whether, *outside the realm of arbitration,*[178] contracting parties are limited to choosing the law of a state or whether

---

[172] Czech codif. art. 21.2.

[173] Argentinean draft codif. art. 2651(b).

[174] Uruguayan draft codif. art. 48(2). *See also* Liechtenstein codif. art. 11 (providing that "in case of doubt," the chosen law does not include the conflicts rules of the chosen state.).

[175] *Restatement (Second)*, § 187, cmt h; La. codif. art. 3540 cmt e; Or. Rev. Stat. § 15.300(1). Although most choice-of-law clauses are phrased in generic terms, some clauses contain express anti-renvoi clauses. *See, e.g.,* Glyka v. New England Cord Blood Bank, Inc., No. 07-10950-DPW, 2009 WL 1816955, at *3 (D. Mass. June 25, 2009) ("[a]ll agreements…are governed by Massachusetts law (excluding conflicts of laws)"); Citgo Petroleum Corp. v. Krystal Gas Marketing Co., Inc., No. 05-CV-0716-CVE-SAJ, 2006 WL 2645133, at *1 (N.D. Okla. Sept. 12, 2006) ("This Agreement…is governed by and construed in all respects in accordance with the substantive laws of the State of Oklahoma, excluding conflict of laws provisions."); Digital Envoy, Inc. v. Google, Inc., 370 F. Supp. 2d 1025, 1029 (N.D. Cal. 2005) (the agreement is to be governed by "the laws of the State of California as it applies to a contract made and performed in such state, excluding conflicts of laws principles.").

[176] *See* Calliess, *Rome Regulations,* 315–317 and authorities cited therein; Bělohlávek, *Rome I,* 1895–1933; Dicey, *Morris & Collins,* 1792–1793.

[177] *Giuliano & Lagarde Report,* at 37 (emphasis added).

[178] In the last three decades, the use of nonstate norms in arbitration has become routine. This chapter does not discuss arbitration.

they are also allowed to choose nonstate norms.[179] The Hague Contracts Principles refer to these norms as "rules of law,"[180] a term that is neither accurate nor neutral.[181] It cannot be accurate because if these norms were really "rules of law," then they should possess the

---

[179] From the vast literature on nonstate norms, *see,* e.g., B. Benson, *The Enterprise of Law: Justice without the State* (1990); K.P. Berger, *The Creeping Codification of the New* Lex Mercatoria (2d ed. 2010); A.C. Cutler, *Private Power and Global Authority: Transnational Merchant Law in the Global Political Economy* (2003); A. López Rodríguez, Lex Mercatoria *and Harmonization of Contract Law in the EU* (2003); D. Oser, T*he UNIDROIT Principles of International Commercial Contracts: A Governing Law?* (2008); J-P. Beraudo, Faut-il avoir peur du contrat sans loi? in B. Ancel et al. (eds.), *Le droit international privé: Esprit et méthodes: Mélanges en l'honneur de Paul Lagarde* 93 (2005); P. Berman, Towards a Cosmopolitan Vision of Conflict of Laws: Redefining Governmental Interests in a Global Era, 153 *U. Pa. L. Rev.* 1819 (2005); P. Berman, Towards a Jurisprudence of Hybridity, 1 *Utah L. Rev.* 11 (2010); M. Bonell, Soft Law and Party Autonomy: The Case of the UNIDROIT Principles, 51 *Loy. L. Rev.* 229 (2005); M. Bonell, Towards a Legislative Codification of the UNIDROIT Principles? 12 *Unif. L. Rev.* 233 (2007); H. Collins, Cosmopolitanism and Transnational Private Law, 8 *Eur. Rev. Contr. L.* 311 (2012); R. Cooter, Decentralized Law for a Complex Economy, 23 *S.W.U. L. Rev.* 443 (1994); R. Cooter, Structural Adjudication and the New Law Merchant: A Model of Decentralized Law, 14 *Int'l Rev. L. & Econ.* 215 (1994); G. Cuniberti, Three Theories of *Lex Mercatoria,* 52 *Col. J. Transn'l L.* (forthcoming 2013); C. Drahozal, Contracting Out of National Law: An Empirical Look at the New Law Merchant, 80 *Notre Dame L. Rev.* 523 (2005); L. Gannagé, Le contrat sans loi en droit international privé, in K. Boele-Woelki & S. van Erp (eds.), *Rapports généraux du XVIIe congrès de L'Academie internationale de droit comparé* 275 (2007), also posted in 11.3 *Electron. J. Comp. L.* (2007), *available at* http://www.ejcl.org/113/abs113-10. html; N. Hatzimihail, The Many Lives, and Faces, of *Lex Mercatoria*: History as Genealogy in International Business Law, *Law & Contemp. Probs.* 169 (2008); N. Jansen & R. Michaels, Private Law beyond the State? Europeanization, Globalization, Privatization, 54 *Am. J. Comp. L.* 843 (2006); F. Juenger, American Conflicts Scholarship and the New Law Merchant, 28 *Vand. J. Transn'l L.* 487, (1995); D. Lawrence, Private Exercise of Governmental Power, 61 *Ind. L.J.* 647 (1986); M. Lehmann, Liberating the Individual from Battles between States—Justifying Party Autonomy in Conflict of Laws, 41 *Vanderbilt J. Transn'l L.* 381 (2008); J. Macey, Public and Private Ordering and the Production of Legitimate and Illegitimate Legal Rules, 82 *Cornell L. Rev.* 1123 (1997); F. Marrella, Choice of Law in the Third-Millennium Arbitrations: The Relevance of the UNIDROIT Principles of International Commercial Contracts, 36 *Vand. J. Transn'l L.* 1137 (2003); R. Michaels, The Re-state-ment of Non-state Law: The State, Choice of Law, and the Challenge from Global Legal Pluralism, 51 *Wayne L. Rev.* 1209 (2005); R. Michaels, The True *Lex Mercatoria*: Law beyond the State, 14 *Ind. J. Global Legal Stud.* 447 (2007); R. Michaels, Rethinking the UNIDROIT Principles: From a Law to Be Chosen by the Parties towards a General Part of Transnational Contract Law, 73 *RabelsZ* 866 (2009); R. Michaels, The Mirage of Non-State Governance, 1 *Utah L. Rev.* 31 (2010); J.A. Moreno Rodríguez, Contracts and Non-State Law in Latin America, 16 *Rev. dr. unif.* 877, 880 (2011); H. Muir Watt, "Party Autonomy" in International Contracts: From the Makings of a Myth to the Requirements of Global Governance, 6 *Eur. Rev. Contr. L.* 250 (2010); N. Oman, Corporations and Autonomy Theories of Contract: A Critique of the New *Lex Mercatoria,* 83 *Denv. U. L. Rev.* 101 (2005); F. Rodi, Private Law beyond the Democratic Order? On the Legitimatory Problem of "Private Law beyond the State," 56 *Am. J. Comp. L.* 743 (2008); F. Sabourin, Le Contrat sans Loi en Droit International Privé, 19 *Rev. quebecoise de droit int'l* 35 (2006); G. Saumier, Designating the Unidroit Principles in International Dispute Resolution, 17 *Unif. L. Rev.* 533 (2012); S. Schwarcz, Private Ordering, 97 *NW. U. L. Rev.* 319 (2002); A. Schwartz & R. Scott, The Political Economy of Private Legislatures, 143 *U. Pa. L. Rev.* 595 (1995); D. Snyder, Private Lawmaking, 64 *Ohio St. L. J.* 371, 385–388 (2003); P. Stephan, The Futility of Unification and Harmonization in International Commercial Law, 39 *Va. J. Int'l L.* 743, 788 (1999); P. Stephan, Accountability and International Lawmaking: Rules, Rents and Legitimacy, 17 *NW. J. Int'l L. & Bus.* 681 (1996); S. Symeonides, Party Autonomy and Private Law-Making in Private International Law: The *Lex Mercatoria* that Isn't, in *Festschrift für Konstantinos D. Kerameus* 1397 (2009).

[180] Hague Contracts Principles, art. 3.

[181] *Cf.* L. Blutman, In the Trap of a Legal Metaphor: International Soft Law, *Int. & Comp. L.Q.* 605 (2010).

same attributes as *real* rules of law, such as the rules of a statute. They do not. They lack the attributes of statutory, judge-made, or customary rules. They do not emanate from the collective will of the people formally expressed through the ordinary, and nowadays democratic, legislative process; they do not result from the pronouncements of the judiciary; and they do not qualify as custom, that is, a usually spontaneous practice repeated for a long time (*longa consuetudo*) and generally accepted as having acquired the force of common and tacit consent (*opinio juris*).[182]

Although some of these norms are drafted by intergovernmental bodies such as UNIDROIT[183] and UNCITRAL,[184] others are drafted by private nongovernmental bodies without any popular participation or approbation, and express the views and predilections of those who draft them. Some of those bodies, such as the Lando Commission,[185] consist of impartial academics with the purest of intentions, but others are far from disinterested. For example, in the United States, nonstate norms are drafted, inter alia, by the American Arbitration Association (AAA), the New York Stock Exchange (NYSE), the American Stock Exchange (AmEx), the National Association of Securities Dealers (NASD), banking clearing-houses, credit card associations, commodities merchants such as diamond dealers, grain merchants, and cotton merchants, and, more recently, Internet service and domain providers.[186]

If these norms were applicable only to disputes between their drafters, for example, grain merchants or diamond dealers, there would be little reason to be concerned. However, many of these norms, such as those drafted by credit card associations, are applicable to credit cardholders who had no participation or input in the drafting of those norms. It is not unreasonable to assume that, in drafting these norms, the "association" was not overly solicitous of the interests of the credit cardholders. These preliminary observations should serve as a check on the unbounded euphoria that seems to pervade much of the recent literature on nonstate norms.

With the possible exceptions of the Venezuelan codification and the Mexico City Convention, which are discussed below, no choice-of-law codification expressly allows the choice of nonstate norms.[187] For example, in the United States, the Restatement

---

[182] *See* E. Kadens, The Myth of the Customary Law Merchant, 90 *Texas L. Rev.* 1153 (2012).

[183] *See UNIDROIT Principles of International Commercial Contracts* (2004), *available at* http://www.unidroit. org/english/principles/contracts/main.htm. For authoritative commentary, *see* M. Bonell, *An International Restatement of Contract Law: The UNIDROIT Principles of International Commercial Contracts* (2d ed. 1997).

[184] *See* http://www.uncitral.org/uncitral/en/uncitral_texts.html.

[185] *See Principles of European Contract Law* (1999), *available at* http://frontpage.cbs.dk/law/commission_on_ european_contract_law. For authoritative commentary by the principal drafters, *see* O. Lando & H. Beale (eds.), *The Principles of European Contract Law, Parts I and II* (1999); O. Lando, E. Clive, A. Prüm & R. Zimmermann (eds.), *Principles of European Contract Law, Part III* (2003).

[186] For citations, *see* Symeonides, *Private Law-Making*, II.A.

[187] Article 2651(d) of the Argentinean draft codification allows the application of the generally accepted commercial usages and practices, customs, and general principles of international commercial law when the parties have "incorporated" them into their contract. As explained *infra*, "incorporation" differs from a choice of law.

(Second), throughout its many provisions, including Section 187, uses the terms "local law" and "law" in a way that ties both terms to a "state," which the Restatement defines as "a territorial unit with a distinct general body of law."[188] This definition, combined with the repeated use of the phrase "law of *the state*" in Section 187, makes it clear that the Restatement's drafters did not contemplate the contractual choice of nonstate norms. This is understandable considering that the Restatement was drafted during the 1950s and early 1960s, a period in which nonstate norms did not have the clarity, maturity, and status they have today.

Nevertheless, the Restatement is not altogether hostile to nonstate norms. To the extent that it recognizes the doctrine of *incorporation* by reference for issues that fall within the parties' contractual power,[189] the Restatement allows the parties to incorporate by reference into their contract the nonstate norms of their choice.[190] The UCC, which employs a similar dichotomy between variable and non-variable rules of the UCC, allows the contractual "incorporation" of nonstate norms with regard to matters governed by variable rules.[191]

Rome I takes the same position. An earlier proposal to allow parties to choose certain well-recognized collections of nonstate norms, such as the UNIDROIT Principles, encountered resistance from several Member States.[192] According to one frustrated commentator, the proposal met "the 'parochial' resentments of a coalition of yesterday-men."[193] The compromise was the insertion of a statement in the Preamble of Rome I allowing for these norms the much lesser status of incorporation by reference. Recital 13 states that Rome I "does not preclude parties from incorporating by reference into their contract a non-State body of law or an international convention."[194] Thus, nonstate norms, which play such a prominent role in the arena of international commercial arbitration, continue to encounter resistance outside that arena.

Professor E. Hernández-Bretón makes a strong argument that the Mexico City Convention and the Venezuelan codification allow the contractual choice of nonstate norms. He bases his argument on certain phrases, quoted below, in Articles 9 and 10 of the Convention, and Articles 30 and 31 of the Venezuelan codification.

---

[188] *Restatement (Second)* § 3.

[189] *See supra* II.B.1 note 47.

[190] *Restatement (Second)* §§ 187 cmt c states that parties may "incorporate into the contract by reference extrinsic material which may, among other things, be the provisions of some foreign law." The "extrinsic material" may be the law of another state, but it can also be a treatise on contract law, or a collection of nonstate norms. Indeed, the Reporter's Note expressly states that the parties "may also stipulate for the application of trade association rules or well known commercial customs." *Id.* at § 187, Reporter's Note to Subsection (1).

[191] *See* Symeonides, *Private Law-Making*, at III.B.1.

[192] For discussion of this issue, *see* O. Lando & P. Nielsen, The Rome I Regulation, 45 *Common Mkt. L. Rev.* 1687, 1694–1698 (2008).

[193] Calliess, *Rome Regulations,* 66.

[194] Rome I, Recital (13). The Argentinean draft codification (art. 2651(d)) has taken the same position. In contrast, the Uruguayan draft codification (art. 51) allows the application of these norms "where appropriate."

Article 9 of the Convention provides that, in the absence of an effective choice of law by the parties, the contract shall be governed by the law of the state that has the closest ties to the contact. The article further provides that, in identifying that state, the court shall take into account all objective and subjective elements of the contract, as well as "the general principles of international commercial law recognized by international organizations."[195]

Article 10 provides that "the guidelines, customs, and principles of international commercial law, as well as commercial usage and practices generally accepted"[196] shall also apply in order to discharge the requirements of justice and equity in the particular case.

Hernández-Bretón concludes that the two phrases quoted above lead to the conclusion that the Convention "allows the contracting parties to submit their contract to the provisions of the new *lex mercatoria*."[197] He reasons that "[i]t would be inconsistent, contradictory and inexplicable that in the absence of a choice a law by the contracting parties, non-state norms would apply as legal rules, while said possibility would be denied if the parties should expressly wish to apply those norms."[198] Because the Mexico City Convention has never entered into force, the correctness of this interpretation has not been tested.[199]

Be that as it may, the first international instrument to take an explicit, favorable position vis-à-vis non-state norms is the Hague Contracts Principles adopted in 2012. The initial draft provided that "[i]n these Principles a reference to law includes rules of law."[200] The accompanying Commentary took the position that (1) the term "rules of law" should not be defined, so as to provide "the maximum support for party autonomy,"[201] and (2) there should *not* be "any restrictive criteria which, for instance, may require the rules of law selected to meet a threshold test of international or regional recognition."[202]

The European Union objected strenuously to this provision on several grounds, including those for which the Union had earlier rejected a similar proposal during the drafting

---

[195] Mexico City Convention art. 9. Article 30 of the Venezuelan codification provides to the same effect.

[196] Mexico City Convention art. 10. Article 31 of the Venezuelan codification provides to the same effect.

[197] E. Hernández-Bretón, *Venezuelan Report*, at XIII.

[198] *Id.*

[199] For support for this interpretation, *see* F. Juenger, Contract Choice of Law in the Americas, 45 *Am. J. Comp. L.* 204, 204–205 (1997); J.A. Moreno Rodríguez, Contracts and Non-State Law in Latin America, 16 *Rev. dr. unif.* 877, 880 (2011); L. Pereznieto Castro, Introducción a la Convención Interamericana sobre derecho aplicable a los contratos internacionales, 30 *Riv. dir. Int'le priv. & proc.* 765, 774–775 (1994). For different interpretations, *see* M.M. Albornoz, Choice of Law in International Contracts in Latin American Legal Systems, 6 *J. Priv. Int'l L.* 23, 27 (2010); D. Fernández Arroyo, La Convention Interaméricaine sur la loi applicable aux contrats internationaux: Certains chemins conduisent au-delà de Rome, 84 *Revue critique* DIP 178, 182–183 (1995). For a full discussion of the issue, *see* J. Samtleben, Los principios generales del derecho comercial internacional y la lex mercatoria en la Convención Interamericana sobre Derecho Aplicable a los Contratos Internacionales, in D. Fernández Arroyo & N. González Martín (eds.), *Tendencias y Relaciones Derecho Internacional Privado Americano Actual* 15 (2010).

[200] Hague Principles, Preliminary Draft, Art. 2.

[201] Hague Principles, Commentary, § 39.

[202] *Id.* § 42.

of Rome I.[203] After intense negotiations that took the better part of a week, a compromise was reached. It is reflected in the new Article 3, which provides as follows: "In these Principles, a reference to law includes rules of law that are generally accepted on an international, supranational or regional level as a neutral and balanced set of rules, unless the law of the forum provides otherwise."[204]

As is often the case, the phrasing of a compromise text leaves much to be desired. It is not accurate to say that, in these Principles, a reference to law *always* "includes rules of law." For example, in Article 3 itself, the reference to the "law of the forum" does *not* include nonstate norms. What the drafters intended to say is that *in Article 2* (which establishes the parties' freedom to choose the applicable law), *the* reference to "law" includes "rules of law."[205]

In other respects, the new text is an improvement because it introduces two important qualifiers for nonstate norms. The first focuses on their attributes: (1) they must be a "set of rules," that is, fairly complete and comprehensive; (2) they must be "neutral and balanced"; and (3) they must be "generally accepted" as such "on an international, supranational, or regional level."

The second qualifier restates the obvious, namely that these norms will not be treated on equal footing with real rules of law if the law of the forum "provides otherwise," for example, by *not* treating these norms as law. This qualifier is obvious because the Principles themselves are "soft law" and thus they apply only to the extent that the law of the forum allows. Even so, this qualifier is necessary in order to avoid uncertainty about preserving the status quo in states that do not recognize these norms. After all, the Principles aspire to be used by courts to "interpret … rules of private international law."[206] Without the phrase "unless the law of the forum provides otherwise," the courts of a Member State of the Hague Conference that acquiesces to this compromise may infer a change in that state's position and begin to interpret their choice-of-law rules accordingly.

Obviously, the "unless" clause does not apply to arbitration. Indeed the divide between arbitration and litigation was omnipresent throughout the week-long session of the Special Commission. While some delegates were thinking primarily in terms of arbitration, others were thinking primarily in terms of litigation. Yet, the two processes are different. For example, nonstate norms have long been applied in arbitration,[207] but in most countries, including the United States and the EU, they have not been applied in litigation.[208] For this reason, a Member State of the Conference that belongs in this category has good reason to object to the elevation of nonstate norms to the status of law *in litigation*, while acquiescing to the status quo in arbitration. After all, when the parties

---

[203] *See supra* text at notes 192–194. This author participated in this meeting as a representative of the then Presidency of the EU Council.

[204] Hague Principles, Art. 3. The Commentary will be changed accordingly and will explain the new text.

[205] This author has suggested to the drafters a redrafting of the article in the next round.

[206] *Principles,* Preamble (3).

[207] *See* Symeonides, *Private Law-Making*, IV.

[208] *See id.*; Hay, Borchers & Symeonides, *Conflict of Laws*, 1135–1136.

opt for arbitration, they know that they opt for private adjudication. It is not far-fetched to assume that they have also opted for, or at least would not object to, private lawmaking. In contrast, parties who have not opted for arbitration have chosen to remain in the arena of public adjudication, and there is no reason to subject them to private lawmaking. Thus, it is appropriate to differentiate between arbitration and litigation and, unlike the Working Group's earlier draft, the final text does just that.

H. SUMMARY

As the above discussion documents, and Figure 3.1 attempts to illustrate, the scope of party autonomy is by no means unlimited in the various choice-of-law codifications; nor are its limitations identical from one system to another. For example, some codifications exempt from the scope of party autonomy certain contracts, such as contracts involving immovables, or consumer and employment contracts. Other codifications allow a choice of law for the latter two contracts, but protect the consumer or employee from the consequences of an adverse choice. Other codifications exempt certain contractual issues, such as capacity or consent, from the scope of a choice-of-law clause, or impose certain limitations on the choice. Most codifications prohibit a pre-dispute choice for non-contractual issues or the choice of another state's procedural law, despite disagreements in drawing the line between substance and procedure; and all codifications agree that ordinarily a

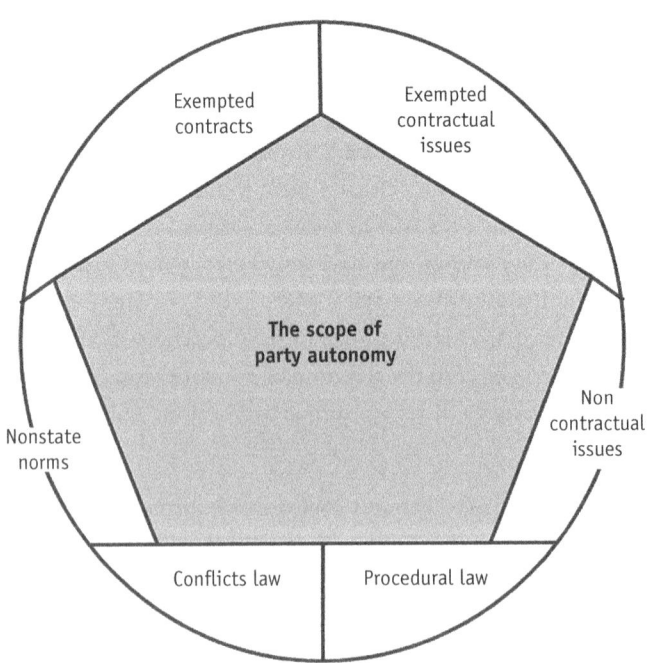

FIGURE 3.1. The Scope of Party Autonomy

choice-of-law clause does not encompass the chosen state's conflicts law. Finally, most codifications limit the parties to choosing state law, as opposed to nonstate norms.

These variations in the scope of party autonomy should be kept in mind in examining the limitations that various codifications impose on party autonomy *within* its defined scope. Generally speaking, the narrower the scope of party autonomy in a particular codification, the fewer its limitations need be, and usually are.

V. The Limitations to Party Autonomy within Its Defined Scope

As already noted, besides their differences in defining the scope of party autonomy, the various codifications also differ on the limitations to which party autonomy is subject, *within* its defined scope. This section discusses those limitations.

The discussion is divided into two questions: (1) which *state's* standards should be used as the measuring stick for determining the limits of party autonomy, namely, which state's law will perform the role of the *lex limitatis*?, and (2) which *threshold* will be used for those limits?

A. DETERMINING THE *LEX LIMITATIS*

Regarding the first question, the standards of three states are candidates for the role of *lex limitatis*: (1) the state whose law is chosen, (2) the state whose law would be applicable in the absence of the clause (*lex causae*), and (3) the state whose courts are called upon to decide the case (i.e., the forum).

In rare cases, these three states, or any two of them, will coincide, or will impose the same limits on party autonomy. The following discussion focuses on cases where they do not. Table 3.2 below illustrates the various possibilities by using lowercase letters to denote a state whose law restricts party autonomy and would not uphold the choice-of-law clause, and uppercase letters to denote a state whose law does not restrict party autonomy and would uphold the choice-of-law clause.

TABLE 3.2. THE POSSIBILITIES

#	*Lex Fori*	*Lex Causae*	Chosen Law
1	state "a"	state "a"	STATE "B"
2	state "a"	state "b"	STATE "C"
3	state "a"	STATE "B"	STATE "B"
4	state "a"	STATE "B"	STATE "C"
5	STATE "A"	state "b"	STATE "A"
6	STATE "A"	state "b"	STATE "C"

In all six patterns portrayed in Table 3.2, the parties have chosen the law that does not restrict party autonomy, but in the first four patterns, the *lex fori* would restrict party autonomy more than the chosen law and thus would not uphold the parties' choice of another state's law. Should this fact alone defeat the parties' choice in all four patterns? In pattern 1, the *lex fori* would have been applicable *but for* the parties' choice of state B law. If this is a strong case for invalidating the parties' choice, is pattern 2 qualitatively different? In pattern 3, the parties have chosen a law that would have been applicable in the absence of choice and that law would uphold their choice. Is it appropriate for the forum qua forum to interfere with such a choice? If not, is pattern 4 qualitatively different? Finally, in patterns 5 and 6, the forum court might be tempted to uphold the parties' choice without even pausing, but would this be appropriate?

The answer to these questions depends on which state's law is assigned the role of the *lex limitatis*. Of the three candidates for this role, namely, the chosen state, the forum state, and the state of the *lex causae*, the chosen state should be eliminated because it would lead to circular, or bootstrapping results. This leaves the states of the *lex fori* and the *lex causae*. The *lex fori* is relevant because party autonomy operates only to the extent that the *lex fori* is willing to permit. The *lex causae* is relevant because, when party autonomy operates, it displaces the *lex causae*.

If the application of the chosen law would exceed the public policy limitations of *both* the *lex fori* and the *lex causae* (as in patterns 1 and 2 of Table 3.2), the chosen law will not be applied.[209] This difficulty arises when the chosen law: (1) exceeds the limits of the *lex fori* but not the *lex causae*, as in patterns 3 and 4; or (2) exceeds limits of the *lex causae* but not the *lex fori*, as in patterns 5 and 6.

The positions of the various codifications and conventions on this issue can be clustered into three groups:

(a) Those that assign the role of *lex limitatis* to the *lex fori* (and thus would uphold the choice of law in patterns 5 and 6, but not in patterns 3 and 4);

(b) Those that assign the role of *lex limitatis* to the *lex causae* (and thus would uphold the choice of law in patterns 3 and 4, but not in patterns 5 and 6); and

(c) Those that follow a combination of the above two positions.

Table 3.3 below portrays the positions of the various codifications and conventions, with the pertinent provisions indicated in parentheses.[210]

---

[209] Conversely, when the application of the chosen law would not exceed the limitations of the *lex fori* or the *lex causae* (a case not depicted in Table 3.2), the chosen law will be applied without problems.

[210] Table 3.3 includes codifications enacted in EU Member States (marked by asterisks), although those codifications are superseded by Rome I for contracts falling within its scope. Conversely, the Table does not include EU Member States that have not enacted a choice-of-law codification within the last 50 years, even though these states are subject to Rome I for contracts falling within its scope.

TABLE 3.3. THE LIMITATIONS OF PARTY AUTONOMY

Codification	*Lex fori* Limits		*Lex causae* Limits	
	Ordre public	Mandatory rules	Public Policy	Mandatory rules
Afghanistan	Yes, 35			
Albania	Yes, 7	Yes, 45.4, 52.2		Yes, 45.4, 52.2
Angola	Yes, 22			
Argentina	Yes, 2600	Yes, 2599.1		Yes, 2599.2
Algeria	Yes, 24			
Armenia	Yes, 1258	Yes, 1259		
Azerbaijan	Yes, 4	Yes, 5.1, 24.4		Yes, 5.2
Belarus	Yes, 1099	Yes, 1100(1)		Yes, 1100(2)
Burundi	Yes, 10			
Cape Verde	Yes, 22			
Central African Rep.	Yes, 47			
Chad	Yes, 72			
China	Yes, 5	Yes, 4		
Cuba	Yes, 21			
East Timor	Yes, 21			
Fyrom	Yes, 5	Yes, 14		
Gabon	Yes, 30			
Georgia	Yes, 5	Yes, 6		Yes, 35.3
Guatemala	Yes, 31			
Guinea-Bissau	Yes, 22			
Japan	Yes, 42			
Jordan	Yes, 29			
Kazakhstan	Yes, 1090	Yes, 1091.1		Yes, 1091.2
Korea (N)	Yes, 5, 13			
Korea (S)	Yes, 10	Yes, 7		
Kyrgyzstan	Yes, 1173	Yes, 1174.1		Yes, 1174.2
Liechtenstein	Yes, 6			
Macau	Yes, 20	Yes, 21		
Mexico	Yes, 15.II			
Moldova	Yes, 1583	Yes, 1584		
Mongolia	Yes? 540.1			
Mozambique	Yes, 22			

Codification	*Lex fori* Limits		*Lex causae* Limits	
	Ordre public	Mandatory rules	Public Policy	Mandatory rules
Paraguay	Yes, 22			
Peru	Yes, 2049			Yes, 2096
Qatar	Yes, 38			
Quebec	Yes, 3081			Yes, 3079
Russia	Yes, 1193	Yes, 1192.1		Yes, 1192.2
Rwanda	Yes, 8			
Serbia	Yes, 39	Yes, 39.1		Yes, 39.2, 144
Somalia	Yes, 28			
Switzerland	Yes, 17	Yes, 18		Yes, 19
Taiwan	Yes, 8	Yes, 7		
Tajikistan	Yes, 1197	Yes, 1198.1		Yes, 1198.2
Tunisia	Yes, 36	Yes, 38.1		Yes, 38.2
Turkey	Yes, 5	Yes, 6		Yes, 31
U.A.E.	Yes, 27			
Ukraine	Yes, 12	Yes, 14.1		Yes, 14.2
Uruguay	Yes, 5.1	Yes, 6.1		Yes, 6.2
Uzbekistan	Yes, 1164	Yes, 1165.1		Yes, 1165.2
Venezuela	Yes, 8	Yes, 10		
Vietnam	Yes, 759.3			
Yemen	Yes, 36			
Rome Convention, Rome I, and 27 Countries under Them				
Rome Conv.	Yes, 16	Yes, 7.2		Yes, 7.1
Rome I	Yes, 21	Yes, 9.2		Yes, 9.3
Belgium*	Yes, 21	Yes, 20(1)		Yes, 20(2)
Bulgaria*	Yes, 45	Yes, 46(1)		Yes, 46(1)
Croatia*	Yes, 4			
Czech Republic*	Yes, 4	Yes, 3		
Estonia*	Yes, 7	Yes, 31		
Germany*	Yes, 6	Yes, 34		
Italy*	Yes, 16	Yes, 17		
Lithuania*	Yes, 11.1	Yes, 1.2		Yes, 1.2
Netherlands*	Yes, 6	Yes, 7.2		Yes, 7.3
Poland*	Yes, 7	Yes, 8.1		Yes, 8.2
Portugal*	Yes, 22			
Romania*	Yes, 8-9			

Codification	*Lex fori* Limits		*Lex causae* Limits	
	Ordre public	Mandatory rules	Public Policy	Mandatory rules
Slovakia*	Yes, 36	Yes, 36		
Slovenia*	Yes, 5			
USA				
Restatement 2d	Yes, 90		Yes, 187(2)	
U.C.C.	Yes		Yes	
Louisiana			Yes, 3540	
Oregon			Yes, 15.355	
Puerto Rico	Yes, 7, 29		Yes, 29	
Conventions				
Hague Sales '55	Yes, 6			
Hague Sales '86	Yes, 18	Yes, 17		
Hague Agency	Yes, 17			Yes, 16
Hague Securities	Yes, 11(1)	Yes, 11(2)		
Hague Principles	Yes, 11.3	Yes, 11.1	Yes, 11.4,"up to *lex fori*"	Yes, 11.2,"up to *lex fori*"
Mexico Conv.	Yes, 18	Yes, 11		Yes, 11 "up to *lex fori*"
Totals	**77**	**40**	**5**	**25**

1. *Lex Fori* Alone

As Table 3.3 indicates, outside the EU, 34 codifications and three conventions assign the role of *lex limitatis* exclusively to the *lex fori*. In 26 of those codifications[211] and one convention,[212] the only limitation is the *ordre public* of the *lex fori*, whereas the remaining eight codifications[213] and two conventions[214] employ, in addition, the mandatory rules of the *lex fori*.

---

[211] See the following codifications and the pertinent articles indicated in parentheses: Afghanistan (art. 35), Angola (art. 22), Algeria (art. 18), Burundi (art. 10), Cape Verde (art. 22), Central African Republic (art. 47), Chad (art. 72), Cuba (art. 21), East Timor (art. 21), Gabon (art. 30), Guatemala (art. 31), Guinea-Bissau (art. 22), Japan (art. 42), Jordan (art. 29), North Korea (arts. 5, 13), Liechtenstein (art. 6), Mexico (art. 12.V), Mongolia (art. 540.1), Mozambique (art. 22), Paraguay (art. 22), Qatar (art. 38), Rwanda (art. 8), Somalia (art. 28), U.A.E. (art. 27), Vietnam (art. 759.3), Yemen (art. 36).

[212] *See* Hague Sales Convention of 1955, art. 6.

[213] *See* the following codifications and the pertinent articles indicated in parentheses: Armenia (arts. 1258, 1259), China (arts. 4, 5), FYROM (arts. 5, 14), South Korea (arts. 7, 10), Macau (arts. 20, 21), Moldova (arts. 1583, 1584), Taiwan (arts. 7, 8), and Venezuela (arts. 8, 10).

[214] *See* Hague Sales Convention of 1986, arts. 17, 18; Hague Securities Convention, arts. 11.1 and 11.2.

Thus, all of these codifications would uphold the choice of law clause in patterns 5 and 6, but not in patterns 1–4 of Table 3.2 above. For the reader's convenience, that table is reproduced again here, with a different heading, and with the addition of a column showing the results under these codifications (Table 3.4).

TABLE 3.4. THE RESULTS IN THE *LEX FORI* STATES

#	*Lex Fori*	*Lex Causae*	Chosen Law	Result
1	state "a"	state "a"	STATE "B"	
2	state "a"	state "b"	STATE "C"	Not
3	state "a"	STATE "B"	STATE "B"	upheld
4	state "a"	STATE "B"	STATE "C"	
5	STATE "A"	state "b"	STATE "A"	Upheld
6	STATE "A"	state "b"	STATE "C"	

In pattern 1, these codifications make the right choice because the law of state "a" would have been applicable *but for* the parties' choice of the law of State "B." Coincidentally, the same is true of pattern 2, at least if the reasons for which both states "a" and "b" restrict party autonomy are the same. The parties' choice of the law of State "C" should not be allowed to evade a public policy that is shared by both states "a" and "b."

On the other hand, in pattern 3, there is absolutely no good reason to disregard the parties' choice of State "B" law, a law that would have been applicable even if the parties had not chosen it. In pattern 4, the parties did not choose the law of a state of the *lex causae* but they chose a law that, like the *lex causae*, does *not* restrict their autonomy. Again, there is no good reason to interpose the more restrictive law of the forum state and disregard the parties' choice, especially if that state's connections to the forum are tenuous. This problem can be avoided in those codifications that require a close connection with the forum before applying the *ordre public* exception. The codifications of Belgium and Bulgaria belong to this category. Unfortunately, both of those codifications are superseded by Rome I.[215]

In patterns 5 and 6, in which the parties chose the law of a state that exceeds the party autonomy limits of the *lex causae,* but not of the *lex fori,* these codifications will uphold the parties' choice. In pattern 5, the chosen state is also the forum state, but even that factor does not necessarily mean that it is appropriate to uphold the parties' choice. The interposition of the liberal limits of the *lex fori* when the *lex causae* would restrict party

---

[215] Article 21(2) of the Belgian codification provides that, in applying the *ordre public* exception, "special consideration is given to the degree in which the situation is connected with the Belgian legal order and to the significance of the consequences produced by the application of the foreign law." Article 45(2) of the Bulgarian codification is substantively identical.

autonomy is particularly problematic in cases in which the forum has only a tenuous connection with the case and its law does not single out weak parties, such as consumers and employees, for protective treatment. This regime enables the economically stronger party to impose well-calculated combinations of choice-of-law-and-forum clauses that deprive the weaker party of any meaningful protection.

2. *Lex Causae* Alone

On the other side of the spectrum, the Louisiana and Oregon codifications assign the role of *lex limitatis* to the *lex causae* rather than to the *lex fori*.[216] Article 3540 of the Louisiana codification provides that the chosen law applies "except to the extent that that law contravenes the public policy of the state whose law would otherwise be applicable" in the absence of that choice.[217] The Oregon codification provides that the law chosen by the parties does not apply "to the extent that its application would…[c]ontravene an established fundamental policy embodied in the law that would otherwise govern the issue in dispute" in the absence of a choice-of-law clause.[218] Neither codification assigns an independent role to the *ordre public* of the *lex fori* as such.

Section 187(2)(b) of the Restatement (Second), which is followed in most other states of the United States, also provides that the state whose public policy may defeat the parties' choice of law is not the forum state qua forum, but rather the state whose law would, under Section 188, govern the particular issue if the parties had not made an effective choice, that is, the *lex causae*.[219] Unlike the Louisiana and Oregon codifications, Section 90 of the Restatement preserves the traditional *ordre public* exception of the *lex fori* as the last shield against the application of a repugnant foreign law, whether that law is chosen by the parties or through the forum's choice-of-law rules. However, the Restatement recognizes the difference between the two public policies, at least as one of degree, by stating that the public policy contemplated by Section 187 "need not be as strong as would be required to justify the forum in refusing to entertain suit upon a foreign cause of action under the rule of § 90."[220]

---

[216] Article 29 of the Puerto Rico draft codification takes the unique position that the chosen law is applied unless it violates restrictions on party autonomy imposed by *both* the *lex fori* and the *lex causae*. For the rationale of this provision, *see* Symeonides, *The Puerto Rico Projet*, 422–424.

[217] La. codif. art. 3540.

[218] Or. Rev. Stat. § 15.355. The same section also provides that the chosen law does not apply to the extent its application would "[r]equire a party to perform an act prohibited by the law of the state where the act is to be performed under the contract" or "[p]rohibit a party from performing an act required by the law of the state where it is to be performed under the contract." *Id.*

[219] In addition, the Restatement provides that the state of the *lex causae* must have "a materially greater interest" than the chosen state in the determination of the particular issue. *Restatement (Second)* § 187(2)(b). In most cases, a conclusion that a state is the state of the *lex causae* is based, at least in large part, on a conclusion that that state has a "materially greater interest" in applying its law.

[220] *Id.* at § 187 cmt g.

The Peruvian codification may be following a similar position depending on how one interprets Article 2096. This article provides that "[t]he law declared applicable under Article 2095 determines the mandatory rules which are to be applied and the limits on the autonomy of the will of the parties."[221] This quoted provision is ambiguous because Article 2095 provides for both the law chosen by the parties and the objectively applicable law. However, it seems more logical to assume that the phrase "declared applicable" refers to the objectively applicable law rather than the contractually chosen law.

As Table 3.5 indicates, in patterns 1 and 2, these codifications would not uphold the parties' choice of law, thus reaching the same result as the codifications that follow the *lex fori* solution. The difference lies in the next four patterns, in which the two groups would reach exactly the opposite results.

TABLE 3.5. THE RESULTS IN THE *LEX CAUSAE* STATES

#	*Lex Fori*	*Lex Causae*	Chosen Law	Result
1	state "a"	state "a"	STATE "B"	Not
2	state "a"	state "b"	STATE "C"	Upheld
3	state "a"	STATE "B"	STATE "B"	
4	state "a"	STATE "B"	STATE "C"	Upheld
5	STATE "A"	state "b"	STATE "A"	Not
6	STATE "A"	state "b"	STATE "C"	Upheld

3. Intermediate Solutions and Combinations

In between the above extremes, one finds several combinations between the standards of the *lex fori* and those of another state, which may be the state of the *lex causae* or a third state. The most widely followed model of such a combination was enunciated by the Rome Convention and is preserved with slight modifications in the Rome I Regulation. Under Rome I, the chosen law must remain within the limitations imposed by the *ordre public* and the "overriding mandatory provisions" of the *lex fori*.[222] However, in consumer and employment contracts, the chosen law must also remain within the limitations imposed by the "simple mandatory rules" of the *lex causae*,[223] and, in all other contracts, within the limitations of the mandatory rules of the country in which "all other elements of the situation" (other

---

[221] Peruvian codif. art. 2096. In addition, Article 2049 restates the *ordre public* exception that operates in favor of the *lex fori*.

[222] *See* Rome I, Art. 21 (*ordre public*); Art. 9(2) ("overriding mandatory provisions" of the *lex fori*). *See also* Art. 9(3), which allows courts to "give effect" to the "overriding mandatory provisions" of the place of performance "in so far as" those provisions "render the performance of the contract unlawful."

[223] *See* Rome I, Arts. 6(2) and 8(1).

than the parties' choice) are located.[224] Several national choice-of-law codifications outside the EU follow this model, at least to the extent that they protect consumers and employees through the mandatory rules of the *lex causae*.[225]

At least a dozen of the codifications that subject the chosen law to the limits of the *ordre public* and mandatory rules of the *lex fori* provide in addition that the court "may" apply or "take into account" the mandatory rules of a "third country" with which the situation has a "close connection."[226] It is safe to assume that the state of the *lex causae* would always qualify as a state that has a "close connection" because, ex hypothesi, it is the state whose law would have been applicable in the absence of a choice-of-law clause. This "close connection" will always render relevant the mandatory rules of the *lex causae* but will not necessarily guarantee their application because the pertinent articles are phrased in discretionary terms.

The Mexico City Convention and the Hague Principles follow a variation of the above position. Article 18 of the Mexico City Convention reiterates the classic *ordre public* exception, while paragraph 1 of Article 11 preserves the application of the mandatory rules of the *lex fori*. Paragraph 2 of Article 11 provides that "[i]t shall be up to the forum to decide when it applies the mandatory provisions of the law of another State with which the contract has close ties."[227]

In a similar fashion, Article 11 of the Hague Principles restates the *ordre public* exception and preserves the application of the mandatory rules of the *lex fori*. The same article also provides that the *lex fori* determines when a court "may or must apply or take into account": (1) the overriding mandatory provisions of another law, or (2) the public policy of the state whose law would be applicable in the absence of a choice of law (*lex causae*).[228]

B. THE THRESHOLDS FOR EMPLOYING THE LIMITATIONS TO PARTY AUTONOMY

After delineating the scope of party autonomy and identifying the state whose standards would define the limits to party autonomy (the *lex limitatis*), the next task of a codifier is to establish the threshold that the parties' choice must exceed before being held

---

[224] *See* Rome I, Art. 3(3). *Cf.* Art. 3(4) (mandatory rules of EU law), Art. 11(5) (mandatory rules of the *lex rei sitae*).

[225] *See* the codifications of Albania (art. 52.2 (consumers only)); FYROM (arts. 24–25); Japan (arts. 11–12); South Korea (arts. 27–28); Liechtenstein (arts. 45, 48); Quebec (arts. 3117–3118); Russia (art. 1212); Serbia (arts. 141–142); Switzerland (arts. 120–121); Turkey (arts. 26–27); Ukraine (art. 45).

[226] *See* the codifications of Argentina (draft arts. 2599–2600); Azerbaijan (arts. 4–5, 24.4); Belarus (arts. 1099, 1100); Georgia (art. 35.3); Kazakhstan (arts. 1090, 1091); Kyrgyzstan (art. 1173, 1174); Quebec (arts. 3079, 3081); Russia (arts. 1192, 1193); Serbia (draft arts. 40.2, 144); Tajikistan (arts.1197–1198); Tunisia (arts. 36, 38); Turkey (arts. 5, 6, 31); Ukraine (arts. 12, 14); Uruguay (arts. 5.1, 6.1–2); and Uzbekistan (arts. 1164, 1165). *See also* Hague Agency Convention, arts. 16, 17. Article 9(3) of Rome I is similar to these articles except that it is limited to the state of performance. It allows courts to "give effect" to the "overriding mandatory provisions" of the place of performance "in so far as" those provisions "render the performance of the contract unlawful."

[227] Mexico City Convention, art. 11.

[228] Hague Principles, art. 11.

unenforceable. If any difference between the *lex limitatis* and the chosen law would defeat the parties' choice, then party autonomy would become a specious gift. As one court noted, "[t]he result would be that parties would have the right to choose the application of another state's law only when that state's law is identical to [the *lex causae*]. Such an approach would be ridiculous."[229]

Thus, there is a general consensus on the need for a higher threshold for multistate contracts than for fully domestic contracts. Predictably, however, the various codifications differ in defining this threshold, the lower the threshold the easier it is to defeat party autonomy, and vice versa. Although it is difficult to quantify the height of the various thresholds, Figure 3.2 attempts to do just that. It depicts in descending order the thresholds used in the various codifications. The following discussion describes these thresholds in the same order.

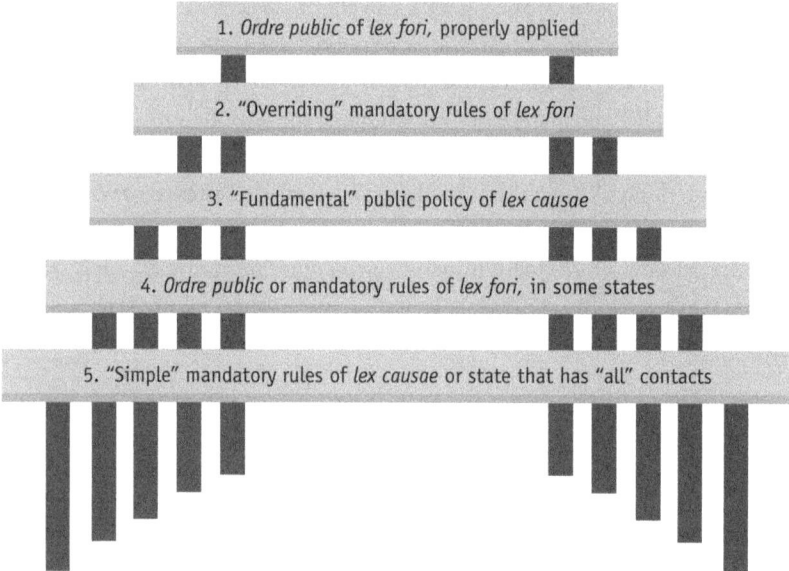

FIGURE 3.2. The Public Policy Thresholds

1. The Ordre Public of the *Lex Fori*

At least theoretically, the highest threshold is the one posed by the *ordre public* exception of the forum state, properly applied. The international literature has developed a consensus, which is reflected in many recent codifications, that a proper application of this exception must be based on the following elements:

(1) *Ordre public* in this context contemplates a strongly held public policy. Some codifications express this notion by referring to "fundamental

---

[229] Cherokee Pump & Equipment, Inc. v. Aurora Pump, 38 F.3d 246, 252 (5th Cir. 1994).

principles,"[230] "fundamental values,"[231] "basic principles of social organization laid down by the Constitution,"[232] or "those principles of the social and governmental system of the [forum state] and its law, whose observance must be required without exception."[233]

(2) *Ordre public* in this context refers to the "international" or "external" public policy rather than the forum's "internal" public policy. The idea is that multistate contracts are entitled to more tolerant treatment than domestic contracts. The codifications of Peru, Portugal, and Uruguay express this concept by specifically referring to the "international" public policy of the forum state,[234] the Quebec codification refers to *ordre public* "as understood in international relations,"[235] and the Tunisian and Romanian codifications refer to the *ordre public* "in the sense of private international law."[236]

(3) What is to be compared is the "effect," "result," or "consequences" of the *application* of the chosen law in the particular case (rather than the chosen law in the abstract) with the public policy of the forum state;[237]

(4) The application of the chosen law must produce a result that is clearly or "manifestly incompatible" with the forum's public policy.[238]

---

[230] German codif. art. 6; Belarus codif. art. 1099; Kyrgyzstan codif. 1173; North Korean codif. art. 13; Mexican codif. art. 15.1.II; Portuguese codif. art. 22; Ukrainian codif. art. 12; Uzbekistan codif. art. 1164.

[231] Liechtenstein codif. art. 6; Tunisian codif. art. 36 ("fundamental choices"); Venezuelan codif. art. 8 ("essential principles").

[232] Croatian codif. art. 4.

[233] Slovak codif. art. 36.

[234] Peruvian codif. art. 2079; Portuguese codif. art. 22; Uruguayan draft codif. art. 5.

[235] Quebec codif. art. 3081.

[236] Tunisian codif. art. 36; Romanian codif. art. 9.

[237] Virtually all codifications contain words to this effect. *See, e.g.,* Polish codif. art. 7 ("A foreign law shall not be applied, if its application would lead to consequences that are incompatible with the public policy of the Republic of Poland."). *See also* the following codifications and the pertinent articles indicated in parentheses: Angola (art. 22), Armenia (art. 1258), Austria (art. 6), Belarus (art. 1099), Belgium (art. 21), Bulgaria (art. 45), Cape Verde (art. 22), Croatia (art. 4), East Timor (art. 21), Estonia (art. 7), FYROM (art. 5), Germany (art. 6), Guinea-Bissau (art. 22); Hungary (art. 7), Italy (art. 16), Japan (art. 42), Kazakhstan (art. 1090), Korea (art. South) (art. 10), Kyrgyzstan (art. 1173), Liechtenstein (art. 6), Lithuania (art. 1.11), Macau (art. 20), Mexico (art. 15.I.II), Moldova (art. 1583), Mozambique (art. 22), Netherlands (art. 6), Peru (art. 2049), Portugal (art. 22), Quebec (art. 3081), Serbia (art. draft. art. 39), Russia (art. 1193), Slovakia (art. 36), Slovenia (art. 5), Switzerland (art. 17), Taiwan (art. 8), Tajikistan codif. art. 1197.1; Ukraine (art. 12), Uruguay (art. 5), Uzbekistan (art. 1164), Venezuela (art. 8). The Russian codification and the codifications bearing Russian influence state specifically that the refusal to apply the foreign law may not be based merely on the difference between the legal, political, or economic system of the two countries. *See* Russian codif. art. 1193; Armenian codif. art. 1258(2); Kazakhstan codif. art. 1090(2); Kyrgyzstan codif. art. 1173(2); Tajikistan codif. art. 1197.2; Ukrainian codif. art. 12(2); Uzbekistan codif. 1164.

[238] The majority of codifications and conventions contain words to this effect. *See, e.g.,* Belgian codif. art. 21; Bulgarian codif. art. 21; Dutch codif. art. 6; South Korean codif. art. 10; Peruvian codif. art. 2079; Rome I, art. 21; Swiss codif. art. 17; Ukrainian codif. art. 12; Venezuelan art. 8; Mexico City Convention art. 18; Hague Agency Convention art. 17; Hague Sales Convention art. 18.

2. The "Overriding" Mandatory Rules of the *Lex Fori*

Rome I distinguishes between "overriding" and "simple" mandatory rules. It defines the latter as rules that "cannot be derogated from by agreement,"[239] and the former as those rules that the enacting state regards as "crucial…for safeguarding its public interests, such as its political, social or economic organisation, to such an extent that they are applicable to any situation falling within their scope, irrespective of the law otherwise applicable."[240] Obviously, the two definitions contemplate a much higher threshold for applying the "overriding" than the "simple" mandatory rules.[241] Rome I ensures that the chosen law may not violate the overriding mandatory rules of the *lex fori* by providing that "[n]othing in this Regulation shall restrict the application of the overriding mandatory provisions of the law of the forum."[242]

As Table 3.3 above indicates, 24 codifications outside the EU and four conventions expressly authorize the application of the overriding mandatory rules of the forum state. Although these codifications do not use the word "overriding," they use phraseology that contemplates an equally high threshold as that of Rome I. They provide that these mandatory rules apply "directly"[243] and "irrespective of,"[244] "regardless of,"[245] or "notwithstanding"[246] the law designated by the codification's choice-of-law rules, including the rules that allow a contractual choice of law.

Table 3.3 also lists 18 codifications outside the EU that authorize the application of the overriding mandatory rules of a "third" state that has a "close" (but not necessarily a closer or the closest) connection with the case. In this context, the "third" state is a state other than the forum state or the chosen state. More likely, it will be the state of the *lex causae*, but it can also be another state, that is, a fourth state. Although the overriding mandatory rules of that state must embody at least the same high level of public policy as those of the forum state, their application is not assured. Whereas the forum's mandatory rules apply automatically, the application of foreign mandatory rules is always discretionary: the court "may" apply or "take into account" the mandatory rules of the third state

---

[239] Rome I, arts. 3(3–4), 6(2), and 8(1).

[240] *Id.*, art. 9(1). The "overriding" mandatory rules are also known as "internationally mandatory" or "super mandatory" rules, while the "simple" mandatory rules are sometimes referred to as "domestic" or "internal" mandatory rules.

[241] *See* Rome I Preamble, Recital 37 ("The concept of 'overriding mandatory provisions' should be distinguished from the expression 'provisions which cannot be derogated from by agreement' and should be construed more restrictively.").

[242] Rome I, art. 9(1).

[243] Chinese codif. art. 5.

[244] Rome I, art. 9(1); Rome II, art. 16; Belgian codif. art. 20; Dutch codif. art. 7; FYROM codif. art. 14; Italian codif. art. 17, South Korean codif. art. 7; Swiss codif. art. 18.

[245] Belarus codif. art. 1100(1); Kyrgyzstan codif. art. 1174(1); Lithuanian codif. art. 1.11(2).

[246] Bulgarian codif. art. 46(1); Venezuelan codif. art. 10; Mexico City Convention, art. 11.

after considering the "nature" and "purpose" of those rules and the "consequences of their application or non-application."[247]

3. The Public Policy of the *Lex Causae*

The few codifications that use the public policy of the *lex causae* as the gauge for policing party autonomy also contemplate a high-level policy. The Louisiana codification conveys this notion by referring to "strongly held" policies[248] of the *lex causae,* the Restatement (Second) uses the qualifier "fundamental,"[249] and the Oregon codification speaks of an "established fundamental" policy.[250]

However, although the word "fundamental" suggests a fairly high threshold, the examples the Restatement provides about rules that embody a fundamental policy—for example, statutes that make certain contracts illegal, and statutes intended to protect one party from "the oppressive use of superior bargaining power,"[251]—suggest a much lower threshold than that of the classic *ordre public.* The same is true of the Oregon codification, which defines a fundamental policy as one that "reflects objectives or gives effect to essential public or societal institutions beyond the allocation of rights and obligations of parties to a contract at issue."[252] Moreover, as noted earlier, the Restatement states that this public policy "need not be as strong" as that contemplated by the traditional *ordre public* exception.[253] Indeed, under the classic American test articulated by Judge Cardozo, the *ordre public* exception should be employed only in exceptional cases in which the applicable foreign law is "shocking" to the forum's sense of justice and fairness.[254]

4. A Low-Level *Ordre Public* in Some States

In some codifications, the *ordre public* exception is phrased in terms that suggest a fairly low threshold. For example, the Chinese codification provides that if the application of a foreign law will "cause harm to the social and public interests of the PRC, the law of the PRC shall

---

[247] Dutch codif. art. 7(3). Identical or similar language exists in all provisions under discussion here. Of course, consideration of the nature, purpose, and consequences of a rule is also necessary for determining whether a rule of the *lex fori* qualifies as a mandatory rule.

[248] *See* La. Codif. art. 3540 cmt f ("only strongly held beliefs of a particular state qualify for the characterization of 'public policy.'").

[249] *Restatement (Second)* § 187(2).

[250] Or. Rev. Stat. § 15.355.

[251] *Id.*

[252] *Id.*

[253] *Restatement (Second)* § 187 cmt g.

[254] *See* Loucks v. Standard Oil Co. of New York, 120 N.E. 198, 201–202 (N.Y. 1918) (the foreign law must "offend our sense of justice or menace the public welfare," or "violate some fundamental principle of justice, some prevalent conception of good morals, some deep-rooted tradition of the common weal," or "shock our sense of justice").

be applied."[255] The codifications of Yemen and the United Arab Emirates provide that foreign law will not be applied if it is contrary to "Islamic law, public policy or good morals,"[256] whereas the Iranian codification provides that "private agreements concluded among parties are valid, if they are not against mandatory laws."[257]

5. The "Simple" Mandatory Rules

Finally, the lowest threshold for defeating party autonomy is that posed by the "simple" mandatory rules, namely rules that, in the words of Rome I, "cannot be derogated from by agreement." As noted earlier, Rome I employs this threshold in two categories of contracts:

(a) Contracts in which "all other elements" other than the parties' choice are "located in a country other than the country whose law has been chosen."[258] In these contracts, the parties' choice "shall not prejudice" the simple mandatory rules of that other country.[259]

(b) Consumer or employment contracts in which the parties chose the law of a state other than the state of the *lex causae*. In these contracts, the parties' choice of another law may not deprive the consumer or the employee of the protection of the simple mandatory rules of the *lex causae*.[260]

Outside the EU, similar rules for consumer contracts are found in the codifications of Albania (art. 52.2), Russia (art. 1212), and the Ukraine (art. 45), and for both consumer and employment contracts in the codifications of FYROM (arts. 24–25), Japan (arts. 11–12), South Korea (arts. 27–28), Liechtenstein (arts. 45, 48), Puerto Rico (arts. 5–36), Quebec (arts. 3117–318), Serbia (arts. 141–142), and Turkey (arts. 256–227).[261]

---

[255] Chinese codif. art. 6. For a discussion of the Chinese codification, *see* W. Chen, *Chinese Report*; J. Liang, Statutory Restrictions on Party Autonomy in China's Private International Law of Contract: How Far Does the 2010 Codification Go?, 8 *J. Priv. Int'l L.* 77 (2012); Y. Xiao & W. Long, Contractual Party Autonomy in Chinese Private International Law, 11 *Ybk Priv. Int'l L.* 193 (2009).

[256] Yemen codif. art. 36; U.A.E codif. art. 27.

[257] Iranian codif. art. 10.

[258] Rome I, art. 3(3). *See also id.,* art. 3(4); Rome Convention art. 3(3).

[259] Outside the EU, similar rules are found in the codifications of Albania (art. 45.4), South Korea (art.25.4), Quebec (art. 3111), and Serbia (draft art. 136.6).

[260] *See* Rome I, arts. 6(2), 8(1). Article 11 of Rome I seems to contemplate an intermediate category between the simple mandatory rules of Articles 6 and 8 and the "overriding" mandatory rules of Article 9. Article 11 provides that in contracts the subject matter of which is an in rem right in immovable property or a tenancy of immovable property, the parties' choice of non-situs law may not derogate from those rules of the situs state that mandate compliance with a particular form if those rules "are imposed . . . irrespective of the law governing the contract."

[261] However, unlike Rome I, the Japanese codification provides that the consumer or employee is entitled to the protection of the mandatory rules of the *lex causae* only if he/she "expresses his/her will to [the other party] to the effect that such mandatory rules should apply." Japanese codif. arts. 11–12.

VI. Comparison

The relative heights of the thresholds described above do not tell the whole story of which systems are more or less liberal toward party autonomy. For example, a high threshold usually implies a liberal regime. Nevertheless, a high public policy threshold, which, for one reason or another is actually employed too frequently in practice, will produce a restrictive regime. Conversely, although a low threshold normally suggests a restrictive regime, a low threshold that courts employ only rarely will produce a liberal regime.

In a similar vein, a system, such as Rome I and the codifications influenced by the Rome Convention, which exempts consumer and/or employment contracts from the scope of party autonomy, can afford to be, and is, more liberal in other contracts. Conversely, a system such as that of the Restatement (Second), which does not exempt any contracts from the scope of party autonomy, appears to be too liberal toward party autonomy.[262] At the same time, the Restatement mitigates that liberality by using a public policy threshold that is both lower and more readily deployable than the threshold or Rome I.

For these reasons, a complete assessment of the "liberality" of a particular regime of party autonomy must consider all pertinent factors and parameters, including:

(a) Which contracts, if any, are exempted from the scope of party autonomy?
(b) Which contractual issues, if any, are exempted from the scope of party autonomy?
(c) Which state's standards are used for determining the limits of party autonomy (*lex limitatis*);
(d) How high is the threshold for employing those limits? and
(e) How often is the threshold employable or employed in practice?

Obviously, these are variable factors and they cannot be quantified. Nevertheless, an attempt at a visual depiction, even if simplistic, can be helpful in conveying the basic differences, at least with regard to their starting points, among various systems. Figure 3.3 below is such an attempt to depict the operative range of party autonomy in three different models: (1) a typical traditional system, (2) Rome I, and (3) the Restatement (Second).

---

[262] Likewise, a system, such as that of the Louisiana, Oregon, and Puerto Rico codifications, which exempts issues of capacity, consent, and formation from the scope of party autonomy can be less circumspect about the parties' choice for other issues.

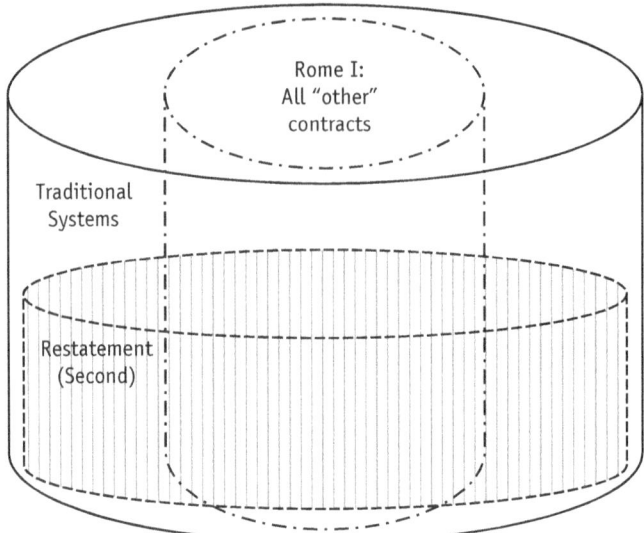

FIGURE 3.3. The Ranges of Party Autonomy in Three Models-Systems

A. TRADITIONAL SYSTEMS

The larger exterior cylinder in Figure 3.3 represents a typical traditional system, such as those reflected in the codifications of Algeria, Armenia, Croatia, Jordan, North Korea, Macau, Mexico, Moldova, Mongolia, Rwanda, Taiwan, Venezuela, and Vietnam.

The cylinder is very wide because these systems do *not* exempt any contracts from the scope of party autonomy, that is, they do not separate for protective treatment contracts involving presumptively weak parties, such as consumers or employees.

The cylinder is also very tall because the only limitation to party autonomy in these systems is that imposed by the *ordre public* of the *lex fori*, a limitation that, if properly applied, requires a very high threshold.[263]

The result of this combination of wide scope and high threshold is that party autonomy enjoys a much wider range of operation in these codifications, both "horizontally" in the sense of the types and numbers of contracts that come within its scope, and "vertically" in the sense of the substantive restrictions to which it is subject.

B. THE RESTATEMENT (SECOND)

The shaded cylinder in Figure 3.3 represents the Restatement (Second). This cylinder is perceptibly shorter than the cylinder representing the traditional systems because the Restatement imposes a much lower and thus more readily employable public policy

---

[263] Obviously, if for whatever reason the courts disregard the high threshold of the *ordre public* exception and apply the exception too frequently, then the range of party autonomy will shrink commensurably.

threshold than the threshold of those other systems. As explained earlier, despite contrary appearances, the Restatement's "fundamental" policy exception contemplates a lower policy level than the classic *ordre public* exception.

However, the Restatement cylinder has the same circumference as that which represents the traditional systems because, like those systems, the Restatement does *not* exempt any contracts (e.g., consumer or employment contracts) from the scope of party autonomy. Instead, the Restatement provides the same party-autonomy rule for all contracts without differentiation and relies on courts to make the necessary differentiations. For similar reasons, the Restatement does not define some critical terms used in Section 187, such as "substantial relationship," "reasonable basis," "fundamental policy," and "materially greater interest."[264] This lack of definitiveness is a deliberate policy choice by the Restatement's drafters. It reflects the lessons learned from the failures of the rigid rules of the first Restatement, a modest degree of confidence in the drafters' ability to provide good a priori solutions for diverse situations, and a high degree of confidence in the courts' ability to do the same on a case-by-case basis.

C. ROME I

The taller and slimmer of the three cylinders in Figure 3.3 above represents the scheme of Rome I, minus its treatment of consumer and employment contracts.[265] As noted earlier, Rome I provides that the parties' choice of law may not deprive the "passive" consumer or the employee of the protection of the *lex causae*. If these contracts were to be represented in Figure 3.3, the Rome I cylinder would have the same circumference as that of the Restatement, but subject to two thresholds. The first would be the threshold of the "simple" mandatory rules of the *lex causae*, which is a lower threshold than the "fundamental" policy of the Restatement. The second threshold would be the same as the ultimate threshold that Rome I imposes on "all other contracts," namely contracts other than consumer and employment contracts.

For these "other contracts," Rome I imposes the same public policy as the traditional systems described earlier, namely the forum's *ordre public*.[266] This is why the cylinder representing Rome I has the same height as the cylinder representing the traditional systems.

---

[264] *Restatement (Second)* § 187.

[265] Another feature not represented by the cylinder is the way Rome I treats domestic contracts, namely contracts in which, except for the parties' choice of law, "all other elements relevant to the situation [...] are located in a country other than the country whose law has been chosen." Rome I, art. 3(3). As noted earlier, in these contracts, the choice of law may not prejudice the application of the "simple" mandatory rules of the country where all the other elements are located. *Id. See also id.* art. 3(4) (providing a similar treatment of contracts in which, except for the country of the chosen law "all other elements [...] are located in one or more Member States" of the EU.).

[266] This includes passenger contracts and small-risk insurance contracts because these contracts are subject to the same *substantive* limitations (as opposed to geographic requirements) as all other contracts.

Although it is true that Rome I imposes, in addition, the limitations embodied in the "overriding" mandatory rules of the *lex fori* (as well as of the state of performance), those rules contemplate an equally high or nearly as high threshold as that of the *ordre public* exception, even if they operate differently.

VII. Assessment

A. A STUDY IN CONTRASTS

1. The Restatement (Second)

A comparison between the Restatement (Second) and Rome I is a study in contrasts, with each document reflecting the legal culture that produced it. The Restatement reflects a typical American skepticism toward categorical a priori rules—a skepticism reinforced by the first Restatement's failure—and a high degree of confidence in the courts' ability to develop appropriate solutions on a case-by-case basis. In a style characteristic of the American legal culture, the Restatement (Second) prefers to err on the side of under-regulation rather than over-regulation. It provides only a single party-autonomy rule (Section 187) for all contracts rather than several rules for different contracts or issues, as it does for contracts that do not contain a choice-of-law clause. Section 187 imposes only two flexible limitations to party autonomy: (1) the easily met requirement for a "substantial relationship" to the chosen state or another "reasonable basis" for the choice, and (2) the requirement that the application of the chosen law should not violate a "fundamental policy" of the *lex causae*.

The Restatement does not define any of the flexible terms quoted above. It relies instead on judges to interpret these terms on a case-by-case basis, confident in the belief that it is better to trust judges than to try to confine them. The fact that American state and federal judges are products of the same legal training and tradition, despite serving different sovereigns, coupled with the rich judicial experience in working with malleable "approaches" rather than black-letter rules, explains the high degree of discretion the Restatement accords judges. The hope is that, over time, judges will develop uniform (or at least similar) solutions and thus will eventually provide a modicum of consistency and predictability. The result of the Restatement's application has been a great degree of judicial flexibility, perhaps at the expense of predictability and consistency.

Admittedly, the fact that the Restatement is not a "code" may explain these attributes. But the UCC, which *is* positive law, also shares the same attributes. The UCC too devotes only one section to party autonomy, Section 1-301, which is even more laconic and elliptical than Section 187 of the Restatement. Section 1-301 provides that "when a transaction bears a reasonable relation to [the forum] state and also to another state or nation the parties may agree that the law of either [the forum] state or of such other state or nation shall govern their rights and duties."[267] Thus, in contracts covered by this provision, a "reasonable relation" with the chosen state is the only express condition for allowing a contractual choice of law.

Moreover, an attempt to add flesh and bones to this laconic provision failed miserably. In 2001, the UCC Commissioners proposed a major detailed revision of Section 1-301, which drew heavily from the Rome Convention. Besides introducing the European concept of "mandatory rules," the proposed revision differentiated between consumer contracts and business-to-business contracts, as well as between international contracts and intra-US interstate contracts, and imposed different party autonomy restrictions for each category.[268] Unfortunately, these ideas proved unpopular with industry leaders and, therefore, state legislatures. By 2008, only the U.S. Virgin Islands had adopted the proposed revision, thus forcing the UCC Commissioners unceremoniously to withdraw it.

2. Rome I

By contrast, legislative timidity has never been a problem on the European continent and certainly not *in Brussels*. Rome I is the culmination of the rich continental experience in crafting a priori rules. The fact that Rome I is designed to serve a plurilegal and multi-ethnic Union—one that brings together uneven legal traditions—may explain why the drafters opted for more black-letter rules and so few escapes. The result is greater predictability and consistency and less judicial flexibility.

Whereas the Restatement deliberately opts for under-regulation, Rome I opts for over-regulation. Rome I is a detailed, sophisticated system employing multiple layers of substantive restrictions on party autonomy and differentiating among three types of contracts: (1) consumer and employment contracts, (2) passenger and insurance contracts, and (3) all other contracts (hereinafter referred to as all "other" contracts). Because the first two categories involve contracts with presumptively weak parties, Rome I imposes party-autonomy restrictions that it does not impose in all other contracts.

In the abstract, the Rome I scheme seems perfectly logical, indeed brilliant, because there is every good reason for a liberal treatment of contracts that do *not* involve weak parties. However, despite its structural and conceptual perfection, this scheme may well be flawed in significant respects. This possibility is discussed below.

---

[267] U.C.C. § 1-301(a). Because the UCC is a statute and the Restatement (Second) is not, Section 1-301 prevails over the Restatement with regard to all contracts falling within the scope of this section, which is coextensive with the scope of the UCC.

[268] For discussion of the proposed revision, *see* E. Scoles, P. Hay, P. Borchers & S. Symeonides, *Conflict of Laws* 983–987 (4th ed. 2004); J. Graves, Party Autonomy in Choice of Commercial Law: The Failure of Revised U.C.C. 1-301 and a Proposal for Broader Reform, 36 *Seton Hall L. Rev.* 59 (2005).

B. CONSUMERS AND EMPLOYEES

The Rome I scheme works perfectly well, perhaps too well, in protecting "passive" consumers and employees from the consequences of an adverse contractual choice of law. As noted earlier, Articles 6(2) and 8(1) provide that a choice-of-law agreement may not deprive a consumer or an employee of the protection of the mandatory rules of the state of the *lex causae*. Thus, these articles essentially allow for the possibility of "double protection," that is, under the chosen law and the *lex causae*. The consumer or employee can enjoy the protection of whichever of the two laws is more protective, and, in some instances, the protection of both laws for different aspects of the contract. This may appear too generous to the consumer or employee, but the other contracting party may easily avoid this generosity simply by not deviating from the *lex causae*.

Moreover, the above provisions may be a bit too generous to passive consumers and to employees by guaranteeing the protection of *all* mandatory rules of the *lex causae* without requiring that those rules embody a strong public policy. This, however, is the policy choice made by the drafters of Rome I. One reason for respecting this policy is that, as a general proposition, it is better to err on the side of overprotecting, rather than under-protecting, weak parties such as consumers or employees.

C. PASSENGERS AND INSUREDS

The Rome I scheme does not seem to work as well in the case of contracts for the carriage of passengers or small-risk insurance contracts. To illustrate the problem, suppose that a Spanish passenger bought an air ticket in Spain for a flight from Madrid to New York operated by a British air carrier headquartered in Liechtenstein. The ticket contains a New York choice-of-law clause that meets the geographical requirements of Article 5(2) because the law of the state of destination is one of the permitted choices. Suppose, however, that New York law deprives the passenger of the protection provided by the mandatory rules of Spain: should the choice-of-law clause be upheld in such a case?

In the absence of Article 5, the answer would probably be negative because this contract would qualify as a consumer contract, and under Article 6(2), the clause would be disregarded to the extent that it deprives the consumer of the protection of Spanish law, which would be the *lex causae*. However, as Article 6(1) expressly declares, Article 5 prevails over Article 6 for passenger contracts, and thus the passenger does not enjoy the protection Article 6 provides for consumers.[269] The passenger can invoke the provisions

---

[269] Rome I, Art. 6(1) provides that Article 6 applies "[w]ithout prejudice" to Article 5. Recital 32 states that "Article 6 should not apply in the context of those [carriage and insurance] contracts."

of Articles 3(3), 3(4), 9(3), 9(2), and 21, but it is doubtful that any of them will lead to the avoidance of the choice-of-law clause. Specifically:

(1) Paragraph 3 of Article 3 would not help the passenger because *not* "all other elements relevant to the situation [...] are located in *a* country other than the country whose law has been chosen."[270] Here, the relevant elements are located not in a *single* country, as the quoted provision contemplates, but rather in four countries;

(2) Similarly, paragraph 4 of Article 3 will also be unavailable to the passenger because *not* "*all*" other elements [...] are located in one or more Member States."[271] The carrier's principal establishment and the place of destination are both located outside the EU. Thus, even if New York law violates existing mandatory rules of Community law, the contractual choice of New York law may not be disregarded;

(3) Paragraph 3 of Article 9 would help the passenger only if: (a) Spain (the country of the passenger's habitual residence and place of departure) qualifies as the state of performance; (b) the pertinent Spanish mandatory rules would qualify as "overriding" mandatory rules; and (c) those rules would render the performance of the contract unlawful. If, as is likely, any one of these conditions is missing, the chosen law must be applied;[272]

(4) Paragraph 2 of Article 9 would help only if: (a) Spain is also the forum state,[273] and (b) its mandatory rules would qualify as "overriding" mandatory rules; and

(5) Article 21 would help only if Spain is the forum state and the application of New York law would be "manifestly incompatible" with Spain's *ordre public*; anything less than that would not defeat the chosen law.

In summary, in most cases, the contractually chosen law will be applied in the above hypothetical despite depriving the passenger of the protection provided by the mandatory rules of the country whose law would have been applicable in the absence of choice (*lex causae*). This result is regrettable. For all practical purposes, the passenger is a consumer who should be protected from the adverse consequences of a contractual choice of law for the same policy and practical reasons for which Article 6 protects other consumers.

The same can be said about small-risk insurance contracts. In many of these contracts, the insured would qualify as a consumer had Article 7 not displaced Article 6. Article 7(3) attempts to protect insureds by limiting the countries whose laws can be chosen in a choice-of-law clause. However, as the above discussion of the passenger contract

---

[270] Rome I, Art. 3(3) (emphasis added).

[271] Rome I, Art. 3(4) (emphasis added).

[272] Even if all conditions are present, the application of the "overriding mandatory rules" is itself permissive, not mandatory.

[273] The carrier will likely impose a choice-of-forum clause, ensuring that the trial will *not* take place in Spain.

illustrates, a geographical limitation does not necessarily guarantee meaningful protection for the insured. For example, in a life insurance contract, a contractual choice of the law of the insured's nationality satisfies the geographical requirement of Article 7(3) (c) but may well deprive the insured of the protection of the mandatory rules of a country that has a closer connection, such as the country where the insured has his habitual residence and where the insurance contract was applied for and delivered, and the risk materialized. For reasons explained above, the tools provided by Articles 3(3)–(4), 9, and 21 would probably not alter this equally regrettable result.

D. OTHER WEAK PARTIES

Other weak parties such as franchisees may find themselves in an equally vulnerable position as passengers and insureds. A franchise contract does not qualify as a consumer contract under Article 6(1) of Rome I because it is not a contract "outside the trade or profession"[274] of either the franchisee or the franchisor. Yet, in many franchise contracts, the franchisee is likely to be in as weak a bargaining position as most consumers. Recognizing this fact, many states of the United States have enacted statutes regulating franchises operating in their territory and usually involving franchisees domiciled there. Typically, these statutes prohibit waivers of the statutes' provisions, either directly or through the contractual choice of another state's law. Thus, when a contract purports to opt out of such a statute through a choice of another state's law, courts routinely strike down the choice-of-law clause. Cases so holding are abundant.[275] In fact, more often than not, such clauses are disregarded even if the statute in question does not expressly prohibit them, at least when the case is litigated in the franchisee's home state.[276]

Unfortunately, Rome I does not seem to provide franchisees with sufficient protection from the consequences of an adverse choice-of-law clause. The only provision of Rome I on franchise contracts is Article 4(1)(e), which provides that, in the absence of a choice-of-law clause, a franchise contract is governed by the law of the country where the franchisee has his habitual residence.[277] Thus, a choice-of-law clause in a franchise contract will be subject only to the infrequently operable limitations of Articles 3(3)–(4), 9, and 21 of Rome I.

---

[274] Rome I, Art. 6(1). For a discussion of franchise contracts and distribution contracts under Rome I, *see* L. García Gutiérrez, Franchise Contracts and the Rome I Regulation on the Law Applicable to International Contracts, 10 *Ybk. Priv. Int'l L.* 233 (2008); M-E. Ancel, The Rome I Regulation and Distribution Contracts, 10 *Ybk. Priv. Int'l L.* 221 (2008). *See also* S. Rammeloo, *Das neue EG-Vetragskollisionsrecht* (1992). For commercial agents, *see* P. Mankowski, Commercial Agents under European Jurisdiction Rules: The Brussels I Regulation Plus the Procedural Consequences of Ingmar, 10 *Ybk. Priv. Int'l L.* 19 (2008). For certain licensing contracts, *see* P. Torremans, Licences and Assignments of Intellectual Property Rights under the Rome I Regulation, 4 *J. Priv. Int'l L.* 397 (2008).

[275] For citations, *see* Hay, Borchers & Symeonides, *Conflict of Laws*, 1123–1125.

[276] *See id.*

[277] This provision is subject to the closest-connection exception of Art. 4(4).

For example, suppose that a franchise contract between Starbucks, a corporation head-quartered in the US state of Washington, and a French franchisee for a Starbucks franchise in France contains a choice-of-law clause selecting the law of the friendly Kingdom of Tonga, as well as a clause allowing the franchisor to unilaterally terminate the franchise under certain circumstances that would not be sufficient under either Washington law or French law. In such a case, the clause would easily pass the test of paragraphs 3 and 4 of Article 3 because one important contact is located in Washington and thus not *all* contract connections are located in a single country (France) or in one or more EU countries. The clause would also pass the test of Article 9 unless the chosen law: (1) violates the "overriding" mandatory rules of France, either in its capacity as the forum state (Art. 9(2)) or as the state of performance, but in the latter case only if those rules render the contract illegal (Art. 9(3)); or (2) is manifestly incompatible with the French *ordre public* (Art. 21). Nothing short of those two high thresholds would prevent the application of Tongan law.

E. CONCLUSIONS

The possibility that the above shortcomings can be cured through the application of some other Regulation or Directive among the myriad that the EU produces every year does not convert these shortcomings into virtues. Even so, one could credibly argue that, in the grand scheme of things, these are minor shortcomings. If nothing else, the drafters of Rome I deserve praise for having the political courage and legal acumen to devise a series of specific rules explicitly designed to protect weak parties, such as consumers, employees, passengers, and insureds. As the discussion in this chapter has highlighted, these rules work quite well for consumers and employees, but not so well for passengers, insureds, and other presumptively weak parties, such as franchisees. Even so, it is preferable to have rules protecting weak parties in *most* cases (even if those rules do not work well in *some* cases) rather than not having any such rules.

One can only hope that someday American drafters will muster the courage to draft similar rules for the United States. Unfortunately, the recent hostility encountered by the proposed pro-consumer revision of the UCC, coupled with the pro-business tilt of American law in general,[278] suggests that this day is not likely to come in the near future. Fortunately, American judges can do what legislatures cannot: a study of the numerous American cases involving choice-of-law clauses in consumer, employment, insurance, and franchise contracts reveals that judges, with their innate sense of justice, do a commendable job in protecting the weak parties in these contracts.[279]

---

[278] *See* P. Borchers, *Categorical Exceptions*, at 1659 ("U.S. law is generally more pro-business and antiregulatory."); *id.* at 1660 ("For a variety of reasons having to do with legal culture and attitudes toward business regulation, it is probably the case that exceptions to party autonomy designed to protect weaker parties in a transaction are not likely to become prevalent in the United States.")

[279] *See* Hay, Borchers & Symeonides, *Conflict of Laws*, 1109–1126.

Thus, in the final analysis, each system plays to its own strengths. The American strength is the strong tradition of judicial independence and creativity. The European strength is a rich tradition in statutory rule crafting. Unfortunately, one rarely finds both of these strengths in the same system.

In any event, as this chapter has documented, the principle of party autonomy has made tremendous strides during the last 50 years, attaining the status of a universal principle. This is certainly a welcome development. After all, party autonomy is like motherhood: nobody is against it, and most commentators enthusiastically endorse it. But party autonomy presupposes the *free will of both parties freely expressed*. Although this is a truism, it is often forgotten amid the euphoria generated by eloquent rhetoric about individual and contractual freedom and other majestic generalities. A codifier's task and challenge is not only to facilitate the unimpeded operation of this principle, but also to ensure the protection of those contracting parties who are least able to take advantage of it. These goals are by definition conflicting, and there are several different ways to accommodate them. Which of those accommodations is more successful depends on not only the text of each codification, but also—if not more importantly—on how each codification is applied *in practice*. But this latter inquiry is a task left for another book.

4   Codification and Flexibility

I. Introduction

Opponents of codification advance several arguments, some of which depend on timing and context, and some of which remain constant. Among the latter are the arguments of petrification and inflexibility. The petrification argument stands for the proposition that codification arrests the smooth development of the law; it freezes it in time and prevents its adaptation to changing needs.[1] The inflexibility argument asserts that codification usually paints with too broad a brush[2] and is too inflexible to properly resolve certain exceptional or unanticipated cases.[3]

One encounters these arguments more frequently in common law systems, where judges are viewed as the principal players, and legislators as only occasional participants in the lawmaking process.[4]

---

[1] *See, e.g.,* B. Currie, Comments on *Babcock v. Jackson,* 63 *Colum. L. Rev.* 1233, at 1241 (1963) ("[N]ew efforts to find short cuts and syntheses should be sternly discouraged. We are beginning to recover from a long siege of intoxication resulting from overindulgence in generalities; for a while, at least, total abstinence should be enforced"); R. Sedler, Reflections on Conflict-of-Laws Methodology, 32 *Hastings L.J.* 1628, 1636 (1981).

[2] *See, e.g.,* D. Trautman, Reflections on Conflict-of-Laws Methodology, 32 *Hastings L.J.* 1612, 1621 (1981) ("[L]egislative direction is inherently incapable of capturing the nuance and sophistication necessary for just and satisfactory choice-of-law solutions.").

[3] *See, e.g.,* W. Reese, Statutes in Choice of Law, 35 *Am. J. Comp. L.* 395, 396 (1987) ("[n]o legislature, no matter how wise it may be, could envisage all of the almost endless possibilities.").

[4] For the United States in particular, these arguments are discussed in Symeonides, *Revolution* 411–419; Symeonides, *A New Conflicts Restatement* 406–422.

The validity of these arguments depends on the style and philosophy of a particular codification. For example, a codification consisting of inflexible mechanical rules (such as those of the Prussian Civil Code of 1763 or the first Conflicts Restatement) is a recipe for petrification and lends credence to the arguments against codification. However, the art or science of codification has advanced significantly in the intervening years and has developed tools for avoiding petrification and ensuring flexibility. This chapter examines the extent to which this is true of modern choice-of-law codifications.

II. The Perennial Tension between the Goals of Legal Certainty and Flexibility

The tension between the need for legal certainty and predictability, on the one hand, and the desire for flexible, equitable, and individualized solutions on the other, is as old as law itself. Aristotle described it more than 23 centuries ago when he spoke of the role of equity as a corrective of the written law.[5] Twenty centuries later, Jean Jacques Rousseau spoke of the legislator's inability to foresee changing circumstances, noting that "[a] thousand cases against which the legislator has made no provision may present themselves."[6] As René David put it, "[t]here is and will always be in all countries, a contradiction between two requirements of justice: the law must be certain and predictable on one hand, it must be flexible and adaptable to circumstances on the other."[7] Private international law is not immune from this contradiction; in fact, it may be particularly susceptible to it.[8]

---

[5] *See* Aristotle, *The Nicomachean Ethics*, V. x 4-7: "[T]he law always speaks in general terms, yet in many cases it is impossible to speak in terms that are both general and correct at the same time. In those cases, then, in which it is necessary to speak in general terms but not possible to do so correctly, the law provides for the majority of cases, with full awareness of the deficiency of its provisions. Thus, when the law pronounces a general rule and thereafter a case arises that is not covered by the general rule, then it is proper, where the legislator's pronouncement is defective because of its over-simplicity, to rectify the defect by deciding in the same way as the legislator would have decided…had he been cognizant of the case.… This is in essence the nature of the equitable (*epieikes*): A corrective of the law when law is defective due to its generality. In fact, this is why it is impossible to legislate about certain matters and why it becomes necessary to address them through [ad hoc] Resolutions. Undefinable matters cannot be regulated by definite rules." (Author's translation).

[6] *See* J.J. Rousseau, *The Social Contract or Principles of Political Right*, Bk. IV, Ch. VI (1762) p. 84 (Kessinger Publ. 2004) ("The inflexibility of the laws, which prevents them from adapting themselves to circumstances, may, in certain cases, render them disastrous.… The order and slowness of the forms they enjoin require a space of time which circumstances sometimes withhold. A thousand cases against which the legislator has made no provision may present themselves, and it is a highly necessary part of foresight to be conscious that everything cannot be foreseen.").

[7] R. David, *English Law and French Law* 24 (1980).

[8] *See, e.g.,* H. Neuhaus, Legal Certainty versus Equity in the Conflict of Laws, 28 *Law & Contemp. Prob.* 795, 795 (1963) (juxtaposing the need for "equal and foreseeable rules of law which enable those who are subject to them to order their behavior in such a manner as to avoid legal conflict or to make clear predictions of their chances in litigation" with the desire "for deciding current, concrete disputes adequately, by giving due weight to the special and perhaps unique circumstances of each case.").

Each legal system has wrestled with this contradiction and has striven to attain an appropriate equilibrium between these two competing yet necessary goals. Naturally, this equilibrium differs not only from system to system, but also from subject to subject, and time to time.

The common assumption is that countries that have not codified their choice of law place a higher premium on flexibility, while countries that have adopted a codification place a higher premium on certainty. As a general proposition, this assumption is not erroneous. After all, a choice-of-law codification is supposed to provide legal certainty by choosing the applicable law in advance, rather than leaving the choice to be made by courts on a case-by-case basis.

III. Codification and Judicial Discretion

However, as centuries of codification experience demonstrate, the decision to adopt statutory rules need not result in outlawing judicial discretion.[9] New codifications, more so than the old ones, are replete with examples of express legislative grants of judicial discretion. In choice of law, the codifier who is favorably inclined toward flexibility can choose from a considerable array of tools to that end. Among these tools are:

(a) The use of alternative connecting factors;
(b) The use of escape clauses authorizing courts to deviate from the choice-of-law rules in appropriate circumstances;
(c) The use (either in choice-of-law rules or in the escapes) of composite or "soft" connecting factors, such as the "closest connection" or "strongest connection," namely, factors that do not depend on the location of a single contact but rather on multiple factors and circumstances to be evaluated in the light of each particular case; or
(d) The use of malleable "approaches" or similar formulas that do not directly designate the applicable law but rather provide a list of factors that the court must consider in choosing that law. In some codifications, these formulas are followed by presumptive rules designating the ordinarily applicable law in specified situations, whereas in other codifications the formulas play a residual role for cases not covered by specific choice-of-law rules.

---

[9] As early as 1804, the redactors of the Code Napoléon recognized the simple truth that had escaped the drafters of the Prussian Code of 1794: that for the *legislateur* "to anticipate everything is a goal impossible of attainment." Portalis, Tronchet, Bigot-Préameneu & Maleville, Texte du discours préliminaire, in J. Locré, *La legislation civile, commerciale et criminelle de la France*, 251, 255 (Vol. 1, 1827). Consequently, the legislator's role is "to set, by taking a broad approach, the general propositions of the law, [and] to establish principles which will be fertile in application.... It is for the judge and the jurist, imbued with the general spirit of the laws to direct their application." *Id.*

Figure 4.1 below shows the position of these tools in the spectrum between extreme rigidity and extreme flexibility. At the one end of the spectrum, one finds the fixed rules of traditional systems, and, at the other extreme, the American-style ad hoc approaches. Between the two extremes, one finds at least three intermediate formulas for controlled flexibility, as well as several combinations among them.

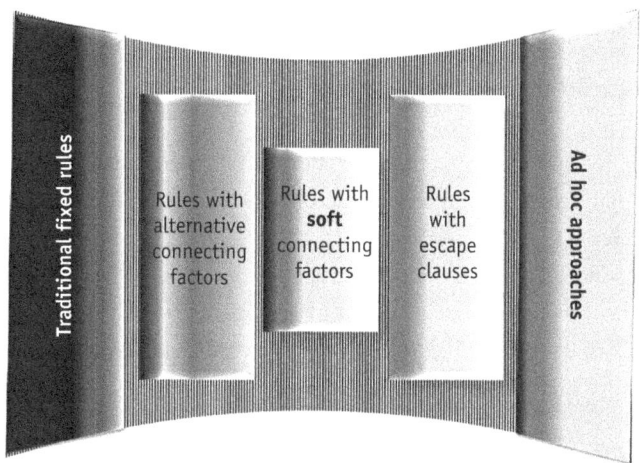

FIGURE. 4.1. The Spectrum and Gradations of Flexibility

IV. Rules with Alternative Connecting Factors

One characteristic feature of traditional choice-of-law systems was their excessive, and often exclusive, reliance on single and mono-directional connecting factors (such as the *locus contractus* or the *locus delicti*), which were intended to leave little or no discretion to the judge in identifying the applicable law. The first small step away from this mind-set was (and remains) the use of "alternative reference rules," namely, rules that give courts a choice between or among more than one connecting factor in certain well-defined cases.

For example, rather than exclusively subjecting the formal validity of a contract to the *lex loci contractus*, an alternative-reference rule authorizes additional choices, such as applying the law that governs the substance of the contract (*lex causae*), the law of the parties' common domicile, habitual residence, or place of business, whichever law upholds the contract. Similarly, rather than a priori fixing the *locus delicti* at the place of the injury, an alternative reference gives the court or victim a choice between the places of the injurious conduct and the resulting injury.

Although a few of these rules appeared as early as the first part of the twentieth century, they have become much more common in recent codifications. Because alternative reference rules are primarily intended to accomplish a particular substantive result, they will be discussed in Chapter 6, *infra*.[10] From the judge's perspective, these rules appear inimical to judicial discretion (and thus to flexibility) in that they deny the judge the freedom to choose a law other than the one that produces the preselected *result* (e.g., upholding the contract). Nevertheless, from a systemic perspective, these rules provide flexibility in that, although they tie the system to a particular result, they do not tie the system to the law of a particular state.

V. Rules with Flexible Connecting Factors

The next step in the movement toward flexibility is the replacement of pre-fixed, mono-directional, and rigid connecting factors (such as the *locus contractus* or the *locus delicti*) with open-ended, poly-directional, and flexible connecting factors. These factors do not depend on the location of a single contact, but rather on multiple contacts and circumstances to be evaluated in light of each particular case. Because of this attribute, these factors allow the judge considerable discretion in identifying the state of the applicable law.

A. THE CLOSER OR CLOSEST CONNECTION

Among recent codifications, the most popular of these flexible connecting factors is the "closer" or "closest" connection. With slight variations in phraseology, several recent national codifications and international conventions, as well as in the Rome I and Rome II Regulations, use this factor as detailed below. The differences in language include the use of a different adjective ("close" or "strong") in either the comparative ("closer" or "stronger") or the superlative ("closest" or "strongest"),[11] as well as the use of a different noun ("connection," "relationship," "link," or "tie").

Despite these phraseological differences, some of which are the result of variations in translation, these formulations have one thing in common: unlike traditional fixed connecting factors that point directly (and often inexorably) to the state of the applicable law, this connecting factor contemplates a more individualized determination of that state. It allows the court to take account of all pertinent contacts and factors, and, when properly applied, it requires the court to explain why one state's contacts are "closer," "more pertinent," or "more significant" than those of another state.

This "closest connection" factor is now ubiquitous. Moreover, it became a "multi-tasker" well before this word became fashionable. It plays several different roles in the

---

[10] *See* Chapter 6 at V, *infra*.

[11] The comparative "closer" is used when the decision-maker is to compare with the connection of one other state, usually the connection with the state of the otherwise applicable law. The superlative is used when the decision-maker is to find the "closest" among several connections.

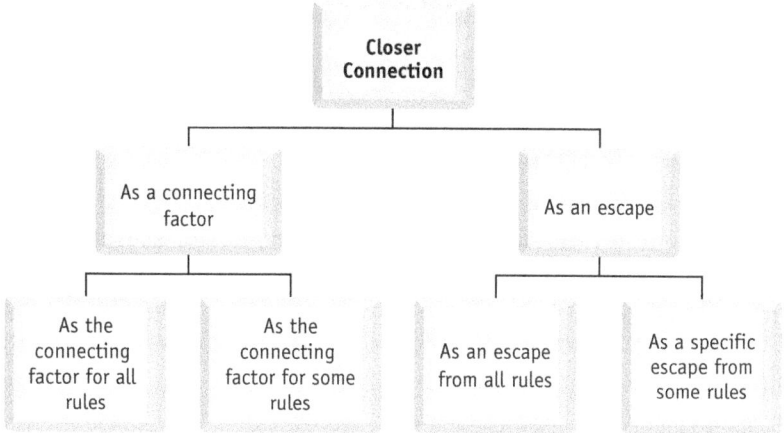

FIGURE 4.2. The Multiple Roles of the "Closer Connection"

various codifications, and often within different rules of the same codification. Figure 4.2 below depicts the most general of these roles, followed by textual documentation and discussion.

1. The Closest Connection as the Principal Connecting Factor

Four codifications (those of Austria, Bulgaria, Burkina Faso, and China) anchor all of their choice-of-law rules on the concept of the closest connection.

The very first article of the Austrian codification provides that multistate cases "shall be judged…according to the legal order with which the strongest connection exists," and that the codification's choice-of-law rules "shall be considered as expressions of this principle."[12]

Likewise, the Bulgarian codification provides in Article 2 that multistate cases are governed by the law of the state with which they are "most closely connected" and that the codification's choice-of-law rules "express this principle." The article also provides that, if the applicable law cannot be determined through those rules, "the law of the State with which the relationship has the closest connection by virtue of other criteria shall apply."[13]

Article 1003 of the Burkina Faso codification provides that multistate cases are governed by the law that has the "strongest connection" and that the codification's choice-of-law rules are "considered as the expression of [this] general principle."[14] The same article also provides that, in cases of gaps or insufficiencies in those rules, the judge should be "inspired" by and draw from this principle.[15]

---

[12] Austrian codif. art. 1, discussed in C. Wenderhost, *Austrian Report,* at B.1
[13] Bulgarian codif. art. 2.
[14] Burkina Faso codif. art. 1003.
[15] *Id.*

Finally, Article 3 of the Chinese codification provides that the law applicable to any civil relationship involving foreign elements "shall have the closest connection" with such relationship, and that if the codification does not provide for a particular relationship, "the law of the country that has the closest connection with the civil relationship involving foreign elements shall be applied."[16]

In many cases, subsequent, more specific articles retract the flexibility that these introductory articles provide. Nevertheless, the closest connection remains the general and residual principle of these codifications and, as explained later, it can serve as both an escape from the specific articles in appropriate cases and as a gap-filler for unprovided-for cases.[17]

2. The Closer Connection as a General Escape

Eleven other codifications (those of Argentina, Belgium, FYROM, South Korea, Lithuania, Netherlands, Quebec, Serbia, Slovenia, Switzerland, and Ukraine)[18] use the closer connection factor as the basis for a general escape from all of their choice-of-law rules, but without explicitly declaring that those rules themselves are based on the closer connection factor. These escapes are discussed later in this chapter.[19]

Many more codifications use the closer-connection factor as the basis for narrower escapes from only some (rather than all) of the codification's rules. These escapes are also discussed later.[20] For now, though, the discussion turns to codifications that use the closer-connection factor as the basis for both a choice-of-law rule and an escape from that rule.

3. The Closer Connection in Specific Roles

Figure 4.3 depicts the various uses of the closer-connection factor in several types of conflicts cases.

a. The Closest Connection as a Presumption in Contract Conflicts, Subject to a Closer-Connection Escape

The closest-connection factor has played a special role in contract conflicts, at least since the days of the 1980 Rome Convention. The Convention provided that contracts that did

---

[16] Chinese codif. art. 3, discussed in W. Chen, *Chinese Report*, at II.

[17] *See infra* VI.A, this chapter.

[18] *See* Argentine draft codif. art. 2597; Belgian codif. art. 19; FYROM codif. art. art. 3; South Korean codif. art. 8(1); Lithuanian codif. art. 1.11(3); Dutch codif. art. 8; Quebec codif. art. 3082; Serbian draft codif. art. 36; Slovenian codif. art. 2(1); Swiss codif. art. 15; Ukrainian codif. art. 4(3).

[19] *See infra* VI.A, this chapter.

[20] *See infra* VI.B.1, this chapter.

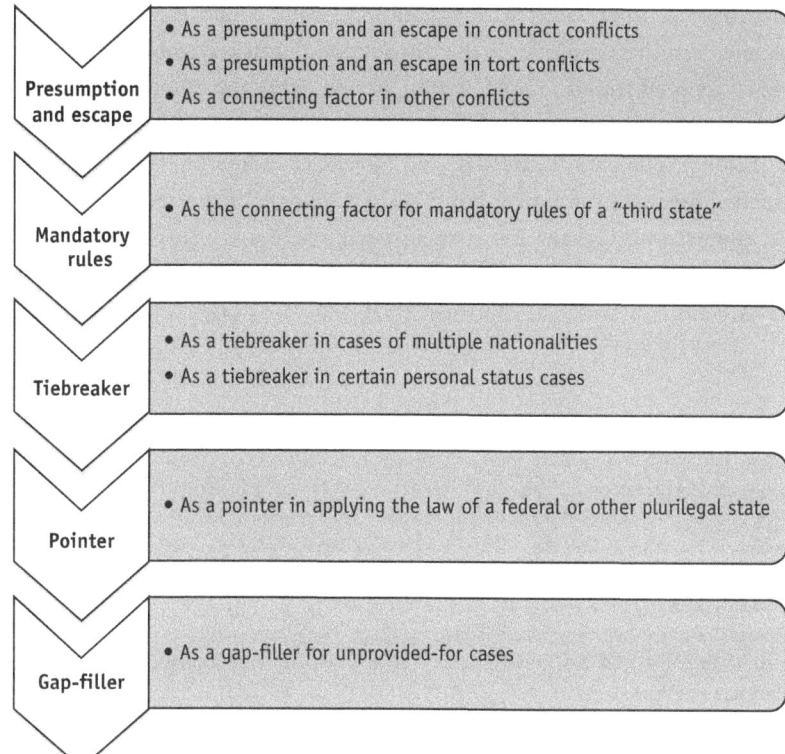

Presumption and escape
- As a presumption and an escape in contract conflicts
- As a presumption and an escape in tort conflicts
- As a connecting factor in other conflicts

Mandatory rules
- As the connecting factor for mandatory rules of a "third state"

Tiebreaker
- As a tiebreaker in cases of multiple nationalities
- As a tiebreaker in certain personal status cases

Pointer
- As a pointer in applying the law of a federal or other plurilegal state

Gap-filler
- As a gap-filler for unprovided-for cases

FIGURE 4.3. The Specific Tasks of the "Closer Connection"

not contain an effective choice-of-law clause were to be governed by the law of the country with which the contract was "most closely connected"[21] and then provided a series of presumptive rules identifying that country for different types of contracts. These rules generally pointed to the habitual residence of the obligor of the "characteristic performance," which itself is another "soft" connecting factor. The Convention also provided, however, that these presumptions were to be disregarded if the contract was "more closely connected with another country."[22]

The Rome I Regulation has since replaced the Rome Convention, but in the meantime several national codifications, as well as in the Mexico City Convention, have emulated

---

[21] Rome Convention art. 4(1) (providing that "[t]o the extent that the law applicable to the contract has not been [validly] chosen…, the contract shall be governed by the law of the country with which it is most closely connected" and that "a severable part of the contract which has a closer connection with another country may by way of exception be governed by the law of that other country.")

[22] Rome Convention art. 4(5) ("the presumptions in paragraphs 2, 3 and 4 shall be disregarded if it appears from the circumstances as a whole that the contract is more closely connected with another country.") *See also id.* art. 6 with regard to employment contracts.

the Convention's scheme, albeit with variations.[23] Some countries, such as Denmark[24] and Germany,[25] which were parties to the Convention as well as members of the European Union, have adopted statutes implementing or emulating the Convention. Emulation was the path chosen by certain countries that later joined the European Union, such as Bulgaria, Estonia, Hungary, Lithuania, and Slovenia.[26] Some EU member states have since amended their codifications to conform to the Rome I Regulation.[27]

Several countries outside the EU have adopted schemes similar to the Convention's or have used the closest-connection factor in similar fashion.[28] These countries include Albania,[29] Argentina,[30] Armenia,[31] Belarus,[32] FYROM,[33] Georgia,[34] Japan,[35] South Korea,[36]

---

[23] *See* Inter-American Convention on the Law Applicable to International Contracts of 1994, art. 9 (providing that "[i]f the parties have not selected the applicable law, or if their selection proves ineffective, the contract shall be governed by the law of the State with which it has the closest ties."). For the text of the convention, *see* http://www.oas.org/juridico/english/treaties/b-56.html. The convention is not yet in force.

[24] *See* Danish Law No. 88 of 9 May 1984, discussed in J. Lookofsky, *Danish Report*, at II.B.

[25] *See* German codif. arts. 28–30. For a discussion of these articles and the reasons they remain in force, *see* P. Mankowski, *German Report*, at I–II, and XIII.

[26] *See* Bulgarian codif. art. 94; Estonian codif. arts. 33, 35, 45; Hungarian codif. art. 29 (in force until 2009); Lithuanian codif. art. 1.37; Slovenian codif. art. 20. These provisions remain applicable to contracts that fall outside the scope of Rome I.

[27] *See, e.g.*, Czech codif. arts. 87–100; Hungarian codif. arts. 24–30.

[28] Before the Chinese codification of 2010, the "closest connection" was also used in the following Chinese laws and China Supreme Court guidelines to the lower courts: Article 5 of the Foreign Economic Contract Law of the People's Republic of China of 1985; Article 145 of the General Principles of Civil Law of 1986, as amended in 2009; Article 269 of the Maritime Code of 1992; Article 188 of the Law of Civil Aviation of 1995 as amended in 2009; Article 126 of the Contract Law of 1999; and Article 5 of the Rules of the Supreme People's Court on Related Issues concerning the Application of Law in Hearing Foreign-Related Contractual Dispute Cases Related to Civil and Commercial Matters of 2007. For pertinent discussion, *see* W. Chen, *Chinese Report*, at XIII.C; Xu Guojian, Contract in Chinese Private International Law, 38 *Int'l & Comp. L.Q.* 648, 651–652 (1989); Tung-Pi Chen, PIL of the People's Republic of China: An Overview, 35 *Am. J. Comp. L.* 445, 462–468 (1987). *See also* Chinese Model Law art. 101 (containing 24 choice-of-law rules for an equal number of contracts but also providing that "[i]f the above contracts apparently have a closer connection with another state or region, the law of that state or region shall apply."). *See also* Chinese Model Law, art. 91 (regarding trusts).

[29] *See* Albanian codif. art. 46 (providing presumptive rules for contracts based on the characteristic performance and the assumed closest connection, and also providing an escape based on the closer connection).

[30] *See* Argentinian draft codif. art. 2653, discussed in M.S. Najurieta & M.B. Noodt Taquela, *Argentinean Report*, at XIII.3.

[31] *See* Armenian codif. art. 1285 (providing that, for contracts not provided for in the article and in which the characteristic performance cannot be determined, the applicable law shall be the law of the state with which the contract is "most closely connected.")

[32] *See* Belarus codif. art. 1125(4).

[33] *See* FYROM codif. art. 22.

[34] *See* Georgian codif. art. 36 (providing presumptive rules for contracts based on the characteristic performance and the assumed closest connection).

[35] *See* Japanese codif. arts. 8, 12 (providing presumptive rules for contracts based on the characteristic performance and the assumed closest connection); T. Kanzaki, *Japanese Report*, at II.2.

[36] *See* South Korean codif. art 26 (providing presumptive rules for contracts based on the characteristic performance and the assumed closest connection); K. Suk, *South Korean Report*, at II.2.

Moldova,[37] Quebec,[38] Russia,[39] Serbia,[40] Switzerland,[41] Taiwan,[42] Turkey,[43] Ukraine,[44] and Venezuela.[45] The codifications of Azerbaijan, Kazakhstan, Kyrgyzstan, Tajikistan, and Uzbekistan use the closest connection in a more limited fashion,[46] while the Japanese, Polish, and Quebec codifications extend the principle of the closest connection to bilateral juridical acts other than contracts, as well as to unilateral acts.[47] Moreover, both codifications articulate the presumption of the characteristic performance in less categorical and more easily rebuttable terms than did the Rome Convention.[48]

Finally, in the Mexico City Convention (as well as the codifications of Venezuela[49] and Macau),[50] the closest connection is the *only* connecting factor, which—unaided

---

[37] *See* Moldovan codif. arts. 1611–1614.

[38] *See* Quebec codif. art. 3112 (providing that, when the parties did not validly choose a law or chose a law that invalidates the contract, the contract is governed by the law of the state of the closest connection) and art. 3113 (providing that a contract is presumed to be closely connected with the state of the characteristic performance). For discussion of these articles and cases applying them, *see* F. Sabourin, *Quebec Report,* at II.b. and c.

[39] *See* Russian codif. art 1211. However, this article provides that its presumptions regarding the closest connection apply "unless it follows otherwise from statute, the terms or nature of the contract, or the totality of the circumstances of the case."

[40] *See* Serbian draft codif. arts. 137–147.

[41] *See* Swiss codif. art. 117 ("In the absence of a choice of law, the contract is governed by the law of the state with which it has the closest connections."). *See also* art. 187 ("The arbitral tribunal decides in accordance with the rules of law chosen by the parties or, in the absence of such choice, in accordance with the rules of law with which the case has the closest connections.").

[42] *See* Taiwanese codif. art. 20 (providing that, in the absence of an effective choice-of-law agreement, a contract "shall be governed by the law which is the most closely connected" and establishing a presumption in favor of the law of the domicile of the obligee of the characteristic performance, if any). *See also id.* arts. 17–18 (agency), 43(1) (bills of lading), 44 (securities), 45 (marriage engagement). For discussion, *see* R. Chen, *Taiwanese Report,* at II, XIII (3).

[43] *See* Turkish codif. art. 24(4) (providing that the article's presumptive rules—which themselves are based on the closest connection and characteristic performance—will be disregarded if the contract has a closer connection with another country). *See also id.* arts. 27 (employment contracts), 28(2) (intellectual property contracts), 29(3) (carriage contracts); Z. Tarman, *Turkish Report,* at II.

[44] *See* Ukrainian codif. arts. 32(2)–(3), 44(2).

[45] *See* Venezuelan codif. art. 30 (providing that, in the absence of a choice of law by the parties, conventional obligations are governed by the law of the state with which they are "most directly linked"); E. Hernández-Bretón, *Venezuelan Report,* at II, XIII.

[46] These codifications provide that the law of the state with the closest connection applies if the characteristic performance cannot be determined, or in contracts that are not provided for in these codifications and in which the parties have not chosen the applicable law. *See* Azerbaijan codif. art. 25.3; Kazakhstan codif. art. 1113.4; Kyrgyzstan codif. art. 1199 3; Tajikistan codif. art 1219; Uzbekistan codif. art. 1190.

[47] *See* Japanese codif. arts. 8–10 (using the term "juridical acts" rather than contracts); Polish. Codif. art. 32 (applicable to unilateral juridical acts); Quebec codif. arts. 3082, 3107, 3112–3113.

[48] Likewise, the Belgian codification has adopted the closest connection as the residual connecting factor for the interpretation or revocation of wills. *See* Belgian codif. art. 84 (providing that, in the absence of a choice of law by the testator, the interpretation or revocation of a testament is governed by the law of the state with which the will or revocation has "the closest connections," and that state is presumed to be the testator's habitual residence "until proof of the contrary is brought."); J. Erauw & M. Fallon, *Belgian Report,* at II.2.b.

[49] *See* Venezuela codif. art. 30 (providing that, in the absence of a valid choice-of-law agreement, the contract is governed by the law of the state with which it is "most directly linked.").

[50] *See* Macau codif. art. 41, discussed in G. Tu, *Macau Report,* at X. *See also id.* regarding maritime contracts.

by presumptive rules—determines the applicable law for contracts that do not contain an effective choice-of-law clause.[51] The Mexico City Convention provides that, in the absence of an effective choice-of-law agreement, the contract is governed by the law of the state with which it has the "closest ties," and that a severable parable part of the contract that has a "closer tie" with another state is governed by the law of the latter state.[52]

The Rome I Regulation has replaced the Rome Convention's presumptive rules with tighter rules and has deleted the Convention's *explicit* statement that these rules are based on the closest-connection factor. Nevertheless, this factor remains omnipresent, albeit in the background. Not only does it remain the residual connecting factor for contracts in which the applicable law "cannot be determined"[53] through the presumptive rules, but it also provides the basis for an exception from all of those rules (albeit an exception phrased in tighter language than in the Convention). Article 4(3) of Rome I provides that, when it is "clear from all the circumstances of the case that the contract is manifestly more closely connected" with a country other than the country designated by those rules, the law of that other country shall apply.[54]

b. The Closest Connection as a Presumption in Tort Conflicts Subject to a Closer-Connection Escape

Many recent codifications assign a similar role to the closest connection in tort conflicts as in contract conflicts. For example, although the text of the Rome II Regulation does not expressly state that its rules are based on the closest connection, Rome II employs several escape clauses based on this factor. These clauses are found in the general rule of Article 4, as well as in articles providing for certain specific torts.[55] The escapes provide that, if it is "clear from all the circumstances of the case" that the tort is "manifestly more closely connected" with a country other than the one whose law is designated as applicable by the above articles, then the law of that country governs.[56]

These escapes are available in all EU countries except Denmark. However, because Rome II does not apply to all possible tort conflicts, the choice-of-law rules of those countries remain

---

[51] Article 9 of the Mexico Convention provides that, in the absence of an effective choice-of-law agreement, the contract is governed by the law of the state with which it has the "closest ties," and that a separable part of the contract that has a "closer tie" with another state is governed by the law of the latter state.

[52] Mexico Conv. art. 9.

[53] Rome I, art. 4(4).

[54] Rome I, art. 4(3). Similar exceptions are found in arts. 5(3) (contracts of carriage), 7(3) (insurance contracts), and 8(4) (individual employment contracts).

[55] In contrast to the preliminary draft, which limited the scope of the escape to cases covered by the general rule, the final text repeats the escape in the articles dealing with products liability (art. 5), unfair competition cases in which the competition affects exclusively the interests of a specific competitor (art. 6(2)), unjust enrichment (art. 10), *negotiorum gestio* (art. 11), and *culpa in contrahendo* (art. 12).

[56] Rome II, arts. 4(3), 5(2), 10(4), 11(4), and 12(2)(c). The first two of these provisions state that a "manifestly closer connection" with another country "might be based in particular on a pre-existing relationship between the parties, such as a contract, that is closely connected with the tort/delict in question."

relevant.[57] Some of these rules differ slightly from the rules of Rome II. Under Article 4 of Rome II, the applicable law is either: (1) the law of the state of injury; or (2) if the tortfeasor and the victim have their habitual residences in the same state, the law of that state. However, both of those laws can be displaced by the law of another state that has a closer connection. Under the Austrian article, the applicable law is the law of the state of conduct, but that law can be displaced by another state's law "if the persons involved have a stronger connection to the law of one and the same state."[58] Under the corresponding Belgian articles, the applicable law is: (1) the law of the parties' common habitual residence; (2) in the absence thereof, the law of the state where both the conduct and the injury occurred; and (3) in all other cases, the law of the state with which the obligation has the closest connection.[59]

Outside the EU, the codifications of Albania,[60] FYROM,[61] Japan,[62] Serbia,[63] Taiwan,[64] and Turkey[65] are among those that employ similar closer-connection escapes in tort conflicts.

c. *The Closest Connection as a Connecting Factor in Other Conflicts*
The closest connection is used as a connecting factor in miscellaneous other cases. The following are some examples:

- The Belgian codification uses this factor for determining the applicable law in certain intellectual property disputes, and for determining rights in certain groups of assets.[66]
- The Czech and Quebec codification use this factor for determining the law applicable to a trust in which the settlor did not choose the applicable law.[67]

---

[57] *See, e.g.,* Austrian codif. art. 48(2); Belgian codif. art. 99; Bulgarian codif. art. 105; Estonian codif. art. 53; German codif. art. 41; Lithuanian codif. art. 1.43; Slovenian codif. art. 30(2).

[58] Austrian codif. art. 48(2).

[59] *See* Belgian codif. art. 99. However, if the obligation has a "close connection" with an existing legal relationship between the parties, the law that governs that relationship displaces these three laws. *See id.* art. 100; J. Erauw & M. Fallon, *Belgian Report,* at II.2.a.

[60] *See* Albanian codif. arts.56.3, 57.3, 63.3, 68.4, 69.4, 70.4.

[61] *See* FYROM codif. art. 33(2) (law of state of closest connection displaces law of state of conduct or injury).

[62] *See* Japanese codif. arts. 20 and 15 (closer connection exception to the choice-of-law rules for torts, *negotiorum gestio,* and unjust enrichment); T. Kanzaki, *Japanese Report,* at II.

[63] *See* Serbian draft codif. art. 161 (general escape applicable to all tort conflicts, except products liability and traffic accidents, which are governed by conventions; *see id.* arts. 162, 168), environmental torts (art. 165), and defamation (art. 170).

[64] *See* Taiwanese codif. art. 25 (law of state of closest connection displaces law of state of conduct). *See also id.* art. 28 (providing that the closer connection determines which of three enumerated laws should govern a tort committed through the media); R. Chen, *Taiwanese Report,* at II.

[65] *See* Turkish codif. art. 34(3) (law of state of closest connection displaces law of state of conduct or injury); Z. Tarman, *Turkish Report,* at II.

[66] *See* Belgian codif. arts. 93 and 87(2); J. Erauw & M. Fallon, *Belgian Report,* at II.2.b.

[67] *See* Czech codif. art. 73; Quebec codif. art. 3107.

- The Czech codification also provides that, in deciding questions of guardianship of minors, the court may apply, in lieu of the *lex fori*, the law of a state that has a "substantial connection," if necessary for the protection of the minor.[68]
- The Ukrainian codification provides that the rights and duties of parents and children are governed by the child's national law or by the law of the state that has a "close connection with the respective relations" if that law is more favorable to the child.[69]
- In the Taiwanese codification, the closest connection is the residual connecting factor for cases involving an agency relationship, bills of lading, and certain rights in securities.[70]
- In the EU Successions Regulation, the closest connection is the unstated connecting factor underlying the general rule of applying the law of the decedent's last habitual residence,[71] the stated basis for an exception from that rule,[72] and the principal connecting factor for agreements involving the succession of several persons.[73]
- Finally, in the codification of Burkina Faso, the closer connection triggers an escape from the national law to the domicile law of the decedent in matters of succession.[74]

d. Close Connection and Mandatory Rules

The close-connection factor is also used in other limited contexts. For example, Article 20 of the Belgian codification allows a court to apply the mandatory rules[75] of a foreign state other than the one whose law is applicable under the codification if the other state has a "*close* connection" with the "situation."[76]

Nearly 20 other codifications use the "close connection" as the vector to the mandatory rules of a third state,[77] as do four Hague conventions,[78] the Mexico City

---

[68] *See* Czech codif. art. 65.

[69] Ukrainian codif. art. 66.

[70] *See* Taiwanese codif. arts. 17–19, 43, 44; R. Chen, *Taiwanese Report*, at II.

[71] *See* Successions Regulation art. 21.1 and recital 23.

[72] *See id.* art. 21.2 (providing that the law of the state of the last habitual residence shall not apply if the decedent was "manifestly more closely connected" with another state); Recital 25.

[73] *See* Successions Regulation art. 25.2 (providing that an agreement regarding the succession of several persons that is admissible under the laws governing the succession of each of those persons is governed by whichever of those laws has the closest connection).

[74] *See* Burkina Faso codif. art. 1043.

[75] The concept of mandatory rules is discussed in Chapter 3 at V.B.2, *supra*, and Chapter 7 at II.B, *infra*.

[76] Belgian codif. art. 20 (emphasis added); J. Erauw & M. Fallon, *Belgian Report*, at II.2.b.V. (c).

[77] *See* the codifications of Argentina (draft art. 2599), Azerbaijan (art. 5.2), Belarus (art. 1100.2), Kazakhstan (art. 1091.2), Kyrgyzstan (art. 1174.2), Lithuania (art. 1.11), Netherlands (art. 7.3), Poland (art. 8.2), Quebec (art. 3079), Serbia (draft art. 40.2), Russia (art. 1192.2), Switzerland (art. 19.1), Tajikistan (art. 1198.2), Tunisia (art. 38), Turkey (art. 31), Ukraine (art. 14), Uruguay (draft art. 6.2), and Uzbekistan (art. 1165).

[78] *See* Hague Convention of 14 March 1978 on the Law Applicable to Agency, Art 16 ("effect may be given to the mandatory rules of any State with which the situation has a significant connection, if and in so far as, under the law of that State, those rules must be applied whatever the law specified by its choice of law rules"); Hague Convention of 1 July 1985 on the Law Applicable to Trusts and on Their Recognition, art. 17; Hague

Convention,[79] the Rome Convention,[80] and the proposed EU Regulations on Matrimonial Property Regimes[81] and on Registered Partnerships.[82]

e. The Closest Connection as a Tiebreaker

Several codifications use the closest-connection factor as a tiebreaker in certain categories of cases, such as those involving persons with multiple nationalities, domiciles, or habitual residences, or those involving the effects of marriage or divorce.

For example, Article 1262 of the Armenian codification provides that the "personal law" of a person is the law of the state of which the person is a citizen and, in the case of multiple citizenships, the law of the state with which the person is "most closely connected." More than 20 other codifications provide a similar rule for persons of multiple nationalities.[83]

Other codifications, such as the Ukrainian, provide an intermediate tiebreaker by referring to the person's domicile or habitual residence before resorting to the closest connection.[84] The codifications of Bulgaria, Croatia, FYROM, Japan, North Korea, Serbia, and Vietnam provide that, in cases of citizenship in multiple countries, the person's habitual residence provides the tiebreaker, but only if the person is a citizen of such country; if not, the closest connection functions as the tiebreaker.[85] The Dutch codification contains similar rules for the law governing a person's capacity and name.[86]

Convention of 1 August 1989 on the Law Applicable to Succession to the Estates of Deceased Persons, art. 6; Hague Convention of 13 January 2000 on the International Protection of Adults, art. 20.

[79] *See* Mexico City Convention, art. 11 (allowing the forum state to decide when to apply the mandatory rules of another state with which the contract has "close ties.")

[80] *See* Rome Convention, art. 7.1 ("effect may be given to the mandatory rules of a country with which the situation has a close connection, if and in so far as, under the law of the latter country, those rules must be applied whatever the law applicable to the contract.").

[81] *See* European Commission Proposal for a Council Regulation on jurisdiction, applicable law and the recognition and enforcement of decisions in matters of matrimonial property regimes, Brussels, 16.3.2011, COM(2011) 126 final 2011/0059 (CNS), art. 22.

[82] *See* European Commission Proposal for a Council Regulation on jurisdiction, applicable law and the recognition and enforcement of decisions regarding the property consequences of registered partnerships, Brussels, 16.3.2011, COM(2011) 127 final, 2011/0060 (CNS), art. 17.

[83] *See, e.g.,* Austrian codif. art. 9; Azerbaijan codif. art. 9.1; Belarus codif. art. 1103; Belgian codif. art. 3(2); Chinese codif. art. 20; Estonian codif. § 11; German codif. art. 5; Greek Civ. Code art. 31; Italian codif. art. 19(2); South Korean codif. art. 3(1); Kazakhstan codif. art. 1094.1; Kyrgyzstan codif. art. 1177; Liechtenstein codif. art. 10(1); Lithuanian codif. art. 1.11 (same rule for multiple or indeterminate domiciles); Moldova codif. art. 1589; Macau codif. art. 52; Polish codif. art. 2.2; Slovenian codif. art. 10; Taiwanese codif. art. 2; Turkish codif. art. 4; Uzbekistan codif. art. 1168; Vietnamese codif. art. 760(3); FYROM codif. art. 11. Some of these codifications contain an exception providing that if one of the nationalities is that of the forum state, that nationality controls.

[84] *See* Ukrainian codif. art. 16. *See also* Albanian codif. art. 8.3.

[85] *See* Bulgarian codif. art 48; Croatian codif. art 11; FYROM codif. art 11(3); Japanese codif. art. 38(1); North Korean codif. art. 7; Serbian codif. art. 7.2; Vietnamese codif. art. 760(2).

[86] *See* Dutch codif. arts. 11.1, 19.2, 146.2.

The closest connection plays a similar role in cases involving the personal or patrimonial effects of marriage or divorce. For example, Articles 36 and 37 of the North Korean codification provide that, if the spouses do not possess the same nationality and do not reside in the same country, the effects of marriage and the availability and effects of divorce shall be determined under the law of the state with which the spouses have the "closest relationship."[87] The Taiwanese codification has the same rules for these two subjects, as well as for engagements to marry and for the matrimonial regime.[88] At least 16 codifications have a similar rule for the effects of marriage,[89] as does the 1987 Hague Convention on the Law Applicable to Matrimonial Property Regimes.[90] Portugal[91] and Poland[92] have a similar rule for the law applicable to adoption, as does Belgium for the filiation of children of same-sex relations.[93]

f. The Closest Connection as a Pointer in Cases involving a Federal or Other Plurilegal State

Several codifications use the closest-connection factor as an orientation vector when a choice-of-law rule refers to the law of a federal or other plurilegal country with sub-national or internal legal systems. These codifications provide that such a reference shall be to the sub-national system chosen by that country's rules, but if those rules are inconclusive or nonexistent, the reference shall be to the sub-national system that has the "closest connection" to the case at hand. For example, Article 18 of the Italian codification provides that "[i]f reference is made to the law of a State having a non-unified legal system as regards territory or persons, the applicable law shall be determined

---

[87] North Korean codif. art. 37.

[88] *See* Taiwanese codif. art. 45(2) (effect of engagement to marry), art. 47 (effects of marriage), art. 48(2) (matrimonial regime), art. 50 (divorce).

[89] *See* Albanian codif. art. 23.3 (personal effects of marriage); Austrian codif. art. 18 (personal effects of marriage); Cape Verde codif. art. 52 (relations between spouses); East Timor codif. art. 51 (relations between spouses); Estonian codif. § 57 (legal consequences of marriage); Finish Marriage Act §§ 128(2) and 129(4) (personal legal effects of marriage and matrimonial regime); German codif. art. 14 (general effects of marriage); Japanese codif. art. 25 (effects of marriage); South Korean codif. art. 37 (general effects of marriage); Macau codif. arts 50 and 58; Dutch codif. art. 36 (personal effects); Polish codif. art. 51.2 (personal relations); Portuguese codif. art. 52 (relations between spouses); Slovenian codif. art. 38(4) (personal and property effects); Swiss codif. art. 48 (effects of marriage); Ukrainian codif. art. 60 (legal consequences of marriage). Some of these codifications use the connecting factor of domicile rather than nationality.

[90] *See* Hague Convention on the Law Applicable to Matrimonial Property Regimes, art.4(3) (1978). The convention is in force in France, Luxemburg, and the Netherlands.

[91] *See* Portuguese codif. art. 60(2) (providing that, if the adoptive parents do not have the same nationality, the applicable law is that of the state with which the family life of the adoptive parents has the closest connection.). For identical provisions, *see* Cape Verde codif. art. 58.2; East Timor codif. art. 57.2; Macau codif. art. 56.2.

[92] *See* Polish codif. art. 57 (providing that if the adoptive parents do not have the same nationality, domicile, or habitual residence, the applicable law is that of the state with which both spouses are most closely connected.).

[93] *See* Belgian codif. art. 62(2) (providing that, in cases of conflict between the filiation rules of more than one country, the law of the state with which the case has the closest connections "among all designated legal regimes" shall govern).

according to the criteria of that State's legal system," but if it is impossible to establish such criteria, "the legal system shall be applied that appears to be most closely connected to the specific case."[94]

Nearly 30 other codifications,[95] as well as the Rome III and Successions regulations,[96] and several Hague Conventions[97] contain similar provisions.

g. *The Closest Connection as a Gap-Filler for Unprovided-For Cases*

Finally, in some codifications, the closest-connection factor plays the role of a gap-filler for cases for which the codification does not provide a choice-of-law rule or for which a particular rule does not provide a clear choice-of-law solution. For example, the Polish codification provides that, if the codification and other Polish statutes or treaties do not designate the applicable law, or if it is impossible to establish the circumstances upon which the application of foreign law depends, the applicable law is the law of the state that has the closest connection.[98] The Russian codification provides that, if it is impossible to determine the applicable law through the rules provided in the codification or elsewhere in Russian statutes or treaties, the law of the country with which the case is "most closely connected" shall be applied.[99] Similar rules exist in other codifications, including those of Armenia, Austria, Belarus, Bulgaria, Burkina Faso, China, the Czech Republic, FYROM, Kazakhstan, Kyrgyzstan, Liechtenstein, Moldova, Poland, Tajikistan, Ukraine, and Uzbekistan.[100]

In a more specific context, the closest-connection factor serves as a residual gap-filler for contracts that do not contain an effective choice-of-law clause and in which the

---

[94] Italian codif. art. 18.

[95] *See* the codifications of Albania (art. 4); Armenia (art. 1256); Austria (art. 5(3)); Azerbaijan (art. 6); Belgium (art. 17); Bulgaria (art. 41.4); Burkina Faso (art. 1007); China (art. 10); Croatia (art. 10); Estonia (art. 3); FYROM (art 10); Georgia (art. 7); Germany (art. 4); Lithuania (art. 1.10.6); The Netherlands (art. 15.3); Japan (art. 38.3); South Korea (art. 3.3); Macau (art. 19); Moldova (art. 1581); Poland (art. 9); Quebec (art. 3077); Russia (art. 1188); Serbia (art. 35.3); Slovenia (art. 9); Taiwan (art. 5); Tunisia (art. 2.2); Turkey (art. 2(5)); Ukraine (art. 9); and Uruguay (draft art. 2(2)).

[96] *See* Rome III, arts. 14 (inter-territorial conflicts) and 15 (interpersonal conflicts); Successions Regulation art. 36(2)b and (3) (inter-territorial conflicts) and art. 37 (inter-personal conflicts).

[97] *See, e.g.,* Hague Convention on the Conflicts of Laws Relating to the Form of Testamentary Dispositions of 5 October 1961, art. 1; Hague Convention of 1 August 1989 on the Law Applicable to Succession to the Estates of Deceased Persons, arts. 19(3)(b), 20; Hague Convention of 19 October 1996 on Jurisdiction, Applicable Law, Recognition, Enforcement and Co-operation in Respect of Parental Responsibility and Measures for the Protection of Children, arts. 47(4), 49(b); Hague Convention of 13 January 2000 on the International Protection of Adults, art. 45(d) and (f) and art. 47(b); Hague Protocol of 23 November 2007 on the Law Applicable to Maintenance Obligations, art. 16(d) and (e).

[98] Polish codif. arts. 67 and 10.

[99] Russian codif. art. 1186(2).

[100] *See* Armenian codif. art. 1253(2); Austrian codif. art. 1(2); Belarus codif. art 1093(3); Bulgarian codif. art. 2(2); Burkina Faso codif. art. 1003(3); Chinese codif. art. 3(2); Czech codif. art. 25; FYROM codif. art. 4; Kazakhstan codif. art. 1084.2; Kyrgyzstan codif. art. 1167(3); Liechtenstein codif. art. 1(2); Moldova codif. art. 1578; Polish codif. art. 10; Tajikistan codif. art. 1191.2; Ukrainian codif. art. 4(2); Uzbekistan codif. art. 1158.

applicable law cannot be determined through other criteria, such as the "characteristic performance." This was the case with the Rome Convention,[101] and remains so with the Rome I Regulation[102] and other codifications influenced by them, as discussed earlier.

It is worth noting that a few other codifications employ an even more malleable concept than the closest connection for choosing the law governing the unprovided-for cases. The Taiwanese codification—which otherwise relies extensively on the closest-connection factor—states that in unprovided-for cases, the applicable law shall be chosen under the principles derived from "the nature of law."[103] The codifications of Jordan, Slovenia, Qatar, U.A.E, and Yemen are only slightly more specific. They provide that the "principles of private international law" apply to conflicts for which these codifications do not designate the governing law.[104] The FYROM codification authorizes resort to the same principles, along with the principles of the codification itself and the forum's legal system as a whole.[105] Finally, the Mongolian codification unhesitantly authorizes resort to unspecified "foreign laws" when Mongolian law is silent or unclear.[106]

B. OTHER SOFT CONNECTING FACTORS

The extensive use of the closest connection in so many codifications injects a considerable amount of flexibility in the judicial choice-of-law process. To be sure, this is primarily a "geographical" flexibility—as opposed to a content-dependent or policy-based flexibility—and is very much in keeping with the Savignian objective of seeking the seat of the relationship. Even so, it is a step forward from the traditional choice-of-law rules, which assigned a priori a seat to each relationship.

Codifications that are less bound to the Savignian tradition feel freer to employ soft connecting factors that are less geographical and more policy-oriented. This is the case with the two American codifications, those of Louisiana and Oregon. The principal "connecting factor" of the Louisiana codification is anything but a geographical pointer. Rather it describes the *objective* of the choice-of-law process: to identify and apply the law of "the state whose policies would be *most seriously impaired* if its law were not applied" to the particular issue.[107] In a similar vein, the objective of the choice-of-law

---

[101] *See* Rome Convention, art. 4(5).

[102] *See* Rome I, art. 4(4) ("Where the law applicable cannot be determined pursuant to paragraphs 1 or 2, the contract shall be governed by the law of the country with which it is most closely connected.").

[103] Taiwanese codif. art. 1.

[104] Jordanian codif. art. 25; Slovenian codif. art 3; Qatar codif. art. 34; U.A.E codif. art. 23; Yemen codif. art. 34. *See also* Slovak codif. art. 10 (providing that, in the absence of an effective choice of law, contracts are governed by the law whose application is "in keeping with a reasonable settlement of the respective relationship.").

[105] *See* FYROM codif. art. 4.

[106] *See* Mongolian codif. art. 540.3 ("Foreign laws and acts can be considered for establishing the legal framework in case Mongolian law does not specify clearly the civil relation's aspect...or it is impossible to decide the case through interpretation of Mongolian law.").

[107] *See* La. codif. arts. 3515, 3519, 3537, and 3542 (emphasis added). For further discussion, *see infra* at VII.

process under the Oregon codification is to identify and apply the law of "the state whose contacts with the parties and the dispute and whose policies on the disputed issues make application of the state's law the *most appropriate* for those issues."[108] Again, this is a qualitative rather than geographical objective.

In the codification of Puerto Rico, a mixed legal system associated with the United States, the objective of the choice-of-law process is to identify and apply the law of the state that has the "most significant connection" ("*la conexión más significativa*")[109] to the parties and the dispute. Reflecting Puerto Rico's cultural equidistance from the two legal traditions, the quoted phrase bears acoustical resemblance with both the "most significant relationship" language of the Restatement (Second)[110] and the "closest" or "stronger" connection of codifications discussed above.[111] Nevertheless, as explained later, the Puerto Rico phrase carries fewer geographical connotations and is intended to invite a more qualitative analysis than the adjectives "stronger" or "closer" used in those codifications.[112]

Finding the "most appropriate law" is also the stated objective of other codifications, albeit in more limited contexts. For example, the Greek Civil Code of 1940 provides that, in the absence of a choice of law by the parties, "a contract is governed by the law which according to all the circumstances is the most appropriate."[113] Although Rome I preempts this provision, it remains applicable for contracts falling outside the scope of Rome I. Likewise, a Portuguese arbitration statute provides that, in the absence of a choice of law by the parties, the arbitrator is free to apply the law "most appropriate" to the dispute.[114]

Finally, as noted earlier, the codifications of Jordan, Slovenia, Qatar, U.A.E, and Yemen use soft connecting factors other than the closest connection for unprovided-for cases.[115] In a different vein, the Slovak codification provides that, in the absence of an effective choice-of-law clause, contracts are governed by the law whose application is "in keeping with a reasonable settlement of the respective relationship."[116]

---

[108] Or. Rev. Stat. § 15.445 (for tort conflicts) (emphasis added). Or. Rev. Stat. 15.360, the corresponding residual provision for contract conflicts, calls for the application of the law that "in light of the multistate elements of the contract…is the most appropriate" for the resolution of the disputed issue.

[109] Puerto Rico draft codif. arts. 2, 8, 13, 21, 33, 36, and 45.

[110] *See, e.g.,* Restatement (Second) §§ 145, 188, 222, 283, 291.

[111] The reasons for choosing this particular phrase and its intended meaning are explained by the drafter in S. Symeonides, *Revising Puerto Rico's Conflicts Law,* 428–429.

[112] *See infra* at VII.

[113] Greek Civ. Code, art. 25.

[114] *See* L. De Lima Pinheiro, *Portuguese Report,* at II.

[115] *See supra* note 104.

[116] Slovak codif. art. 10(1). For discussion of an identical provision in the Czechoslovakian codification, *see* M. Pauknerová, *Czech Report,* at II.

VI. Escape Clauses

As Aristotle recognized so many centuries ago, any pre-formulated rule, no matter how carefully or wisely drafted, may, "because of its generality,"[117] or because of its specificity, produce results that are contrary to the purpose for which it was designed. In the words of Peter Hay, this "is a natural consequence of the difference between *law making* and *law application*."[118]

With some notable exceptions, most modern legislatures seem to be fully aware of the inherent limitations in their ability to anticipate everything. In recent years, those that have codified choice of law have recognized these limitations and have taken the previously unprecedented step of expressly granting judges the authority to adjust (or avoid altogether) the application of a rule when the circumstances of the individual case so dictate. In addition to traditional escapes, such as *ordre public* or *fraude à la loi*, this grant of authority takes the form of escape clauses attached to the rules.[119] This section discusses these escapes.

It is an open question whether escape clauses are a bolder step toward flexibility than rules containing flexible connecting factors such as those discussed above. Obviously, much depends on the language, number, and especially the breadth of the escape clauses. For example, escape clauses phrased in terms that make them employable only in statistically rare cases are clearly a smaller step toward flexibility than escapes phrased in less categorical language. One suspects, however, that although judges would welcome both rules containing flexible connecting factors and escapes attached to fixed rules, if forced to, they would probably choose the former.

Escape clauses can be divided into two categories:

(1) General escapes, namely those that apply to all (or most) choice-of-law rules in a comprehensive choice-of-law codification; and

(2) Specific escapes, namely those that are attached to a particular choice-of-law rule, or small group of rules, so as to provide an exception to that rule or rules.

---

[117] Aristotle, *Nicomachean Ethics, supra.*

[118] P. Hay, Flexibility versus Predictability and Uniformity in Choice of Law, 226 *Recueil des cours* 281, 291 (1991-I).

[119] Escape clauses in PIL were the subject of the XIVth International Congress of Comparative Law held in Athens in 1994. The general and national reports on this subject were published in D. Kokkini-Iatridou, *Les Clauses d'Exception en matière de Conflits de Lois et de Conflits de Juridictions—ou le principe de proximité* (1994). *See also* Cézar E. Dubler, *Les clauses d' exception en droit international privé* (1983); C. Adesina Okoli & G. Omoshemime Arishe, The Operation of the Escape Clauses in the Rome Convention, Rome I Regulation and Rome II Regulation, 8 *J. Priv. Int'l L.* 514 (2012); P. Hay & Ellis, Bridging the Gap between Rules and Approaches in Tort Choice of Law in the United States: A Survey of Current Case Law, 27 *Int'l Lawyer* 369 (1993); F. Mosconi, Exceptions to the Operation of Choice of Law Rules, 217 *Recueil des cours*, 9, 189–195 (1989-V); K. Nadelmann, Choice of Law Resolved by Rules or Presumptions with an Escape Clause, 33 *Am. J. Comp. L.* 297 (1985); S. Symeonides, Exception Clauses in American Conflicts Law, 42 *Am. J. Comp. L.* 813 (1994-Supp.); A.E. von Overbeck, Les questions générales du droit international privé à la lumière des codifications et projets récents, 176 *Recueil des cours* 9, 186–207 (1982-III).

The line between general and specific escapes is blurred in the case of partial choice-of-law codifications (such as those limited to contracts or torts) that contain escapes applicable to all or most choice-of-law rules of that codification. Rome I, Rome II, and the Oregon statutes for contract and tort conflicts are examples of this situation. For the purposes of this chapter, all escape clauses contained in partial, as opposed to comprehensive, codifications are considered specific rather than general escapes.

A. GENERAL ESCAPES

Article 15 of the Swiss codification is the prime example of a general escape. It provides that the law designated as applicable by any of the codification's rules is "by way of exception" not to be applied if, "from the totality of the circumstances, it is manifest that the particular case has only a very slight connection to that law and has a much closer relationship to another law."[120]

Article 19 of the Belgian codification contains a two-prong escape. It provides that the law designated as applicable by the codification should not be applied if "it manifestly appears from the totality of the circumstances" that the matter has "only a very slight connection" with the state of the designated law but is "very closely connected" to another state. In such case, the law of the latter state governs.[121] The article also provides more guidance for the judicial deployment of the escape. In applying this escape, the court should give due consideration to "the need of predictability of the applicable law" and "the circumstance that the relevant legal relationship was validly established in accordance with the private international law of the States with which the legal relationship was connected when it was created."[122]

In a similar vein, Article 8 of the Dutch codification provides that the law designated as applicable by a Dutch statutory choice-of-law rule that is "based on the presumption of a close connection with that law" shall exceptionally not be applied "if, given all circumstances, the presumed close connection is hardly existent and a much closer connection exists to another law."[123]

---

[120] Swiss codif. art. 15. The second paragraph of the article provides that the escape is not applicable in cases of choice of law by the parties. In the words of Professor Siehr, "[t]his escape clause…replaces overgeneralized hard and fast conflicts rules with new specific conflict-of-law rules. As a safety valve, Article 15(1) tries to adjust specific situations to new rules, and it is understood that this adjustment is made *modo legislatoris*, according to the Aristotelian tradition of Article 1(2) Swiss Civil Code…." K. Siehr, *Swiss Report*, at IV.15, in S. Symeonides, *Progress or Regress* 383, 391. For a discussion of this article and cases applying it, *see* A. Bonomi, *Swiss Report*, at II; A.E. von Overbeck, The Fate of Two Remarkable Provisions of the Swiss Statute on Private International Law, 1 *Ybk. Priv. Int'l L.* 119 (1999); A. Bucher, La clause d'exception dans le contexte de la partie générale de la LDIP, in A. Bonomi & E. Cashin Ritaine (eds.), *Vingt ans LDIP* 59 (2009).

[121] Belgian codif. art. 19 of the Belgian. For discussion, *see* J. Erauw & M. Fallon, *Belgian Report*, at II.2(d).

[122] Belgian codif. art. 19(2). The article also provides that this escape does not apply when there is a valid contractual choice of law, or when the codification's designation of the applicable law is "based on its content." *Id.* art. 19(3).

[123] Dutch codif. art. 8. For discussion, *see* K. Boele-Woelki & D. van Iterson, *Dutch Report*, at 4.1.4. This provision does not apply when the parties have made a valid choice of the applicable law. *Id.*

Similar general escapes, with slight variations in phraseology, exist in other codifications, including those of Argentina,[124] FYROM,[125] South Korea,[126] Lithuania,[127] Quebec,[128] Serbia,[129] Slovenia,[130] and Ukraine.[131]

Although the above escapes differ in their wording, they nevertheless possess several common substantive features that are noted below, together with their differences.

- All of these escapes, except the Lithuanian one, can displace not only a foreign law, but also the law of the forum.
- None of these escapes apply when the applicable law is validly chosen by the parties.[132]
- All of these escape clauses require a comparative evaluation—specifically, a comparison between the connections of the case to the state whose law is designated

---

[124] Article 2597 of the Argentine draft codification provides that the designated law should not be applied when, based on all the circumstances of the case, it is clear that the situation does not have "relevant ties" with that law and instead has very close ties with another state's law whose application provides predictability and under whose rules the relationship was validly established. This exception does not apply to cases of contractual choice of law.

[125] See FYROM codif. art. 3(1) (providing that the designated law shall not apply when it has no "significant connection" with the case and there is a "manifestly closer connection" with another law).

[126] Article 8(1) of the South Korean codification provides that if the law designated as applicable by the codification is "only slightly connected with the legal relationship concerned, and it is evident that the law of another country is most closely connected with the legal relationship," the law of the other country shall apply. The second paragraph of the article provides that this escape does not apply in cases of contractual choice of law. For a discussion of this article, see K. Suk, South Korean Report, at II.

[127] Article 1.11(3) of the Lithuanian codification provides that "the applicable foreign law may not be given effect where, in the light of all attendant circumstances of the case, it becomes evident that the foreign law concerned is clearly not pertinent to the case or its part, with the case in question being more closely connected with the law of another state." (emphasis added). This provision does not apply where the applicable law is determined by the agreement of the parties. Id.

[128] Article 3082 of the Quebec codification provides that the law designated as applicable by the codification shall not apply "if, in the light of all attendant circumstances, it is clear that the situation is only remotely connected with that law and is much more closely connected with the law of another country...." For discussion of this article and cases applying it, see F. Sabourin, Quebec Report, at II(a).

[129] Article 36 of the Serbian draft codification provides that law designated as applicable by the codification does not apply "if from all circumstances it appears manifestly that the matter has only a very slight connection" with that law "but is very closely connected to another state," in which case the law of that other state shall be applied. This article also provides that this escape does not apply in cases of choice of law by the parties or if the codification's choice of law "is meant to produce a substantive legal result." Id. This escape also does not apply in cases of infringement of intellectual property rights (art. 129), contracts involving real rights in immovable property (art. 138), consumer contracts (art. 141), and environmental torts (art. 165).

[130] Article 2(1) of the Slovenian codification provides that the law designated as applicable by the codification shall not apply "in exceptional cases where, having regard for all circumstances of the case, it is evident that the connection with that law is not of greatest importance and that the case is more closely connected with another law."

[131] Article 4(3) of the Ukrainian codification provides that the law of the designated state does not apply if that state has an "insignificant connection" with the case and another state has a "closer connection." This exception does not apply in cases of a valid choice of law by a party or parties.

[132] Each of the escapes contains language to this effect.

as applicable by the codification (e.g., state A) and the connections to another state (e.g., state B). If the connections to state A are "too slight" or attenuated and the connections to state B are "manifestly...much closer," then the law of state B displaces that of state A. As the quoted words indicate, the threshold for employing these escapes is intended to be quite high. The escapes are to be employed only in exceptional cases, when the connections of the case to the two states are "manifestly" and highly unequal.

- This required comparison of "connections" suggests that these escapes are intended to provide an exception from only those choice-of-law rules that are themselves based on the principle of the closest connection (known as the "principle of proximity") and not rules that are based on other factors, such as the substantive content of the applicable law. Some commentators have taken exactly this position.[133] However, the wording of most of the escapes is much broader. They speak of "the law designated as applicable" by the codification's other rules, without any particular limitation. Only three escapes use language that expresses the intention suggested above:

(1) The Dutch escape, which provides that the law designated as applicable by a choice-of-law rule *"based on the presumption of a close connection with that law"* shall exceptionally not be applied if *"the presumed close connection"* is not in fact close and there exists a much closer connection with another law;[134]

(2) The Belgian escape, which is inoperable against rules that designate the applicable law "based on its content";[135] and

(3) The Serbian escape, which is also inoperable when the codification's choice of law "is meant to produce a substantive legal result."[136]

- The reference to "connections" and its geographic connotations suggest that the escapes are intended to operate only within the confines of "conflicts justice" and should not be employed solely because of dissatisfaction with the substantive quality of the result the applicable law produces ("material justice").[137] This is the prevailing view among Swiss scholars.[138] The Belgian and Serbian escapes quoted above do not necessarily support a contrary argument. The fact that the Belgian and Serbian drafters declared these escapes inoperable against rules in

---

[133] For the view that the Swiss escape should be so limited, *see* Bucher, *supra* note 120, at 61–62. For a contrary opinion, *see* von Overbeck, *supra* note 120, at 130. *See also* K. Boele-Woelki & D. van Iterson, *Dutch Report*, at 4.1.4 (stating that the Explanatory Report to the Dutch draft states that the escape cannot displace choice-of-law rules based on the "favour principle" or the "protection principle").

[134] Dutch codif. art. 8 (emphasis added).

[135] Belgian codif. art. 19(3).

[136] Serbian codif. art. 36.3.

[137] The concepts of "conflicts justice" and "material justice" are discussed in Chapter 6, *infra*.

[138] *See* A. Bonomi, *Swiss Report*, at II.1.

which *the drafters* chose the applicable law based on its content ("material justice") does not necessarily mean that the drafters would wish the courts to deviate from other rules based *on the courts'* sense of material justice. Nevertheless, at least in Switzerland, courts have employed the escapes in ways motivated by considerations of material justice.[139] The drafters of the Dutch escape rejected a broader escape based on unfairness or unreasonableness for fear that it may lead to a "better law approach."[140] It remains to be seen, however, whether Dutch courts will adhere to the spirit of the adopted text.

Article 1 of the Austrian codification provides a more subtle escape, at least potentially. The first paragraph of this article states the operating principle of the entire codification by providing that "[f]actual situations with foreign contacts shall be judged…according to the legal order to which the strongest connection exists."[141] The second paragraph provides that the codification's choice-of-law rules "shall be considered as expressions of this principle."[142] This paragraph can be interpreted in two different ways. The first is that this provision is no more than a gap-filler to be employed only in cases for which the codification does not designate the applicable law.[143] The second and more logical interpretation is that this provision is a genuine (albeit oblique) general escape from all of the codification's rules. Such an escape would authorize the court to deviate from a particular rule if the court determines that, in the circumstances of a particular case, the rule would lead to a result that is inconsistent with the general principle of the strongest connection. Austrian court decisions support both of these interpretations.[144]

Article 2 of the Bulgarian codification is similar but arguably more capable of functioning as a general escape. Paragraph 1 of the article provides that multistate relationships are governed by the law of the state that has the closest connection with the legal relation at stake, and that the codification's choice-of-law rules "express this principle."[145] Paragraph 2 then states that, if the governing law cannot be determined through those rules, "the law of the State with which the relationship has the closest connection by virtue of other criteria shall apply."[146] The fact that Paragraph 2 expressly addresses the

---

[139] *See id.* at II.1 (discussing the three Swiss court decisions that have applied the Swiss escape thus far). *See also* J. Erauw & M. Fallon, *Belgian Report*, at II.2(d).

[140] K. Boele-Woelki & D. van Iterson, *Dutch Report*, at IV.A.d.25.

[141] Austrian codif. art. 1.

[142] *Id.*

[143] Other codifications contain provisions that function as gap-fillers. For example, Article 26 of the Tunisian codification provides that if the codification does not provide a rule for a particular situation, "il dégagera la loi applicable par une détermination objective de la catégorie juridique de rattachement." Article 1253(2) of the Armenian codification provides that if the codification does not provide a choice-of-law rule for a particular subject, the court should apply "the law most closely connected" with that subject.

[144] For a discussion of these cases, *see* C. Wendehorst, *Austrian Report*, at B.I.

[145] Bulgarian codif. art. 2.1.

[146] *Id.* art. 2.2.

gap-filling function of the closest-connection principle would render the reference to the same principle in Paragraph 1 superfluous, unless that reference was intended to serve as an authorization for an escape when the state designated by a choice-of-law rule turns out *not* to have the closest connection in the particular case.

Article 1003 of the Burkina Faso codification[147] and Article 3 of the Chinese codification have the same capacity to function as general escapes. The Chinese article provides that the law governing a multistate civil relationship "shall have the closest connection" with such relationship, and if the codification does not provide for a particular relationship, "the law of the country that has the closest connection with [that] relationship...shall be applied."[148] As Professor Weizuo Chen astutely observes,

> an escape clause may be derived from this general clause, authorizing Chinese courts to deviate from the choice-of-law rules contained in the codification, *i.e.*, if a civil relationship involving foreign elements has manifestly loose connections with the applicable law designated by the choice-of-law rules of the [codification], but has the closest connection with the law of another country, the law of the latter shall be applied in those exceptional circumstances.[149]

B. SPECIFIC ESCAPES

Specific escapes, namely, escapes that qualify fewer than all of the choice-of-law rules of a particular codification, are much more numerous than general escapes. This is not surprising; after all, the need for legal certainty varies from one area of the law to another. For this reason, the adoption of escape clauses encounters less resistance in some areas of the law (such as torts) than in other areas (such as property), thus making the adoption of specific escapes more palatable to legislators who are less trusting of judges.

1. Escapes Based on the "Closer Connection"

The majority of specific escape clauses are based on the principle of the "closer connection" ("proximity principle"). This is not surprising because most of the escapes accompany choice-of-law rules that themselves are based on the principle of closest connection. The typical escape provides that, if the state whose law is designated as applicable by a particular choice-of-law rule (based on the closest connection) turns out to have an

---

[147] Article 1003 of the Burkina Faso codification provides that multistate legal relationships are governed by the law that has the "strongest connection" and that the codification's choice-of-law rules are "considered as the expression of [this] general principle." The same article also provides that, in the case of a gap or insufficiency in those rules, the judge should be "inspired" by, and draw from, this principle.

[148] Chinese codif. art. 3.

[149] W. Chen, *Chinese Report*, at II.

attenuated connection, and another state has a manifestly much closer connection, the law of the latter state shall govern.

Escape clauses based on this principle can be found in the Rome Convention and now the Rome I Regulation for contracts, and the Rome II Regulation for torts. Article 4(5) of the Rome Convention provided that the presumptive rules of that article "shall be disregarded if it appears from the circumstances as a whole that the contract is more closely connected" with a country other than the country designated by those rules.[150] Paragraph 3 of Article 4 of Rome I contains the same escape in slightly tighter language. It provides that if it is "clear from all the circumstances of the case" that a contract that does not contain a choice-of-law clause is "manifestly more closely connected" with a country other than that indicated by the preceding paragraphs of that article, the law of that other country shall apply.[151]

Rome II contains similar escapes in its general rule of Article 4, as well as in the articles dealing with products liability (art. 5), unfair competition cases in which the competition exclusively affects the interests of a specific competitor (art. 6(2)), unjust enrichment (art. 10), *negotiorum gestio* (art. 11), and *culpa in contrahendo* (art. 12). The escapes provide that, if it is "clear from all the circumstances of the case" that the tort is "manifestly more closely connected" with a country other the one whose law is designated as applicable by the above articles, then the law of that country governs.[152]

The above escapes are now available in the 27 EU countries in which Rome I and Rome II are in force, whether or not those countries have similar escapes in their own codifications.[153]

Outside the EU, escapes similar to those of the Rome Convention or Rome I can be found in the Hague Sales Convention,[154] and the codifications of Albania, Argentina,

---

[150] Also, paragraph 2(b) of Article 6 provided that, in the absence of an effective choice of law by the parties, employment contracts in which the employee does not habitually carry out his work in any one country are to be governed by the law of the country in which the place of business through which he was engaged is situated, "unless it appears from the circumstances as a whole that the contract is more closely connected with another country, in which case the contract shall be governed by the law of that country."

[151] A similar escape is found in arts. 5(3) (contracts of carriage), 7(2) (insurance contracts), and 8(4) (individual employment contracts).

[152] Rome II, arts. 4(3), 5(2), 10(4), 11(4), and 12(2)(c). The first two of these provisions state that a "manifestly closer connection" with another country "might" be based on a preexisting relationship between the parties, such as a contract, that is "closely connected with the tort/delict in question."

[153] *See, e.g.,* Austrian codif. §§ 35(3) for contracts and 48(2) for torts; Bulgarian codif. arts. 94(8) for contracts and 105(3) for torts; Czech codif. arts. 84 and 87 for contracts, and arts. 84 and 101 for torts; Estonia, art. 34(6) for contracts, 36(3) for employment contracts, 53(1) for torts; German codif. arts. 28(5) for contracts, 30(2), last sentence, and 41 for torts; Hungarian codif. arts. 24–35 for contracts and torts; Lithuania codif. art. 1.37(4) for contracts; Romanian codif. art. 78(2) for contracts.

[154] *See* art. 8(3) of the Hague Convention for the Law Applicable to the International Sales of Goods (1986) (providing that "where, in the light of the circumstances as a whole…, the contract is manifestly more closely connected with a law which is not the law which would otherwise be applicable to the contract…, the contract is governed by that other law."). This convention is not yet in force.

Serbia, Taiwan, and Turkey.[155] For torts, escapes similar to those of Rome II can be found in the codifications of Albania, FYROM, Japan, Serbia, Taiwan, and Turkey.[156]

In the area of successions, specific escapes based on the closer connection are found in the EU Successions Regulation,[157] the Hague Convention on the Law Applicable to Estates,[158] the Finnish Inheritance Code,[159] and the Burkina Faso codification.[160]

In other areas, escapes based on the closer connection are found in the provisions of the German codification dealing with property,[161] and the provisions of the Polish codification dealing with goods in transit.[162] The Hague conventions dealing with maintenance,[163] and the protection of children,[164] and adults[165] also employ similar (and indeed

---

[155] *See* Albanian codif. arts. 45.4 and 46.3 for all contracts, and 50.4 for carriage contracts; Argentinean draft codif. art. 2653; Serbian draft codif. arts. 137.4, 149.3; Taiwanese codif. art. 20; and Turkish codif. art. 24(4) for contracts, art. 27(4) for employment contracts, and art. 28 for contracts relating to intellectual property.

[156] *See* Albanian codif. arts. 56.4 (torts in general), 57.3 (party autonomy), 63.3 (products liability), 68.4 (unjust enrichment), 69.4 (industrial action), and 70.3 (pre-contractual liability); FYROM codif. art. 33(2); Japanese codif. art. 15 (*negotiorum gestio* and unjust enrichment), art. 20 (torts); T. Kanzaki, *Japanese Report*, at II; Serbian codif. art. 161 (torts in general), art. 163 (unfair competition), art. 167 (industrial action); Taiwan codif. arts. 25, 28; R. Chen, *Taiwanese Report*, at XII; Turkish codif. art. 34; Z. Tarman, *Turkish Report*, at II, XII.

[157] Article 21 of the Succession Regulation provides that, unless the decedent had chosen another law (art. 22), the succession is governed by the law of the state of the decedent's last habitual residence. However, if the decedent was "manifestly more closely connected" with another state, the law of the latter state governs.

[158] Article 3 of the 1989 Hague Convention on the Law Applicable to the Estates of Deceased Persons provides that, "in exceptional circumstances," the principle of the closest connection may lead to the application of a law other than the one designated by the Convention. This convention is not yet in force.

[159] *See* Finnish Code Inheritance § 5(3) (providing that although the law of the decedent's nationality governs in certain cases, that law will be displaced by the law of another state with which the decedent had "an essentially closer connection ... taking all circumstances into account").

[160] *See* Burkina Faso codif. art. 1043 (providing that the law of the decedent's last domicile displaces the otherwise applicable national law if the decedent had a closer connection with the domiciliary state).

[161] *See* German codif. art. 46 ("If there is a substantially closer connection with the law of a country other than that which would apply under articles 43 and 45, then that law shall apply.").

[162] *See* Polish codif. art. 43 (providing that rights in goods in transit are governed by the law of the state of dispatch, unless another state has a closer connection, in which case the latter law applies).

[163] *See* Hague Protocol of 23 November 2007 on the Law Applicable to Maintenance Obligations, art. 5 (providing that the court may deviate from the otherwise applicable law if one of the parties objects and "the law of another state, in particular the state of the spouses' last common habitual residence, has a closer connection with the marriage."). This protocol has been ratified by the European Union

[164] *See* Hague Convention of 19 October 1996 on Jurisdiction, Applicable Law, Recognition, Enforcement, and Co-operation in Respect of Parental Responsibility and Measures for the Protection of Children, art. 5(2) (providing that "in so far as the protection of the person or the property of the child requires," a court may "exceptionally apply or take into consideration" the law of a state other than that of the otherwise applicable law if the other state has a "substantial connection" with "the situation"). This convention is in force in 21 countries.

[165] *See* Hague Convention of 13 January 2000 on the International Protection of Adults, art. 13(2) (providing that "in so far as the protection of the person or the property of the adult requires," a court may "exceptionally apply or take into consideration" the law of a state other than that of the otherwise applicable law if the other state has a "substantial connection" with "the situation"). This convention is in force in four countries.

more malleable) escapes. These escapes authorize courts to deviate from the otherwise applicable law and apply the law of another state that has a "*substantial* connection" with the case.[166]

2. Escapes Based on Other Factors

Among the escapes that are based on factors other than the closer connection, Article 1213 of the Russian codification stands out because it is phrased as an *exception* to the closest-connection factor. Article 1213 provides that contracts that do not contain an effective choice-of-law clause are governed by the law of the country with which the contract is "most closely connected." The article then provides several rules presumptively identifying the most closely connected country. However, each of these rules is accompanied by the phrase "unless it otherwise follows from a statute, the terms or the nature of the contract, or *the totality of the circumstances of the case.*"[167] The FYROM codification uses a similar escape.[168]

Article 10 of the Slovak codification begins by stating that contracts that do not contain an effective choice-of-law clause are governed by the law whose application is "in keeping with a reasonable settlement of the respective relationship"[169] and then designates that law for various types of contracts through seven different paragraphs. However, these paragraphs are introduced with the phrase "as a rule," thus allowing courts to deviate from those rules in appropriate cases. In a similar fashion, Article 20 of the Croatian codification introduces 20 rules designating the applicable law for various contracts with the phrase "if … special circumstances of the case do not refer to another law,"[170] thus allowing courts to deviate from these rules if the circumstances of the case so warrant.

Article 9 of the Dutch codification provides a general, renvoi-type escape from its rules in order to protect certain rights acquired under foreign law. Based on the "doctrine of the accomplished fact," Article 9 provides that when a foreign law that is applicable under the choice-of-law rules of an involved foreign state attributes certain consequences to a particular fact, a Dutch court may attribute the same consequences in deviation from its own choice-of-law rules, if failure to do so would constitute "an unacceptable violation of the parties' legitimate expectations or of legal certainty."[171]

---

[166] *See* notes 162–165, *supra* (emphasis added).

[167] Russian codif. art. 1211 (emphasis added). Articles 1203, 1213, 1217, and 1222 contain similar escapes for cases involving, respectively, certain foreign juridical persons, immovable property contracts, unilateral juridical acts, and unfair competition.

[168] *See* FYROM codif. art. 22(2) (providing that a contract is presumed as most closely connected with the home state of the party who is to effect the characteristic performance "unless special circumstances refer to another law.").

[169] Slovak codif. art. 10. For discussion of an identical provision in the Czechoslovakian codification, *see* Pauknerová, *Czech Report,* at II(1)–(2), XII.

[170] Croatian codif. art. 20. For discussion, *see* D. Babić, *Croatian Report,* at C.II.

[171] Dutch codif. art. 9, discussed in Boele-Woelki & Van Iterson, *Dutch Report,* at IV.A.e.

The English statute of 1995, which applied to tort conflicts other than defamation before the adoption of Rome II, contains a general rule in Section 11 and a multifactor escape in Section 12. The escape provides that the law applicable under the general rule of Section 11 will be displaced

> [i]f it appears, in all the circumstances, from a comparison of (a) the significance of the factors which connect a tort or delict with the country whose law would be the applicable law under the general rule; and (b) the significance of any factors connecting the tort or delict with another country, that it is substantially more appropriate for the applicable law for determining the issues arising in the case, or any of those issues, to be the law of the other country[.][172]

Article 3547 of the Louisiana codification provides an escape from all of the codification's articles dealing with tort conflicts (arts. 3543–3546). This article provides that the law applicable under these articles shall not apply if, "from the totality of the circumstances of an exceptional case," it is "clearly evident"[173] under the principles of Article 3542 (the general article for tort conflicts) that the policies of another state would be "more seriously impaired if its law were not applied to the particular issue." In such a case, the law of the latter state applies.[174]

The Oregon codification for contract conflicts articulates its general rule for contracts that do not contain an effective choice-of-law clause in Section 15.360, and then provides a series of presumptive rules for particular types of contracts in Section 15.380. However, the latter section allows a court to deviate from the law designated by those rules if a party demonstrates that the application of that law would be "clearly inappropriate under the principles of [Section] 15.360."[175]

The Oregon codification for tort conflicts articulates its general approach in Section 15.445 and provides particular choice-of-law rules for certain product liability cases in Section 15.435 and for non-product torts in Section 15.440. Both of the latter sections

---

[172] U.K. codif. § 12; C. Roodt, *English Report*, at B.I(b). For critical discussion, *see* R. Fentiman, *English Report* (at 3.v), in S. Symeonides (ed.), *Progress or Regress*, 165, 186, concluding as follows:

> [T]he ambiguity of section 12 has the effect of leaving the design of the exception which it contains— and thus (in effect) of the new choice of law rule in tort—to the courts. This is an arresting example of English law's pragmatic approach to choice of law. Certainly, it reflects the assumption that legal principles should be derived from decided cases over time, as distinct from the view that judicial decisions should reflect pre-ordained principles. Whatever the general merits of such a view it is hard to defend legislation which so conspicuously abstains from offering guidance as to the approach to be adopted.

[173] The word "clearly" and the tautology it produces ("clearly evident") was inserted at the insistence of legislators who wanted to further tighten the escape.

[174] For the history, meaning, and subsequent application of this article, *see* Symeonides, *Louisiana Exegesis*, 763–766; Symeonides, *Two Surprises*, 517–522. For a critique, *see* R. Weintraub, The Contributions of Symeonides and Kozyris to Making Choice of Law Predictable and Just: An Appreciation and Critique, 38 *Am. J. Comp. L.* 511 (1990).

[175] Or. Rev. Stat. § 15.380. For discussion, *see* Symeonides, *Oregon Contracts Exegesis*, 235–245.

contain escapes that allow the court to deviate from the law designated by these sections if a party demonstrates that the application of the law of another state to a disputed issue is "substantially more appropriate under the principles of [Section] 15.445,"[176] in which case the law of the other state would govern that issue.

Section 15.440 contains one additional escape for torts in which both the injurious conduct and the resulting injury occurred in a state other than the home state of either the tortfeasor or the victim and in which the laws of those states conflict. In such cases, the applicable law is the law of the state of conduct and injury. However, an escape provides that if a party demonstrates that, under the circumstances of the particular case, the application of that law to a disputed issue will "not serve the objectives of that law," that issue will be governed by the law selected under the general approach of Section 15.445.[177]

The Puerto Rico draft code contains several escapes, including one for tort conflicts that is modeled after the Louisiana escape. The escape provides that when the code's rules for tort conflicts would produce a result that is "clearly contrary to the objectives"[178] of Article 39 (which articulates the code's general approach for tort conflicts), the applicable law should be selected under the approach of Article 39. For contract conflicts, the draft code provides a general approach in Article 30, followed by presumptive rules for certain types of contracts in Article 31. The latter article also provides, however, that a party may prevent the application of the law designated by these presumptive rules by demonstrating that, with regard to the issue in question, another state has a "manifestly more significant connection to the parties and the transaction in accordance with the principles of Article 30."[179] For child custody cases, Article 20 calls for the application of forum law, unless, under the general article for issues of status, another state has "a more significant connection" to the child and the dispute and the application of the law of that state would "serve the best interest of the child."[180] For matrimonial regimes, Article 24 provides that if the law applicable upon termination of the regime would result in unfairly depriving one spouse of protection accorded by the law previously governing the regime, the court may make "appropriate exceptions or adjustments in order to accord that spouse substantially equivalent protection."[181] Finally, Article 4 provides a general

---

[176] Or. Rev. Stat. §§ 15.435(3) and 15.440(4). For discussion by the article's dafter, *see* Symeonides, *Oregon Torts Exegesis*, 997–1044.

[177] Or. Rev. Stat. § 15.440(3)(b).

[178] Puerto Rico draft codif. art. 39.

[179] *Id.* art. 31. For discussion, *see* Symeonides, *The Puerto Rico Projet*, 424–434.

[180] Puerto Rico draft codif., art. 20.

[181] *Id.* art. 24. With regard to marriage, Article 11 provides that the starting point is the law of the state of the marriage or the state of the first matrimonial domicile. If the marriage was valid in either of those states, the marriage is considered valid, unless it violates a "strong" public policy of the state that, under the general article for status, has a "substantially more significant connection" to the parties and the dispute. *Id.* If the marriage was not valid in either of the two states, the marriage may nevertheless be considered valid "if it would be so considered in another state" that, under the general article, has a "more significant connection" to the parties and the dispute. *Id.*

exception from rules that call for the application of the law of a person's domicile. The exception provides that, when a person's connection to the state of his domicile is "attenuated" and his connections to another state are "significantly stronger and more pertinent to the particular issue," that person may be treated as a domiciliary of the latter state for the purposes of that issue, "provided such treatment is appropriate" under the principles of the code's general article (art. 2).[182]

C. ASSESSMENT OF ESCAPES

It is clear that the introduction of escape clauses is a significant step in the right direction of choice-of-law flexibility and a sign of progress in the art of codification. It is equally clear, however, that not all escapes are born equal. Some escapes promise more than they can deliver. They are phrased in such a tight way as to be employable only in the most extreme of cases. This is particularly true of the escapes based on the closest connection. A good example is the general escape of Rome II, found in paragraph 3 of Article 4, which provides an escape from both the *lex loci* rule of paragraph 1 and the common-domicile rule of paragraph 2. As noted earlier, the escape authorizes the court to apply the law of another country if "it is clear from all the circumstances of the case that the tort/delict is manifestly more closely connected with [that other] country."[183] The two problematic features of this escape are that: (1) it is phrased in exclusively geographical or quantitative terms that are not correlated to an overarching principle, and (2) it does not permit an issue-by-issue evaluation.

1. Too Much Geography, Too Little Principle

The reliance on geography is symbolized by the drafters' choice of the adjective "closer" to qualify the word "connection," rather than, for example, "more significant," which is the critical adjective in the English statute[184] and the Restatement (Second).[185] The finding of a "closer connection" must be based on consideration of "all the circumstances," but, in the absence of any non-quantitative qualifiers, judges will comprehend the quoted phrase primarily if not solely in geographical terms. In one sense, it is almost inevitable that a system of geographically based rules would also rely on geography when formulating escapes from those rules. Rome II is such a system because most of its dispositive rules depend on the place in which a single critical event occurred, or in which one or both parties reside. Very few non-geographical factors affect the choice, and the content of the conflicting laws is a factor that appears only in a few narrow exceptions.[186] Having

---

[182] *Id.* art 4(c).

[183] Rome II, art. 4(3).

[184] *See supra* text at note 172.

[185] *See, e.g., Restatement (Second)* § 146, *infra* at text accompanying note 187.

[186] *See* Symeonides, *Rome II*, 181–183.

relied on geography in erecting this system, the drafters of Rome II may have felt bound to likewise rely on geography to handle the exceptional cases and overcome the inevitable impasses.

The benefits of such logic, however, will rarely overcome its shortcomings. Escapes should be designed to cure the rule's deficiencies, not to reproduce them. To intelligently employ an escape, the court must know the reasons for which the drafters made the choices the rule embodies and the goals it seeks to promote. To simply say that one should look for a "closer" connection gives courts little meaningful guidance and creates the risk of degenerating into a mechanical counting of physical contacts. This risk decreases when the escape is correlated to the overarching principles underlying the rules, and/or when the escape allows an issue-by-issue evaluation.

On this point only, a comparison with the Restatement (Second) can be instructive. Section 6 of the Restatement articulates the overall goal of the choice-of-law process as one of identifying the state that has the "most significant relationship" with the case. Although literally the quoted phrase appears to contemplate a determination based on geography, the content of Section 6 negates any such inference because it lists a series of substantive policies intended to guide this determination. The subsequent sections of the Restatement provide specific rules, most of which contain an escape authorizing the judge to apply the law of another state if, *"with respect to the particular issue,"* that state has a more significant relationship *"under the principles stated in § 6."* [187]

Similarly, Article 3542 of the Louisiana codification enunciates the general goal of the choice-of-law process for tort conflicts as one of identifying the state whose policies would be most seriously impaired if its law were not applied. After establishing specific rules based on that goal, the codification also provides an escape clause in Article 3547 that authorizes the judge to apply the law of another state if, *"under the principles of Article 3542,"* the policies of that other state *"would be more seriously impaired if its law were not applied to the particular issue."* [188]

The italicized phrases signify what is missing from the escape of Article 4(3) of Rome II: issue-by-issue evaluation and correlation to non-geographical overarching principles. The absence of these two elements will lead courts to a mere quantitative employment of the escape, which will help only in the simplest of conflicts.

Let us return to the hypothetical used in Chapter 2, involving a French hunter who, while hunting in Kenya, injured a Belgian hunter with whom he had no preexisting relationship. [189] Suppose that Kenya limits the amount of damages to the equivalent of five thousand euros, while France and Belgium impose no ceiling and define the amount of damages in identical ways. In such a case, there is no reason to apply the

---

[187] *Restatement (Second)* § 146 (emphasis added).

[188] La. codif. art. 3547 (emphasis added). For discussion by the article's drafter, *see* Symeonides, *Louisiana Exegesis,* 763–766.

[189] *See supra* Chapter 2, at IV.D.

Kenyan ceiling and every good reason to apply either Belgian or French law. Yet, in such a case: (1) Article 4(1) of Rome II would mandate the application of the Kenyan ceiling, (2) the common-domicile rule of Article 4(2) would be inoperable, and (3) the escape of Article 4(3) would not correct this wrong choice because neither France nor Belgium would be considered to have a "manifestly closer connection" than Kenya. In contrast, the much briefer and simpler escape found in the unenacted Benelux law would have allowed a court to avoid the application of Kenya law by finding that, with regard to the issue of damages, "the *consequences* of a wrongful act belong to the legal sphere of a country other than [Kenya] where the act took place."[190] Likewise, under the escape of the English statute, a court would compare the "*significance* of the factors" connecting the case with the three countries and conclude that it would be "substantially *more appropriate*" to apply either French or Belgian law "for determining the *issues* arising in the case, or any of those *issues,*" here, the issue of damages.[191]

2. Issue-by-Issue Deployment

The failure to allow an issue-by-issue deployment and evaluation is the second major problem with the Rome II escape (and similar escapes). The escape avoids not only the dirty word "issue," but also the phrase "*obligation* arising out of a tort/delict," which is used earlier in the same article.[192] For the escape to apply, the entire "tort/delict" must be "manifestly more closely connected" with another state, in which case the law of that state will apply to the entire "tort/delict," not to parts or aspects of it. Thus, this is an "all or nothing" proposition, and therein lies its most serious flaw. For example, in the Kenyan hypothetical, one cannot credibly argue that the *entire tort* is "manifestly more closely connected" with either France of Belgium; but one can credibly, indeed persuasively, argue that *one* aspect of the dispute that arises from this tort, that is, the *issue* of the amount of damages, is so connected.

In another publication, this author has attempted to illustrate these flaws through six hypothetical scenarios.[193] That discussion will not be repeated here. Its conclusion was and remains that, although the inclusion of an escape clause in Rome II is a significant step in the right direction, the escape would have benefited from more nuanced and flexible drafting. The drafters' preference for a tight escape that does not swallow the rules is understandable. However, an escape that is so tight as to be rarely utilized, or one that is phrased in broad all-or-nothing terms, is only slightly better than no escape at all.

---

[190] Traité Benelux portant loi uniforme relative au droit international privé, art. 14 (1969) (emphasis added), discussed *supra* Chapter. 2 at IV.A.

[191] English codif. § 12 (emphasis added).

[192] Rome II, art. 4(1) (emphasis added). This phrase could allow a separate evaluation of the potentially multiple obligations that may arise from the same facts, such as (but not only) when the case involves multiple tortfeasors or multiple victims.

[193] *See* Symeonides, *Reciprocal Lessons*, 1773–1782.

The reasons for the EU Council and Commission's political preference for certainty over flexibility are obvious. The primary motive behind the movement to draft Rome II, as well as the choice of the particular instrument for its implementation (a regulation as opposed to a directive), was the need to ensure uniformity of choice-of-law decisions within the European Union.[194] These two bodies must have concluded that uniformity would be in jeopardy if Rome II were to include too many flexible rules or escape clauses. Although this is plausible, it is not necessarily the best conclusion. The argument that a codification intended for application by the courts of different countries cannot afford to be flexible is highly overrated. For example, whatever its other faults, the Rome Convention did not fail for being too flexible.

Moreover, although no one would question the desirability of uniformity and certainty, one can question the extent to which these values should displace all other values of the choice-of-law process, such as the need for sensible, rational, and fair decisions in individual cases. If the American experience has something to offer, it is a reminder that a system that is too rigid (as the First Restatement was) ultimately fails to deliver the promised predictability because, in a democratic society, no system can "mechanize judgment";[195] to the extent that a system attempts to do so, judges will largely ignore it.[196] To be sure, it would be unfair to characterize Rome II as a mechanical system. Its drafters were conscious of the need for flexibility and attempted to provide some degree of it. The question is whether they provided enough of it, a question on which reasonable minds can differ.

VII. "Approaches"

As used in this context, a choice-of-law "approach" is the antithesis of a choice-of-law "rule." Whereas a rule directly designates the applicable law, an approach does so only indirectly (if at all) by providing a list of principles, policies, and factors through which the court will choose the applicable law after considering the circumstances of the individual case. A rule reflects the legislature's a priori choice of law, whereas an approach empowers judges to make the choice a posteriori and ad hoc within certain general parameters.

---

[194] *See* Rome II, recital (6) ("The proper functioning of the internal market creates a need, in order to improve the predictability of the outcome of litigation, certainty as to the law applicable and the free movement of judgments, for the conflict-of-law rules in the Member States to designate the same national law irrespective of the country of the court in which an action is brought.").

[195] D. Cavers, Restatement of the Law of Conflict of Laws, 44 *Yale L.J.* 1478, 1482 (1935).

[196] In Professor Weintraub's words, "[i]ronically Rome II is more likely to succeed in providing reasonable foreseeability if its rules provide sufficient flexibility." R. Weintraub, Rome II and the Tension between Predictability and Flexibility, 19 *Riv. dir. int'le priv. e process.* 561, 561 (2005).

The paradigmatic model of an approach is Section 6 of the Restatement (Second). It sets forth the guiding principles of the choice-of-law process by stating that

> the factors relevant to the choice of the applicable rule of law include (a) the needs of the interstate and international systems, (b) the relevant policies of the forum, (c) the relevant policies of other interested states and the relative interests of those states in the determination of the particular issue, (d) the protection of justified expectations, (e) the basic policies underlying the particular field of law, (f) certainty, predictability, and uniformity of result, and (g) ease in the determination and application of the law to be applied.[197]

These factors—which are not listed in a hierarchical order and may in fact point in different directions in a given case—provide a guiding, as well as a validating, test for applying almost all other sections of the Restatement, most of which incorporate Section 6 by reference.[198]

This clearly is a very open-ended formula. Conventional wisdom suggests that such a formula has no place in a legislative text. Arguably, a codification is not worth undertaking if the legislature is not prepared to provide more specific direction than restating generalities such as those found in Section 6. However, this does not mean that an approach is *incompatible* with codification; an approach is compatible, provided that it is combined with rules. Indeed, the combination of an approach with rules provides a much more versatile tool for attaining an appropriate equilibrium between the competing needs of certainty and flexibility than either an approach or rules alone can accomplish. Rules can provide certainty for those areas of the law (such as property) where certainty is most needed, as well as other areas in which there is a sufficient accumulation of experience to allow articulation of safe and relatively noncontroversial rules. An approach can cover areas in which such experience is lacking and in which the need for certainty is not as pressing. Moreover, an approach can provide the best basis on which to anchor any escapes from the rules for handling exceptional cases.

This combination of rules and approaches is the methodology followed in the two American codifications of Louisiana and Oregon, as well as in the Puerto Rico draft codification. The Louisiana codification employs an approach in Article 3515, the general and residual article for the entire codification. Article 3515 provides that (1) conflicts cases are to be governed by the law of "the state whose policies would be most

---

[197] *Restatement (Second)* § 6.

[198] *See,* e.g., *Restatement (Second)* § 145, which provides that a tort issue is governed by the law of the state that, with respect to that issue, has the most significant relationship to the occurrence and the parties "under the principles stated in § 6."

seriously impaired if its law were not applied" to the particular case, and (2) that state is determined by:

> evaluating the strength and pertinence of the relevant policies of all involved states in the light of: (1) the relationship of each state to the parties and the dispute; and (2) the policies and needs of the interstate and international systems, including the policies of upholding the justified expectations of parties and of minimizing the adverse consequences that might follow from subjecting a party to the law of more than one state.[199]

Similarly, the titles on status, contracts, and torts contain one general, residual, and flexible article[200] that enunciates the general approach for that title, and then a varying number of specific articles that implement the general approach for particular fact situations. The residual article applies to cases and issues not covered by (or disposed of under) the specific articles of that title.

In the titles on status and contracts, the specific articles are few and far between, thus allowing ample room for judicial discretion expressly authorized by the flexible articles dominating those titles. In the all-important Title VII on torts, the specific articles are more numerous, but they are purposefully narrow.[201] They cover only those case patterns that appeared susceptible to relatively noncontroversial rules derived from the accumulated experience of Louisiana and American jurisprudence. The remaining cases have been left for judicial determination under the codification's general approach.[202]

The Oregon codification for torts articulates its general and residual approach in Section 15.445, which calls for the application of the law of the state "whose contacts with the parties and the dispute and whose policies on the disputed issues make application of the state's law the most appropriate for those issues."[203] The section also provides that the "most appropriate law" is determined by:

(1) Identifying the states that have a relevant contact with the dispute, such as the place of the injurious conduct, the place of the resulting injury, the domicile, habitual residence or pertinent place of business of each person, or the place in which the relationship between the parties was centered;

(2) Identifying the policies embodied in the laws of these states on the disputed issues; and

---

[199] La. codif. art. 3515.

[200] *See* La. codif. arts. 3519, 3537, and 3542, respectively.

[201] For specifics, *see* Symeonides, *Louisiana Exegesis*, 729–731, 749–757.

[202] In the other titles of the codification, the same interrelationship exists between specific articles and a residual article, but the residual article is more in the nature of a classic choice-of-law rule. This is the case, for example, in the Titles on marital property and successions because the need for certainty is greater in those areas than in other areas.

[203] Or. Rev. Stat. § 15.445.

(3) Evaluating the relative strength and pertinence of these policies with due regard to: (a) The policies of encouraging responsible conduct, deterring injurious conduct and providing adequate remedies for the conduct; and (b) The needs and policies of the interstate and international systems, including the policy of minimizing adverse effects on strongly held policies of other states.[204]

The codification provides specific choice-of-law for many (but not all) possible tort conflicts or issues. Cases or issues not covered by the specific rules are governed by the law chosen under the general approach of the above-quoted Section 15.445, which also provides the anchor for the escapes contained in some of the specific rules.

The Puerto Rico draft Code follows a similar combination of approach and rules as the Louisiana codification. The general approach is to identify the state of the "most significant connection" by

(a) considering the policies embodied in the particular rules of law claimed to be applicable, as well as any other pertinent policies of the involved states; and

(b) evaluating the strength and pertinence of these policies in the light of: (1) the relationship of each involved state to the parties and the dispute; and (2) the policies and needs of the interstate and international systems."[205]

The state of the "most significant connection" is legislatively identified through the codification's specific rules, and is to be judicially determined in all cases and issues not covered by those rules.

The English choice-of-law statute discussed earlier also employs a rules/approach combination, except that the approach element is confined to the escape from the rules. Section 11 of the statute states the general rule, which calls for the application of the "country in which the events constituting the tort or delict in question occur."[206] Section 12 contains the escape, which is phrased as an approach in the sense that it calls for an individualized evaluation of a series of factors for determining whether to displace the general rule in a particular case.[207]

For cultural and historical reasons, such rules-and-approaches combinations are uncommon in the rest of the world; but they do exist. For example, Article 7 of the 1985 Hague Trust Convention provides that a trust that does not contain a valid choice-of-law

---

[204] *Id.* For discussion of this approach, *see* Symeonides, *Oregon Torts Exegesis*, 1032–1038. The Oregon codification for contracts follows a similar combination of rules and approach as the torts codification. For discussion, *see* Symeonides, *Oregon Contracts Exegesis*, 235–245.

[205] Puerto Rico draft codif. art. 2. For discussion, *see* Symeonides, *The Puerto Rico Projet*, 424–426; Symeonides, *Revising Puerto Rico's Conflicts Law*, 427–433.

[206] Private International Law (Miscellaneous Provisions) Act § 11(c. 42) (1995).

[207] The text of Section 12 is partly reproduced at text accompanying note 172, *supra*.

stipulation is governed by the law with which it is "most closely connected."[208] That law is identified by considering the place of administration of the trust designated by the settlor, the situs of the trust assets, the trustee's place of residence or business, and the "objects of the trust and the places where they are to be fulfilled."[209] The fact that this is a fairly open-ended approach has not prevented 11 countries, including some civil law countries such as Italy and Switzerland, from ratifying the convention.[210] In addition, the Czech and Quebec codifications have adopted the very same approach.[211]

The Mexico City Convention and the Venezuelan codification also employ an approach of sorts for contracts that do not contain a valid choice-of-law clause. Article 9 of the Convention and Article 30 of the Venezuelan codification provide, respectively, that such a contract is governed by the law of the state with which it has the "closest ties" or is "most directly linked," after considering "all objective and subjective elements" of the contract. The Convention provides that the court will also consider the "general principles of international commercial law recognized by international organizations," and the "guidelines, customs, and principles of international commercial law as well as commercial usage and practices…in order to discharge the requirements of justice and equity in the particular case."[212] The Venezuelan codification calls for consideration of the "General Principles of Business Law accepted by international organizations" and the "norms, customs, and principles of International Business Law, as well of generally accepted trade uses and practices, with the purpose of reifying the requirements imposed by justice and fairness in the solution of a concrete case."[213]

VIII. A Comparison with Uncodified Choice-of-Law Systems

By definition, countries that choose to not codify their choice of law allow a greater degree of judicial discretion and thus greater flexibility than is available in countries with codified choice of law. As an Australian author observed, "[b]y their very nature, judge-made rules are much more flexible than rules enshrined in legislation."[214] There is "a much greater degree of judicial discretion that can be exercised when it comes to

---

[208] Hague Convention of 1 July 1985 on the Law Applicable to Trusts and on Their Recognition, art. 7. For the text, see http://www.hcch.net/index_en.php?act=conventions.text&cid=59.

[209] Id.

[210] The Convention is in force in 11 countries: Australia, Canada, Italy, Liechtenstein, Luxemburg, Malta, Monaco, Netherlands, San Marino, Switzerland, and the United Kingdom.

[211] See Czech codif. art. 73; Quebec codif. art. 3107.

[212] Mexico City Convention, arts. 9 and 10.

[213] Venezuelan codif. arts. 30 and 31; E. Hernández-Bretón, *Venezuelan Report*, at XIII. For partly similar provisions, *see* Uruguayan Draft arts. 51 and 13(3) (the latter regarding international trade law); C. Fresnedo de Aguirre, *Uruguayan Report*, at XI.3.

[214] A. De Jonge, *Australian Report,* at II.A.

applying, escaping from, or altering common law choice of law rules than where such rules are enshrined in legislation."[215]

Nevertheless, uncodified choice-of-law systems cannot entirely avoid the tension between certainty and flexibility and the quest for the "right" equilibrium between them. One means of accomplishing this equilibrium is by enacting statutory choice-of-law rules in some areas[216] and then confronting the tension in the remaining areas by following, distinguishing, evading, or overruling existing judicial precedent. Moreover, over time, uncodified choice-of-law systems also experience similar cyclical movements from certainty to flexibility, and vice versa, as do codified systems.

A. THE AMERICAN CONFLICTS EXPERIENCE: FROM CERTAINTY TO REVOLUTION, AND THEN?

American conflicts law graphically illustrates such a movement. Although never codified, American conflicts law acquired at one point all the characteristics of a rigid system. This occurred in the 1930s, when the American Law Institute promulgated the first Restatement of Conflict of Laws, which was drafted by Professor Joseph Beale.[217] Technically, a Restatement is not a statute, much less a code. Rather, it is a private document that courts may choose to adopt or not adopt, in whole or in part, with or without modifications.[218] However, American courts decided to adopt the Restatement wholesale, perhaps preferring the certainty of a clear but flawed document rather than the uncertainty of the common law. Indeed, although academic commentators criticized the Restatement from its very inception, most American courts eventually adopted it, albeit with varying degrees of enthusiasm. As late as the middle of the twentieth century, the Restatement enjoyed an almost universal judicial following.

1. The Certainty of Rules

The Restatement was a complete, organized, and disciplined network of bilateral, fixed, neutral, and detailed choice-of-law rules designed to provide solutions for every conflicts case, and aspiring to eliminate forum shopping and to foster international or interstate uniformity.

---

[215] *Id. See also* G. Cordero Moss, *Norwegian Report,* at II ("The mere circumstance that conflict rules are mainly not codified, and that those rules that are codified are the result of international obligations of the State rather than of an internal process, testify that the legal system traditionally has not considered certainty of the law in this field as a main priority.").

[216] Australia, Denmark, England, Finland, Israel, and Norway, are among the countries that have followed this path. *See, respectively,* A. De Jonge, *Australian Report,* at II.A; J. Lookofsky, *Danish Report,* at II.; C. Roodt, *English Report,* at B.I; U. Liukkunen, *Finish Report,* at II; T. Einhorn, *Israeli Report,* at II; G. Cordero Moss, *Norwegian Report,* at II.

[217] *See supra* Chapter 2 at I, II.A and Chapter 3 at I.

[218] Moreover, as its name suggests, a restatement is not supposed to create new law but rather to restate and recast the existing common law. However, the first Conflicts Restatement was more of a pre-statement of Beale's

Unfortunately, these rules were also mechanical and rigid. They completely sacrificed flexibility in favor of certainty and an ill-conceived ideological purity. This was not their only flaw. Among their many other ones was an excessive reliance on territoriality and a relative indifference to the content of the territorially chosen law. But most of these flaws could have been cured if the rules were accompanied by exceptions allowing judicial deviation in appropriate atypical cases. It is precisely the lack of such exceptions, the lack of an escape hatch, that built up the pressure for a judicial "revolution."

2. Discontent and Revolution

In the beginning, judicial discontent with the Restatement was quiet and oblique. In the late 1950s, judges began deviating from the Restatement's rules by inventing their own escapes, such as the manipulation of the characterization and localization processes, and an expansive application of the only authorized exception, the *ordre public* exception.[219]

Gradually, however, even these escapes proved inadequate to relieve the pressure, prompting many courts to totally abandon the *lex loci delicti* and *lex loci contractus* rules in favor of flexible, open-ended "approaches." What later came to be known as a revolution began in the 1960s, caught fire in the 1970s, spread in the 1980s, and finally declared victory in the 1990s.[220] The result was the demolition of the traditional system, at least in tort and contract conflicts. Today, only 10 US jurisdictions follow the traditional system in tort conflicts, and only 11 do so in contract conflicts.[221]

3. The Demise of Rules

The revolution changed American conflicts law in many beneficial, and some inevitable, ways.[222] However, one change that was neither beneficial nor inevitable was the denouncement of not only the particular rules of the First Restatement, but also *all* choice-of-law rules in general. Brainerd Currie, the revolution's chief protagonist, proclaimed that "we are better off without choice of law rules."[223]

This extreme position, which initially found many followers, was problematic both within the context of a single state and at the national level. In the context of a single state, this position dealt a decisive blow to legal certainty. From a national perspective, this

---

own views rather than a restatement of the common law. *See* S. Symeonides, *The First Conflicts Restatement*, 57–62, 66–78.

[219] *See* Hay Borchers & Symeonides, *Conflict of Laws*, 145–175; Symeonides, *American PIL* 74–85.

[220] For documentation and discussion of this movement, *see* Symeonides, *Revolution*, 37–62, *et passim*.

[221] *See* Symeonides, *Choice of Law in 2012*, at 279; Symeonides, *Revolution*, 38–50.

[222] *See* Symeonides, *Revolution*, 419–421.

[223] *See* Currie, *Selected Essays* 180 ("The [traditional] rules […] have not worked and cannot be made to work […]. But the root of the trouble goes deeper. In attempting to use rules we encounter difficulties that stem not from the fact that the particular rules are bad, […] but rather from the fact that we have such rules at all."). *See also id.* at 183 ("We would be better off without choice-of-law rules.").

position destroyed the unity, or at least uniformity, of American choice of law by replacing Beale's cacophonous system with an uncoordinated dissonant polyphony of "approaches."

4. Excessive Flexibility and Its Price

The revolution did not aspire to and did not produce a new rule system to replace the old one. Instead, the revolution offered conflicting and open-ended "approaches," all of which required an individualized handling of each case. The result was that, in a relatively short time, American conflicts law began looking like "a tale of a thousand-and-one-cases" in which "each case [was] decided as if it were unique and of first impression."[224]

Just as the Restatement had gone too far toward certainty to the exclusion of flexibility, the revolution went too far in its infatuation with flexibility. This move had its own price tag. Although flexibility is preferable to uncritical rigidity, too much flexibility can be as problematic as no flexibility at all.[225] Besides increasing litigation costs[226] and wasting judicial resources,[227] too much flexibility often leads to judicial subjectivism and dissimilar handling of similar cases, which tests the citizens' faith in the legal system and tends to undermine its very legitimacy.[228]

5. Disillusionment and Hope

Gradually, the initial euphoria surrounding the revolution subsided and gave way to disillusionment. Judges, particularly federal judges who often adjudicate complex

---

[224] P.J. Kozyris, Interest Analysis Facing Its Critics, 46 *Ohio St. L.J.* 569, 578, 580 (1985).

[225] *See id.* ("any system calling for open-ended and endless soul-searching on a case-by-case basis carries a high burden of persuasion"); M. Rosenberg, Comments on *Reich v. Purcell*, 15 *UCLA L. Rev.* 641, 644 (1968) ("The idea that judges can be turned loose in the three-dimensional chess games we have made of [conflicts] cases, and can be told to do hand-tailored justice, case by case, free from the constraints or guidelines of rules, is a vain and dangerous illusion.").

[226] *See* P. Borchers, Empiricism and Theory in Conflicts Law, 75 *Ind. L.J.* 509 (2000) ("[T]he extreme flexibility of the modern approaches probably brings increased litigation costs, in particular through the need to prosecute appeals. [...]. [T]he ever-present wild card of choice of law may discourage settlement.").

[227] *See* P.J. Kozyris, The Conflicts Provisions of the ALI's Complex Litigation Project: A Glass Half Full?, 54 *La. L. Rev.* 953, 956 (1994) ("Conflicts theorists [...] have been notoriously indifferent to the issue of efficiency, treating every case as a unique specimen calling for custom-made handling on the tacit assumption that litigation resources are infinite"); P. Borchers, Back to the Past: Anti-pragmatism in American Conflicts Law, 48 *Mercer L. Rev.* 721, 724 (1997); E. O'Hara & L. Ribstein, From Politics to Efficiency in Choice of Law, 67 *U. Chi. L. Rev.* 1151 (2000); S. Wiegand, Fifty Conflict of Laws "Restatements": Merging Judicial Discretion and Legislative Endorsement, 65 *La. L. Rev.* 1 (2004). *See also* Kaczmarek v. Allied Chem. Corp., 836 F. 2d 1055, 1057 (7th Cir. 1987) (Posner, J.).

[228] *See* P.J. Kozyris, Conflicts Theory for Dummies: Après le Deluge, Where Are We on Producers Liability?, 60 *La. L. Rev.* 1161, 1162 (2000) ("[T]elling the courts in each conflicts case to make a choice and fashion the applicable law 'ad hoc' and 'anew' [...] as is often done under the prevailing conflicts theories, appears to me to be not only inconsistent with the basic principles of separation of powers, not only burdensome and potentially arbitrary beyond reason, not only disorienting to the transacting person, but also essentially empty of meaning. [...] [U]npredictable law is not law to begin with.").

multidistrict cases, began advocating the enactment of federal choice-of-law legislation for such cases.[229] At least one judge has described modern American conflicts law as "a veritable jungle, [in] which, if the law can be found out, leads not to a 'rule of action' but a reign of chaos dominated in each case by the judge's 'informed guess.' "[230] The influential New York Court of Appeals, which had led the revolution, boldly confronted this "chaos" by enunciating, in a quasi-legislative fashion, a set of rules (the *Neumeier* rules) for resolving certain tort conflicts.[231]

Even some of the revolution's scholastic protagonists eventually recognized the need for new rules. For example, David Cavers spoke eloquently of the need to provide rules "under which the same cases will be decided the same way no matter where the suit is brought."[232] He led the way by proposing his own "principles of preference" for tort and contract conflicts.[233] Willis Reese, the chief drafter of the Restatement (Second), also proclaimed that "the formulation of rules should be as much an objective in choice of law as it is in other areas of law."[234] Other scholars have also advocated the development of rules,[235] and some have proposed their own rules.[236]

---

[229] *See, e.g., In re* Air Crash Disaster at Stapleton Int'l Airport, Denver, 720 F. Supp. 1445, 1454–1455 (D. Colo. 1988); J. Weinstein, Mass Tort Jurisdiction and Choice of Law In a Multinational World Communicating by Extraterrestrial Satellites, 37 *Willamette L. Rev.* 145, 153 (2000) ("A federal statute would help. An international treaty would be even better.").

[230] *In re* Paris Air Crash of 3 March 1974, 399 F. Supp. 732, 739 (C.D. Cal. 1975).

[231] *See* Neumeier v. Kuehner, 286 N.E.2d 454 (N.Y. 1972), appeal after remand, 43 A.D. 2d 109, 349 N.Y.S. 2d 866 (1973).

[232] Cavers, *Choice of Law Process,* 22 ("We will not […] fulfill the objectives of the conflict of laws unless we can provide rules […] under which the same cases will be decided the same way no matter where the suit is brought.").

[233] *See id.* at 139–203.

[234] *See* W. Reese, General Course on Private International Law, 150 *Recueil des cours* 1, 61 *et passim* (1976). As early as 1976, Reese argued that the conflicts experience since the revolution had "reached the stage where most areas of choice of law can be covered by general principles subject to imprecise exceptions. We should press on, however, beyond these principles to the development, as soon as our knowledge permits, of precise rules." *Id.* at 62.

[235] *See, e.g.,* Hay, Borchers & Symeonides, *Conflict of Laws,* 873–874, 950–951, 973–974, 1071–1080; M. Gottesman, Draining the Dismal Swamp: The Case for Federal Choice of Law Statutes, 80 *Geo. L.J.* 1 (1991); A. Hill, For a Third Conflicts Restatement: But Stop Trying to Reinvent the Wheel, 75 *Ind. L.J.* 535 (2000); L. Kramer, On the Need for a Uniform Choice of Law Code, 89 *Mich. L. Rev.* 2134 (1991); M. Rosenberg, Two Views on *Kell v. Henderson*: An Opinion for the New York Court of Appeals, 67 *Colum. L. Rev.* 459 (1967); R. Whitten, Curing the Deficiencies of the Conflicts Revolution: A Proposal for National Legislation on Choice of Law, Jurisdiction, and Judgments, 37 *Willamette L. Rev.* 259 (2000); S. Wiegand, Fifty Conflict of Laws "Restatements": Merging Judicial Discretion and Legislative Endorsement, 65 *La. L. Rev.* 1 (2004).

[236] *See, e.g.,* Symeonides, *Revolution,* 207–210, 233–236, 259–263, 346; Hay, Borchers & Symeonides, *Conflict of Laws,* 1075–1080 (product-liability rules proposed by Cavers, Weintraub, Juenger, and Kozyris); R. Sedler, Choice of Law in Conflicts Torts Cases: A Third Restatement or Rules of Choice of Law?, 75 *Ind. L.J.* 615, 619–622 (2000); Wiegand, *supra* note 235.

One of them, the undersigned author, initiated a debate for a new conflicts Restatement[237] and proposed for discussion purposes a set of rules for tort conflicts.[238] He did not proffer the rules that he drafted for the Louisiana and Oregon codifications, which, unlike purely academic proposals, have survived the sobering realities of the legislative process. But he did argue (1) that conditions were ripe for a new process of consolidation and standardization (which could take the form of a new Restatement); and (2) that it is now feasible to construct a new breed of smart evolutionary choice-of-law rules that reflect the lessons learned from the American conflicts experience, both from and since the conflicts revolution, without repeating the mistakes of the first Restatement.[239]

In 1994, the American Law Institute (ALI) proposed for enactment by the US Congress a comprehensive set of choice-of-law rules for mass torts and mass contracts cases.[240] And, in 1999, American conflicts professors devoted their annual meeting to discussing the need for a Third Conflicts Restatement.[241] However, Congress is decidedly uninterested in entering the "dismal swamp" of conflicts law,[242] state legislatures are equally reluctant, and the ALI is more interested in juicier topics.[243]

The irony is that while legislatures and restaters alike continue to maintain their negative stance toward choice-of-law rules, American courts have been converging to results that are perfectly capable and ready to produce such rules. As Chapter 2 documents, American courts have reached surprisingly uniform results in resolving most categories of tort conflicts, despite using different approaches or rationales.[244] Unfortunately, without the aid of legislatures, or at least the ALI's restaters, this unconfirmed uniformity is not very helpful to courts. Without the compass of a rule, courts have to reinvent the wheel in each case, after interminable discussions on the relative weight of contacts, policies, and interests.

---

[237] *See* S. Symeonides, The Judicial Acceptance of the Second Conflicts Restatement: A Mixed Blessing, 56 *Md. L. Rev.* 1246 (1997).

[238] *See* S. Symeonides, *The Need for a Third Conflicts Restatement*, 449–474. For subsequent refinements of, or additions to, these rules, *see* Symeonides, *Revolution*, 207–210, 233–236, 259–263, 346–364; Symeonides, *Cross-Border Torts*, 403–411.

[239] *See id.*; S. Symeonides, *A New Conflicts Restatement*, 383.

[240] *See* American Law Institute, *Complex Litigation: Statutory Recommendations and Analysis* (1994).

[241] *See* Symposium: Preparing for the Next Century, A New Restatement of Conflicts, 75 *Ind. L.J.* 399 (2000) (containing an introduction by Shreve; articles by Juenger, Richman and Reynolds, Symeonides, and Weinberg; and commentaries by Borchers, Dane, Gottesman, Hill, Maier, Peterson, Posnak, Reimann, Reppy, Sedler, Silberman and Lowenfeld, Simson, Singer, Twerski, and Weintraub). The debate continued the following year. *See* Symposium: American Conflicts Law at the Dawn of the 21st Century, 37 *Willamette L. Rev.* 1 (2000) (containing articles by Symeonides, Juenger, Kay, von Mehren, Weinstein, and Weintraub and commentaries by Cox, Nafziger, Sedler, Shreve, and Whitten).

[242] *See* W. Prosser, Interstate Publications, 51 *Mich. L. Rev.* 959, 971 (1953) ("The realm of the conflict of laws is a dismal swamp, filled with quaking quagmires, and inhabited by learned but eccentric professors who theorize about mysterious matters in a strange and incomprehensible jargon. The ordinary court, or lawyer, is quite lost when engulfed and entangled in it.").

[243] For a list of the topics currently on ALI's agenda, *see* http://www.ali.org/index.cfm?fuseaction=projects. main.

[244] *See supra* Chapter 2, at II.C.1–3.

6. The Benefits of Comparison

A major reason for the American reluctance to adopt a system of choice-of-law rules, even soft Restatement-type rules, is that the only experience Americans have had with a rule system was with the rigid and spectacularly bad rules of the first Restatement. This reluctance is understandable. However, some familiarity with foreign choice-of-law codifications, particularly the European ones, can help overcome it. Such familiarity can be reassuring because it can show that codification is not incompatible with flexibility and judicial discretion. As this chapter has demonstrated, most modern choice-of-law codifications have found ways to combine certainty with flexibility. They provide flexibility through a combination of soft connecting factors and escape clauses. Even if some of these combinations do not provide enough flexibility for the American taste, one can easily remedy this by changing the dosages in the combination.

B. THE EUROPEAN EXPERIENCE: A CAUTIOUS EVOLUTION

During the same period as the American choice-of-law revolution, other choice-of-law systems have also moved between certainty and flexibility, albeit in a much slower and deliberate fashion.

For example, until the 1960s, most European countries had statutory choice-of-law rules (such as the *lex loci delicti* for torts) that were almost as rigid and flawed as those of the first Restatement. As a European scholar recently recalled, his peers were equally "dissatisfied with mechanical, inflexible rules," and the ideas generated by the American choice-of-law revolution were "hotly debated" as a "viable alternative."[245]

However, that debate did not have the transformative effect that the "scholastic revolution" had in the United States, where it precipitated and guided the judicial revolution.[246] Even in England, the ultimate reaction was cautious. As a knowledgeable English scholar observed:

> [U]nlike their counterparts in the United States, English lawyers have never—or have never entirely—lost faith in the effectiveness and validity of traditional conceptions of legal reasoning. Certainly, English law never experienced the challenge (and response) to formalism represented by the American realist movement.... [I] f the American conflicts revolution is a realist revolution, it is striking how little English conflicts scholarship owes to both.[247]

---

[245] de Boer, *Living Apart Together*, 202 ("Initially, a new generation of conflicts scholars, dissatisfied with mechanical, inflexible rules, set great store by the fresh approach laid open by Currie and his kindred spirits. In Europe, in the 1970s and 1980s, interest analysis was hotly debated, a sure sign that it was considered by some as a viable alternative to the allocation method, by others as a serious threat to the universalist ideals they still cherished.")

[246] *See* Symeonides, *Revolution*, 9–35 (scholastic revolution) and 37–62 (judicial revolution).

[247] R. Fentiman, English Private International Law at the End of the 20th Century: Progress or Regress?, in Symeonides, *Progress or Regress?* 165, 169. *See also id.* at 173–174.

European judges and eventually legislators also paid attention to this debate.[248] In the end, however, they used some of these ideas but rejected the means. They chose evolution over revolution, gradually and carefully repairing the old rules rather than jettisoning them.

For example, when the German Federal Court confronted a tort case involving the same common-domicile pattern as *Babcock v. Jackson*[249] (the case that marked the beginning of the choice-of-law revolution in the United States), the German court reached the same *result* as *Babcock*.[250] The court applied the law of the parties' common domicile rather than the law of the place of the tort. However, the court also made it clear that this decision was to serve as a mere exception to the *lex loci delicti* rule, which was to remain the basic rule for tort conflicts. Eventually, the 1999 German codification preserved this very scheme. The *lex loci* remained the rule,[251] and the *lex domicilii communis* became the exception,[252] along with other exceptions such as the "closer connection."[253] As this chapter documents, other European and non-European codifications, including Rome II, have followed the same careful path, *and*, as Chapter 2 documents, they have essentially arrived at the same results as those reached by American courts.

The training and mindset of European judges and legislators, as well as European legal history in general, can explain the choice of evolution instead of revolution better than any other factor. A contributing factor might be that, as a German commentator observed, "European judges," and indeed legislators, "took advantage of the fact that they

---

[248] For the influence of the American conflicts revolution in Europe, but also for the reasons for which European choice-of-law systems did not follow in the revolution's path, at least in degree, *see, e.g.,* B. Audit, A Continental Lawyer Looks at Contemporary American Choice-of-Law Principles, 27 *Am. J. Comp. L.* 589 (1979); J. Dolinger, Evolution of Principles for Resolving Conflicts in the Field of Contracts and Torts, 283 *Recueil des cours* 189, 381–386, 468–482 (2000); G. Kegel, Paternal Home and Dream Home: Traditional Conflict of Laws and the American Reformers, 27 *Am. J. Comp. L.* 615 (1979); E. Jayme, The American Conflicts Revolution and Its Impact on European Private International Law, in Univ. van Amsterdam Centrum voor Buitenlands Recht en IPR (eds.), *Forty Years On: The Evolution of Postwar Private International Law in Europe*, 15 (1992); K. Siehr, Ehrenzweigs lex-fori-Theorie und ihre Bedeutung für das amerikanische und deutsche Kollisionsrecht, 34 *RabelsZ* 583 (1970); F. Vischer, New Tendencies in European Conflict of Laws and the Influence of the US-Doctrine: A Short Survey, in J. Nafziger and S. Symeonides (eds.), *Law and Justice in a Multistate World: Essays in Honor of Arthur T. von Mehren,* 459 (2002); E. Vitta, The Impact in Europe of the American "Conflicts Revolution," 30 *Am. J. Comp. L.* 1 (1982). *See also* S. Symeonides, *An Outsider's View of the American Approach to Choice of Law: Comparative Observations on Current American and Continental Conflicts Doctrine* 159–374 (1980).

[249] 191 N.E.2d 279 (N.Y. 1963) (*discussed supra,* Chapter 2, at II.A).

[250] *See* BGH, 8.1.1985, *JZ* 144 (1985), note Werner Lorenz. A similarly smooth evolution occurred in England. The House of Lords faced its own *Babcock* scenario in *Boys v. Chaplin,* [1969] 3 WLR 322 (HL), and reached the same result, which eventually found its way into the 1995 statute for tort conflicts as a flexible exception to the *lex loci* rule. *See supra* note 172.

[251] *See* German codif. art. 40(1).

[252] *See id.,* art. 40(2).

[253] *See id.* art. 41, which authorizes displacement of the law designated by Articles 38–40, "[i]f there is a substantially closer connection to the law of [another] state."

were to decide later than their American colleagues,"[254] and thus they could selectively draw from the American experience without repeating its excesses.

It is true that "American thinking has pervaded [European PIL] by osmosis"[255] and has contributed to a healthy skepticism toward rules, but this skepticism led to their repair rather than their demise. While American conflicts law careened from the one extreme of the first Restatement's rigidity to another extreme of total flexibility, European and other codified choice-of-law systems in the rest of the world slowly, but steadily, proceeded from certainty to flexibility.[256] They experienced no revolutions, did not undertake drastic changes, and have not abandoned rules in favor of ad hoc "approaches." Instead, they injected small controlled doses of flexibility through some new devices, as well as through some old and tested ones. As another German author noted, as a result of these developments,

> the original severity of [PIL's] forms has been mitigated; the previous strictness of its structures has been moderated; the former rigidity of the rules has been loosened; the old crampedness of the principles has been broken. The conflict rules...and the connecting factors...have become decidedly more diverse and flexible than before...and sophisticated exception clauses, elaborate evasion clauses and intricate escape clauses have been designed.[257]

Many European scholars recognize that these beneficial changes "can be attributed...to the reverberations the American conflicts revolution had in the rest of the world."[258] Now, the new choice-of-law codifications in Europe and elsewhere are sending their own reverberations in the opposite direction. For those willing to listen, the message is clear: statutory choice-of-law rules are not evil, and they need not be inflexible. To repeat Sir Peter North's words: "Codes are not monsters. Even if they are, they can be trained."[259]

---

[254] E. Jayme, *supra* note 248, at 22.

[255] *Id.*, at 24. Although Jayme's statement refers only to the German codification, the statement can also be made about European conflicts law in general.

[256] One could argue that the countries that did not have statutory rules at the beginning of the century but have acquired them in the meantime have moved from flexibility to certainty. However, as this chapter illustrates, the certainty to which they aspired and which they attained is much more pliable than the uncompromising certainty of the first Restatement.

[257] Martinek, *Seven Pillars of Wisdom*, § 61.

[258] de Boer, *Living Apart Together*, 203:

> In short, the dissatisfaction with traditional choice of law may have caused a methodological revolution in the United States, but it did not fail to affect the development of choice of law in other jurisdictions, especially in Europe, even if they remained faithful to traditional choice-of-law conceptions. Their conflicts rules no longer depend on abstract geographical factors alone. There is room for flexibility in the designation of the applicable law. Substantive values and policies have been translated into connecting factors focusing on the weaker party, or into alternative reference rules favoring a specific substantive result. These changes can be attributed, I think, to the reverberations the American conflicts revolution had in the rest of the world.

[259] P. North, Problems of Codification in a Common Law System, 46 *RabelsZ* 490, 500 (1982).

IX. Codification and Flexibility

The tension between the conflicting needs for certainty and flexibility is an innate feature of both codified and uncodified choice-of-law systems. Each system, codified or uncodified, reacts differently to this tension and strikes a different equilibrium between certainty and flexibility at different points in time. Moreover, because of changing circumstances and societal needs, what may be the "right" equilibrium for one period is not necessarily so for the next period. Thus, the quest for the golden mean is perpetual.

As the preceding discussion demonstrates, codification in general and choice-of-law codification in particular need not petrify the law nor render it unduly inflexible for exceptional cases. Codification does not necessarily outlaw judicial discretion. Modern choice-of-law codifications employ various tools such as soft connecting factors, escape clauses, or a combination of rules and residual approaches that inject controlled dosages of flexibility, and thus help attain an equilibrium between certainty and flexibility.

To be sure, one may question whether this equilibrium is the "right" one in every case. For example, the same German author quoted above concluded that, although in recent years the law of conflict of laws "has enormously gained refinement, flexibility, diversity and sophistication," certainty and foreseeability have nevertheless "suffered, and so has the old ideal of an international harmony.... [T]he dangers of such an *over-flexibility*, however, are at hand."[260]

Conversely, one can argue that, viewed from the American perspective, most modern choice-of-law codifications do not provide enough flexibility because the rules and escapes of these codifications are phrased not in terms of issues and policies but rather in terms that are either (1) too holistic, that is, geared to the whole case rather than to aspects or issues of it; or (2) too geographic (e.g., "closer" connection).[261]

Certainly, this is a matter on which reasonable minds can differ. Gains in flexibility will always produce corresponding losses in certainty, and vice versa, and questions will always exist on whether the losses outweigh the gains; the search for the "right" equilibrium is as perpetual as the tension identified by Aristotle 23 centuries ago. But in the meantime, let us agree that, as a result of the developments discussed in this chapter, the choice-of-law process "has enormously gained refinement, flexibility, diversity and sophistication."[262]

---

[260] Martinek, *Seven Pillars of Wisdom,* § 6.1 (emphasis added).

[261] For a detailed discussion of this point, *see* Symeonides, *Reciprocal Lessons,* 1773–1782.

[262] Martinek, *supra* note 260, at *id.*

5 Broad or Narrow Choice of Law: Issue-by-Issue Choice and *Dépeçage*

I. Introduction

A. BROAD RULES

Related to the general theme of flexibility, which is discussed in the previous chapter, is the question of the scope of choice-of-law rules—the narrower the scope, the more precise and apt the choice of law will be. Many traditional choice-of-law rules were formulated around broad "legal categories" borrowed from domestic law, such as tort, contract, status, succession, etc. Old codifications usually provided one choice of law for each of those categories, for example just one rule for torts (e.g., *lex loci delicti*), one rule for contracts (e.g., *lex loci contractus*), and so forth. Broad rules such as these were inimical to flexibility and aptness because they required courts to make wholesale choices rather than narrow choices tailored to the needs of individual cases.

In the United States, the excessive breadth of the first Restatement's rules was one of the reasons for the choice-of-law revolution. In the seminal case *Babcock v. Jackson,*[1] which marked the beginning of the revolution in tort conflicts, the court asked an important question: whether the *lex loci delicti* should "*invariably* govern the availability of relief for the tort or [whether] the applicable choice of law rule [should] also reflect a consideration of other factors which are relevant to the purposes served by the enforcement or denial of the remedy."[2] The court ultimately answered this question by deciding to apply the law of the state that, "because of its relationship or contact with the occurrence of the parties, has the greatest concern with the *specific issue* raised in the litigation."[3]

B. ISSUE-BY-ISSUE ANALYSIS

The italicized words in the above-quoted phrases illuminate one important feature of the court's approach—what is now known as "issue-by-issue analysis." The word "invariably" suggests that the court did not seek a wholesale abandonment of the *lex loci* rule, but rather sought to narrow the scope of the rule depending on the *particular issue* on which the laws of the involved states actually conflicted. In *Babcock,* the conflict was confined to a single issue—the driver's immunity from suit because of the Ontario guest statute, and the absence of such an immunity statute in New York. The court was no longer thinking in broad global terms, such as what law should apply to the tort *as a whole*. Rather, the

---

[1] 191 N.E.2d 279 (N.Y. 1963).

[2] *Id.* at 280–281 (first emphasis in original, second emphasis added).

[3] *Id.* at 283 (emphasis added).

court isolated the particular issue that presented a conflict of laws and focused its analysis on the conflicting laws.

This mode of issue-by-issue analysis is one of the few breakthroughs of choice-of-law thinking in the United States. It is based on the elementary realization that, in many cases, the conflict is confined to only one or less than all aspects or "issues" of the case and that the involved states may be interested in different issues. Consequently, rather than seeking to choose a law as if all aspects of the case are contested, one should focus on the narrow issues about which a conflict actually exists and proceed accordingly. This issue-by-issue analysis has become an integral feature of all of the approaches produced by the American choice-of-law revolution. It is a return to the familiar schemes of common-law decision-making, temporarily submerged by Bealian systematics, which typically proceeds with small, cautious steps of inductive reasoning. At least in the abstract, such an analysis is more conducive to a nuanced, individualized, and thus more rational resolution of conflicts problems.

C. *DÉPEÇAGE*

1. Definition

Issue-by-issue analysis means that, if a case (or, more precisely, a cause of action) comprises more than one issue on which the laws of the involved states conflict, each issue should be subjected to a separate choice-of-law analysis. If such an analysis leads to the application of different states to the different issues, then the resulting phenomenon is called *dépeçage*. Thus, dépeçage is the application of the laws of different states to different parts, aspects, or "issues" of the same *cause of action*.[4]

Dépeçage is not the *purpose* or goal of issue-by-issue analysis but rather its potential and occasional *result*. Although issue-by-issue analysis is generally a good thing because, as noted earlier, it introduces the needed flexibility into the choice-of-law process, dépeçage in the abstract is neither good nor bad, neither a panacea nor anathema. When dépeçage occurs—and it occurs less frequently than commonly assumed—it is innocuous in many cases and inappropriate in a few cases. Table 5.1 below depicts the various possibilities.

As the table indicates:

(1) In some instances, there is only one disputed choice-of-law issue. In those instances, the court applies one law and thus there is no dépeçage.

---

[4] If the case consists of two causes of action, for example, a contract cause of action, which is governed by the law of state A, and also a tort cause of action, which is governed by the law of state B, this phenomenon is *not*, properly speaking, dépeçage. Conversely, if the law of state C governs some aspects of the contract cause of action (e.g., issues of form), while the law of state D governs other aspects (e.g., issues of capacity, or performance), the resulting phenomenon *is* dépeçage.

TABLE 5.1. THE POSSIBILITIES FOR *DÉPEÇAGE*

Choice-of-Law Issues	Applicable Law	Dépeçage
1. Only one	One law	No
2. More than one	Same laws	No
3. More than one	Different laws	Yes, but innocuous
4. More than one	Different laws	**Yes, and potentially inappropriate**

(2) In other instances, there are two or more disputed choice-of-law issues but the court applies the same law to all issues. Again, there is no dépeçage.

(3) Finally, in some instances, the court applies the laws of different states to two or more disputed choice-of-law issues. In those cases, and only in those cases, there is dépeçage. In some of those cases, dépeçage is totally unproblematic and innocuous because the applicable laws are entirely congruent.

(4) In the remaining cases, dépeçage may be problematic and dangerous if the applicable laws are incongruent and the circumstances are such that the picking and choosing between laws can defeat the policies of both states and produce an anomalous result. As explained below, in those cases dépeçage should be avoided.

In any event, the fact that in *some* cases issue-by-issue analysis may lead to dépeçage and that in *some* of those cases the dépeçage may be inappropriate is not a good reason for rejecting issue-by-issue analysis in general and returning to the wholesale choices of the traditional system. Rather than precluding issue-by-issue analysis, the better solution is to guard against the possibility of an inappropriate dépeçage and to provide tools for avoiding it in the few situations where it may occur.

2. When Dépeçage Is Problematic

Brainerd Currie, one of the chief proponents of issue-by-issue analysis, acknowledged the fact that in some cases dépeçage may be problematic. He noted that "modern conflict-of-laws analysis can make no more serious mistake than to indulge in an unprincipled eclecticism, picking and choosing from among the available laws in order to reach a result that cannot be squared with the interests of any of the related states."[5] He stated that issue-by-issue analysis "should not result in the cumulation of negative policies to produce a result not contemplated by the law of either state."[6] This would be like a "synthetic hybrid" of "half a donkey and half a camel."[7]

---

[5] Currie "J." in Cavers, *Choice-of-Law Process*, 38.

[6] *Id.*

[7] *Id.* at 39.

The question then is how to avoid this "synthetic hybrid" of incongruous laws, or in other words, how to distinguish between a permissible and an inappropriate dépeçage and how to avoid the latter. In this context, it helps to remember that the term "dépeçage" can be paraphrased in English as "picking and choosing." Generally speaking, *picking and choosing is inappropriate when the rule of the one state that is chosen is so closely interrelated to a rule of the same state that is not chosen that applying the one rule without the other would drastically upset the equilibrium established by the two rules and would distort and defeat the policies of that state.* In those cases, dépeçage is inappropriate and must be avoided.

Suppose for instance that state A, a northern state, requires that cars driven in the state during the winter months use snow tires and consider the failure to use such tires as "negligence per se." State B, a southern state, does not require the use of snow tires. While driving in state A without snow tires, a state B domiciliary causes an accident resulting in the death of his passenger, also a state B domiciliary. In such a case, there is little argument that state A has a legitimate reason to insist on adherence to its snow-tire rule and on defining the consequences of noncompliance, and that state B's no–snow-tire rule is simply irrelevant with regard to driving outside its borders. Suppose further that the two states differ in designating the beneficiaries of the victim's survival action. State A designates the victim's spouse as the exclusive beneficiary, while state B includes as beneficiaries the victim's children. Here again, there is little argument that state B has the better claim to apply its law to this issue of loss distribution.

In this case, the resulting *dépeçage* is not inappropriate because the snow-tire rule of state A is not closely related, and perhaps not related at all, to the survival-action rule of the same state. The application of the former rule and the non-application of the latter would neither distort nor defeat the policies of that state, nor would it disturb whatever equilibrium these two rules might establish between deterrence and compensation. The same is true with regard to the application of state B's survival-action rule without state B's snow-tire rule.

A different conclusion would follow if, in the same hypothetical, the conduct-regulating rule and the loss-distributing rule of state A are closely interrelated and intended to be applied together. Suppose, for example, that state A's snow-tire rule is coupled with a rule that reduces or increases by 10 percent the amount of damages that can be recovered from a defendant, depending on whether the defendant used snow tires. In such a case, it would be inappropriate to apply the snow-tire rule without its intended companion rule regarding the amount of recoverable damages.

The next question to consider is how to avoid an inappropriate dépeçage. Such avoidance is easy in the United States because the general absence of statutory or other inflexible choice-of-law rules leaves the courts considerable flexibility. The same is true in the two American codifications—Louisiana's and Oregon's— which employ issue-by-issue analysis, but also provide flexible tools for avoiding a potentially inappropriate dépeçage.[8] In

---

[8] *See infra* at IV.1.a, 2, IV.B.4, and V.

other choice-of- law codifications, such avoidance may not be as easy and this may be the reason that these codifications are generally hostile to dépeçage, at least in theory.

Before examining the extent to which dépeçage appears in those systems, it is necessary to clarify what is, and what is not, dépeçage as this term is used here.

II. Dépeçage in Codified Choice-of-Law Systems

In codified choice-of-law systems, dépeçage may result from (exclusive or partial) legislative, judicial, or private action, or a combination thereof.

(1) A *legislative or statutory dépeçage* occurs when the statutory choice-of-law rule or rules, properly applied, lead to the application of the substantive laws of different states to different aspects of the same cause of action. It is immaterial whether the application of these different laws:

   (a) Is specifically intended or acknowledged by the legislature;

   (b) Results from the application of a choice-of-law rule or an exception therefrom (such as the *ordre public* reservation or the mandatory rules exception),[9] or a specific or general escape (such as those discussed in Chapter 4, *supra*);[10] or

   (c) Results from the application of one or more choice-of-law rules and, in the latter case, whether those rules cover different and established "legal categories" (such as contractual capacity, form, or performance),[11] as long as those categories are parts of the same cause of action.

(2) A *judicial dépeçage* occurs when a court applies the laws of different states to different aspects of the same cause of action in an uncodified choice- of-law system, or in a codified system that does not mandate a dépeçage for the particular cause of action.[12]

(3) A *voluntary or subjective dépeçage* occurs when the application of the laws of different states to different aspects of the same cause of action results from the legally permissible expression of the volition of one party (such as a testator) or more than one party (such as the parties to a contract).

The prevailing opinion is that most choice-of-law codifications are hostile to issue-by-issue analysis and therefore to dépeçage. As two Belgian authors observe, "[i]t does not rhyme with the traditional European approach to allow an ad hoc splitting up of

---

[9] In some countries, this is not considered dépeçage. *See, e.g.,* K. Boele-Woelki & D. Van Iterson, *Dutch Report*, at 4.4 (stating that, in Dutch literature, "the fact that overriding mandatory rules may claim application in a case which is otherwise governed by one particular law is not regarded as dépeçage.").

[10] *See* Chapter 4 at VI.A–B, *supra*.

[11] In some countries, a narrower definition prevails. *See infra* notes 14–16.

[12] If the system authorizes such an application, then the resulting dépeçage is both statutory and judicial.

issues."[13] However, the keywords in the quoted phrase are the words "ad hoc." What the Europeans seem to object to is the "ad hoc" *judicial* splitting of the issues, not the legislative splitting. In other words, this hostility is limited to the *legislatively unauthorized* issue-by-issue analysis, apparently because of concerns that it may lead to an undisciplined or inappropriate *judicial* dépeçage. Contrary to the definition of this chapter, they do not consider legislative issue-splitting to be dépeçage. Instead, they call it "fragmentation,"[14] "differentiation,"[15] or "branching out into detail."[16]

Nonetheless, legislative issue-splitting is at least as likely as a judicial issue-by-issue analysis to lead to the application of the laws of different states to different issues, and thus to statutory dépeçage as defined in this chapter. As a Croatian author observes, "[t]he more the legal categories used in the conflict of laws rules are fragmented, the more likely it is that courts will have to apply several laws in the same cause of action (dépeçage)."[17]

Moreover, as Sections III and IV of this chapter document, legislative issue-splitting is far more frequent than commonly assumed. Indeed, it occurs even in traditional codifications. For example, in contracts, these codifications typically provide one choice-of-law rule for contractual capacity (e.g., *lex patriae* or *domicilii*), another rule for formal validity (e.g., *lex regit actum*), and another rule for substantive validity. Thus, when a case involves more than one of the above issues and the pertinent connecting factors are

---

[13] J. Erauw & M. Fallon, *Belgian Report*, at III.1. *See also* D. Babić, *Croatian Report*, at III ("Croatian conflict of laws rules typically refer to general, broadly phrased categories of private law relationships (such as capacity, rights in rem, contract, tort) which normally cover the entire cause of action."); P. Mankowski, *German Report*, at III ("German PIL rules generally pursue a unitary approach and negate any issue-by-issue choice."); T. Kanzaki, *Japanese Report*, at III ("The [Japanese PIL] Act provides a single choice-of-law rule for the law applicable to an entire cause of action or a legal relationship as a whole. The Act does not allow dépeçage on its face."); C. Esplugues Mota & C. Azcárraga Monzonís, *Spanish Report*, at III.1 (noting that Spanish choice-of-law rules are "characterized by the broadness of their scope."); A. Bonomi, *Swiss Report,* at III ("The general approach in the [Swiss codification] is to adopt a single choice-of-law rule for the law applicable to the entire cause of action and thus limit dépeçage."); Z. Tarman, *Turkish Report*, at III.1 ("The Turkish PIL Code is principally dedicated to apply a single law to the entire cause of action for the sake of consistency…").

[14] As the Dutch reporters state, such a "fragmentation of conflict of laws rules is a very common phenomenon in Dutch PIL," but "[b]y contrast, there are few examples of conflict of laws rules which allow…dépeçage." K. Boele-Woelki & D. Van Iterson, *Dutch Report*, at 4.4. According to the authors,

> In the Dutch legal literature the mere fact that different aspects or issues of a certain type of cross-border legal relationship fall within different PIL categories and are therefore governed by different laws is not regarded as dépeçage.… Dépeçage only occurs when the parties designate different laws to be applicable to different issues falling within a single PIL category… or when, in the absence of such a designation by the parties, a court determines that different rules apply to different aspects in such a case.
> *Id.*

[15] *See* P. Mankowski, *German Report*, at III (noting that "[a] proper dépeçage ought to be distinguished from … [a] differentiation of issues," such as "contracting the marriage, issues of matrimonial property; maintenance; marital name; other effects of the marriage.").

[16] *See* J. Erauw & M. Fallon, *Belgian Report*, at III.1 (referring to the Belgian codification's separate choice-of-law rules on different aspects of the same relationship as "a branching out into detail, which is a substitute for dépeçage.").

[17] D. Babić, *Croatian Report*, at III.

located in different states, these rules *mandate* the application of the laws of different states to each of the issues and consequently lead to dépeçage.

Similarly, for succession cases, traditional codifications typically provide one choice-of-law rule for testamentary capacity (e.g., *lex patriae* or *domicilii*), another rule for testamentary form (e.g., an alternative-reference rule such as those described in Chapter 6),[18] and another rule for succession to immovables (e.g., *lex rei sitae*). Again, when a given case involves more than one of the above issues and the pertinent connecting factors (or the immovables) are located in different states, the application of these rules will inevitably lead to dépeçage.

As discussed below, modern codifications retain, and considerably expand, these instances of legislatively authorized dépeçage. Before examining the various national codifications, we turn to two influential and recent multinational codifications, the Rome I and Rome II Regulations.

III. *Dépeçage* in the Rome Convention and the Rome Regulations

A. ROME CONVENTION AND ROME I REGULATION

In contrast to other codifications of its time, the Rome Convention took an *officially* hospitable stance on dépeçage by, inter alia, authorizing in its general Articles 3 and 4 both voluntary dépeçage and judicial dépeçage.

Article 3(1) authorized a voluntary dépeçage by allowing contracting parties to choose the law applicable to the whole "or a part only" of the contract.[19] Obviously, such a partial choice produces dépeçage if the parties choose a law other than that which would govern the contract under the Convention's other articles. Moreover, the quoted phrase implicitly allowed the parties to choose one law for some parts of the contract and another law for other parts of the contract, thus leading even more directly to dépeçage.

Article 4(1) provided that "[t]o the extent that" the parties had not chosen the applicable law, the contract was to be governed by the law of the country with which it was most closely connected.[20] The italicized phrase would lead to dépeçage in two circumstances. First, when the parties choose a law for only part of the contract, as noted above, and second, when they choose a law for the whole contract, but their choice is only partly valid. Even more directly, Article 4(1) authorized judicial dépeçage through an escape clause. This escape clause provided that, although a contract was to be governed by the most closely connected law, "a severable part" of the contract that had a closer connection with another country would be governed by the law of that other country.[21]

---

[18] *See* Chapter 6 at V.A.1, *infra*.
[19] Rome Convention, art. 3(1).
[20] *Id*., art. 4(1) (emphasis added).
[21] *Id*.

The Rome I Regulation continues to allow a voluntary dépeçage by reproducing without change Article 3(1) of the Rome Convention, and allowing the contracting parties to choose the applicable law for a part (or parts) of the contract.[22]

However, Rome I has not reproduced the above-quoted escape of Article 4(1) of the Convention, which allowed a severable part of the contract to be governed by a law other than the law that governs the rest of the contract. Instead, paragraph 3 of Article 4 of Rome I allows an escape only when "the contract" is manifestly more closely connected with a country other than the country designated by the previous paragraphs of the article.[23] Similarly, most other provisions of Rome I speak of the law applicable to "the contract" as a whole. These changes suggest a partial retreat from the Convention's pro-dépeçage stance, although some scholars express doubts on whether European courts will be as eager to follow suit.[24]

In any event, dépeçage is still possible under several other articles of Rome I that single out certain issues and assign them to a law that, depending on the location of the pertinent connecting factors, may be different from the law governing the rest of the contract. The following are among those articles:

(1) *Form.* Paragraphs 1 and 2 of Article 11 provide that a contract is formally valid if it satisfies the formal requirements of the law that governs the substance of the contract (*lex causae*) or the law of at least one other state. That other state is the state in which all parties expressed their assent to the contract and, in cross-border contracts, the state in which at least one party expressed its assent or had its habitual residence.[25] Under this alternative reference rule, if a particular contract is formally invalid under the *lex causa* but valid under one of the other laws, the other law will govern the issue of formal validity, and the *lex causae* will govern the rest of the contract, thus producing a dépeçage.[26]

(2) *Consent.* Paragraph 1 of Article 10 provides that the existence and validity of a contract are both governed by the *lex causae*. However, paragraph 2 of the

---

[22] *See* Rome I, art. 3(1).

[23] *Id.*, art. 4(3). This paragraph corresponds partly with paragraph 5 of Article 4 of the Rome Convention.

[24] *See, e.g.,* J. Erauw & M. Fallon, *Belgian Report*, at III.1 (expressing doubts on whether the judges in European countries "will be able to resist the temptation to split up a relationship and apply two different national laws to different issues under a contract, if the need were to occur."); P. Mankowski, *German Report*, at III (considering it an "open question" whether the judicial dépeçage authorized by Article 4(3) of the Rome Convention has survived the conversion to the Rome I Regulation).

[25] *See* Rome I, art. 11(1)–(2). Paragraph 3 provides a similar rule for unilateral juridical acts. These paragraphs do not apply to consumer contracts.

[26] A dépeçage may also occur in a contract in which the subject matter is "a right in rem in immovable property or a tenancy of immovable property." Paragraph 5 of Article 11 requires observance of the formal requirements of the law of the situs (which according to Article 4(1)(c) is the *lex causae*), but only if those requirements qualify as mandatory rules. If not, the formal validity of the contract may be governed by the law of one of the other states listed in paragraphs 1 or 2 of Article 11, while its substantive validity will be governed by the law of the *situs-causae*, thus again producing a dépeçage.

same article allows a party, under certain conditions, to invoke the law of her habitual residence (which may be in a state other than that of the *lex causae)* in order to establish that she did not consent to the contract. Again, a dépeçage is possible under these circumstances.

(3) *Capacity.* Similarly, Article 13 provides that, in a contract concluded between persons who are in the same country, a natural person who is capable of contracting under the law of that country may, under certain conditions, invoke his incapacity under the law of another country. If those conditions are met, that party is held incapable under the law of that other country, but the "consequences of [this] nullity" are governed by another law—the *lex causae* selected under Articl2 12(1)(e) of Rome I.[27]

(4) *Performance.* Article 12 provides that, although performance in general is governed by the *lex causae*, nevertheless, with regard to the "manner of performance" and the steps to be taken in the event of defective performance, "regard shall be had" to the law of the country in which performance takes place. If the court *applies* that law rather than simply give it "regard," a dépeçage will occur.

(5) *Insurance Contracts.* Paragraph 5 of Article 7 provides that, when an insurance contract that meets certain conditions specified therein covers risks located in more than one EU Member State, "the contract shall be considered as constituting several contracts each relating to only one Member State."[28] This provision may lead to dépeçage because, under paragraph 3 of the same article, these insurance contracts are governed by the law of the state where the risk is situated, unless the parties have validly chosen another law.

(6) *"Simple" Mandatory Rules.* Article 3(3) provides that a contractually chosen law will not be applied *to the extent* it conflicts with the "simple" mandatory rules of the country where "all other elements relevant to the situation ... are located."[29] Articles 6(2) and 8(1) provide that, in consumer contracts and employment contracts, respectively, a contractually chosen law will not be applied *to the extent* it deprives the consumer or employee of the protection of the "simple" mandatory rules of the otherwise applicable law.

(7) *Overriding Mandatory Rules.* Article 9(2) and (3) provide that the court will not apply the contractually or judicially chosen law *to the extent* that it conflicts with the "overriding mandatory provisions"[30] of the law of the forum, or the law of the place of performance insofar as the latter provisions render performance of the contract unlawful.

(8) *Ordre Public.* Article 21 allows displacement of the applicable law *to the extent* that it is manifestly incompatible with the forum's *ordre public.*

---

[27] Rome I, art. 12(1)(e).

[28] Rome I, art. 7(5).

[29] *Id.,* art. 3(3). *See also* art. 3(4) regarding the mandatory rules of EU law.

[30] *Id.,* art. 9(2) and (3).

B. ROME II

Unlike the Rome Convention (and to a lesser extent the Rome I Regulation), Rome II takes a negative stance on issue-by-issue analysis, apparently because of the drafters' desire to avoid the possibility of dépeçage. Indeed, the EU Council and Commission specifically rebuffed the Parliament's attempts to introduce issue-by-issue analysis. These attempts are reflected in one of Parliament's amendments, which attached the following concluding sentence to what became the general rule of Article 4: "In resolving the question of the applicable law, the court seised shall, where necessary, subject each specific issue of the dispute to separate analysis."[31] The Council and Commission rejected this amendment. In the end, most of Rome II's articles were phrased in broad terms designating the law that would govern the case as a whole, the "tort/delict." Article 15 reaffirms this holistic approach by providing a long list of issues that comprise the scope of the law applicable under these articles.[32]

Nevertheless, a closer look at some of the other articles reveals that Rome II does not—because it cannot—entirely avoid an issue-by-issue analysis and thus the application of different laws in the same case. This is possible under the following articles of Rome II, in numerical order.

(1) Article 4 and most of Rome II's operative articles speak of the law applicable to the "obligation"[33] arising out of a tort or delict, rather than to the tort or delict as a whole. A tort may give rise to multiple obligations, such as when a tortfeasor's single act injures multiple victims. In such a case, a different law may govern the different obligations arising from the same act. For example, if one victim has the same habitual residence as the tortfeasor and another victim does not, the tortfeasor's obligation toward the first victim will be governed by the law of the common habitual residence under paragraph 2 of Article 4, while the tortfeasor's obligation toward the second victim will be governed by the law of the state of injury under paragraph 1 of Article 4.[34]

---

[31] Eur. Parl. Final A6-0211/2005 (27 June 2005) 19/46.

[32] Article 15 of Rome II provides that the scope of the applicable law encompasses virtually all issues likely to arise in tort litigation, including the basis and extent of liability, the grounds for exemption from liability, any limitation of liability and any division of liability, the existence, the nature and the assessment of damage or the remedy claimed; injunctive relief, the proper beneficiaries of the right to claim damages, and its transferability or heritability, respondeat superior, and the extinction or prescription of the obligation (statutes of limitation).

[33] *See, e.g.*, Rome I, arts. 4.1, 5.1, 6, 7, and 8.

[34] One could argue that this case consists of two torts, one against each victim, or two causes of action, one by each victim, and that, technically, the application of two laws does not amount to dépeçage. Nevertheless, this case presents the same problems of potential incongruence between the two laws as a technical dépeçage.

(2) Recital 33 purports to authorize the application of the law of the habitual residence of the victim of a traffic accident in quantifying the recoverable damage,[35] even when the law of the accident state governs all the other issues resulting from the accident.[36]

(3) Article 8(2), which deals with certain intellectual property rights, can lead to the application of Community law to some issues and national law to other issues.[37]

(4) Article 14 on choice-of-law agreements can lead to the same dépeçage possibilities as those discussed above under Rome I.[38] For example, the parties may choose different laws for different aspects of the case, or they may choose one law for some issues and none for others. Even when they choose one law for all issues, that law will not be applied to the extent it violates the mandatory rules described in Article 14(2) of Rome II or the Community rules described in Article 14(3).

(5) Articles 16 and 26 allow displacement of the applicable law *to the extent* necessary to satisfy the mandatory rules of the forum state, or to the extent that law is incompatible with the forum's *ordre public*.

(6) Article 17 allows the court to "take account" of the rules of "safety and conduct" of the state of conduct when the remainder of the case is governed by the law of another state.[39] If the court chooses to apply the rules of conduct and safety (instead of merely "taking account" of them), a dépeçage will occur.

(7) Article 18 allows the tort victim to sue the tortfeasor's insurer directly under the law governing the insurance contract, even if another law governs the tort.[40]

---

[35] This recital states that "when quantifying damages for personal injury in cases in which the accident takes place in a State other than that of the habitual residence of the victim," the court should "take into account all the relevant actual circumstances of the specific victim, including in particular the actual losses and costs of after-care and medical attention." Rome II, recital (33).

[36] In fact, the possibility of dépeçage is the main reason cited by the Council and Commission for rejecting Parliament's express rule to that effect. Although the recital does not enjoy the same status as an express rule in the Regulation's main body, the recital either means what it says, in which case the possibility of dépeçage remains, or it does not mean what it says, in which case Parliament did not get anything from the purported compromise.

[37] Article 27 of Rome II can also lead to the same phenomenon by recognizing that a case may be governed partly by the law designated by Rome II and partly by the law designated by other choice-of-law rules contained in other community instruments.

[38] Article 14 allows choice-of-law agreements entered either before or after the occurrence of the tort, but subject to different conditions. It applies to all non-contractual claims other than those arising from unfair competition, restrictions to competition, and infringement of intellectual property rights. *See* Rome II, arts. 6(4) and 8(3).

[39] Rome II, art. 17.

[40] One could argue that the victim's claims against the tortfeasor, on the one hand, and against the tortfeasor's insurer, on the other hand, constitute two causes of action and thus the application to them of different laws

(8) Articles 19 and 20 provide that the rights of subrogation, indemnification, and contribution between the parties mentioned in these articles may be governed by a law other than the law governing the victim's claims against these parties.[41]

The above list is much longer than the opponents of dépeçage would ordinarily tolerate. This is not a criticism. After all, more often than not, dépeçage is not inappropriate and, when it is, there are tools for avoiding it. Unfortunately, Rome II provides no such tools because, as discussed in Chapter 4, its all-important general escape of Article 4(3) is also phrased in wholesale, geographic terms that, inter alia, preclude an issue-by-issue deployment.[42] Thus, Rome II ends up with the worse of both worlds: (1) no issue-by-issue analysis with its attendant benefits, and (2) no tools for avoiding an inappropriate dépeçage.

IV. Dépeçage in Other Modern Codifications

The fact that the Rome Convention has been emulated in many non-EU countries,[43] coupled with the fact that the Rome I Regulation is in force in 27 of the 28 EU countries,[44] demonstrates that the receptive stance these two instruments take toward dépeçage has been accepted in a significant number of countries.

The fact that Rome II, which is also in force in 27 EU countries, is replete with dépeçage possibilities despite the drafters' official disapproval of issue-by-issue analysis also confirms the inevitability of dépeçage.

A careful examination of other choice-of-law codifications would produce a very extensive list of provisions that could lead to dépeçage. The text below provides a merely illustrative list.

---

does not amount to dépeçage. This argument is questionable, but even if it is valid, this case presents the same problems of potential incongruence between the two laws as a technical dépeçage.

[41] Again, one could argue the claims of some of these parties involve different causes of action. Even if this is true, the application of different laws presents the same problems of potential incongruence between the two laws as a technical dépeçage.

[42] *See supra* Chapter 4 at VI.C.

[43] See *supra* Chapter 3.

[44] The only exception is Denmark, which, however, applies the Rome Convention. *See* J. Lookofsky, *Danish Report,* at I.

A. STATUTORY OR VOLUNTARY *DÉPEÇAGE*

1. Contracts

a. *Statutory Dépeçage*

In addition to the 27 EU countries that are bound by Rome I, several other countries have emulated the Rome Convention in their codifications, in whole or in part. These codifications present similar possibilities for dépeçage.

The same is true of many other codifications outside the EU, at least with regard to issues of capacity, form, and all other contractual issues. Table 5.2 below provides an alphabetical listing of these non-EU codifications and of the separate articles they contain for issues of contractual capacity, form, and other issues, respectively.

TABLE 5.2. NON-EU CODIFICATIONS AND THEIR SEPARATE RULES FOR CERTAIN CONTRACTUAL ISSUES

Codification	Capacity	Form	Other Issues
Afghanistan	art. 17	art. 28	art. 27
Albania	art. 11	art. 18	arts. 45–52
Algeria	art. 10	art. 19	art. 18
Angola	arts. 27–28	art. 36	arts. 41–42
Argentina	arts. 2616–2617	art. 2649	arts. 2651–2652
Armenia	arts. 1265–1266	art. 1281	arts. 1284–1285
Azerbaijan	art. 10	art. 17	arts. 24–25
Belarus	arts. 1104, 1112	art. 1116	arts. 1124–1127
Burundi	art. 2	art. 5.1	art. 5.2
Cape Verde	arts. 27–28	art. 36	arts. 41–42
China	art. 12		arts. 41–43
East Timor	arts. 26–27	art. 35	arts. 40–41
FYROM	arts. 15–16	art. 7	arts. 21–22, 26–27
Gabon	art. 32	arts. 57–58	art. 55
Georgia	art. 23	art. 29	arts. 35–36
Guatemala	art. 21	arts. 29–30	art. 31
Guinea-Bissau	arts. 27–28	art. 36	arts. 41–42
Japan	art. 4	art. 10	art. 7
Jordan	art. 12	art. 21	art. 20
Kazakhstan	art. 1095	arts. 1104–1105	arts. 1112–1114
N. Korea	art. 18	art. 26	art. 24

Codification	Capacity	Form	Other Issues
S. Korea	arts. 13, 15	art. 17	arts. 25–29
Kyrgyzstan	art. 1178	art. 1190	arts. 1198–1201
Liechtenstein	art. 12	art. 8	arts. 39–49
Macau	art. 24	art. 35	arts. 40–41, 34
Madagascar	art. 28	art. 33	art. 30
Mauritania	art. 7		art. 10
Mexico	art. 13.II	art. 13.IV	art. 13.V
Moldova	arts. 1589–1590	arts. 1610, 1614	arts. 1611–1613
Mongolia	art. 543	art. 548	art. 549
Mozambique	arts. 27–28	art. 36	arts. 41–42
Paraguay	arts. 11–14	arts. 23, 699	art. 297
Peru	arts. 2070, 2073	art. 2094	art. 2095
Qatar	art. 11	art. 29	arts. 27–28
Quebec	arts. 3083–3087	arts. 3109–3110	arts. 3111–3113
Russia	art. 1197	art. 1209	arts. 1210–1216
Rwanda	arts. 10–11	art. 14.1	art. 14.2
Serbia	arts. 54–55, 147	arts. 41, 146	arts. 136–137
Slovenia	art. 13	art. 7	arts. 19-20
Somalia	art. 11	art. 20	art. 19
Sudan	art. 11.1	art. 11.13c	art. 11.13a
Switzerland	arts. 35–36	art. 124	arts. 116–117, 123, 125
Taiwan	arts. 10, 13–14	art. 16	art. 20[45]
Tajikistan	art. 1201	arts. 1210–1211	arts. 1218–1221
Tunisia	arts. 40, 43	art. 68	arts. 62–64
Turkey	art. 9	art. 7	art. 24, 33
U.A.E	art. 11	art. 19	art. 19
Ukraine	arts. 18–19	art. 31	art. 32, 43–44
Uruguay	art. 20	art. 43	arts. 44–50
Uzbekistan	art. 1169	arts. 1181–1182	arts. 1189–1190
Venezuela	arts. 16–20	art. 37	arts. 29–31
Vietnam	arts. 762–763, 765	arts. 770–771	art. 769
Yemen	art. 25	art. 31	art. 30

---

[45]. *See also id.* arts. 17–19 (agency), 21–22 (particular contracts).

The simple fact that these codifications provide different choice-of-law rules for the three categories of issues shown in the last three columns of the Table suggests that these codifications accept the possibility that, in a given case, these rules may lead to the laws of different states. Obviously, and despite contrary protestations, this is nothing other than the very dépeçage that the prevailing academic doctrine seems to despise.

In contrast to this hostility, the codifications of Louisiana, Oregon, and Puerto Rico officially mandate an issue-by-issue analysis and thus they are entirely content with the possibility of dépeçage. In addition to providing separate choice-of-law rules for issues of form,[46] capacity,[47] and consent,[48] the three codifications also require that the judicial search for the law applicable to any other issue must focus on "that issue."[49]

The Mexico City Convention does not use the word "issue" but it too is also issue-oriented. Besides also providing separate choice-of-law rules for form, capacity, and consent,[50] the Convention allows the court to apply different laws to "separable" parts of a contract.[51]

b. Voluntary Dépeçage

Like the Rome Convention and the Rome I Regulation,[52] many recent codifications allow contracting parties to choose a law for only part of the contract, or to choose different laws for different parts of the contract. Obviously, if the parties either make a partial choice of law or choose multiple laws, their choice will produce a dépeçage. In addition to the 27 EU countries that are bound by Rome I, such partial or multiple choice is expressly authorized by the Mexico City Convention, the Hague Sales Convention, and the Hague Contracts Principles,[53] by more than 20 codifications outside the EU,[54] and by judicial practice in other countries.[55]

---

[46] See La. codif. art. 3538; Or. Rev. Stat. § 15.325; Puerto Rico draft codif. art. 32.

[47] See La. codif. art. 3539; Or. Rev. Stat. § 15.330; Puerto Rico draft codif. art. 33.

[48] See Or. Rev. Stat. § 15.335; Puerto Rico draft codif. art. 34.

[49] See La. codif. art. 3537 ("...the law of the state whose policies would be most seriously impaired if its law were not applied to that issue"); Or. Rev. Stat. § 15.360 ("...the law...that is the most appropriate for a resolution of that issue."); Puerto Rico draft codif. art. 30 ("...the law of the state which, with regard to the issue in question, has the most significant connection").

[50] See Inter-American Convention on Law Applicable to International Contracts, arts. 13 and 12.

[51] See id. art. 9(3).

[52] See Rome Convention, art. 3(1); Rome I, art. 3(1).

[53] Inter-American Convention on Law Applicable to International Contracts, art. 7; Hague Convention of 22 December 1986 on the Law Applicable to Contracts for the International Sale of Goods, art. 7(1); Hague Principles on the Choice of Law in International Contracts, art. 2.2.

[54] See Albanian codif. art. 45.1; Argentine draft codif. art. 2651; Armenian codif. art. 1284(2); Azerbaijan codif. art. 24.1; Belarus codif. art. 1124(4); FYROM codif. art. 15(3); Kazakhstan codif. art. 112.3; South Korean codif. art. 25(2); Kyrgyzstan codif. art. 1198 (2); La. codif. art. 3540, cmt. (e); Moldova codif. art. 1611. Or. Rev. Stat. § 15.350(1); Puerto Rico draft, art. 28; Quebec codif. art. 3111(3); Russian codif. art. 1210(4); Serbian codif. art. 136.3; Tajikistan codif. art. 1218.3; Turkish codif. art. 24(2); Ukrainian codif. art. 5.3; Uruguayan draft, art. 48.3; Uzbekistan codif. art. 1189.2.

[55] See, e.g., W. Chen, Chinese Report, at III; T. Einhorn, Israeli Report, at III.3; A. Bonomi, Swiss Report, at III.3.

2. Torts

The possibilities of dépeçage in tort conflicts under the Rome II Regulation, which binds 27 EU countries, were discussed earlier.[56] Similar possibilities exist in certain national codifications and international conventions. One of them involves the "conduct and safety" rules of the state of conduct. As seen in Chapter 2, many other codifications (six within the EU[57] and 10 outside the EU[58]) and two Hague Conventions[59] have a provision similar to Article 17 of Rome II. They provide that the court shall "take account" of the conduct and safety rules of the conduct state when the tort is governed by the law of another state, such as the state of injury or the parties' common home state. Some of these codifications use mandatory language requiring the application of the conduct rules, while others use more flexible language instructing the court to "consider" or "take account" of (and perhaps not necessarily *apply*) those rules. If the court applies the conduct rules of the conduct state, side by side with the other rules of another state, then a judicial dépeçage occurs.

Another possibility is that of the dépeçage in codifications that follow the Rome II model; it involves pre-dispute choice-of-law agreements. Two recent codifications (those of Albania and Serbia) have adopted an identical article to Article 14 of Rome II, which allows such agreements.[60] As noted earlier, that article creates the possibility of a voluntary dépeçage because nothing in the article prohibits a partial choice of law or the choice of multiple laws, and, even if the parties choose a single law for the entire cause of action, the possibility of a judicial dépeçage remains.

Outside the sphere of Rome II, some codifications mandate a statutory dépeçage between the issues of liability and damages. As seen in Chapter 2, these codifications provide that the victim of a tort governed by foreign law may not recover more damages than those allowed by the law of the forum. Seven codifications (Estonia, Germany, Hungary, Japan, North Korea, and South Korea) do so for all torts,[61] and three (Romania, Switzerland, and Turkey) do so only for certain torts.[62]

---

[56] *See supra* at III.B.
[57] *See* Belgian codif. art. 102; Bulgarian codif. art. 115; Hungarian codif. art. 34.1; Dutch Torts Act of 2001, art. 6; Portuguese codif. art. 45(3); Romanian codif. art. 110.
[58] *See* the codifications of Albania (art. 59), Angola (art. 45.3), Cape Verde (art. 45.3), East Timor (art. 44.3), Guinea-Bissau (art. 45.3), Macau (art. 44.3), Mozambique (art. 45.3), Serbia (draft art. 176), Switzerland (art. 142.2), and Tunisia (art. 75).
[59] *See* Hague Convention on the Law Applicable to Traffic Accidents of 1971, art. 7; Hague Convention on the Law Applicable to Products Liability of 1972, art. 9.
[60] *See* Albanian codif. art. 57; Serbian draft codif. art. 158.
[61] *See* Chapter 2 at IV.G, *supra*.
[62] *See* Romanian codif. art. 116 ("The Romanian courts can grant damages, [for products liability], based on a foreign law, only within the limits fixed by the Romanian law for appropriate damages."); art. 119 (same for unfair competition); Swiss codif. art. 135(2) ("When claims based on a defect in, or a defective description of, a

The Louisiana codification and the Puerto Rico draft have different choice-of-law rules for issues of "conduct regulation" and issues of "loss distribution," respectively,[63] but also provide tools, such as an escape clause,[64] that can be used to avoid an inappropriate dépeçage. The tort choice-of-law statutes of Oregon and the United Kingdom can also lead to dépeçage because they are built on issue-by-issue analysis, but they too provide similar avoidance tools.[65]

3. Marriage

In the law of marriage, there is a possibility of statutory dépeçage in all systems that apply the personal law of each spouse to determine whether that spouse meets the requirements for a valid marriage. For example, Article 48 of the Polish codification provides that "[t]he ability to conclude a marriage is determined towards each of the parties by the law of his or her nationality as of the day when the marriage is concluded."[66] At least 30 other codifications have similar rules.[67]

Like many other codifications, the Polish codification contains two additional choice-of-law rules applicable to the formal validity and personal effects of marriage, respectively. Article 49 provides that the law of the state in which the marriage is concluded governs its formal validity.[68] Article 51 provides that the personal relations between the spouses are governed by the law of their common nationality, domicile, or habitual residence, if any, and, in the absence of such commonality, by the law of the state with which both spouses are "otherwise most closely connected."[69]

Real life tends to be less complicated than the hypothetical scenarios used in the classroom. Nevertheless, it is not inconceivable that in a given situation the three Polish articles can lead to the application of three (or even four) different laws to the issues of capacity, formal validity, and personal relations, respectively. If the three laws are incongruous, the resulting dépeçage would be inappropriate, but the codification does not provide any vehicle for avoiding that result. The dépeçage possibilities are

---

product are governed by foreign law, no damages other than those that would be awarded under Swiss law for such injury may be awarded in Switzerland."), art. 137(2) (same for obstructing competition); Turkish codif. art. 38(2) (same for obstruction to competition).

[63] *See* La. codif. arts. 3543–3544; Puerto Rico draft, arts. 40–41.

[64] *See* La. codif. art. 3547; Puerto Rico draft, art. 39(3).

[65] *See* Or. Rev. Stat. §§ 15.400–15.455; Private International Law (Miscellaneous Provisions) Act of 8 November 1995 (c 42).

[66] Polish codif. art. 48.

[67] *See* the codifications of Albania (art. 21); Algeria (art. 11); Angola (art. 49); Austria (art. 17.1.); Belgium (art. 46); Bulgaria (art. 79); Burkina Faso (art. 1022); Cape Verde (art. 49); Czech Republic (art. 48.1); East Timor (art. 48); FYROM (art. 38.1); Georgia (art. 44.1); Germany (art. 13); Italy (art. 27); Guinea-Bissau (art. 49); Japan (art. 24); Jordan (art. 13); North Korea (art. 35); South Korea (art. 36.1); Liechtenstein (art. 18); Macau (art. 48); Mozambique (art. 48); Peru (art. 2075); Portugal (art. 49); Romania (art. 18); Serbia (art. 61); Slovakia (art. 19); Slovenia (art. 24); Taiwan (arts. 45–46); Turkey (art. 13); U.A.E. (art. 12); Venezuela (art. 21).

[68] Polish codif. art. 49.1.

[69] *Id.* art. 51.

even higher if the case also involves a dispute about the spouses' property relations, for which the Polish codification, along with many other codifications, allows the spouses to choose the applicable law.[70] This possibility is discussed in the next subsection.

4. Matrimonial Property Regimes

A matrimonial property regime can be contractual, or legal (i.e., by operation of law when the parties have not agreed otherwise), or partly contractual and partly legal. In all three types of regimes, a statutory or voluntary dépeçage is quite common, and in some instances inevitable. The following are some examples.

(1) Certain systems differentiate between movable and immovable assets and subject them to different laws,[71] or allow the parties to subject immovables to the law of the situs when a different law governs the regime.[72]

(2) Regardless of the type of the regime, the rights of third parties, such as creditors, are subject to a different choice-of-law rule, which may lead to the application of a different law than the law governing the regime as between the spouses.[73]

(3) The formal validity of the agreement establishing or modifying a regime is often subject to a different choice-of-law rule, which may lead to the application of a different law than that which governs the regime's substantive validity.[74]

(4) Most systems allow spouses to agree on the law governing the regime, but this choice may be held ineffective *to the extent* it violates the public policy limits of the otherwise applicable law.[75]

---

[70] *See id.* arts. 52–53.

[71] For example, the Turkish codif. art. 15(2) and Taiwanese codif. art. 48.3 allow a choice of law by the parties but mandatorily exempt from it immovables situated in a state other than the chosen state. *See also* Family Law (Scotland) Act 2006 asp 2 § 39. In the United States, the differentiation between movables and immovables is the norm. *See, e.g.,* Uniform Disposition of Community Rights at Death Act of 1971; Calif. Civ. Code §§ 5110, 4800, 4800.5, 4803; Calif. Prob. Code §§ 28, 100–102, 120. See also La. codif. arts. 3523–3527.

[72] *See, e.g.,* Hague Convention on the Law Applicable to Matrimonial Property Regimes, arts. 3(4), 6(4); Albanian codif. art. 24.2.c; Chinese codif. art. 26; FYROM codif. art. 43(2)3. German codif. art. 15(2)3; South Korean codif. art. 38(2)3.

[73] *See, e.g.,* Hague Convention on the Law Applicable to Matrimonial Property Regimes, art. 9; Belgian codif. art. 54; Bulgarian codif. art. 81; Estonian codif. art. 59; German codif. art. 16; Finish Law 1226/2001 § 135; Italian codif. art. 30.3; Japanese codif. art. 26(3); South Korean codif. art. 38(3)–(4); Lithuanian codif. art. 1.28(3)–(4); Portuguese codif. art. 54.2; Puerto Rico draft codif. art. 25; Serbian draft codif. art. 75.2; Swiss codif. art. 57; Taiwanese codif. art. 49; Turkish codif. art. 15(2).

[74] *See, e.g.,* Hague Convention on the Law Applicable to Matrimonial Regimes, arts. 12–13; Belgian codif. art. 52; Estonian codif. art. 58(2); German codif. arts. 15(3) and 14(4); Finish Law 1226/2001 § 130(3); Italian codif. art. 30.2; Lithuanian codif. art. 1.28(2); Romanian codif. art. 21(3); Serbian draft codif. art. 74.1; Swiss codif. art. 57.

[75] *See, e.g.,* Bulgarian codif. art. 79(4); Finish Law 1226/2001 §§ 134, 139(2).

(5) Some systems allow spouses: (a) to choose a governing law for only some of their assets; (b) to subject certain assets (e.g., immovables) to a different law than the law governing the rest of the regime; (c) to otherwise (e.g., in terms of time) choose more than one law; or (d) to change the governing law prospectively or retrospectively.[76] For example, the Serbian codification provides that "[u]nless the spouses agree otherwise, a change of the law applicable to the matrimonial property regime made during the marriage shall, be effective only in the future."[77] Conversely, the Swiss codification provides that a choice of law made after the celebration of the marriage has retroactive effect to the date of the marriage, but only "[i]n the absence of a contrary agreement."[78] The Swiss codification also provides that, when the spouses change their domicile from one state to another, the law of the new domicile applies and has retroactive effect to the date of the marriage, but the spouses may "agree in writing to exclude this retroactivity."[79]

(6) The Belgian codification seeks to prohibit a contractual dépeçage by providing that the spouses' choice of law must cover all of their assets.[80] However, if the spouses agree to change the applicable law, they may do so only prospectively, *unless* they agree to change it retroactively.[81] Finally, the Hague Convention on the Law Applicable to Matrimonial Property Regimes allows spouses, either before marriage (art. 3) or during marriage (art. 6), to choose the law governing the regime. Although, the chosen law must govern "the whole of their property,"[82] the spouses may exempt from that chosen law (or from the law that would be applicable in the absence of choice) all or some of their (present or future) immovables, and to subject them to the law or laws of the respective situses.[83]

5. Successions

As noted earlier, in testamentary succession conflicts, the possibility of dépeçage between form, capacity, and other issues was present even in traditional choice-of-law codifications. The same possibilities exist in modern codifications. However, what is new is the possibility of voluntary dépeçage. Voluntary dépeçage is now possible because of the

---

[76] *See, e.g.,* Hague Convention on the Law Applicable to Matrimonial Regimes, Arts. 7–8; Chinese codif. art. 26; German codif. art. 15(2)3; Finish Law 1226/2001 § 137(2); FYROM Codification, art. 43(2)3; South Korean codif. art. 38(2)3; Puerto Rico draft codif. art. 23; Serbian draft codif. art. 73; Uruguayan draft codif. art. 25.7.

[77] Serbian draft codif. art. 73.3.

[78] Swiss codif. art. 53.2.

[79] *Id.* art. 55.

[80] Belgian codif. art. 50 §2.

[81] *See id.* art. 50 § 3. ("The change of applicable law resulting from a choice by the spouses will only have effect for the future. The spouses may depart from this rule by agreement without adversely affecting third parties' rights."). *See also* Finish Law 1226/2001 § 129.

[82] Hague Convention on the Law Applicable to Matrimonial Property Regimes, arts. 3(3), 6(3).

[83] *Id.,* arts. 3(4), 6(4).

relatively new idea of allowing a testator to choose, within certain geographical and substantive limits, the law that will govern his or her succession upon death. Rules to this effect exist in: (1) the Hague Convention on the Law Applicable to Estates, the Successions Regulation in the EU, the Uniform Probate Code and other statutes in the United States;[84] and (2) more than 20 codifications in other countries.[85]

In addition to respecting the testator's volition, these rules can help accomplish an important goal of the substantive law of successions: treating the estate as a single unit under a single law regardless of the location of the assets. However, this goal can be accomplished only if the particular rule prohibits a partial choice of law or the choice of more than one law. In fact, very few rules contain such an express prohibition, and some specifically allow partial or multiple choices.

For example, the Hague Convention provides that the testator's choice of law "is to be construed as governing succession as a whole," but only "in the absence of a contrary provision by the deceased."[86] In fact, another article expressly allows the testator to choose the law of "one or more States to govern the succession to particular assets in his estate."[87] The Serbian codification provides that "[w]ith regard to the succession as a whole," a testator may choose the law of his nationality or habitual residence, but "[w]ith regard to the succession of his immovable estate," a testator may choose the law of the situs.[88]

Finally, a New York statute provides that, with regard to immovable *or movable* property situated in New York, a testator with no other connections to that state may elect to have New York law govern the disposition of the New York property,[89] while the rest of the testator's property will be governed by another law.

Even if the some of the aforementioned provisions are interpreted as prohibiting a partial or multiple testamentary choice of law, or even when a testator chooses a single law, there is no guarantee that a single law will ultimately govern the estate. If there are other disputed issues (such as issues of form or capacity) that are controlled by a different law, or if the chosen law violates certain provisions of the otherwise applicable law (such as those guaranteeing a compulsory share for the surviving spouse or children), then a dépeçage will be inevitable.

---

[84] *See* Hague Convention on the Law Applicable to Estates, art. 5; EU Successions Regulation, art. 22; Uniform Probate Code § 2-602; New York Estate Powers and Trusts Law § 3-5.1(h).

[85] *See* Albanian codif. art. 33.3; Azerbaijan codif. art. 29; Armenian codif. art. 1292; Belarus codif. arts. 1133, 1135; Belgian codif. art. 79 (testaments) and 124 (trusts); Bulgarian codif. art. 89; Burkina Faso codif. art. 1044; Estonian codif. art. 25; Italian codif. art. 46 (successions) and art. 56 (donations); Kazakhstan codif. art. 1121; South Korean codif. art. 49; Kyrgyzstan codif. art. 1206; Liechtenstein codif. art. 29.3; Moldovan codif. art. 1624; Dutch codif. art. 145; Polish codif. art. 64.1; Puerto Rico draft codif. art. 48; Quebec codif. arts. 3098–3099; Romanian codif. art. 68(1); Serbian codif. art. 104; Swiss codif. arts. 90(2), 91(2), 87(2), 95(2)(3); Tajikistan codif. arts. 1231–1232; Ukrainian codif. art. 70; Uzbekistan codif. art. 1197.

[86] Hague Estates Convention, art. 5(4).

[87] *Id.,* art. 6.

[88] Serbian draft codif. art. 104.

[89] New York Estate Powers and Trusts Law § 3-5.1 (h).

6. Trusts

The Hague Trusts Convention, which is in force in 11 countries,[90] expressly authorizes dépeçage. Chapter II of the Convention, which deals with the applicable law, provides that a trust is governed by the law chosen by the settlor and, in the absence of such a choice, by the law with which the trust is "most closely connected."[91] Article 9 provides that "[i]n applying this Chapter, a severable aspect of the trust, particularly matters of administration, may be governed by a different law."[92] The Czech and Quebec codifications have adopted a similar scheme, including the last-quoted provision, which authorizes a judicial and perhaps a voluntary dépeçage.[93]

B. JUDICIAL *DÉPEÇAGE*

A judicial dépeçage may occur in other codifications, such as those of Louisiana and Oregon, which employ "approaches" and issue-oriented rules. However, it can also occur under other codifications, inter alia: (1) through the handling of the incidental question, (2) by employing the *ordre public* reservation, (3) in applying the mandatory rules of the law of the forum or of a state other than the state of the otherwise applicable law, or (4) by employing an escape clause.

1. Incidental Question

Very few choice-of-law codifications address the question of what law governs the "incidental question." Among the few codifications that do contain an article on this point are the Dutch, Uruguayan, and Venezuelan codifications, and the Inter-American Convention on General PIL Rules.

The Dutch codification provides:

> Where the question of whether legal consequences ensue from a fact arises as a preliminary question in connection with another question that is subject to foreign law, the preliminary question shall be regarded as an autonomous question.[94]

---

[90] See Hague Convention of 1 July 1985 on the Law Applicable to Trusts and on Their Recognition (in force in: Australia, Canada, Italy, Liechtenstein, Luxemburg, Malta, Monaco, Netherlands, San Marino, Switzerland, and the United Kingdom).

[91] Hague Trusts Convention, art. 7

[92] *Id*. art. 9. Article 10 provides that the law applicable to the validity of the trust determines whether that law or the law governing a severable aspect of the trust may be replaced by another law.

[93] *See* Czech codif. art. 73; Quebec codif. art. 3107.

[94] Dutch codif. art. 4.

The clear implication of this provision is that the incidental question will be governed by the law designated by the choice-of-law rule applicable to this "autonomous" question, and that may *or may not* be the same law as that which governs the principal question.

The Inter-American Convention and the Venezuelan codification directly confirm this inference. They provide:

> Previous, preliminary or incidental issues that may arise from a principal issue need not necessarily be resolved in accordance with the law that governs the principal issue.[95]

Indeed, they "need not" be governed by the same law; and, when they are not, the result is, of course, dépeçage.

In other systems, there is no hard-and-fast rule on what law governs the incidental question. The available options are to apply: (1) the law governing the principal issue (*lex causae*), (2) the law designated by the choice-of-law rules of the *lex causae*, (3) the law designated by the choice-of-law rules of the forum state, or (4) the law of the forum qua forum.[96] A dépeçage is possible under the last three options.

2. *Ordre Public*

In virtually all choice-of-law systems, a court may refuse to apply the otherwise applicable foreign law *to the extent* that its application is manifestly incompatible with the public policy of the forum state. For example, Rome II provides that the application of "a provision" of the law of any country specified by Rome II may be refused if such application is manifestly incompatible with the public policy of the forum.[97]

In many cases, the objectionable provision of the foreign law must be replaced by another provision from either the same law (if possible)[98] or, more likely, from the law of the forum. Several codifications expressly authorize the application of the *lex fori* without qualification in place of the discarded provision of foreign law,[99] while other codifications authorize such application "if necessary."[100] For example, the Serbian codification

---

[95] Inter-American Convention on General Rules of Private International Law, art. 8. The Venezuelan article is virtually identical. *See* Venezuelan codif. art. 6. The Uruguayan draft codification (art. 10) provides directly that preliminary or incidental questions that arise in connection with the principal issue are governed by the law applicable to them.

[96] *See, e.g.,* C. Wendehorst, *Austrian Report*, at III.

[97] Rome II, art. 26.

[98] *See, e.g.,* Bulgarian codif. art. 45 (providing that "another appropriate provision of the same foreign law shall be applied" and, "[i]n the absence of such a provision, a provision of Bulgarian law shall apply, if necessary…"); Macau codif. art. 20; Portuguese codif. art. 22.2.

[99] *See, e.g.,* the codifications of: Albania (art. 7); Congo (Brazzaville) (art. 829); Kazakhstan (art. 1090.1); Kyrgyzstan (art. 1173); Moldova (art. 1583); Qatar (art. 38); Senegal (art. 851); Tajikistan codif. art. 1197.1; Togo (art. 730); Tunisia (art. 36.5); Ukraine (art. 12.1); and Uzbekistan (art. 1164.1).

[100] See Austrian codif. art. 6 (providing that "the corresponding provision of Austrian law shall be applied, if necessary."); Estonian codif. § 7 ("In such case, Estonian law applies."); Russian codif. art. 1193 ("In such a

provides that "[w]here *a provision* of a foreign law cannot be applied due to the violation of public policy, *a provision* of the law of the Republic of Serbia shall apply instead of it, if necessary."[101] Obviously, a dépeçage occurs whenever a court applies a foreign law for one part of a case and a provision of forum law for another part of the case for which the foreign law is repugnant to the forum's public policy.

3. Mandatory Rules

As Chapter 7 documents: (1) more than 40 codifications and conventions contain general provisions that expressly require the application of the mandatory rules of the forum state, and (2) nearly 30 codifications and conventions authorize the application of the mandatory rules of a third state (other than the forum state or the state of the *lex causae*) with which the case has a "close connection" in lieu of the provisions of the otherwise applicable foreign law.[102]

Moreover, as Chapter 3 documents, the Rome I Regulation and several codifications in countries outside the EU provide that a choice-of-law clause in a consumer contract or an employment contract may not deprive the consumer or employee, respectively, of the protection afforded by the mandatory rules of the country whose law would govern the contract in the absence of such a clause.[103] Rome I and the same codifications also provide that a contractually chosen law may not displace the mandatory rules of the country in which "all other elements relevant to the situation ... are located."[104]

In all instances where a court applies the mandatory rules of one state along with the non-displaced provisions of another state (the state of the otherwise applicable law), the court engages in dépeçage.

4. Escape Clauses

As the discussion in Chapter 4 documents, the use of escape clauses such as those based on the "closer connection" has become quite common in modern codifications.[105] For purposes of this topic, escape clauses can be divided into two categories. The first category consists of escape clauses that are directed at broad legal categories, such as contract or tort. The escape clauses in the majority of codifications, including those of Rome I and Rome II, belong to this category.[106] The second category consists of escapes clauses, such

---

case, if necessary, the respective norm of Russian law shall be applied."); Turkish codif. art. 5. ("where deemed necessary, Turkish law shall apply.").

[101] Serbian draft codif. art. 39(3) (emphasis added).

[102] *See* Chapter 7 at II.B.3, *infra*.

[103] *See* Chapter 3 at IV.B.2, V.A.3, and VII.B, *supra*.

[104] *See* Chapter 3, at II.A, *supra*.

[105] *See* Chapter 4 at VI, *supra*.

[106] *See id.* at VI.A–B.1.

as those found in the English tort statute and the Louisiana and Oregon codifications, which are directed toward particular *issues* within a contract or tort.[107]

The escape clauses of the second category can lead to dépeçage if the court employs them as to a particular issue rather than to the entire contract or tort. In contrast, the escape clauses of the first category are not supposed to lead to dépeçage because they may be employed only when the entire contract or tort is more closely connected with a state other than that of the otherwise applicable law. However, whether judges will in fact employ these clauses in such a wholesale fashion remains an open question.[108]

V. Assessment

This chapter is not intended to, and does not, prove that dépeçage is either a good or a bad thing. Rather, the chapter documents that dépeçage (1) is potentially as frequent in codified as in uncodified choice-of-law systems, and (2) it is much more frequent than commonly assumed. Although most codifications (such as Rome II) do not allow a judicial issue-by-issue analysis, they are replete with countless instances of legislative issue-splitting, which is at least as likely to lead to dépeçage as a judicial issue-by-issue analysis. Worse yet, most codifications do not provide the necessary tools to avoid a statutory dépeçage in those cases in which it may be inappropriate. This is somewhat ironic because a judicial issue-by-issue analysis carries with it judicial discretion to avoid an inappropriate dépeçage, whereas legislative issue-splitting usually does not unless the codification specifically grants it.

Unfortunately, very few codifications provide preventive or corrective tools against an inappropriate statutory dépeçage. Among the few exceptions are the codifications of Louisiana, Oregon, Puerto Rico, Venezuela, Uruguay, Burkina Faso, and the Inter-American Convention on General PIL Rules.

The first three codifications consist of flexible rules and escapes that give courts the ability to avoid an inappropriate dépeçage.[109] The Louisiana codification contains at least one provision, Article 3529, which is specifically designed to avoid an inappropriate statutory dépeçage. This provision is found in the title on successions, which consists of relatively fixed rules. Article 3529 contains two separate choice-of-law rules for issues of testamentary capacity and vices of consent, respectively. It provides that a person is capable of making a testament if, at the time of making the testament, he possessed that capacity under the law of the state in which he was domiciled either at that time or at the time of death. Article 3529 also provides that, if the testator possessed capacity under the law

---

[107] *See id.* at VI.B.2.

[108] *See, e.g.,* J. Erauw & M. Fallon, *Belgian Report,* at III.1 (expressing doubts on "whether the judges in European countries will be able to resist the temptation to split up a relationship and apply two different national laws to different issues under a contract, if the need were to occur.").

[109] For detailed discussion, *see* Symeonides, *Mixed Jurisdiction,* 472–476.

of only one of the above states, then "his will contained in the testament shall be held free of vices only if it would be so held under the law of *that* state."[110] The quoted provision is intended to avoid a dépeçage on the issues of testamentary capacity and consent because, in most systems, the rules on these two issues are closely interrelated so that applying one set of rules without the other would disturb the equilibrium accomplished by them and would distort the policies of both involved states.

The Inter-American Convention on General PIL Rules provides a more general admonition for avoiding an inappropriate *dépeçage*. Article 9 of the Convention provides that: (1) "[t]he different laws that may be applicable to various aspects of one and the same juridical relationship shall be applied harmoniously in order to attain the purposes pursued by each of such laws"; and that (2) "[a]ny difficulties that may be caused by their simultaneous application shall be resolved in the light of the requirements of justice in each specific case."[111]

The codifications of Venezuela,[112] Burkina Faso,[113] and Uruguay[114] also contain similar articles.

Unfortunately, most other codifications do not provide such tools and, for this reason, end up with the worst of both worlds:

(1) Out of concern that issue-by-issue analysis may lead to an inappropriate judicial dépeçage in some cases, these codifications avoid this analysis and thus deprive themselves of the benefits such an analysis provides in terms of flexibility and rationality.

(2) Yet these codifications produce countless cases of statutory dépeçage, and they do not provide the tools to avoid it in those cases in which it is inappropriate.

---

[110] La. codif. art. 3529 (emphasis added). For an in-depth discussion of the rationale and operation of this article, *see* Symeonides, *The "Dismal Swamp,"* 1057–1060.

[111] Inter-American Convention on General Rules of Private International Law, art. 9.

[112] *See* Venezuelan codif. art. 7 (providing that "[t]he several Laws that may be competent to govern the different aspects of a juridical relationship, shall be applied harmoniously, aiming at reaching the goals sought by each of those laws," and that "[p]ossible difficulties resulting from their simultaneous application shall be solved considering the requirements imposed by equity in the specific case.")

[113] *See* Burkina Faso codif. art. 1009 ("Lorsqu'un rapport juridique est, dans ses différents aspects, régit par des droits différents, ceux-ci doivent être appliqués d'une manière harmonieuse en vue de la réalisation des buts poursuivis par chacun de ces droits.")

[114] *See* Uruguay draft codif. art. 11 (providing that "[t]he different laws applicable to different aspects of a given situation must be applied harmoniously, taking into account the aims pursued by each law" and that any resulting difficulties should be resolved by "taking into account the equities of the case."). An earlier version of the Argentinean draft codification contained a similar provision, Article 12, which provided that "[t]he different laws applicable to different aspects of the same or different legal relationships involved in a case shall be applied harmoniously, with the aim of reaching the objectives pursued by each one of those laws." This article was omitted from the latest draft of 2011.

6   Codification and Result Selectivism

I. Introduction

One of the basic dilemmas of the choice-of-law process is whether, in choosing the law applicable to cases involving conflicts of laws, one should aim for: (1) the proper *law,* namely, the law of the *proper state* in the sense of the state with the most pertinent *contacts,* without concern for the "justness" of the particular result that the law produces ("conflict justice"); or (2) the proper *result,* that is, a result that produces the same quality of justice in the individual case as is expected in fully domestic, non-conflicts cases ("material justice").

II. The Classical View: "Conflicts Justice"

The classical, traditional view of PIL, going as far back as Savigny and Story, is grounded on the basic premise that the function of PIL is to ensure that each multistate legal dispute is resolved according to the law of the state that has the "most appropriate" relationship with that dispute. Opinions on defining and assessing the "propriety" of such a relationship have differed over the years from one legal system to another and from one subject to the next. Despite such differences, however, all versions of the classical school have remained preoccupied with choosing the proper *state* to supply the applicable law, rather than directly searching for the proper *law* (or, much less, for the proper *result*).

Indeed, the implicit, if not explicit, assumption of the classical school is that, in the great majority of cases, the law of the proper state *is* the proper law. In this context, however, "propriety" is defined not in terms of the content of that law, or the quality of the solution it produces, but rather in geographical or spatial terms.[1] If the contacts between the state from which that law emanates and the multistate dispute at hand are such as to meet certain predefined choice-of-law criteria, then the application of that law is considered proper, regardless of the qualities of the solution it produces. Whether the solution is "good" or "bad" depends on the inherent goodness or badness of the applicable law, and this is something beyond the domain of conflicts law. After all, conflicts exist because different societies have laws reflecting different value judgments on how to resolve legal disputes.[2] As long as multistate disputes are resolved by choosing the law of one state over the other, such a choice is bound to satisfy one society and one party and aggrieve another. This being so, the choice of the applicable law cannot afford to be motivated by whether it produces a "good" or "just" resolution of the actual dispute. Hence, although conflicts law should strive to ensure the application of the law of the proper state (conflicts justice), it cannot expect to ensure the same type and quality of justice as is pursued in fully domestic situations (material justice). In Gerhard Kegel's words, conflicts law "aims at the *spatially* best solution… [while] substantive law aims at the *materially* best solution."[3]

III. The Second View: "Material Justice"

A second view begins with the premise that multistate cases are not qualitatively different from domestic cases, and thus judges should not abdicate their responsibility to resolve disputes *justly and fairly* when they discover that the case contains foreign elements. Resolving such disputes in a manner that is substantively fair and equitable to the litigants should be an objective of conflicts law as much as it is of internal law. Justice should not be dispensed in gradations, and conflicts law should not accept a lesser quality of justice. Thus, this view rejects the classical presumption that the law of the proper state is necessarily the proper law and directly scrutinizes the applicable law to determine whether it actually produces the proper *result*. Again, opinions differ on defining the "propriety" of the result, but all versions of this view agree that the propriety should be determined in material terms (rather than spatial ones).

---

[1] *See* G. Kegel, The Crisis of Conflict of Laws, 112 *Recueil des cours* 91, 184–185 (1964) ("[W]hat is considered the best law according to its content, that is, *substantively*, might be far from the best spatially").

[2] *See* A. von Mehren, American Conflicts Law at the Dawn of the 21st Century, 37 *Willamette L. Rev.* 133, 134 (2000) ("[T]he difficulties posed for instrumental or teleological analysis are far greater when the controversies to be resolved are not localized in a single legal order that holds shared values and policies and has a unified administration of justice that can authoritatively weigh competing values and decide which shall prevails when conflicts arise."). *See also id.* at 137 ("[T]he same degree of justice usually cannot be given in matters that concern more than one society as is provided in matters that concern only one society and its legal order"); A. von Mehren, Choice of Law and the Problem of Justice, 41 *Law & Contemp. Prob.* 27, 42 (1977).

[3] G. Kegel, Paternal Home and Dream Home: Traditional Conflict of Laws and the American Reformers, 27 *Am. J. Comp. L.* 615, 616–617 (1979).

This view is much older than is generally believed. Historical precedents include the Byzantine commentators' preference for the *philanthropoteron* result,[4] the Italian statutists' preference for the forum's *statuta favorabilia* over foreign *statuta odiosa*,[5] and Magister Aldricus's call for the application of the *potior et utilior* law.[6] However, for at least seven centuries, this view has remained in the periphery of choice-of-law thinking until the twentieth century, when it found a more hospitable climate.

In the United States,[7] the material justice view is chiefly associated with Professor Robert A. Leflar. In the 1960s, Leflar proposed the following five "choice-influencing considerations" to guide the judicial choice of the applicable law: (1) predictability of results, (2) maintenance of interstate and international order, (3) simplification of the judicial task, (4) advancement of the forum's governmental interest, and (5) the application of the "better rule of law."[8] Although the "better-law" factor was, in Leflar's words, "only one of five" factors and "more important in some types of cases than in others, almost controlling in some but irrelevant in others,"[9] nothing prevented that factor from becoming decisive in all of the cases (and they are many) in which the other four factors are not dispositive. This is precisely how courts employed this factor (at least in the early years), treating it as dispositive while paying lip service to the other four. Consequently, Leflar's approach is deservedly known as "the better-law approach" and may be criticized or praised on that basis. The main criticisms are that a better-law approach can become a euphemism for a *lex fori* approach and that it provides convenient cover for judicial subjectivism. Although Leflar admonished against subjective choices, arguing that judges are capable of recognizing when foreign law is better than forum law,[10] there is considerable evidence to support the conclusion that the risks of such an approach are real.[11]

---

[4] *See* M. Maridakis, L'inaplicabilité du droit étranger à Byzance, 2 *Mélanges Fredericq* 79 (1965). The Greek word *philanthropoteron* is the comparative form of the word *philanthropos*, which is the root of the English word *philanthropic*. It would loosely translate as the more philanthropic, humane, benevolent, or merciful result.

[5] *See* 1 A. Lainé, *Introduction au droit international privé*, 146, 264 (1888).

[6] *See* Code cisianus E.VIII. 218 § 46.

[7] For other countries, *see, inter alia*, T.M. de Boer, Facultative Choice of Law: The Procedural Status of Choice-of-Law Rules and Foreign Law, 257 *Recueil des cours* 223, 293–297 (1996); K. Zweigert, Zur Armut des internationalen Privatrechts an sozialen Werten, 37 *RabelsZ* 435 (1973). *See also* C. Joerges, *Zum Functionswandel des Kollisionsrecht, Die "Governmental Interest Analysis" und die "Krise des Internationalen Privatrechts"* (1971); J. González Campos, Diversification, spécialisation et matérialisation des règles de droit international privé, 287 *Recueil des cours* 9 (2000); P. Gutzwiller, Von Ziel und méthodes des "IPR," *Ann. Suisse droit int'l* 161 (1968).

[8] *See* R. Leflar, Choice-Influencing Considerations in Conflicts Law, 41 *N.Y.U. L. Rev.* 367 (1966); R. Leflar, Conflicts of Law: More on Choice Influencing Considerations, 54 *Cal. L. Rev.* 1584 (1966).

[9] R. Leflar, L. McDougal & R. Felix, *American Conflicts Law* 300 (4th ed. 1986).

[10] *See id.* at 298–299. ("Judges can appreciate…the fact that their forum law in some areas is anachronistic…or that the law of another state has these benighted characteristics").

[11] *See* Symeonides, *American PIL* §§ 243–247.

The material justice view has also had other adherents among American scholars, including Professors Friedrich Juenger,[12] Luther McDougal,[13] and, to a lesser extent, Professors David Cavers,[14] Russell Weintraub,[15] and, recently, Joseph Singer.[16]

Juenger advocated a type of better-law approach that was less conventional than Leflar's version. Unlike Leflar, who argued for choosing the better between the existing laws of the involved states, Juenger argued that the court should construct and apply to the case at hand a new substantive rule derived from the laws of the involved states.[17] For example, in product liability conflicts, Juenger proposed that the court should draw from among the laws of the states of conduct, injury, product acquisition, and domicile of the parties, and then construct a substantive rule that "most closely accords with modern standards of products liability."[18] Not coincidentally, Juenger called his approach a "substantive-law" approach,[19] a purposefully chosen term that evokes the most ancient approach to resolving conflicts problems, the approach of the Roman *praetor peregrinus*, who, in resolving disputes between Roman and non-Roman citizens, constructed ad hoc substantive rules derived from the laws of the involved countries. Indeed, Juenger rejected both unilateralism and multilateralism, the two branches of the conflictual method, in favor of the third and oldest method, substantivism.[20]

Luther McDougal took a step beyond both Leflar and Juenger when he proposed his "best" law approach. Unlike Leflar and Juenger, who thought that the courts' choices, albeit different, should be confined to the laws of the states involved in the conflict, McDougal argued that "[c]ourts are not so limited in their choice"[21] and that they should, in principle, be free to look beyond those states in constructing the "best" rule of law. McDougal described the best rule as "one that best promotes net aggregate long-term

---

[12] *See* Juenger, *Multistate Justice* 145–173, 191–208, 233–237.

[13] *See* L. McDougal, Towards the Application of the Best Rule of Law in Choice of Law Cases, 35 *Mercer L. Rev.* 483 (1984).

[14] *See* Cavers, *Critique*, 47 *Harv. L. Rev.* 173, *et seq.* (arguing that "justice in the individual case" should be an important consideration in choice-of-law decisions); Cavers, *Choice of Law Process* 180 (proposing result-oriented principles of preference for contracts); D. Cavers, The Proper Law of Producer's Liability, 26 *Int'l & Comp. L.Q.* 703 (1977) (proposing a result-oriented principle for product-liability conflicts).

[15] *See* R. Weintraub, *Commentary on the Conflict of Laws* 360, 397–398 (3d ed. 1986) (proposing a plaintiff-favoring rule for tort conflicts and a rule of validation for contract conflicts).

[16] *See* J. Singer, Pay No Attention to That Man Behind the Curtain: The Place of Better Law in a Third Restatement of Conflicts, 75 *Ind. L.J.* 659 (2000); J. Singer, Justice and the Conflict of Laws, 48 *Mercer L. Rev.* 831 (1997); J. Singer, A Pragmatic Guide to Conflicts, 70 *B.U. L. Rev.* 731 (1990).

[17] Juenger, *Multistate Justice*, 236.

[18] *Id.* at 197.

[19] *See id.* at 172 (advocating "an unabashedly teleological substantive law approach.").

[20] For the difference between these methods, *see* Symeonides, *At the Dawn of the 20th Century*, 4, 11–16; Symeonides, *Accommodative Unilateralism*, 417 *et seq.*

[21] McDougal, *supra* note 13, at 483–484.

common interests,"[22] and provided examples of such rules.[23] Unlike Leflar's approach, the approaches of Juenger and McDougal have not gained any appreciable judicial following.

IV. "Only in America"?

The foregoing brief description of American result-selective approaches may cause readers from other countries to conclude that "only in America" could such approaches take roots. Maybe so, but this does not mean that other choice-of-law systems are oblivious to material-justice considerations. Although the classical view remains very much the prevailing view outside the United States, the material justice view has made significant inroads into the classical view. Put another way, the classical view of conflicts justice has accepted the corrective function of material justice in many more instances than, say, 50 years ago, and in more instances than it is generally believed.

To begin with, as discussed elsewhere, material-justice considerations play a significant, albeit covert, role in the judicial resolution of conflicts cases in uncodified choice-of-law systems.[24] What is more surprising, however, is the degree to which codified choice-of-law systems have accepted material-justice considerations and have compressed them into choice-of-law rules that structurally fit the traditional mold. This chapter focuses first on codified choice-of-law systems in which the classical view is supposed to dominate, and then examines the degree to which these systems *officially* sanction the pursuit of material justice in the choice-of-law process. Although most of these systems are unlikely to endorse ideas such as those advanced by Juenger or McDougal, or to entrust judges with the same degree of open-ended discretion envisioned by Leflar, nothing prevents the pursuit of material justice through other means, such as statutory rules designed for such a purpose. This chapter surveys a representative number of recent conflicts codifications from five continents and identifies a fairly high number of choice-of-law rules that are *specifically* designed[25] to produce a particular substantive result.

---

[22] *Id.* at 484

[23] For non-economic loses, McDougal proposed a rule that permits "complete recovery of all losses, pecuniary and nonpecuniary, and of all reasonable costs incurred in obtaining recovery, including reasonable attorney's fees and litigation costs." *Id.* at 533. For claims concerning punitive damages, he proposed a rule that imposes such damages "on individuals who engage in outrageous conduct and who are not adequately punished in the criminal process." *Id.*

[24] *See* Symeonides, *Progress or Regress?* 46–48.

[25] Material justice can also be pursued through other rules or techniques that are not specifically designed for this purpose. Among them are: (1) open-ended choice-of-law rules, (2) rules that rely on soft or indeterminate connecting factors, (3) content-oriented choice-of-law rules, (4) statutory escape clauses, (5) the *ordre public* reservation, (6) the characterization process, and (7) renvoi. For a comparative discussion of these rules or techniques, *see* Symeonides, *Progress or Regress?* 26–34, 37–42.

It should be noted that these rules are classic *choice-of-law* rules rather than substantive rules insofar as they authorize courts to choose the existing substantive law of one of the involved states, rather than directly providing a substantive solution to the conflict at hand. At the same time, they are *result-selective*, or result-oriented, rules because they instruct courts to choose a law that produces a particular substantive result, such as upholding a juridical act or favoring a particular party, as explained below. In this sense, the French terminology of *"règles de conflit à coloration matérielle"* is particularly apt.

This chapter compiles an illustrative list of such rules and then attempts to determine how their existence should inform the continuing debate between the proponents of the conflicts-justice and material-justice views.

V. Result-Selective Statutory Choice-of-Law Rules

Result-selective rules appear in varying shapes and forms. Their common characteristic, however, is that they are specifically designed to accomplish a certain substantive result that is considered a priori desirable. More often than not, this result is favored by the domestic law of not only the enacting state, but also the majority of states that partake in the same legal tradition. This result may be one of the following:

(1) Favoring the formal or substantive validity of a juridical act, such as a testament, a marriage, or an ordinary contract;

(2) Favoring a certain status, such as legitimacy or filiation, the status of a spouse, or even the dissolution of a status (divorce); or

(3) Favoring a particular party, such as a tort victim, the owner of stolen movable property, a consumer, an employee, a maintenance obligee, or any other party whom the legal order considers weak or whose interests are considered worthy of protection.

The first two objectives (favoring the validity of a juridical act or favoring a certain status) are accomplished by choice-of-law rules that contain a list of alternative references to the laws of several states connected with the case (*"alternative-reference" rules*) and authorize the court to select a law that validates the juridical act or confers the preferred status.

The third objective (protecting a particular party) is accomplished through choice-of-law rules that: (1) grant alternative choices to the court as above; (2) allow the protected party, either before or after the events that give rise to the dispute, to choose the applicable law from among the laws of certain designated states; or (3) protect that party from the adverse consequences of a potentially coerced or uninformed choice-of-law.

A. RULES FAVORING THE VALIDITY OF CERTAIN JURIDICAL ACTS (*FAVOR VALIDITATIS*)

Result-selective rules that are designed to favor the validity of a certain juridical act were not unknown at the beginning of the twentieth century. However, by the end of the century, these rules proliferated, and their scope expanded. As the following discussion indicates, these rules (1) can be found in almost every country, (2) apply to more juridical acts than ever before, and (3) encompass not only issues of form but issues of substance as well.

One of the broadest rules of this type is Article 22(2) of the Paraguayan Civil Code, which, although it is a unilateral rule, encompasses *all* juridical acts. It provides that foreign laws shall not be applied if they are less favorable to the validity of a juridical act than the Code's own provisions.[26] However, as shown below, most other rules are bilateral yet narrower in scope because they encompass only certain juridical acts.

1. Testaments (*favor testamenti*)

The policy of *favor testamenti* is an old policy of the substantive law of succession.[27] This policy has also been projected to the multistate level by choice-of-law rules that, through a list of alternative references to several laws, are designed to preserve the validity of the testament whenever possible by authorizing the court to apply whichever one of the listed laws would uphold the testament.

a. Formal Validity

One of the longer lists of alternative references is contained in the Hague Convention on the Conflicts of Laws Relating to the Form of Testamentary Dispositions (1961).[28] Article 1 of the Convention provides that a testament shall be considered formally valid if it conforms to the internal law of any one of the following places:

a) The place where the testator made it, or
b) A nationality possessed by the testator, either at the time when he made the disposition, or at the time of his death, or
c) A place in which the testator had his domicile either at the time when he made the disposition, or at the time of his death, or

---

[26] Paraguayan Civ. Code art. 22(2) ("No se aplicarán las leyes extranjeras cuando las normas de este Código sean más favorables a la validez de los actos.")

[27] *See* Symeonides, *The "Dismal Swamp,"* 1048, 1046; *See also* E. Rabel, *Conflict of Laws: A Comparative Study* 287 (1958) ("invalidity of a will, discovered after the testator's death is irreparable.")

[28] For the text of the convention and a list of the countries in which it is in force, *see* http://www.hcch.net/index_en.php?act=conventions.text&cid=40 (last visited Dec. 2, 2013). For an authoritative discussion of this convention by its *Rapporteur, see* A.E. von Overbeck, *L'unification des règles de conflits de lois en matière de forme de testaments* (1961).

d) The place in which the testator had his habitual residence either at the time when he made the disposition, or at the time of his death, or

e) Insofar as immovables are concerned, of the place where they are situated.[29]

In the majority of cases, the court's choices under this article will be no more than a couple. However, in cases involving dual nationals or testators who changed their domiciles or nationalities between the time of making the testament and the time of death, the court's choices will be far more numerous, indeed, as many as the *eight* possibilities depicted in Table 6.1 below.

TABLE 6.1. CHOICES OF VALIDATING LAWS UNDER HAGUE CONVENTION

1. Place of making		
2. Testator's nationality	(a) at time of testament	
	(b) at time of death	
3. Testator's domicile	(a) at time of testament	
	(b) at time of death	
4. Testator's habitual residence	(a) at time of testament	
	(b) at time of death	
5. Situs (for immovables)		

A similar rule had been proposed in the United States at a much earlier time in the 1909 Uniform Wills Act. The Act was gradually adopted in the majority of the states of the United States and was eventually replaced by a similar result-oriented provision contained in the Uniform Probate Code. Section 2-506 of the Code provides that a testament that meets certain minimum requirements is valid "if its execution complies with the law at the time of execution of the place where the will is executed, or of the law of the place where, at the time of execution or at the time of death the testator is domiciled, has a place of abode, or is a national."[30]

The EU Regulation on Successions of 2012 has followed a similar path as that of the Hague Convention by adopting an even more liberal rule for matters of testamentary form. This rule is more liberal because it also applies to "agreements as to succession."

---

[29] Hague Testaments Convention, art. 1 (emphasis added).

[30] Uniform Probate Code § 2-506 (2010 version). For the text of the Code, *see* http://uniformlaws.org/Act. aspx?title=Probate Code (Last visited Dec. 2, 2013). This version of the Code has been adopted in the following 17 states: Alaska, Arizona, Colorado, Hawaii, Idaho, Maine, Massachusetts, Michigan, Minnesota, Montana, Nebraska, New Jersey, New Mexico, North Dakota, South Carolina, South Dakota, and Utah, and Wisconsin. Virtually all other states of the United States have adopted similar validation rules. *See* Symeonides, *The "Dismal Swamp,"* 1043.

Article 27 provides that a *mortis causa* disposition made in writing shall be valid as to form if it complies with the law of:

(a) The state in which the disposition was made or the succession agreement concluded;

(b) The nationality, domicile, or habitual residence of the testator or of at least one party to the agreement, at either the time of the disposition or agreement or the time of death; or

(c) With regard to immovables, the situs state.[31]

The Hague Convention is in force in 41 countries. These countries are listed on the left-hand column of Table 6.2 below, with the pertinent provisions of implementing or parallel internal legislation shown in parentheses. The right-hand column of the Table lists codifications that contain rules with similar or (usually) shorter lists or alternative validating references.

TABLE 6.2. RESULT-SELECTIVISM FOR TESTAMENTARY FORM

Countries in which the Hague Convention is in force	Countries with implementing or similar legislation
Antigua & Barbuda	Afghanistan (art. 25)
Armenia	Albania (art. 35)
Australia	Algeria (art. 16)
Austria (art. 30)	Angola (art. 65)
Belgium (art. 83)	Argentina (draft art. 2645)
Bosnia	Azerbaijan (art. 30)
Botswana	Belarus (art. 1135)
Brunei	Bulgaria (art. 90.2)
Croatia (art. 31)	Burkina Faso (art. 1047)
Denmark	Cape Verde (art. 63)
Estonia (art. 27)	China (art. 34)
Fiji	Congo (Brazzaville) (art. 826)
Finland (Inheritance Code arts. 9, 18)	Czech Republic (art. 76.2)
France	East Timor (art. 62)
FYROM (art. 37)	European Union (Succ. Reg. art. 27)
Germany (art. 26)	Georgia (art.56)

---

[31] Article 27 of Regulation (EU) No 650/2012 of the European Parliament and of the Council of 4 July 2012 on jurisdiction, applicable law, recognition and enforcement of decisions, and acceptance and enforcement of authentic instruments in matters of succession and on the creation of a European Certificate of Succession.

Countries in which the Hague Convention is in force	Countries with implementing or similar legislation
Greece	Guinea-Bissau (art. 65)
Grenada	Hungary (art. 36(2))
Ireland	Jordan (art. 18.2)
Israel (Succession Law art. 140)	Italy (art. 48)
Japan	Kazakhstan (art. 1122)
Lesotho	North Korea (art. 46.2)
Luxembourg	South Korea (art. 50.3)
Mauritius	Kyrgyzstan (art. 1207)
Moldova (art. 1624.2)	Liechtenstein (art. 30)
Montenegro	Lithuania (art. 1.61)
Netherlands (art. 151)	Louisiana (art. 3528)
Norway	Macau (art. 62)
Poland (art. 66)	Mongolia (art. 552.2–3)
Serbia (draft art. 108)	Mozambique (art. 65)
Slovenia (art. 33)	Paraguay (art. 2626.2)
South Africa	Portugal (art. 65.1)
Spain (arts. 8, 11.1)	Puerto Rico (draft art. 43)
Swaziland	Qatar (art. 24)
Sweden	Quebec (art. 3109.3)
Switzerland (art. 93)	Romania (art. 68.3)
Tonga	Senegal (art. 848)
Turkey (arts. 20.4, 7)	Somalia (art. 17)
Ukraine (art. 72)	Sudan (art. 11(11))
United Kingdom	Taiwan (art. 61)
	Tajikistan (art. 1232)
	Togo (art. 722)Tunisia (art. 55)
	United Arab Emirates (art. 17.4)
	United States (Unif. Probate Code)

b. Substantive Validity

Rules designed to favor the validity of a testament with regard to matters other than form are less common, but they do exist. For example, regarding testamentary capacity, the Argentinean, Austrian, Louisiana, and Puerto Rico codifications provide alternative references to the laws of the testator's domicile either at the time of the testament's making or the time of the testator's death.[32] The Serbian codification limits the choices to the time of making the testament but authorizes the application of the law of either the

---

[32] *See* Argentine draft codif. art. 120; Austrian codif. art. 30; Louisiana codif. art. 3529; Puerto Rico draft codif. art. 44.

testator's habitual residence or nationality.[33] The Swiss codification limits the choices to the time of the testator's death but expands them to "the law of the state of his domicile or of his habitual residence, or the law of one of the states of which he is a national."[34] The Finnish Inheritance Code adopts the same solution with regard to time but adds to these choices the "law applicable to the inheritance."[35]

Other codifications extend this liberality to other matters affecting substantive validity. For example, the Liechtenstein codification provides that a *mortis causae* disposition is valid as to capacity "and other conditions or validity" if it satisfies the requirements of the laws of the decedent's nationality or habitual residence at either the time of disposition or the time of death, or of the law of Liechtenstein with regard to proceedings in that country.[36] The Chinese codification allows the same choices with regard to the "effects" of a testament, although not phrased explicitly in validating terms.[37]

2. Other Juridical Acts (*favor negotii*)

a. Formal Validity

Many codifications provide similar validating rules for contracts and other inter vivos juridical acts. As noted earlier, the broadest rule in this regard is Article 22.2 of the Paraguayan codification, which provides that foreign law does not apply if the rules of "this code," that is, the Paraguayan Civil Code, are "more favorable to the validity of juridical acts."[38] Most other codifications have narrower rules that differentiate between matters of form and substantive matters.

Article 11 of the European Union's Rome I Regulation stands out as one characteristic example of a validation rule for matters of form. The article provides that a contract is formally valid if it satisfies the requirements of the law of the state that governs the substance of the contract (hereinafter *lex causae*).[39] The article also provides that: (1) a contract concluded between persons who are in the same country is formally valid if it satisfies the requirements of that country, and (2) a contract between persons who are in different countries is formally valid if it conforms to the law of "either of the countries where either of the parties or their agent is present at the time of conclusion, or of the law of the country where either of the parties had his habitual residence at that time."[40]

---

[33] See Serbian draft codif. art. 107.

[34] Swiss codif. art. 94.

[35] Finnish Code of Inheritance § 10.

[36] *See* Liechtenstein codif. art. 30.

[37] *See* Chinese codif. art. 35. However, the choices do not include the *lex fori* as such. The Chinese Model Law adds the law of the place of the testament's making, and allows the same choices for the "contents and effect" of a will. It first gives the testator a choice from among the above four laws and then provides that, in the absence of such a choice, the law "most favorable to the formation" of the will shall govern. *See* Chinese Model Law arts. 142, 144.

[38] Paraguayan codif. art. 22.2.

[39] It should be noted that in Rome I, as well as in many other codifications, this law might well be the law designated in a choice-of-law clause.

[40] Rome I, art. 11. For a similar provision, *see* Rome Convention, art. 9.

Rome I supersedes identical or similar rules found in EU Member States, such as Bulgaria, Estonia, Germany, Italy, Lithuania, the Netherlands, Poland, and Romania,[41] although those rules remain in force for juridical acts other than contracts falling outside the scope of Rome I. Parallel provisions are found in the Hague Sales Convention, as well as in the codifications of Albania, South Korea, Moldova, Oregon, Puerto Rico, Serbia, Switzerland, Taiwan, Tunisia, and Ukraine.[42]

The Mexico City Convention provides that contracts between parties who are in different states are valid if they conform to: (1) the law of either state, (2) the law that governs the substance of the contract (*lex causae*), or (3) the law of the place of performance (*lex loci solutionis*).[43] However, for contracts between parties who are in the same state, the Convention provides a somewhat curious rule. Such contracts are valid if they meet the requirements of (1) the *lex causae*, (2) the *lex loci solutionis*, or (3) "the law of the State in which the contract is valid."[44] It is to be noted that the quoted phrase does not require any connection between "the State" and the contract or the parties.

Many other codifications have also adopted contract validation rules with shorter or longer lists of alternative references in multiple combinations, including the following:[45]

(1) The *lex loci actum* or the *lex loci causae*;[46]

(2) The *lex loci actum*, the *lex causae*, or—in contracts between parties not acting in the same state—either party's presence or habitual residence;[47]

(3) The *lex loci actum* or the common national law of the contracting parties;[48]

(4) The foreign *lex loci actum* or the *lex fori*;[49]

---

[41] *See* Bulgarian codif. art. 98; Estonian codif. § 37; German codif. art. 11; Italian codif. art. 57; Lithuanian codif. arts. 1.38 (contracts) and 1.41 (donations); Dutch codif. art. 12; Polish codif. art. 25; Romanian codif. art. 86 (for other juridical acts, *see id.* art. 71)

[42] *See* art. 11 of the Hague Convention for the Law Applicable to the International Sales of Goods (1986); Albanian codif. art. 18; South Korean codif. art. 17; Moldova codif. art. 1610; Oregon contracts codif. § 15.325; Puerto Rico draft codif. art. 32; Serbian draft codif. art. 146; Swiss codif. arts. 124 (contracts), art. 178(2) (arbitration agreements), and art. 56 (formalities of matrimonial agreements); Taiwanese codif. Art 16; Tunisian codif. art. 68; Ukrainian codif. art. 31.

[43] Inter-American Convention on the Law Applicable to International Contracts, Art 13(2) (1994).

[44] *Id.* art. 13(1).

[45] Some of these codifications allow an additional reference to the law of the situs with regard to immovables located in the situs state.

[46] *See* Argentinian draft art. 2649; Croatian codif. art. 7; Japanese codif. arts. 10, 34; North Korean codif. art. 26; Peruvian codif. art. 2094; Portuguese codif. art. 36.2; Serbian codif. art. 41; Turkish codif. art. 7.

[47] *See* the provisions of Rome I and the codifications of Bulgaria, Estonia, Germany, Italy, Lithuania, the Netherlands, Poland, and Romania cited at notes 40–41 *supra*, and those of Albania, South Korea, Moldova, Oregon, Puerto Rico, Serbia, Switzerland, Taiwan, Tunisia, and Ukraine, cited at note 42, *supra*.

[48] *See* Algerian codif. art. 19; Burundi codif. art. 5; Rwanda codif. art. 14.

[49] *See* Azerbaijan codif. art. 17.1; Belarus codif. art. 1116; Guinea-Conakry codif. art. 9; Kazakhstan codif. art. 1104; Kyrgyzstan codif. art. 1190 (but subject to an exception for cases involving forum citizens); Russian codif. art. 1209.1 (with same exception); Tajikistan codif. art. 1210 (with same exception); Uzbekistan codif. art. 1181 (with same exception); Vietnamese codif. art. 770(1).

(5) The *lex loci actum, lex causae,* or *lex solutionis;*[50]

(6) the *lex loci actum,* the *lex causae,* the *lex solutionis,* the law of the parties' common domicile or place of business, or the law chosen by the parties;[51]

(7) The *lex loci actum,* the *lex causae,* or the law of the parties' common domicile or nationality;[52]

(8) The *lex loci actum, lex causae, lex fori,* or law of place of intended effect of contract;[53]

(9) The *lex loci actum,* the *lex causae,* the *lex rei sitae,* or the law of the domicile of one of the parties;[54]

(10) The *lex loci,* the *lex causae,* or the law of the domicile of the executing party;[55]

(11) The *lex causae,* the *lex loci,* or the law designated by the choice-of-law rule of the *lex loci.*[56]

Table 6.3 below depicts these combinations of validating alternative references used by various codifications, as well as the number of codifications adopting each combination.

TABLE 6.3. ALTERNATIVE VALIDATING REFERENCES FOR FORMALITIES OF JURIDICAL ACTS

Number of codifications following	*Lex loci actus*	*Lex causae*	*Lex solutionis*	*Lex fori*	Common dom. or nationality	Either party's dom.	Dom. of executing party	Either party's presence	Other
8	X	X							
19	X	X				X		X	
8	X			X					
3	X			X					
1	X	X	X						
1	X	X	X		X				X
5	X	X			X				
1	X	X		X					X
1	X	X				X			
4	X	X					X		
1	X	X							X

---

[50] *See* Slovenian codif. art. 7.

[51] *See* Louisiana codif. art. 3538.

[52] *See* Jordanian codif. art. 21; Qatar codif. art. 29; Somalian codif. art. 20; Sudanese codif. art. 11(13c); Yemen codif. art. 31.

[53] *See* Hungarian codif. art. 29(2).

[54] *See* Quebec codif. art. 3109 (1)(2).

[55] *See* Moldova codif. art 1610; Mongolian codif. art. 548; Spanish codif. art. 11; Venezuelan codif. art. 37.

[56] *See* Macau codif. art. 35.

The common denominator among these codifications is that they all subscribe to the notion that validation, rather than invalidation, is the desired substantive policy. Nevertheless, as the above table reveals, they differ widely on the degree of preference that policy should enjoy and on the means used to attain it.

b. Capacity

The trend of favoring validation of juridical acts has even been carried over to issues of capacity, although validation in this context is placed within narrower parameters than is the case with regard to issues of form. For example, even traditional European Civil codes, such as those of Greece and Spain, contain rules that reflect the solution reached in the well-known nineteenth-century *Lizardi* case[57] and favor validation by applying the validating rule of the *lex fori* as the *lex loci actum* in lieu of the otherwise applicable personal law of the actor.[58] This rule, in its unilateral iteration, is reproduced in more than 20 recent codifications.[59]

Other codifications have bilateralized this rule by authorizing the application of the validating law of the *locus actum* even when that *locus* is not in the forum state. For example, Article 12 of the Chinese codification provides that, although a person's capacity to enter into juridical acts is governed by the law of her habitual residence, a person who lacks such capacity under that law is nevertheless considered capable if she possesses such capacity under the law of the place of the act.[60] Similar rules are found in more than 20 other codifications.[61]

In a similar vein, the Venezuelan codification provides that a person who lacks capacity under the law of his domicile shall be considered capable if he possesses capacity under the law governing the substance of the act.[62] The Louisiana codification contains a similar but more precise rule providing that a person is considered capable of contracting if she possesses such capacity under the law of the state in which she is domiciled or under the

---

[57] Req., 16 Jan. 1861, in *Dalloz Périodique* 1.193 (1861), *Sirey* 1.305 (1805).

[58] *See, e.g.,* Greek Civ. Code. arts. 7, 9; Spanish Civ. Code art. 10(8). These rules contain exceptions making them inapplicable to matters of family law and successions.

[59] *See* the codifications of: Algeria (art. 10); Angola (28.1); Cape Verde (art. 28.1); East Timor (art. 27.1); Guinea-Bissau (art. 28.1); Hungary (art. 15(2)(3)); Jordan (art. 12); North Korea (Art 18); Latvia (art. 8); Macau (art. 27); Mauritania (art. 7); Peru (art. 2070); Portugal (art. 28(1)); Qatar (art. 11); Slovakia (art. 3.2); Somalia (art. 11); Sudan (art. 11.1); Taiwan (art. 10(3)); U.A.E (art 11.1); and Yemen (art. 25). In contrast, a rule such as Article 762(2) of the Vietnamese codification is *not* a result-selective *validating* rule. It provides that Vietnamese law governs the capacity of foreigners acting in Vietnam (rather than the otherwise applicable law of the actor's nationality), regardless of whether Vietnamese law would validate or invalidate the act.

[60] Chinese codif. art. 12.

[61] *See* the codifications of: Albania (art. 12); Armenia (art. 1265); Bulgaria (art 50(2)); Burkina Faso (art. 1018); Croatia (art. 14); Estonia (art. 12.2); FYROM (art. 15); Germany (art. 12); Italy (art. 23.2(3)); Japan (art. 4); South Korea (arts. 13, 15.1); Liechtenstein (art. 12); Oregon (§ 15.330); Polish (arts. 11–12); Puerto Rico draft codif. (art. 33); Quebec (art 3086); Romania (art. 17); Russia (art. 1197); Serbia (draft art. 55); Switzerland (art. 36); Tunisia (art. 40.); Slovenia (art. 13); Turkey (art. 9.2); Ukraine (art. 18).

[62] Venezuelan codif. art. 18.

law applicable to the *particular issue* under the codification's general flexible approach for contract conflicts.[63]

The Puerto Rico and Oregon codifications reproduce the same rule, and also provide that a person may invoke her incapacity under the law of her domicile only against a party that "knew or should have known" of the incapacity.[64] This is a similar test as that provided in the Rome Convention and later the Rome I Regulation. Article 13 of Rome I provides that, in contracts concluded between persons who are in the same country, a natural person who would have capacity under that country's law may invoke his incapacity resulting from another law only if the other party was "aware of that incapacity … or was not aware thereof as a result of negligence."[65] More than 15 other codifications also contain similar rules that narrowly favor validation by limiting the circumstances under which a party may invoke the provisions of a law that declares that party incapable of contracting.[66]

Finally, in the United States, one author has extracted a similar "rule of validation" from the case law,[67] and two other authors have proposed explicit validation rules encompassing, inter alia, issues of contractual capacity. Thus, subject to certain exceptions, Professor Russell Weintraub would uphold a contract that is considered valid under the law of "any state having a contact with the parties or with the transaction sufficient to make that state's validating policies relevant."[68] Similarly, in his Principle of Preference no. 6, Professor David Cavers would apply the invalidating law of a state only if the party protected by that law is domiciled in that state *and* the transaction is centered there.[69]

B. RULES FAVORING A CERTAIN STATUS

1. Legitimacy (*favor legitimationis*)

At least until the middle of the twentieth century, illegitimacy carried discriminatory and stigmatizing legal and social effects in virtually every country. Because of these dire consequences, the domestic law of most countries contained several rules designed to ensure that all ambiguities and doubts would be resolved in favor of legitimacy. Because legitimacy was the preferred status in domestic law, it also became the favored status in PIL. This preference was reflected in choice-of-law rules that, within certain narrow

---

[63] *See* La. codif. art. 3539.

[64] *See* Oregon contracts codif. § 15.330; Puerto Rico Draft Code art. 33.

[65] Rome I, art. 13. *See also* Rome Convention art. 11.

[66] *See* the codifications of: Argentina (draft art. 2617); Armenia (art. 1265); Bulgaria (art. 50.2); Burkina Faso (art. 1018); Estonia (art. 12.2); Germany (art. 12); Italian (art. 23.2(3)); South Korea (arts. 13, 15.1); Liechtenstein (art. 12); Moldova (art. 1592); Netherlands (art. 11.2); Polish (art. 12); Puerto Rico (draft art. 33); Quebec (art. 3086); Romania (art. 17); Switzerland (art. 36); Tunisia (art. 40).

[67] *See* A. Ehrenzweig, The Statute of Frauds in the Conflict of Laws: The Basic Rule of Validation, 59 *Colum. L. Rev.* 874, 875–880 (1959); A. Ehrenzweig, "Choice of Law: Current Doctrine and True Rules," 49 *Cal. L. Rev.* 240 (1961).

[68] R. Weintraub, *Commentary on the Conflict of Laws* 397 (3d ed. 1986)

[69] *See* Cavers, *Choice of Law Process,* 180.

parameters, were designed to lead to the application of a law that afforded the status of legitimacy.

By now, these rules have multiplied, even though the discriminatory treatment of illegitimate children is decreasing, having been declared unconstitutional in many countries. For example, Article 2083 of the Peruvian Civil Code provides that "[m]atrimonial filiation is governed by the law of the place where the marriage was celebrated or of the conjugal domicile at the time the child is born, whichever is more favorable to legitimacy."[70]

The Japanese, South Korean, and Taiwanese codifications also favor legitimacy by providing that a child is legitimate if the child enjoys that status under the national law of either parent or of the child.[71] The Liechtenstein codification provides that legitimacy at birth and legitimation by subsequent marriage are governed by the common personal law of the spouses and, in the absence thereof, by the law of that spouse which favors the child's legitimacy or legitimation.[72] The Portuguese codification, and the codifications based on it, favor legitimacy by prohibiting an otherwise permissible renvoi if it would lead to a law that would consider the child illegitimate.[73]

Finally, the Slovenian codification provides that legitimacy is governed by the law of the parents' common nationality and, in the absence thereof, by the national law of that parent, whichever favors legitimacy.[74] The Croatian codification takes the next step. It provides that if neither parent's national law would consider the child legitimate, the law of the forum applies, provided that the child and the parents are domiciled in the forum.[75]

2. Filiation (*favor infantis*)

Even if the distinction between legitimacy and illegitimacy were to disappear, the consequences that flow from the status of a child (legitimate or illegitimate) will continue to provide justification for other result-oriented rules favoring that status. An example of such a rule is Article 3091 of the Quebec codification, which provides that filiation is governed by "the law of the domicile or nationality of the child or one of his parents…whichever is more beneficial to the child."[76] The Serbian codification provides that parentage is determined by the law of the child's habitual residence at the time of the proceedings, but "if it is in the best interest of the child" parentage is determined by the

---

[70] Peruvian codif. art. 2083. *See also* Italian codif. art. 33(2) (legitimacy governed by the national law of either parent); art. 34 (legitimation by subsequent marriage governed by the child's national law or the national law of either spouse).

[71] Japanese codif. art. 30; South Korean codif. art. 42; Taiwanese codif. art. 51.

[72] *See* Liechtenstein codif. arts. 22–23.

[73] *See* Portuguese codif. art. 19(1); Angola codif. art. 19.1; Cape Verde codif. art. 19.1; East Timor codif. art. 18.1; Guinea-Bissau codif. art. 19.1; Macau codif. art. 17; Mozambique codif. art. 19.1.

[74] *See* Slovenian codif. art. 45.

[75] *See* Croatian codif. art. 43.

[76] Quebec codif. art. 3091. *See also* Austrian codif. art. 25(1) (authorizing the application of the personal law of the child at either the time of birth or later, whichever favors paternity).

law of the child's nationality or the nationality or habitual residence of the parent whose parentage is at issue.[77]

Similar examples abound, including the following:

- The Tunisian codification allows the court to choose the most favorable from among the laws of the nationality or domicile of the defendant or of the child;[78]
- The Czech, Polish, Puerto Rico, Romanian, and Slovak codifications also authorize the court to choose between two laws the one that favors the filiation;[79]
- The Burkina Faso codification provides that if paternity cannot be established under the national law of the father, it can be established under the law of the common domicile of the parents or, failing that, under the law of forum;[80]
- The German codification provides that parentage is determined by alternative references to the law of the child's habitual residence, the parent's national law, and the law that governs the effects of the marriage;[81]
- The Argentinian and Uruguayan draft codifications authorize the court to choose from among three laws the one that favors filiation;[82]
- The Albanian and Bulgarian codifications provide four choices;[83] and
- The Lithuanian and Turkish codifications provide *six* choices.[84]

---

[77] Serbian draft codif. art. 85.1. For a similar rule regarding the acknowledgment of the child of a "common law marriage," *see id*. art. 85.2.

[78] *See* Tunisian codif. Art 52.

[79] Article 55 of the Polish codification provides alternative references to the laws of the child's nationality at the time of birth or at the time of (judicial) determination. Article 28 of the Romanian codification provides that the filiation of a child who has dual foreign citizenship is governed by whichever of two laws is more favorable to the child. Article 23 of the Slovak codification provides that paternity is determined under the law of the state of the child's nationality at birth, but if the child lives in the forum state, paternity may be determined under forum law, "if this is in the child's interest." Article 54 of the new Czech codification adds the mother's habitual residence to these choices. Articles 15 and 16 of the Puerto Rico Draft Code provide that a child is filiated to a parent who, at the time of birth, is considered a parent under the law of the state in which the child was born or that parent was domiciled, and to a parent who, subsequent to the child's birth, has entered into a marriage that, under the law of the state in which either that parent or the child was domiciled resulted in filiating the child.

[80] Burkina Faso codif. art. 1031.

[81] *See* German codif. art. 19. *See also* Italian codif. art. 13(3) (providing that renvoi shall be taken into account only if it leads to the application of a law that allows filiation to be established).

[82] *See* Argentine draft codif. art. 2632 (alternative references to the laws of the domicile of the child or parent or the place of celebration of the marriage); Uruguayan draft codif. art. 28 (alternative reference to the laws of (1) the matrimonial domicile, and in the absence of such domicile, the mother's domicile; (2) the child's domicile if the child is a major, or habitual residence if the child is a minor), and (3) the defendant's domicile).

[83] *See* Albanian codif. art 28 (alternative references to the laws of the child's nationality at birth, or nationality or habitual residence at time of establishment, or the law governing the parents' personal relationship); Bulgarian codif. art. 83 (alternative references to the laws of the child's nationality at birth or nationality or habitual residence at time of establishment, or the law governing the parents' personal relationship).

[84] *See* Lithuanian codif. Art 1.31 (alternative reference to the laws of the child's nationality or domicile, or either parent's nationality or domicile); Turkish codif. art. 16 (alternative references to the laws of the child's nationality, habitual residence, or place of birth, the national law of either parent, or the law of the parents' common habitual residence).

The Chinese codification provides more generally that the "personal and property relations of parent and child" are governed by the law of their common habitual residence and, in the absence thereof, by the law of either party's habitual residence or nationality, "whichever is more favourable to the protection of the weaker party's rights and interests."[85]

Finally, reflecting the changing social mores on this issue, the latest codification of this period, the Dutch codification, contains a rule (Article 93) that favors the contestation of legal filiation presumably in favor of biological filiation. Article 92 provides that the establishment of filiation is governed by the law of the common nationality of the mother and the alleged father, and in the absence thereof, the law of their habitual residence, and in the absence thereof by the law of the child's habitual residence. Article 93 provides that the annulment or denial of filiation is governed by the same law, but if such "a denial is not or no longer possible, the court may, where it is in the best interest of the child and upon the joint application of the parents and the child for such a purpose, apply another law mentioned in Article 92 ..."[86]

3. Acknowledgment

The Swiss codification also raises to six the number of potentially different laws under which the acknowledgment of a child can be validly made in Switzerland,[87] or under which an acknowledgment or legitimation made abroad may be recognized in Switzerland.[88] The Puerto Rico draft provides for acknowledgment under four different laws;[89] the Dutch codification under three;[90] and the Argentinean, Polish, Japanese, and Taiwanese codifications under two laws, whichever favors the acknowledgment.[91]

4. The Common Denominator

Table 6.4 below depicts the result-selective solutions adopted by these codifications in order to facilitate the filiation, legitimacy, or acknowledgment of a child.

---

[85] Chinese codif. art. 25.

[86] Dutch codif. art. 93.

[87] *See* Swiss codif. art. 72. These laws are the law of the child's habitual residence or nationality, or the law of the domicile or nationality of either parent. The same article provides that the contestation of acknowledgment is governed exclusively by Swiss law. *See also* Italian codif. art. 35 (acknowledgment, wherever made, is governed by the national law of the child or of the acknowledging parent, whichever is more favorable to acknowledgment).

[88] *See* Swiss codif. arts. 72–73.

[89] *See* Puerto Rico Draft codif. art. 16 (the four choices are the laws of the state in which the act of acknowledgment took place, the state in which either the acknowledging parent or the child was domiciled, or any other state whose law is applicable under the Code's general principles).

[90] *See* Dutch codif. art. 95 (the three laws are those of the acknowledging parent's nationality, the child's habitual residence, and the parent's habitual residence, with intermediate solutions in cases of multiple nationalities).

[91] *See* Argentinean codif. art. 2633 (alternative references to the laws of the domicile of the child or of the acknowledging parent, whichever favors acknowledgment); Polish codif. art. 55.3 (alternative reference to the law of the child's nationality at either the time of birth or at the time of acknowledgment).

TABLE 6.4. ALTERNATIVE REFERENCE RULES FAVORING LEGITIMACY, FILIATION, AND ACKNOWLEDGMENT

Codification	Child's contacts					Father		Mother		Parent's common Nat.	Matrim. Dom.	Marriage law	Place of marriage	Lex fori
	Birth place	Nat. at birth	Nat. later	Dom. at birth	Dom. later	Nat.	Dom.	Nat.	Dom.					
LEGITIMACY														
Croatia						X		X		X				X
Italy						X		X						
Japan		X				X		X						
S. Korea		X				X		X						
Liechtenstein						X		X		X				
Peru										X	X		X	
Slovenia						X		X		X				
Taiwan		X				X		X						
FILIATION														
Albania		X	X		X							X		
Argentina				X			X						X	
Bulgaria		X	X		X							X		
Burk. Faso		X				X					X			X
Czech Rep.		X					X							X
Germany					X	X		X						X
Italy			X			X		X						X

Codification	Child's contacts					Father		Mother		Parent's common Nat.	Matrim. Dom.	Marriage law	Place of marriage	Lex fori
	Birth place	Nat. at birth	Nat. later	Dom. at birth	Dom. later	Nat.	Dom.	Nat.	Dom.					
Lithuania				X		X	X	X	X		X			
Poland		X	X											
Puerto Rico	X				X		X							
Quebec		X		X	X	X	X	X	X					
Serbia			X		X	X	X							
Slovakia		X												X
Turkey				X		X	X	X	X		X			
Tunisia		X		X		X	X							
Uruguay					X				X		X			
ACKNOWLEDGMENT														
Argentina					X	X	X							
Japan			X			X								
Switz.			X		X	X	X	X						
Netherlands					X	X	X							
Poland		X	X											
Puerto Rico					X		X							X
Taiwan			X			X								

A perusal of the table reveals a wide geographic and cultural diversity among the countries that have adopted such result-oriented solutions, as well as a significant diversity in their choice of connecting factors in order to produce the desired result. Indeed, the only thing these codifications have in common is their willingness to subordinate "conflicts justice" in order to accomplish the same material result of favoring the child.

5. Adoption

The Belgian experience with adoption offers another example of material-justice considerations making inroads into conflicts justice in a country known for its strong adherence to the classical view. A 1969 Belgian law that required compliance with the national laws of both parents for a valid adoption was subjected to repeated manipulation by Belgian courts. In 1987, that law was replaced with a new law that favors adoption by providing that compliance with either the national law of the adopting parent or with Belgian law will suffice for a valid adoption in Belgium by parties maintaining stable Belgian connections.[92] The Belgian codification of 2004 provides that the conditions for adoption are governed by the personal law of "the adopter or both adopters," but also authorizes the application of Belgian law if the foreign law is "clearly harmful to the higher interest of the adoptee" and either the adoptee or the adopters have certain contacts with Belgium.[93]

Czechoslovakia had adopted a similar solution, which remains in effect in Slovakia and is the new Czech codification,[94] as did the German, and later the Dutch codification.[95] The Inter-American Convention on Conflict of Laws Concerning Adoption of Minors provides that the law of the domicile of "the adopter (or adopters)" governs the requirements for adoption, unless that law imposes "manifestly less strict" requirements than the law of the adoptee's habitual residence, in which case the latter law applies.[96] In contrast, the Lithuanian codification applies the law of the adoptee's domicile, but also

---

[92] *See* M. Fallon & J. Meeusen, Belgian Report, in Symeonides, *Progress or Regress?*, 110–111.

[93] Belgian codif. art. 67. *See also id.* art. 68 (providing that consent to adoption is governed by the law of the adoptee's habitual residence, but also authorizing application of Belgian law if the foreign law does not require consent or does not know the institution of adoption). *Cf. id.* art. 62 (providing that filiation by voluntary act is governed by the law of nationality but if such law does not require consent then the law of habitual residence governs).

[94] *See* Slovak codif. art. 26.3 (providing that if the applicable law does not permit adoption or does so under "extremely difficult conditions," forum law shall be applied, provided that the adopter or at least one of the adopting spouses has been living in the forum state for a "longer period of time."); Czech codif. art. 61.

[95] *See* German codif. art 23 (providing that the necessity and the granting of the consent to adopt is governed by the child's national law, but "[if] the best interest of the child so requires, German law shall be applied instead."); Dutch codif. art. 105 (providing that a parent's consent to adoption of his or her child is governed by the child's national law, but, if that law "does not recognize the concept of adoption, Dutch law applies.").

[96] Inter-American Convention on Conflict of Laws Concerning Adoption of Minors art. 4. For the text of the convention, *see* http://www.oas.org/juridico/english/treaties/b-48.html (last visited Dec. 2, 2013).The convention is in force in Belize, Brazil, Chile, Colombia, Honduras, Mexico, Panama, and Uruguay.

allows the application of the law of the adopter's domicile or nationality under certain conditions "if this will not prejudice the best interest of the child."[97]

6. Marriage (*favor matrimonii*)

Until the middle of the twentieth century, most countries imposed strict requirements on the substantive validity of marriages and on the granting of divorce, and PIL did likewise. The substantive validity of a marriage was judged either exclusively under a single law or cumulatively under the personal laws of both prospective spouses. Divorce was also exclusively governed by a single law, usually the law of the spouses' common domicile or nationality. By the end of the twentieth century, the substantive law of most countries had become more liberal, and so has PIL.

Regarding marriage, the notion of *favor matrimonii* has gained wider acceptance and is pursued through choice-of-law rules with alternative connecting factors. With regard to the form of a marriage, the most generous rule is probably found in the Chinese codification. Article 24 provides that a marriage is valid as to form if it complies with the requirements of the *lex loci celebrationis,* or the *lex patriae,* or the law of the law of habitual residence of *one* party.[98] The corresponding provisions of the Finnish, Lithuanian, and Quebec codifications give essentially the same choices.[99] The Albanian codification provides that a marriage is valid if it is valid under the *lex loci celebrationis* or the law of a state that has a "connection" with the marriage.[100] The Italian and Qatari codifications provide for slightly narrower or at least specific choices (alternative validation references to the *lex loci celebrationis*, the national law of either spouse, or the law of their common habitual residence).[101] Also narrower are the corresponding provisions of: the Polish codification (*lex loci celebrationis*, or the law of the spouses' common nationality, domicile, or habitual residence);[102] Japanese and Taiwanese codifications (*lex loci celebrationis* or the national law of either spouse);[103] and the Austrian, Jordanian, and U.A.E codifications (*lex loci celebrationis* or the personal law of each spouse).[104]

With regard to substantive requirements, the Swiss codification provides that a marriage between foreigners in Switzerland is to be considered valid if it conforms to the substantive requirements prescribed by Swiss law or by the national law of *either* prospective

---

[97] Lithuanian codif. Art 1.33.

[98] Chinese codif. art. 23.

[99] *See* Finnish Marriage Act § 115; Lithuanian codif. art. 1.26; Quebec codif. art. 3088.

[100] *See* Albanian codif. art. 22.

[101] Italian codif. art. 28; Qatari codif. art. 14.

[102] *See* Polish codif. art. 49.2 (applicable to marriages concluded outside Poland).

[103] *See* Japanese codif. art. 24; Taiwanese codif. art. 46. *See also id.* art. 45.1 (giving the same choices for the law governing marriage engagements).

[104] Austrian codif. art.16; Jordanian codif. art. 13.2; U.A.E codif. art. 12.2; *See also* Louisiana codif. art. 3520 and Puerto Rico draft codif. art. 11 (applicable to both formal and substantive validity and providing alternative validation reference to the *lex loci celebrationis* and the state where the parties were first domiciled as husband and wife, but subject to a public policy limitation).

spouse.[105] The corresponding German provision begins by requiring compliance with the national law of *each* prospective spouse, but if neither law allows the marriage, then German law applies if either spouse is a resident or citizen of Germany and the foreign law is "incompatible with freedom of marriage."[106] The Albanian and Bulgarian codifications follow a similar approach,[107] as does, to a lesser extent, the Romanian codification.[108] The Austrian codification subjects the personal legal effects of marriage and of a registered domestic partnership to the spouses' common personal law, but if, under that law, the marriage is not valid or the partnership is not given legal effect, Austrian law governs.[109]

The Dutch codification adopts a more complex scheme designed to ensure that marriages that have both foreign and Dutch contacts will conform to certain Dutch substantive conceptions of marriage. Article 28 provides that a marriage will be solemnized if: (1) each of the spouses meets the requirements of Dutch law and one of them has a Dutch nationality or habitual residence, or (2) each of the spouses meets the requirements of his or her national law. However, Article 29 introduces several exceptions to the application of foreign law under item (2) above. It prohibits a marriage if the prospective spouses have not reached the age of 15, or they are related within the second degree by birth or by adoption; if the free consent of a prospective spouse is lacking; or if one is party to an existing marriage or registered partnership. Conversely, Article 29 provides that the solemnization of a marriage may not be refused because of an impediment imposed by the national law of one of the future spouses that is contrary to Dutch public policy.[110]

At the other end of the spectrum, the Gabonese codification also begins with the principle that the substantive requirements of marriage are governed by the national law of each prospective spouse, but also provides that a foreigner who acquires Gabonese nationality may opt for polygamy.[111] The codification also provides that if the otherwise applicable foreign law prohibits a marriage because of an impediment that violates Gabonese public policy, the marriage may be solemnized in Gabon if the marriage would meet the requirements of Gabonese law.[112]

---

[105] Swiss codif. art. 44. The corresponding Dutch provision (art. 28) allows compliance with either Dutch law (if one of the spouses is a Dutch citizen or habitual resident) or the national law of each spouse.

[106] German codif. art. 13. This article also provides that the prospective spouses must have taken reasonable steps to comply with their national law. The article also gives examples of foreign laws that violate the principle of freedom to marry by providing that "a marriage shall not be prevented by a previous marriage of either engaged person, if the validity of the previous marriage has been set aside by a decision made or recognized within the country, or, if the spouse of either engaged person has been declared dead."

[107] *See* Albanian codif. art. 21; Bulgarian codif. art. 76.

[108] *See* Romanian codif. of 1992 art. 18 (providing that if a foreign law imposes an impediment to the marriage that is incompatible with the right to marry under Romanian law, the impediment may not prevent a marriage in Romania if one of the prospective spouses is a Romanian citizen).

[109] *See* Austrian codif. arts. 18 and 27b. Also, Article 17(2) provides that if the marriage was dissolved or annulled by a judgment recognizable in Austria, a new marriage may not be prohibited solely because the personal law of one or both of the spouses does not recognize the judgment. For a similar provision, *see* Estonian codif. § 56(3).

[110] Dutch codif. art 29.

[111] Gabonese codif. art. 34.

[112] *Id.* art. 35.

7. Same-Sex Unions

States that allow same-sex marriages or unions, often called "registered partnerships" accord them the same pro-validation treatment they accord traditional marriages. For example, the Dutch codification provides that Dutch law governs the capacity of each of the partners to enter into a registered partnership in the Netherlands, even in the absence of any other Dutch connections.[113] The Belgian codification provides that the national law of each prospective spouse governs the substantive requirements of marriage, but if one of those laws prohibits same-sex marriages, that law shall not be applied if the other spouse is a national of a state that allows such marriages, or maintains his or her habitual residence there.[114]

8. Divorce (*favor divortii*)

The liberalization of the substantive law of divorce in many countries is reflected in the proliferation of pro-divorce choice-of-law rules in those countries. These rules pursue a policy of *favor divortii* through a variety of devices, such as: (1) applying, as a principal or default choice, the pro-divorce law of the forum; (2) providing a list of laws and authorizing the application of whichever of them allows divorce; or (3) allowing the parties to choose the applicable law (which can work only in consensual divorces). The following are some examples:

- In the United States, the pro-divorce law of the forum applies to all cases subject to its jurisdiction. This includes cases in which only the plaintiff is domiciled in the forum state and cases in which neither spouse is domiciled in the forum state, as long as the defendant files an appearance.[115]
- In Finland, courts have jurisdiction to grant a divorce under Finland's pro-divorce law if the plaintiff "has been" domiciled in Finland or otherwise has a "close link" to Finland and he or she cannot without "unreasonable inconvenience" obtain a divorce in the foreign state where either spouse is domiciled.[116]
- The Chinese codification provides that a contested divorce is governed by the law of the forum,[117] and that the parties may agree to submit an uncontested divorce to the law of either party's habitual residence or nationality.[118]
- The Dutch codification provides that the requirements for a divorce or termination of a registered partnership are governed by Dutch law, and that the law of

---

[113] Dutch codif. art. 60.

[114] Belgian codif. art. 46. For discussion, *see* M. Fallon & J. Erauw, *Belgian Report,* at IV.c and V.

[115] *See* Symeonides, *American PIL* §§ 534–541.

[116] Finnish Marriage Act §§ 119(2), 120.

[117] Chinese codif. art. 27.

[118] Chinese codif. art 26. In the absence of such an agreement, the law of the parties' common habitual residence applies and, in the absence thereof, the law of their common nationality and, in the absence thereof, the law of the forum.

a common foreign nationality of the spouses or partners may be applied only exceptionally.[119]

- The Belgian and Serbian codifications preclude the application of a foreign law that does not allow divorce, and also allow the parties to opt for the application of the law of the forum.[120]
- The codifications of Albania, Bulgaria, Estonia, the Czech Republic, Germany, Lithuania, Romania, Slovakia, Slovenia, and Switzerland provide that the *lex fori* displaces the otherwise applicable foreign law if that law does not allow or severely restricts divorce and one of the spouses is a citizen or domiciliary of the forum state.[121]
- The codifications of Austria, Estonia, Hungary, Italy, North Korea, Spain, and Uruguay also favor divorce through alternative reference rules.[122]

Finally, the Rome III Regulation, which is in force in 15 EU countries, including some of the countries mentioned above,[123] allows the parties to choose the law applicable to divorce from a list of five potentially different laws, one of which is the law of the

---

[119] *See* Dutch codif. arts. 56 for marriages, and 87 for partnerships. The law of the foreign common nationality may be applied only upon a joint petition of the spouses or partners, or the petition of one of them if there exists a "real societal connection" with the state of the common nationality. *Id.*

[120] *See* Belgian codif. art. 55. This article provides that divorce is governed by the law designated in a priority list of four laws, the last of which is the law of the forum as such. The article also provides, however, that: (1) if the applicable foreign law does not allow divorce, then the law next in line applies, as long as it allows divorce; and (2) the parties can always agree to the application of the law of their common nationality or the law of the forum. The Belgian codification also contains a special rule (art. 57) regarding the narrow conditions under which a foreign unilateral repudiation of a marriage by the husband (*talaq*) may be recognized in Belgium. For discussion, *see* J. Erauw & M. Fallon, *Belgian Report,* at IV.c. Articles 81–83 of the Serbian draft codification are substantively similar.

[121] *See* Albanian codif. art. 25; Bulgarian codif. art 82; Czech codif. art. 50.2; Estonian codif. art. 60(2); German codif. art. 17; Lithuanian codif. art. 1.29; Romanian codif. art. 22; Slovak codif. art. 22; Slovenian codif. art. 37; Swiss codif. art. 61.

[122] *See* Austrian codif. Art 20 (providing that if the law governing personal effects of marriage does not allow divorce, then divorce shall be judged according to the plaintiff's personal law); Hungarian codif. art. 41(a) (a marriage can be dissolved under the *lex fori* even if the applicable foreign law does not allow dissolution); Italian codif. art. 31 (divorce is governed by the law common to both spouses and, in the absence of such commonality, by the law of the state "in which the matrimonial life is mainly located," but if that law does not allow divorce or separation, then Italian law governs); North Korean codif. art. 38 (North Korean law may displace the otherwise applicable law if one spouse is a citizen and resident of North Korea); Spanish codif. art. 107 (Spanish law displaces otherwise applicable law under certain narrow conditions); Uruguayan draft codif. art. 26 (providing that, in the absence of a common matrimonial domicile, the plaintiff can choose between the laws of the domicile of either spouse).

[123] *See* Council Regulation (EU) No 1259/2010 of 20 December 2010 implementing enhanced cooperation in the area of the law applicable to divorce and legal separation ("Rome III") (OJ L 343, p. 10 ff.) (2010), in force in Belgium, Bulgaria, Germany, Spain, France, Italy, Latvia, Lithuania, Luxembourg, Hungary, Malta, Austria, Portugal, Romania, and Slovenia.

forum.[124] In the absence of such an agreement (which is not very likely in cases of contested divorces), these same five laws apply in priority order.[125] However, Rome III also provides that if the applicable law does not allow divorce or "does not grant one of the spouses equal access to divorce or legal separation on grounds of their sex," then the law of the forum applies.[126] It should be noted that, under the applicable jurisdiction rules of the Brussels II Regulation, the plaintiff's latitude in choosing the forum is fairly broad, and that in some cases the chosen forum may have no connection with the defendant.[127]

At the other end of the spectrum, the Paraguayan codification provided that (1) a marriage celebrated in Paraguay "is not dissolved except by the death of one spouse,"[128] (2) a marriage celebrated abroad may not be resolved by divorce in Paraguay if the spouses are domiciled there,[129] and (3) a foreign dissolution by divorce of a marriage celebrated in Paraguay does not entitle either spouse to remarry except as provided by Paraguayan law.[130]

In a similar vein, the Ecuadorian codification provides that (1) a marriage that can be dissolved under the law of the place of celebration may not be dissolved in Ecuador except in conformity with Ecuadorian law,[131] and (2) the dissolution of a marriage in a foreign country according to the laws of that country does not enable either spouse to marry in Ecuador until the marriage is validly dissolved in Ecuador.[132]

C. RULES FAVORING ONE PARTY: CHOICE OF LAW BY, OR FOR THE BENEFIT OF, ONE PARTY

By favoring the validity of a juridical act or a certain status, the choice-of-law rules described above also favor, directly or indirectly, the party or parties whose interests depend on the particular act or status. Other rules, however, are even more explicitly and directly designed to benefit one of the parties to a legal dispute, such as: a tort victim, a maintenance obligee, a consumer, an employee, an insured, or any other party whom the legal order considers weak or whose interests are considered worthy of protection.

---

[124] *See* Rome III art. 5. The five laws are: (1) the law of the spouses' current habitual residence; (2) the law of the state in which the spouses were last habitually resident, insofar as one of them still resides there; (3) the national law of either spouse; and (4) the law of the forum.

[125] *See* Rome III art. 8. The only difference is that the law of the state in which the spouses were last habitually resident applies only if the period of residence did not end more than one year before the court is seized. *Id.*

[126] Rome III art. 10.

[127] *See* Brussels II art. 3. One of the plaintiff's choices is the plaintiff's habitual residence provided such residence began at least a year immediately before the filing of the action, or even six months if the plaintiff is also a national of the forum state. *Id.*

[128] Paraguayan codif. art. 163. In 1991, this article was amended to allow divorce for the first time. See Article 22 of Law No. 45 of 1991.

[129] Paraguayan codif. art. 164.

[130] *Id.* art. 165.

[131] Ecuadorian codif. art. 93

[132] *Id.* art. 92.

This party is favored through one or more of the following means: (1) granting that party, either before or after the events that give rise to the dispute, the right to choose the applicable law from among the laws of more than one state, or allowing the court to make a choice for the benefit of that party; or (2) protecting that party from the adverse consequences of a potentially coerced or uninformed choice of law. These means are described below.

1. Pre-dispute Choice by One Party

Rules that allow one party[133] the right to select the applicable law are par excellence result-oriented because that party is likely to choose the law that he or she considers best. Although this is clearer when the choice is exercised after the dispute (see below), it is also true when the choice is made in advance, as in the case of testate succession.

Indeed, a testator chooses a law to govern his or her succession for certainty and peace of mind, but he chooses a *particular* law, in large part, because of the substantive solutions it ensures, for example, avoiding forced heirship. Rules that mandate enforcement of such a choice reflect a societal substantive choice in favor of testamentary freedom at the expense of other substantive succession policies, such as protecting heirs.[134]

In this sense, the new choice-of-law rules that allow a testator to select the law that will govern his or her succession provide another example of a recent concession to material-justice considerations. Such rules are found in the Hague Convention on the Law Applicable to Trusts,[135] the Hague Convention on the Law Applicable to Estates,[136] the European Union's Successions Regulation,[137] and the Uniform Probate Code in the United States,[138] as well as in the codifications of many countries, including: Albania, Azerbaijan, Armenia, Belarus, Belgium, Bulgaria, Burkina Faso, Estonia, Italy, Kazakhstan, South Korea, Kyrgyzstan, Liechtenstein, Moldova, The Netherlands, Poland, Puerto Rico, Quebec, Romania, Serbia, Switzerland, Tajikistan, Ukraine, and Uzbekistan.[139] Indeed, the acceptance of principle of party autonomy in the law of

---

[133] Rules that allow both parties to a bilateral act (such as an ordinary contract) to pre-select the applicable law should not be considered result-oriented (although they are content-oriented) in that they are motivated primarily (or at least as much) by conflicts-justice consideration as by material-justice considerations. *See* Symeonides, *Progress or Regress?*, 38–39.

[134] *See* A. Bonomi, Testamentary Freedom or Forced Heirship? Balancing Party Autonomy and the Protection of Family Members, 2010 *Nederl. Int'l Priv.* 605 (2010).

[135] *See* Art. 6 of Hague Convention of 1 July 1985 on the Law Applicable to Trusts and on Their Recognition. This convention is in force in Australia, Canada, Italy, Luxembourg, Malta, Monaco, the Netherlands, Switzerland, and the United Kingdom.

[136] *See* Art. 5 of the Hague Convention of 1 August 1989 on the Law Applicable to Succession to the Estates of Deceased Persons. This convention is not in force.

[137] *See* Art. 22 of Regulation (EU) No. 650/2012 of the European Parliament and of the Council of 4 July 2012 on jurisdiction, applicable law, recognition and enforcement of decisions and acceptance and enforcement of authentic instruments in matters of succession and on the creation of a European Certificate of Succession.

[138] Uniform Probate Code § 2-703.

[139] *See* Albanian codif. art. 33.3; Azerbaijan codif. art. 29; Armenian codif. art. 1292; Belarus codif. arts. 1133, 1135; Belgian codif. art. 79 (testaments) and 124 (trusts); Bulgarian codif. art. 89; Burkina Faso codif. art. 1044; Estonian codif. art. 25; Italian codif. art. 46 (successions) and art. 56 (donations); Kazakhstan codif. art.

successions has been sufficiently widespread to make credible the claim that it can be "a starting point for a global consensus."[140]

To be sure, this result-selectivism is not unlimited because in all of these codifications, the testator's choice of law is subject to geographical and substantive limitations. In some codifications, however, these limitations are very loose or nonexistent, For example, a New York statute imposes no substantive and virtually no geographic limitations on the testator's choice of law. The statute provides that, with regard to immovable *or movable* property situated in New York, a testator with no other connections to that state may elect to have New York law govern "*the intrinsic validity, including the testator's general capacity, effect*, interpretation, revocation or alteration of any such disposition" of the New York property.[141] In so providing, the statute enables a foreign testator who deposits money in a New York bank to evade the laws of his or her own country. The statute is clearly result-selective. The validation of the testament is simply a means to an end. That the end is far from laudable is another matter.

2. Post-dispute Choice by One Party

Result selectivism is even more prevalent in choice-of-law rules that allow one party to choose the applicable law *after* the occurrence of the events giving rise to the dispute, such as in cross-border torts in which conduct in one state caused injury in another.

a. *Victim's Choice in Cross-Border Torts and Products Liability*

As documented in Chapter 2, many recent codifications allow the victim of a cross-border tort to choose between the laws of the place of the injurious conduct and the place of the resulting injury. For example, Article 40(1) of the German codification provides in part:

> Claims arising from tort are governed by the law of the state in which the person liable to provide compensation acted. The injured person may demand, however, that the law of the state where the result took effect be applied instead.[142]

Likewise, Article 62 of the Italian codification provides in reverse that torts are governed by the law of the state of injury, but "the person suffering damage may request the application of the law of the State in which the event causing the injury took place."[143]

[1121]; South Korean codif. art. 49; Kyrgyzstan codif. art. 1206; Liechtenstein codif. art. 29.3; Moldovan codif. art. 1624; Dutch codif. art. 145; Polish codif. art. 64.1; Puerto Rico draft codif. art. 48; Quebec codif. arts. 3098-99; Romanian codif. art. 68(1); Serbian draft codif. art. 104; Swiss codif. arts. 90(2), 91(2), 87(2), 95(2)(3); Tajikistan codif. arts. 1231–1232; Ukrainian codif. art. 70; Uzbekistan codif. art. 1197.

[140] C. Roodt, Party Autonomy in International Law of Succession: A Starting Point for a Global Consensus, 2 *J. So. African L.* 241 (2009).

[141] New York Estate Powers and Trusts Law § 3-5.1(h) (emphasis added).

[142] German codif. art. 40(1).

[143] Italian codif. art. 62(1).

(1) ALL CROSS-BORDER TORTS Like the German and Italian codifications, seven other codifications give this choice in all cross-border torts—those of Estonia, FYROM, Lithuania, Oregon, Tunisia, Uruguay, and Venezuela.[144]

(2) PRODUCTS LIABILITY Sixteen codifications and one international convention that is in force in 11 countries provide that, in products liability conflicts, the victim may, within certain parameters, choose the applicable law. Specifically:

- The codifications of Italy, Quebec, Switzerland, and Turkey allow the victim to choose from among the laws of either (a) the tortfeasor's place of business or habitual residence; or (b) subject to a proviso, the place in which the product was acquired.[145]
- The codifications of Azerbaijan, Belarus, Kazakhstan, Kyrgyzstan, Russia, Tajikistan, Ukraine, and Uzbekistan add the plaintiff's domicile to these choices.[146]
- The codifications of Tunisia and Taiwan add the state of injury to the victim's choices.[147]
- The codifications of Moldova and Romania allow plaintiffs to choose between the laws of their home state and the place of the product's acquisition.[148]
- The Chinese codification provides for the application of the law of the state of the victim's habitual residence, unless the defendant has not conducted related business in that state, in which case the victim may choose between the laws of the state of injury, or the defendant's principal place of business.[149]
- The Hague Convention on the Law Applicable to Products Liability allows the plaintiff to choose between the laws of the tortfeasor's principal place of business and the law of the place of injury, if certain contingencies are met.[150]

---

[144] *See* Estonian codif. § 50; FYROM codif. art. 33; Lithuanian codif. art. 1.43(1); Or. Rev. Stat. § 15.440(3) (c); Tunisian codif. art. 70; Uruguayan draft codif. art. 52(1); Venezuelan codif. art. 32.

[145] *See* Argentinean Draft codif. art. 91; Italian codif. art. 63; Quebec codif. art. 3128; Swiss codif. art. 135(1); Turkish codif. art. 36.

[146] *See* Azerbaijan codif. art. 27; Belarus codif. art. 1130; Kazakhstan codif. art. 1118; Kyrgyzstan codif. art. 1203; Russian codif. art. 1221; Tajikistan codif. art. 1227; Ukrainian codif. art. 50; Uzbekistan codif. art. 1195.

[147] *See* Tunisian codif. art. 72; Taiwanese codif. art. 26 (same except that the victim's choice includes the law of nationality (rather than domicile) of the tortfeasor or the victim).

[148] *See* Moldova codif. art. 1618; Romanian codif. art 114.

[149] *See* Chinese codif. art. 48.

[150] *See* arts. 6 and 4–5 of the Hague Convention on the Law Applicable to Products Liability (1973). This convention is in force in Croatia, Finland, FYROM, France, Luxemburg, Montenegro, the Netherlands, Norway, Serbia, Slovenia, and Spain.

(3) OTHER CROSS-BORDER TORTS The following 10 codifications and Rome II, which is in force in 28 countries, allow the victim to choose the applicable law in the cross-border torts shown in parentheses:

- Albania (environmental torts, infringement of rights of personality, and certain cases involving anticompetitive restrictions);[151]
- Belgium (defamation);[152]
- Bulgaria (defamation, environmental torts, and direct action against insurer);[153]
- Moldova (injury to rights of personality);[154]
- Poland (injury to rights of personality);[155]
- Romania (defamation, and unfair competition);[156]
- Rome II and all countries to which it applies (environmental torts, direct actions against insurers, and certain cases involving anticompetitive restrictions);[157]
- Serbia (environmental torts and defamation);[158]
- Switzerland (cases involving emissions and injury to rights of personality);[159]

---

[151] *See* Albanian codif. arts. 66.2, 67, 64.5.

[152] *See* Belgian codif. art. 99(2) (1) (allowing plaintiff to choose between the laws of the state of conduct and, subject to a foreseeability proviso, the state of injury).

[153] *See* Bulgarian codif. art. 108 (defamation, victim's choice among laws of victim's or tortfeasor's habitual residence or place of injury); art. 109 (environmental torts, victim's choice between laws of place of conduct or place of injury); and 116 (direct action against insurer, victim's choice between the law that governs the tort and the law that governs the insurance contract).

[154] *See* Moldova codif. art. 1617 (injury to rights of personality; victim may choose from among the laws of the victim's or the defendant's domicile, or the place of injury).

[155] *See* Polish codif. art. 16 (victim's choice between the laws of state of conduct and state of injury).

[156] *See* Romanian codif.] art. 112 (applicable to defamation; allowing victim to choose between the laws of the defendant's domicile or residence and—subject to a foreseeability proviso—the plaintiff's domicile or residence, or the state of injury); arts. 117–118 (applicable to unfair competition; applying the law of the state of injury but also allowing the victim to choose another law in certain cases).

[157] *See* "Rome II" art. 7 (environmental torts; applying the law of the state of injury, unless the plaintiff opts for the law of the place of conduct); art. 6(3) (b) (allowing the plaintiff to choose between the otherwise applicable law and the law of the forum in certain cases involving anticompetitive restrictions); art. 18 (authorizing a direct action against the insurer if such action is allowed by either the law applicable to the tort or the law applicable to the insurance contract).

[158] *See* Serbian draft codif. art. 165 (applicable to environmental torts; allowing victim to choose between the laws of the state of conduct and the state of injury), and art. 170 (applicable to defamation; allowing plaintiff to choose between the laws of the defendant's habitual residence; and, subject to a foreseeability proviso, the states of the victim's domicile or injury). *See also id.* art. 164 (applicable to cases involving anticompetitive restrictions; allowing choice of forum law if the forum's market is one of the affected markets).

[159] *See* Swiss codif. art. 138 (applicable to emissions; allowing victim to choose between the laws of the state of conduct and the state of injury); art. 139 (injury to rights of personality; giving victims a choice from among the laws of the tortfeasor's habitual residence or place of business, and—subject to a foreseeability defense—the victim's habitual residence or the place of the injury).

- Taiwan (unfair competition and direct actions against tortfeasor's insurer);[160] and
- Turkey (defamation and direct actions against insurer).[161]

b. Choice by Owner of Stolen Property

The codifications of Albania, Belgium, Serbia, and Bulgaria extend the concept of post-dispute choice by one party to the owner of stolen cultural property. They provide that a state seeking to recover cultural property illegally exported from its territory may choose between its own law and the law of the state in which the property is found at the time of the claim.[162]

The first three codifications also provide that, if the claimant state chooses its own law and that law does not grant any protection to good faith possessors, the defendant may invoke the protection accorded such possessors by the law of the state in which the property is located at the time of the claim.[163] In addition, Article 92 of the Belgian codification gives the same choices to the owner of other stolen goods.[164]

The Romanian codification also contains two interesting articles applicable to movable things claimed by usucapion or acquisitive prescription. Article 145 of the Act provides that prescription is governed by the law of the state in which the thing was located at the beginning of the applicable prescriptive period. Article 146 provides that, if the thing is moved to another state in which the prescriptive period expires, "the owner" can request the application of the law of the latter state "if all the conditions required by the...law [of the former state], beginning from the date of the removal of the thing, are met."[165] It seems that the quoted word "owner" refers not to a previous owner of the thing but rather to the possessor who claims to have acquired ownership of it through acquisitive prescription.[166] If this interpretation is correct, then, in contrast to the Belgian article discussed above, the Romanian article favors possessors over owners. In any event, even if these articles favor different outcomes, both provide good examples of result-selective choice-of-law rules.

---

[160] *See* Taiwanese codif. art. 27 (unfair competition: choice between the law governing the tort or the contract, if any), art. 29 (choice between the law governing the tort and the law governing the insurance contract).

[161] *See* Turkish codif. art. 35 (applicable to defamation; allowing plaintiff to choose between the laws of the defendant's habitual residence or place of business and, subject to a foreseeability proviso, the states of the victim's domicile or injury); art. 34(4) (applicable to direct actions against the tortfeasor's insurer; providing that the action will be allowed if it is allowed by either the law governing the tort or the law governing the insurance contract).

[162] *See* Albanian codif. art. 40.1; Belgian codif. art 90.1; Serbian draft codif. art. 121.1; Bulgarian codif. art. 70.

[163] *See* Albanian codif. art. 40.2; Belgian codif. art 90.2; Serbian draft codif. art. 121.2.

[164] *See* Belgian codif. art. 92 (allowing the owner to choose between the laws of the state from which the goods were stolen or the state in which the goods are located at the time of revindication but allowing the defendant to invoke the protection accorded good faith possessors by the law of the former state if the owner opts for the law of the latter state).

[165] Romanian codif. art. 146.

[166] Also, the phrase "*all* conditions" apparently means all conditions other than the length of the prescriptive period.

c. Choice by Unwed Mother

Finally, the Czech codification grants an unwed mother a choice of law in disputes with the with the child's father. The applicable law is the law of the mother's habitual residence at the time of birth, unless she opts for the law of her nationality. If the child is not yet born, the mother may choose between the laws of her habitual residence and her nationality at the time of filing the petition.[167]

3. Post-dispute Choice by the Court

Allowing one party to choose the applicable law after the dispute has arisen is simply the most direct and overt way of favoring that party. A less direct but equally overt way is when the legislature chooses in advance the party that needs particular protection and then constructs choice-of-law rules that require the court to apply the law that will provide that protection. This section discusses these rules.

a. Court Choice for the Benefit of Tort Victims

As documented in Chapter 2, several codifications favor the victim of a cross-border tort through choice-of-law rules that require the court to choose between the laws of the state of conduct and the state of injury the one that favors the victim.[168] For example, as early as 1966, the Portuguese codification provided that cross-border torts are governed by the law of the state of conduct, except when that law does not hold the actor liable but the state of injury does. In such a case, the law of the state of injury governs "provided the actor could foresee the occurrence of injury in that country as a consequence of his act or omission."[169]

Since then, 20 other codifications have adopted the same rule. For example, the Croatian codification provides that torts are governed by the law of the place of conduct or the law of place of injury, "depending on which is most favourable for the injured party."[170] Similar rules are found in the codifications of the former Portuguese colonies of Angola, Cape Verde, East Timor, Guinea-Bissau, Macau, and Mozambique,[171] as well as in the codifications of Georgia, Hungary, Peru, and Slovenia.[172]

Moreover, as also documented in Chapter 2, seven other codifications contain rules that have been interpreted as authorizing, or which are capable of producing, the same pro-victim

---

[167] *See* Czech codif. art. 59.1.

[168] See Chapter 2, at III.C.

[169] Portuguese codif. art. 45(2).

[170] Croatian codif. art. 28.1.

[171] *See* Angola codif. art. 45.2; Cape Verde codif. art. 45.2; East Timor codif. art. 44.2, Guinea-Bissau codif. art. 45.2; Macau codif. art. 44.2; Mozambique codif. art. 45.2.

[172] *See* Georgian codif. art. 42.1; Hungarian codif. arts. 33(2), 33(4), and 10(3); Peruvian codif. art 2097(2); Slovenian codif. art. 30(1).

result for all issues in all cross-border torts,[173] and two codifications that mandate the same result for conduct regulation issues.[174]

b. Court Choice for the Benefit of Maintenance Obligees

In areas other than torts, choice-of-law rules expressly designed to favor one party are fairly common in domestic relations matters. In addition to the rules involving status discussed earlier, other rules of this kind are those that, in child and spousal support disputes, authorize the court to choose from among several laws the one most favorable to the obligee.

One example is Article 18 of the German codification, which, subject to certain qualifications, allows a choice of the law most favorable to the maintenance obligee from among the laws of (1) the obligee's habitual residence, (2) the common nationality of the obligor and the obligee, and (3) the law of the forum. Other codifications, including those of Albania,[175] Burkina Faso,[176] Georgia,[177] Spain,[178] and Ukraine,[179] give the same choices to the court, whereas the French Civil Code gives similar choices directly to the obligee.[180] Several countries have identical or similar rules, including Belgium,[181] Bulgaria,[182] Estonia,[183] Hungary,[184] South Korea,[185] Lithuania,[186] Quebec,[187] and Switzerland.[188]

---

[173] *See* Chapter 2, at III.C.2–3, *supra*, regarding the codifications of China, Japan, South Korea, Quebec, Russia, and Switzerland, as well as the Slovak, and Vietnamese codifications.

[174] *See* Louisiana codif. art. 3543 and Puerto Rico draft codif. art. 40 (law of state of conduct applies unless injury occurred in another state imposing a higher standard of conduct and the occurrence of the injury in that state was objectively foreseeable).

[175] *See* Albanian codif. art. 26 (applicable law is that of the obligee's habitual residence, or the country of the common nationality and residence of the obligor and obligee, but if those laws do not grant maintenance, then the *lex fori* governs).

[176] *See* Burkina Faso codif. art. 1041 (alternative references to laws of obligee's domicile, common national law of obligor and obligee, or Burkina Faso law).

[177] Georgian codif. art. 48.1 (applicable law is that of the obligee's habitual residence, or the country of the common nationality and residence of the obligor and obligee, but if those laws do not grant maintenance, then the *lex fori* governs).

[178] *See* Spanish codif. art. 9.7.

[179] *See* Ukrainian codif. art. 67.

[180] *See* French civ. code arts. 311–318.

[181] *See* Belgian codif. art. 74 (applicable law is that of the obligee's habitual residence, or the country of the common nationality of obligor and obligee if the obligor is habitually resident in that country, but if those laws do not grant maintenance, then the law of common nationality applies, and if that law does not grant maintenance, then Belgian law governs).

[182] *See* Bulgarian codif. 87 (alternative references to law of obligee's habitual residence or nationality, common national law of obligor and obligee, or Bulgarian law).

[183] *See* Estonian codif. § 61 (choice from among the laws of the forum, the obligee's habitual residence, or the common national law of the obligor and the obligee).

[184] *See* Hungarian codif. art. 46 (with regard to the status, family relationships, and maintenance rights of children living in Hungary, Hungarian law applies whenever it is more favorable to the child than the otherwise applicable law).

[185] *See* South Korean codif. art. 46(1) (choice between laws of obligee's habitual residence and parties' common national law).

[186] *See* Lithuanian codif. art. 1.35.

[187] *See* Quebec codif. art. 3094 (choice between the law of the domicile of the obligee or the obligor).

[188] *See* Swiss codif. arts. 49 and 83.

The Argentinean codification provides that: (1) actions for (non-spousal) maintenance may be brought, at the option of the obligee, in the courts of his or her domicile or habitual residence, the courts of the defendant's domicile, or, "if reasonable under the circumstances," in the courts of any place where the defendant has assets;[189] and (2) that the court may apply the law of either the obligee's or the obligor's domicile, whichever is more favorable to the obligee.[190] The Uruguayan codification gives directly to the maintenance obligee the option of choosing between the law of the habitual residence of either the obligor or the obligee.[191] The Tunisian codification allows the court to choose from among four potentially different laws the one most favorable to the obligee. The four laws are those of the obligee's nationality or domicile or the obligor's nationality or domicile.[192] The Chinese codification includes those four as well and adds the law of the state in which the maintenance property is situated.[193]

In the meantime, several international instruments have adopted the same or similar pro-obligee choices. Specifically:

- The 1956 Hague Convention on the Law Applicable to Maintenance Obligations Towards Children give a choice between the *lex fori* and the law of the child's habitual residence;[194]
- The 1973 Hague Convention on the Law Applicable to Maintenance Obligations gives a sequential choice from among the laws of the obligee's habitual residence, or the common national law of the obligor and the obligee, or the law of the forum;[195]
- The 1989 Inter-American Convention on Support Obligations provides that the right to support is governed by the law of the domicile or habitual residence of the creditor or the law of the domicile or habitual residence of the debtor, "whichever … [is] most favorable to the creditor."[196]
- The 1996 Hague Child Protection Convention gives the court a choice between the law of the forum state and the law of another state "with which the situation has a substantial connection" but only "in so far as the protection of the person or the property of the child requires."[197]

---

[189] Argentinean draft codif. art. 2629.1.

[190] *Id.* art. 2630.1.

[191] *See* Uruguayan draft codif. art. 29.

[192] *See* Tunisian codif. art. 51.

[193] *See* Chinese codif. art. 29.

[194] *See* Hague Convention 24 October 1956 on the Law Applicable to Maintenance Obligations Towards Children, arts. 1–3. This convention is in force in: Austria, Belgium, France, Germany, Italy, Japan, Liechtenstein, Luxemburg, the Netherlands, Portugal, Spain, Switzerland, and Turkey.

[195] *See* Hague Convention of 2 October 1973 on the Law Applicable to Maintenance Obligations, arts. 4–6. The convention is in force in: Albania, Estonia, France, Germany, Greece, Italy, Japan, Lithuania, Luxemburg, the Netherlands, Poland, Portugal, Spain Switzerland, and Turkey.

[196] Inter-American Convention on Support Obligations, art. 6. The convention is in force in Argentina, Belize, Bolivia, Brazil, Costa Rica, Ecuador, Guatemala, Mexico, Panama, Paraguay, Peru, and Uruguay.

[197] *See* Hague Convention of 19 October 1996 on Jurisdiction, Applicable Law, Recognition, Enforcement and Co-operation in Respect of Parental Responsibility and Measures for the Protection of Children, art. 15. This

- The 2007 Hague Maintenance Protocol Convention[198] and the 2009 EU Regulation on Maintenance,[199] which makes the Hague Protocol applicable throughout the EU, gives a choice among the laws of the child's habitual residence, the forum state, or the state of the common nationality of the child and the obligor.[200]

c. Court Choice for the Benefit of Children and Other Weak Parties

The following are some additional examples of choice-of-law rules designed to accomplish the material result of protecting children or other persons in need of protection, such as persons under guardianship or curatorship.

- The Belgian codification provides that parental authority and guardianship are governed by the law of the state of the habitual residence of the child or the person under guardianship, and if that law does not provide sufficient protection, by the law of that person's nationality. In either case, Belgian law applies if it is materially or legally impossible to take the protective measures provided for by the applicable foreign law.[201]
- The Argentinean codification provides that matters of parental responsibility are governed by the law of the child's habitual residence, but the court may also take into account—"to the extent required by the interests of the child"—the law of another state with which the situation has "relevant links."[202]
- In guardianship proceedings, the Serbian codification authorizes the court to deviate from the normally applicable law and apply a law of another state "with which the situation is closely connected," if this is "necessary to protect the personality or property of the protégé."[203]

---

convention is in force in Albania, Armenia, Australia, Austria, Bulgaria, Cyprus, Czech Republic, Denmark, Ecuador, Estonia, Finland, France, Germany, Greece, Hungary, Ireland, Luxemburg, Malta, Latvia, Lesotho, Lithuania, Monaco, Montenegro, Morocco, Netherlands, Poland, Portugal, Romania, Russia, Slovakia, Slovenia, Spain, Sweden, Switzerland, Ukraine, United Kingdom, and Uruguay.

[198] See Hague Protocol of 23 November 2007 on the Law Applicable to Maintenance Obligations. The Protocol is in force in the European Union and in Serbia.

[199] Council Regulation (EC) N1 4/2009, of 18 December 2008, on Jurisdiction, Applicable Law, Recognition and Enforcement of Decisions and Cooperation in Matters Relating To Maintenance Obligations, *OJ* L 7/1 of 1 January 2009.

[200] See Hague Maintenance Protocol, arts. 3–4. With regard to spouses, the applicable law is the law of the obligee's habitual residence, but subject to an exception in favor of the law of another state—in particular, the state of the spouses' last common habitual residence—if such other state has a "closer connection with the marriage." *Id.* art. 5.

[201] Belgian codif. art. 35.

[202] Argentinean draft codif. art. 2639.

[203] Serbian draft codif. art. 51.2.

- The Armenian codification provides that Armenian law displaces the otherwise applicable foreign law if it is more protective of a person under guardianship or curatorship and that person lives in Armenia.[204] The codifications of Belarus, Kazakhstan, Moldova, Russia, Tajikistan, and Ukraine provide the same with regard to persons under guardianship or curatorship who live in those countries, respectively.[205] The Chinese codification allows more choices, even if the person under guardianship is not domiciled in China. The applicable law is the law of the habitual residence or the *lex patriae* of *one* party that most favorably protects the rights and interests of the person under guardianship.[206]

- The Ukrainian codification provides that the duties of parents and children are governed by the personal law of the child or the law of the country that has a close connection with the relationship, whichever is more favorable to the child.[207] The Albanian codification provides that the relationship between parents and child are governed by the law of the child's nationality or habitual residence, whichever is more favorable to the child.[208] The Chinese codification provides that in the absence of a common habitual residence, the personal and property relationship between parents and children are governed by "the law of habitual residence or the *lex patriae* of *one* party that most favorably protects the rights and interests of the weaker party."[209]

- The Dutch codification provides that, if a spouse enjoys a benefit because of the application of the law of the situs as directed by a foreign choice-of-law rule, and the spouse would not have enjoyed such a benefit under the law applicable under the Dutch choice-of-law rule, the other spouse is entitled to compensation upon termination of the matrimonial regime.[210]

- The Hungarian codification provides that Hungarian law applies to the status of family relationship and maintenance rights of a Hungarian child or a child residing in Hungary, if that law is more favorable to the child than the otherwise applicable law.[211]

- Article 15 of the 1996 Hague Convention for the Protection of Children provides that a state that has jurisdiction under the convention shall apply its own law. The article also provides, however, that "in so far as the protection of the person or the property of the child requires" the court may "exceptionally" apply or "take into consideration" the law of another state "with which the situation

---

[204] Armenian codif. art. 1268.

[205] *See* Belarus codif. art. 1109(3); Kazakhstan codif. art. 1124.3; Moldova codif. art. 1595.4; Russian codif. art. 1199.3; Tajikistan codif. art. 1234; Ukrainian codif. art. 24.

[206] Chinese codif. art. 32.

[207] Ukrainian codif. art. 65.

[208] Albanian codif. art. 29.

[209] Chinese codif. art. 25 (emphasis added).

[210] Dutch codif. art. 47.

[211] Hungarian codif. art. 46.

has a substantial connection."[212] The Hague Convention on the International Protection of Adults contains an identical rule (Article 13) applicable to adults who "by reason of an impairment or insufficiency of their personal faculties, are not in a position to protect their interests."[213]

d. Protecting Consumers or Employees from the Consequences of an Adverse Choice-of-Law Clause

In contrast to the above rules that protect tort victims by granting them the right to choose the applicable law, other rules seek to protect consumers and employees from the adverse consequences of their own, potentially coerced or uninformed, assents to choice-of-law clauses.

The best-known examples are Articles 5 and 6 of the Rome Convention, which are reproduced without material changes in the new Rome I regulation.[214] These articles provide that a choice-of-law clause in a consumer contract or an employment contract may not deprive the consumer or employee, respectively, of the protection afforded by the mandatory rules of the country whose law would govern the contract in the absence of such a clause (*lex causae*). Thus, a choice-of-law clause can expand but cannot contract the protection available to consumers or employees.

Similar provisions are found in the laws of many countries, both within the EU[215] and outside the EU, including Albania, FYROM, Georgia, South Korea, Liechtenstein, Puerto Rico, Quebec, Russia, Serbia, Switzerland, Turkey, Ukraine, and Uruguay.[216] The corresponding Japanese rules deserve special mention because they give directly to consumers and employees a post-dispute choice of whether to invoke the protection of the mandatory rules of the *lex causae*.[217] Again, the materially desirable result of protecting members of a protected class is given preference over conflicts-justice considerations.

---

[212] Hague Convention of 19 October 1996 on Jurisdiction, Applicable Law, Recognition, Enforcement and Co-operation in Respect of Parental Responsibility and Measures for the Protection of Children, art. 15. This convention is in force in 22 countries. *See supra* note 197.

[213] Hague Convention of 13 January 2000 on the International Protection of Adults, art. 1. Article 13 provides that, although a state that has jurisdiction under the convention shall apply its own law, it may also, "in so far as the protection of the person or the property of the adult requires," apply or take into consideration the law of another state with which the situation has a "substantial connection." This convention is in force in seven countries (Czech Republic, Estonia, Finland, France, Germany, Switzerland, and the United Kingdom).

[214] *See* Rome Convention Arts 5–6 and Rome I arts. 6 and 8.

[215] *See* Austrian codif. § 41; Bulgarian codif. arts 95–96; Estonian codif. §§ 34(1), 35(1); German codif. arts. 29–30; Lithuanian codif. art. 1.39; Romanian codif. arts. 101–102 (employment contracts); Slovenian codif. arts. 21–22.

[216] *See* Albanian codif. art. 52; FYROM codif. arts. 25–26; Georgia codif. art. 38; South Korean codif. arts. 27–28; Liechtenstein codif. arts. 45, 48; Puerto Rico codif. arts. 35–36; Quebec codif. arts. 3117–3118; Russian codif. art. 1212; Serbian draft codif. arts. 141–142; Turkish codif. arts. 26–27; Ukrainian codif. art. 45.

[217] *See* Japanese codif. arts. 11–12.

VI. Result-Selectivism in the Courts and in Uncodified Systems

The fact that the above discussion has focused on the influence of material-justice considerations in the process of drafting choice-of-law rules should not leave the impression that only legislatures are susceptible to such influence. If anything, judges are more likely to be influenced by such considerations because they have a close-up view of the facts and circumstances of the parties and can easily discern where the equities lie. In turn, such awareness can influence a judge's decision of whether to invoke one of the escape clauses discussed in Chapter 4,[218] or whether to use any of the old mechanisms, such as characterization, *ordre public*, or renvoi, in order to avoid the result dictated by a content-blind jurisdiction-selecting rule. As a Professor Siehr observed in discussing the general escape of Article 15(1) of the Swiss codification:

> Although not enacted for this purpose but rather to correct a generalizing "jurisdiction-selecting" rule, such a correction may be influenced by a certain "touch" for material justice. If a law not designated by the regular conflicts rule is less "just" than another law with close connections to the case, the latter as the law of the much closer connection is likely to replace the former. Although everybody agrees that Article 15 (1) does not codify a "better-law approach," it cannot be excluded that this escape clause also will serve as a safety valve for "material justice."[219]

Twelve years later, Professor Bonomi confirmed this very use of the escape clause. He described several Swiss court decisions to that effect and concluded that the escape clause of Article 15 has been "sometimes used by courts to favor a certain material result, though it was not originally intended to be for that purpose."[220]

Other authors from countries with codified PIL give examples of cases in which a court deviated from the normally applicable law to achieve a result the court considered more appropriate in the particular case. For example, Professors Fallon and Erauw note that Belgian courts had used renvoi "to deviate from the choice-of-law rule before the entry into force of the [new] Belgian code...especially...in the field of tort, in reaction against the hard and fast rule designating the law of the place of the tort."[221] Likewise, Professor Pauknerová notes the result-oriented function of the *ordre public* reservation in Czech judicial practice,[222] as do Professors Esplugues Mota and Azcárraga Monzonís with regard to Spain, concluding that public policy is "used as a tool to protect our values after

---

[218] *See supra* Chapter 4, at VI.
[219] K. Siehr, *Swiss Report*, in S. Symeonides (ed.), *Progress or Regress?*, 383, 387.
[220] A. Bonomi, *Swiss Report*, at IV.3(e) and II.
[221] J. Erauw & M. Fallon, *Belgian Report*, at II.2(e).
[222] M. Pauknerová, *Czech Report*, at IV.

the 'blind' choice-of-law rule has pointed out the law applicable to the controversy."[223] Several other authors have also made the same points with regard to other countries, such as France, Greece, and Australia.[224]

For equally obvious reasons, the pursuit of material justice is both easier and more likely in choice-of-law systems that do not adhere to preestablished choice-of-law rules but instead resolve conflicts problems on a case-by-case basis. In such systems, the judge has the freedom—and is more likely to have the predilection—to aim for a result that is not only spatially but also materially proper.

For example, it is generally believed that, even during the heydays of the traditional approach in the United States, American judges were motivated by considerations of material justice in their frequent utilization of "escape devices."[225] Gradually, the need for such escape devices decreased as more and more states of the United States abandoned the traditional rule-based system in favor of flexible ad hoc approaches.[226] Some of these approaches explicitly advocate the pursuit of material justice. Although only one of those approaches (Leflar's better-law approach) has received judicial sanction,[227] the multiplicity and eloquent advocacy of so many result-oriented approaches demonstrates a growing de facto acceptance of the material-justice view in the United States. As important, however, is the fact that the pursuit of material justice is equally possible, though not expressly advocated, under many of the other flexible American approaches, such as the Restatement (Second)'s most significant relationship formula.[228]

The situation is not much different in other countries in which judges are not restrained by statutory choice-of-law rules. For example, as an Australian author notes:

Since not generally constrained by statutory choice of law rules, Australian courts have exercised a fair degree of freedom in being able to take into account the content, aims and objectives of potentially conflicting laws....[although] [i]t is only

---

[223] C. Esplugues Mota & C. Azcárraga Monzonís, *Spanish Report*, at IV.2.

[224] *See* B. Audit, *Rapport Français*, in S. Symeonides (ed.), *Progress or Regress?*, 191 at 202–210 (discussing the French use of characterization, renvoi, and *ordre public* as vehicles for material justice); S. Vrellis, *Rapport grec*, in *id.* 243 at 245–246, discussing efforts to characterize employment accidents as contractual rather than delictual in nature so as to make them fall within the scope of the flexible article governing contracts, rather than the inflexible article governing torts, with the ultimate objective being to choose "*la loi matérielle la plus juste (la 'meilleure')*."; J. Chen, *Australian Report*, in *id.* 83 at 88–89 ("Australian courts have, on occasions and through manipulation of classification techniques and choice of law rules, made direct choice of the most desirable law or result, sometimes quite openly.").

[225] *See* Hay, Borchers & Symeonides, *Conflicts of Law*, 145–175.

[226] According to the latest count, more than 40 American states have opted for such approaches. *See* Symeonides, *Choice of Law in 2012*, 279.

[227] Five states follow Leflar's better-law approach in tort conflicts and two states do so in contract conflicts. *See id.*

[228] *See* C. Peterson, *United States Report*, in S. Symeonides (ed.), *Progress or Regress?*, 413 at 425 ("The modern [American] theories…all purport in one way or another to take substantive justice into account.…[S]ome form of pursuit of the objective of substantive justice is the prevailing view.")

rarely that judges openly admit that they are applying the forum or foreign law because it produces justice in the particular case. In many international cases, nevertheless, the result is one which appeals intuitively to a sense of justice, and material justice certainly appears to have been an underlying, though unspoken, aim of the approach adopted by the court.[229]

A Danish author makes a similar point:

Although Danish judges rarely reveal the philosophy which guides their decision-making, some available evidence supports the claim that Danish judges consider the content and purpose of competing substantive rules, at least where no inflexible PIL codification stands in their way.[230]

The "Scandinavian legal pragmatism"[231] noted by the Danish author is also confirmed by a Norwegian author who notes that:

The pragmatic, case-oriented approach of Norwegian courts tends to address the question of governing law from the point of view of the scope of applicability of Norwegian law, having in mind what would be the best solution under those particular circumstances.[232]

VII. Summary and Conclusions

A. SUMMARY

As Table 6.5 indicates, result-selective choice-of-law rules come in different shapes and forms. These rules are designed to ensure a particular substantive result, such as upholding the validity of specified juridical acts, according the benefits of a particular status, or protecting one party in an actual or potential dispute.

---

[229] A. De Jonge, *Australian Report*, at IV. *See also* J. Chen, *Australian Report*, in S. Symeonides (ed.), *Progress or Regress?*, 83 at 87 (characterizing a decision of the High Court of Australia as being "clearly an acceptance of the US emphasis on achieving justice, fairness and the best practical result").

[230] J. Lookofsky, *Danish Report*, at IV (footnote omitted). *See also* Lookofsky, *Danish Report* in S. Symeonides (ed.), *Progress or Regress?*, 147 at 150: "[M]ost Danish judges would also agree with the proposition that multistate cases are not qualitatively different from fully domestic cases and that a judge's duty to resolve disputes justly and fairly does not disappear the moment the judge encounters a case with foreign elements." (internal quotation marks omitted).

[231] J. Lookofsky, *Danish Report*, at IV.

[232] G. Cordero Moss, *Norwegian Report*, at IV. *See also* K. Boele-Woelki, C. Joustra & G. Steenhoff, *Dutch Report*, in S. Symeonides (ed.), *Progress or Regress?*, 295 at 307 ("Nowadays, it is generally recognized that

TABLE 6.5. RESULT-SELECTIVE STATUTORY CHOICE-OF-LAW RULES

A. Rules favoring the validity of juridical acts (*favor validitatis*)		
	1. Testaments (*favor testamenti*)	
	2. Contracts and other juridical acts (*favor negotii*)	
B. Rules favoring a certain status		
	1. Legitimacy (*favor legitimationis*)	
	2. Filiation (*favor infantis*)	
	3. Acknowledgment	
	4. Adoption	
	5. Marriage (*favor matrimonii*)	
	6. Divorce (*favor divortii*)	
C. Rules favoring one party		
	1. Pre-dispute choice of law by one party	
	2. Post-dispute choice of law by one party	
		a. Victim's choice in cross-border torts and products liability
		b. Choice by owner of stolen property
		c. Choice by unwed mother
	3. Post-dispute choice by the court	
		a. For the benefit of tort victims
		b. For the benefit of maintenance obligees
		c. For the benefit of children and other weak parties
		d. For the benefit of consumers
		e. For the benefit of employees

As this chapter documents, these rules are not only numerous, but they also exist in virtually every country that has enacted a choice-of-law codification in the last 50 years. In fact, of the 84 codifications reviewed in this book, *only four* codifications do *not* contain result-selective choice-of-law rules—those of the Central African Republic, Chad, Cuba, and Madagascar. All four of them were enacted in the earlier part of the 50-year period, and they are very brief.[233]

---

substantive values should be integrated into the choice of law process."); *id.* at 309–310 (describing one of the approaches followed in the Netherlands, the "favour approach," which "comes close to the American doctrine of better law.")

[233] The codification of the Central African Republic was enacted in 1965 and consists of 10 articles. The codification of Chad was enacted in 1967 and consists of one article with six subdivisions. The Cuban codification was enacted in 1987 and consists of 14 articles placed in the civil code. The codification of Madagascar was enacted in 1962 and consists of 16 articles.

B. NOT "ONLY IN AMERICA"

The fact that 80 other countries, on five continents, saw fit to enact myriad result-selective choice-of-law rules answers the rhetorical question of whether material-justice views prosper "only in America." The long list of countries and result-selective rules demonstrates that, despite significant differences among themselves and from the American system, choice-of-law systems around the world are far from indifferent to material-justice considerations.

This is true of codified conflicts systems, which were previously considered bastions of conflicts justice. Authors from those systems now routinely confirm the "integration of value considerations into private international law."[234] They acknowledge that "conflicts rules no longer depend on abstract geographical factors alone," and that "[s]ubstantive values and policies have been translated into connecting factors focusing on the weaker party, or into alternative reference rules favoring a specific substantive result."[235]

In turn, this development suggests that the classical conception of the choice-of-law process (statutory or judicial) as a blindfolded, value-neutral exercise is either wrong or outdated. During the last 50 years, the material-justice view has gained significant ground over the classical view. Indeed, we have moved from an era in which material justice was officially unmentionable to an era in which it has become an important, and, in some instances, almost coequal, goal with conflicts justice. Today, the dilemma is no longer (and perhaps it never should have been) an "either/or" choice between conflicts justice and material justice. Rather, it is a question of *when, how*, and *how much* the desideratum of material justice should temper the search for conflicts justice.[236]

C. THE DIFFERENCE: CONFLICTS JUSTICE TEMPERED BY MATERIAL JUSTICE

To be sure, there are qualitative differences between result-selectivism in legislation as exemplified by the rules described in this chapter and result-selectivism in adjudication as advocated by American scholars such as Leflar or, especially, Juenger. The most important difference is *not* that these rules are few and far between. As this chapter documents, they are not.

---

[234] Martinek, *Seven Pillars of Wisdom* § 6.1 (2001). *See also id.* ("It is no longer and not alone the determination of the geographically better law that governs private international law unreservedly and independently from substantive value judgments.")

[235] de Boer, *Living Apart Together*, at 203. *See also* T. Pajor, *Polish Report*, in S. Symeonides (ed.), *Progress or Regress?*, 329 at 346–347 ("[S]olutions in the area of conflict of laws should aim to protect individual interests not only by a proper allocation of legal relationships, but also by making choice of law decisions dependent upon obtaining the appropriate substantive result (so-called material justice).").

[236] *Cf.* B. Audit, *Rapport Français*, in S. Symeonides (ed.), *Progress or Regress?*, 191 at 194 ("La simple justice des conflits est susceptible de degrés."); *id.* at 195 ("Il y a donc une 'justice de répartition.'").

The most important difference is that, in legislative selectivism, the desirable substantive result is identified in advance and *in abstracto* through the consensus mechanisms of the democratic legislative processes. These rules are designed to produce results that the *collective* will consider desirable and noncontroversial. By contrast, in judicial selectivism, the substantive result is chosen ex post facto and *in concreto* and often by a single individual who, with the best of intentions, cannot easily avoid the dangers of subjectivity. As the late Peter Nygh pointed out, "one court's better law may be another's worse."[237]

Nevertheless, the existence of these result-selective choice-of-law rules demonstrates that, although PIL continues to aim primarily for conflicts justice, it is not indifferent to material-justice considerations. Moreover, the fact that these rules are so numerous and exist in so many and diverse countries means that they cannot be dismissed as minor exceptions in the operation of choice-of-law systems. Conflicts justice may remain the official goal, but, for better or worse, this goal is often tempered by considerations of material justice.

---

[237] P.E. Nygh, *Conflict of Laws in Australia* 29 (6th ed. 1995) ("[O]ne court's better law may be another's worse. It is only by reference to an ideology that a court can in some cases make a choice as to which is the better law; there needs to be a commitment in some cases to allowing the 'collective good' to prevail.")

7   The Publicization of PIL: Unilateralism, State
       Interests, and International Uniformity

I. Introduction

How "private" is private international law? How *international* is the law of conflict of laws? Is international uniformity still the supreme goal of PIL? Is the debate between multilateralism and unilateralism still relevant? Must a PIL codification choose one or another? To what extent, in drafting choice-of-law rules, do modern codifiers consider the interests of the involved states, and to what extent do they give preference to the interests of the forum state? How do codifiers reconcile the lofty ideal of internationalism with the instinctive urge of protectionism? This chapter examines how modern choice-of-law codifications answer these and related questions.

A. WHAT'S IN A NAME: PRIVATE OR PUBLIC LAW?

For historical reasons, our subject is known by different names in different parts of the world. The term *private international law*, which was coined by an American writer,

Joseph Story,[1] is the most widely used name, although it is not used in the United States. The term *conflict of laws*, which was coined by a European writer, Ulrich Huber,[2] is the prevailing term in the United States and some common law countries, but it is not used in Europe. Each of the two names reflects different and also debatable assumptions about the nature and function of this subject and this branch of the law. These assumptions are reflected in the adjectives *international* and *private* in the first name and in the word *conflict* in the second name.

1. International

The adjective *international* in PIL describes the cases that fall within the scope of the subject, namely cases that have a significant international (or multistate) dimension. But this adjective can also be misleading because it allows the uninitiated to infer that PIL emanates from a supranational source. Reality is much different: Other than the few international conventions that avoid or resolve conflicts problems through substantive or choice-of-law rules, international law imposes few restraints and provides little guidance on the subject. Thus, PIL is very much *national* law.[3]

At the same time, the adjective *international* reflects the internationalist aspirations of this field as expressed by Mancini and especially Savigny in the nineteenth century.[4] In entering this field, national lawmakers are supposed to act as surrogates of a nonexistent international legislature. They should (1) aim for international harmony and uniformity; (2) act unselfishly, impartially, and evenhandedly; (3) treat equally foreign and forum law, as well as foreign and domestic litigants; (4) and adopt only those choice-of-law rules that are sufficiently appealing to be adopted by other nations, thus producing an international consensus.[5]

---

[1] *See* J. Story, *Commentaries on the Conflict of Laws* (1834).

[2] *See* U. Huber, De conflictu legum diversarum in diversis imperiis, in U. Huber, *Praelectiones Juris Romani et Hodierni* (1689).

[3] *See* de Boer, *Living Apart Together,* 195 ("Today, no conflicts scholar of note would suggest that public and private international law are branches of the same tree. Contemporary conflicts theory does not hold that the choice between *lex fori* and foreign law is dictated by universal rules or principles. States are still deemed to be completely free to enact their own rules of jurisdiction, choice of law, or recognition and enforcement—subject, of course, to federal restraints or supranational limitations.").

[4] *See* P.S. Mancini, *Della nazionalità come fondamento del diritto delle genti: Prelezione al corso di diritto internazionale e marittimo pronunziata nella R. Università de Torino nel dì 22 gennaio 1851* (1851); E. Jayme, *Pasquale Stanislao Mancini, Internationales Privatrecht zwischen Risorgimento und praktischer Jurisprudenz* (1980); F.C. von Savigny, *System des heutigen Römischen Rechts,* v. 8, §§ 348, 360–361 (1849).

[5] *See* H. Batiffol, Réflexions sur la coordination des systèmes nationaux, 120 *Recueil des Cours* 165 (1967-I); P. Vallindas, Les principes de la bilatéralité et de la possibilité d'internationalization des règles du droit international privé, 1 *Rev. Hellénique dr. int'l.* 327 (1948).

2. Private

The adjective *private* in PIL echoes the private-public law distinction prevalent in the civil law world; it assumes that the cases that fall within the scope of this subject are garden-variety private-law disputes that implicate *only* the interests of the litigants and not the interests of their respective home states or the states that have other pertinent contacts with the case.[6] However, precisely because of their multistate dimension, conflicts cases implicate the laws of more than one state, and these laws may embody different objectives, values, or policies. Although these states are not the actual disputants as in a public international law dispute, is it realistic to assume that they are entirely indifferent to the way these conflicts cases are resolved?

The term *conflict of laws* seems to assume that, in all multistate cases, each involved state has an active or passive desire, claim, or *interest* in applying its own law, and that these desires *conflict* in the sense of always pulling in opposite directions. If these assumptions are accurate, then PIL is not only strictly national rather than international law, but it is also by nature ethnocentric and antagonistic. Are these assumptions accurate? Is a state really *interested* in the outcome of disputes between private persons? If yes, does this encompass all disputes or only disputes with strong *public law* characteristics? If states do have interests in the outcome of PIL disputes, then is it realistic to continue to consider international uniformity as one of the principal goals of PIL?

B. INTERNATIONALIST HERITAGE AND ASPIRATIONS

Until relatively recently, the differences reflected in the above nomenclature were pushed to the background because of the dominance of the classical theory of PIL articulated primarily by Friedrich Carl von Savigny in Europe and Joseph Story in the United States.[7] Despite their other differences, both scholars subscribed to the same private-law premises and internationalist aspirations and postulated that the supreme goal of PIL was international (or interstate) uniformity in choice-of-law decisions regardless of where litigation occurs.

In this idealistic environment, any assertion or even serious discussion of state interests was frowned upon. There was little room for favoritism of forum law or protectionism of forum litigants. Choice-of-law rules and decisions were supposed to be neutral and evenhanded, treating equally foreign and forum law, and foreign and domestic litigants.

---

[6] *See* G. Rühl, Unilateralism, in J. Basedow, K. Hopt & R. Zimmermann (eds.), *Max Planck Encyclopedia of European Private Law* (2012) (" [P]rivate law—unlike public law—is neutral and apolitical. It does not incorporate state interests and has no socially constitutive functions. Instead, it orders personal activities and freedoms and regulates interests of private parties. Cases with ties to multiple legal orders are, therefore, not a matter of conflicts between states and state interests but clashes between private intentions and individual spheres of freedom.").

[7] *See* Savigny, *supra,* note 4; Story, *supra* note 1.

Despite occasional disagreements on the margins, this conception of PIL was firmly entrenched in the PIL of most countries until the middle of the twentieth century.

C. PROTECTIONIST URGES

Gradually, however, many authors and later many courts, especially in the United States, concluded that the goal of international uniformity, although laudable, was also unattainable. This conclusion turned attention to other choice-of-law goals and led to an increasing recognition, or perhaps a reawakening, of the notion that conflicts of laws can implicate conflicting interests that extend beyond the interests of the immediate parties to the conflict—broader societal, public, and thus *state* interests. Thus, PIL could not be as apolitical as Savigny conceived it to be, and states could not be as uninterested or unprovincial as Story portrayed them to be. In the United States, where the private-public law distinction never took hold, conflicts law began to be viewed again as being at least as policy-laden or "political" as any other branch of the law.[8]

In the rest of the world, particularly in the civil law world, where the public-private law distinction continues to prevail, the official view continues to consider PIL as primarily private law. The seemingly inevitable corollary is that PIL does not implicate public interests except in certain exceptional cases such as those involving taxation, antitrust, or other public laws. Savigny continues to be revered and his classical theory of PIL continues to hold sway, as does the international uniformity rhetoric.

This chapter attempts to determine the extent to which modern choice-of-law codifications reflect the two opposing trends of internationalism and protectionism and how they reconcile them. The traditional literature associates internationalism with multilateralism and protectionism with unilateralism. Accepting this association for the moment and only for purposes of discussion,[9] this chapter begins by cataloguing what may be characterized as unilateralist inroads in recent choice-of-law codifications.

II. Unilateralist Inroads in Choice-of-Law Codifications

A review of the codifications enacted in the last 50 years leaves no doubt that multilateralism continues to be the preferred and indeed dominant method in the drafting of choice-of-law codifications. Nevertheless, a closer examination reveals that, although all modern codifications employ the multilateral method, they also selectively employ several unilateralist techniques, which are discussed below.

Moreover, choice-of-law codifications coexist with numerous substantive statutes that also apply unilaterally to multistate cases. Thus, when one looks at the totality of a PIL

---

[8] *See infra* at III.C.

[9] For this author's views on this matter, *see* Symeonides, *Accommodative Unilateralism*, 417, *et seq.*

system, rather than only at a choice-of-law codification, the emerging picture is much more complex. As antithetical as they may have been at their inception, multilateralism and unilateralism now coexist in many choice-of-law systems. It should be unsurprising that modern legislatures value practicality over methodological purity and are, therefore, as eclectic on this issue as they are on many other methodological issues.

This section catalogues the inroads of unilateralism into multilateralism. These inroads materialize through four different types of rules that are listed below and explained in the following subsections.

(1) "Localizing rules" contained in substantive statutes (other than choice-of-law codifications). These rules *expressly* delineate the spatial reach of the particular statute so as to ensure its applicability to certain multistate cases;

(2) "Rules of immediate application" or "mandatory rules." These rules have the same effect as localizing rules, even in the absence of such express language;

(3) Unilateral choice-of-law rules contained in PIL codifications; and

(4) Certain multilateral rules that, despite their multilaterality and resulting appearance of neutrality, are designed to lead to the application of the *lex fori* in the majority of cases and thus to ensure compliance with important public policies of the enacting state.

Together, the four types of rules form a perimeter designed to protect the interests and values of the forum state (Figure 7.1).

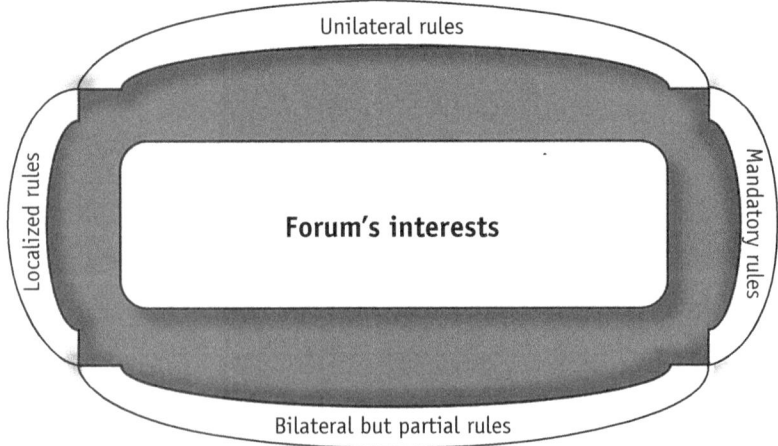

FIGURE 7.1. Unilateralist Tools Protecting the Forum's Interests

A. LOCALIZING RULES IN SUBSTANTIVE STATUTES

A choice-of-law codification always coexists with many other statutes that regulate particular areas of substantive law. Some of these statutes contain *express* provisions making the statute applicable to multistate situations that have certain prescribed connections to the enacting state. For example, a Quebec statute provides that traffic-accident victims domiciled in Québec are entitled to compensation under the statute "whether the accident occurs in Québec or outside Québec."[10]

These provisions are referred to hereafter as "localizing rules" and the statutes that contain them as "localized statutes."[11] Under standard principles of statutory interpretation (e.g., the principle *lex specialis derogat legi generali*), these statutes, being more specific, override the choice-of-law rules of a choice-of-law codification, which usually has a general and residual character.

Localizing rules are also found in statutes enacted in states that, like most states of the United States, do not have a choice-of-law codification. In these states, the localized statutes preempt the judicial choice-of-law process, which usually follows the bilateral method.

1. Consumer Contracts

A plethora of EU Directives require the Member States of EU to accord consumers a certain level of substantive-law protection specified in the directives and "to ensure that the consumer does not lose the protection granted by th[ese] Directive[s] by virtue of the choice of law of a non-Member country as the law applicable to the contract if the latter has a close connection with the territory of the Member States."[12]

The quoted localizing provision is from Council Directive 93/13/EEC of 5 April 1993 on Unfair Terms in Consumer Contracts, but other EU Directives also contain almost identical provisions, including: Directive 2008/48/EC on credit agreements for consumers,[13] Directive 97/47/EC on time-sharing contracts,[14] Directive 97/7/EC on distance contracting,[15] Directive 1999/44/EC on the sale of consumer goods and associated guarantees,[16] and Directive 2000/31/EC on electronic commerce.[17]

---

[10] Quebec Automobile Insurance Act § 7. For similar Quebec statutes covering other fields, *see* Act Respecting Industrial Accidents and Occupational Diseases §§ 7–8; Act Respecting Labour Standards § 2, discussed in F. Sabourin, *Quebec Report,* at V.2.

[11] Another term used for the same concept is *spatially conditioned substantive rules. See* A. Nussbaum, *Principles of International Law* 69–73 (1943). *See also* B. Audit & L. d'Avout, *DIP,* 107 (using the terms "règles substantielles auto-limitées.")

[12] Council Directive 93/13/EEC of 5 April 1993 on Unfair Terms in Consumer Contracts.

[13] *See* Art. 22(4) ("Member States shall take the necessary measures to ensure that consumers do not lose the protection granted by this Directive by virtue of the choice of the law of a third country as the law applicable to the credit agreement, if the credit agreement has a close link with the territory of one or more Member States.").

[14] *See* Article 9 ("Member States shall take the measures necessary to ensure that, whatever the law applicable may be, the purchaser is not deprived of the protection afforded by this Directive, if the immovable property concerned is situated within the territory of a Member State.").

[15] *See* Art. 12(2) ("Member States shall take the measures needed to ensure that the consumer does not lose the protection granted by this Directive by virtue of the choice of the law of a non-member country as the law applicable to the contract if the latter has close connection with the territory of one or more Member States.").

[16] *See* Art. 7(2) ("Member States shall take the necessary measures to ensure that consumers are not deprived of the protection afforded by this Directive as a result of opting for the law of a nonmember State as the law applicable to the contract where the contract has a close connection with the territory of the Member States.").

[17] *See* Directive 2000/31/EC of 8 June 2000 on electronic commerce, arts. 3, 8.

When an EU country implements these Directives, that country adopts similar local-ized statutes. For example, in implementing the above-quoted Directive, the United Kingdom enacted the Unfair Contract Terms Act, providing that it applies "notwith-standing any contract term which applies or purports to apply the law of any country outside the United Kingdom."[18] Likewise, the Polish codification provides that the con-tractual choice of the law of a state that is not a member of the European Economic Area in a contract that has a "close connection with at least one member state" may not deprive a consumer of the protection provided by the provisions of Polish law that implement the above-listed EU Directives.[19]

Many other countries, as well as states of the United States, have enacted similar local-ized statutes for consumer protection. For example, an Indiana statute requires the appli-cation of Indiana law to consumer credit transactions that have certain connections to that state, and prohibits a contractual choice of another state's law.[20]

2. Insurance Contracts

A Nevada statute provides that it applies to "(1) *All* insurers authorized to transact insur-ance in this state; (2) *All* insurers having policyholders resident in this state; [and] (3) *All* insurers against whom a claim under an insurance contract may arise in this state."[21] Many other states have similar statutes,[22] and many of them expressly prohibit the contractual choice of another state's law. For example, an Oregon statute provides that, for an insur-ance policy "delivered or issued for delivery in" Oregon, any "condition, stipulation or agreement requiring such policy to be construed according to the laws of any other state or country . . . shall be invalid."[23]

---

[18] Unfair Contract Terms Act 1977, § 27(2).

[19] Polish codif. art. 30.

[20] *See* Ind. Code § 24-4.5-1-201. For similar statutes in other states, *see, e.g.,* La. Rev. Stat. Ann. §§ 9:3511, 9:3563, 51:1418.

[21] Nev. Rev. Stat. § 696B.020 (emphasis added).

[22] For example, a Texas statute provides: "Any contract of insurance payable to any citizen or inhabitant of this State by any insurance company . . . doing business within this State shall be . . . governed by [the laws of this State] notwithstanding such . . . contract . . . may provide that the contract was executed and the premi-ums . . . should be payable without this State." Tex. Ins. Code Ann. § 21.42. A North Carolina Statute pro-vides: "All contracts of insurance on property, lives, or interests in this State shall be deemed to be made therein, and all contracts of insurance the applications for which are taken within the State shall be deemed to be made within this State and are subject to the laws thereof." N.C. Gen. Stat. § 58-3-1. A Wisconsin statute provides that "[e]very insurance against loss or destruction of or damage to property in this state or in the use of or income from property in this state is governed by the law of this state." Wis. Stat. § 632.09. For other similar statutes, *see* Minn. Stat. § 60A.08(4) ("All contracts of insurance on property, lives, or interests in this state, shall be deemed to be made in this state"); Colo. Rev. Stat. § 10-4-711; Fla. Stat. ch. 627.727; Okla. Stat. tit. 36 § 3636; La. Rev. Stat. Ann. §§ 22:611, 22:655, 22:1406(D).

[23] Or. Rev. Stat. §§ 742.001, 742.018. For similar statutes, *see, e.g.,* La. Rev. Stat. Ann. 22:629; Tex. Ins. Code Ann. § 21.42.

Another Oregon statute provides that, in cases of insurance for environmental contamination, Oregon law "shall be applied in all cases where the contaminated property to which the action relates is located within the State of Oregon."[24] Statutes in other states also require the application of forum law to cases arising from trans-boundary pollution within the forum state.[25]

Within the European Union, Directive 2009/103/EC on motor vehicle insurance requires each EU Member State to provide a certain level of protection for insureds, victims of traffic accidents, and the general public for vehicles normally based in its territory. Article 7 of the Directive also requires each Member State to ensure that vehicles from third countries shall not be used in its territory unless they are insured for the minimum liability coverage required by the Directive.

3. Franchise, Distributorship, and Commercial Agency Contracts

Localized statutes protecting franchisees, distributors, and commercial agents are also quite common. For example, an Iowa statute mandates the application of forum law to franchises operated in that state,[26] prohibits a contractual choice of another state's law,[27] and provides that a contractual choice of Iowa law does not alone render that statute applicable.[28] Other states have enacted similar statutes.[29]

A Belgian statute provides that Belgian law governs the sanctions for a unilateral breach of a distribution agreement of unlimited duration that covers Belgian territory, in whole or in part.[30] A Portuguese statute provides that the termination of an agency contract to be performed exclusively or primarily in Portugal may be governed by foreign law only if that law is more favorable to the agent than Portuguese law.[31] Finally, the Turkish Commercial Code provides that its rules on agency apply to persons carrying on transactions in Turkey on behalf of foreign principals who have no branch office in Turkey.[32]

---

[24] Or. Rev. Stat. § 465.480(2)(a). The statute continues as follows: "Nothing in this section shall be interpreted to modify common law rules governing choice of law determinations for sites located outside the State of Oregon." *Id.*

[25] *See, e.g.*, Mich. Comp. Laws § 324.1804 ("The law to be applied in an action or other proceeding brought pursuant to this part, including what constitutes 'pollution' is the law of this state, excluding choice of law rules."). For identical provisions, *see* Colo. Rev. Stat. §§13-1.5-104, 51-351b; NJ Stat. Ann. § 2A:58A-5; Wis. Stat. § 299.33(4).

[26] *See* Iowa Code § 523H.2.

[27] *See id.* § 523H.14.

[28] *See id.* § 523H.2.

[29] *See, e.g.*, Minn. Stat. § 80C.21 (franchises); *id.* § 325.064 (farm equipment dealerships); § 325.064 (heavy equipment dealerships).

[30] *See* Law of 27 July 1961, discussed in M. Fallon & J. Erauw, *Belgian Report,* at V.

[31] *See* art. 38 of the Decreto-Lei no 178/86, of 3/7, discussed in L. De Lima Pinheiro, *Portuguese Report* at V.

[32] *See* art. 117/3 of Turkish Commercial Code, discussed in Z. Tarman, *Turkish Report* at V.

4. Employment Contracts

In the United States, every state's worker's compensation statute contain provisions authorizing its extraterritorial application to injuries sustained outside the forum state if the employee or the employment relationship have certain connections with the forum state.[33]

In the European Union, there is a similar interplay between EU employee-protecting directives and implementing national legislation as described above with regard to consumers. For example, the United Kingdom's Employment Rights Act provides that its anti-discrimination provisions apply to UK employees, regardless of the law applicable to the employment contract.[34] A Spanish statute provides that Spanish employment law applies to Spanish workers working abroad but hired in Spain by Spanish employers.[35] A Greek statute provides that in individual employment contracts concluded by Greek employees working in Asia or Africa, the contractual choice of a foreign law is valid only if that law is more favorable to the employee than Greek law, and that the clauses regarding salary and working conditions must provide at least the same level of protection as mandated by Greek law.[36]

5. Other Contracts

A Louisiana statute requires the application of forum law to construction contracts to be performed in that state and prohibits the contractual choice of another state's law.[37]

Australia's Carriage of Goods by Sea Act provides that all parties to a sea carriage document relating to the carriage of goods from any place in Australia to any place outside Australia "are taken to have intended to contract according to the laws in force at the place of shipment," and prohibits the contractual choice of a non-Australian law. The Act also prohibits the choice of a non-Australian forum for trips to and from Australia.[38] Argentina's Navigation Act provides that its provisions on the carrier's liability toward the passenger apply to any contract of carriage of passengers by water if the contract is made in Argentina or the trip begins or ends in an Argentinean port.[39]

---

[33] *See, e.g.,* Ala. Code § 25-5-35; Ariz. Rev. Stat. § 23-904; Cal. Lab. Code § 3600.5; Ind. Code § 22-3-2-20; Ga. Code Ann. § 34-9-242; Ky. Rev. Stat. Ann. § 342.670; La. Rev. Stat. Ann. § 23:1035.1; Md. Code. Ann. Lab. & Empl. § 9-203; Okla. Stat. tit. 85 § 4; Tenn. Code Ann. § 50-6-115; Tex. Code Ann. § 406.071.

[34] *See* Employment Rights Act 1996, § 204(1). According to Professor Roodt, "the implicit territorial limitation [is] that the employee must be working in the UK." C. Roodt, *English Report,* at IV.

[35] *See* Article I.4 of the Spanish Workers Statute, discussed in C. Esplugues Mota & C. Azcárraga Monzonís, *Spanish Report,* at V.

[36] *See* Greek Law No 1429/1984, art. 2(1), discussed in E. Vassilakakis, *Greek Report,* at 4.

[37] *See* La. Rec. Stat. § 9:2779. *See also id.* §§ 9:2778, 38:2196 (same with regard to contracts involving the state and its agencies or subdivisions).

[38] Australian Carriage of Goods by Sea Act 1991 (Cth), § 11, discussed in A. De Jonge, *Australian Report,* at V.

[39] Argentina's Navigation Act 20.094 (1973), art. 604; discussed in M. Najurieta & M. Noodt Taquela, *Argentinean Report,* at V.

The Uruguayan Commercial Code applies to charter contracts involving foreign vessels, even if the contract was made elsewhere, as long as it involves performance in Uruguay.[40]

6. Antitrust

The United States, along with many countries and the European Union, have judicially interpreted their antitrust laws as reaching anticompetitive conduct occurring abroad but intended to have, and having, detrimental effects within their territories.[41] Some countries have expressly adopted this "effects doctrine" in their antitrust legislation. For example, South Korea's Capital Market Integration Act provides that its provisions apply extraterritorially to acts abroad that produce detrimental effects in South Korea.[42] Likewise, a Spanish statute provides that it applies to any acts of unlawful competition, wherever committed, which actually produce or may produce substantive effects on the Spanish market.[43]

B. MANDATORY RULES OR RULES OF IMMEDIATE APPLICATION

1. The Concept

Mandatory or *imperative* rules, or rules of *immediate* or *necessary* application,[44] are substantive legal rules that embody important state interests and that, for this reason, are intended to necessarily, mandatorily, and *directly* apply to multistate situations—that is, regardless of whether a choice-of-law rule authorizes their application, and even if a choice-of-law rule calls for the application of another law.[45]

Many localized statutes described in the preceding section would also qualify as mandatory rules or rules of immediate or necessary application.[46] The difference is that

---

[40] *See* art. 1270 of the Uruguayan Commercial Code, discussed in C. Fresnedo de Aguirre, *Uruguayan Report*, at V.

[41] *See, e.g.*, Hartford Fire Ins. Co. v. California, 509 U.S. 764 (1993); F. Hoffman-La Roche Ltd. v. Empagran S.A., 542 U.S. 155 (2004); S. Symeonides & W. Perdue, *Conflict of Laws: American, Comparative, International*, 707–708 (3d ed. 2012).

[42] *See* art. 2 of the South Korean Act concerning Capital Market and Financial Investment Business Act of 4 February 2009, discussed in K. H. Suk, *South Korean Report*, at V.

[43] *See* art. 4 of Act 3/1991 of 10.01.1991 on Unfair Competition, discussed in C. Esplugues Mota & C. Azcárraga Monzonís, *Spanish Report*, at V.

[44] The rules are known as *règles d'application immédiate*, *normes d'intervention*, or *lois de police* in France, *normes d'applicacione necessaria* in Italy, *normas de aplicación necesaria* in Spain, *Eingriffsnormen*, in Germany, and *voorrangsregels* in the Netherlands.

[45] *See* B. Audit & L. d'Avout, *DIP* 171–172 ("On parle de loi d'application immédiate lorsqu'une règle interne est appliquée à une situation internationale indépendamment de sa désignation par une règle de conflit.").

[46] Localizing rules also resemble the unilateral choice-of-law rules discussed in the next section. The difference is that, rather than being part of a choice-of-law codification, the localizing rules are embedded in special substantive statutes.

a localizing provision *expressly* declares its applicability to a particular multistate situation and, for this reason, it displaces a choice-of-law rule *without* the need to determine whether the provision reflects an important public interest. In contrast, a rule that embodies a significant public interest may qualify as a mandatory rule even if it does not contain language declaring its applicability to a particular multistate situation. Stated another way, localized statutes and mandatory rules have the same operative effect of displacing choice-of-law rules, but (1) localized statutes do so because of their express wording and without the need to examine whether they embody a high level of public policy, whereas (2) mandatory rules qualify as mandatory only if they embody a high level of public policy.

2. Scholastic Discovery

To be sure, mandatory rules are not a new phenomenon. As early as the middle of the nineteenth century, Savigny, the intellectual father of multilateralism, alluded to their existence when he said that the principle of equality between forum and foreign law did not apply to those rules that are of a strictly positive, binding nature (*Gesetze von streng positiver, zwingender Natur*).[47] However, it was only during the second half of the twentieth century that these rules received wider recognition by academic doctrine, primarily due to the classic writings of Phocion Francescakis.[48]

Francescakis observed that, in dealing with certain kinds of cases with foreign elements, French courts bypassed the pertinent choice-of-law rule and instead applied directly certain rules of French substantive law. These rules were referred to as *lois de police et de sûreté* (in reference to Article 3(1) of the French Civil Code) or as *lois d'ordre public*. Francescakis renamed both categories *règles d'application immédiate*. This term described more precisely the way these rules operated while also disassociating them from both the notion of territoriality (with which the term *lois de police* was traditionally linked) and the concept of *ordre public* (which was traditionally seen as having a defensive rather than an affirmative function).

Indeed, quite apart from territoriality, the rules of immediate application embody an affirmative public policy of the enacting state in safeguarding its overall political and economic organization and promoting important public interests. Reflecting the increasing

---

[47] 8 F.C. Savigny, *System des heutigen Römischen Rechts* 33 (1849).

[48] *See* Ph. Francescakis, *La théorie du renvoi et les conflits de systèmes en droit international privé*, 11 *et seq.* (1958); Ph. Francescakis, Quelques précisions sur les "lois d'application immédiate" et leurs rapports avec les règles de conflits de lois, 55 *Revue critique DIP* 1 (1966); Ph. Francescakis, Lois d'application immédiate et règles de conflit, 3 *Riv. dir. int'le priv. e process.* 691 (1967); Ph. Francescakis, Conflits de Lois (principes généraux), in *Répertoire de droit international*, vol. 1, 470, 480 (no. 128) (1968). *See also* R. De Nova, Conflict of Laws and Functionally Restricted Substantive Rules, 54 *Calif. L. Rev.* 1569 (1966); P. Gothot, Le renouveau de la tendance unilatérale en droit international privé, 60 *Rev. critique DIP* 1, 209, 415 (1971); P. Graulich, Règles de Conflit et règles d'application immédiate, in 2 *Melanges Dabin* 629 (1963); G. Sperduti, Norme di applicazione necessaria e ordine publico, 12 *Riv. dir. Int'le priv. e process.* 769 (1976).

state intervention in contemporary society, these rules are found not only in traditionally public-law fields (such as taxation or currency regulation) that express important economic policies, but also in fields such as labor law, which involve important social policies, and family law, which reflect certain moral beliefs. Because of the importance of the interests they embody, these rules have priority over other rules of substantive law, and, a fortiori, over any otherwise applicable foreign law. Thus, whenever a case with foreign elements falls within the ambit of a rule of immediate application, the rule applies directly (*immédiatement*)—that is, without considering whether such rule is made applicable by a choice-of-law rule. In such a case, there is no question of applying foreign law and, therefore, no need to consider choice-of-law rules. The interests reflected in the rules of immediate application are simply too important to be jeopardized by subjecting these rules to the ordinary choice-of-law process, which may point to the application of a foreign law. These rules deserve a privileged status both domestically and internationally because they preserve the very identity of the state, an identity that international law does not deny but takes as its premise.

The unilateralist tenet of this thought is apparent, but it is only a partial unilateralism, for two reasons. First, unlike the unilateralism of the statutists, this type of unilateralism is confined to a particular class of substantive rules, that is, those of *police et de sûreté* and those of an *ordre public* character and, at least as originally conceived, it extends only to the law of the forum. Second, it does not reject the value of a bilateral system, to which it resorts in two categories of cases, namely: (1) cases that do not fall within the ambit of any forum rule of immediate application, and (2) for the "remaining part" of those cases that fall only partly within the ambit of a rule of immediate application.

Francescakis did not discuss a question that later acquired importance, namely whether the forum should ever apply a rule of immediate application that does not belong to either the *lex fori* or the *lex causae*,[49] but rather to a third state. To a unilateralist, this question is not difficult to answer because, whenever forum law is inapplicable, a unilateralist looks to the laws of all potentially implicated states. To a bilateralist, who looks at only two laws, the *lex fori* and the *lex causae* (and who tends to despise *dépeçage*), this question is almost inconceivable.

Surprisingly, however, the first writer to answer this question in the affirmative was a bilateralist jurist, Professor Wilhelm Wengler, as early as 1941. In discussing contract conflicts, Wengler proposed his theory of "special connections" (*Sonderanknüpfungen*).[50] According to his theory, when a foreign imperative rule that is not part of the *lex contractus* claims application to a contract, the court should consider such application if the enacting state has a "sufficiently close connection" with the contract, such as when that

---

[49] A rule of immediate application of the state whose law applies to a case (*lex causa*) is always applicable as part of the *lex causae*, unless of course the application of that rule is prevented by a contrary rule of immediate application of the *lex fori* or offends the forum's *ordre public*.

[50] *See* W. Wengler, Die Anknknüpfüng des zwingended Schuldrechts im IPR: Eine Rechtsvergleichende Studie, 54 *ZvglRW* 168, 194–195 (1941).

state is physically in a position to impose its policies. Many years later, Wengler's idea found its way into what became Article 7 of the Rome Convention, which is discussed later.[51]

3. Legislative Sanction

Article 13 of the unenacted Benelux Uniform Law on PIL of 1969 was the first codification expressly to provide for "imperative" rules, defining them as rules "whose peculiar nature and object exclude the application of any other law."[52] However, Article 13 was limited to the narrow context of party autonomy, stating that, under certain circumstances, mandatory rules would override a *contractual* choice of law.[53] In contrast, Article 7 of the 1972 E.E.C. Draft Convention on the Law Applicable to Contractual and Non-Contractual Obligations broadened the scope of mandatory rules by providing that, under certain conditions, these rules could override not only a contractual, *but also a legislative or judicial* choice of law. With small modifications, this provision survived as Article 7 of the 1980 Rome Convention on Contractual Obligations, which is reproduced below.[54]

The 1978 Hague Convention on the Law Applicable to Agency contained a similar article, providing that "effect may be given to the mandatory rules of any State with which the situation has a significant connection, if and in so far as, under the law of that State, those rules must be applied whatever the law specified by its choice of law rules."[55] This convention did not go into effect until 1992. In the meantime, the Rome Convention went into effect in 1980 and differentiated between the mandatory rules of the forum state and those of another state.[56]

Since then, several choice-of-law codifications have also followed suit by providing express statutory sanction to mandatory rules, including (in chronological order) the codifications of:

Switzerland (1987), Germany (1989), Quebec (1991), United Kingdom (1995), Italy (1995), Uzbekistan (1997), Armenia (1998), Belarus (1998), Georgia (1998), Kyrgyzstan (1998), Tunisia (1998), Venezuela (1998), Kazakhstan (1999), Macau (1999), Azerbaijan (2000), Lithuania (2000), South Korea (2001), Estonia (2002), Moldova (2002), Russia (2002), Belgium (2005), Bulgaria (2005), Tajikistan (2005), Ukraine (2005), FYROM (2005), Turkey (2007), Uruguay (draft 2009),

---

[51] *See infra* at II.B.4.

[52] Benelux Law, art. 13.

[53] Article 13 of the Benelux Law provided that "[i]f the contract is clearly located in a certain country, provisions of the law of that country whose peculiar nature and object exclude the application of any other law cannot be excluded by the will of the parties."

[54] *See infra* at II.B.4.

[55] Hague Convention of 14 March 1978 on the Law Applicable to Agency, art. 16.

[56] *See* Rome Convention, art. 7 (reproduced *infra*). *See also id.* art. 3(3).

China (2010), Taiwan (2010), Poland (2011), Netherlands (2011), Argentina (draft 2011), and Serbia (draft 2012).[57]

In addition, the Rome I, Rome II, and Successions Regulations,[58] the Mexico City Convention,[59] and at least five Hague Conventions in addition to the Agency convention,[60] have also provided for the application of mandatory rules.[61]

---

[57] *See* Swiss codif. arts. 18, 19; German codif. art. 34; Quebec codif. arts. 3076, 3079, 3129; English tort statute § 14(4); Italian codif. art. 17; Uzbekistan codif. art. 1165; Armenian codif. art. 1259; Belarus codif. art. 1100; Georgia codif. art. 6; Kyrgyzstan codif. art. 1174; Tunisian codif. art. 38; Venezuelan codif. art. 10; Kazakhstan codif. art. 1091; Macau codif. art. 21; Azerbaijan codif. art. 5; Lithuanian codif. art. 1.11; South Korean codif. art. 7; Estonian codif. art. 31; Moldovan codif. art. 1584; Russian codif. art. 1192; Belgium codif. art. 20; Bulgarian codif. art. 46; Tajikistan codif. art. 1198; Ukrainian codif. art. 14; FYROM codif. art. 14; Turkish codif. arts. 6, 31; Uruguay draft codif. art 6; Chinese codif. art. 5; Taiwan codif. art. 7; Polish codif. art. 8; Uruguay Draft codif. art 6; Dutch codif. art. 7; Argentinean draft codif. art. 2599; Serbian draft codif. art. 40.

[58] *See* Rome I, arts. 9, 3(3)–(4); Rome II, art. 16; Successions Regulation art. 30. *See also* European Commission Proposal for a Council Regulation on jurisdiction, applicable law and the recognition and enforcement of decisions in matters of matrimonial property regimes, Brussels, 16.3.2011, COM(2011) 126 final 2011/0059 (CNS), art. 22; European Commission Proposal for a Council Regulation on jurisdiction, applicable law and the recognition and enforcement of decisions regarding the property consequences of registered partnerships, Brussels, 16.3.2011, COM(2011) 127 final, 2011/0060 (CNS), art. 17.

[59] *See* Inter-American Convention on the Law Applicable to Contracts, art. 11.

[60] *See* Hague Convention of 1 July 1985 on the Law Applicable to Trusts and on Their Recognition, art. 17; Hague Convention of 22 December 1986 on the Law Applicable to Contracts for the International Sale of Goods, art. 17; Hague Convention of 1 August 1989 on the Law Applicable to Succession to the Estates of Deceased Persons, art. 6; Hague Convention of 13 January 2000 on the International Protection of Adults, art. 20; Hague Convention of 5 July 2006 on the Law Applicable to Certain Rights in Respect of Securities Held with an Intermediary, art. 11, Hague Principles for Choice of Law in International Contracts, art. 11.

[61] From the voluminous recent literature on these rules, *see* A. Bonomi, *Le norme imperative nell diritto internazionale privato* (1998); B. Remy, *Exception d'ordre public et mécanisme des lois de police en droit international privé* (2008); K.A.S. Schäfer, *Application of Mandatory Rules in the Private International Law of Contracts: A Critical Analysis of Approaches in Selected Continental and Common Law Jurisdictions* (2010); U. Liukkunen, *The Role of Mandatory Rules in International Labour Law: A Comparative Study in the Conflict of Laws* (2004); Z. Papassiopi-Passia, *Rules of Immediate Application and Substantive Choice of Law Rules* (in Greek) (1989); C. Tsouka, *Les lois etrangeres d'application immédiate et leur impact sur la nature méthodologiques du droit international privé* (1997); N. Voser, *Die Theorie Der Lois D'application Immediate Im Internationalen Privatrecht* (1993); A. Bonomi, Mandatory Rules in Private International Law: The Quest for Uniformity of Decisions in a Global Environment, 1 *Ybk. Priv. Int'l L.* 219 (1999); A. Bonomi, Overriding Mandatory Provisions in the Rome I Regulation on the Law Applicable to Contracts, 10 *Ybk. Priv. Int'l L.* 285 (2008); A. Chong, The Public Policy and Mandatory Rules of Third Countries in International Contracts, 2(1) *J. Priv. Int'l L.* 27 (2006); M. Davies, Forum Selection, Choice of Law and Mandatory Rules, 2011 *Lloyd's Marit. & Comm. L.Q* 237; A. Dickinson, Third-Country Mandatory Rules in the Law Applicable to Contractual Obligations: So Long, Farewell, Auf Wiedersehen, Adieu?, 3(1) *J. Priv. Int'l L.* 53 (2007); D. Einsele, Overriding Mandatory Provisions in Capital Market Law: Does the Rome I Regulation Need a Special Rule Regarding Harmonized European Law?, *IPRax* 481 (2012/6); J. Fawcett, Evasion of Law and Mandatory Rules in Private International Law, 49 *Cambridge L J.* 44 (1990); Y. Gan, Mandatory Rules in Private International Law in the People's Republic of China, 14 *Ybk. Priv. Int'l L.* 305 (2012–2013); T. Guedj, The Theory of the *Lois De Police*,

Moreover, the concept of mandatory rules has been recognized by special statutes, judicial practice, or academic doctrine in many countries (1) that have not recently enacted a comprehensive choice-of-law codification, or (2) whose codification does not contain an express statutory rule giving priority to mandatory rules. Australia, Finland, Israel, and Norway are some of the countries in the first group,[62] and Austria, Croatia, Greece, Portugal, and Spain are some of the countries in the second group.[63] France belongs to a special category, as it is the intellectual motherland of the modern doctrine of mandatory rules.[64]

Table 7.1 below shows the codifications and conventions that contain express and *general* provisions giving priority to mandatory rules. The table does *not* include codifications that provide for mandatory rules only as limitations to party autonomy,[65] or countries that recognize mandatory rules only through special statutes, judicial decisions, or academic doctrine.[66]

---

a Functional Trend in Continental Private International Law: A Comparative Analysis with Modern American Theories, 39 *Am. J. Comp. L.* 661 (1991); J. Harris, Mandatory Rules and Public Policy under the Rome I Regulation, in F. Ferrari & S. Leible (eds.), *Rome I Regulation: The Law Applicable to Contractual Obligations in Europe* 269 (2009); T. Hartley, Mandatory Rules in International Contracts: The Common Law Approach, 266 *Recueil des Cours* 337(1998); M. Hellner, Third Country Overriding Mandatory Rules in the Rome I Regulation: Old Wine in New Bottles?, 5(3) *J. Priv. Int'l L.* 447 (2009); S. Knöfel, Mandatory Rules and Choice of Law: A Comparative Approach to Article 7(2) of the Rome Convention, 1999 *J. Bus. L.* 239 (1999); P. Malaurie, Lois de police et méthodes de conflits de lois en matière de commerce exterieur, 8 *J. Soc. legisl. comp.* 541 (1986); P. Mayer, Les lois de police, *Travaux Com. Français Dr. Int'l Priv.* 105 (1988); Y. Nakanishi, New Private International Law of Japan: Protection of Weaker Parties and Mandatory Rules, 50 *Japan. Ann. Int'l L.* 60 (2007); A. Nuyts, L'application des lois de police dans l'espace: Réflexions au depart du droit belge de la distribution commerciale et du droit communautaire, 88 *Rev. critique DIP* 31 (1999); S. Sanchez Lorenzo, Choice of Law and Overriding Mandatory Rules in International Contracts after Rome I, 12 *Ybk. Priv. Int'l L.* 67 (2010); J. Schultsz, Les lois de police etrangeres, *Trav. Com. Français Dr. Int'l Priv. 1982–83*, 39 (1983); K. Siehr, False conflicts, lois d'application immediate und andere "Neuentdeckungen" im IPR: Zu gewissen Eigengesetzlichkeiten kollisionsrechtlicher Systeme, in J. Basedow et al., (eds.) *Festschrift fur Ulrich Drobnig zum siebzigsten Geburtstag* 443 (1998); M. Storme, Freedom of Contract: Mandatory and Non-mandatory Rules in European Contract Law, 15 *Eur. Rev. Priv. L.* 233 (2007); C. Tillman, The Relationship between Party Autonomy and the Mandatory Rules in the Rome Convention, 2002 *J. Bus. L.* 45 (2002); F. Vischer, Lois d'application immediate als Schranken von Gerichtsstands-und Schiedsvereinbarungen, in A. Overbeck et al. (eds.), *Collisio Legum: Studi di diritto internazionale privato per Gerardo Broggini*, 577 (1997); M. Wojewoda, Mandatory Rules in Private International Law, 7 *Maastricht J. Eur. & Comp. L.* 183 (2000).

[62] *See* A. De Jonge, *Australian Report*, at V (discussing Australian cases); U. Liukkunen, *Finnish Report*, at V (discussing several Finnish statutes); T. Einhorn, *Israeli Report*, at VII.2; G. Cordero Moss, *Norwegian Report, passim* (discussing Norwegian statutes on commercial agency, insurance and consumer sales, as well as cases applying these statutes).

[63] *See* C. Wendehorst, *Austrian Report*, at B.II; D. Babić, *Croatian Report*, at V; E. Vassilakakis, *Greek Report*, at II,4; L. de Lima Pinheiro, *Portuguese Report*, at V, V.II; C. Esplugues Mota & C. Azcárraga Monzonís, *Spanish Report*, at V.

[64] *See* Francescakis, *supra* note 48; B. Remy, *French Report*, at V.

[65] *See infra* note 77; Chapter 3, *supra*, at V.B.

[66] *See supra* notes 62–64.

TABLE 7.1. CODIFICATIONS AND CONVENTIONS EXPRESSLY AUTHORIZING THE
APPLICATION OF MANDATORY RULES

Codifications	Forum rules	Foreign rules
Argentina	X	X
Armenia	X	—
Azerbaijan	X	X
Belarus	X	X
Belgium	X	X
Bulgaria	X	X
Czech Republic	X	—
China	X	—
England	X	X
Estonia	X	—
FYROM	X	—
Georgia	X	—
Germany	X	—
Italy	X	—
Kazakhstan	X	X
South Korea	X	—
Kyrgyzstan	X	X
Lithuania	X	X
Macau	X	—
Moldova	X	—
Netherlands	X	X
Poland	X	X
Quebec	X	X
Serbia	X	X
Russia	X	X
Switzerland	X	X
Taiwan	X	—
Tajikistan	X	X
Tunisia	X	X
Turkey	X	X
Ukraine	X	X
Uruguay	X	X
Uzbekistan	X	X
Venezuela	X	—
Rome I	X	X
Rome II	X	—

Conventions	Forum rules	Foreign rules
Reg. on Successions	X	X
Rome Convention	X	X
Mexico City Convention	X	X
Hague Agency Conv.	X	X
Hague Trusts Conv.	X	X
Hague Sales Conv.	X	—
Hague Successions Conv.	X	X
Hague Protection of Adults	X	X
Hague Securities Conv.	X	—
Hague Contracts Principles	X	X
Totals	46	30

Perhaps the most widely discussed provision on mandatory rules is Article 7 of the Rome Convention. Article 7 defined mandatory rules in the first paragraph and then differentiated between foreign and forum mandatory rules in its two paragraphs, as follows:

1. When applying…the law of a country, effect may be given to the mandatory rules of the law of another country with which the situation has a close connection, if and in so far as, under the law of the latter country, those rules must be applied whatever the law applicable to the contract….
2. Nothing in this Convention shall restrict the application of the rules of the law of the forum in a situation where they are mandatory irrespective of the law otherwise applicable to the contract.[67]

Although the second paragraph was met with universal approval, the part of the first paragraph that authorized the application of foreign mandatory rules proved controversial.[68] The controversy continued during the deliberations for converting the Convention into the Rome I Regulation. As a compromise, Article 7 of the Convention was replaced with Article 9 of Rome I, which narrowed significantly the circumstances in which foreign mandatory rules may be applied. Instead of referring to the mandatory rules of a state with a "close connection," paragraph 3 of Article 9 of Rome I refers only to the state of the contract's performance and authorizes the application of that state's mandatory rules only to the extent they render the performance "unlawful."[69]

---

[67] Rome Convention art. 7.

[68] As a result, seven countries filed a reservation to that paragraph, as allowed by the Convention. The seven countries were Ireland, Germany, Latvia, Luxembourg, Portugal, Slovenia, and the United Kingdom.

[69] Rome I, art. 9(3). For an identical provision, *see* Serbian draft codif. art. 144. A similar controversy led to the deletion of an earlier reference to foreign mandatory rules in Rome II, although Article 17 contemplates such rules when it authorizes consideration of the rules of "safety and conduct" of the state in which the conduct occurred.

Be that as it may, paragraph 1 of Article 9 of Rome I provides a clearer, albeit narrow, definition of mandatory rules: They are those rules that the enacting country regards as "crucial…for safeguarding its public interests, such as its political, social or economic organisation, to such an extent that they are applicable to any situation falling within their scope, irrespective of the law otherwise applicable."[70] Article 9 characterizes these rules as "overriding" mandatory rules[71] because they override, preempt, or displace the ordinary choice-of-law rules and the substantive law that would apply under those rules.

Rome I, which is confined to contract conflicts, distinguishes between the "overriding" mandatory rules (Article 9) and "simple" mandatory rules, which it defines in Articles 3(3), 6, and 8 as rules that "cannot be derogated from *by agreement*."[72] Article 3(3) provides that, when "all other elements" are located in a country other than the country whose law the parties have chosen, that choice "shall not prejudice" the application of the "simple" mandatory rules of that country.[73] Articles 6 and 8 provide that a choice-of-law clause in a consumer contract or an employment contract may not deprive the consumer or employee, respectively, of the protection afforded by the mandatory rules of the *lex causae*. Similar provisions are found in the laws of many states, both within the EU[74] and outside the EU, including FYROM, Japan, South Korea, Liechtenstein, Puerto Rico, Quebec, Russia, Serbia, Turkey, Ukraine, and Uruguay.[75]

One difference between the "simple" and the "overriding" mandatory rules is that the former override a contractual choice of another law, whereas the latter override both a contractual and a legislative or judicial choice of another law. Another difference is that the threshold for applying the "overriding" rules is higher than for applying the "simple"

---

[70] Rome I, art. 9(1). This definition is drawn from a decision of the Court of Justice of the European Communities in Cases C-369/96 and C-374/96 Arblade [1999] ECR 1-8453, para 30 (rendered 23.11.1999) (*Arblade* case). However, the Court used narrower language to the extent it referred to rules that "require compliance…by all persons present on the national territory…and all legal relationships within that State." For discussion of recent case law under Article 9, *see* O. Remien, Variationen zum Thema Eingriffsnormen nach Art. 9 Rom I-VO und Art. 16 Rom II-VO unter Berücksichtigung neuerer Rechtsprechung zu Art. 7 Römer Übereinkommen, in H. Kronke & K. Thorn (eds.), *Grenzen überwinden, Prinzipien bewahren: Festschrift für Bernd von Hoffmann* 334 (2012).

[71] Rome I, art. 9(1).

[72] Rome I, arts. 3(3–4), 6(2), and 8(1) (emphasis added). The "overriding" mandatory rules are also known as "internationally mandatory" or "supermandatory" rules, whereas the "simple" mandatory rules are sometimes referred to as "domestic" or "internal" mandatory rules.

[73] Rome I, art. 3(3). *See also id.* art. 3(4), which provides that when all other elements are located in one or more Member States, the parties' choice of applicable law other than that of a Member State "shall not prejudice" the application of the mandatory rules of Community law.

[74] *See* Austrian codif. art. 41; Bulgarian codif. arts 95–96; Estonian codif. arts. 34(1), 35(1); German codif. arts. 2930; Lithuanian codif. art. 1.39; Romanian codif. arts. 101–102 (employment contracts); Slovenian codif. arts. 21–22.

[75] *See* FYROM codif. arts. 25–26; Japanese codif. arts. 11–12; South Korean codif. arts. 27–28; Liechtenstein codif. arts. 45, 48; Puerto Rico draft codif. arts. 35–36; Quebec codif. arts. 3117–3118; Russian codif. art. 1212; Serbian draft codif. arts. 141–142; Turkish codif. arts. 26–27; Ukrainian codif. art. 45.

mandatory rules[76] because the former reflect a higher grade of public policy than the latter,[77] although both types of rules embody important *public* interests.

In any event, outside the field of contract conflicts, the distinction between the two categories of mandatory rules is inapplicable. This is why, outside the field of contracts, other codifications or conventions do not use the adjective "overriding,"[78] even though, by their nature, mandatory rules always override choice-of-law rules. As these codifications provide, mandatory rules apply "directly"[79] and "irrespective of,"[80] "regardless of,"[81] or "notwithstanding"[82] the law designated by the codification's choice-of-law rules.

For example, the Italian codification provides that its choice-of-law rules "do not prejudice" those provisions of Italian law that "because of their object and purpose, are applicable irrespective of the reference made to a foreign law."[83] Similarly, the Swiss codification provides for the mandatory provisions of Swiss law[84] and then provides that, under certain circumstances, a mandatory provision of a law other than the one designated as applicable by the codification "may be taken into consideration if the situation at hand has a close connection to that law"[85]

The Russian codification provides that its choice-of-law rules "do not affect the effectiveness of those imperative norms of [Russian] law ... that, in view of an indication in the imperative norms themselves or in view of their special significance ... regulate the respective relations regardless of the otherwise applicable law"[86] The codification also provides that courts "may take into consideration" the imperative norms of another country "having a close connection," if, "according to the law of that country such norms must regulate the respective relations regardless of the [otherwise] applicable law."[87]

---

[76] *See* Rome I Preamble, Recital 37 ("The concept of 'overriding mandatory provisions' should be distinguished from the expression 'provisions which cannot be derogated from by agreement' and should be construed more restrictively.").

[77] Another difference is that in Rome I: (1) the simple mandatory rules that can defeat a contractual choice of law are (a) those of the *lex causae* in consumer and employment contracts (*see* arts. 6.2 and 8.1), and (b) those of the country in which "all other elements" of the situation are located—which may or may not be the *lex causae*—in all other contracts (*see* art. 3.3–4); whereas (2) the "overriding" rules that may defeat either a contractual or a judicial choice of another law are those of the *lex fori* (art. 9.2) or the law of the place of performance, but only if they render performance unlawful (art. 9.3).

[78] The only exception is Article 7 of the Dutch codification, which uses the adjective *overriding* for all mandatory rules, without differentiating between "overriding" and "simple" ones.

[79] Chinese codif. art. 5.

[80] Rome I, art. 9(1); Rome II, art. 16; Belgian codif. art. 20; Dutch codif. art. 7; FYROM codif. art. 14; Italian codif. art. 17, South Korean codif. art. 7; Serbian draft codif. art. 40.1; Swiss codif. art. 18.

[81] Belarus codif. art. 1100(1); Kyrgyzstan codif. art. 1174(1); Lithuanian codif. art. 1.11(2).

[82] Bulgarian codif. art. 46(1); Venezuelan codif. art. 10; Inter-American Contracts Convention, art. 11.

[83] Italian codif. art. 17.

[84] *See* Swiss codif. art. 18 ("The present statute does not prejudice those mandatory provisions of Swiss law, which, in light of their particular purpose, are applicable irrespective of the law designated by the present statute.").

[85] Swiss codif. art. 19(1).

[86] Russian codif. art. 1192(1).

[87] *Id.* art. 1192(2).

Finally, the Belgian codification provides that its choice-of-law rules "do not prejudice" the application of the "mandatory or public policy rules" of Belgian law, which, "by virtue of the law or their manifest purpose, are aimed to govern an international situation irrespective of the law designated by the choice-of-law rules."[88] The codification also provides that "effect may be given to the mandatory or public policy rules" of a state with which the situation has a "close connection," if and insofar as, "under the law of [that] state, those rules apply irrespective of the law otherwise applicable" under the codification's choice-of-law rules.[89]

As Table 7.1 above indicates, 37 codifications (including three EU Regulations) and nine international conventions expressly sanction the concept of mandatory rules. Twenty-three codifications (including two EU Regulations), and seven conventions expressly authorize the application of the mandatory rules of both the forum state and a *third* foreign state in addition to the state of the *lex causae*,[90] while 14 codifications (including Rome II), and two conventions do so for only the mandatory rules of the forum state.[91] In virtually all codifications, the third state is a state that has a "close" (but not necessarily a closer or the closest) connection with the case.[92] The standard for applying foreign mandatory rules is usually different from the standard for applying the forum's corresponding rules.[93] Whereas the forum's mandatory rules apply automatically, the application of foreign mandatory rules is always discretionary—the court "may" apply the mandatory rules of a third country after considering the "nature" and "purpose" of those rules and the "consequences of their application or non-application."[94]

---

[88] Belgian codif. art. 20(1).

[89] *Id.* art. 20(2).

[90] Obviously, if a mandatory rule is part of the *lex causae*, the rule applies as part of the *lex causae*. It applies *because,* rather than "irrespective," of the choice-of-law rule that designates the *lex causae*.

[91] The Quebec codification contains—in addition to a general article for the mandatory rules of the forum qua forum (art. 3076) and a general article for foreign mandatory rules (art. 3079)—a special article (art. 3129) mandating the application of Quebec law "in matters of civil liability for damage suffered in or outside Québec as a result of exposure to or the use of raw materials, whether processed or not, originating in Québec." Also, the codification provides for mandatory rules as a limitation to party autonomy in consumer and employment contracts (*see* arts. 3117–3118) and contracts in general (art. 3111).

[92] Except as noted below, all pertinent provisions use the phrase "close connection." Tunisia uses the phrase "strong" connection; Lithuania uses the phrase "most closely related"; the Hague Agency Convention uses the phrase "a significant connection"; Rome I, art. 9, refers only to the state of the performance of the contract and only insofar as the law of that state renders performance of the contract illegal; the proposed Regulations on Matrimonial Regimes and on Registered partnerships simply refer to a "Member State"; and the English tort statute simply refers to rules that have effect "notwithstanding the rules of private international law."

[93] The only exceptions are the English tort statute, the Hague Agency Convention, and the EU Succession Regulation.

[94] Dutch codif. art. 7(3). Identical or similar language exists in all provisions under discussion here. Of course, consideration of the nature, purpose, and consequences of a rule is also necessary for determining whether a rule of the *lex fori* qualifies as a mandatory rule.

4. Mandatory Rules, Unilateralism, and State Interests

As the above survey illustrates, the advent of mandatory rules is widespread. It represents a small but clear victory of unilateralism over multilateralism, even if it is not "unilateralism triumphant," as one author proclaimed.[95] Indeed, the very definition of mandatory rules relies on unilateralist thinking. To determine whether a rule qualifies as mandatory, the court must examine the "purpose" of the rule and the "consequences of its application or nonapplication."[96] The notion that, by examining the purpose of a substantive legal rule, one can determine whether the rule was intended to apply to a particular case is by no means unique. It is, after all, the characteristic feature of old and well-established methods of statutory interpretation, such as the teleological method or the functional method. However, in the context of PIL, this notion is a uniquely unilateralist insight. It recognizes that, by examining the purpose of substantive legal rules, one can determine their intended *spatial* reach. In this sense, this notion is not much different from the basic tenets of policy analysis as practiced in the United States.[97]

Moreover, the advent of mandatory rules reflects a recognition that states do have interests in the outcome of choice-of-law disputes, and that the laws embodying those interests should override the (usually) multilateral choice-of-law rules.[98]

It can be argued that this recognition applies only to interests embodied in *public* laws and, if so, this is something that multilateralists have always acknowledged. The narrow definition of mandatory rules in Article 9(1) of Rome I may provide support for this argument insofar as it speaks of rules safeguarding a country's "public interests, such as its political, social or economic organisation."[99] However, as the words "such as" indicate, the quoted phrase is merely illustrative. It is true that, within the regime of Rome I, there is an ongoing debate about whether Article 9 encompasses only *Eingriffsnormen*

---

[95] P. Nygh, *Reasonable Expectations,* 378 (referring to mandatory rules as "unilateralism triumphant").

[96] The quoted words appear in most codifications.

[97] *See* Symeonides, *Revolution* 396–398.

[98] *See* K. Siehr, *Swiss Report,* in S. Symeonides (ed.), *Progress or Regress?,* 389 (characterizing mandatory rules as rules intended to "promote State or national interests."); H. Sonnenberger, *Rapport Allemand,* in *id.* at 225 (referring to mandatory rules as means "par lesquelles l'Etat défend ou promeut les intérêts collectifs."). *See also id.* at 225–226 (referring to these norms as "destinées à garantir des intérêts de la communauté sans distinguer s'il s'agit d'intérêts propres à l'Etat, d'intérêts économiques, culturels, concernant l'éducation ou la politique de la famille ou de la vie sociale."); K. Boele-Woelki, C. Joustra & G. Steenhoff, *Dutch Report,* in *id.,* at 299 ("rules which should be applied in order to safeguard the general interests of the forum…irrespective[ly] of the law otherwise applicable to the [case]."); S. Vrellis, *Rapport grec,* in *id.* at 248: ("La théorie des règles d'application immédiate reflète la prédominance des intérêts étatiques"); R.M. Moura Ramos, *Rapport Portugais,* in *id.,* at 381 (referring to "le cas de l'affirmation de certaines valeurs matérielles, qui se sont imposées soit par des règles d'application nécessaire et immédiate (ici en rupture avec le principe d'égalité de traitement entre les différents ordres juridiques), soit par des règles de droit international privé matériel, soit par un choix de la loi *effect-oriented.*").

[99] Rome I, art. 9(1).

or also *Parteischutzvorschriften;*[100] and that sometimes the debate follows a tripartite distinction of rules into: (1) rules that protect only purely public interests, (2) rules that protect both public and private interests, and (3) rules that protect only private interests.[101] These distinctions may be meaningful within the framework of Rome I because of Article 9(1)'s restrictive phraseology, and also because Articles 6 and 8 secure the priority of pro-consumer and pro-employee "simple" mandatory rules regardless of whether they protect public or private interests. However, outside Rome I, the validity of this tripartite distinction is very much in doubt.

First, in most other codifications, the definition of mandatory rules is not as restrictive as that of Article 9(1) of Rome I. Most of these codifications simply require that the rule's "purpose" be such as to mandate its application "regardless" of the otherwise applicable law. At least three codifications expressly refer to rules that safeguard "the rights of private parties to participate in civil relations."[102] Moreover, as one commentator noted,

> [T]he underlying assumption that there is a contradiction between public and private interests is highly debatable. All public interests are built upon the interests of individuals, as only individuals exist in the real world. On the other hand, all private interests, at least those that affect a sufficient number of individuals, can also be said to be public interests.[103]

As another commentator concluded, rules that protect consumers or other presumptively weak parties "can also have a fundamental importance for the political, social and economic organisation of a country" and, hence, their a priori exclusion from the category of overriding mandatory rules is "overly strict and unacceptable."[104]

It can also be argued that mandatory rules are merely a particular application of the traditional *ordre public* reservation, which is a characteristic feature of multilateral choice-of-law systems. However, although mandatory rules embody the enacting state's strong public policy, they operate differently than the *ordre public* reservation. The *ordre public* reservation operates defensively as a shield against a repugnant foreign law and, more often than not, leads to the application of forum law. In contrast, a mandatory rule

---

[100] *See* the discussion in A. Bonomi, Overriding Mandatory Provisions in the Rome I Regulation on the Law Applicable to Contracts, 10 *Ybk. Priv. Int'l L.* 285, 291 (2008).

[101] *See* Hellner, *Third Country Overriding Mandatory Rules,* 459.

[102] *See* Russian codif. art. 1192(1) (defining imperative norms as those that "in view of an indication in the imperative norms themselves or in view of their special significance, including for ensuring the rights and interests of participants in civil dealings, regulate the respective relations regardless of the [otherwise applicable] law…"); Armenian codif. art. 1259; Kazakhstan codif. art. 1091,

[103] M. Hellner, *Third Country Overriding Mandatory Rules,* 459.

[104] A. Bonomi, *Overriding Mandatory Provisions,* 293. *See* also A. Bonomi, Mandatory Rules in Private International Law: The Quest for Uniformity of Decisions in a Global Environment, 1 *Ybk. Priv. Int'l L.* 219, 232 (1999) ("even if they rely on [a] public policy reason, internationally mandatory rules are private law rules, which directly affect private relations.").

operates offensively as an "imperialistic" sword[105] of the enacting state—be it the forum state or a foreign state—that demands respect for its public interests.

One misleading similarity is that the application of mandatory rules is supposed to be as exceptional in practice as the application of the *ordre public* reservation.[106] In reality, this is true only for mandatory rules of a *third foreign* state, not the mandatory rules of either the *lex causae* or the *lex fori*.

Similarly, the fact that, in a given codification, there is usually only one article on mandatory rules and several dozens of articles containing multilateral choice-of-law rules does not mean that mandatory rules are of marginal significance. After all, that single article establishes the priority of mandatory rules over multilateral choice-of-law rules and acts as the gateway for the application of mandatory rules. Whether that gateway is utilized rarely or frequently is another question, the answer to which varies from country to country.

Finally, one should bear in mind that, even if mandatory rules are *methodologically*, or even statistically, exceptional, they are not the only unilateralist tools in a legislature's choice-of-law toolbox. They are complemented by other unilateralist tools such as the localized statutes described earlier and the unilateral choice-of-law rules discussed below.

C. UNILATERAL CHOICE-OF-LAW RULES

This section discusses unilateral *choice-of-law* rules found in PIL codifications, as opposed to the localizing rules found in substantive statutes, which, as discussed earlier, also function as unilateral rules.[107] Unilateral rules can be divided into two categories: inward-looking and outward-looking.

Inward-looking rules subject certain multistate cases that have specified forum contacts to the law of the forum (thereby excluding the application of foreign law) without authorizing the application of foreign law to analogous cases that lack the specified forum contacts.

Outward-looking rules do the reverse; they subject certain multistate cases that have specified contacts with a foreign state to the law of that state, without designating the applicable law for cases that lack those contacts.[108] Such rules are relatively rare and, most often, they are paired with inward-looking rules so as to produce the same effect as a bilateral rule. The discussion below focuses primarily on inward-looking unilateral rules.

---

[105] *See* Y. Loussouarn, Cours général de droit international privé, 139 *Recueil des cours* 275, 333 (1973) ("Cet impérialisme de la loi de police").

[106] *See* G. Rühl, *Unilateralism* ("[F]rom a methodological point of view they represent exceptions that prove the rule, namely the validity and supremacy of multilateralism.").

[107] *See supra* II.A.

[108] For examples of outward-looking unilateral rules, *see infra* at II.C.2.b.

1. Old-Fashioned, General Unilateral Rules

The primary example of an inward-looking unilateral choice-of-law rule is Article 3 of the French Civil Code. It provides that: (1) French "laws of police and safety are binding on all those inhabiting the [French] territory"; (2) "Immovables [situated in France] are governed by French law, even when owned by aliens"; and (3) French "[l]aws concerning the status and capacity of persons govern French persons, even those residing in a foreign country."[109]

Unilateral rules such as these were not uncommon among nineteenth century codifications, such as the Spanish Civil Code of 1889.[110] However, they fell into disfavor with the advent of bilateralism during the twentieth century, although they have survived in some codifications enacted in postcolonial Africa. For example, Article 9 of the codification of Guinea-Conakry provides that (1) the laws of police and security are binding on all those found in the national territory; (2) Guinean immovables, including those possessed by foreigners are governed by Guinean law; and (3) Guinean laws concerning status and capacity of persons apply to Guineans even when they reside abroad.[111] Similar rules are found in the codifications of the Central African Republic, Congo-Brazzaville, Gabon, Madagascar, Mauritania, Rwanda, Senegal, and Togo.[112] However, even in some of these codifications, these rules are surrounded and outnumbered by bilateral rules.

2. Unilateral Rules for Tort Conflicts

a. Inward-Looking Rules

Indeed, in modern codifications, unilateral provisions are the exceptions rather than the norm. For example, virtually all codifications regulate tort conflicts through bilateral rules.[113] Nevertheless, several codifications also contain inward-looking unilateral rules phrased as exceptions from the bilateral rules.

The adoption of an inward-looking unilateral rule is a clear signal that important public interests are at stake, which the codification's drafters do not want to jeopardize by

---

[109] *Code Civil* art. 3:
   Les lois de police et de sûreté obligent tous ceux qui habitent le territoire.
   Les immeubles, même ceux possédés par des étrangers, sont régis par la loi française.
   Les lois concernant l'état et la capacité des personnes régissent les Français, même résidant en pays étranger.

[110] *See* Spanish Civil Code of 1889, art. 8; Puerto Rico Civil Code of 1890, art. 9; Civil Code of the Philippines, arts. 14–16.

[111] Guinea-Conakry codif. art. 9 Loi no 51-62 du 14 avril 1962 relative a la theorie generale de la loi (promulguee, D. no 197, 4 janv. 1962, J. off. Rep. Guinee, 1er juill. 1962).

[112] *See* Central African Republic codif. art. 39; Congo-Brazzaville codif. art. 820; Gabon codif. arts. 40, 43; Madagascar codif. art. 27; Mauritania codif. art. 9; Rwanda codif. arts. 7, 10; Senegal codif. art. 841; Togo codif. art. 708.

[113] For example, even some (but not all) of the African codifications that contain a unilateral rule requiring the application of the forum's laws of "police and security" also contain a bilateral *lex loci delicti* rule for tort conflicts. *See, e.g.*, Central African Republic codif. art. 42(2); Gabon codif. art. 41; Madagascar codif. art. 30.2; Mauritania codif. art. 11.

allowing the application of foreign law. The Quebec codification provides a very clear example of this phenomenon. Its bilateral choice-of-law rules for torts (art. 3126) and products liability (art. 3128) generally favor plaintiffs by, inter alia, giving them a choice between the laws of the place of conduct or the place of injury in cross-border torts, and between the laws of the manufacturer's home state and the state of the product's acquisition in products liability cases. However, Articles 3151 and 3129 single out cases involving an injury caused by raw materials originating in Quebec. The first article subjects these cases to the exclusive jurisdiction of Quebec authorities, while the second article "imperative[ly]" subjects these cases to Quebec law. Article 3129 provides that the application of the rules of the Quebec Civil Code "is imperative in matters of civil liability for damage suffered in or outside Québec as a result of exposure to or the use of raw materials, whether processed or not, originating in Québec."[114]

Another example is provided by the so-called "double-actionability rules" in countries that otherwise adhere to multilateralism. As noted in Chapter 2,[115] these rules provide that, for a tort victim to recover from the tortfeasor, the tortfeasor's conduct must have been actionable under both: (1) the foreign law ordinarily applicable to the tort, and (2) the law of the forum qua forum. In addition to the United Kingdom, which continues to follow this rule only in defamation cases,[116] these countries include: Afghanistan, Algeria, Belarus, Japan, Jordan, Kazakhstan, North Korea, Kyrgyzstan, Qatar, Somalia, Sudan, Tajikistan, Ukraine, the U.A.E., and Uzbekistan.[117] By superimposing forum law on a tort that is otherwise governed by foreign law, these rules protect forum domiciliaries who are always subject to jurisdiction in the forum country and are more likely to be sued there.

Article 551 of the Mongolian codification is more direct in protecting domestic defendants. The article provides that torts are governed by the law of the country of the injury, but if the injury occurred outside Mongolia and the tortfeasor is a Mongolian natural or legal person, then Mongolian law governs.[118]

Rules that limit the amount or types of damages to the standards of the *lex fori* are another example of inward-looking unilateral rules designed to primarily protect domestic

---

[114] Quebec codif. art 3129. For a critique of this article and Article 3151, *see* H.P. Glenn, La guerre de l'amiante, 80 *Rev. critique DIP* 41, 59 (1991). According to Professor Talia Einhorn, a provision in Israel's products liability statute that *prevents* its application to foreign injuries was "intended to shield Israeli manufacturers from the application of strict liability," which apparently the statute imposes, in cases involving foreign injuries. T. Einhorn, *Israeli Report,* at V.

[115] *See* Chapter 2 at IV.F, *supra.*

[116] *See* C. Roodt, *English Report,* at C.I.(a),(c).

[117] *See* Afghanistan codif. art.29.2; Algerian codif. art 20(2); Belarus codif. art. 1129(3); Japanese codif. art. 22; Jordanian codif. art. 22(2); Kazakhstan codif. art. 1117.3; North Korean codif. art. 31(2); Kyrgyzstan codif. art. 1203(3); Qatar codif. art. 30(2); Somali codif. art. 21.2; Sudanese codif. art. 11(14)(b); Tajikistan codif. art. 1225.3; U.A.E codif. art. 20(2); Ukrainian codif. art. 49.3; Uzbekistan codif. art. 1194.4. In addition, Hungary follows the double actionability rule for torts committed before its adoption of Rome II. *See* Hungarian codif. art. 34.1

[118] Mongolian codif. art. 551.

defendants. These rules provide that, when a foreign law governs a tort action, the amount or type of damages to be awarded will not differ, or at least not differ significantly, from the damages available under the *lex fori*. At least seven codifications contain such rules.

For example, the Swiss codification provides that in products liability and obstruction to competition cases governed by foreign law "no damages may be awarded in Switzerland beyond those that would be awarded … under Swiss law."[119] The Turkish codification has a similar rule regarding the amount of damages in cases of obstruction to competition.[120] The Romanian codification provides that Romanian courts may award damages under the applicable foreign law, but "only within the limits fixed by Romanian law."[121] The Estonian codification provides that, in such cases, the amount of damages shall not be "significantly greater" than the amount allowed under Estonian law.[122]

The German and South Korean damages-limiting rules are slightly more subtle. The German rule provides that damages claims for a tort governed by foreign law "cannot be raised insofar as they (1) go substantially beyond what is necessary for an adequate compensation of the injured party, [or] (2) obviously serve purposes other than an adequate compensation of the injured party[.]"[123] The South Korean rule provides that damages for a tort governed by foreign law "shall not be awarded if the nature of the damages is clearly not appropriate to merit compensation to the injured party or if the extent of the damages substantially exceeds appropriate compensation to the injured party."[124]

From a methodological perspective, the German and South Korean provisions differ in some respects from the Swiss provisions and those of the other countries described above. For example, strictly speaking, the German and South Korean provisions are not unilateral choice-of-law rules (or for that matter choice-of-law rules); they do not mandate the automatic application of forum law to the exclusion of foreign law. Rather, they are substantivist provisions authorizing the judge to scrutinize foreign law through the lenses of the forum's substantive law and to reject claims considered excessive or punitive under that law. In this sense, these provisions may be characterized as specialized *ordre public* exceptions clauses.[125] At the same time, however, these provisions dramatically lower the threshold for interjecting the forum's public policy and are likely to produce the same pro-forum results as the above Swiss provision.

---

[119] Swiss codif. arts. 135(2), 137(2). The French text of these articles use the words *other than* in lieu of the word *beyond*, which is used in the German text quoted above. Thus, the French text may be interpreted to preclude both higher damages than those allowed by Swiss law, and types of damages that are not available under Swiss law, such as punitive damages.

[120] Turkish codif. art. 38(2).

[121] Romanian codif. art. 119.

[122] Estonian codif. art. 52.

[123] German codif. art. 40(3).

[124] South Korean codif art. 32(4).

[125] A draft of what later became Rome II provided specifically that the application of a foreign law that imposed exemplary or punitive damages was contrary to Community public policy. This provision was dropped in the final text on the assumption that the generic *ordre public* reservation would likely produce the same result in most cases without mandating it in all cases.

b. Outward-Looking Rules

Outward-looking unilateral rules are much rarer than the inward-looking ones, but they exist. As documented in Chapter 2, 41 recent codifications have adopted the common-domicile exception to the *lex loci delicti*, which calls for the application of the law of the tortfeasor and the victim to torts committed in another state.[126] In 32 of these codifications, this exception is bilateral; namely it applies to both domestic and foreign torts and authorizes the application of either foreign or domestic law, depending on the location of the parties' common domicile.

However, nine codifications (those of Azerbaijan, Belarus, Kazakhstan, Kyrgyzstan, Russia, Tajikistan, Ukraine, Uzbekistan, and Vietnam)[127] have phrased their exception in unilateral terms that make it applicable only to *foreign* torts. The operation of this exception together with the *lex loci* rule ensures a much wider range for the law of the forum than for foreign law. It means, for example, that a Ukrainian court will apply foreign law to a foreign tort involving foreign co-domiciliaries, but will apply Ukrainian law to *both* a foreign tort involving Ukrainian co-domiciliaries and a Ukrainian tort involving foreign co-domiciliaries.[128]

3. Multiple Nationalities

Many choice-of-law codifications continue to use nationality or citizenship as a connecting factor for choice-of-law purposes. When a person has more than one nationality, these codifications encounter a "conflict of nationalities" from which they must choose the controlling nationality. Such a choice is necessary for determining, inter alia, which law governs: (1) a person's status (e.g., general legal capacity, right to a name, filiation); (2) a person's capacity to act (e.g., to contract); and (3) a person's relationship with another person when the applicable law depends on whether the two have a "common nationality," as in the case of marriage, divorce, or personal or property relations between spouses.

Most codifications differentiate between cases in which one of the multiple nationalities is that of the forum state and those in which it is not. In the latter case, most codifications choose the controlling or "effective" nationality through a bilateral rule that usually is based on the "closest connection" or a similar concept.[129] In the former case, that is, when one of the nationalities is that of the forum state, most codifications employ a unilateral rule providing that the effective nationality is that of the forum state. For example, the Algerian codification provides that, in cases of multiple nationalities, the court applies the law of the effective nationality, but if one of the nationalities is Algerian, that

---

[126] *See* Table 2.4 in Chapter 2, at IV.C.2, *supra*.

[127] *See* Azerbaijan codif. art. 26.2; Belarus codif. art. 1129.2; Kazakhstan codif. art. 1117.2; Kyrgyzstan codif. art. 1203.2; Russian codif. art. 1219.2; Tajikistan codif. art. 1225.2; Ukraine codif. art. 49.2; Uzbekistan codif. art. 1194.2; Vietnamese codif. art. 773.3.

[128] *See* Chapter 2, at IV.C.2.c, *supra*.

[129] *See* Chapter 4 at V.A.3.e, *supra*.

nationality prevails.[130] At least 25 other codifications contain similar rules.[131] The Dutch codification adopts the same solution with regard to a person's name.[132]

4. Capacity

Many choice-of-law codifications distinguish between general civil capacity (i.e., capacity to have rights and duties, also known as "personality"), and capacity to enter into contracts and other juridical acts. Regarding the former type of capacity, the most common choice-of-law rule is a bilateral rule applying the "personal law" of the person whose capacity is at issue.[133] However, some codifications, such as the Swiss codification, have adopted a unilateral rule mandating the application of the *lex fori* for both forum and non-forum domiciliaries.[134] This rule is benevolent rather than xenophobic because it is intended to accord foreigners the same rights as Swiss citizens rather than to deprive foreigners of the rights they possess in their home countries. Other codifications express this idea more directly by providing that, subject to some exceptions, foreigners enjoy the same rights within the forum state as the citizens of that state.[135]

Regarding a person's capacity to enter into juridical acts, most codifications employ a bilateral rule, calling for the application of the "personal law" of the party whose capacity is at issue. A few codifications provide an exception that is also phrased as a bilateral rule in favor of the state in which all contracting parties acted.[136] However, several other codifications provide an exception phrased as a unilateral rule in favor of the forum state. This rule provides that, if a person who lacks capacity under her personal law enters into a juridical act in

---

[130] Algerian codif. art. 22.

[131] *See* Albanian codif. art. 8; Austrian codif. art. 9(1); Belarus codif. art. 1103(1); Belgian codif. art. 3(2); Bulgarian codif. art 48(2); Congolese codif. art. 827; Croatian codif. art. 11(1); Czech codif. art. 28.1; FYROM codif. art. 11(1); Hungarian codif. art. 11(2); Italian codif. art. 19(2); Japanese codif. art. 38(1); Jordanian codif. arts. 15, 26; North Korean codif. art. 7(1); South Korean codif. art. 3(1); Liechtenstein codif. art. 10(1); Qatar codif. arts. 13, 35; Russian codif. art. 1195(2); Senegal codif. arts. 843.4, 849; Serbian draft codif. art. 7.1; Slovak codif. art. 33.1; Slovenian codif. art. 10.1; Somalian codif. art. 25.2; Swiss codif. art. 23(1); Togo codif. art. 727; Tunisian codif. art. 39; U.A.E codif. arts. 14, 24; Yemen codif. art. 35. For a provision following the same solution in cases of multiple residences, *see* Macau codif. art. 35.4.

[132] *See* Dutch codif. art. 25.

[133] In defining the personal law, different codifications use different connecting factors, such as nationality, domicile, or habitual residence.

[134] *See* Swiss codif. art. 34(1) ("The capacity to be the subject of rights and obligations is governed by Swiss law.").

[135] *See, e.g.,* Burundi codif. art. 1; Congo-Brazzaville codif. art. 819; Gabonese codif. art. 25; Kazakhstan codif. art. 1095.1; Lithuanian codif. art. 1.15; Mongolian codif. art. 543; Russian codif. art. 1196; Senegalese codif. art. 840; Togo codif. art. 707; Vietnamese codif. art. 761(1).

[136] *See, e.g.,* Rome I, art. 13; Rome Convention, art. 11; Armenian codif. art. 1265; Bulgarian codif. art 50(2); Burkina Faso codif. art. 1018; Chinese codif. art. 12; Croatian codif. art. 14; Estonian codif. § 12(3); FYROM codif. art. 15; German codif. art. 12; Italian codif. art. 23(2)(3); Japanese codif. art. 4; South Korean codif. arts. 13, 15(1); Moldovan codif. art. 1592.2; Liechtenstein codif. art. 12; Oregon contracts codif. § 15.330; Polish codif. arts. 11–12; Puerto Rico draft codif. art. 33; Quebec codif. art 3086; Romanian codif. art. 17; Russian codif. art. 1197; Swiss codif. art. 36; Tunisian codif. art. 40; Slovenian codif. art. 13; Turkish codif. art. 9(2); Ukrainian codif. art. 18. These articles provide that a person who is considered capable of contracting under

the forum state for which she would have capacity under the *lex fori*, then that person will be deemed to have capacity. Unilateral rules to this effect are found in nearly 30 codifications.[137] All of these rules apply the law of the forum only when it validates the juridical act,[138] and most of them do not apply to juridical acts relating to family law or successions. These limitations suggest that the real purpose of these rules is to promote the security of transactions in the forum state rather than to favor foreigners.

5. Marriage

Most modern choice-of-law codifications have adopted a bilateral rule providing that the substantive requirements for a valid marriage are governed, with regard to each prospective spouse, by the personal law of that spouse. In many codifications, however, this rule is subject to exceptions phrased as unilateral rules in favor of the *lex fori*. The *lex fori* exceptions are designed to guard against foreign laws that may be either too restrictive or not restrictive enough regarding the right to marry.

The codifications of Albania, Austria, Belgium, Bulgaria, Estonia, Germany, and Romania are among those that employ unilateral rules to guard against restrictive foreign laws. For example, the German codification begins by requiring compliance with the national law of each prospective spouse, but if neither law allows the marriage, then German law applies if one spouse is a resident or citizen of Germany and the foreign law is "incompatible with freedom of marriage."[139] The Bulgarian codification also requires compliance with the national law of each prospective spouse, but also provides that if one of those laws imposes a marriage impediment that under Bulgarian law is "incompatible with the freedom to marry" and the other prospective spouse is a Bulgarian national or resident, the impediment "shall be disregarded."[140] The Romanian and Albanian codifications have a similar unilateral rule.[141] The Austrian codification provides that if the

---

the law of the place of the making may invoke his incapacity resulting from another law only if the other party knew or should have known of the incapacity at the time of the contract.

[137] *See* the codifications of: Algeria (art. 10); Angola (art. 28.1); Cape Verde (art. 28.1); Guinea-Bissau (art. 28.1); Hungary (art. 15.2–3); Israel (Law 5722/1962 § 77); Jordan (art. 12); North Korea (art. 18); Latvia (art. 8); Lithuania (art. 1.17); Macau (art. 27); Mauritania (art. 7); Mozambique (art. 28.1); Peru (art. 2070); Portugal (art. 28.1); Qatar (art. 11); Slovakia (art. 3.2); Somalia (art. 11); Sudan (art. 11.1); Spain (art. 10(8)); Taiwan (art. 10.3); U.A.E codif. (art 11.1); Yemen (art. 25).

[138] For exceptions, see the corresponding rules of the Belarus (art. 1104.3) and Vietnam (art. 762.2) codifications, which apply the law of the forum to the capacity of foreigners acting in the forum state even when that law does not validate the juridical act.

[139] German codif. art. 13. This article also provides that the prospective spouses must have taken reasonable steps to comply with their national law. The article also gives examples of foreign laws that violate the principle of freedom to marry. It provides that "a marriage shall not be prevented by a previous marriage of either engaged person, if the validity of the previous marriage has been set aside by a decision made or recognized within the country, or, if the spouse of either engaged person has been declared dead."

[140] *See* Bulgarian codif. art. 76.

[141] *See* Romanian codif. art. 18 (providing that if a foreign law imposes an impediment to the marriage that is incompatible with the right to marry under Romanian law, the impediment may not prevent a marriage in

marriage was dissolved or annulled by a foreign judgment recognizable in Austria, a new marriage may not be prohibited solely because the judgment is not recognized by the personal law of one or both of the spouses.[142] The Estonian and Liechtenstein codifications also contain a similar provision.[143]

Recently, several codifications have adopted similar solutions for same-sex marriages and unions. The Belgian codification provides that the substantive requirements of marriage are governed by the national laws of each prospective spouse, but if one of those laws prohibits same-sex marriage, then that law does not apply if one of the spouses (1) is a national of a state that allows such marriages, or (2) maintains his or her habitual residence in such a state.[144] The Dutch codification provides that Dutch law governs the capacity of each of the partners to enter into a registered partnership in the Netherlands, even in the absence of any other Dutch connections.[145]

Some codifications take a more direct road to the *lex fori* by making it the basic rule. For example, the Swiss codification provides that a marriage between foreigners in Switzerland need only conform to the substantive requirements of Swiss law, although conformity with the requirements prescribed by the national law of either prospective spouse would also suffice.[146] The Lithuanian codification takes a similar, albeit indirect, road to the *lex fori*.[147] The Ukrainian codification requires compliance with Ukrainian substantive law for all marriages celebrated in Ukraine, even those involving foreigners, and for all marriages celebrated abroad in which one of the spouses is a Ukrainian

---

Romania if one of the prospective spouses is a Romanian citizen); Albanian codif. art. 21 (providing that, according to the national law of each of the prospective spouses one or more of the substantive requirements of marriage are lacking, Albanian law governs if one of the spouse is an Albanian national or habitual resident).

[142] Austrian codif. art. 17(2). The Austrian codification subjects the personal legal effects of marriage and of a registered domestic partnership to the spouses' common personal law, but if, under that law, the marriage is not valid or the partnership does not have legal effect, Austrian law governs. *See* Austrian codif. arts. 18 and 27b.

[143] *See* Estonian codif. 56(3) ("A previous marriage of a prospective spouse shall not hinder contraction of a new marriage if the previous marriage has been terminated on the basis of a decision made or recognised in Estonia, even if such decision is not in accordance with the [governing] law of the state of residence of the prospective spouse."); Liechtenstein codif. art. 18(2).

[144] Belgian codif. art. 46. This unilateral rule "push[es] this 'Belgian' governmental policy forward; imposing [it] as a superior solution." M. Fallon & J. Erauw, *Belgian Report,* at V.a. The authors point out that "[t]his certainly made same-sex marriage easily permissible in Belgium based on the Belgian nationality of one partner or on one partner living in Belgium." *Id.*

[145] Dutch codif. art. 60. *See also* Hungarian codif. art. 41/A (in force since 21 June 2012) (providing that a person may enter into a civil union in Hungary even if his or her personal law does not allow it, if the other partner is a Hungarian citizen or either partner is domiciled in Hungary.)

[146] Swiss codif. art. 44. The corresponding Dutch provision (art. 28) allows compliance with either Dutch law (if one of the spouses is a Dutch citizen or habitual resident) or the national law of each spouse.

[147] *See* Lithuanian codif. art. 1.25 (providing that: (1) "[m]atrimonial capacity and other conditions to contract marriage" are governed by Lithuanian law; (2) Lithuanian authorities have jurisdiction to perform a marriage if either prospective spouse is a Lithuanian citizen or domiciliary; and (3) for foreigners, matrimonial capacity and other conditions to contract marriage "may" be determined by the law of the state of domicile of both prospective spouses "if such marriage is recognized in the state of domicile of either of them.").

national.[148] The Algerian, Slovakian, and Turkish codifications assign a subsidiary, but not insignificant, role to the *lex fori*. They provide that the substantive requirements of marriage are governed by the common personal law of the prospective spouses, but if there is no such common law (a usual phenomenon in multistate cases), then the *lex fori* governs.[149]

The Dutch codification imposes *lex fori* exceptions against both foreign laws that are too restrictive of the right to marry and laws that are too permissive. Article 29 provides that: (1) the solemnization of a marriage may not be refused because of an impediment imposed by the national law of one prospective spouse that is contrary to Dutch public policy,[150] and (2) a marriage may not be solemnized in the Netherlands in violation of certain impediments prescribed by Dutch substantive law.[151] The codifications of Croatia, FYROM, Hungary, and North Korea also employ a unilateral rule to guard against foreign laws that are more permissive than the *lex fori*.[152] For example, the Hungarian codification provides that a marriage may not be celebrated in Hungary if there is an "unavoidable impediment according to the Hungarian law."[153]

At the other end of the spectrum, the Gabonese codification also begins with the principle that the substantive requirements of marriage are governed by the national law of each prospective spouse, but also provides that a foreigner may opt for polygamy if he acquires Gabonese nationality.[154] The codification also provides that if the otherwise applicable foreign law prohibits a marriage because of an impediment that violates Gabonese public policy, the marriage may be solemnized in Gabon if the marriage would meet the requirements of Gabonese law.[155]

6. Divorce

Regarding the right to obtain a divorce, unilateral rules pointing to the *lex fori* have become more prevalent in recent decades. In some countries, the *lex fori* applies directly and exclusively. For example, in the United States, the forum state routinely applies its pro-divorce law to all cases subject to its jurisdiction. This includes cases in which only the *plaintiff* is domiciled in the forum state, but also cases in which neither spouse is

---

[148] *See* Ukrainian codif. arts. 55, 58.

[149] *See* Algerian codif. art. 13; Slovak codif. art. 21.1; Turkish codif. art. 13.

[150] Dutch codif. art 29.2.

[151] *Id.* art 29.1 (prohibiting marriages in which the prospective spouses have not reached the age of 15, or they are related within the second degree by birth or by adoption; if the free consent of a prospective spouse is lacking; or if one of them is party to an existing marriage or registered partnership.).

[152] The Croatian and FYROM codifications define more specifically the impediments as those arising from an existing marriage, consanguinity, and mental incapacity. *See* Croatian codif. art. 32(2); FYROM codif. art. 38(2). In the North Korean codification, an existing marriage and consanguinity are mere examples of such impediments. *See* North Korean codif. art. 35.

[153] Hungarian codif. art. 38(2).

[154] Gabonese codif. art. 34.

[155] *Id.* art. 35.

domiciled there so long as the defendant appears and fails to contest jurisdiction.[156] Other examples include the Chinese codification, which provides that a "contested divorce" is governed by the *lex fori*,[157] and the Rwandan codification, which provides that foreigners may obtain a divorce in Rwanda "in cases provided by Rwandan law."[158]

The Dutch codification provides that the requirements for a divorce or termination of a registered partnership are governed by Dutch law, and that the law of a common foreign nationality of the spouses or partners may be applied only exceptionally.[159] A Finnish statute also calls for the application of the *lex fori*, but restricts the jurisdiction of Finnish courts to cases in which either spouse is domiciled in Finland or the petitioner has a "close link" to Finland.[160]

Other codifications resort to the *lex fori* when the otherwise applicable foreign law (which usually is the common personal law of the spouses) does not allow, or severely restricts, divorce. However, these codifications require that at least one of the spouses must have a specified affiliation with the forum state, such as nationality or habitual residence. Included in this group are the codifications of Bulgaria, Croatia, the Czech Republic, Estonia, FYROM, Germany, Lithuania, Romania, Slovakia, Slovenia, and Switzerland.[161] The Italian, Belgian, and Serbian codifications do not require such an affiliation (other than what is necessary for jurisdictional purposes).[162] The last two codifications also allow spouses to agree to the application of the law of the forum.[163]

The Japanese, North Korean, South Korean, and Polish codifications apply the *lex fori* if *one* of the spouses is a national or habitual resident of the forum[164] Other codifications

---

[156] *See* Symeonides, *American PIL* §§ 534–541.

[157] Chinese codif. art. 29.

[158] Rwandan codif. art. 295. This article provides that, as an exception to the codification's general rule, which provides that the family relations of foreigners are governed by their national law, a divorce may be granted in Rwanda "*only* in cases provided by Rwandan law." (emphasis added). The italicized word *only* functions as a limitation in cases in which Rwanda law is more restrictive than the foreign law. However, in the converse situation in which Rwanda law is more permissive than the foreign law, a foreigner may obtain a divorce in Rwanda even if his national law would not allow it.

[159] *See* Dutch codif. arts. 56 for marriages, and 87 for partnerships. The law of the foreign common nationality may be applied only upon a joint petition of the spouses or partners, or the petition of one of them, provided there exists a "real societal connection" with the state of the common nationality. *Id.*

[160] *See* Law 1226/2001, §§ 119–120.

[161] *See* Bulgarian codif. art. 82(3); Croatian codif. art. 35(3); Czech codif. art. 50.2; Estonian codif. § 60(2); FYROM codif. art. 41(3); German codif. art. 17(1); Lithuanian codif. art. 1.29(3); Romanian codif. art. 22(2); Slovak codif. art. 22.2; Slovenian codif. art. 37(3); Swiss codif. art. 61(3). *See also* Spanish Civ. Code art. 107 (Spanish law displaces the otherwise applicable law under certain narrow conditions).

[162] *See* Belgian codif. art. 55(3); Italian codif. art. 31; Serbian draft codif. art. 83. *See also* Hungarian codif. art. 41(a) (in force until 21 June 2009).

[163] *See* Belgian codif. art. 55, discussed in J. Erauw & M. Fallon, *Belgian Report*, at IV.c.; Serbian draft codif. art. 80. An Israeli draft law provides that a "divorce of persons domiciled abroad, even if invalid under that law, will be valid if [it is] valid under Israeli law." Draft Bill on Persons and Family Law § 193, discussed in T. Einhorn, *Israeli Report*, at I.2.B(3).

[164] *See* Japanese codif. art. 27; North Korean codif. art. 38; South Korean codif. art. 39; Polish codif. arts. 54 and 2(3). *See also* Liechtenstein codif. art. 21(3).

do so when the spouses do not possess the same nationality[165] or domicile,[166] or have neither a common nationality nor a common habitual residence.[167]

The codifications of Paraguay and Ecuador occupy the other end of the spectrum. The Paraguayan codification provides that: (1) a marriage celebrated abroad may not be resolved by divorce in Paraguay if the spouses are domiciled there,[168] and (2) a foreign dissolution by divorce of a marriage celebrated in Paraguay does not entitle either spouse to remarry except as provided by Paraguayan law.[169] The Ecuadorian codification provides that (1) a marriage, which can be dissolved under the law of the place where it was contracted, may not be dissolved in Ecuador except in conformity with Ecuadorian law;[170] and (2) the dissolution of a marriage in a foreign country according to the laws of that country does not enable either spouse to marry in Ecuador until the marriage is validly dissolved in Ecuador.[171]

Finally, Rome III defers to the law of the forum, both when that law allows divorce and when it does not. Article 13 provides that "[n]othing in [Rome III] shall oblige the courts of a participating Member State whose law does not provide for divorce or does not deem the marriage in question valid for the purposes of divorce proceedings to pronounce a divorce by virtue of the application of [Rome III]."[172] Article 10 provides that when the applicable law "makes no provision for divorce or does not grant to one of the spouses equal access to divorce or legal separation on grounds of their sex, the law of the forum shall apply."[173]

7. Adoption

The Belgian codification provides that, although the establishment of filiation by adoption is governed by the law of the adopter's nationality, a Belgian court should instead apply Belgian law if the application of the foreign law is "clearly harmful to the higher interest of the adoptee and if the adoptee or the adopters have manifestly close links with Belgium."[174] The same codification also provides that the law of the adoptee's habitual residence governs the consent of the adoptee and the adoptee's parents, but Belgian law

---

[165] *See* Slovak codif. art. 22.

[166] *See* Togo codif. art. 714(2).

[167] *See* Burkina Faso codif. art. 1028; Congo-Brazzaville codif. art. 822; Senegalese codif. art. 843; Turkish codif. art. 14(1).

[168] Paraguayan codif. art. 164.

[169] *Id.* art. 165. Until 1991, Article 163 of the Paraguayan codification provided that a marriage celebrated in Paraguay "is not dissolved except by the death of one spouse." This article was amended in 1991 to allow divorce. *See* Article 22 of Law No. 45 of 1991.

[170] Ecuador codif. art. 93.

[171] *Id.* art. 92.

[172] Council Regulation (EU) No 1259/2010 of 20 December 2010 implementing enhanced cooperation in the area of the law applicable to divorce and legal separation OJ L 343/10 29.12.2010 ("Rome III"), art. 13.

[173] Rome III, art. 10.

[174] Belgian codif. art. 67.

governs if the foreign law "does not provide for the necessity of such consent or ignores the institution of adoption."[175]

The Dutch codification provides that Dutch law governs all issues of an adoption pronounced or revoked in the Netherlands, except the issue of parental or institutional consent to adoption, which is governed by the child's national law. If that law does not recognize the concept of adoption, Dutch law again governs.[176]

The Swiss codification provides that Swiss law governs the requirements for adoption in Switzerland. However, if it appears that the state of domicile or nationality of the adopter(s) would not recognize the adoption and that the child would be "seriously prejudiced thereby," the court should consider that law and "[if] recognition does not appear to be assured, the adoption must not be granted."[177] The codification also provides that an adoption granted in a foreign country may be annulled in Switzerland "only if there also exists a ground for annulment under Swiss law."[178]

8. Maintenance

As noted in Chapter 6, many codifications have adopted alternative-reference rules designed to favor the maintenance obligee.[179] However, sometimes the foreign law that is applicable under those rules does not provide for maintenance. In such cases, some of those codifications authorize the application of the *lex fori*. Among them are the codifications of Albania, Belgium, Burkina Faso, Germany, Hungary, and Switzerland.[180] The Hungarian codification provides that Hungarian law applies to the status and maintenance rights of a Hungarian child or a child residing in Hungary if that law is more favorable to the child than the otherwise applicable law.[181] Strictly speaking, these are not

---

[175] *Id.* art. 68.
[176] Dutch codif. art. 105.
[177] Swiss codif. art. 77(1).
[178] *Id.* art. 77(2).
[179] *See* Chapter 6, at V.C.3.b, *supra*.
[180] *See* Albanian codif. art. 26.3 (applicable law is that of the obligee's habitual residence, or the country of the common nationality and residence of obligor and obligee, but if those laws do not grant maintenance, then Albanian law governs); Belgian codif. art. 74 (applicable law is that of the obligee's habitual residence, or the country of the common nationality of obligor and obligee if the obligor is habitually resident in that country; but if those laws do not grant maintenance, then the law of common nationality applies, and if that law does not grant maintenance, then Belgian law governs); Bulgarian codif. 87 (alternative references to law of obligee's habitual residence or nationality, common national law of obligor and obligee, or Bulgarian law); Burkina Faso codif. art. 1041 (alternative references to laws of obligee's domicile, common national law of obligor and obligee, or Burkina Faso law); German codif. art. 18 (subject to certain qualifications, the court may choose the law most favorable to the maintenance obligee from among the laws of (1) the obligee's habitual residence, (2) the common nationality of the obligor and the obligee, and (3) the law of the forum); Swiss codif. arts. 49 and 83.
[181] Hungarian codif. art. 46. In 2011, this article was amended to exclude maintenance, which is now governed by the EU Maintenance Regulation. But the article remains applicable to the status of the child and "the family law relationships between him and his parents."

unilateral rules because the *lex fori* is applied as a last resort, but these rules do reflect the forum's desire to protect important public interests when the foreign law does not do so.

9. Successions

Many codifications employ bilateral rules providing that succession is governed by the law of the decedent's last domicile or nationality, but also subject these rules to unilateral exceptions ensuring the application of the *lex fori* to immovable, and in some instances movable, property situated in the forum state. In some codifications, such as those of Argentina, Gabon, Paraguay, the U.A.E., and Uruguay, these exceptions apply only to immovable property situated in the forum state, even if that state has no other connections with the case.[182]

The Venezuelan codification provides that if the decedent owned immovable *or* movable property situated in Venezuela, the decedent's descendants, ascendants, and surviving spouse have a claim against the Venezuela property in order to satisfy their forced share guaranteed by Venezuelan law.[183] It is unclear whether the forced share is to be calculated on the basis of the entire estate (i.e., including property situated outside Venezuela) or only on the basis of the property situated in Venezuela. The Taiwanese codification follows the second option but it does not limit it to forced heirs. It provides that succession is governed by the decedent's national law, but also provides that a person who qualifies as a "successor" under Taiwanese law "can succeed [in] the estate situated within the Republic of China (Taiwan)."[184]

The Italian codification provides that succession is governed by the decedent's national law, but also allows a testator to choose instead the law of his or her residence. However, if the testator is an Italian national, his or her choice of law "shall not affect the rights that Italian law confers on the heirs who are resident in Italy."[185]

The Louisiana codification contains two unilateral rules: Article 3533 for immovables situated in Louisiana and Article 3544 for immovables situated outside Louisiana. Both articles call for the application of the law of the situs state, but each is subject to different exceptions. For Louisiana immovables, the exception from the situs rule operates *against* the *lex fori*. Article 3533 provides that the application of Louisiana law to Louisiana immovables does not include that state's forced heirship law if at the time of death the deceased was domiciled outside Louisiana and left no forced heirs domiciled in Louisiana. For foreign immovables, the exception from the situs rule operates in favor of the *lex fori*. Article 3544 provides that, if the deceased was domiciled in Louisiana at death and was survived by forced heirs, any of whom were at the time domiciled in

---

[182] *See* Argentine draft codif. art. 2644; Gabon codif. art. 54; Paraguay codif. art. 2447; U.A.E codif. art. 19.5; Uruguay draft codif. art. 30.1(a).
[183] Venezuelan codif. arts. 34–35.
[184] Taiwanese codif. art. 58.
[185] Italian codif. art. 46(2).

Louisiana, then the value of the foreign immovables is included in calculating the decedent's disposable portion and in satisfying the heirs' forced shares.[186]

The Successions Law of Israel provides that "where foreign law confers rights of interstate succession upon anyone who is not related to the deceased by blood, marriage, affinity, or adoption, such law shall not be followed except in so far as it recognizes rights of succession as aforesaid which are conferred by Israel law."[187]

10. Formal Validity

As noted in Chapter 6, most codifications have adopted alternative-reference rules of validation for the formal validity of contracts and other juridical acts. These rules authorize the application of the law of whichever one of several states connected to the act would validate the act.[188] However, some codifications have adopted much narrower validation rules that operate only in favor of the *lex fori*. For example, the Russian codification provides that the form of a juridical act, including a power of attorney, is governed by the law of the country where the act was made. However, if the act was made in a foreign country and is formally invalid under that country's law but valid under Russian law, then the act shall be treated as valid, apparently even if Russia has no relevant connections other than the jurisdictional ones.[189] Thus, the law of the forum qua forum applies to validate an act made elsewhere, but foreign law does not apply to validate an act made in the forum state. Identical rules are found in the codifications of Armenia, Azerbaijan, Belarus, Kazakhstan, Kyrgyzstan, Tajikistan, and Uzbekistan.[190]

These same codifications have also adopted similar narrow unilateral rules for testamentary formalities. The rules provide that the form of a testament is governed by the law of the state in which the testator was domiciled at the time of making the testament. However, if the testament was formally invalid under that law but valid under the law of the forum qua forum, then the testament shall be treated as formally valid.[191]

---

[186] For an explanation of the rationale of these articles by their drafter, *see* Symeonides, *The "Dismal Swamp,"* 1092–1097. The Louisiana codification also employs unilateral rules in the area of matrimonial regimes: Article 3525 deals with foreign immovables acquired by a spouse while domiciled in Louisiana; and Articles 3526–3527 deal with Louisiana immovables acquired by a spouse while domiciled in another state. For discussion of these articles by their drafter, *see* S. Symeonides, Louisiana's Draft on Successions and Marital Property, 35 *Am. J. Comp. L.* 259 (1987); S. Symeonides, In Search of New Choice-of-Law Solutions to Some Marital Property Problems of Migrant Spouses: A Response to the Critics, 13(3) *Comm. Prop. J.* 11 (1986).

[187] Law 5765/1965 § 144.

[188] *See* Chapter 6 at V.A.2, *supra*.

[189] *See* Russian codif. art. 1209(1).

[190] *See* Armenian codif. arts. 1281(1), 1282; Azerbaijan codif. arts. 17–18; Belarus codif. arts. 1116–1117; Kazakhstan codif. arts. 1104–1105; Kyrgyzstan codif. arts. 1190–1191; Tajikistan codif. arts. 1210–1211; Uzbekistan codif. arts. 1181–1182. *See also* Vietnamese codif. art. 770(1).

[191] *See* Russian codif. art. 1224(2); Armenian codif. art. 1292(2); Belarus codif. art. 1135; Kazakhstan codif. art. 1122; Kyrgyzstan codif. art. 1207; Tajikistan codif. art. 1232; Uzbekistan codif. art. 1198.

The Russian codification also contains another unilateral rule not found in the other three codifications. This rule applies to transactions in which at least one participant is either a Russian legal person or natural person engaging in commercial activity. The rule provides that Russian law governs the formal validity of such a transaction "regardless of the place of conclusion of the transaction."[192] The Armenian codification provides that a foreign transaction in which at least one party is an Armenian legal or natural person must be in written form.[193]

11. Contracts

As seen in Chapters 3 and 6, many modern choice-of-law codifications protect weak parties (such as consumers or employees) through bilateral, result-selective rules that protect those parties from the adverse consequences of a potentially coerced or uninformed assent to choice-of-law clauses.[194] These codifications provide that a choice-of-law clause may not deprive the consumer or employee of the protection afforded by the mandatory rules of the country whose law would govern the contract in the absence of such a clause.

Some codifications provide this protection only for consumers or employees domiciled in the forum state, by exempting contracts involving them from the scope of party autonomy and, expressly or implicitly, subjecting them to the *lex fori*. For example, the Ukrainian codification provides that Ukrainian law governs contracts for employment to be performed in Ukraine, or contracts between Ukrainian employers and employees for employment outside Ukraine.[195]

The Puerto Rico draft code provides similar protection through three unilateral rules that apply to consumers, insureds, and employees, respectively. For consumer contracts, the draft code provides that "unless the consumer requests otherwise," the law of Puerto Rico governs if (1) the consumer was domiciled or resided in Puerto Rico at the time of contracting; and (2) his assent to the contract was obtained, or was induced in substantial measure by an invitation or advertisement, in Puerto Rico.[196]

The draft code provides a similar rule for contracts of life, health, or disability insurance "if the policy or its renewal was delivered or issued for delivery in Puerto Rico or the insured was there domiciled at the time the relevant issuance or renewal occurred"; and for all other insurance contracts (except contracts for ocean marine or foreign trade insurance) if, at the time the policy was issued or renewed, the insurer "knew or should have known that the insured risk was or would be located primarily in Puerto Rico."[197]

---

[192] Russian codif. art. 1209(2).

[193] *See* Armenian codif. art. 1281(2).

[194] *See supra* Chapter 3, at V.A.3, V.B.5, and VII.B, and Chapter 6, at V.C.3.c.

[195] *See* Ukrainian codif. arts. 52–55.

[196] Puerto Rico draft codif. art. 35. If the consumer "requests otherwise," the applicable law is chosen through the bilateral rules of the draft code. For discussion, *see* Symeonides, *The Puerto Rico Projet*, 433–434.

[197] Puerto Rico draft codif. art. 37.

Puerto Rico law also applies to employment contracts for services to be rendered primarily in Puerto Rico, "unless the employee requests otherwise."[198] In contracts for services to be rendered outside Puerto, the draft code provides that a person domiciled or residing in Puerto Rico and hired there "may not be deprived of the protection provided by those mandatory rules of Puerto Rican law whose application is appropriate regardless of the place where the services are rendered."[199]

Similarly, the Oregon contracts codification contains unilateral rules for certain Oregon contracts and contracts with the State of Oregon. The codification provides that Oregon law applies to: (1) contracts for construction work to be performed primarily in Oregon; (2) contracts for services to be rendered primarily in Oregon by an Oregon resident; (3) consumer contracts, if the consumer is an Oregon resident and the consumer's assent to the contract is obtained there or the consumer is induced to enter into the contract in substantial measure by an invitation or advertisement in Oregon; and (4) contracts for services to be rendered in Oregon, or for goods to be delivered there, if the State of Oregon or any of its agencies or subdivisions is a party to the contract.[200]

The Quebec codification protects Quebec insureds through a unilateral rule. Article 3119 provides that "[n]otwithstanding any agreement to the contrary," a contract insuring property or "an interest" situated in Québec or "subscribed in Québec by a person resident in Québec" is governed Québec law "if the policyholder applies therefor in Québec or the insurer signs or delivers the policy in Québec."[201] The article also provides that Québec law governs a group insurance contract if "the participant has his residence in Québec at the time he becomes a participant."[202]

12. Rights in Movables

The Taiwanese codification provides that Taiwanese law governs real rights established on a movable before its importation to Taiwan.[203] The Estonian codification provides that if a movable is brought into Estonia and the creation or extinction of a real right in it has not been completed abroad, "the events which occurred abroad shall be deemed to have occurred in Estonia."[204]

---

[198] *Id.* art. 36(1).

[199] *Id.* art. 36(2).

[200] *See* Or. Rev. Stat. § 15.320(1) –(4). In the last case, the contract may waive the application of Oregon law. For the rationale of these provisions, *see* Symeonides, *Oregon Contracts Exegesis,* 212–214. The Hungarian codification provides that "the legal relationships of the Hungarian State shall be governed by its own law," except when the state expressly consents to the application of foreign law or when the legal relationship concerns foreign real property owned by the state or participation in a foreign economic organization. Hungarian codif. art. 17.

[201] Quebec codif. art. 3119.

[202] *Id.*

[203] Taiwanese codif. art 40.

[204] Estonian codif. art. 18(3).

The North Korean codification provides that rights in intellectual property, such as copyright and patents, are governed by North Korean law and, if North Korea does not have a rule on the subject, by international treaties.[205]

13. *Mea Culpa*

This author has no criticism for choice-of-law rules designed to protect important interests or values of the forum state. In fact, he is guilty of being associated with protectionist unilateral rules. One example is the third paragraph of Article 3543 of the Louisiana Civil Code. As originally drafted by the undersigned as Reporter, this article was a bilateral rule consisting of two paragraphs. The paragraphs provided that issues of conduct regulation are governed (1) by the law of the state of conduct; but (2) if the injury foreseeably occurred in another state that imposes a higher standard of conduct, then by the law of the state of injury. However, during the legislative process, and despite the Reporter's strenuous objections, a third paragraph was added consisting of a unilateral protectionist rule. The rule provides that conduct in Louisiana by a person domiciled in, or having another significant connection with, Louisiana is to be judged according to Louisiana standards of conduct and safety, even if it violates the higher standards of another state where the injury occurs.[206] As the Reporter later conceded, the adoption of this paragraph "is a typical example of hometown protectionism which should be neither vilified nor, of course, idealized, but can be understood as a very common part of the legislative process in this imperfect world."[207]

This author has also drafted other protectionist unilateral rules, this time without coercion. In addition to the Puerto Rico rules described earlier, one such rule is found in the Oregon tort codification, which generally consists of bilateral rules. One of these rules (Section 15.440(3)(c)) provides that in cross-border torts the plaintiff may choose between the laws of the state of conduct or the state of injury, subject to certain conditions specified in that rule. However, in derogation from that and other rules, Section 15.430 contains a unilateral rule designed to protect Oregon public entities and certain Oregon defendants from the application of foreign law. This rule mandates the application of Oregon law to: (1) actions against a "public body of the State of Oregon"; (2) actions against the owner of an Oregon immovable that "seek to recover for, or to prevent, injury on that property and arising out of conduct that occurs in Oregon"; and (3) actions for professional malpractice arising from "services rendered entirely in Oregon by personnel licensed to perform those services under Oregon law."[208] Thus, a plaintiff

---

[205] North Korean codif. art. 23.

[206] It is worth noting that an identical article drafted by the same author for the Puerto Rico Draft Code does not contain this third paragraph.

[207] Symeonides, *Louisiana Exegesis*, 714.

[208] Or. Rev. Stat. § 15.430. For an explanation of the rationale of these provisions by their drafter, see Symeonides, *Oregon Torts Exegesis*, 983–986.

who is injured in the neighboring state of Washington as a result of the Oregon conduct of the afore-mentioned defendants will not have the option of choosing Washington law under Section 15.440(3)(c).[209]

At the same time, and again drawing from this author's drafting experience, it is important to stress that not all unilateral rules are protectionist in the narrow sense. For example, two outward-looking unilateral rules drafted for the Louisiana codification are designed to protect *foreign* decedents and *foreign* surviving spouses. The first rule is found in Article 3533 dealing with successions. It provides that Louisiana's forced heir-ship law shall *not* apply to the succession of Louisiana immovables owned by a foreign decedent who left no forced heirs domiciled in Louisiana at the time of his death.[210] The second outward-looking unilateral rule is found in Article 3527 on matrimonial regimes. It provides that, upon the death of a spouse domiciled outside Louisiana, any Louisiana immovables that he acquired while domiciled in another state and which do not qualify as community property will be subject to the same rights in favor of the surviving spouse as provided by the law of the decedent's last domicile.

The legislative passage of these unilateral rules was extremely difficult politically. One reason for this difficulty is that they are an unselfish derogation from the bilateral situs rule, which is sacrosanct in the United States and which remains the basic rule in Louisiana.

D. MULTILATERAL BUT NON-IMPARTIAL CHOICE-OF-LAW RULES

Multilateral rules are supposed to treat forum and foreign law evenhandedly. Conceptually, this is true with regard to the *traditional*, state-selecting multilateral rules (namely those that select the applicable law through neutral connecting factors), as opposed to content-oriented or result-selective rules that select the applicable law through factors that depend on the substantive content of that law or the quality of the solution it pro-duces.[211] However, a conceptually equal treatment does not necessarily produce equality of results. Contemporary codifiers know how to draft multilateral choice-of-law rules that appear neutral on their face but are calculated to lead to the application of forum law more frequently than foreign law.

---

[209] The Oregon and Louisiana codifications also provide unilateral rules for certain product liability conflicts that have enumerated connections with the forum state. *See* La. codif. art. 3545; Or. Rev. Stat. § 15.435. However, these unilateral rules are paired with bilateral rules that cover all product liability cases falling outside the reach of the unilateral rules. For discussion, see Symeonides, *Louisiana Exegesis*, 749–759, and *Oregon Torts Exegesis*, 986–993.

[210] *See* La. codif. art. 3533 (providing that, although succession to immovables situated in Louisiana is governed by Louisiana law, "[t]he forced heirship law of [Louisiana] does not apply if the deceased was domiciled out-side [Louisiana] at the time of death and at the time he acquired the immovable and he left no forced heirs domiciled in [Louisiana] at the time of his death.").

[211] Content-oriented or result-selective rules may be biased toward a particular result, but they can be even-handed as between forum and foreign law.

Even in the idealistic pre-war years of the twentieth century, it was widely acknowledged that the debate on whether to use nationality or domicile as a connecting factor for matters of status and succession, though phrased in lofty deontological terms, was essentially a pragmatic debate about conflicting national interests of countries with emigrating and countries with immigrating populations.[212] Countries with emigrating populations opted for nationality as the connecting factor that would maintain a bond with their emigrating citizens, whereas countries with immigrating populations opted for domicile as a means of assimilating the immigrants living in their territory while also avoiding the application of foreign laws. As Professor Babić observes in commenting on the PIL codification of the former Yugoslavia, "[n]ationality…was chosen as the prime connecting factor for matters of personal status, family and succession law issues, with the awareness that, because former Yugoslavia was a country of emigration rather than immigration, the nationality criterion would favour the application of local law."[213] The same codification also provides that the law of the licensee or transferee governs license and technology transfer agreements. According to Babić, this "clear deviation from the principle of characteristic performance…was introduced because Yugoslavia was mostly an importer rather than an exporter of technology, and…this provision would protect local enterprises by favouring the application of Yugoslav law."[214]

To use an example from contemporary reality, suppose that for product liability conflicts: (1) country A, a net exporter of large quantities of products and having a pro-manufacturer substantive law, adopts a choice-of-law rule calling for the application of the law of the producer's home state; and (2) country B, a net importer of products, adopts a rule that gives consumers a choice among the laws of the victim's home state, the place of injury, the place of the product's acquisition, or the producer's home state. Both of these rules would be bilateral and thus ostensibly neutral; yet, in their actual operation, the first rule would serve the exporting country's interest in protecting its manufacturers through the application of its pro-manufacturer substantive law, whereas the second rule would serve the importing country's interest in protecting its consumers by giving them maximum choices on the applicable law.

As Chapter 2 on torts documents,[215] several countries that are net importers rather than exporters of products have adopted pro-consumer choice-of-law rules similar to the hypothetical rule of country B. For example, Tunisia provides the consumer four choices from among the laws of the defendant's principal place of business or domicile,

---

[212] See, e.g., S. Vrellis, *Rapport grec,* in S. Symeonides (ed.), *Progress or Regress?,* 247–248 ("Sous certains aspects, le choix du législateur en ce qui concerne le facteur de rattachement prépondérant, qui reste encore en Grèce…la nationalité, est un choix imposé par le souci de satisfaire aux intérêts nationaux ou étatiques, à une époque où la Grèce était un pays d'émigration, donc un pays qui cherchait à maintenir ses liens avec ses ressortissants qui s'installaient à l'étranger ainsi qu'avec les descendants").

[213] D. Babić, *Croatian Report,* at VI.

[214] *Id.*

[215] See Chapter 2, at VII.B, *supra.*

the state in which the product was acquired, the victim's habitual residence, and the state of injury.[216] The codifications of Azerbaijan, Belarus, Kazakhstan, Kyrgyzstan, Tajikistan, and Uzbekistan allow the first three choices,[217] whereas the Quebec codification gives consumers "only" two choices: (1) the state of the defendant's principal place of business or, in the absence thereof, habitual residence; and (2) the state in which the product was acquired.[218] However, the same codification also provides that Quebec law "imperative[ly]" applies to product liability actions for injury outside (or within) Quebec "as a result of exposure to or the use of raw materials…originating in Quebec."[219] Thus, Quebec protects both Quebec consumers injured by foreign producers *and* Quebec producers injuring foreign consumers.

No country has adopted a rule that favors manufacturers as blatantly as the rule of country A described above. However, Japan, a major product exporter, has come very close. The new Japanese codification calls for the application of the law of the state of the product's delivery and, if delivery in that state was not foreseeable, then the law of the state of the producer's principal establishment.[220] This rule does not unduly favor Japanese manufacturers because it does subject them to the laws of the states in which their products are foreseeably delivered. But the protectionist element surfaces in two unilateral rules to which this rule is subject. The first rule is the double actionability rule, which provides that when a foreign law governs a tort, the victim may not claim damages or "any other remedies" under that law if the injurious conduct is not "unlawful" under Japanese law.[221] This means, for example, that if an erroneous description of the product's qualities is not "unlawful" under Japanese law but is unlawful under the otherwise applicable foreign law, the consumer would not be entitled to any remedies in Japan. The second unilateral rule provides that, even if the injurious conduct is unlawful under both foreign law and Japanese law, the victim "may not claim any greater recovery of damages or any other remedies than those available under Japanese law."[222] Thus, a Japanese manufacturer may not be forced to provide remedies or damages that are more favorable to the consumer than those provided by Japanese law.[223]

---

[216] *See* Tunisian codif. art. 72.

[217] See Azerbaijan codif. art. 27; Belarus codif. art. 1130; Kazakhstan codif. art. 1118; Kyrgyzstan codif. art. 1203; Tajikistan codif. art. 1227; Ukrainian codif. art. 50; Uzbekistan codif. art. 1195.

[218] Quebec codif. art. 3128.

[219] *Id.* art. 3129. For a critique of this article and Article 3151, *see* H.P. Glenn, La guerre de l'amiante, 80 *Rev. critique DIP* 41, 59 (1991).

[220] *See* Japanese codif. art. 18.

[221] *Id.* art. 22(1).

[222] *Id.* art. 22(2).

[223] The converse phenomenon is one of a country that has a pro-consumer substantive law that it makes unavailable to foreign consumers. As noted earlier, *see supra* note 114, a provision in Israel's apparently pro-consumer products liability statute, which *prevents* the statute's application to foreign injuries, may have precisely that effect.

The drafters of Rome II avoided both a pro-defendant rule such as the Japanese formula and an overtly pro-plaintiff rule such as the rules previously adopted in some European countries, such as Italy and Switzerland, which give plaintiffs two choices on the applicable law. Instead, Rome II has adopted a very complex provision, Article 5, which is based on a sequential combination of contacts and cascading connecting factors. On its face, Article 5 seems perfectly neutral. Nonetheless, for reasons explained in detail elsewhere, this article will lead in the majority of cases to the application of the law of the victim's habitual residence.[224] This too is a seemingly neutral result. However, this result means that when the plaintiff is a resident of an EU country with a generous pro-consumer law (e.g., France) and the manufacturer is based in a state with a pro-manufacturer law (e.g., Germany), the plaintiff will be protected under French law. But if the plaintiff is a habitual resident of an African country (e.g., Chad), the same article will ensure that the German defendant will be held accountable (or perhaps unaccountable) under the lower standards of the plaintiff's foreign residence. Thus, like the Quebec rules described above, this seemingly neutral bilateral rule protects both EU consumers injured by foreign (or EU) manufacturers and EU manufacturers injuring foreign consumers. It confirms the astute observation that "[a]n apparently blind choice of law rule…can hide a firm substantive policy goal."[225]

III. Assessment

A. A PARADIGM SHIFT

As the preceding survey demonstrates, contemporary legislatures employ a whole panoply of devices designed to protect specific values or interests of the forum state in the international or interstate arena. Besides multilateral rules that are facially neutral but are crafted in a way that frequently leads to the application of *lex fori*,[226] these devices include:

(1) Unilateral choice-of-law rules. There is hardly any choice-of-law codification that does not contain some unilateral choice-of-law rules, even if they are far less numerous than bilateral rules;

(2) Rules of immediate application or mandatory rules. There is almost no country in which mandatory rules are not given priority over choice-of-law rules (either bilateral or unilateral), whether or not such priority is expressly recognized by a choice-of-law codification; and

---

[224] *See* Symeonides, *Rome II*, 207–209.

[225] M. Fallon & J. Meeusen, *Belgian Report,* in S. Symeonides (ed.), *Progress or Regress?*, 112. *See also* F. Pocar & C. Honorati, *Italian Report,* in *id.* at 289 ("[T]he use of a specific connecting factor could achieve (or jeopardize) certain results of substantive law.").

[226] *See supra* at II.D.

(3) Localizing rules contained in substantive statutes and mandating the application of those statutes to an increasingly expanding range of multistate cases. Under the principle of *lex specialis derogat legi generali*, these statutes, being more specific, override the choice-of-law rules of a PIL codification, without regard to whether the statutes embody the high level of public policy required for mandatory rules.

All three types of rules are examples of unilateralist techniques—they all mandate the application of forum law and exclude the possibility of even considering foreign law. This mandate is express in unilateral and localizing rules and implied but clear in the rules of immediate application.

These rules exist in virtually every country. They are employed in diverse fields of law, not only in traditional public-law fields such as antitrust, but also in traditional private-law fields such as contracts, marriage, divorce, maintenance, property, and successions. Moreover, they protect not only economic interests of the enacting state, but also certain strongly held societal values and beliefs. For example, ensuring gender equality in marriage or facilitating divorce, as some of these rules do, does not protect an economic interest but it does promote a society's sense of equality and freedom to marry

The multiplication of these rules in the last 50 years has produced a perceptible change in the PIL landscape. Multilateralism is no longer the sole actor; it shares the stage with unilateralism. This is a significant paradigm shift because the previous history of these two schools has been one of successive mutual displacement, not coexistence.

B. METHODOLOGICAL IMPLICATIONS: FROM ANTAGONISM TO CO-EXISTENCE

Heretofore, the conventional wisdom has been that multilateralism and unilateralism are entirely antithetical and mutually exclusive.[227] This assumption finds some justification in the historical antagonism between the two schools. Historically, unilateralism preceded multilateralism. Initially developed by the Italian statutists of the late twelfth century and subsequently improved by their French and Dutch successors, unilateralism prevailed until the nineteenth century when it succumbed to the devastating attacks of Savigny.[228] Savigny's influence launched a new era in which multilateralism displaced unilateralism and dominated the scene until the middle of the twentieth century.

---

[227] *See, e.g.*, F. Juenger, A Third Conflicts Restatement?, 75 *Ind. L.J.* 403, 410 (2000) ("[U]nilateralism and multilateralism are antithetical.").

[228] *See* Hay, Borchers & Symeonides, *Conflict of Laws*, 10–18; S. Symeonides & W. Perdue, *Conflict of Laws: American, Comparative, International*, 10–15 (3d ed. 2012).

That is when unilateralist literature began reappearing, first in the writings of Jean-Paul Niboyet, Alexander Pilenko, and Rolando Quadri in Europe,[229] and then in the writings of Brainerd Currie in the United States.[230] Especially the last two of these authors fiercely attacked both multilateralism as a method and the very concept of choice-of-law rules, be they multilateral or unilateral.

Looking back at the real world of legislation, it is clear that these neo-unilateralists did not win the war against multilateralism, not even the battle, but they forced significant concessions. As a European author recently acknowledged, "the unilateral islands in the sea of multilateral international private law have grown in the last years."[231] Unilateralism now occupies a respectable position, side by side with multilateralism, as a mainstream method of resolving conflict of laws. As the preceding discussion illustrates, there is now ample evidence of de facto coexistence, and even amalgamation. In fact, what distinguishes this period from previous periods in PIL history is that the relation between the multilateral and the unilateral approaches is no longer as antagonistic as it once was. Rather they coexist peacefully, and they complement each other.

This coexistence is particularly pronounced in the United States where multilateralism and unilateralism cohabit within the confines of each of several modern choice-of-law approaches, and where localized, unilateral state statutes are becoming commonplace. After more than a century of domination, Story's multilateral method ran into an impasse, particularly in the hands of one of his successors, Joseph Beale. Moving to the other extreme, Professor Brainerd Currie proposed his unilateral method as a complete substitute, but it too ran into its own impasses, especially in confronting the true-conflict and no-interest paradigms. Currie did not win the war against multilateralism, but he succeeded in forcing other approaches to adopt significant elements of his unilateralist approach.

The Restatement (Second) provides the most conspicuous example of blending multilateralist and unilateralist elements. Its all-important Section 6 employs the basic tools of unilateralism insofar as it directs the court to consider both the forum and non-forum states' interests. At the same time, Section 6 directs the court to be mindful of values and factors with a peculiarly cosmopolitan and thus multilateral bent. These factors include

---

[229] *See* 2 J.-P. Niboyet, *Cours de droit international privé français* 349 ff., 443 ff., 478 ff. (1949); 3 J.P. Niboyet, *Traité de droit international privé français* 243 *ff.* (1944); R. Quadri, *Lezioni di diritto internazionale privato* (3d ed. 1961); A. Pilenko, Le droit spatial et le droit international privé dans le projet du nouveau Code civil français, 6 *Rev. Hellénique dr. int'l* 319 (1953); A. Pilenko, Droit spatial et droit international privé, 5 *Jus gentium* 35 (1954). For an excellent exposition of European neo-unilateralism, *see* P. Gothot, Le renouveau de la tendance unilatérale en droit international privé, 60 *Rev. critique DIP* 1, 209, 415 (1971).

[230] *See* Currie, *Selected Essays*. Another unilateralist, albeit less influential than Currie, was Professor Albert Ehrenzweig. For his voluminous work, *see, inter alia*, A. Ehrenzweig, *A Treatise on the Conflict of Laws* (1962); A. Ehrenzweig, *Private International Law*, Vol. I (1967); A. Ehrenzweig, Specific Principles of Private Transnational Law, 125 *Recueil des cours* 170 (1969); A. Ehrenzweig, A Proper Law in a Proper Forum: A "Restatement" of the "*Lex Fori* Approach," 18 *Okla. L. Rev.* 340 (1965).

[231] Rühl, *supra* note 6.

"(a) the needs of the interstate and international systems ... (d) the protection of justified expectations ... [and] (f) uniformity of result."[232] Whether this blend of unilateralism and multilateralism is a successful one is a matter of opinion, but the success or failure of the Restatement has not depended on the fact that it drew from both of these schools of thought. Rather it has depended on the merits of the particular choices the drafters made in formulating the Restatement's specific sections.

In other countries, unilateralism has resurfaced not as a substitute for, but rather as a complement to, multilateralism. The resulting blending of the two methods may be less conspicuous than in the United States, but as this chapter demonstrates, it is very much real. As a prominent European author recently observed,

> [C]ontemporary conflicts law is not impervious to the influence of unilateralist theories. Legislative intent does play a part in the choice-of-law process where the spatial reach of forum law is delineated in a unilateral choice-of-law rule, or where policies and interests must be assessed under the doctrine of overriding mandatory rules or pursuant to policy-oriented choice-of-law considerations.[233]

These examples of unilateralism's resilience suggest that unilateralism will continue to be with us for the foreseeable future. Rather than ignoring this reality, academic writers can help shape its development by using their persuasive powers to steer legislatures and courts toward a non-parochial use of unilateralism. A preliminary step in that direction would be to begin seeing this symbiosis of the multilateral and unilateral methods as a sign of maturity, rather than as a symptom of decline.[234]

C. UNILATERALISM AND STATE INTERESTS

The proliferation of unilateral rules and other unilateralist devices is a clear confirmation that contemporary legislatures understand that many categories of conflicts cases implicate not only the private interests of the disputing parties but also *public* or *state* interests.

This should not come as a surprise. Legislation is the formal expression of the sovereign will, which in a democratic country is the collective will of its people. If a code or statute regulating domestic cases is supposed to protect and promote broad societal interests (among other values), is a choice-of-law code or statute intended for multistate cases supposed to ignore the enacting state's interests? So stated, the question can only be answered in the negative. Throughout history, "[w]hether cloaked in terms of

---

[232] *Restatement (Second),* § 6 (2).

[233] de Boer, *Living Apart Together,* 205.

[234] As Professor Roodt notes, "[t]o assume that [these two methods] exist in opposition or compete is to miss the mark. The fact that Rome I accommodates both types and integrates supermandatory rules into the same structure is an indication of the maturity of the conflicts system at this point." C. Roodt, *English Report,* at IV(c) (footnotes omitted).

territoriality, public policy, governmental interests, or *Sonderanknüpfung*, the protection of national public interests has always outweighed any other choice-of-law consideration."[235] Hence, the question is not whether the drafting of a choice-of-law codification considers the national interest, but how, and how much, it does so.

The term and concept of state interest is often misunderstood, primarily because of its association with Brainerd Currie and his strong and unnecessarily provocative rhetoric. The criticism from both continental and American scholars has been intense.[236] For example, Friedrich Juenger argued that the very notion of a state interest in this context is "a highly implausible construct."[237] He rejected Currie's hypothesis that states have such an interest, or, as Juenger put it, that states have "a deep-seated concern in the implementation of their legal rules."[238] He criticized Currie and his followers for "[not] adducing empirical evidence for this hypothesis."[239]

In fact, at least in the United States, there is a plethora of empirical evidence about both the existence and the assertion of state interest in the outcome of choice-of-law disputes.[240] Interestingly, European governments, and recently the European Union on their behalf, are among those foreign governments that file *amicus* briefs asserting their respective interests in the outcome of disputes litigated in American courts.[241]

However, Juenger was right to attack Currie's *particular* conception of state interests. Indeed, Currie spoke as if states have an active desire to apply their laws and, worse, a proclivity to assert such desires in an aggressive, imperialistic, "beggar thy neighbor" fashion.[242] In so doing, Currie either erred or exaggerated. States do not have *active* desires regarding the outcome of private disputes. But the policies, purposes, and values embodied in a state's law *can* be adversely affected when that law is *not* applied to a case that the law was intended to reach. In this sense, speaking of a state's "interest" in applying its law

---

[235] de Boer, *Living Apart Together,* at 204.
[236] Among the early critics, *see* A. Ehrenzweig, *Private International Law* 63 (v. I, 1967); P. Graulich, *Principes de droit international privé* 14 (1961); D. Evrigenis, Tendances doctrinales actuelles en droit international privé, 118 *Recueil des cours* 313 (1966); G. Kegel, The Crisis of Conflict of Laws, 112 *Recueil des Cours* 91, 180–182 (1964); M. Rheinstein, How to Review a Festschrift, 11 *Am. J. Comp. L.* 632, 664 (1962).
[237] F. Juenger, *Multistate Justice* 135.
[238] *Id.*
[239] *Id.*
[240] For documentation, *see* Symeonides, *Revolution,* 370–373, *et passim.* Symeonides, *At the Dawn of the 21st Century,* 21–26, 28–32.
[241] *See* S. Symeonides, Maritime Conflicts of Law from the Perspective of Modern Choice of Law Methodology, 7 *Maritime Lawyer,* 223, 224–225, 228, 247 (1982). For more recent cases, *see* Kiobel v. Royal Dutch Petroleum Co., ___ U.S. ___, 133 S. Ct. 1659 (2013); J. McIntyre Machinery, Ltd. v. Nicastro, 564 U.S. __, 131 S. Ct. 2780 (2011); Goodyear Dunlop Tires Operations, S.A. v. Brown, 564 U.S. ___, 131 S. Ct. 2846 (2011); Sosa v. Alvarez-Machain, 542 U.S. 692 (2004); Am. Ins. Ass'n v. Garamendi, 539 U.S. 396 (2003); Hartford Fire Ins. Co. v. California, 509 US 764 (1993); F. Hoffman-La Roche Ltd. v. Empagran S.A., 542 U.S. 155 (2004); Attorney General of Canada v. R.J. Reynolds Tobacco Holdings, Inc., 268 F.3d 103 (2d Cir. 2001).
[242] *See* S. Symeonides, Revolution and Counter-revolution in American Conflicts Law: Is There a Middle Ground?, 46 *Ohio St. L.J.* 549, 558–563 (1985).

is simply a shorthand way of describing these *adverse consequences*.[243] In this sense, states are far from indifferent to the resolution of conflicts between their respective laws.

This conclusion does not carry with it a wholesale, or even a partial, subscription to Currie's particular value-system—especially the narrow, selfish perspective that Currie ascribed to the forum state—and to his assumption that states are only interested in protecting their own citizens but not similarly situated out-of-staters (the "personal law" principle).[244] To paraphrase John Donne, *no state is an island*, even if geographically it is. The selfish pursuit of the forum's interests is inimical to individual justice and state coexistence, as well as detrimental to the forum's own interests in the long run.

At the same time, a state has every reason to prevent adverse consequences to policies and values about which it feels strongly. As the preceding discussion of modern choice-of-law codifications illustrates, many countries have taken this lesson to heart. Although they continue to use the international-uniformity rhetoric, they have adopted rules and mechanisms designed to protect the forum's interests, in derogation of the official desideratum of international uniformity.

The adoption of supranational codifications such as Rome II may restrain the assertion of national interests of EU Member States against each other, but not the assertion of shared interests against third countries.[245] Rome II articulates these shared interests (which of course are *state* interests), even though none of Rome II's articles refer to state interests. For example, its Preamble describes Rome II's goal as one of "ensur[ing] a reasonable balance between the interests of [the *parties*, i.e.,] the person claimed to be liable and the person who has sustained damage."[246] Yet, a closer examination reveals that Rome II recognizes that many tort conflicts implicate not only the interests of the litigants but also broader societal, public, and thus state interests. For example, with regard to products liability, Recital 20 of Rome II speaks of the policies of "fairly spreading the risks, … protecting consumers' health, stimulating innovation, securing undistorted competition and facilitating trade."[247] With regard to unfair competition, Recital 21 speaks of the need to "protect competitors, consumers and the general public and ensure that the market economy functions properly."[248] Recital 25, concerning environmental torts, states that

---

[243] This is the overarching principle of the Louisiana codification. It is built on the premise that the choice-of-law process should aim to identify—and apply—the law of the state that, "in light of its relationship to the parties and the dispute and its policies rendered pertinent by that relationship, would bear the most serious legal, social, economic, and other *consequences* if its law were not applied to that issue." La. codif. art. 3515 cmt. (b) (emphasis added). Relying on the quoted phrase, Professor Weintraub called this a "consequences-based approach." R. Weintraub, *Commentary on the Conflict of Laws* 355 (4th ed. 2001). The codification's drafter agreed with this characterization. *See* S. Symeonides, The Conflicts Book of the Louisiana Civil Code: Civilian, American, or Original?, 83 *Tul. L. Rev.* 1041, 1053–1054 (2009).

[244] *See* Currie, *Selected Essays,* 705; Symeonides, *Revolution,* 16–17.

[245] Like other EU Regulations, Rome II has "universal application." *See* Rome II, art. 3 ("Any law specified by this Regulation shall be applied whether or not it is the law of a Member State.").

[246] Rome II, recital (16).

[247] *Id.* recital (20).

[248] *Id.* recital (21).

the need for a "high level of [environmental] protection" and the "principle that the polluter pays" justify a choice-of-law rule "discriminating in favour of the person sustaining the damage."[249] Finally, Recital 31 recognizes the need to impose certain restrictions on the parties' power to choose the governing law in order to protect weaker parties.[250]

More important, some of Rome II's dispositive articles can only be explained in terms of public (and thus state) interests, rather than in terms of private interests. Besides Article 26, which codifies the traditional *ordre public* exception, and Article 16, which allows the forum to interpose its own mandatory rules, many other provisions of Rome II are designed to be sensitive to certain preferred substantive polices. The clearest example is Article 7, which in cross-border environmental torts serves the substantive policy of "polluter pays" by allowing the plaintiff to choose the more favorable law of either the state of conduct or the state of injury.[251] Another example is Article 5 on products liability, which is discussed in Chapter 2.[252] Other less obvious examples are: Articles 6(4) and 8(3), which prohibit choice-of-law agreements in cases of unfair competition, restriction to competition, and infringement of intellectual property rights; Article 14(2)–(3), which prohibits choice-of-law clauses to the extent they violate certain mandatory rules of a non-chosen state or of the EU; and Article 14(1)(b), which allows pre-tort choice-of-law clauses only in contracts between commercial parties and subjects them to certain limitations.

Except for Articles 16 and 26, all of the other afore-mentioned Rome II articles: (1) consist of bilateral rules, and (2) are not designed to protect the policies or interests of the forum state as such. Instead, they are designed to protect important state policies and thus interests, such as a pro-environment or pro-competition policy. In turn, this suggests that to recognize that conflicts cases implicate public interests need not lead to parochialism. This topic is addressed in the next section.

In sum, although modern unilateralist devices are generally more subtle or exceptional than Currie's unabashedly parochial approach, their existence and numerosity signify that foreign legislatures, no less than American scholars or judges, are well aware of and sensitive to the fact that conflicts cases implicate broader interests beyond those of the private litigants.

D. UNILATERALISM AND PAROCHIALISM

The re-emergence of unilateralism in choice-of-law codifications and the legislative employment of other unilateralist devices are often greeted with regret as a parochial

---

[249] *Id.* recital (25).

[250] *Id.* recital (31).

[251] For discussion of this article, *see* S. Symeonides, Rome II and Tort Conflicts: A Missed Opportunity, 56 *Am. J. Comp. L.* 173, 209–211 (2008).

[252] *See* Chapter 2, *supra* at VII.A.

"step backward."[253] The assumption that unilateralism is necessarily parochial can find justification in the apparent parochialism of certain outspoken unilateralists such as Currie and Ehrenzweig.[254] However, although unilateralism and parochialism tend to travel together, they can also travel separately just as well. Parochialism is neither inseparable from unilateralism nor antithetical to multilateralism.

For example, Leflar's better-law approach is multilateral in appearance,[255] but can be parochial in its operation, if in applying that approach judges routinely conclude that forum law is better.[256] Conversely, although a strong partiality toward the forum's interests was central in Currie's own thinking, that partiality is severable from the remainder of his basic analysis. Many cases employing interest analysis demonstrate that, in the hands of enlightened judges, even Currie's approach can shed its pro-forum bias.[257] Other American approaches such as those of von Mehren and Trautman,[258] and to a lesser extent comparative impairment,[259] illustrate that one can adopt some of unilateralism's basic postulates (such as inquiring into state interests, "concerns," or "impairments" before choosing the applicable law) without falling into the pit of parochialism.

In fact, one can argue that, by inquiring into the interest of both the forum and the foreign state before choosing the applicable law, unilateralism has the *potential* of being more solicitous of foreign interests than a multilateral system, which chooses that law a priori based solely on the forum's assumptions. Although Currie's unilateral method scorned this potential, other unilateral methods, both before and after Currie's, have not done so. For example, the statutists did not oppose the application *in foro* of a foreign personal statute. Likewise, as documented above, the majority (indeed two thirds) of the codifications that have sanctioned the concept of *règles d'application immédiate* have also authorized the application of foreign mandatory rules in appropriate circumstances.[260]

---

[253] *See, e.g.,* M. Martinek, *The Seven Pillars of Wisdom,* § 5.1 ("The private international law codifications which are in force today in Germany and in Switzerland rightfully neglect or even ignore (if not rebut) the political approach. The political school of private international law is today regarded as a step backwards into the direction of a destructive politisation and towards a medieval neo-statutism.")

[254] *See supra* note 230, and S. Symeonides, Revolution and Counter-revolution, *supra* note 242, at 566–567. For Ehrenzweig's forum bias, *see* Hay, Borchers & Symeonides, *Conflict of Laws,* 41–45.

[255] *See* R. Leflar, Choice-Influencing Considerations in Conflicts Law, 41 *N.Y.U. L. Rev.* 367 (1966); R. Leflar, Conflicts of Law: More on Choice Influencing Considerations, 54 *Calif. L. Rev.* 1584 (1966).

[256] For evidence to this effect, see Symeonides, *Revolution,* 82–83.

[257] *See, e.g.,* People v. One 1953 Ford Victoria, 311 P. 2d 480 (Cal. 1957) (California court applying Texas law, which favored a Texas mortgagee at the expense of a California state entity); Bernkrant v. Fowler, 360 P. 2d 906 (Cal. 1961) (California court applying Nevada law, which favored a Nevada claimant at the expense of a California estate); Eger v. Du Pont DeNemours Co., 539 A. 2d 1213 (N.J. 1988) (applying South Carolina law, which favored a foreign defendant at the expense of a forum plaintiff); Kaiser-Georgetown Comm. Health Plan, Inc. v. Stutsman, 491 A. 2d 502 (D.C. 1985) (applying forum law, which favored a foreign plaintiff at the expense of local defendants).

[258] *See* A. von Mehren & D. Trautman, *The Law of Multistate Problems* (1965).

[259] *See* W.F. Baxter, Choice of Law and the Federal System, 16 *Stan. L. Rev.* 1 (1963).

[260] *See* Table 7.1, at II.B.3, *supra.*

Moreover, some of the countries that have enacted inward-looking unilateral rules have paired them with mirror-like outward-looking unilateral rules.

An example of the latter phenomenon is the Louisiana codification, which contains several such pairings,[261] as well as the Swiss codification, which offers an example of a double pairing. Articles 90 and 91 of the Swiss codification consist of four unilateral rules designating the law governing the succession of: (1) Swiss citizens domiciled in Switzerland, (2) foreigners domiciled in Switzerland, (3) Swiss citizens domiciled abroad, and (4) foreigners domiciled abroad. The four rules provide different choices to decedents in each category and together they produce a carefully crafted, sophisticated scheme that could not have been constructed through bilateral rules. These and other examples illustrate that the unilateral technique is a high precision tool that allows the drafting of more focused and nuanced rules than the bilateral technique.

Moreover, one should keep in mind that an inward-looking unilateral rule, even when not paired with a corresponding outward-looking unilateral rule, does not operate in isolation, particularly when it is surrounded by multilateral rules. Another example from the Louisiana codification illustrates this point. Article 3545 contains an inward-looking unilateral rule in its first paragraph. This rule calls for the application of forum law to product liability cases that have certain connections to the forum state (subject to a foreseeability exception provided in the second paragraph). The third paragraph then provides that [a]ll cases not disposed of by the preceding paragraphs are governed by the other Articles of the [torts] Title.[262] The latter articles consist of bilateral rules, most of which provide the court with ample, but guided discretion in choosing the applicable law.[263] Again, the use of the unilateral technique allows the drafter to delineate with precision the reach of the law of the forum but without prejudging the reach of foreign law, and to do so in a non-parochial fashion.[264]

Even when an inward-looking unilateral rule is neither paired with a corresponding outward-looking rule nor complemented by a bilateral rule, the result is not necessarily parochialism. For example, a rule such as Article 3 of the French *Code Civil* (which provides that forum law governs torts committed in the forum's territory) does not foreclose—and indeed, it suggests—the possibility of applying foreign law to torts committed outside the forum. Rather, the rule relegates the latter torts to the judicial case-by-case

---

[261] *See supra* II.C.9 and II.C.13; Symeonides, *Les grands problèmes*, 260–263.

[262] La. codif. art. 3545 (3).

[263] One of these articles, Article 3547, contains an escape that can displace even the unilateral rule of the first paragraph of Article 3545. For a detailed discussion of this scheme and its rationale, see S. Symeonides, Problems and Dilemmas in Codifying Choice of Law for Torts: The Louisiana Experience in a Comparative Perspective, 38 *Am. J. Comp. L.* 431, 464–469 (1990); S. Symeonides, *Louisiana Exegesis*, 749–757.

[264] The Oregon and Puerto Rico codifications follow the same combination of unilateral and multilateral rules. *See* Or. Rev. Stat. § 15.435; Puerto Rico draft codif. art. 42.

revolution, which may or may not be parochial and which can lead to a judicial "bilateral-ization" of the rule, as it has in France.[265]

Another example is the previously quoted Oregon statute that mandates the application of Oregon law to insurance conflicts arising from contaminated environmental sites located in Oregon.[266] That statute does not address the question of which law applies to non-Oregon sites. Instead, it states that "[n]othing in this section shall be interpreted to modify common law rules governing choice of law determinations for sites located outside the State of Oregon."[267] Thus, the statute wisely preserves the use of the ordinary choice-of-law process for non-forum sites and, with it, the courts' freedom to apply either forum law or foreign law, depending on all of the choice-of-law factors that are pertinent in the particular case.

E. THE UNILATERALITY OF MULTILATERALISM

In contrast to unilateralism's negative reputation, multilateralism has enjoyed a very positive image from the very beginning. In large part, this was a result of the stature of its founder, who was also the slaughterer of unilateralism, the great Friedrich Carl von Savigny. Unlike the unilateralists who focused on the conflicting laws and tried to ascertain their intended spatial reach, Savigny focused on "legal relationships" and sought to identify the state in which each relationship had its "seat," or in whose legislative jurisdiction it "belonged." But the important questions are not only *how* to decide where each relationship belonged but also *who* would do the deciding. Savigny's hopes for an international consensus never materialized and, in the absence of a supranational legislature, each country claimed for itself the task of *unilaterally* enacting bilateral rules assigning a seat to each relationship.

Herein lies the de facto unilaterality of multilateralism. Multilateralism purports to aspire to international uniformity, yet it leaves to each country to define it and to choose the means of pursuing it. It vaguely admonishes the forum country to respect the interests of other countries, yet by generally disfavoring renvoi, it does nothing specific to encourage consideration, much less accommodation, of those interests. It is supposed to be a forum-neutral system, but in reality it is more of a *forum-knows-best* system. For example, when the forum adopts a bilateral choice-of-law rule such as the *lex loci contractus* rule, the forum assumes that the law of the country in which the contract was made is the most appropriate law to govern all disputes arising from that contract, even if the latter country holds the view that its law is the *least* appropriate. Indeed, except in the limited circumstances in which it allows renvoi, multilateralism is totally indifferent to the views of countries other than the forum. Moreover, as noted earlier, in some cases,

---

[265] *See* B. Audit & L. d'Avout, *DIP* 171–172.

[266] *See supra* note 24.

[267] Or. Rev. Stat. § 465.480(2)(a).

the neutral bilateral rules, of which multilateralism prides itself, may conceal deliberate policy choices designed to promote the forum's national interest.[268]

F. COMPARISON

Some labels can be simplistic or misleading. In PIL, the labels of *unilateralism* and *multilateralism* are simplistic. As one author put it, "equating unilateralism with an unwillingness to apply foreign law and multilateralism with a willingness to apply foreign law is a poor way to use those terms."[269]

The truth is that unilateralism is not unwilling to apply foreign law in general, not even the unilateral rules of that law in particular. But unlike multilateralism, unilateralism examines the applicability of foreign law only after concluding that forum law is inapplicable. In this sense, unilateralism is forum-centered, but whether it is also parochial depends on how frequently it reaches the conclusion that forum law applies and on what grounds. Although some unilateralists such as Currie reach that conclusion rather frequently, others are far more accommodating of foreign law.[270]

On the other hand, multilateralism does not always live up to its commitment to treat forum and foreign law equally. For example, as noted earlier, some bilateral choice-of-law rules that are facially neutral are actually calculated to lead to the application of forum law much more frequently than foreign law. Second, there is always the *ordre public* exception that—whether used only exceptionally and defensively (as it should), or frequently and offensively—results in the exclusion of foreign law.[271] Third, the old favorite devices of characterization[272] and renvoi[273] can also be used to the same end, even if they are not designed for this purpose. Fourth, the various escape clauses and soft connecting factors discussed in Chapter 4 provide ample flexibility and the ability to favor the law of the

---

[268] *See supra* at II.D.

[269] W. Dodge, Extraterritoriality and Conflict-of-Laws Theory: An Argument for Judicial Unilateralism, 39 *Harv. Int'l L.J.* 101, 109 (1998).

[270] For a proposal for an "accommodative unilateralism," *see* Symeonides, *Accommodative Unilateralism*, 431–434.

[271] *See*, e.g., J. Chen, *Australian Report*, in S. Symeonides (ed.), *Progress or Regress?*, 103 ("In effect, the doctrine of the *ordre public* has been used defensively as well as offensively."); T. Pajor, *Polish Report*, in *id.*, at 337–338 (criticizing a Polish Supreme Court decision for this reason); M. Fallon & J. Meeusen, *Belgian Report*, in *id.*, at 122 (commenting on the "remarkably 'positive' color" of the Belgian Cour de Cassation's definition of *ordre public*). *Cf.* B. Audit, *Rapport Français*, in *id.* at 206–207 (describing how French lower courts have used the *ordre public* device to apply French law to cases like *Babcock v. Jackson*, that is, cases arising out of accidents occurring outside France but involving French parties only).

[272] *See*, e.g., J. Chen, *supra* note 271, at 104: "[C]haracterisation has also been used by courts…to enable them to apply the forum law"; B. Audit, *supra* note 271, at 203:
En fait, ce conflit de qualifications n'est que la manifestation d'un conflit de politiques législatives, c'est-à-dire d'un 'vrai conflit' de lois, au sens de Currie. En effet, le choix par un système donné d'une qualification reflète les considérations sous-jacentes à la matière en cause en droit interne; de sorte que la solution affirmée exprime simplement qu'un tel conflit est résolu en faveur de la politique législative du for.

[273] *See*, e.g., M. Fallon & J. Meeusen, *Belgian Report*, in S. Symeonides (ed.), *Progress or Regress?*, 122: "[T]he admission of *renvoi* in Belgium is also, and probably for the most part, inspired by the wish to apply the *lex*

forum. For example, although the term *closest connection* appears to contemplate a geographical relationship, it does not specifically discourage an inquiry into state interests; in fact, it may provide legitimacy for such an inquiry if the judge is willing to undertake it. As Professor de Boer has noted in commenting on the application of the pertinent provision of the Rome Convention by Dutch courts, "[w]hether it is motivated by a wish to avoid unfamiliar foreign law or by a vague better law notion or by a principled preference for a certain substantive policy, the choice is easily wrapped in the objective geographical terms of closest connection."[274] Last, there is the selective use of unilateral rules such as the ones described earlier in this chapter. Thus, even if each of the above devices alone is exceptional, they add up to many forum-favoring opportunities and devices.

G. THE LOSS OF INNOCENCE

This long chapter could have been as long as a book, and yet it could not have exhausted the many issues upon which it touches. In the final analysis, however, most of these issues can be compressed into one question. It is an ontological rather than a deontological question—what sort of beings *are* states, and how do they *act,* not how *should* they act in the PIL arena. Are states as selfish as Currie assumed them to be, or are they as altruistic as Savigny had hoped they would be? Based on the choice-of-law codifications of the last 50 years, the answer is squarely in the middle.

Clearly, in dealing with multistate *private*-law disputes, states are not as selfish as Currie assumed. Nevertheless, this does not mean that they are indifferent to the outcome of those disputes. Equally clearly, however, states are not as concerned with international uniformity as Savigny had hoped. PIL is no longer as "private,"[275] neutral,[276] or "innocent"[277] as it was supposed to be half a century ago. International uniformity remains the *official* desideratum of the choice-of-law process, but only as long as it does not stand in

---

fori."; L. Burián, *Hungarian Report,* in *id.,* at 274: "The Hungarian PIL Code...accepts reference back, but rejects reference to another legal system. So it serves the homeward trend."

[274] T.M. de Boer, The EEC Contracts Convention and the Dutch Courts, 54 *RabelsZ* 24 (1990).

[275] "The old dichotomies between public law and private law, and between national law and international law, are gradually fading. Conflicts law is not exclusively concerned with international relationships between private parties." T.M. de Boer, *Living Apart Together,* 195.

[276] *Cf.* V. van Den Eeckhout, Private International Law, *Quo Vadis:* PIL as a Perfect Conductor for Achieving Political Objectives? A Tale of Lost Innocence (Oct. 14, 2011), *available at* SSRN: http://ssrn.com/abstract=1944020 and http://dx.doi.org/10.2139/ssrn.1944020.

Is PIL "neutral" in the sense that PIL rules are supposed to result in the application of the legal system that is "most closely connected" in any case—following on from the "neutral PIL" as expounded by Von Savigny? Or is PIL "neutral" in quite a different sense by now, namely that PIL is apparently unable to resist attempts to use this branch of law instrumentally and to mould it into a shape that best suits the result needed? Is PIL degenerating into a political tool, with the resulting loss of its innocence?

[277] "Le droit international privé a perdu son innocence." S. Vrellis, *Rapport grec,* in S. Symeonides (ed.), *Progress or Regress?,* 247. *See also* A. Lüderitz, Anknüpfung im Parteiinteresse, in G. Kegel, H-J. Musielak & K. Schurig (eds.), *Festschrift für Kegel* 31 (1977) ("Das Internationale Privatrecht hat seine Unschuld verloren.").

the way of other, less exalted forum objectives.[278] "[W]e preach the equivalence of all legal systems of the world, [while] at the same time applying our own law as often as we can."[279]

In other words, since Savigny's time, the theory and practice of PIL have come to recognize other goals that should be pursued, either in parallel with uniformity or in derogation from it. In the United States, this rearrangement of goals has been openly and honestly debated, thanks primarily to Currie's prompting. Currie would have placed the pursuit of state interests at the top, and uniformity in the basement, of the conflicts pyramid. This extreme idea was soundly and properly rejected, even in its country of origin, but Currie did score a partial victory by making the pursuit of state interests a legitimate goal of the choice-of-law process, side by side with the loftier goal of interstate uniformity.

In the rest of the world, Currie's ideas would never have received serious consideration. Nevertheless, a similar though less transparent rearrangement of values and goals has occurred there as well. The resurgence of unilateralism and its coexistence with multilateralism is one manifestation of this rearrangement. It signifies a recognition that sometimes choice-of-law disputes implicate important public interests and that countries no longer shy away from protecting those interests. The difference then may be only one of degree. In these systems, the protection, or at least the assertion of state interests is, or is supposed to be, the exception rather than the rule, and it is disguised rather than openly undertaken and explained.

Although the "loss of innocence" is regrettable, it would be even more regrettable if we pretended that it has not occurred. A good understanding of reality is the first precondition for successfully addressing the problem at hand. As we proceed into the twenty-first century, we can expect that states will, even more boldly, assert their interest in multistate private-law disputes. Our discipline can serve the interstate and international legal order by recognizing the existence of state interests, by recognizing when they truly conflict, and by articulating the principles and mechanisms that will provide a reasonable accommodation between these interests.

---

[278] *Cf.* T.M. de Boer, *Facultative Choice of Law*, 285 ("If Savigny's theory was meant to bring about uniformity of result, or decisional harmony, it has failed miserably.").

[279] *Id.* at 419.

8 Conclusions

This book was written in 2013, a year that coincidentally marked the 700th anniversary of the birth of Bartolus of Saxoferrato (1613–1357), the progenitor of modern or at least post-ancient PIL. During the intervening seven centuries, the world has grown denser and more complex, the art of law codification has become a science, and PIL has come a long way. Some periods have been more productive than others, but progress was made in each century. In terms of the quality of the gray matter devoted to this discipline, the best period was probably the first part of the nineteenth century, when both Friedrich Carl von Savigny (1779–1861) and Joseph Story (1779–1845) taught and wrote on this subject.

However, in terms of legislative activity, the 50-year period covered by this book is by far the most productive, not only more productive than any previous 50-year period, but also more productive than all of the previous 650 years since Bartolus. During this period, we have witnessed the adoption of 91 choice-of-law codifications and four final drafts in 86 states; 15 EU Regulations; and 86 international conventions, protocols, and similar instruments.

This tremendous increase in codification activity can be attributed only in part to the emergence of new independent states following the decolonization of Africa and parts of Asia,[1] and then the fall of communism in Eastern Europe.[2] For the rest, the reasons must be sought in other factors, such as the momentous upsurge of cross-border activity and mobility, even before the phenomenon now known as globalization. Whatever the

---

[1] Twenty-one of these codifications have been enacted in former colonies in Africa (19) and Asia (2).

[2] The dissolution of the former Soviet Union led to the establishment of 14 new states (in addition to Russia), and all but one of them (Turkmenistan) enacted new choice-of-law codifications. The split of Yugoslavia added three new codifications, and the split of Czechoslovakia added one. In addition, three other Eastern European countries enacted a choice-of-law codification after the fall of communism.

reasons, however, this dramatic increase has definitively answered the old question of whether PIL is susceptible to codification, even if the debate regarding the resultant costs and benefits will continue.

Inevitably, there is a fair degree of emulation, borrowing, and transplantation, especially from the sophisticated Western European codifications and the Rome Convention to eastern European and Asian codifications. However, this borrowing is rarely subservient or mechanical. It is often accompanied by shrewd adjustments carefully crafted to accommodate the particular values, needs, or interest of the borrowing country.

The codifications of this period are not only more numerous but also much different from those of the previous generation. They are more comprehensive, complex, flexible, pragmatic, pluralistic, and eclectic. They also provide new and, in some respects, surprising answers to some of the fundamental questions, tensions, and dilemmas of private international law.

One of these old tensions was between two grand principles invoked to explain the operation of laws beyond the territory of the enacting state—territoriality and personality. Historically, personality was the older principle, but it was largely displaced by territoriality well before the beginning of the 50-year period covered by this book. In the area of tort conflicts, territoriality was the exclusive principle insofar as virtually all countries adhered to the *lex loci delicti* rule for all torts. By the end of the 50-year period, the principle of personality recaptured some significant ground from personality. Although all but one of the new codifications have retained the *lex loci delicti* rule, most of them have also introduced a major exception to it based on the principle of personality—the common-domicile exception. According to this exception, when the tortfeasor and the victim are domiciled in the same state, the law of that state governs a tort occurring in another state.[3] Many codifications have also introduced other exceptions to the *lex loci delicti* rule, such as the *favor laesi* principle, which mitigates the harshness of that rule in cross-border torts.[4]

In the area of contract conflicts, territoriality was not the exclusive principle insofar as many countries applied the parties' personal law to certain contractual issues such as capacity. For the rest, however, the choice of the applicable law was based on territorial contacts, such as the place of the contract. In particular, relatively few countries recognized the principle of party autonomy. By the end of the period, there is virtually no country that does not allow, indeed encourage, contracting parties to agree in advance on the applicable law.[5] This widespread endorsement of party autonomy has become one of the unifying principles of contemporary PIL, although differences remain about the modalities and limitations of this autonomy (especially as it affects weak parties).[6]

---

[3] *See* Chapter 2 at IV.C, *supra*.

[4] *See* Chapter 2 at III.C, *supra*.

[5] *See* Chapter 3 at I, *supra*.

[6] *See* Chapter 3 at III–V, *supra*.

One key argument of codification opponents has always been that whatever gains it procures in terms of certainty are largely offset by the loss of flexibility. The choice-of-law codifications of this period provide ample evidence that such a loss is not inevitable. If carefully crafted, a codification need not petrify the law, nor render it unduly inflexible for unanticipated or exceptional cases. The new codifications have developed several different tools, such as alternative or "soft" connecting factors and escape clauses, which provide controlled dosages of flexibility. One is hard-pressed to find a new codification that does not employ one or more of these tools, such as the ubiquitous "closer connection."[7] By enabling courts to aptly resolve atypical cases, these tools help attain the desired equilibrium between the perpetually competing needs for certainty.

Another way of facilitating apt solutions is by providing narrower rules that are closely tailored to specific categories of cases and, better yet, to specific aspects or *issues* in these cases. Although the new codifications do not necessarily endorse an American-style judicial issue-by-issue analysis, they do provide rules that are narrower than those of the old codifications. For example, rather than having a single broad rule for all contracts or torts, the new codifications provide narrower rules for different types of contracts or torts *and,* in many instances, different rules for different issues in a contract or tort. By narrowing and concentrating the focus of the choice of law, these rules are far more likely than the old rules to produce apt solutions to individual cases and issues. Thus, besides being more flexible, the new codifications are also more nuanced. However, in cases that involve more than one disputed issue, the new, narrow rules may lead to the application of the laws of different states (a phenomenon known as *dépeçage*)[8] and, in *some* of those cases, this may produce incongruous or inharmonious results. Some, but by no means all, codifications provide direct or indirect means for avoiding such incongruities.

One of the old philosophical, and nowadays pragmatic, questions of PIL is whether the choice-of-law process should aim for the law of the *state* that has the "proper" connection(s) to the case, regardless of the quality of the result in the particular case ("conflicts justice"), or whether the process should aim directly for the law that will produce the "right" result ("material justice"). In the new codifications, the "material justice" view, which was previously considered heretical, has gained significant ground at the expense of "conflicts justice." For the most part, the new codifications continue to aim for "conflicts justice" insofar as most of their rules are geared toward *state*-selection rather than a content-dependent *law* selection. However, most codifications have also made serious and targeted concessions to the desideratum of "material justice." These concessions take the form of result-selective rules mandating the application of a law that produces a particular substantive result, such as favoring the validity of a juridical act,

---

[7] *See* Chapter 4, *supra.*
[8] *See* Chapter 5, *supra.*

a particular status, or a particular party. There is virtually no codification that does not contain at least one, and usually many more, result-selective choice-of-law rules.[9]

The final group of questions that the new codifications can answer involve the very nature of PIL and the goals it should serve: whether PIL is really "private" law in the sense of involving only the private interests of the disputing parties, or whether it also implicates the interests of the states connected to the dispute; whether the old principle of equality between forum law and foreign law is realistic; and whether international uniformity is still the supreme goal of PIL, or whether that goal is illusory.

Once again, the answers that the new codifications provide are mixed. Although international uniformity remains an official desideratum, it is no longer the supreme goal. Rather, it is coequal with, and often subordinated to, other goals and values. PIL may still be viewed as "private" law, but as one that often implicates important public interests. In theory, the new codifications purport to subscribe to the principle of equality of forum law and foreign law. However, they also subtly, and sometimes not so subtly, protect the forum's values and interests in selected areas. Although the new codifications consist primarily of bilateral rules, they also selectively employ several unilateral rules and other unilateralist devices whenever important forum interests are at stake. They also give priority to mandatory rules and other localizing rules contained in substantive statutes that reflect important forum policies and interests. These developments suggest that PIL is no longer as "private," neutral, or "innocent" as it was supposed to be at the beginning of this period. If these codifications are accurate reflections of the way states behave in the international arena, then states are neither as impartial and altruistic as Savigny had hoped, or as selfish as Brainerd Currie had assumed them to be.

As the above summary makes clear, today's codifications cannot claim methodological or philosophical purity; and it is doubtful that they have aspired to it, or that they should.[10] Indeed, if one were to define the dominant feature of contemporary codifications, it would have to be *eclecticism*, or at least methodological and philosophical pluralism. This is particularly obvious to anyone who takes seriously the polemical academic literature, which often gives the impression of a virtual civil war among rival schools of thought. Unlike academic authors, the drafters of new codifications have no qualms about combining ideas that their proponents have posited as polar opposites, such as multilateralism with unilateralism, and conflicts justice with material justice. Four decades ago, Henry Batiffol spoke approvingly of a *"pluralisme des méthodes"*[11] in PIL, and Bernard Audit later characterized this pluralism as "the dominant trend" in the evolution

---

[9] *See* Chapter 6, *supra.*

[10] *Cf.* M. Martinek, *Seven Pillars of Wisdom*, at § 6.1 (noting that in the drafting of German and Swiss codification, "[n]o conceptional [sic] purism could be sustained; compromises had to be made.").

[11] H. Batiffol, Le pluralisme des méthodes en droit international privé, 139 *Recueil des cours* 75, 106 (1973);

of private international law during the twentieth century.[12] The two authors could well have concluded with the exclamation "*vive le pluralisme!*"[13]

Admittedly, eclecticism has a bad reputation. When eclecticism is the result of subservient imitation or intellectual laziness, this reputation is justified. Uncritical, undigested, and uncoordinated "picking and choosing" can lead to internal contradictions and incoherence. But a studied, adapted, and thoughtful eclecticism can combine the "best of both worlds." It can live up to the true meaning of this Greek word, which literally means "choosing *well*."[14]

Moreover, eclecticism is often the most practical response to the complexity of the modern world and a sensible choice between opposing perceptions of the same reality. Take for example the epic clash between the idealistic vision of the classic school of PIL and Currie's realpolitik protectionist vision and its more moderate equivalents in other countries.[15] The classic school saw PIL as an impartial mediator of multistate disputes that implicate only the private interest of the disputants. In this context and upon this premise, the doctrine of equality between forum and foreign law was simply a natural corollary of that impartiality, and international uniformity could be seen as not only desirable but also achievable. Currie, on the other hand, saw conflicts law as a means of resolving actual conflicts between states, almost akin to those falling within the ambit of public international law. He therefore saw nothing wrong with actively promoting the interests of the forum state at almost every juncture, because to do otherwise would be to "suppress[] the natural instincts of community self-interest" and endorse a "purposeless self-denial."[16]

None of the modern codifications has accepted Currie's assumptions and his overtly "political"[17] and polemical approach. However, most codifications have recognized that

---

[12] B. Audit, *Rapport Français*, in S. Symeonides (ed.), *Progress or Regress?*,191 at 210 ("[L]e pluralisme des méthodes constitue une tendance dominante de l'évolution du droit international privé français au cours du XXᵉ siècle"). Although Professor Audit was referring to French PIL, his comment applies equally to PIL in general.

[13] Methodological pluralism was also one of the central themes of Professor Bucher's excellent "general course" at The Hague Academy of International Law in 2009. *See* A. Bucher, *La dimension sociale du droit international privé* (2011).

[14] The word *eclecticism* derives from the Greek words εκλεκτικός *(eklektikos)*, which means the one who chooses well, and εκλεκτός *(eklektos)*, which means the well chosen.

[15] *See, e.g.*, C. Joerges, *Zum Funktionswandel des Kollisionsrechts* (1971); R. Quadri, *Lezioni di diritto internazionale privato* (3d ed. 1961); C. Joerges, Vorüberlegungen zu einer Theorie des internationalen Wirtschaftsrechts, 43 *RabelsZ* 6 (1979); A. Heini, Neuere Strömungen im amerikanischen internationalen Privatrecht, 19 *Schweizerisches Jahrbuch für Internationales Recht* 31 (1962); R. Wiethölter, Vorbemerkungen zum IPR, in Deutscher Rat für IPR Erbrechtskommission, *Internationales Nachlaßverfahrensrecht, Vorschläge und Gutachten zur Reform des deutschen internationalen Erbrechts*, 142 (1969); R. Wiethölter, Begriffs- und Interessenjurisprudenz -falsche Fronten im IPR, in G. Kegel, H-J. Musielak & K. Schurig, *Festschrift für Kegel*, 213, 224, 233, 239, 260 (1977).

[16] Currie, *Selected Essays*, 525.

[17] *See* M. Martinek, *Seven Pillars of Wisdom*, at §5.1 (referring to "the wrongfulness of a decidedly and expressly political approach like the governmental interest analysis approach (Currie) which once was fashionable in the U.S.A.").

some categories of conflicts cases, indeed, a significant number, *do* implicate important interests of the forum state, and have accordingly adopted unilateral rules designed to protect *those* interests. The result is an eclectic combination of multilateralism and unilateralism, which the purists may find unprincipled and inconsistent, but which is a practical and workable response to contemporary realities.[18]

A pragmatic eclecticism also characterizes the position of new codifications on the other major clash between the proponents of conflicts justice and material justice. In the eyes of proponents of conflicts justice, PIL is more concerned with geographic propriety and symmetry—placing the "seat" of each legal relationship in the right *state*—rather than with the result such placement produces. In their view, the choice-of-law process should lead to the application of the law of the state that has the proper contacts with the case, regardless of the material quality of the result the application of that law will produce. At the other end of the spectrum, the proponents of the material-justice or "better law" view, such as Leflar and Juenger, want the judge to always "choos[e] law with an eye on the prize."[19]

Modern codifications would never go that far; nor should they have to. However, they have recognized that, in a significant number of cases, such as those involving children, maintenance obligees, consumers, tort victims, and other weak parties, the geographic propriety of the choice of law is far less important than the substantive propriety of the result that law would produce in the particular case. Accordingly, modern codifications have adopted result-selective rules that authorize the court, and in some instances the weak party, to choose the law (from among geographically connected laws) that produces the proper result. The proliferation of such result-selective rules and their coexistence with state-selective, content-neutral rules may offend the purists, but it is another example of a sensible, pragmatic eclecticism that enables PIL to serve justice not preceded by an adjective.

In the final analysis, the modern legal mind has come to realize that the complexity of contemporary conflicts problems requires a toolbox approach—the more tools the better—rather than a single tool or method; that no single theory or school of thought has all the right solutions to all conflicts problems, but each school has something valuable to contribute; and that, rather than choosing a single school or method wholesale, it is better to draw the best ideas from each and properly combine them into a workable system. As this book documents, most codifications of this period have engaged in such an eclecticism. Whether they have chosen well is a matter of opinion; this author's opinion is that most of them have.

---

[18] *See* T. Pajor, *Polish Report,* in S. Symeonides (ed.), *Progress or Regress,* 346 (noting that "the return in PIL to recognition of a multiplicity of regulatory methods must be viewed as progress. This return may be seen, for example, in the existence of both multilateral and unilateral approaches in the same legal system, allowing choice of law solutions to be adapted to the variety of substantive law regulations.").

[19] R. Weintraub, Choosing Law with an Eye on the Prize, 15 *Mich. J. In'l L.* 705 (1994) (*reviewing* F. Juenger, *Choice of Law Multistate Justice* (1993)).

It is also this author's opinion that, 700 years after the birth of Bartolus, PIL is not only alive and well, albeit being less idealistic and less "pure," but it is also richer, more vibrant, sophisticated, flexible, and pluralistic.

However, what matters more than any academic author's opinion is the *reality* of PIL, whether good or bad. As the late Professor Russell Weintraub wrote, "[m]ore important than what the commentators are up to as they deforest the land with the mountains of conflicts articles, is the results that the courts are reaching."[20] Indeed, in countries such as the United States, which do not have statutory choice-of-law rules, judicial decisions represent the entire reality of PIL. But in other countries, such as those whose codifications this book reviews, these codifications represent the major and most authentic part of this reality. The judicial decisions that apply them to actual cases represent the remaining part. But that is a project for another book.

---

[20] R. Weintraub, *Commentary on the Conflict of Laws* 347 (4th ed. 2001).

Codifications, Regulations, and Conventions: Alphabetical List and Bibliography

I. CODIFICATIONS

Afghanistan

CODIFICATION: Civil Code of the Republic of Afghanistan, arts. 3–35, Official Gazette No. 353, published 1977/01/05 (1355/10/15 A.P.); English Translation by the Afghanistan Rule of Law Project (AROLP)/USAID 2006, *available at* http://www.asianlii.org/af/legis/laws/toc-1977.html

Albania

CODIFICATION: Law No. 10428 of 2 July 2011 on Private International Law. German translation with and introduction by Wolfgang Stoppel, 53 *Jahrbuch fur Ostrecht* 357 (2012).

SECONDARY SOURCES: A. Kalia, *E drejta ndërkombëtare private* (Private International Law) (2008).

Algeria

CODIFICATION: Algerian Civil Code arts. 9–24 as amended by Ordinance No. 75-58 of 26 September 1975. French text in 66 *Rev. critique DIP* 380 (1977), and at: http://www.droit.mjustice.dz/code%20civile.pdf.

SECONDARY SOURCES: (1) ARTICLES: B. Dutoit, Le droit international privé algérien dans le nouveau Code civil du 26 septembre 1976, *Festschrift für Günter Beitzke* 462 (1979); D. Nelle, Neues Kollisionsrecht in Algerien, *IPRax* 548 (2007); G. Peyrard, La solution des conflits de lois en Algérie, 66 *Rev. critique DIP* 382 (1977); (2) BOOKS: Mohand Issad, *Droit international privé: v. I—Les règles de Conflits* (2d ed. 1983); Mohand Issad, *Droit international privé, v. II.—Les règles matérielles* (1986).

Angola

CODIFICATION: Civil Code of Angola, arts. 14–63, Law-Decree 496 of 25 November 1977, renewing the force of Portuguese Civil Code initially adopted by Portuguese Decree-Law No. 47,344 of 25 November 1966 and extended to then Overseas Provinces by Ordinance No. 22,869, of 4 September 1967. Portuguese text and German translation, in J. Kropholler et al., *Aussereuropäische IPR-Gesetze* 36 (1999).

Argentina

DRAFT CODIFICATION: Anteproyecto de Código Civil y Commercial de la Nación (2012) by Commisión de Reformas decreto presidencial 191/2011, Arts. 2594–2671. *Available at* https://guillermoberto.files.wordpress.com/2012/03/codigo-civil-anteproyecto-articulado. pdf. Explanatory Report: Fundamentos Del Anteproyecto De Código Civil Y Comercial De La Nación, *available at* http://www.jdsupra.com/legalnews/anteproyecto-cx00f3digo-civil-2 012-ar-18982/.

SECONDARY SOURCES: (1) ARTICLES: M.S. Najurieta & M.B. Noodt Taquela, *Argentinean Report;* A. Dreyzin de Klor, *Republic of Argentina*, in *International Encyclopedia of Laws: Private International Law*, v. 1 (2011); G. Lucas Sosa, Las Normas Generales de Derecho Internacional Privado en el Proyecto de Codificacion del Derecho Internacional Privado en Argentina, in J. Kleinheisterkam & G.A. Lorenzo Idiarte, (eds.), *Avances Del Derecho Internacional Privado En America Latina: Liber Amicorum Jürgen Samtleben* 192 (2002); (2) BOOKS: A. Boggiano, *Derecho internacional privado* (5th ed. 2006); A. Dreyzin de Klor & D. Fernández Arroyo, *Derecho internacional privado argentino: Tratados en vigor y otros textos relevantes* (2009); M.B. Noodt Taquela, *Derecho Internacional Privado:Libro De Casos* (2d ed. 2006); W. Goldschmidt, *Derecho internacional privado* (10th ed. updated by A. Perugini Manetti, 2009); I. Weinberg De Roca, *Derecho internacional privado* (2d ed. 2004).

Armenia

CODIFICATION: Civil Code of Armenia as adopted in 1998, Division 12, arts. 1253–1293. English translation at http://www.parliament.am/legislation.php?sel=show&ID=1556&lang =eng; German translation in 29 *IPRax* 96 (2009).

Austria

CODIFICATION: Bundesgesetz vom 15. 6. 1978 über das internationale Privatrecht (IPR-Gesetz), BGBl I 1978/304. For subsequent amendments, *see* BGBl I No. 119/1998, I No. 18/1999, I No. 135/2000, I No. 117/2003, I No. 58/2004, I No. 109/2009, I No. 135/2009. English translation and discussion, E. Palmer, The Austrian Codification of Conflicts Law, 28 *Am. J. Comp. L.* 197 (1980).

SECONDARY SOURCES: (1) ARTICLES: Christiane Wendehorst, *Austrian Report;* G. Beitzke, Neues österreichisches Kollisionsrecht, 43 *RabelsZ* 245 (1979); (2) BOOKS: T. Borič (ed.), *Internationales Privatrecht und Zivilverfahrensrect* (4th ed. 2008); A. Duchek & F. Schwind, *Internationales Privatrecht* (1979); F. Kerschner, *Internationales Privatrecht* (3d ed. 2010); F. Mänhardt, *Die Kodifikation des österreichischen internationalen Privatrechts* (1978); F. Mänhardt & W. Posch, *Internationales Privatrecht, Privatrechtsvergleichung, Einheitsprivatrecht* (1999);W. Posch, *Bürgerliches Recht, v. VII. Internationales Privatrecht* (2010); M. Schwimann. *Internationales Privatrecht* (2001); F. Schwind, *Internationales Privatrecht* (1990); B. Verschraegen, *Internationales Privatrecht* (2012).

Azerbaijan

CODIFICATION: Law of 6 June 2000 on Private International Law. English translation, *available at* http://cis-legislation.com/document.fwx?rgn=2633; German translation in 23 *IPRax* 386 (2003).

Belarus

CODIFICATION: Civil Code of Belarus (Law of 7 December 1998, as amended as of 28 December 2009), Section VII, comprising arts. 1093–1136. English translation available at the legal portal of the Republic of Belarus http://www.law.by/work/englportal.nsf/0791c722ea4cdeb5c225716600 472038/a6f0bfbf7d5ce1abc2257226004222a5?OpenDocument.

SECONDARY SOURCES: (1) ARTICLES: D. Solenik, Attempting a "Judicial Restatement" of Private International Law in Belarus, 10 *Ybk Priv. Int'l L.* 505 (2008); (2) BOOKS: A. Danilevich, *Private International Law in Belarus* (2012).

Belgium

CODIFICATION: Code de droit international privé (Loi du 16 juillet 2004), Moniteur Belge 27 Juillet 2004; J. Carlier, M. Fallon, B. Martin-Bosly (eds.), *Code de droit international privé* (2004); English translation by C. Clijmans & P. Torremans, 6 *Ybk. Priv. Int'l L.* 319 (2004).

SECONDARY SOURCES: (1) ARTICLES: Marc Fallon & Johan Erauw, *Belgian Report;* Barnich, Présentation du nouveau code de droit international privé, *Rev. notarial belge* 6 (2005); J. Carlier, Le code belge de droit international privé, 94 *Rev. critique DIP* 11 (2005); J. Erauw, Brief Description of the Draft Belgian Code of Private International Law, 4 *Ybk. Priv. Int'l L.* 145 (2002); M. Fallon, Le droit international privé belge dans les traces de la loi italien dix ans après, *Riv. dir. int. proc.* 318 (2005); M. Fallon, La loi belge de droit international privé, pour un bicentenaire, *Trav. Com. français dr. int'l priv.* (2004–2006), 90 (2008); A. Fiorini, The Codification of Private International Codification: The Belgian Experience. 54 *Int'l & Comp. L. Q.* 499 (2005); S. Francq, Das belgische IPR-Gesetzbuch, 70 *RabelsZ* 235 (2006); N. Watté & C. Barbé, Le nouveau droit international privé belge: Étude critique des fondements des règles de conflit de lois, *J. dr. int'l (Clunet)* 851 (2006); N. Watté, Les enjeux de la codification du droit international privé belge, in *Mélanges Delnoy* 1133 (2005); (2) BOOKS: J. Erauw & M. Fallon (eds.), Het Wetboek

Internationaal Privaatrecht becommentarieerd—Le Code de droit international privé commenté (2006); J. Erauw & M. Fallon, *De nieuwe wet op het internationaal privaatrecht/La nouvelle loi sur le droit international privé (Recueil de travaux préparatoires)* (2004); F. Rigaux & M. Fallon, *Droit international privé* (3d ed. 2005).

Bosnia-Herzegovina

CODIFICATION: [Former Yugoslav] Act of 15 July 1982 on the Resolution of Conflicts of Laws with Laws and Regulations of Other Countries in Certain Matters. English translation by Ž. Matić in 30 *Neth. Int'l L. Rev.* 220 (1983).

SECONDARY SOURCES: *See* Yugoslavia, *infra.*

Bulgaria

CODIFICATION: Bulgarian Private International Law Code (Law No. 42 of 2005 as amended by Law No. 59 of 2007). English translation at http://solicitorbulgaria.com/index.php/bulgarian-private-intern and http://www.ifrc.org/Docs/idrl/868EN.pdf.

SECONDARY SOURCES: (1) ARTICLES: C. Jessel-Holst, The Bulgarian Private International Law Code of 2005, 9 *Ybk. Priv. Int'l L.* 375 (2007); J. Zidarova & V. Stančeva-Minčeva, Gesetzbuch über das Internationales Privatrecht der Republik Bulgarien, *RabelsZ* 398 (2007); B. Musseva, Das neu internationale Zivilverfahrensrecht Bulgariens in Zivil- und Handelssachen 27 *IPRax* 256 (2007); (2) BOOKS: P. Maesch, *Kodifikation und Anpassung des bulgarischen IPR an das Europäische Recht* (2010); S.P. Parvanov, *New Private International Law Code of Bulgaria* (2006).

Burkina Faso

CODIFICATION: Code of Persons and Family arts. 988–1050 (Law VII 0013 of 19 November 1989, effective 4 August 1990). French text and commentary by P. Meyer, 80 *Rev. critique DIP* 220 (1990); French and German text in J. Kropholler, et al., *Aussereuropäische IPR-Gesetze* 122 (1999).

SECONDARY SOURCES: P. Mayer, *Droit international privé burkinabè et comparé* (1933).

Burundi

CODIFICATION: Code of Persons and Family arts. 1–10, 94, Decree-Law No. 1/1 of 15 January 1980 as revised by Decree-Law No. 1/024 of 28 April 1993, *available at* http://www.ligue-iteka.africa-web.org/article.php3?id_article=36.

Cape Verde

CODIFICATION: Civil Code of Cape Verde, arts. 14–63, adopted by Legislative Decree No. 12-C/97 of 30 June 1997, renewing the force of the Portuguese Civil Code, initially adopted by [Portuguese] Decree-Law No. 47,344 of 25 November 1966 and extended to then Overseas Provinces by Ordinance No. 22,869, of 4 September 1967; *available at* http://www.wipo.int/edocs/lexdocs/laws/pt/cv/cv024pt.pdf (in Portuguese).

Central African Republic

CODIFICATION: Law No. 65-71 of 3 June 1965 regarding the obligatory force of laws and the conflict of laws in time and space, effective on 1 July 1965, arts. 38–45. French text in *Revue critique DIP*, 394 (1973).

Chad

CODIFICATION: Ordinance No. 6 of 21 March 1967 for the Reform of Judicial Organization, arts. 70–72. French and German translations in J. Kropholler et al., *Aussereuropäische IPR-Gesetze* 850 (1999).

China

CODIFICATION: Statute of Application of Law to Foreign Civil Relations, adopted at the 17th session of the Standing Committee of the 11th National People's Congress on 28 October 2010, effective 1 April 2011; English translation by W. Chen & K. Moore, 12 *Ybk. Priv. Int'l L.* 669 (2010). For previous drafts, *see* Draft Statute of the Law Applicable to Civil Relationships Involving Foreign Elements (formerly Book Nine of the Draft Civil Code of 2002). *See also* Chinese Society of Private International Law, Model Law of Private International Law of the People's Republic of China (6th Draft, 2002), 3 *Ybk. Priv. Int'l L.* 349 (2001).

SECONDARY SOURCES: (1) ARTICLES: Weizuo Chen, *Chinese Report*; W. Chen, Chinese Private International Law Statute of 28 October 2010, 12 *Ybk. Priv. Int'l L.* 27 (2010); Y. Gan, Mandatory Rules in Private International Law in the People's Republic of China, 14 *Ybk. Priv. Int'l L.* 305 (2012–2013); Y. Guo, Legislation and Practice on Proof of Foreign Law in China, 14 *Ybk. Priv. Int'l L.* 289 (2012–2013); Q. He, The EU Conflict of Laws Communitarization and the Modernization of Chinese Private International Law, 76 *RabelsZ* 47 (2012); Q. He, Recent Developments with Regards to Choice of Law in Tort in China, 11 *Ybk Priv. Int'l L.* 211 (2009); Q. He, Changes to Habitual Residence in China's *Lex Personalis*, 14 *Ybk. Priv. Int'l L.* 323 (2012–2013); J. Huang, Creation and Perfection of China's Law Applicable to Foreign-Related Civil Relations, 14 *Ybk. Priv. Int'l L.* 269 (2012–2013); J. Huang & H. Du, Chinese Judicial Practice in Private International Codification: 2003, 6 *Chinese J. Int'l L.* 227 (2007); Z. Huo, Reshaping Private International Law in China: The Statutory Reform of Tort Conflicts, 5 *J. of East Asia & Int'l L.* 93 (2012); Z.I. Huo, An Imperfect Improvement: The New Conflict of Laws Act of the People's Republic of China, 60 *Int'l & Comp. L.Q.* 1065 (2011); J. Liang, Statutory Restrictions on Party Autonomy in China's Private International Law of Contract: How Far Does the 2010 Codification Go?, 8 *J. Priv. Int'l L.* 77 (2012); W. Liang, The Applicable Law to Rights in rem under the Act on the Law Applicable to Foreign-Related Civil Relations of the People's Republic of China, 14 *Ybk. Priv. Int'l L.* 353 (2012–2013); W. Long, Act of the People's Republic of China on Application of Law in Civil Relations with Foreign Contacts, *IPRax* 203 (2012); W. Long, The First Choice-of-Law Act of China's Mainland: An Overview, *IPRax* 273 (2012); A.V.Y. Ong, Issues in the Application of Dépeçage in Chinese Private International Law, *Chin. J. Int'l. L* 637 (2009); K.B. Pissler, Das neue Internationale Privatrecht der Volksrepublik China: Nach den Steinen tastend den Fluss überqueren, 76 *RabelsZ* 1 (2012); G. Tu & M. Xu, Contractual Conflicts in the People's Republic of China: The

Applicable Law in the Absence of Choice, 7 *J. Priv. Int'l L.* 179 (2011); G. Tu, China's New Conflicts Code: General Issues and Selected Topics, 59 *Am. J. Comp. L.* 563 (2011); G. Tu, The Codification of Conflict of Laws in China: What Has/Hasn't Yet Been Done for Cross-Border Torts?, 14 *Ybk. Priv. Int'l L.* 341 (2012–2013); Y. Xiao & W. Long, Contractual Party Autonomy in Chinese Private International Law, 11 *Ybk. Priv. Int'l L.* 193 (2009); Y. Xiao & Z. Hou, *Ordre Public* in China's Private International Law, 53 *Am. J. Comp. L.* 653 (2005); T. Xue & G. Zou: Gesetz der Volksrepublik China über die Rechtsanwendung auf Zivilbeziehungen mit Auslandsberührung, *IPRax* 199 (2012); S. Yu, Y. Xiao & B. Wang, The Closest Connection Doctrine in the Conflict of Laws in China, *Chin. J. Int'l L.* 423 (2009); M. Zhang, Codified Choice of Law in China: Rules, Processes and Theoretic Underpinnings, 37 *N.C. J. Int'l L. & Com. Reg.* 83 (2011); M. Zhang, Choice of Law in Contracts: A Chinese Approach, 26 *NW. J. Int'l L. & Bus.* 289 (2006); W. Zhu, The New Conflicts Rules for Family and Inheritance Matters in China, 14 *Ybk. Priv. Int'l L.* 369 (2012–2013); W. Zhu, Codification of Private International Law: The Latest Development in China, 48 *Codicillus* 11 (2007); W. Zhu, China's Codification of the Conflict of Laws: Publication of a Draft Text, 3 *J. Priv. Int'l L.* 283 (2007); (2) BOOKS: R. Cavalieri & P. Franzina, *Il nuovo diritto internazionale privato della Repubblica Popolare Cinese* (2012).

Congo-Brazzaville

CODIFICATION: Family Code, arts. 38–39, 155, 819–832 of Law No. 073/1984 of 17.10.1984. French and German text in J. Kropholler, et al., *Aussereuropäische IPR-Gesetze* 428 (1999).

Costa Rica

CODIFICATION: Civil Code of Costa Rica arts. 23–30, as revised by Law No. 7020 of 6 January 1986.

SECONDARY SOURCES: W. Antillón & G. Trejos, *International Encyclopedia of Comparative: Law, National Reports* 1-C—Costa Rica (1980); J.J. Obando Peralta, *International Encyclopedia of Laws: Private International Law—Republic of Costa Rica* (2013); G. Ortiz Martín, *El Derecho Internacional Privado de Costa Rica* (1969); D. Rissel, *Das internationale Privatrecht von Costa* Rica (2001); F. Rodríguez Serrano, *Introducción al Derecho Internacional Privado* (1988); J. Rosabal Camarillo, *Jurisprudencia sobre Derecho Internacional Privado Costarricense* (2002).

Croatia

CODIFICATION: [Former Yugoslav] Act of 15 July 1982 on the Resolution of Conflicts of Laws with Laws and Regulations of Other Countries in Certain Matters. English translation by Ž. Matić in 30 *Neth. Int'l L. Rev.* 220 (1983).

SECONDARY SOURCES: Davor Babić, *Croatian Report*; P. Bosnić, Hrvatsko medunarodno privatno pravo—obrazloženje i komentar zakona [Croatian Private Interrnational Law—Commentary of the Conflict of Laws Act] (Part 1-1999, Part 2-2003); Ž. Matić, Medunarodno privatno pravo: posebni dio [Private International Law: Special Part] (1982); K. Sajko, Medunarodno privatno pravo [Private International Law] (5th ed. 2009). *See also* Yugoslavia, *infra*.

Cuba

CODIFICATION: Civil Code of 1987, arts. 11–21, adopted by Law No. 59 of 16 July 1987, Gaceta Oficial Extraordinaria of 15 October 1987, effective 12 April 1988.

SECONDARY SOURCES: E. Huzel, Neues internationales Privatrecht in Kuba, 10 *IPRax* 416 (1990); K.S. Tuininga, Cuban Private International Law: Some Observations, Comparisons, and Suppositions, 40 *U. of Miami Inter-Amer. L. Rev.* 401 (2009).

Czech Republic

CODIFICATION: (1) Until 1 January 2014: Czechoslovak Act 97 of 1963 (effective April 1964) on Private International law and Procedure, as amended by Acts No. 158/1969, 234/1992, 264/1992, 125/2002, 37/2004, 257/2004, 361/2004, 377/2005, 57/2006, 70/2006, 233/2006, 296/2007, 123/2008, 7/2009 and 409/2010 Coll.; (2) After 1 January 2014: Law No. 91 of 25 January 2012 on Private International Law, effective 1 January 2014, *available at* http://www.czechlegislation. com/en/91-2012-sb.

SECONDARY SOURCES: (1) ARTICLES: Monika Pauknerová, *Czech Report*; M. Pauknerová, Private International Law in the Czech Republic: Tradition, New Experience and Prohibition of Discrimination on Grounds of Nationality, 4 *J. Priv. Int'l L.* 83 (2008); (2) BOOKS: Z. Kučera, *Mezinárodní právo soukromé* (2009); M. Pauknerová, *Private International Law in the Czech Republic* (2011).

Czechoslovakia

CODIFICATION: Act 97 of 1963 (effective April 1964) on Private International law and Procedure. French translation in 54 *Rev. critique DIP* 614 (1965).

SECONDARY SOURCES: (1) ARTICLES: R. Bystricky, Les traits généraux de la codification tchéco-slovaque sur le droit international privé, 123 *Recueil des Cours* 409 (1968); (2) BOOKS: P. Kalenský, *Trends of Private International Law* (1971); Z. Kučera & L. Tichý, *Zákon o mezinárodním právu soukromém a procesním: Komentář* (1989).

East Timor

CODIFICATION: Civil Code of East Timor, arts. 13–62, enacted by Law No. 10/2011 of 14 September 2011 approving the Civil Code, *available at* http://www.dh-cii.uminho.pt/o_content/investigao/ files_CRDTLA/leis/2011/lei_n._degrees_10-2011_de_14_de_setembro-aprova_o_codigo_civil.pdf.

Ecuador

CODIFICATION: Ecuador Civil Code as revised by Law of 10 May 2005, arts. 13–17, 43, 91–93, 103, 129, 137, 139, 1019, 1057–1058, 1087–1089, and 2337, *available at* http://www.ecuamundo1.com/ lex-dura-lex/c%C3%B3digo-civil-ecuatoriano/.

SECONDARY SOURCES: J. Larrea Holguín, *Derecho internacional privado* (1986); J. Larrea Holguín & M.A. Gómez de la Torre, *Sistema ecuatoriano de derecho internacional privado* (1980); D. Kadner, *Das internationale Privatrecht von Ecuador* (1999); C. Salazar Flor, *Derecho Civil Internacional* (1976).

El Salvador

CODIFICATION: Civil Code of El Salvador, arts. 14–18, 53-55, 617, 740, 966, 994–995, 1021, 1333, and 2160, as revised by Decreto Ley No 724, 30/09/1999, published in Diario Oficial No. 198, T. 345, 23/10/1999.

SECONDARY SOURCES: A. Tiedemann, Neue Kollisionsnormen in El Salvador, 51 *RabelsZ* 120 (1987).

Estonia

CODIFICATION: Private International Law Act of 27 March 2002, effective 1 July 2002, The State Gazette, "Riigi Teataja" I 2002, 35, 217. English translation *available at* http://www.legaltext.ee/etandmebaa/tekst.asp?loc=text&dok=X30075K1&keel=en&pg=1&ptyyp=RT&tyyp=X&query=rahvusvahelise+era%F5iguse.

SECONDARY SOURCES: I. Nurmela, Developments in Estonian Private International Law: Private International Law Act: A Revival of Private International Law?, 7 *Juridica Int'l* 467 (2002); K. Sein, The Development of Private International Law in Estonia, 10 *Ybk. Priv. Int'l L.* 459 (2008); K. Sein, Law Applicable to Persons Pursuant to Draft Private International Law Act, 6 *Juridica Int'l* 135 (2001); M. Torga, Characterisation in Estonian Private International Law: A Proper Tool for Achieving Justice between the Parties?, 18 *Juridica Int'l* 84 (2011).

Finland

CODIFICATION: Hallituksen esitys Eduskunnalle kansainvälisluonteisiin sopimuksiin sovellettavaa lakia koskevaksi lainsäädännöksi, HE 44/1987 vp, p. 25; Act on Law Applicable to Sale of Goods of International Character of 1964, *available at* http://www.finlex.fi/en/laki/kaannokset/196-4/en19640387.pdf; Marriage Act (Act 234/1929, with amendments up to Act 1226/2001), *available at* http://www.finlex.fi/en/laki/kaannokset/1929/en19290234.pdf; Code of Inheritance (Act 40/1965 with amendments up to Act 1228/2001), *available at* http://www.finlex.fi/en/laki/kaannokset/1965/en19650040.pdf.

SECONDARY SOURCES: (1) ARTICLES: Ulla Liukkunen, *Finnish Report*; K. Buure-Hägglund, Codification of Private International Law Rules on Employment Contracts, 24 *Scandin. Stud. L.* 133 (1980); K. Buure-Hägglund, New Finnish Legislation on Law Applicable to Contracts, *IPrax* 407 (1989); E. Jayme, Zur Kodifikation des internationalen Namensrechts in Finnland, *IPRax* 319 (1986); T. Mikkola, A New Map for a Shrinking World: Comparative and Private International Law in Finland, 25 *Retfaerd* 19 (1998); T. Mikkola, The Present Situation of Private International Law in European Union: Finland, *Eur. Leg. Forum* 6 (2005); T. Mikkola, Pleading and Proof of Foreign Law in Finland, 14 *Ybk. Priv. Int'l L.* 465 (2012–2013); A-K. Reich, Neue Kollisionsnormen im finnischen Erbgesetzbuch, *IPrax* 548 (2002); (2) BOOKS: H.T. Klami & E. Kuisma, *Finnish Law as an Option: Private International Law in Finland* (2000); U. Liukkunen, *The Role of Mandatory Rules in International Labour Law—A Comparative Study in the Conflict of Laws* (2004).

FYROM (Former Yugoslav Republic of Macedonia)

CODIFICATION: Private International Law Act of 4 July 2007, effective on 19 July 2008, of the Former Yugoslav Republic of Macedonia. German translation in *IPRax* 579 (2013).

SECONDARY SOURCES: T. Deskoski, The New Macedonian Private International Law Act of 2007, 10 *Ybk Priv. Int'l L.* 441 (2008); C. Jessel-Holst, Zum Gesetzbuch über internationales Privatrecht der Republik Mazedonien, 28 *IPRax* 154 (2008); C. Jessel-Holst, Approximation of the Macedonian Law with the Rome II-Regulation, *IPRax* 572 (2013).

Gabon

CODIFICATION: Civil Code arts. 25–77, Law No. 15/1972 of 29.7.1972 adopting Part I of Civil Code. Official J. Rep. Gabon of 20.12.1972 p.1. Text *available at* http://www.wipo.int/wipolex/en/text.jsp? file_id=209873#LinkTarget_225; French and German text in J. Kropholler, et al, *Aussereuropäische IPR-Gesetze* 246 (1999).

Georgia

CODIFICATION: Act No. 1362 of 29 April 1998 on Private International Law, effective 1 October 1998, *available at* http://laws.codexserver.com/all.htm (in Georgian).

SECONDARY SOURCES: (1) ARTICLES: S. Gamkrelidze, The Law of Georgia on Private International Law, [Rep. of] *Ga. L. Rev. 2nd & 3rd Q.* 20 (1998); (2) BOOKS: R. Knieper, L. Chanturia & H-J. Schramm, *Das Privatrecht im Kaukasus und in Zentralasien: Bestandsaufnahme und Entwicklung* (2010)

Germany

1986 CODIFICATION: Gesetz zur Neuregelung des IPR vom 25.7.1986, Bundesgesetzblatt I/1986, 810. English translation with an introduction by G. Wegen, 27 *I.L.M.* 1, 18 (1988).

SECONDARY SOURCES: Peter Mankowski, *German Report*, also published under the title "The Codification of Private International Law since the 1960s," in J. Basedow, U. Kischel & U. Sieber, U. (eds.), *German National Reports to the 18th International Congress of Comparative Law*, 133 (2010); P. Dopffel, U. Drobnig & K. Siehr, *Reform des deutschen internationalen Privatrechts* (1980); J. Basedow, Die Neuregelung des Internationalen Privat- und Prozeßrechts, *Neue Juristische Wochenschrift*, 2971 (1986); C. Böhmer, Das deutsche Gesetz zur Neuregelung des Internationalen Privatrechts von 1986, 50 *RabelsZ* 646 (1986); B. Dickson, The Reform of Private International Law in the Federal Republic of Germany, 34 *Int'l & Comp. L.Q.* 231 (1985); R. Gildeggen & J. Langkeit, The New Conflict of Laws Code Provisions in the Federal Republic of Germany: Introductory Comment and Translation, 17 *Ga. J. Int'l & Comp. L.* 229 (1987); E. Jayme, Das neue IPR-Gesetz-Brennpunkte der Reform, 6 *IPRax* 265 (1986); A. Lüderitz, Internationales Privatrecht im Übergang-Theoretische und praktische Aspekte der deutschen Reform, in *Festschrift für Kegel* II, 343 (1987); K. Siehr, Codification of Private International Law in the Federal Republic of Germany, 31 *Neth. Int'l L. Rev.* 92 (1984); H. Sonnenberger, Le droit international privé allemand à la fin du vingtième siègle, in S. Symeonides, *PIL at the End of the 20th Century: Progress or Regress?*, 221 (2000); W. Wengler, Zur Technik der internationalprivatrechtlichen Rechtsanwendungsanweisungen des IPR-"Reform" gesetzes von 1986, 53 *RabelsZ* 409 (1989).

1999 CODIFICATION: Gesetz zum IPR für außervertragliche Schuldverhältnisse und das Sachenrecht vom 21.5.1999, Bundesgesetzblatt 1999, I, 1026. English translation by Peter Hay, 47 *Am. J. Comp. L.* 650 (1999); French translation in 88 *Rev. critique DIP* 870 (1999).

SECONDARY SOURCES: (1) ARTICLES: Peter Mankowski, *German Report*; P. Hay, From Rule-Orientation to "Approach" in German Conflicts Law: The Effect of the 1986 and 1999 Codifications, 47 *Am. J. Comp. L.* 633 (1999); K. Kreuzer Die Vollendung der Kodifikation des deutschen Internationalen Privatrechts durch das Gesetz zum Internationalen Privatrecht der außervertraglichen Schuldverhältnisse und Sachen vom 21. 5. 1999, 65 *RabelsZ* 383 (2001); M. Reimann, Codifying Tort Conflicts: The 1999 German Legislation in Comparative Perspective, 60 *La. L. Rev.* 1297 (2000); H. Sonnenberger, La loi allemande du 21 mail 1999 sur le droit international privé des obligations non contractuelles et des biens, 88 *Rev. critique DIP* 647 (1999); (2) BOOKS: D. Looschelders, *Internationales Privatrecht, Art. 3–46 EGBGB* (2004); G. Kegel & K. Schurig, *Internationales Privatrecht* (2004); J. Kropholler, *Internationales Privatrecht* (6th ed. 2006); T. Rauscher, *Internationales Privatrecht* (3d ed. 2009); H. Sonnenberger & R. Birk, *Münchener Kommentar zum Bürgerlichen Gesetzbuch*, v. 10 (5th ed. 2010); C. von Bar & P. Mankowski, *Internationales Privatrecht*, v. 1 (2d ed. 2003), v. 2 (2d ed. 1991); B. von Hoffmann & K. Thorn, *Internationales Privatrecht* (9th ed. 2007).

Guatemala

CODIFICATION: Ley del Organism Judicial, arts. 21–35, Decreto 2-89, of 18.3.1989, *available at* www.oj.gob.gt/.../index.php?option=com.

SECONDARY SOURCES: C. Larios Ochaita, *Derecho Internacional Privado* (1998); C. Hall Lloreda, *Concepto, Caracteres y Funciones del Derecho Internacional Privado* (1964).

Guinea-Bissau

CODIFICATION: Civil Code of Guinea-Bissau, arts. 14–65, initially enacted by Portuguese Ordinance No. 22,869, of 4 September 1967 and renewed by Guinea-Bissau Law No. 1/73 of 27 September 1973, published in Boletim Oficial No. 1, of 4 January 1975; *available at* http://www. fdbissau.org/PDF_files/cod[1]-leg-ultimaversao.pdf (in Portuguese).

Hungary

CODIFICATION: Law-Decree No. 13 of 1979 on Private International Law; published in English in *The Statutes of the Hungarian People's Republic* (1982), with an introduction by F. Mádl. For another English translation and discussion, *see* F. Gabor, A Socialist Approach to Codification of Private International Law in Hungary: Comments and Translation, 55 *Tul. L. Rev.* 63 (1980). For a consolidated version incorporating all amendments adopted after Hungary's membership in the EU, see C.I. Nagy, *Hungary*, in *International Encyclopedia of Laws: Private International Law* 151 (2012).

SECONDARY SOURCES: (1) ARTICLES: Katalin Raffai & Sarolta Szabó, *Hungarian Report*, published under the title "Selected Issues on Recent Hungarian Private International Law Codification" in 51 *Acta Jurid. Hungarica* 136 (2010); G. Roman, Conflict of Laws Solutions in the Hungarian New Private International Law, 10 *Int'l J. Leg. Inform.* 169 (1982); L. Burián, Hungarian PIL at the End of the 20th Century, in S. Symeonides, *PIL at the End of the 20th Century: Progress or Regress?* 263 (2000); L. Burián, Private International Law in Hungary, 2 *Ybk. Priv. Int'l L.* 157 (2000); L. Kecskés, European Union Legislation and Private International Law: A View from Hungary, in P. Hay et al. (eds.), *Resolving International Conflicts: Liber*

Amicorum Várady Tibor, 165 (2009); F. Mádl, System and Principles of the Hungarian Code of Private International Law, 44 *Rev. Hellénique dr. int'l* 227 (1991); G.P. Palásti, The Future Impact of the Rome Convention on Hungarian Conflict Rules, 3(1) *European Integration Studies* 57 (2004); O. Zoltan Odon, La nouvelle réglementation hongroise du droit international privé, 32 *Rev. int'le dr. comp.* 87 (1980); (2) BOOKS: L. Burián, L. Kecskés & I. Vörös, *Magyar nemzetközi kollíziós magánjog* (2005); C. Jessel, *Zur Kodifikation des ungarischen Internationalen Privatrechts* (1979); F. Mádl & L. Vékás, *Nemzetközi magánjog és nemzetközi gazdasági kapcsolatok joga* (2004); F. Mádl & L. Vékás, *The Law of Conflicts and of International Economic Relations* (1998); C.I. Nagy, *Private International Law in Hungary* (2012).

Italy

CODIFICATION: Act No. 218 of 31 May 1995 (Riforma del sistema italiano di diritto internazionale privato). For Italian text, see *Riv. dir. Int'le priv. & proc.* 905 (1995), with a commentary by several authors. English translations 35 *I.L.M.* 765 (1995) (with introduction by A. Giardina); A. Montanari & V. A. Narcisi, *Conflict of Laws in Italy* (1997).

SECONDARY SOURCES: (1) ARTICLES: T. Ballarino & A. Bonomi, The Italian Statute on Private International Law, 2 *Ybk. Priv. Int'l L.* 99 (2000); T. Ballarino, Personnes, famille, régimes matrimoniaux et successions dans la loi de réforme du droit international privé, 85 *Rev. critique DIP* 21 (1996); A. Giardina, Les charactères généraux de la réform, 85 *Rev. critique DIP* 1 (1996); A. Giardina, Criteri ispiratori e tecniche di un'eventuale riforma di diritto internazionale privato, *Riv. Dir. Int. Priv. Proc.* (1995); P. Mengozzi, *International Encyclopedia of Laws: Private International Law—Italy* (v. 3, 2005); F. Pocar & C. Honorati, Italian PIL at the End of the 20th Century, in S. Symeonides, *Progress or Regress?*, at 279; F. Pocar, Le droit des obligations dans le nouveau droit international privé italien, 85 *Rev. critique DIP* 41 (1996); (2) BOOKS: T. Ballarino, *Diritto internazionale privato: La Legge n. 218/95(riforma del dip) esplicata articolo per articolo, il diritto internazionale privato dell'Unione europea, altre convenzioni internazionali* (2006); T. Ballarino, *Diritto internazionale privato italiano* (11th ed. 2011); N. Boschiero, *Appunti sulla riforma del sistema italiano di diritto internazionale privato* (1996); CEDAM, *Le nuove leggi civili commentate* (1995); G. Conetti, S. Tonolo & F. *Vismara, F., Commento alla riforma del diritto internazionale privato italiano* (2nd ed. 2009); G. Gaja & E. Vitta, *La riforma del Diritto internazionale privato e processuale: Raccolta in riccordo di Edoardo Vitta* (1994); P. Mengozzi, *Italy*, in *International Encyclopedia of Laws: Private International Law* (2004); P. Mengozzi, *La riforma del diritto internazionale privato italiano* (2000); F. Pocar, T. Treves, S.M. Carbone, A. Giardia, R Luzzatto, F. Mosconi & R. Clerici, *Commentario Del Nuovo Diritto Internazionale Privato* (1996); F. Mosconi & C. Campiglio, *Diritto internazionale privato e processuale: Parte generale e obbligazioni* (2010); P. Picone, *La riforma italiana del diritto internazionale privato* (1998); F. Pocar, *Il nuovo diritto internazionale privato* (2002);

Japan

CODIFICATION: Law No. 10 of 1898 as Newly Titled and Amended on 21 June 2006, effective 1 January 2007, on the General Rules of Application of Laws [Hô no tekiyô ni kan suru tsûsoku-hô]. English translation by K. Anderson & Y. Okuda, 8 *Ybk Priv. Int'l L.* 427 (2006) and 8 *Asian-Pacific L. & Pol'y J.* (2006); German translation in 27 *IPRax* 560 (2007).

SECONDARY SOURCES: (1) ARTICLES: Tadashi Kanzaki, *Japanese Report;* R. Brand & T. Fish, An American Perspective on the New Japanese Act on General Rules for Application of Laws, *Japan. Ybk. Int'l L.* 298 (2009); M. Dogauchi, New Private International Law of Japan: An Overview, 50 *Japan. Ann. Int'l L.* 3 (2007); Y. Hayakawa, New Private International Law of Japan: General Rules on Contracts, 50 *Japan. Ann. Int'l L.* 25 (2007); T. Kanzaki, New Private International Law of Japan: Persons, 50 *Japan. Ann. Int'l L.* 15 (2007); A. Kitazawa, New Private International Law of Japan: Assignment of Receivables and Set-Off, 50 *Japan. Ann. Int'l L.* 77 (2007); Y. Nishitani, New Private International Law of Japan: Protection of Weaker Parties and Mandatory Rules, 50 *Japan. Ann. Int'l L.* 40 (2007); Y. Okuda, Reform of Japan's Private International Law: Act on the General Rules of the Application of Laws, 8 *Ybk Priv. Int'l L.* 145 (2006); Y. Okuda, A Short Look at Rome I on Contract Conflicts from a Japanese Perspective, 10 *Ybk. Priv. Int'l L.* 301 (2008); Y. Okuda, New Provisions on International Jurisdiction of Japanese Courts, 13 *Ybk. Priv. Int'l L.* 367 (2011); Y. Sakurada & E. Schwittek, The Reform of Japanese Private International Law, 76 *RabelsZ* 86 (2012); R. Yamakawa, Transnational Dimension of Japanese Labor and Employment Laws: New Choice of Law Rules and Determination of Geographical Reach, 31 *Comp. Lab. L. & Pol'y J.* 347 (2010). For the previous law, *see* Horei Application of Laws (General) Act No.10, as amended by 1986 No.84; Chin Kim, New Japanese Private International Law: The 1990 Horei, 40 *Am. J. Comp. L.* 1 (1992); (2) BOOKS: J. Basedow, H. Baum & Y. Nishitani (eds.), *Japanese and European Private International Law in Comparative Perspective* (2008); K. Ishiguro, *Kokusaishiho* (Private International Law) (2d ed. 2007); T. Kanzaki, *Kaisetsu Ho no Tekiyo ni kansuru Tsusoku Ho* (The Outline of the Act on General Rules for Application of Laws) (2006); S. Kidana, H. Matsuoka & S. Watanabe, *Kokusaishiho Gairon* (Private International Law in Outline) (5th ed. 2007); K. Koide et. al.,*Chikujou Kaisetsu Ho no Tekiyo ni kansuru Tsusoku Ho* (Article-by-Article Commentary on the Act on General Rules for Application of Laws) (2009); H. Matsuoka, *Gendai Kokusaishiho Kogi* (Lecture on Private International Law Today) (2008); Y. Sakurada, *Kokusaishiho* (Private International Law in a Nutshell) (5th ed. 2006); T. Sawaki & M. Dogauchi, *Kokusaishiho Nyumon* (Introduction to Private International Law) (6th ed. 2006).

Jordan

CODIFICATION: Jordanian Civil Code of 1 August, 1976 arts. 1–3, 11–29 (effective 1 Jan. 1977) J.O. no 2645 of 1 Aug. 1976. French translation with comments by S. Aldeeb Abu-Sahlieh in 76 *Rev. critique DIP* 643 (1987).

SECONDARY SOURCES: H. Krüger, Jordanische Rechtsprechung zum Kollisionsrecht, *IPRax* 539 (2009).

Kazakhstan

CODIFICATION: Civil Code of the Republic of Kazakhstan, arts. 1158–1124, enacted by Law No. 409-1 ZRK of 1 July 1999. English translation in W.E. Butler (ed.), *Civil Code of the Republic Kazakhstan* (4th ed. 1999).

SECONDARY SOURCES: A. Weishaupt, Neues Kollisions- und Internationales Zivilprozessrecht in der Republik Kasachstan, *IPRax* 53 (2002).

Korea (North)

CODIFICATION: Minju-juui innin konghwaguk tae'oe minsa kwan'gye bop (The Law of the Democratic People's Republic of Korea on External Civil Relations) adopted by Resolution No. 62 of the Standing Committee of the Supreme People's Assembly on 6 September 1995, and amended by Decree No. 251 of the Presidium of the Supreme People's Assembly on 10 December 1998; *available at* http://www.nkeconwatch.com/nk-uploads/Compilation-of-laws.pdf; English translation and discussion by Chin Kim, The 1995 Private International Law of North Korea, 29 *Cal. West. Int'l L. J.* 205 (1998).

Korea (South)

CODIFICATION: Law 6465 of 7 April 2001, effective 1 July 2001, Amending the Conflict of Laws Act of the Republic of Korea. English translation by K.H. Suk, 5 *Ybk. Priv. Int'l L.* 315 (2003); German translation in 27 *IPRax* 479 (2007).

SECONDARY SOURCES: (1) ARTICLES: Kwang Hyun Suk, *South Korean Report*; K.H. Suk, The New Conflict of Laws Act of the Republic of Korea, 5 *Ybk. Priv. Int'l L.* 99 (2003); K.B. Pissler, Das neue IPR der Republik Korea, 70 *RabelsZ* 279 (2006); (2) BOOKS: Beopmubu (Ministry of Justice), *Gukjesabeip Haeseol* (Commentary on the New Conflict of Laws of Korea) (2001); K.H. Suk, *Gukjesabeop Haeseol* (Commentary on Private International Law) (2d ed. 2003).

Kyrgyzstan

CODIFICATION: Law of 5 January 1998 revising Civil Code arts. 1167–1208. German translation in 24 *IPRax* 274 (2004); English translation at http://www.libertas-institut.com/de/Mittel-Osteuropa/Civil%20Code%20part%20II.pdf.

SECONDARY SOURCES: H. Krüger & J. Braun, Das Kollisionsrecht der Republik Kirgisistan, *IPRax* 270 (2004).

Latvia

CODIFICATION: Latvian Civil Code of 1993, arts. 8–25. English translation *available at* http://www.ebrd.com/downloads/legal/core/latvia.pdf.

SECONDARY SOURCES: J.R. Bojars, *Starptautiskās privāttiesības* (2010).

Liechtenstein

CODIFICATION: Private International Law Act of 1996, Liechensteinisches Landesgesetzblatt 1996 No. 194; also published in *RabelsZ* 545 (1997) and *17 IPrax* 364 (1997), with a note by C. Kohler, at *id.* 209; French translation in 86 *Rev. critique DIP* 858 (1997).

SECONDARY SOURCES: (1) ARTICLES: A. Appel, Reform und Kodifikation des Liechtensteinischen Internationalen Privatrechts, 61 *RabelsZ* 510 (1997); H. Heiss, Zur Kodifikation des liechtensteinischen internationalen Privatrechts, in K. Ebert (ed.), *Pro Justitia et Scientia: Festgabe zum 80 Geburtstag von Karl Kohlegger* 263 (2001); C. Kohler, Kodifikation und Reform des Internationalen Privatrechts in Liechtenstein, *IPRax* 309 (1997); (2) BOOKS: F. Sturm, *Das neue Internationale Privatrecht Liechtensteins* (1997).

Lithuania

CODIFICATION: Civil Code of the Republic of Lithuania of 2000, arts. 1.10–1.62. English translation at http://www3.lrs.lt/pls/inter3/dokpaieska. showdoc_l?p_id =245495; German translation in 23 *IPRax* 298 (2003), with a note by Pavluševičius at *id*. 272.

SECONDARY SOURCES: (1) ARTICLES: V. Mikelėnas, Reform of Private International Law in Lithuania, 7 *Ybk. Priv. Int'l L.* 161 (2005); (2) BOOKS: V. Mikelėnas, *Tarptautinės privatinės teisės* (An Introduction to Private International Law) (2001).

Louisiana

CODIFICATION: Book IV of the Louisiana Civil Code, enacted into law by La. Act No. 923 of 1991, effective 1 January 1992. French translation in 81 *Rev. critique DIP* 223 (1992); German translation in 57 *RabelsZ* 508 (1993), and 13 *IPRax* 56 (1993-1).

SECONDARY SOURCES: P. Borchers, Louisiana's Conflicts Codification: Some Empirical Observations regarding Decisional Predictability, 60 *La. L. Rev.* 1061 (2000) E. Jayme, Neue Kodifikation des Internationalen Privatrechts in Louisiana, 13 *IPRax* 56 (1993-1); J.P. Kozyris, Values and Methods in Choice of Law for Products Liability: A Comparative Comment on Statutory Solutions, 38 *Am. J. Comp. L.* 475 (1990); R.A. Sedler, The Louisiana Codification and Tort Rules of Choice of Law, 60 *La. L. Rev.* 1331 (2000); S. Symeonides, The Conflicts Book of the Louisiana Civil Code: Civilian, American or Original, 83 *Tul. L. Rev.* 1041 (2009); S. Symeonides, Private International Law Codification in a Mixed Jurisdiction: The Louisiana Experience, 57 *RabelsZ* 460 (1993); S. Symeonides, Les grands problèmes de droit international privé et la nouvelle codification de Louisiane, 81 *Rev. critique DIP* 223 (1992); S. Symeonides, La nuova normativa della Louisiana sul diritto internazionale privato in tema di responsabilità extracontrattuale, 29 *Riv. dir. Int'le priv. e proc.* 43 (1993); S. Symeonides, Louisiana's New Law of Choice of Law for Tort Conflicts: An Exegesis, 66 *Tul. L. Rev.* 677 (1992); S. Symeonides, Louisiana Conflicts Law: Two "Surprises," 54 *La. L. Rev.* 497 (1994); R. Weintraub, The Contributions of Symeonides and Kozyris in Making Choice of Law Predictable and Just: An Appreciation and Critique, 38 *Am. J. Comp. L.* 511 (1990); R. Weintraub, Courts Flailing in the Waters of the Louisiana Conflicts Code: Not Waving but Drowning, 60 *La. L. Rev.* 1365 (2000).

Macau

CODIFICATION: Civil Code of Macau, arts. 13–62, Approved by Law-Decree No. 39/99 of 3 August 1999, *available at* http://www.al.gov.mo/lei/codigo/civil/po/p0001-0200.htm. Portuguese text and English translation by A. Marques dos Santos, see 2 *Ybk Priv. Int'l L.* 329, 343 (2000).

SECONDARY SOURCES: (1) ARTICLES: Tu Guangjian, *Macau Report*, published under the title "The Conflict of Laws System in Macau" in 40 *Hong Kong L.J.* 85 (2010); R.M. Moura Ramos, The Private International Law Rules of the New Special Administrative Region of Macau of the People's Republic of China, 60 *La. L. Rev.* 1281 (2000); A. Marques Dos Santos, The New Private international Law Rules of Macao, 2 *Ybk. Priv. Int'l L.* 133 (2000); (2) BOOKS: Jin Huang & Huacheng Guo, *General Part of Private International Law in Macau* (1997).

Madagascar

CODIFICATION: Arts. 20–35, Ordonnance No. 62-041 du 19 septembre 1962 relative aux dispositions générales de droit interne et de droit international privé (J.O no. 244 du 28-9-62, p1989), complétée par la loi no. 98-019 du 2 décembre 1998 (J.O. no. 2549 du 15.12.98, p. 3642 et 3654; Errata: J.O. no. 2571 du 26.04.99, p.1060), *available at* http://www.jafbase.fr/docAfrique/Madagascar/LoiDIP.pdf.

Mauritania

CODIFICATION: Code des Obligations et des Contrats, arts. 6–11, Ordonnance no. 89-126 du 14 septembre 1989, JO of the Islamic Republic of Mauritania no. 739 of du 25 octobre 1989. French text and German translation in J. Kropholler, et al, *Aussereuropäische IPR-Gesetze* 522 (1999).

SECONDARY SOURCES: H. Krüger, Das internationale Privat- und Zivilverfahrensrecht Mauretaniens, *RIW* 988 (1990).

Mexico

CODIFICATION: Arts. 12–15, 29–34, 2736–2738 of Civil Code for the Federal District in Ordinary Matters and for the Entire Republic in Federal Matters, as amended by Decree of 11 December 1987 (effective 8 January 1988), Diario official, 7Jan. 1988, p.2.

SECONDARY SOURCES: (1) ARTICLES: J. Alberto Silva, Derecho internacional privado en México su estado actual, in N. Gonzalez Martin & D. Fernández Arroyo (eds.), *Tendencias y relaciones del derecho internacional privado americano actual* 135 (2010); D. Fernández Arroyo, What's New in Latin American Private International Law?, 7 *Ybk Priv. Int'l L.* 85 (2005); L. Pereznieto Castro, The Revolution of Private International Law in the World at Present, Regarding the Mexican Case, in *A Commitment to Private International Law: Essays in Honour of Hans Van Loon* 453 (2013); J. Vargas, Conflict of Laws in Mexico: The New Rules Introduced by the 1988 Amendments, 28 *Int'l Lawyer* 659 (1994); (2) BOOKS: F.A. Vázquez Pando, *El nuevo derecho internacional privado mexicano: Introducción y selección de fuentes* (1990); F. Cuevas Cancino, *Manual de Derecho Internacional Privado Mexicano* (1997); L. Pereznieto Castro, *Derecho internacional privado. Parte General* (9th ed. 2011); J.A. Silva, *Derecho internacional privado sobre el proceso* (3d ed. 2011).

Moldova

CODIFICATION: Moldova Civil Code (Law 1107 of 6 June 2002), arts. 1578–1625. Romanian text at http://lex.justice.md/index.php?action=view&view=doc&lang=1&id=325085. English translation at http://cis-legislation.com/document.fwx?rgn=3244, http://www.ebrd.com/downloads/legal/core/moldova.pdf and http://www.docstoc.com/docs/134775627/MOLDOVA-CIVIL-CODE-EBRD.

SECONDARY SOURCES: N. Osoianu, Application of Foreign Law in the International Private Law of the Republic of Moldova, 3–4 *Riv. Stud. Jurid. Univ.* (2010), *available at* http://studiijuridice.md/revista-nr-3-4-2010/application-of-foreign-law-in-the- international- private-law-of-the-republic-of-moldova.

Mongolia

CODIFICATION: Mongolian Civil Code, arts. 539–552, enacted 2 January 2002, effective 1 September 2002. English translation *available at* http://www.investmongolia.com/law04.pdf; German translation in 23 *IPRax* 381 (2003), with a note by D. Nelle, at *id.* 378.

Montenegro

CODIFICATION: [Former Yugoslav] Act of 15 July 1982 on the Resolution of Conflicts of Laws with Laws and Regulations of Other Countries in Certain Matters. English translation by Ž. Matić in 30 *Neth. Int'l L. Rev.* 220 (1983).

SECONDARY SOURCES: M. Kostič-Mandić, M. Stanivukovič & M. Zivkovič, *International Encyclopaedia of Laws: Private International Law—Montenegro* (2010). *See also* Yugoslavia, *infra*.

Mozambique

CODIFICATION: Mozambique Civil Code, arts. 14–65, adopted by Portuguese Law-Decree No. 47,344 of 25 November 1966, and extended to Mozambique by ordinance No. 22,869 of 4 September 1967. Portuguese text and German translation in J. Kropholler et al. (eds.), *Aussereuropäische IPR-Gesetze* 566 (1999).

Netherlands

CODIFICATION: Act of 19 May 2011 adopting and implementing Book 10 (Private International Law) of the Dutch Civil Code, Bulletin of Acts and Decrees 2011, 272. Decree of 28 June 2011 fixing the time of entry into force of the Adoption and Implementation Act of Book 10, Bulletin of Acts and Decrees 2011, 340; English translation by M.H. Ten Wolde, J.G. Knot & N.A. Baarsma, at 13 *Ybk. Priv. Int'l L.* 654 (2011); French text in *Rev. critique DIP* 1058 (2012).

SECONDARY SOURCES: Katharina Boele-Woelki & Dorothea Van Iterson, *Dutch Report*, posted under the title "The Dutch Private International Law Codification: Principles, Objectives and Opportunities," 14.3 *Electron. J. Comp. L.* (Dec. 2010), http://www.ejcl.org/143/art143-3.pdf; T.M. de Boer, Naar een gecodificeerd internationaal privaatrecht, 101 *Consult. Rpts. for the Netherlands Soc'y Int'l L.* 3 (1990); H.U. Jessurun d'Oliveira, Is een codificatie van het Nederlandse IPR nog zinvol? Oftewel, geloven we nog in Boek 10 BW? *NTBR* 425 (2005); M.V. Polak, Naar een gecodificeerd internationaal privaatrecht, 101 *Consult. Rpts. for the Netherlands Soc'y Int'l L.* 51 (1990); P. Vlas, On the Development of Private International Law in the Netherlands: From Asser's Days to the Codification of Dutch Private International Law (1910–2010), 57 *Netherlands Int'l L. Rev.* 167 (2010); P. Vlas, Boek 10 BW (IPR): lang verwacht, toch gekomen: wetsvoorstel Boek 10 BW (IPR), 6819 *WPNR* 893 (2009); A.P.M.J. Vonken, Boek 10 BW: meer—incomplete—consolidatie dan codificatie van het Nederlandse internationaal privaatrecht, *Ned. IPR* 399 (2010); M.H. Ten Wolde, Codification and Consolidation of Dutch Private International Law: The Book 10 Civil Code of the Netherlands, 13 *Ybk. Priv. Int'l L.* 389 (2011); M.H. Ten Wolde, De mysteries van het fait accompli en boek 10 BW, *Ned. IPR* 430 (2010); (2) BOOKS: K. Boele-Woelki, *Internationaal Privaatrecht: verordeningen, verdragen & wetten 2011/2013* (2013); L. Strikwerda, *Inleiding tot het Nederlandse Internationaal Privaatrecht* (9th ed. 2008); P. Vlas, *Hoofdlijnen Boek 10 BW (internationaal privaatrecht)* (2011).

Oregon

CODIFICATION: (1) For contracts: Or. Rev. Stat. §§ 15.300–15.380 (2001); (2) For torts: Or. Rev. Stat. §§ 15.400–15.460 (2009).

SECONDARY SOURCES: J. Nafziger, Oregon's Conflicts Law Applicable to Contracts, 38 *Willamette L. Rev.* 397 (2002); S. Symeonides, Codifying Choice of Law for Contracts: The Oregon Experience, 67 *RabelsZ* (2003); S. Symeonides, Oregon's Choice-of-Law Codification for Contract Conflicts: An Exegesis, 44 *Willamette L. Rev.* 205 (2007); S. Symeonides, Oregon's New Choice-of-Law Codification for Tort Conflicts: An Exegesis, 88 *Or. L. Rev.* 963 (2009); S. Symeonides, Codifying Choice of Law for Tort Conflicts: The Oregon Experience in Comparative Perspective, 12 *Ybk Priv. Int'l L.* 17 (2011); H. Stoll, Die Kodifikation des internationalen Privatrechts der außerverträglichen Haftung im Staate Oregon, 2009, in H. Kronke & K. Thorn (eds.), *Grenzen überwinden, Prinzipien bewahren: Festschrift für Bernd von Hoffmann zum 70. Geburtstag am 28. Dezember 2011*, 448 (2012).

Panama

CODIFICATION: Panama Civil Code, arts. 1, 5–8, 631–632, 765–770, as revised by Law No. 18 of 1992; Panama Family Code, arts. 6–11, as revised by Law No. 3 of 17 May 1994. Spanish text and German translation in J. Kropholler et al. (eds.), *Aussereuropäische IPR-Gesetze* 630 (1999).

SECONDARY SOURCES: G. Boutin, *Derecho Internacional Privado* (2002); G. Boutin, *De los conflictos de leyes en el derecho de familia en el Código de Bustamante y en el derecho panameno* (1987).

Paraguay

CODIFICATION: Civil Code of Paraguay as revised by Law No. 1183 of 18 December 1985, arts. 11–26, 101, 132–136, 163–167, 177–178, 297, 699, 1196, 1199, 2184, 2447–2448, 2609, and 2626. French translation in *Rev. critique DIP* 469 (1987); German translation in *RabelsZ* 454 (1987).

SECONDARY SOURCES: (1) ARTICLES: M. Baus, Der neue Código Civil von Paraguay und seine Kollisionsnormen, 51 *RabelsZ* 440 (1987); A. Sánchez Mussi, El derecho internacional privado del Paraguay, in N. Gonzalez Martin & D. Fernandez Arroyo (eds.), *Tendencias y relaciones del derecho internacional privado americano actual* 121 (2010); (2) BOOKS: J.A. Moreno Rodríguez, *Dos Tesis Sobre Contratos* (2007); R. Ruiz Díaz Labrano, *Derecho Internacional Privado* (2010); R. Silva Alonso, *Derecho Internacional Privado* (2012).

Peru

CODIFICATION: Peruvian Civil Code of 1984, Book X (arts. 2046–2111). Spanish text, in 129 Normas Legales, 128 (Oct. 1984). English translation with an introduction by Alejandro Garro, 25 *I.L.M.* 997 (1985).

SECONDARY SOURCES: (1) ARTICLES: J. Samtleben, Neues Internationales Privatrecht in Peru, 49 *RabelsZ* 486 (1985); (2) BOOKS: J. Basadre Ayulo, *Derecho Internacional Privado* (2000); C. Delgado Barreto, M.A. Delgado Menéndez & C.L. Candela Sanchez, *Introducción Al Derecho Internacional Privado* v. 1 (2004), v. 2 (2008); D. Revoredo, *Código Civil Peruano, Tomo VI. Exposición de Motivos y Comentarios* (1985); M. del Carmen Tovar Gil & J. Tovar Gil, *Derecho Internacional Privado* (1987).

Poland

CODIFICATION: Act of Private International Law of 4 February 2011, Ustawa z dnia 4 lutego 2011 r. Prawo prywatne międzynarodowe, Dz U. z dnia 15 kwiethnia 2011 r. nr 80, poz. 432; English translation in 13 *Ybk. Priv. Int'l L.* 641 (2011). For the old codification, *see* Act of 12 November 1965, effective 1 July 1966, on Private International Law.

SECONDARY SOURCES: (1) ARTICLES: M. Pazdan, *Polish Report;* U. Ernst, The Polish Private International Law Act of 2011—National Recodification in Times of Exercise of Supranational Competences, 76 *RabelsZ* 597 (2012); T. Pajor, Introduction to the New Polish Act on Private International Law of 4 February 2011, 13 *Ybk. Priv. Int'l L.* 381 (2011); T. Pajor, La nouvelle loi polonaise de droit international privé, 101 *Rev. critique DIP* 5 (2012); M. Pazdan, Das neue polnische Gesetz über das internationale Privatrecht, *IPRax* 77 (2012). For the 1964 codification, *see* D. Lasok, The Polish System of Private International Law, 15 *Am. J. Comp. L.* 330 (1967); J. Rajski, The New Polish Private International Law 1965, 15 *Int'l & Comp. L.Q.* 457 (1966); T. Pajor, Polish PIL at the End of the 20th Century, in S. Symeonides, *Private International Law at the End of the 20th Century: Progress or Regress?* 329 (2000); (2) BOOKS: M. Pazdan, *Prawo prywatne międzynarodowe* (12th ed. 2009); J. Kosik, *Zagadnienia prawa rzeczowego prawie prywatnym międzynarodowym z 1965* (1976).

Portugal

CODIFICATION: Portuguese Civil Code, arts. 14–65, as revised in 1966. French translation, Asser Instituut, *Les legislations de droit international privé* 157 (1971), with an introductory note by A. Ferrer-Correia and Baptista-Machado; and 57 *Rev. Critique DIP* 369 (1968); Law no. 496/77 (revising 1966 codification in line with Portugal's new constitution). French translation in 67 *Rev. Critique DIP* 598 (1978).

SECONDARY SOURCES: (1) ARTICLES: Luís de Lima Pinheiro, *Portuguese Report*; A. Ferrer Correia, Les problèmes de codification en droit international privé, 145 *Recueil des Cours* 55 (1975); L. de Lima Pinheiro, Algumas reflexões sobre a codificação portuguesa do Direito Internacional Privado, in J. Miranda (ed.), *Estudos em Homenagem ao Prof. Doutor Sérvulo Correia* 743 (2011); R.M. Moura Ramos, Le droit international privé portugais, in S. Symeonides, *Progress or Regress?*, at 349; R.M. Moura Ramos, Portugal Droit de la famille Dispositions intéressant le droit international privé, 67 *Rev. critique DIP* 598 (1978); Almeno de Sá, A revisão do Código Civil e a Constituição, 3 *Rev. Dir. e Econ.* 425 (1977); (2) BOOKS: J. Baptista Machado, *Lições de Direito Internacional Privado* (2d ed. 1982); A. Ferrer Correia, *Direito Internacional Privado I: Alguns Problemas* (1981); A. Ferrer Correia, *Lições de Direito Internacional Privado* (2000); I. Garcia Velasco, *Conception del derecho internacional privado en el nuevo Código civil portuques* (1971); L. de Lima Pinheiro, *Direito Internacional Privado* (2d ed. 2008); L. de Lima Pinheiro, *Direito Internacional Privado, v. I—Introdução e Direito de Conflitos: Parte Geral* (2013), v. II *Direito de Conflitos: Parte Especial* (2009); A. Marques Dos Santos, *Direito Internacional Privado* (2001).

Puerto Rico

DRAFT CODIFICATION: Proyecto de Ley para la Revisión y Reforma del Código Civil De Puerto Rico, Libro Séptimo (Derecho Internacional Privado), por Symeon Symeonides, 25 de mayo 2002, available at http://www.codigocivilpr.net/. For an earlier version, *see* Academia Puertorriqueña de Jurisprudencia y Legislacion, Proyecto para la Codificación del Derecho internacional privado de Puerto Rico (S. Symeonides & A. von Mehren, Rapporteurs, 1991).

SECONDARY SOURCES: M. Figueroa-Torres, Recodification of Civil Law in Puerto Rico: A Quixotic Pursuit of the Civil Code for the New Millennium, 23 *Tul. Eur. Civ. L.F.* 143 (2008); S. Symeonides, Revising Puerto Rico's Conflicts Law: A Preview, 28 *Colum. J. Transnat'l L.*, 413 (1990); S. Symeonides, Codifying Choice of Law for Contracts: The Puerto Rico Projet, in J. Nafziger & S. Symeonides eds., *Law and Justice in a Multistate World: Essays in Honor of Arthur T. von Mehren*, 419 (2002).

Qatar

CODIFICATION: Arts. 10–38 of the Civil Code of Qatar, as amended by law 22/2004 of 8 August 2004. English translation *available at* Qatar Legal Portal http://xn--mgba6a9dfiz.xn--wgbl6a/LawArticles.aspx?LawTreeSectionID=8880&LawID=2559&language=en.

SECONDARY SOURCES: M. Najm, Codification of Private International Law in the Civil Code of Qatar, 8 *Ybk. Priv. Int'l L.* 249 (2006).

Quebec

CODIFICATION: L.Q. 1991, ch. 64 (adopted in 1991, effective 1994) and composing Book Ten of the Quebec Civil Code (arts. 3076–3168). *available a*t http://www2.publicationsduquebec.gouv.qc.ca/dynamicSearch/telecharge.php?type=2&file=/CCQ_1991/CCQ1991_A.html.

SECONDARY SOURCES: (1) ARTICLES: Frédérique Sabourin, *Quebec Report;* E. Groffier, *La réforme du droit international privé québécois* (1993); J.G. Castel, Commentaire sur certaines dispositions du Code civil du Québec se rapportant au droit international privé, *Clunet* 625 (1992); H.P. Glenn, Codification of Private International Law in Quebec, 60 *RabelsZ* 231 (1996); H.P. Glenn, Réflexions sur la codification du droit international privé au Quebec et en Europe, 11 *Rev. Dr. Univ. Sherbrooke* 231 (1980); G. Goldstein, Les règles générales du statut des obligations contractuelles dans le droit international privé du nouveau Code Civil du Québec, (1993) 53 *R. du B. 197*, 205 (1993); A. Prujiner, Canadian PIL at the End of the 20th Century, in S. Symeonides, *Progress or Regress?*, at 127 A. Prujiner & S. Guillemard, La codification internationale du droit international privé: Un échec? 46 *Les Cahiers de Droit* 175 (2005); J. Talpis & G. Goldstein, The Influence of Swiss Law on Quebec's 1994 Codification of Private International Law, *Ybk. Priv. Int'l L.* 339 (2009); (2) BOOKS: J.G. Castel, *Droit international privé québécois* (1980); C. Emanuelli, *Droit international privé québécois* (2d ed. 2006); E. Groffier, *La réforme du droit international privé québécois: Supplément au Précis de droit international privé québécois* (1993); G. Goldstein, *De l'exception d'ordre public aux règles d'application nécessaire* (1996); G. Goldstein & E. Groffier, *Droit international privé, v. 1, Théorie générale* (1998); J.A. Talpis & J.G. Castel, *Le Code civil du Québec: Interprétation des règles du droit international privé, in La réforme du Code civil* (1993).

Romania

CODIFICATION: Law No. 105 of 22 September 1992, effective 26 October 1993, on the Settlement of Private International Law Relations, Official Gazette of Romania No. 245 of 1 October 1992, German translation in *RabelsZ* 534 (1994).

SECONDARY SOURCES: (1) ARTICLES: C. Avasilencei, La codification des conflits de lois dans le nouveau Code civil roumain: Une nouvelle forme en attente d'un contentieux, 101 *Rev. critique DIP* 247 (2012); O. Căpătină, Das neue rumänische Internationale Privatrecht, 58 *RabelsZ* 465 (1994); O. Căpătină, La réforme du droit international privé roumain, *Rev. critique DIP* 167 (1994); C. Mindach, Rumänisches Internationales Privat- und Zivilverfahrensrecht, *ROW* 349 (1993); (2) BOOKS: R. Bogdan Bobei, *Legea nr. 105/1992 cu privire la reglementarea raporturilor de Drept International Privat* (2005); D. Lupascu & D. Ungureanu, *Drept international privat* (2012); S. Stanescu, *Drept international privat: Practica judiciara* (2008).

Russia

CODIFICATION: Civil Code of the Russian Federation, Part III, arts. 1186–1224, enacted by Federal law no. 146 of 26 November 2001, Rossyiskaya Gazeta, n. 49 item 4553, 28/11/2001, effective 1 March 2002. English translation in W. Butler, *Civil Code of the Russian Federation* 437 (2002); P. Maggs, *The Civil Code of the Russian Federation: Part 3*, 37–50 (2002); 4 *Ybk. of Priv. Int'l L.* 349 (2002); French translation with commentary by Bogdanova & Litvinski in 91 *Rev. critique DIP* 182 (2002).

SECONDARY SOURCES: (1) ARTICLES: M.R. Badykov, The Russian Civil Code and the Rome Convention: Implied Choice of the Governing Law, 33 *Rev. Cent. & East Euro. L.* 181 (2008); N. Bogdanova & D. Litvinski, Les nouvelles règles de conflit du droit international privé russe, *Rev. critique DIP* 191 (2002); N. Erpyleva & I. Getman-Pavlova, Improving Russian Legislation on Private International Law, 2009 *Russ. L. Theory & Pract.* 204 (2009); E.V. Kabatova, Fundamentals of Civil Legislation and Draft Law on International Private Law, 2 *J. Int'l Priv. L.* 14 (1993); S. Lebedev, A. Muranov, R. Khodykin & E. Kabatova, New Russian Legislation on Private International Law, 4 *Ybk. Priv. Int'l L.* 117 (2002); P. Maggs, Special Section on the Fundamentals of Civil Law: Choice of Law, 6(2) *Soviet & East Euro. L.* (1991); A.L. Makovskii, A New Stage in the Development of Private International Law in Russia, 22 *Rev. Cent. & E. Eur. L.* 595 (1996); O. Sadikov, Die Kodifikation des Internationalen Privatrechts Rußlands, 67 *RabelsZ* 318 (2003); V.P. Zvekov, The New Civil Code of the Russian Federation and Private International Law, 44 *McGill L.J.* 525 (1999); (2) BOOKS: M.M. Boguslavskii, *Private International Law: The Soviet Approach* (1988); L.A. Lunts, *Kurs mezhdunarodnogo chastnogo práva: Obshchaya chast* (1973); L.A. Lunts, *Kurs mezhdunarodnogo chastnogo práva: Osobennaya chast* (1975); L.A. Luntz, *Course on Private International Law* (repr. 2002); A.L. Makovskii & E.A. Sukhanov (eds.), *Kommentarii k chasti tret'ei Grazhdanskogo kodeska Rossiiskoi Federatsii* (2002); O. Vorobieva, *Private International Law in Russia* (2012); P. Maggs, W. Burnham & G. Danilenko, *Law and Legal System of the Russian Federation* (4th ed. 2009); A. Trunk, R. Knieper & A.G. Svetlanov (eds.), *Russland im Kontext der Internationalen Entwicklung: Internationales Privatrecht, Kulturgüterschutz, geistiges Eigentum, Rechtsvereinheitlichung: Festschrift für Mark Moiseevič Boguslavskij* (2004).

Rwanda

CODIFICATION: Law no. 42/1988 (Preliminary Title and First Book of the Civil Code) in force since 1 May 1992. French text *available at* http://www.jafbase.fr/docAfrique/Rwanda/CodeCiv.htm#458.

Senegal

CODIFICATION: Family Code of Senegal, arts. 840–854, Law No. 76-61 of June 1972, Official Journal of Republic of Senegal No. 4243 of 12.8.1972, 1295, *available at* http://www.justice.gouv. sn/droitp/CODE%20FAMILLE.PDF.

SECONDARY SOURCES: (1) ARTICLES: P. Bourel, Le nouveau droit international privé sénégalais de la famille, 7(13) *Rev. sénegalaise de dr.* 5 (1973); S. Guinchard, Réflexions critiques sur les grandes orientations du Code sénégalais de la famille, 87 *Recueil Pénant*, 175 (1978); (2) BOOKS: A-K. Boye, *Les mariages mixtes en droit international privé sénégalais* (1981).

Serbia

CODIFICATION: Serbian Ministry of Justice Draft of 20 July 2012 on Private International Law Code, *available at* http://arhiva.mpravde.gov.rs/cr/news/vesti/zakon-o-medjunarodnom–privatnom -pravu-radna-verzija.html.

SECONDARY SOURCES: M. Stanivukovič, & M. Zivkovič, *International Encyclopaedia of Laws: Private International Law—Serbia* (2008); Council of Europe (C. Jessel-Holst & R. Farrugia), Opinion on the Draft Private International Law Code of the Republic of Serbia (22 October 2012). *See also* Yugoslavia, *infra*.

Slovakia

CODIFICATION: Czechoslovakian Act 97 of 1963 (effective 12 April 1964) on Private International law and Procedure, as amended by Acts Nos. 158/1969, 234/1992, 264/1992, 48/1996, 510/2002, 589/2003, 382/2004, 36/2005, 336/05, 273/07, 384/2008, 388/2011 Coll.

SECONDARY SOURCES: Miloš Hatapka & Bea Verschraegen, *Pramene medzinárodného práva súkromného a procesného—Legal Sources of Private International Law* (2010); F. Poredoš, M. Ďuriš & P. Lysina, *Základy medzinárodného práva súkromného* (2005); Z. Valentovič & Elena Júdová, *Príručka pre štúdium medzinárodného práva súkromného* (1999).

Slovenia

CODIFICATION: Private International Law and Procedure Act of 30 June 1999 (Zakon o mednarodnem zasebnem pravu in postopku—ZMSPP) (Ur.l. RS, no. 56/1999) in Official Gazette of the Republic of Slovenia 1999/56. English translation in *26 Riv. dir. int'l priv. proc.* 829 (2000); German translation in 23 *IPRax* 163 (2003) with a note by Rudolf at *id.* 158.

SECONDARY SOURCES: G. Conetti, La lege sul diritto internazionale privato della Repubblic di Slovenia, 26 *Riv. dir. int'l priv. proc.* 569 (2000); M. Geč-Korošec, Die Reform des slowenischen Internationalen Privat- und Verfahrensrechts und seine Anpassung an das Recht der Europäischen Union, 66 RabelsZ 710 (2002); M. Geč-Korošec, Neuordnung des Internationalen Privatrechts in der Republik Slowenien, in J. Basedow (ed.), *Aufbruch nach Europa: 75 Jahre Max-Planck-Institut für Privatrecht* 633 (2001); K. Puharič, Private International Law in Slovenia, 5 *Ybk. Priv. Int'l L.* 155 (2003).

Somalia

CODIFICATION: Civil Code of Somalia, arts. 10–28, Law no. 37 of 2 July 1973, Off. Bul. of Democratic Republic of Somalia, 2 July 1973, n.6. Italian and German text in J. Kropholler et al., *Aussereuropäische IPR-Gesetze* 750 (1999).

Spain

CODIFICATION: Spanish Civil Code, arts. 8–16, as revised in 1974. English translation in J.L. de San Pio, *Civil Code of Spain: Bilingual Edition* (2009); German translation in 39 *RabelsZ* 724 (1975); French translation in 32 *Ann. suisse dr. int'l* 400 (1976).

SECONDARY SOURCES: (1) ARTICLES: Carlos Esplugues Mota & Carmen Azcárraga Monzonís, *Spanish Report*; J.A. Carrillo Salcedo, Le nouveau droit international privé español, 32 *Ann. suisse dr. int'l* 9 (1976); B. von Hoffmann & A. Ortiz-Arce, Das neue spanische internationale Privatrecht, 39 *RabelsZ* 647 (1975); (2) BOOKS: P. Abarca Junco (ed.), *Derecho internacional privado* (vol. I, 6th ed. 2008, vol. II, 3d ed. 2009); M. Aguilar Benítez de Lugo, et al., *Lecciones de Derecho civil internacional privado* (2d ed. 2006); S. Álvarez González, et al., *Legislación de Derecho internacional privado* (10th ed. 2007); A. Borrás, et al., *Legislación básica de Derecho internacional privado* (17th ed. 2007); A.L. Calvo Caravaca & J. Carrascosa González, *Legislación de Derecho internacional privado comentada y con jurisprudencia* (12th ed. 2011); A.L. Calvo Caravaca & J. Carrascosa González, *Derecho internacional privado* (13th ed. 2012); J. A. Carrillo Salcedo, *Derecho internacional privado* (3d ed. 1983); Centro de Estudios Superiores, Sociales y Jurídicos Ramón Caranda, *España y la codificación internacional del derecho internacional privado* (1993); J.M. Espinar Vicente, *Teoría general del Derecho internacional privado* (2000); C. Espluques Mota & J. Iglesias Buhigues, *Derecho internacional privado* (6th ed. 2012); D.P. Fernández Arroyo, P. Maestre Casas & M. Checa Martínez, *International Encyclopaedia of Laws: Private International Law—Spain* (v. 4, 2008); J.C. Fernández Rozas & S. Sánchez Lorenzo, *Derecho internacional privado* (5th ed. 2009); F.J. Garcimartín Alférez, *Derecho internacional privado* (2012); J.D. González Campos et al., *Derecho internacional privado. Parte especial* (6th ed. 1995); J.L. Iriarte Angel et al., *Derecho internacional privado* (5th ed. 2007); A. Marín López, *Derecho internacional privado español* (vol. 1 9th ed. vol. 2 8th ed. 1994); E. Pérez Vera (ed.), *Derecho internacional privado* (3d ed. 2001).

Sudan

CODIFICATION: Civil Code of Sudan, arts. 10–16, 655, 684, Law of 24 May 1971 as amended by Law of 14 February 1984, Off. J. Democratic Republic of Sudan no. 1340 of 16 February 1984. German translation in J. Kropholler, et al, *Aussereuropäische IPR-Gesetze* 762 (1999).

SECONDARY SOURCES: S. Aldeeb Abu-Sahlieh, Dispositions relatives au droit international privé du Soudan, traduction et commentaire, 81 *Rev. critique DIP* 165 (1992); O. Elwan, Die kollisionsrechtlichen Bestimmungen im Gesetz über den zivilrechtlichen Geschäftsverkehr der Demokratischen Republik Sudan, *IPRax* 56 (1986).

Switzerland

CODIFICATION: Bundesgesetz über das Internationale Privatrecht (IPRG) vom 18. Dezember 1987—Loi féderale sur le droit international privé (LDIP) du 18 décembre 1987, 1988 BB I 5

(German, French and Italian text); English translation with an introduction by S. Symeonides in 37 *Am. J. Comp. L.* 193 (1989); A. Bucher & P. Tschanz, *Private International Law and Arbitration, Switzerland, Basic Documents*, 1 (1996).

SECONDARY SOURCES: (1) ARTICLES: Andrea Bonomi, *Swiss Report*; A. Samuel, The New Swiss Private International Law Act, 37 *Int'l & Comp. L.Q.* 681 (1988); K. Siehr, Swiss PIL at the End of the 20th Century, in S. Symeonides, *Progress or Regress?*, at 383; A.E. von Overbeck, Der schweizerische Entwurf eines Bundesgesetzes über das internationale Privatrecht, 42 *RabelsZ* 601 (1978); F. Vischer, Drafting National Legislation on Conflict of Laws: The Swiss Experience, 41 *Law & Contemp. Prob.* 31 (1977); F. Vischer, "Revolutionary Ideas" and the Swiss Statute on Private International Law, in K. Boele-Woelki, T. Einhorn, D. Girsberger & S. Symeonides (eds.), *Convergence and Divergence in Private International Law: Liber Amicorum Kurt Siehr*, 101 (2010); (2) BOOKS: G. Broggini (ed.), *Il nuovo diritto internazionale privato in Svizzera* (1990); A. Bucher, *Droit international privé suisse*, vol. I.1 (1998), vol. I.2 (1995), vol. II (1992); A. Bucher & A. Bonomi, *Droit international privé* (2d ed. 2004); F. Dessemontet (ed.), *Le nouveau droit international privé suisse* (1988); B. Dutoit, *Droit international privé suisse: Commentaire de la loi fédérale du 18 décembre 1987* (4th ed. 2004); E. Geisinger & P. Patocchi, *Code de droit international privé suisse annoté. La loi fédéral sur le droit international privé* (1995); A. Heini, M. Keller, K. Siehr, F. Vischer & P. Volken, *Kommentar zum Bundesgesetz über das Internationale Privatrecht (IPRG) vom 1. January 1989* (2d ed. 2004); H. Honsell, P. Vogt & A. Schnyder (eds.), *Kommentar zum schweizerischen Privatrecht, Internationales Privatrecht* (2d ed. 2007); P. Karrer, K. Arnold & P. Patocchi, *Switzerland's Private International Law* (2d ed. 1994); M. Keller & K. Siehr, *Einführung in die Eigenart des internationalen Privatrechts* (3d ed. 1984); F. Knoepfler, P. Schweizer & S. Othenin-Girard, *Droit International Privé Suisse* (3d ed. 2005); J. Kren-Kostkiewicz, *Internationales Privatrecht* (2004); A. Schnyder, *Das neue IPR-Gesetz* (2d ed. 1990); A.K. Schnyder & M. Liatowitsch, *Internationales Privat- und Zivilverfahrensrecht* (2000); I. Schwander, *Einführung in das internationale Privatrecht: Allgemeiner Teil* (2d ed. 1990); K. Siehr, *Das internationale Privatrecht der Schweiz* (2002); F. Vischer & A. von Planta, *Internationales Privatrecht* (2d ed. 1982); F. Vischer, L. Huber & D. Oser, *Internationales Vertragsrecht* (2d ed.2000).

Taiwan

CODIFICATION: Act Governing the Application of Laws in Civil Matters Involving Foreign Elements, promulgated on 26 May 2010, effective on 26 May 2011. English translation by Rong-chwan Chen, in Chen, *Taiwanese Report*.

SECONDARY SOURCES: (1) ARTICLES: Rong-chwan Chen, *Taiwanese Report*; R.C. Chen, New Directions of Private International Law: A Birdview of the Revising Draft for the Act on Application of Laws in Civil Matters Involving Foreign Elements, 57 *Taiwan L. J.* 207 (2004) (in Chinese); R.C. Chen, New Way of Thinking in Private International Law Legislation: Material Justice in Conflicts Rules, 89 *Taiwan L. Rev.* 50 (2002) (in Chinese); H.H.P. Ma, *Private International Law of the Republic of China: Past, Present and Future*, in J. Basedow et al. (eds.), *Private Law in the International Arena: Liber Amicorum Kurt Siehr* 413 (2000); (2) BOOKS: T.C. Liu & R.C. Chen, *Private International Law* (4th ed. 2008) (in Chinese); H.H.P. Ma, *Private International Law: General and Special Parts* (2004) (in Chinese).

Tajikistan

CODIFICATION: Civil Code of the Republic of Tajikistan, Section VII, Chapters 63–64, comprising articles 1191–1234, enacted by Law No. 3 of 1 March 2005, *available at* http://www.wipo.int/wipolex/en/text.jsp?file_id=236010#LinkTarget_1157 (in Russian), and at http://www.wipo.int/wipolex/en/text.jsp?file_id=237334 in Tajik.

Togo

CODIFICATION: Code of Persons and Family, arts. 707–734 (Law 80-16 of 31 January 1980 as revised by Law of 29 June 2012), *available at* http://togo.eregulations.org/media/loi-portant-modification-du-code-des-personnes-et-de-la-famille_1.pdf.

Tunisia

CODIFICATION: Code of Private International Law (Law No. 98-97 of 27 November 1998), Official Journal of the Republic of Tunisia, 1 December p. 2332. French text in 88 *Rev. critique DIP* 382 (1999) and http://www.jurisitetunisie.com/tunisie/codes/cdip/menu.html http://www. jurisitetunisie.com/tunisie/codes/cdip/cdip1055.htm; English translation in *Riv. dir. Int'l priv. proc.* 541 (2000).

SECONDARY SOURCES: (1) ARTICLES: S. Bostanji, Les survivances du communautarisme dans l'application judiciaire du droit international privé tunisien, *Rev. critique DIP* 251 (2009); S. Bostanji, L'incidence de la Constitution sur les nouvelles solutions de conflits de lois, in *Mouvements du droit contemporain, Mélanges offerts à Sassi Ben Halima* 281 (2005); S. Bostanji, L'émergence d'un statut privilégié de l'enfant en droit international privé tunisien, 16 *Actualités jurid.* 125 (2001); A. Mezghani, Les innovations du code tunisien de droit international privé, 65 *RabelsZ* 78 (2001); (2) BOOKS: A. Mezghani (ed.), *Commentaires du Code de droit international privé* (1999); K. Meziou & M. Ghazouani (eds.), *Le code tunisien de droit international privé deux ans après* (2003).

Turkey

CODIFICATION: Law No. 5718 of 27 November 2007 adopting the Turkish Code of Private International Law and International Civil Procedure. English translation by A. Odman Boztosun, in 9 *Ybk. Priv. Int'l L.* 583 (2007), German translation in 28 *IPRax* 283(2008).

SECONDARY SOURCES: (1) ARTICLES: Zeynep Derya Tarman, *Turkish Report*; T. Ansay, The Anatomy of Turkey's New Private International Law Regime, 74 RabelsZ 393 (2010); E. Nomer, N.A. Odman & G. Tekinalp, *International Encyclopaedia of Laws: Private International Law—Turkey* (v. 4, 2000); Z.D. Tarman, The Applicable Law to Contractual and Non-contractual Obligations under Turkish Private International Law, 27(1) *Ned. Int'l Priv.* 15 (2009); Z.D. Tarman, The International Jurisdiction of the Turkish Courts on Personal Status of Turkish Nationals, 14 *Ybk. Priv. Int'l L.* 477 (2012–2013); G. Tekinalp, The 2007 Turkish Code concerning Private International Law and International Civil Procedure, 9 *Ybk. Priv. Int'l L.* 313 (2007). For the previous codification of 1982, see Law No. 2675 of Nov. 22, 1982, on Private International Law and Procedure, reprinted in German, with comment by Krüger, in 2 *IPRax* 252 (1982); 46 *RabelsZ* 184 (1982); A. Sakmar, Le nouveau droit international privé turc, *Recueil des Cours* 313 (1990-IV); G. Tekiÿnalp, Das Türkishe Gesetz über internationals Privatrecht vom 22.5.1982,

47 *RabelsZ* 131 (1983); N. Uluocak, Réformes en droit international privé turk, 27 *Ann. Fac. Dr. d'Istanbul* 211 (1980); (2) BOOKS: R. Aybay & E. Dardağan, *Uluslararası Düzeyde Yasaların Çatışması* (2008); A. Çelikel & B. Erdem, *Milletlerarasi Özel Hukuk* (10th ed. 2010); V. Doğan, *Milletlerarasi Özel Hukuk* (2010); E. Nomer, *Devletler Hususi Hukuku* (19th ed. 2011);

U.A.E. (United Arab Emirates)

CODIFICATION: Arts. 1–3, 10–28 of Code of Civil Transactions of the United Arab Emirates (J.O. of U.A.E. no 185, December 1985, p. 11-361); French translation and commentary by M.S. Aldeeb Abu-Sahlieh in 75 *Rev. critique DIP* 390 (1986); English translation by James Whelan *available at* http://translex.uni-koeln.de/touch/document.php?docid=605600 and at http://lexemiratidotnet. files.wordpress.com/2011/07/uae-civil-code-_english-translation_.pdf.

SECONDARY SOURCES: S.A. Aldeeb Abu Sahlieh, Dispositions relatives au droit international privé dans le code des transactions civiles des Emirats Arabes Unis, Rev. critique DIP 393 (1986); A.M. Elhawary, Regulation of Conflict of Laws in the United Arab Emirates, 27 *Arab L. Q.* 1 (2013); H. Krüger Grundzüge des internationalen Zivilverfahrensrechts der Vereinigten Arabischen Emirate, *RIW* 384 (1993); H. Krüger, Zur Praxis des internationalen Privatrechts in den Vereinigten Arabischen Emiraten, in *Festschrift für Erik Jayme*, v. 1, 477 (2004).

Ukraine

CODIFICATION: Law of 23 June 2005 No. 2709-IV on Private International Law, as amended by Law of 21 January 2010, No. 1837-VI, and Law of 19 May 2011, No. 3390-VI. English translation *available at* http://cis-legislation.com/document.fwx?rgn=16954 and in W.E. Butler (ed.), *Civil Code of Ukraine and Law of Ukraine on Private International Law* (2011).

SECONDARY SOURCES: A. Dovgert, Codification of Private International Law in Ukraine, 7 *Ybk Priv. Int'l L.* 131 (2005).

United Kingdom

CODIFICATION: Private International Law (Miscellaneous Provisions) Act of 8 November 1995 (c 42) (codifying conflicts rules for torts). For other statutes, *see* J. Chuah & R. Earle, *Statutes and Conventions on Private International Law* (2d ed. 2004).

SECONDARY SOURCES: (1) ARTICLES: Christa Roodt, *English Report*; R. Fentiman, English PIL at the End of the 20th Century, in S. Symeonides, *PIL at the End of the 20th Century: Progress or Regress?* 165 (2000); C.G.J. Morse, Torts in Private International Law: A New Statutory Framework, 45 *Int'l & Comp. L.Q.* 888 (1996); A. Reed, The Private International Law (Miscellaneous Provisions) Act 1995 and the Need for Escape Devices, 15 *Civ. Just. Q.* 305 (1996); B.J. Rodger, Ascertaining the Statutory *Lex Loci Delicti*: Certain Difficulties under the Private International Law (Miscellaneous Provisions) Act 1995, 47 *Int'l & Comp. L.Q.* 205 (1998); (2) BOOKS: P. Beaumont & P. McEleavy, *Anton's Private International Law* (3d ed. 2011); A. Briggs, *The Conflict of Laws* (3d ed. 1013); L. Collins, *Dicey, Morris and Collins on the Conflict of Laws* (15th ed. 2012); C. Clarkson & J. Hill, *The Conflict of Laws* (2011); J.J. Fawcett & J.M. Carruthers, *Cheshire, North & Fawcett Private International Law* (14th ed. 2008); D. McClean, *Morris on the Conflict of Laws* (5th ed. 2000); P. Rogerson & J. Collier, *Collier's Conflict of Laws* (4th ed. 2013).

Uruguay

DRAFT CODIFICATION: Proyecto de Ley General de Derecho Internacional Privado, 19.1.2009 (Draft General Law of Private International Law of 19 January 2009), *available at* http://www.par-lamento.gub.uy/indexdb/Repartidos/ListarRepartido.asp?Id=6052, with Exposición De Motives.

SECONDARY SOURCES: (1) ARTICLES: Cecilia Fresnedo de Aguirre, *Uruguayan Report*; C. Fresnedo de Aguirre & G. Lorenzo Idiarte, El Proyecto de Ley General de Derecho Internacional Privado de la República Oriental del Uruguay, 11 *DeCITA* 429 (2009); G. A. Lorenzo Idiarte, C. González Pedrouzo & A. Fernández Pereiro, *International Encyclopaedia of Laws: Private International Law-Uruguay* (v. 4, 2013); D. Opertti Badán & C. Fresnedo de Aguirre, The Latest Trends in Latin American Law: The Uruguayan 2009 General Law on Private International Law, 11 *Ybk. Priv. Int'l L.* 305 (2009); D. Opertti Badán & C. Fresnedo de Aguirre, El derecho comercial internacional en la nueva Ley General de Derecho Internacional Privado Uruguayo: Una primera aproximación, in D.P. Fernández Arroyo & J.A. Moreno Rodríguez (eds.) *Cómo se codifica hoy el derecho comercial internacional?* 385 (2010); (2) BOOKS: C. Fresnedo de Aguirre, C., *Curso de derecho internacional privado* (2007); C. Fresnedo de Aguirre, *La Autonomía de la Voluntad en la Contratación Internacional* (1991); D. Opertti Badán & C. Fresnedo de Aguirre, *Contratos comerciales internacionales* (1997).

Uzbekistan

CODIFICATION: Civil Code of the Republic of Uzbekistan, arts. 1158–1199, enacted by Law 257-I of 29.08.1996, effective 1 March 1997. English translation in W.E. Butler (ed.), *Civil Code of the Republic of Uzbekistan* (1997).

Venezuela

CODIFICATION: Act of 6 August, 1998 on Private International Law (Official Gazette No. 36,511) effective 6 February 1999; English translation in 1 *Ybk. Priv. Int'l L.* 341 (1999), and at http://www.reference-global.com/doi/abs/10.1515/9783866537125.5.341; French translation in 88 *Rev. critique DIP* 392 (1999).

SECONDARY SOURCES: (1) ARTICLES: Eugenio Hernández-Bretón, *Venezuelan Report*; E. Hernández-Bretón, Recientes desarrollos del derecho internacional privado venezolano, in D.P. Fernández Arroyo & N. González Martín (eds.), *Tendencias y Relaciones Derecho Internacional Privado Americano Actual* (2010); T. de Maekelt, Venezuelan PIL at the End of the 20th Century, in S. Symeonides, *Progress or Regress?*, at 445; G. Parra-Aranguren, The Venezuelan Act of Private International Law of 1998, 1 *Ybk. Priv. Int'l L.* 103 (1999); G. Parra-Aranguren, Topics of Procedure in the Venezuelan 1998 Act of Private International Law, 60 *La. L. Rev.* 1241 (2000); G. Parra-Aranguren, La loi vénézuélienne de 1998 sur le droit international privé, 88 *Rev. critique DIP* 3209 (1999); (2) BOOKS: E. Hernández-Bretón, *Problemas Contemporáneos del Derecho Procesal Civil Internacional Venezolano* (2004); T. de Maekelt, I. Esis Villaroel & C. Resende (eds.), *Ley de Derecho Internacional Privado Comentada* (2005); T. de Maekelt, *Ley venezolana de Derecho Internacional Privado: Tres años de su vigencia* (2002); T.B. de Maekelt, H. Barrios, Z. Marín Vargas, & M. Méndez Zambrano (eds.), *Derecho Procesal Civil Internacional, In Memoriam Tatiana B. de Maekelt* (2010); J. María Bouvier, El nuevo sistema venezolano de derecho internacional privado (2001); N. Monleón, *Das neue internationale Privatrecht von*

Venezuela (2008); F. Parra-Aranguren (ed.), *Libro homenaje a Gonzalo Parra-Aranguren, Ley de Derecho Internacional Privado de 6 de Agosto de 1998,* vols. I, II, III (2001), v. IV (2002).

Vietnam

CODIFICATION: Civil Code of the Socialist Republic of Vietnam of 1995, Arts. 826–838. French translation by Que & Luong in 89 *Rev. critique DIP* 298 (2000). For a subsequent revision, see Law of 14 June 2005, Civil Code of Socialist Republic of Viet Nam, Arts. 758–777; English translation *available at* http://moj.gov.vn/vbpq/en/Lists/Vn% 20bn%20php%20lut/View_Detail. aspx?ItemID=6595. For the rules on international jurisdiction, *see* Vietnamese Code of Civil Procedure (2004), Arts. 405–418. For recognition and enforcement of foreign judgments and arbitration awards, see id. arts. 342–374.

SECONDARY SOURCES: S. Cavet, Choice of Law in Vietnam and the New Civil Code: Is Choice of Law Available for Your Type of Contract? (And Why It Matters), 9 *East Asian Exec. Reports* 9 (1996); Q. Nguyen, Cross-Border Transactions in Vietnam and the Vietnam-US Bilateral Trade Agreement, 8 *Int'l Trade & Bus. L. Ann.* 159 (2003); P. Nicholson & Q. Nguyen, Vietnamese Law: A Guide to Sources and Commentary, 2 *J. Comp. L.* 219 (2007).

Yemen

CODIFICATION: Law of 29 March 1992 on Private International Law; French translation in *82 Rev. critique* DIP 363 (1993). For the former North Yemen, *see* Arts. 1–11, 20, 23–35 of Civil Code of the Arab Republic of Yemen, promulgated by law 10 of 21 April 1979 in J.O. of 30 April 1979, French translation with comments by S. Aldeeb Abu-Sahlieh in 76 *Rev. critique DIP* 650 (1987). *See also id.* at 654 for the codification in the then South Yemen (without any indication as to date of enactment).

SECONDARY SOURCES: S. Aldeeb Abu-Sahlieh, Dispositions relatives au droit international privé de la République arabe yéménite, 76 *Rev. critique DIP* 650 (1987); S. Aldeeb Abu-Sahlieh, Dispositions relatives au droit international privé de la République démocratique populaire du Yémen, 76 *Rev. critique DIP* 654 (1987); S. Aldeeb Abu-Sahlieh, Dispositions relatives au droit international privé du Yémen, 82 *Rev. critique DIP* 363 (1993); H. Krüger & N. Küppers, Das internationale Privat- und Zivilverfahrensrecht der Arabischen Republik Jemen, 7 *IPrax* 39 (1987); H. Krüger, Internationales Zivilverfahrensrecht in der Republik Jemen, *RIW* 470 (1993); H. Krüger, Allgemeiner Rechtszustand und internationales Privatrecht der Republik Jemen, *RIW* 28 (1993); H. Krüger, Neues internationales Privatrecht in der Republik Jemen, *IPRax* 370 (2004).

Yugoslavia (Bosnia-Herzegovina, Croatia, Montenegro, Serbia)

CODIFICATION: Act of 15 July 1982 on the Resolution of Conflicts of Laws with Laws and Regulations of Other Countries in Certain Matters. English translation and Note by Ž. Matić in 30 *Neth. Int'l L. Rev.* 220 (1983); German translation and Note by Firsching in 49 *RabelsZ* 544 (1985). *See also* 27 *Neth. Int'l L. Rev.* 121 (1980) for English translations of two earlier installments by Ž. Matić.

SECONDARY SOURCES: (1) ARTICLES: P. Sarcevic, The New Yugoslav Private International Law Act, 38 *Am. J. Comp. L.* 283 (1985); M. Stanivukovič, Yugoslav PIL at the End of the 20th

Century, in S. Symeonides (ed.), *PIL at the End of the 20th Century: Progress or Regress?*, 461 (2000); T. Varady, *Some Observations on the New Yugoslav Private International Law Code*, 19 *Riv. dir. int'le priv. e process.* 69 (1983); (2) BOOKS: M. Dika, G. Knežević & S. Stojanović, *Komentar Zakona o medunarodnom privatnom i procesnom pravu* (Commentary of the PIL Code) (1991); A. Jakšić, *Medunarodno privatno pravo* (2008); D. Mitrović & A. Kupman, *Osnovi medunarodnog privatnog prava* (2007); M. Pak, *Medunarodno privatno pravo* (4th rev. ed. 2000); M. Roćkomanović, M., *Medunarodno privatno pravo* (4th rev. ed. 2006); M. Stanivukovič & M. Zivkovič, *International Encyclopaedia of Laws: Private International Law—Serbia* (2008); M. Stanivukovič & M. Zivkovič, *Medunarodno privatno pravo, opčti deo* (General Part, 2008); M. Stanivukovič & P. Đundič, *Medunarodno privatno pravo, posebni deo* (Special Part, 2008); T. Varadi, B. Bordaš, G. Knežević & V. Pavič, *Medunarodno privatno právo* (2007).

II. EU REGULATIONS (AND CONVENTIONS)

Brussels Convention

TEXT: Brussels Convention of 27 September 1968 on jurisdiction and the enforcement of judgments in civil and commercial matters, OJ [1990] C 189, *available at* http://eur-lex.europa.eu/LexUriServ/LexUriServ.do?uri=CELEX:41968A0927%2801%29:EN:HTML.

SECONDARY SOURCES: A.L. Calvo Caravaca (ed.), *Comentario al convenio de Bruselas relativo a la competencia judicial y a la ejecución de resoluciones judiciales en material civil y mercantile* (1994); D. Czernich & S. Tiefenthaler, *Die Übereinkommen von Lugano und Brüssel: Europäisches Gerichtsstands- und Vollstreckungsrecht—Kurzkommentar* (1997); G.A.L. Droz, *Pratique de la Convention de Bruxelles du 27 septembre 1968* (1973); P. Gothot & D. Holleaux, *La. Convention de Bruxelles du 27 septembre 1968* (1985); K. Hertz, *Jurisdiction in Contract and Tort under the Brussels Convention* (1998); P. Jenard, *La Convention de Bruxelles du 27 septembre 1968 et ses prolonguements* (1994); L. Mari, *Il diritto processuale civile delta Convenzione di Bruxelles I: Il sistema della competenza* (1999); F. Pocar, *La Convenzione di Bruxelles sulla giurisdizione e l'esecuzione delle sentence* (3d ed. 1995); M. Weser, *Convention communautaire sur la compétence judiciaire et l'exécution des decisions* (1975).

Lugano Convention

TEXT: Convention on Jurisdiction and the Enforcement of Judgments in Civil and Commercial Matters, Done at Lugano on 16 September, 1988, OJ [1988] L 319/9, *available at* http://curia.europa.eu/common/recdoc/convention/en/c-textes/lug-idx.htm; Lugano Convention of 30 October 2007on Jurisdiction and the Recognition and Enforcement of Judgments in Civil and Commercial Matters, [2007] O.J. L 393/3, *available at* http://www.eda.admin.ch/etc/medialib/downloads/edazen/topics/intla/intrea/depch/misc/conlug2.Par.0014.File.tmp/mt_090325_en.pdf.

SECONDARY SOURCES: (1) ARTICLES: D. Mavromati & R. Rodriguez, *The Revised Lugano Convention from a Swiss Perspective*, Eur. Bus. L. Rev. 87 (2009); F. Pocar, *The New Lugano Convention on Jurisdiction and the Recognition and Enforcement of Judgments in Civil and Commercial Matters*, 10 Ybk. Priv. Int'l L. 1 (2008); (2) BOOKS: P. Byrne, *The European Union and Lugano Conventions on Jurisdiction and the Enforcement of Judgments* (1994); M. Carpenter et al., *The Lugano and San Sebastian Conventions* (1990); Y. Donzallaz, *La Convention de Lugano du 16 septembre 1988 concernant la compétence judiciaire et l'execution des décisions en matière civile et commerciale*, vol. I–III (1996–1998); T. Fisknes, *Luganokonvensjonen og dens betydning I sjørettslige twister* (1991); N. Gillard (ed.), *L'espace judiciaire européen: La Convention de Lugano du 16 septembre 1988* (1992); L. Killias, *Die Gerichtsstandsvereinbarungen nach dem Lugano-Übereinkommen* (1993); U. Klinke, *Brüsseler Übereinkommen und Übereinkommen von Lugano über die gerichtliche Zuständigkeit und die Vollstreckung gerichtlicher Entscheidungen in Zivil- und Handelssachen* (1993); S.A. Mädder, Die Anwendung des Lugano- Übereinkommens im gewerblichen Rechtsschutz (1999); P. Mercier & P. Dutoit, *L'Europe judiciaire: Les Conventions de Bruxelles et de Lugano* (1991); T. Schmidt-Parzefall, *Die Auslegung des Parallelübereinkommens von Lugano* (1995); L.W. Valloni, *Der Gerichtsstand des Erfüllungsortes nach Lugano- und Brüsseler- Übereinkommen* (1998).

Brussels I Regulation

TEXT: European Community Council Regulation (EC) No. 44/2001 of 22 December 200 on Jurisdiction and the Recognition of Judgments in Civil and Commercial Matters, [2001] Official Journal L.12/1, 16.1, 1001, effective 1 March 2002. RECAST: Regulation (EU) No 1215/2012 of the European Parliament and of the Council of 12 December 2012 on jurisdiction and the recognition and enforcement of judgments in civil and commercial matters (recast) OJ 20 December 2012, L 351/1, effective on 10 January 2015.

SECONDARY SOURCES: (1) ARTICLES: A. Briggs, Recognition of Foreign Judgments: A Matter of Obligation, *L Q. Rev.* 87 (2013); G.A.L. Droz & H. Gaudemet-Tallon, La transformation de la Convention de Bruxelles du 27 septembre 1968 en Réglement du Conseil concernant la competence judiciaire, la reconnaissance et exécution des decisions en matière civile et commerciale, *Rev. critique DIP* 601 (2001); M. Fallon & T. Kruger, The Spatial Scope of the EU's Rules on Jurisdiction and Enforcement of Judgments: From Bilateral Modus to Unilateral Universality?, 14 *Ybk. Priv. Int'l L.* 1 (2012–2013); L. Gillies, Creation of Subsidiary Jurisdiction Rules in the Recast of Brussels I: Back to the Drawing Board?, *J. Priv. Int'l. L.* 489 (2012); J. Harris, Agreements on Jurisdiction and Choice of Law: Where Next?, *Lloyds Mar. Comp. L.Q.* 537 (2009); L. Merrett, Article 23 of Brussels I Regulation: A Comprehensive Code for Jurisdiction Agreements?, *Int'l Comp. L.Q.* 545 (2009); M. Pohl, The Recast of Brussels I—Striking the Balance between Trust and Control, *IPRax* 109 (2013); M. Requejo Isidro, The Use of Force, Human Rights Violations and the Scope of the Brussels I Regulation, 14 *Ybk. Priv. Int'l L.* 113 (2012–2013); K. Takahashi, Review of the Brussels I Regulation: A Comment from the Perspectives of Non–Member-States (Third States), *J. Priv. Int'l. L.* 1 (2012); (2) BOOKS: B. Hess, T. Pfeiffer & P. Schlosser, *The Brussels I Regulation (EC) No 44/2001: The Heidelberg Report on the Application of Regulation Brussels I in 25 Member States* (2009); U. Magnus & P. Jankowski (eds.), *Brussels I Regulation* (2d rev. ed. 2012); J. Meeusen et al. (eds.), *Enforcement of International Contracts in the European Union. Convergence and Divergence between Brussels I and Rome I* (2004); J. Newton, *The Uniform Interpretation of the Brussels and Lugano Conventions* (2002).

Brussels IIbis

TEXT: Council Regulation (EC) No 2201/2003 of 27 November 2003 concerning jurisdiction and the recognition and enforcement of judgments in matrimonial matters and the matters of parental responsibility, [2003] Official Journal L 338/1 (also known as "Brussels IIa" or

"Brussels *IIbis*"), *available at* http://eur-lex.europa.eu/Result.do?T1=V2&T2= 2003&T3= 2201&RechType=RECH_naturel&Submit=Search.

SECONDARY SOURCES: (1) ARTICLES: B. Ancel & H. Muir Watt, L'intérêt supérieur de l'enfant dans le concert des jurisdictions: Le Règlement de Bruxelles II Bis, *Rev. critique DIP* 569 (2005); W. Kennett, The Treaty of Amsterdam; The Brussels II Convention, 48 *Int'l & Comp. L.Q.* 465 (1999); P. McEleavy, Brussels IIbis: Matrimonial Matters, Parental Responsibility, Child Abduction and Mutual Recognition, 53 *Int'l & Comp. L Q.* 503 (2004); (2) BOOKS: K. Boele-Woelki & C. Gonzalez-Beilfuss, *Brussels II Bis: Its Impact and Application in the Member States* (2007); N. Lowe, N. Lowe & M. Nicholls, *The New Brussels II Regulation: A Supplement to International Movement of Children* (2005); U. Magnus & P. Jankowski (eds.), *Brussels IIbis Regulation* (2012); M. Shúilleabháin, *Cross-Border Divorce Law: Brussels II Bis* (2010).

Insolvency:

TEXT: Council Regulation (EC) No 1346/2000 of 29 May 2000 on Insolvency Proceedings, OJ L 160/1, 30.6.2000.

SECONDARY SOURCES: (1) ARTICLES: E. Aasaru, The Desirability of Centre of Main Interest as a Mechanism for Allocating Jurisdiction and Applicable Law in Cross-Border Insolvency Law, *Eur. Bus. L. Rev.* 349 (2011); E. Consalvi, The Regime for Circulation of Judgements under the EC Regulation on Insolvency Proceedings, 15 *Int'l Insolv. Rev.* 147 (2006); M.N. Jobard-Bachellier, Les procédures de surendettement et de faillite internationales ouvertes dans la communauté européenne, *Rev. critique DIP* 491 (2002); I. Mevorach, Jurisdiction in Insolvency: A Study of European Courts' Decisions, 6 *J. Priv. Int'l L.* 327 (2010); P. Rogerson, International Insolvency: Law Applied to Distribution, 67 *Cambridge L.J.* 476 (2008); (2) BOOKS: B. Hess et al., *External Evaluation of Regulation No 1346/2000/EC on Insolvency Proceedings* (2013) (Heidelberg-Vienna Report) and extensive bibliography provided therein, *available at* http://ec.europa.eu/justice/civil/files/evaluation_insolvency_en.pdf; I.F. Fletcher, *Insolvency in Private International Law* (2d ed. 2007); G. Moss, L. Fletcher & S. Isaacs (eds.), *The EC Regulation on Insolvency Proceedings: A Commentary and Annotated Guide* (2d ed. 2009); P.J. Omar, *International Insolvency Law: Themes and Perspectives* (2008); P.S. Smart, *Cross-Border Insolvency* (2d ed. 2007); M. Tsvengrosh, *Arbitration and Insolvency—Conflict of Laws Issues* (2011); B. Wessels & J. Kilbornn, *International Cooperation in Bankruptcy and Insolvency Matters* (2009); B. Wessels, *International Insolvency Law* (2012).

Maintenance

TEXT: Council Regulation (EC) No 4/2009 of 18 December 2008 on Jurisdiction, Applicable Law, Recognition and Enforcement of Decisions and Cooperation in Matters Relating to Maintenance Obligations L 7/1 [2009] O.J. 10.1.2009, effective in 2011, *available at* http://eur-lex.europa.eu/ Result.do?T1=V2&T2=2009&T3=4&RechType=RECH_naturel&Submit=Search.

SECONDARY SOURCES: B. Ancel & H. Muir Watt, Aliments sans frontières. Le règlement CE No 4/2009 du 18 décembre 2008 relatif à la compétence, la loi applicable, la reconnaissance et l'exécution des décisions et la coopération en matière d'obligations alimentaires, *Rev. critique DIP* 457 (2010); P. Beaumont, The Maintenance Project, the Hague Conference and the

EC: A Triumph of Reverse Subsidiarity, 73 *RabelsZ* 509 (2009); R. Wagner, Der Wettstreit um neue kollisionsrechtliche Vorschriften im Unterhaltsrecht, *FamRZ* 979 (2006).

Rome I

TEXT: Regulation (EC) No. 593/2008 of the European Parliament and of the Council of 17 June 2008 on the Law Applicable to Contractual Obligations (Rome I), [2008] OJ L 177/6.

SECONDARY SOURCES: (1) ARTICLES: B. Ancel, The Rome I Regulation and Distribution Contracts, 10 *Ybk. Priv. Int'l L.* 221 (2008); B. Ancel & H. Muir Watt, The Relevance of Substantive International Commercial Norms for Choice of Law in Contract: The Rome and Mexico City Conventions Compared, in *Festschrift Juenger* 1 (2006); M.R. Badykov, The Russian Civil Code and the Rome Convention: Implied Choice of the Governing Law, 33 *Rev. Cent. & East Eur. L.* 181 (2008); T. Ballarino, Dalla Convenzione di Roma del 1980 al regolamento Roma I, *Riv. dir. Int'l* 40 (2009); J. Basedow & W. Wurmnest et al. (eds.), Comments on the European Commission's Proposal for a Regulation of the European Parliament and the Council on the Law Applicable to the Contractual Obligations, 71 *RabelsZ* 225 (2007); V. Behr, Rome I Regulation: A-Mostly-Unified Private International Law of Contractual Relationships within-Most-of the European Union, 29 *J.L. & Com.* 233 (2011); B. Bierman & T. Struycken, Rome I on Contracts Concluded within Multilateral Systems, 2009 *Nederl. IPR.* 416 (2009); M. Bogdan, The Rome I Regulation on the Law Applicable to Contractual Obligations and the Choice of Law by the Parties, 2009 *Nederl. IPR.* 407 (2009); A. Bonomi, The Rome I Regulation on the Law Applicable to Contractual Obligations: Some General Remarks, 10 *Ybk. Priv. Int'l L.* 165 (2008); A. Bonomi, Overriding Mandatory Provisions in the Rome I Regulation on the Law Applicable to Contracts, 10 *Ybk. Priv. Int'l L.* 285 (2008); P. Borchers, Categorical Exceptions to Party Autonomy in Private International Law, 82 *Tul. L. Rev.* 1645 (2008); A.L. Calvo Caravaca, El Reglamento Roma I sobre la ley aplicable a las obligaciones contractuales: Cuestiones escogidas, 1 *Cuad. Der. Transn'l* 52 (2009); T.D. Czigler & I. Takacs, Chaos Renewed: The Rome I Regulation vs. Other Sources of EU Law: A Classification of Conflicting Provisions, 14 *Ybk. Priv. Int'l L.* 539 (2012–2013); De Miguel Asensio, Applicable Law in the Absence of Choice to Contracts Relating to Intellectual or Industrial Property Right, 10 *Ybk. Priv. Int'l L.* 199 (2008); J.C. Fernandez Rozas, Comunitarización del derecho internacional privado y derecho aplicable a las obligaciones contractuales, *Rev. esp. seg.* 595 (2009); S. Francq, Le règlement "Rome I" sur la loi applicable aux obligations contractuelles, *Clunet* 41 (2009); F. Garcimartín Alférez, Hermeneutic Dialogue between Rome I and Rome II: General Principles and Argumentative Rules, in *A Commitment to Private International Law: Essays in Honour of Hans Van Loon* 169 (2013); F. Garcimartín Alférez, The Rome I Regulation: Much Ado about Nothing?, *Eur. Legis. F.* 61 (2008-2); F. Garcimartín Alférez, New Issues in the Rome I Regulation: The Special Provisions on Financial Market Contracts, 10 *Ybk. Priv. Int'l L.* 245 (2008); F. Garcimartín Alferez, The Rome I Regulation: Exceptions to the Rule on Consumer Contracts and Financial Instruments, 5 *J. Priv. Int'l L.* 85 (2009); L. García Gutiérrez, Franchise Contracts and the Rome I Regulation on the Law Applicable to International Contracts, 10 *Ybk. Priv. Int'l L.* 233 (2008); P. Hay, Flexibility versus Predictability and Uniformity in Choice of Law, 226 *Recueil des Cours* 281 (1991-I); H. Heiss, Insurance Contracts in Rome I: Another Recent Failure of the European Legislature, 10 *Ybk. Priv. Int'l L.* 261 (2008); J. Kuipers, Party Autonomy in the Brussels I Regulation and Rome I Regulation and the European Court of Justice, 10 *German L J.* 1055 (2009); P. Lagarde & A.

Tenebaum, De la convention de Rome au règlement Rome I, 97 *Rev. critique DIP* 727 (2008); P. Lagarde, Remarques sur la proposition de règlement sur la loi applicable aux obligations contrac-tuelle, 96 *Rev. critique DIP* 331 (2006); O. Lando & P. Nielsen, The Rome I Regulation, 45 *Comn. Mkt. L. Rev.* 45 (2008); S. Leible & M. Lehmann, Die Verordnung über das auf vertragliche Schuldverhältnisse anzuwendende Recht ("Rome I"), *Recht der internationalen Wirtschaft* 528 (2008); E. Lein, The New Rome I/Rome II/Brussels I Synergy, 10 *Ybk. Priv. Int'l L.* 177 (2008); L. de Lima Pinheiro, Rome I Regulation: Some Controversial Issues, in *Festschrift für Bernd von Hoffmann* 242 (2011); D. Martiny, Europäisches Internationales Vertragsrecht in Erwartung der Rom I-Verordnung, *Zeitschrift für Europäisches Privatrecht* 79 (2008); C. Okoli & G. Arishe, The Operation of the Escape Clauses in the Rome Convention, Rome I Regulation and Rome II Regulation, 8 *J. Priv. Int'l L.* 512 (2012); Y. Okuda, A Short Look at Rome I on Contract Conflicts from a Japanese Perspective, 10 *Ybk. Priv. Int'l L.* 301 (2008); A. Reed, The Rome I Regulation and Reapprochement of Anglo-American Choice of Law in Contract: A Heralded Triumph of Pragmatism over Theory, 23 *Fla. J. Int'l L.* 359 (2011); D. Solomon, The Private International Law of Contracts in Europe: Advances and Retreats, 82 *Tul. L. Rev.* 1709 (2008); S. Symeonides, Party Autonomy in Rome I and II from a Comparative Perspective, 28(2) *Ned. IPR* 191 (2010); R. Wagner, Der Grundsatz der Rechtswahl und das mangels Rechtswahl anwendbare Recht (Rom I-Verordnung), *IPrax* 377 (2008); R. Weintraub, How to Choose Law for Contracts and How Not To: The EEC Convention, 17 *Tex. Int'l L.J.* 155 (1982); M. Wethmar-Lemmer, Party Autonomy and International Sales Contracts, 3 *J. So. Afr. L.* 431 (2011); (2) BOOKS: A.J. Bělohlávek, *Rome Convention, Rome I Regulation* (2010); E. Cashin Ritaine & A. Bonomi (eds.), *Le nouveau règlement européen "Rome I" relatif à la loi applicable aux obligations contractuelles* (2008); E. Castellanos Ruiz, *El Reglamento Roma I sobre la ley aplicable a los contratos inter-nacionales y su aplicación por los tribunales españoles* (2009); S. Corneloup & N. Joubert (eds.), *Le règlement communautaire "Rome I" et le choix de loi dans les contrats internationaux* (2011); F. Ferrari & S. Leible, *Rome I Regulation: The Law Applicable to Contractual Obligations in Europe* (2009); U. Magnus & P. Mankowski, *Rome I Regulation* (2009); R. Plender & M. Wilderspin, *The European Private International Law of Obligations* (3d ed. 2009); G. Calliess (ed.), *The Rome Regulations: Commentary on the EC Regulations on Conflict Laws* (2010); T. Rauscher (ed.), *Europäisches Zivilprozess- und Kollisionsrecht EuZPR/EuIPR. Kommentar Rom I-VO, Rom II-VO* (2011); U. Villani, *La Convenzione di Roma sulla legge aplicabile ai contratti* (1997).

Rome II

TEXT: Regulation (EC) No. 864/2007 of the European Parliament and of the Council of 11 July 2007 on the Law Applicable to Non-contractual Obligations (Rome II), [2007] OJ L 199/40.

SECONDARY SOURCES: (1) ARTICLES: J. Basedow, Federal Choice of Law in Europe and the United States: A Comparative Account of Interstate Conflicts, 82 *Tul. L. Rev.* 2119 (2008); P. Beaumont & Z. Tang, Classification of Delictual Damages—*Harding v Wealands* and the Rome II Regulation, 12 *Edinb. Rev.* 131 (2008); T.M. de Boer, The Purpose of Uniform Choice-of-Law Rules: The Rome II Regulation, *Neth. Int'l L. Rev.* 295 (2009); T.M. de Boer, Party Autonomy and Its Limitations in the Rome II Regulation, 9 *Ybk. Priv. Int'l L.* 19 (2008); L. de Lima Pinheiro, Choice of Law on Non-contractual Obligations between Communiterization and Globalization: A First Assessment of EC Regulation Rome II, *Riv. dir. int. priv. proc.* 5 (2008);

A. Chong, Choice of Law for Unjust Enrichment/Restitution and the Rome II Regulation, 57 *Int'l & Comp. L.Q.* 863 (2008); T.W. Dornis, "When in Rome, Do as the Romans Do?" A Defense of the *Lex Domicilii Communis* in the Rome-II Regulation, 4.1 *Eur. Legis. F.* 152 (2007); M. Fallon, La relation du règlement Rome II avec d'autres règles de conflit de lois, Rev. dr. comm. Belge 549 (2008); C. Fresnedo de Aguirre & D. Fernandez Arroyo, A Quick Latin American Look at the Rome II Regulation, 9 *Ybk. Priv. Int'l L.* 193 (2008); F. Garcimartin Alferez, The Rome II Regulation: On the Way towards a European Private International Code, 2007(3) *Eur. Legis. F.* 77 (2007); G. Garriga, Relationship between Rome II and Other International Instruments: A Commentary on Article 28 of the Rome II Regulation, 9 *Ybk. Priv. Int'l L.* 137 (2008); Hamburg Group of Private International Law, Comments on the European Commission's Draft Proposal for a European Council Regulation on the Law Applicable to Non-contractual Obligations (29/10/2002), 67 *RabelsZ* 1 (2003); T. Hartley, Choice of Law for Non-contractual Liability: Selected Problems under the Rome II Regulation, 57 *Int'l & Comp. L.Q.* 899 (2008); P. Hay, Contemporary Approaches to Non-contractual Obligations in Private International Law (Conflict of Laws) and the European Community's "Rome II" Regulation, 4(1) *Eur. Legis. F.* 137 (2007); G. Hohloch, Place of Injury, Habitual Residence, Closer Connections and Substantive Scope—The Basic Principles, 9 *Ybk. Priv. Int'l L.* 1 (2008); P. Huber & M. Illmer, International Product Liability: A Commentary on Article 5 of the Rome II Regulation, 9 *Ybk. Priv. Int'l L.* 31 (2008); T. Kadner Graziano, Le nouveau droit international privé communautaire en matière de responsabilité extracontractuelle, 97 *Rev. critique DIP* 445 (2008); P.J. Kozyris, Rome II: Tort Conflicts on the Right Track! A Postscript to Symeon Symeonides' "Missed Opportunity," 56 *Am. J. Comp. L.* 471 (2008); R. Michaels, The New European Choice-of-Law Revolution, 82 *Tul. L. Rev.* 1607 (2008); C.I., Nagy, The Rome II Regulation and Traffic Accidents: Uniform Conflict Rules with Some Room for Forum Shopping—How So?, *J. Priv. Int'l L.* 93 (2010); E. O'Hara & L. Ribstein, Rules and Institutions in Developing a Law Market: Views from the United States and Europe, 82 *Tul. L. Rev.* 2147 (2008); G. Palao Moreno, The Law Applicable to a Non-contractual Obligation with Respect to an Industrial Action: A Commentary on Article 9 of the Rome II Regulation, 9 *Ybk. Priv. Int'l L.* 115 (2008); W. Reppy, Eclecticism in Methods for Resolving Tort and Contract Conflict of Laws: The United States and the European Union, 82 *Tul. L. Rev.* 2053 (2008); S. Symeonides, Rome II and Tort Conflicts: A Missed Opportunity, 56 *Am. J. Comp. L.* 173 (2008); S. Symeonides, Tort Conflicts and Rome II: A View from Across, in *Festschrift für Erik Jayme* 935 (2004); J. von Hein, Something Old and Something Borrowed, but Nothing New? Rome II and the European Choice-of-Law Evolution, 82 *Tul. L. Rev.* 1663 (2008); C. Wadlow, Trade Secrets and the Rome II Regulation on the Law Applicable to Non-contractual Obligations, 30 *Eur. Intell. Prop. Rev.* 309 (2008); R. Weintraub, The Choice-of-Law Rules of the European Community Regulation on the Law Applicable to Non-contractual Obligations: Simple and Predictable, Consequences-Based, or Neither?, 43 *Tex. Int'l L.J.* 401 (2008); (2) BOOKS: J. Ahern & W. Binchy, *The Rome II Regulation on the Law Applicable to Non-contractual Obligations: A New International Litigation Regime* (2009); G. Calliess (ed.), *The Rome Regulations: Commentary on the EC Regulations on Conflict Laws* (2010); S. Corneloup & N. Joubert (eds.), *Le règlement communautaire "Rome II" sur la loi applicable aux obligations non contractuelles* (2008); A. Dickinson, *The Rome II Regulation: A Commentary* (2009); Huber, P. (ed.), *Rome II Regulation Pocket Commentary* (2011); A. Malatesta (ed.), *The Unification of Choice of Law Rules on Torts and Other Non-contract Obligations in Europe. The "Rome II" Proposal* (2006); R. Plender & M. Wilderspin, *The European Private International Law of Obligations* (3d ed. 2009).

Rome III

TEXT: Council Regulation (EU) No 1259/2010 of 20 December 2010 implementing enhanced cooperation in the area of the law applicable to divorce and legal separation (OJ L 343, p. 10 ff.) (2010), *available at* http://eur-lex.europa.eu/Result.do?direct=yes&lang=en& where= EURO VOC:000483&whereihm=EUROVOC:divorce. (Applicable in Belgium, Bulgaria, Germany, Spain, France, Italy, Latvia, Luxembourg, Hungary, Malta, Austria, Portugal, Romania, and Slovenia).

SECONDARY SOURCES: N.A. Baarsma, European Choice of Law on Divorce (Rome III): Where Did It Go Wrong?, 27 *Nederl. Int'l PrvR.* 9 (2009); K. Boele-Woelki, For Better or for Worse: The Europeanization of International Divorce Law, 12 *Ybk. Priv. Int'l L.* 1 (2010); B. Campuzano Díaz, The Coordination of the EU Regulations on Divorce and Legal Separation with the Proposal on Matrimonial Property Regimes, *Ybk. Priv. Int'l L.* 233 (2011); M. Fallon, Le nouveau droit du divorce international selon le règlement Rome III: Une évolution tranquille, *Rev. Trim. Dr. Fam.* 313 (2012); A. Fiorini, Rome III—Choice of Law in Divorce: Is the Europeanization of Family Law Going Too Far?, 22 *Int'l J.L. Pol'y & Fam.* 178 (2008); C. Henricot, Droit applicable au divorce international: Mise en application du règlement "Rome III," *J. des Trib.* 57 (2012); C. Kohler, Le choix de la loi applicable au divorce—Interrogations sur le règlement "Rome III" de l'Union européene, in *Festschrift für Bernd von Hoffmann* 208 (2011); B. Nascimbene, Jurisdiction and Applicable Law in Matrimonial Matters: Rome III Regulation?, 2009 *Eur. Leg. For.* 1 (2009); M. Torga, Party Autonomy of the Spouses under the Rome III Regulation in Estonia: Can Private International Law Change Substantive Law?, *Ned IPR* 547 (2012); P.W. von Mohrenfels, Die Rom III-VO und die Parteiautonomie, in *Festschrift für Bernd von Hoffmann* 527 (2011).

Successions

TEXT: Regulation (EU) No 650/2012 of the European Parliament and of the Council of 4 July 2012 on jurisdiction, applicable law, recognition and enforcement of decisions and acceptance and enforcement of authentic instruments in matters of succession and on the creation of a European Certificate of Succession (OJ n. L 201, p. 107 ff.)

SECONDARY SOURCES: (1) ARTICLES: S. Altmeyer, Vereinheitlichung des Erbrechts in Europa: Der Entwurf einer "EU-Erbrechts-Verordnung" durch die EU-Kommission, in *Z. für Eur. Stud.* 475 (2010); M. Álvarez Torné, Key Points on the Determination of International Jurisdiction in the New EU Regulation on Succession and Wills, 14 *Ybk. Priv. Int'l L.* 409 (2012–2013); J. Basedow et al., Comments on the European Commission's Proposal for a Regulation of the European Parliament and of the Council on Jurisdiction, Applicable Law, Recognition and Enforcement of Decisions and Authentic Instruments in Matters of Succession and the Creation of a European Certificate of Succession, *RabelsZ* 524 (2010); M. Bogdan, Some Reflections on Multiculturalism, Application of Islamic Law, Legal Pluralism and the New EU Succession Regulation, in *A Commitment to Private International Law: Essays in Honour of Hans Van Loon* 59 (2013); A. Bonomi, Conférence De La Haye et Union Européenne—Synergies Dans Le Domaine du Droit des Successions, in *A Commitment to Private International Law: Essays in Honour of Hans Van Loon* 69 (2013); A. Bonomi, Successions internationales: Conflits de lois et de juridictions, 350 *Recueil des cours* 71 (2010); A. Bonomi, The Interaction among the Future EU Instruments on Matrimonial Property, Registered Partnerships and Successions, 13 *Ybk. Priv. Int'l L.* 217

(2011); A. Dutta, Succession and Wills in the Conflict of Laws on the Eve of Europeanisation, 73 *RabelsZ* 547 (2009); J. Fitchen, "Recognition," Acceptance and Enforcement of Authentic Instruments in the Succession Regulation, 8 *J. Priv. Int'l L.* 323 (2012); E. Jayme, Party Autonomy in International Family and Succession Law: New Tendencies, 11 *Ybk Priv. Int'l L.* 1 (2009); J. Harris, The Proposed EU Regulation on Succession and Wills: Prospects and Challenges, 22 *Trust L. Int'l* 181 (2008); P. Kindler, La legge regolatrice delle successioni nella proposta di regolamento dell'Unione Europea: Qualche riflessione in tema di carattere universale, rinvio e professio iuris, *Riv. dir. Int'le* 422 (2011); P. Lagarde, Les principes de base du nouveau règlement européen sur les successions, *Rev. critique DIP* 691 (2012); K.W. Lange, Die geplante Harmonisierung des Internationalen Erbrechts in Europa, *Z. für Vergleichende Rechtswissenschaft*, 426 (2011); E. Lein, Further Step towards a European Code of Private International Law: The Commission Proposal for a Regulation on Succession, 11 *Ybk Priv. Int'l L.* 107 (2009); S. Marino, La proposta di regolamento sulla cooperazione giudiziaria in materia di successioni, *Riv. dir. int'le*, 463 (2010); É. Ralser, Les principes de base du nouveau règlement européen sur les successions, 101 *Rev. critique DIP* 691 (2012); C. Roodt, Party Autonomy in International Law of Succession: A Starting Point for a Global Consensus, 2 *J. So. African L.* 241 (2009); K. Schurig, Das internationale Erbrecht wird europäisch: Bemerkungen zur kommenden Europäischen Verordnung, in J. Bernreuther et al (eds.), *Festschrift für Ulrich Spellenberg* 343 (2010); A. Wysocka, How Can a Valid "Professio Juris" Be Made under the EU Succession Regulation?, *Ned. IPR* 566 (2012); (2) BOOKS: G. Khairallah & M. Revillard (eds.), *Perspectives du droit des successions européennes et internationales: Étude de la proposition de règlement du 14 octobre 2009* (2010); H. Bosse-Platière, N. Damas & Y. Dereu (eds.), *L'avenir européen du droit des successions internationales* (2011).

III. HAGUE CONVENTIONS

AGENCY: Hague Convention of 14 March 1978 on the Law Applicable to Agency.

Hague Conference on Private International Law, *Actes et documents de la Treizième session (1976)—Agency* (1979); I.G.F. Karsten, *Explanatory Report on the 1978 Hague Agency Convention* (1978).

SECONDARY SOURCES: M. Arguas, Derecho de los intermediarios. Convención sobre ley aplicable a los contractos de intermediarios y la representación, *Rev. Der. com. de las Obligaciones* 467 (1978); R. Baldi, *Le droit de la distribution commerciale dans l'Europe communautaire* (1988); J. Basedow, Das Vertretungsrecht im Spiegel konkurrierender Harmonisierungsentwürfe, *RabelsZ* 196 (1981); R. De Quenaudon, Quelques remarques sur le conflit de lois en matière de représentation volontaire, *Rev. critique DIP* 413, 597 (1984); P. Hay, & W. Müller-Freienfels, Agency in the Conflict of Laws and the 1978 Hague Convention, *Am. J. Comp. L.* 1 (1979); C.A.J.F.M. Hensen. Het Europees IPR in botsing met Haagse Verdragen, problemen van samenloop, *Eenvormig en Vergelijkend Priv.* 199 (1990); P. Lagarde, La Convention de La Haye sur la loi applicable aux contrats d'intermédiaires et à la representation, *Rev. critique DIP* 31 (1978); M.C. Mestre, *La Convention de La Haye du 14 mars 1978 sur la loi applicable aux contrats d'intermédiaires et à la representation* (1981); W. Müller-Freienfels, Der Haager Konventionsentwurf, über das auf die Stellvertretung anwendbare Recht, *RabelsZ* 80 (1979); W. Müller-Freienfels, *Stellvertretungsregelungen in Einheit und Vielfalt. Rechtsvergleichende Studien zur Stellvertretung* (1982); M.G. Pfeifer, The Hague Convention on the Law Applicable to Agency, *Am. J. Comp. L.* 434 (1978); A. Takakuwa, The Convention on the Law Applicable to Agency, 648 *Jurist* 112

(1977); H.L.E. Verhagen, *Agency in Private International Law—The Hague Convention on the Law Applicable to Agency* (1995).

CHOICE OF COURT: Hague Convention of 30 June 2005 on Choice of Court Agreements
  Hague Conference on Private International Law, *Proceedings of the Twentieth Session; vol. III Choice of Court* (2010); Trevor Hartley & Masato Dogauchi, *Explanatory Report on the 2005 Hague Choice of Court Agreements Convention* (2007).

SECONDARY SOURCES: M.H. Adler & M.C. Zarychta, The Hague Convention on Choice of Court Agreements: The United States Joins the Judgment Enforcement Band, 27 *NW J. Int'l L. & Bus.* 1 (2007); R. Amin, International Jurisdiction Agreements and the Recognition and Enforcement of Judgments in Australian Litigation: Is There a Need for the Hague Convention on Choice of Court Agreements?, 17 *Australian Int'l L.J.* 113 (2010); B. Audit, Observations sur la Convention de La Haye du 30 juin 2005 relative aux accords d'élection de for, *Vers de nouveaux équilibres entre ordres juridiques. Liber Amicorum Hélène Gaudemet-Tallon* 17 (2008); P. Beaumont, Hague Choice of Court Agreements Convention 2005: Background, Negotiations, Analysis and Current Status, 5 *J. Priv. Int'l L.* 125 (2009); M.B. Berlin, The Hague Convention on Choice of Court Agreements: Creating an International Framework for Recognizing Foreign Judgments, *B.Y.U. Int'l L. & Mgmt. Rev.* 43 (2006); M. Bläsi, *Das Haager Übereinkommen über Gerichtsstandsvereinbarungen—Unter besonderer Berücksichtigung seiner zu erwartenden Auswirkungen auf den deutsch-amerikanischen Rechtsverkehr* (2010); R.A. Brand & P. Herrup, *The 2005 Hague Convention on Choice of Court Agreements: Commentary and Documents* (2008); R.A. Brand, Forum Selection and Forum Rejection in US Courts: One Rationale for a Global Choice of Court Convention, *Reform and Development of Private International Law, Essays in Honour of Sir Peter North* 51 (2002); R.A. Brand, U.S. Implementation *vel non* of the 2005 Hague Convention on Choice of Court Agreements, 12 *Ybk. Priv. Int'l L.* 107 (2010); R.A. Brand, A Tea Party at The Hague?, 18 *SW J. Int'l L.* 101 (2012); P. Briza, Choice-of-Court Agreements: Could the Hague Choice of Court Agreements Convention and the Reform of the Brussels I Regulation Be the Way Out of the *Gasser-Owusu* Disillusion?, 5 *J. Priv. Int'l L.* 537 (2009); A. Bucher, La Convention de La Haye sur les accords d'élection de for, 16 *Rev. suisse dr. int'l & eur.* 29 (2006); S.B. Burbank, Federalism and Private International Law: Implementing the Hague Choice of Court Convention in the United States, 2 *J. Priv. Int'l L.* 287 (2006); M. Dogauchi, The Hague Convention on Choice of Court Agreements (2005), K. Shindo & K. Yamamoto eds., *Civil Procedure and Business Law Practice* 251 (2006); M. Dogauchi, Japanese Concerns in the Process of Drafting the Hague Convention on Choice of Court Agreements, 2005, 58 *Doshisha L. Rev.* 243 (2006); C. Edsall, Implementing the Hague Convention on Choice of Court Agreements in the United States: An Opportunity to Clarify Recognition and Enforcement Practice, 120 *Yale L J.* 397 (2010); C. Forrest, The Hague Convention on Choice of Court Agreements: The Maritime Exceptions, 5 *J. Priv. Int'l L.* 491 (2009); R. Garnett, The Hague Choice of Court Convention: Magnum Opus or Much Ado about Nothing?, 5 *J. Priv. Int'l L.* 161 (2009); E. González de Castilla del Valle, The Hague Convention on Choice of Court Agreements of 30 June 2005: A Mexican View, 27 *SW J.L. & Trade in the Americas* 1 (2006); T.C. Hartley, The Hague Choice-of-Court Convention, 31 *Eur. L. Rev.* 414 (2006); T.C. Hartley, The International Scope of Choice-of-Court Agreements under the Brussels I Regulation, the Lugano Convention and the Hague Convention, *Liber Amicorum Ole Lando* 197 (2012); W. Heiser, The Hague

Convention on Choice of Court Agreements: The Impact on *Forum non Conveniens*, Transfer of Venue, Removal, and Recognition of Judgments in United States Courts, 31 *U. Pa. Int'l Law*. 1013 (2010); B. Keri, The Hague Convention on Choice-of-Court Agreements: Is the Public Policy Exception Helping Click-Away the Security of Non-negotiated agreements?, 37 *Brooklyn J. Int'l L*. 1103 (2007); C. Kessedjian, La Convention de La Haye du 30 juin 2005 sur l'élection de for, *Clunet* 813 (2006); M. Keyes, Jurisdiction under the Hague Choice of Courts Convention: Its Likely Impact on Australian Practice, 5 *J. Priv. Int'l L*. 181 (2009); T. Kruger, The 20th Session of the Hague Conference: A New Choice of Court Convention and the Issue of EC Membership, *Int'l & Comp. L.Q.* 447 (2006); G.S. Lipe & T.J. Tyler, The Hague Convention on Choice of Court Agreements: Creating Room for Choice in International Cases, 33 *Hous. J. Int'l L*. 1 (2010); R. Michaels, Some Fundamental Jurisdictional Conceptions as Applied in Judgments Conventions, *Conflict of Laws in a Globalized World* 29 (2007); R. Mortensen, The Hague and the Ditch: The Trans-Tasman Judicial Area and the Choice of Court Convention, 5 *J. Priv. Int'l L*. 213 (2009); V. Nanda, The Landmark 2005 Hague Convention on Choice of Court Agreements, 42 *Tex. Int'l L.J.* 773 (2007); P.A. Nielsen, The Hague Judgments Convention, 80 *Nordic J. Int'l L*. 95 (2011); M. Pertegás & L.E. Teitz, Prospects for the Convention of 30 June 2005 on Choice of Court Agreements, *A Commitment to Private International Law. Essays in Honour of Hans van Loon* 465 (2013); D. Sancho Villa, Jurisdiction over Jurisdiction and Choice of Court Agreements: Views on the Hague Convention of 2005 and Implications for the European Regime, 12 *Ybk. Priv. Int'l L*. 399 (2010); A. Schulz, The Hague Convention of 30 June 2005 on Choice of Court Agreements, 21 *J. Priv. Int'l L*. 243 (2006); N. Sievi, Enforceability of International Choice of Court Agreements: Impact of the Hague Convention on the US and EU Legal System, *Hague Ybk. Int'l L*. 95 (2011); J.L. Siqueiros, La Convención de La Haya sobre Acuerdos de Elección de Foro. Version Final, 6 *An. Mex. Der. Int'l* 817 (2006); D.J.B. Svantesson, The Choice of Courts Convention: How Will It Work in Relation to the Internet and E-Commerce?, 5 *J. Priv. Int'l L*. 517 (2009); J. Talpis & N. Krnjevic, The Hague Convention on Choice of Court Agreements of 30 June 2005: The Elephant That Gave Birth to a Mouse, 13 *SW J. Law & Trade in the Americas* 1 (2006); C. Tate, American *Forum non Conveniens* in Light of the Hague Convention on Choice-of-Court Agreements, 69 *U. Pitt. L. Rev.* 165 (2007); D. Taylor, Reflections on a Critical Aspect of CISG-Governed International Sale of Goods Transactions: The Impact of the Hague Convention on Choice of Court Agreements on Forum Selection, 15 *Int'l Trade & Bus. L. Rev.* 42 (2012); L.E. Teitz, The Hague Choice of Court Convention: Validating Party Autonomy and Providing an Alternative to Arbitration, 53 *Am. J. Comp. L.* 543 (2005); C. Thiele, The Hague Convention on Choice-of-Court Agreements: Was It Worth the Effort?, *Conflict of Laws in a Globalized World* 63 (2007); P. Trooboff, Proposed Principles for United States Implementation of the New Hague Convention on Choice of Court Agreements, 42 *N.Y.U. J. Int'l L. & Pol'y* 237 (2009); G. Tu, The Hague Choice of Court Convention—A Chinese Perspective, 55 *Am. J. Comp. L.* 347 (2007); L. Usunier, La Convention de La Haye du 30 juin 2005 sur les accords d'élection de for. Beaucoup de bruit pour rien? *Rev. critique DIP* 37 (2010); R. Wagner, Das Haager Übereinkommen vom 30.6.2005 über Gerichtsstandsvereinbarungen, 73 *RabelsZ* 100 (2009); R. Wagner & J.M. Schüngeler, Das Haager Übereinkommen vom 30.6.2005 über Gerichtsstandsvereinbarungen und die Parallelvorschriften in der Brüssel I-Verordnung (EuGVVO), *ZfVR* 399 (2009); W.J. Woodward, Saving the Hague Choice of Court Convention, 29 *U. Pa. J. Int'l Econ. L.* 657 (2008).

CONTRACTS: Hague Principles on Choice of Law for International Contracts, adopted by the Special Commission on 12–16 November 2012, *available at* http://www.hcch.net/index_en.php?act=text.display&tid=49.

SECONDARY SOURCES: A. Dickinson, A Principled Approach to Choice of Law in Contract?, *Butterworths J. Int'l Bank. & Fin. L.* 151 (2013); L. Gama Jr, & N. De Araujo, A escolha da lei aplicável aos contractos do comércio internacional: os futuros principos da Haia e perspectivas para o Brasil, 34 *Rev. Arbitrageme e Mediacao*, 11 (2012); T. Kadner Graziano, Solving the Riddle of Conflicting Choice of Law Clauses in Battle of Forms Situations: The Hague Solution, 14 *Ybk. Priv. Int'l L.* 71 (2012–2013); O. Lando, The Draft Hague Principles on the Choice of Law in International Contracts and Rome I, in A *Commitment to Private International Law: Essays in Honour of Hans van Loon* 299 (2013); W. Long, The Feasibility of Parties' Choice of the PICC in Sino-European Commercial Contracts: An Overview of the Chinese Legal Framework, *Unif. L. Rev.* 1 (2013); B.A., Marshall, Reconsidering the Proper Law of the Contract, 13 *Melbourne J. Int'l L.* 1 (2012); J.A. Moreno Rodríguez, Los contratos y La Haya ¿ancla al pasado o puente al futuro? *Contratación y Arbitraje: Contribuciones recientes*, 3 (2010); J.M. Moreno Rodríguez & M.M. Albornoz, Reflections on the Mexico Convention in the Context of the Preparation of the Future Hague Instrument on International Contracts, 7 *J. Priv. Int'l L.* 491 (2011); J. Neels, J. & E.A. Fredericks, Tacit choice of law in the Hague Principles on Choice of Law in International Contracts, 1 *De Jure L. J.* 101 (2011); Conférence de La Haye de Droit International, Bureau Permanent, Choix de la loi applicable aux contrats du commerce international: Des Principes de La Haye? 99 *Rev. critique DIP* 83 (2010); M. Pertegás, Les travaux de la Conference de La Haye sur un instrument non contraignant favorisant l'autonomie des parties, in *Le Règlement communautaire "Rome I" et le choix de loi dans les contrats Internationaux* 19 (2011); L.G. Radicati Di Brozolo, Non-national rules and Conflicts of Laws: Reflections in light of the UNIDROIT and Hague Principles, 48 *Riv. dir. int'le priv. e proc.* 841 (2012); G. Saumier, Designating the Unidroit Principles in International Dispute Resolution, 17 *Unif. L. Rev.* 533 (2012); G. Saumier & L. Gama, Non-state Law in the (Proposed) Hague Principles on Choice of Law in International Contracts, in D.P. Fernandez Arroyo & J.J. Obando Peralta (eds.), *El derecho internacional-privado en los procesos de integracion regional*, 41 (2011); S. Symeonides, The Hague Principles on Choice of Law for International Contracts: Some Preliminary Comments, 61 *Am. J. Comp. L.* 873 (2013).

MAINTENANCE: Hague Convention of 2 October 1973 on the Law Applicable to Maintenance Obligations.

Michel Verwilghen, *Explanatory Report on the 1973 Hague Maintenance Conventions* (1975).

SECONDARY SOURCES: H. Batiffol, Obligations alimentaires, *Rev. critique DIP* 261 (1973); P. Bellet, Les nouvelles Conventions de La Haye en matière d'obligations alimentaires, *Clunet* 1 (1974); C. Biscaretti Du Ruffia, Commento alle convenzioni in materia di obbligazioni alimentari, *Le nuove leggi civili commentate* 83 (1983); A. Bonomi, La réforme des règles de conflit en matière d'obligations alimentaires: Quelques observations sur les travaux en cours à La Haye et à Bruxelles, *L'arbre de la méthode et ses fruits civils. Recueil de travaux en l'honneur du Professeur Suzette Sandoz* 201 (2006); A. Borrás & C. Parra, Conferencia de La Haya de Derecho internacional privado: Comisión especial para la preparación de un Convenio en materia de alimentos (19–28 de junio de 2006), 53 *Rev. Esp. Der. Int'l* 600 (2006); M.H. Carson, United States Perspective on the New Hague Convention on the International Recovery of Child Support and Other Forms of Family Maintenance, 43 *Fam. L.Q.* 21 (2009); D.F. Cavers, Recognition and Enforcement of Decisions Relating to Maintenance Obligations; Report of the US Delegation to the Twelfth Session of the Hague Conference on Private International Law, 12 *I.L.M.* 869 (1973); D.F. Cavers, International Enforcement of Family Support, 81 *Col. L. Rev.* (1981); F.A. Ferreira Pinto, *Do conflito de leis em matéria de obrigação de alimentos: estudo de DIP convencional* (1992); W. Galster, Zur Vollstreckung übergeleiteter Unterhaltstitel im Ausland nach dem Haager Übereinkommen, *IPRax* 146 (1990); F. Herzfelder, *Les obligations alimentaires en droit international privé—Les deux Conventions de La Haye du 2 octobre 1973* (1985); Y. Kikuchi, Japan's acceptance of the Hague Convention on the Law Applicable to Maintenance Obligations, *Japan. Ann. Int'l L.* 36 (1987); P. Lagarde, Observations sur l'articulation des questions de statut personnel et des questions alimentaires dans l'application des conventions de droit international privé, *Conflits et harmonisation: Mélanges Alfred E. von Overbeck* 511 (1990); A. Marín López, Proyecto de convenio de la Conferencia de La Haya sobre obligaciones alimenticias con los mayores, *Rev. gen. der.* 546, 658 (1972); D. Martiny, Maintenance Obligations in the Conflict of Laws, 247 *Recueil des Cours* 131 (1994); E. Pérez-Vera, La XIIe sesión de la Conferencia de La Haya, su aportación en materia de alimentos, 2 *An. estudo. soc. & jurid.* 315 (1973); G.E. Schmidt, Equal Treatment of the Parties in International Maintenance Cases, *Private Law in the International Arena: From National Conflict Rules towards Harmonization and Unification. Liber Amicorum Kurt Siehr* 657 (2000); M. Schwimann, Unterhaltszumessung als "Schutzmassnahme" im Sinne des Haager Minderjährigenschutzabkommens? *IPRax* 81 (1982); R.G. Spector, Maintenance in Private International Law in the United States: Harmonization of Divergent Rules and the Proposed Hague Maintenance Convention, 7 *Ybk. Priv. Int'l L.* 63 (2005); A.E. von Overbeck, Les nouvelles Conventions de La Haye sur les obligations alimentaires, 29 *Ann. suisse dr. int'l* 135 (1973); A.E. von Overbeck, Obligations "alimentaires" entre époux après divorce: Autonomie ou rattachement objectif?, *Le rôle de la volonté dans les actes juridiques. Etudes à la mémoire du Professeur Alfred Rieg* 839 (2000).

MAINTENANCE PROTOCOL: Hague Protocol of 23 November 2007 on the Law Applicable to Maintenance Obligations.

Andrea Bonomi, *Explanatory Report on the Hague Protocol of 23 November 2007 on the Law Applicable to Maintenance Obligations* (2009).

SECONDARY SOURCES: B. Ancel & H. Muir Watt, Aliments sans frontières. Le règlement CE No 4/2009 du 18 décembre 2008 relatif à la compétence, la loi applicable, la reconnaissance et l'exécution des décisions et la coopération en matière d'obligations alimentaires, *Rev. critique DIP* 457 (2010); M. Andrae, Zum Verhältnis der Haager Unterhaltskonvention 2007 und des Haager Protokolls zur geplanten EU-Unterhaltsverordnung, *FPR* 196 (2008); A. Bonomi, The Hague Protocol of 23 November 2007 on the Law Applicable to Maintenance Obligations, 10 *Ybk. Priv. Int'l L.* 333 (2008); R. Fucik, Das neue Haager Unterhaltsprotokoll: Globales Einheitskollisionsrecht gezeichnet, *Interdisziplinäre Z. für FamR* 90 (2008); J. Hirsch, Neues Haager Unterhaltsübereinkommen—Erleichterte Geltendmachung und Durchsetzung von Unterhaltsansprüchen über Ländergrenzen hinweg, *FamRB int'l* 70 (2008); U. Janzen, Die neuen Haager Übereinkünfte zum Unterhaltsrecht und die Arbeiten an einer EG-Unterhaltsverordnung, *FPR* 218 (2008); M. Levante, Die Reform des internationalen Unterhaltsrechts—das Haager Unterhaltsübereinkommen und das Protokoll über das auf Unterhaltspflichten anwendbare Recht von 2007, *Innovatives Recht, Festschrift für Ivo Schwander* 729 (2011).

MATRIMONIAL PROPERTY: Hague Convention of 14 March 1978 on the Law Applicable to Matrimonial Property Regimes.

Hague Conference on Private International Law, *Actes et Documents De La Treizième Session (1976)—Matrimonial Property Regimes* (1978); Alfred E. von Overbeck, *Explanatory Report on the 1978 Hague Matrimonial Property Regimes Convention* (1978).

SECONDARY SOURCES: G. Beitzke, Die 13 Haager Konferenz und der Abkommensentwurf zum ehelichen Güterrecht, 41 *RabelsZ* 457 (1977); A. Bonomi & M. Steiner (eds.), *Les Régimes Matrimoniaux en Droit Comparé et en Droit International Privé, Actes du Colloque de Lausanne du 30 septembre 2005* (2006); G. A. L. Droz, Les régimes matrimoniaux en droit international privé comparé, 143 *Recueil des Cours* 9 (1974); G.A.L. Droz, Les principaux traités multilatéraux relatifs aux régimes matrimoniaux, successions et libéralités, Rapport général, 1 *Régimes matrimoniaux, successions et libéralités* 205 (1979); B. Dutoit, La Treizième session de la Conférence de La Haye de droit international privé sous le signe du droit de la famille, 14 *Riv. dir. int'le priv. & proc.* 449 (1978); H.P. Glenn, Conflict of Laws. The 1976 Hague Conventions on Marriage and Matrimonial Property Regimes, 55 *Can. Bar Rev.* 586 (1977); E. Jayme & H. von Olshausen, Gleichberechtigungsgrundsatz und Haager Ehewirkungsabkommen-speziell zum Ehegüterrecht, 20 *Zeitschrift für das gesamte Familienrecht* 281 (1973); M. Lienard-Ligny, Régime matrimonial en droit international privé et la Convention de La Haye du 14 mars 1978, *Ann. Fac. droit de Liège* 311 (1981); F. López Ramón, Consideraciones sobre el régimen jurídico de las marismas, *Rev. Adm. Públ.* 83 (1981); Y. Loussouarn, La Convention de La Haye sur la loi applicable aux régimes matrimoniaux, *Clunet* 5 (1979); A. Pérez-Vera, El Convenio de La Haya sobre la ley aplicable a los regímenes económicos matrimoniales, *Mélanges Miaja de la Muela* 1167 (1979); A. Philip, Hague draft Convention on Matrimonial Property, 24 *Am. J. Comp. L.* 307 (1976); M. Revillard, Premier bilan d'application de la Convention de La Haye du 14 mars 1978 sur la loi applicable aux régimes matrimoniaux, *E Pluribus Unum. Liber Amicorum Georges A.L. Droz* 369 (1996); A.V.M. Struycken, Régimes matrimoniaux—banc d'essai de la codification internationale du droit international privé, *E Pluribus Unum. Liber Amicorum Georges A.L. Droz* 445 (1996); C. von Bar, Die eherechtlichen Konventionen der Haager Konferenz(en), *RabelsZ* 63 (1993); A.E. von Overbeck, La Convention de La Haye sur la loi applicable aux régimes matrimoniaux, 33 *Ann. suisse dr. int'l* 105 (1977); N. Watte, La détermination de la loi applicable au régime matrimonial en vertu de la Convention de La Haye du 14 mars 1978 sur la loi applicable aux régimes matrimoniaux, 101 *J. des Trib.* 661 (1982).

PRODUCTS LIABILITY: Hague Convention of 2 October 1973 on the Law Applicable to Products Liability.

Hague Conference on Private International Law, *Actes et documents de la Douzième session (1972)—Responsabilité du fait des produits* (1974); W.L.M. Reese, *Explanatory Report on the 1973 Hague Products Liability Convention* (1974).

SECONDARY SOURCES: H. Batiffol, La loi applicable à la responsabilité du fait des produits, *Rev. critique DIP* 252 (1973); D.F. Cavers, The Proper Law of Producer's Liability, *Int'l & Comp. L.Q.* 703 (1977); P. Cavin, La Convention sur la loi applicable à la responsabilité du fait des produits, 18 *Ann. suisse dr. int'l* 45 (1972); M. De Angulo Rodriguez, El Convenio de La Haya sobre la ley aplicable a la responsabilidad por daños derivados de los productos, *An. Der. Civil* 930 (1974); J.A. De Ment Jr., International Products Liability: Toward a Uniform Choice of Law Rule, 5 *Cornell Int'l L.J.* 75 (1972); R. De Nova, La Convenzione dell'Aja sulla legge applicabile alla responsabilità per danni derivanti da prodotti, *Riv. dir. int'le priv. & proc.* 297 (1973); H. Duintjer Tebbens, *International Product Liability. A Study of Comparative and International Legal Aspects of Product Liability* (1979); B. Durham, Hague Convention on the Law Applicable to Products Liability, 4 *Ga. J. Int'l & Comp. L.* 178 (1974); A. Dyer, The Hague Convention on the Law Applicable to Products Liability After One Fifth of a Century, 9(4) *Int'l Litig. Q.* 42 (1993); M. Fallon, Le projet de convention sur la loi applicable à la responsabilité du fait des produits, 89 *J. des Trib.* (Belgique) 73 (1974); J.J. Fawcett, Products Liability in Private International Law: A European Perspective, 238 *Recueil des Cours* 9 (1993); H. Fischer, The Convention on the Law Applicable to Products Liability, 79 *McGill L.J.* 44 (1974); E. Gottschalk, *Allgemeine Lehren des IPR in kollisionsrechtlichen Staatsverträgen* (2002); Kadner Graziano, T., *La responsabilité délictuelle en droit international privé européen* (2004); T. Kadner Graziano, La coordination des règlements européens et des conventions internationales en matière de droit international privé, *Rev. suisse dr. int'l & eur.* 279 (2006); P.J. Kozyris, Values and Methods in Choice of Law for Products Liability: A Comparative Comment on Statutory Solutions, 38 *Am. J. Comp. L.* 475 (1990); K. Kreuzer, Apfelschorf im "Alten Land"—Kollisionsrechtliche Probleme der Produkthaftung, *IPRax* 1 (1982); J. Kropholler, Zur Kodifikation des internationalen Deliktsrechts, 16 *ZfRV* 256 (1975); W. Lorenz, Der Haager Konventionsentwurf über das auf die Produktenhaftpflicht anwendbare Recht, *RabelsZ* 317 (1973); Y. Loussouarn, La responsabilité des fabricants dans les relations internationales et le droit conventionnel, *Etudes A. Jauffret* 483 (1974); Y. Loussouarn, La Convention de La Haye sur la loi applicable à la responsabilité du fait des produits, 101 *Clunet* 32 (1974); W.W. Park, International Products Liability Litigation: Choosing the Applicable Law, 17 *Int'l Lawyer* 845 (1978); W.L.M. Reese, Products Liability, Report of the United States Delegation to the Twelfth Session of the Hague Conference on Private International Law, 12 *I.L.M.* 859 (1973); W.L.M. Reese, Draft Convention on the Law Applicable to Products Liability, 21 *Am. J. Comp. L.* 149 (1973); W.L.M. Reese, Products Liability and Choice of Law: The United States Proposals to the Hague Conference, 25 *Vanderbilt L. Rev.* 29 (1972); W.L.M. Reese, Further Comments on the Hague Convention on the Law Applicable to Products Liability, 8 *Ga. J. Int'l & Comp. L.* 311 (1978); M.L. Saunders, An Innovative Approach to International Products Liability: The Work of the Hague Conference on Private International Law, 4 *L. & Pol'y Int'l Bus.* 187 (1972); H. Stoll, Anknüpfungsgrundsätze bei der Haftung für Strassenverkehrsunfälle und der Produktenhaftung nach der neueren Entwicklung des internationalen Deliktsrechts, *Mélanges Kegel* 113 (1977); M.H. van Hoogstraten, La Convention de La Haye sur la loi applicable à la responsabilité du fait des produits, 4 *Dr. & pratique du com. Int'l* 61 (1978); E. Zabaro Escudero, La ley aplicable a la responsabilidad por daños derivados de los productos en el derecho internacional privado español, *Rev. Esp. Der. Int'l* 75 (1991); H. Ziebold, Die Haftung für schadenverursachende Waren, *Aktuelle Beiträge der Staats- und Rechtswissenschaft* 136 (1981).

SALES: Hague Convention of 22 December 1986 on the Law Applicable to Contracts for the International Sale of Goods.

Hague Conference on Private International Law, *Proceedings of the Extraordinary Session (1985)—Diplomatic Conference on the Law Applicable to Sales Contracts* (1987); Arthur T. von Mehren, *Explanatory Report on the 1986 Hague Sales Convention* (1987).

SECONDARY SOURCES: N. Boschiero, La Nuova Convenzione dell'Aja sulla legge applicabile alla vendita internazionale, *Riv. dir. int'le priv. & proc.* 507 (1986); K. Finke, *Die Bedeutung der internationalen Handelsklauseln für Gefahrübertragung nach deutschem und US-amerikanischem*

Recht. Eine rechtsvergleichende Studie unter Berücksichtigung des Haager Einheitlichen Kaufrechts nach der UNCITRAL-Kaufrechts am Beisp. d. Klauseln CIT, FOB und den Klauseln des Ankunftsvertrages (1984); F. Gabor, Emerging Unification of Conflict of Laws Rules Applicable to the International Sale of Goods: UNCITRAL and the New Hague Conference on Private International Law, *NW J. Int'l L. & Bus.* 696 (1986); P. Lagarde, La nouvelle Convention de La Haye sur la loi applicable aux contrats de vente internationales de merchandises,7 *Rev. int'le dr. comp.* 327 (1985); O. Lando, The 1955 and 1985 Hague Conventions on the Law Applicable to the International Sale of Goods, *RabelsZ* 155 (1993); M. Lopez de Gonzalo, La Convenzione dell'Aja del 1985 sulla legge applicabile ai contratti di vendita internazionale, *Dir. comm. Int'le* 49 (1988); Y. Loussouarn, La Convention de La Haye d'octobre 1985 sur la loi applicable aux contrats de vente internationale de merchandises, *Rev. critique DIP* 271 (1986); Z. Matic, The Hague Convention on the Law Applicable to Contracts for the International Sale of Goods—Rules on the Applicable Law, *International Contracts and Conflicts of Laws—A Collection of Essays* 51 (1990); C. McLachlan, The New Hague Sales Convention and the Limits of the Choice of Law Process, *L.Q. Rev.* 591 (1986); G. Napoletano, Il progretto di una nuove convenzione sulla legge applicabile alla compravendita internazionale di merci, 24 *Dir. com. degli scambi int'li* 19 (1985); M. Pelichet, La vente internationale de marchandises et le conflit de lois, 201 *Recueil des Cours* 9 (1987); M. Pelichet, Les rapports entre la Convention de Vienne et la Convention de La Haye de 1986 sur la loi applicable aux contrats de vente internationale de marchandises, *Les ventes internationales, Journée d'étude en l'honneur du prof. Karl H. Neumayer* 57 (1998); L.S. Rossi, Il problema dei conflitti fra le convenzioni promosse dalla CEE e della Conferenza permanente dell'Aja sulla disciplina internazionalprivatistica delle vendite internazionali, 25 *Dir. com. degli scambi int'li* 347 (1986); G. Sacerdoti, I criteri di applicazione della convenzione di Vienna sulla vendita internazionale: Diritto uniforme, diritto internazionale privato e autonomia dei contraenti, *Riv. Trim. Dir. & Proc. Civ.* 733 (1990); J.A. Tomás Ortiz de La Torre, Sur la Convention de La Haye du 22 décembre 1986 sur la loi applicable aux contrats de vente internationale de marchandises, *Rev. Jur. Esp. La Ley* 6 (1987); P. Winship, Private International Law and the UN Sales Convention, 21 *Cornell Int'l L.J.* 487 (1988).

SUCCESSIONS: Hague Convention of 1 August 1989 on the Law Applicable to Succession to the Estates of Deceased Persons.

Hague Conference on Private International Law, *Proceedings of the Sixteenth Session (1988)— Succession to Estates, Applicable Law* (1990); D.W.M. Waters, *Explanatory Report on the 1989 Hague Succession Convention* (1990).

SECONDARY SOURCES: A. Borrás, La Convention de La Haye de 1989 sur la loi applicable aux successions à cause de mort et l'Espagne, *E Pluribus Unum. Liber Amicorum Georges A.L. Droz* 67 (1996); A. Bonomi, Conférence De La Haye et Union Européenne—Synergies Dans Le Domaine du Droit des Successions, in *A Commitment to Private International Law: Essays in Honour of Hans Van Loon* 69 (2013); F. Boulanger, Codifications nationales et convention de La Haye du 1er août 1989: L'improbable unification du droit international des successions, *Le droit international privé: Esprit et méthodes, Mélanges Paul Lagarde* 155 (2005); T. Brandi, *Das Haager Abkommen von 1989 über das auf die Erbfolge anzuwendende Recht* (1996); C.S. Bruch, The Hague Convention on the Law Applicable to Succession to the Estates of Deceased Persons: Do Quasi-community Property and Mandatory Survivorship Laws Need Protection?, *L. & Contemp. Probs.* 309 (1993); T. Frantzen, Europäisches internationales Erbrecht, *Festschrift für Erik Jayme* 187 (2004); E. Gottschalk, *Allgemeine Lehren des IPR in kollisionsrechtlichen Staatsverträgen* (2002); D. Hayton, The Significance of the Hague Conventions on Trusts and on Succession: A Common Law Perspective, *E Pluribus Unum. Liber Amicorum Georges A.L. Droz* 121 (1996); K-H. Kunz, Wandel oder Ruhe im deutschen internationalen Erbrecht? *Zeitschrift für Rechtspolitik* 212 (1990); P. Lagarde, La nouvelle Convention de La Haye sur la loi applicable aux successions, *Rev. critique DIP* 249 (1989); J. Schoenblum, Choice of Law and Succession to Wealth: A Critical Analysis of the Ramifications of the Hague Convention on Succession to Decedents' Estates, 32 *Va. J. Int'l L.* 83 (1991); E.F. Scoles, The Hague Convention on Succession, *Am. J. Comp. L.* 85 (1994); J.H.A. van Loon, The Hague Convention on the Law Applicable to Succession to the Estates of Deceased Persons, *Hague Ybk. Int'l L.* 48 (1989); E. Vassilakakis, La *professio juris* dans les successions internationales, *Le droit international privé: Esprit et méthodes, Mélanges Paul Lagarde* 803 (2005); A.E. von Overbeck, La Convention du 1er août 1989 sur la loi applicable aux successions pour cause de mort, *Ann. suisse dr. int'l* 138 (1989).

TESTAMENTARY FORM: Hague Convention of 5 October 1961 on the Conflicts of Laws Relating to the Form of Testamentary Dispositions.

Hague Conference on Private International Law, *Actes et documents de la Neuvième session* (1960)—Forme des testaments (1961); Henri Batiffol, *Explanatory Report on the 1961 Hague Form of Wills Convention* (1961).

SECONDARY SOURCES: H. Batiffol, Une succession de méthodes. La forme des testaments en droit international privé, *Festschrift Günther Beitzke* 409 (1979); J.A., Carrillo Salcedo, La ley aplicable a la forma de las disposiciones testamentarias. Nota sobre el proyecto de convenio adoptado por la Conferencia de La Haya de DIP, IXa sesión, 1960, *Rev. Esp. Der. Int'l* 169 (1961); J.J. Curtis Jr., The Convention on International Wills: A Reply to Kurt Nadelmann, 23 *Am. J. Comp. L.* 119 (1975); H.U. Jessurun D'oliveira, Vormperikelen bij internationale testamenten, *Weekblad voor Privaatrecht, Notaris-ambt en Registratie* 209, 232, 245 (1967); I. Kisch, Convention sur les conflits de lois en matière de forme des dispositions testamentaires, *Rev. Henri Maigret* 155 (1961); H. Köhler, Ausländisches Testamentrecht, 2 *Schriftenreihe für internationales Recht* 118 (1974); A. Maczynski, La révocation du testament à la lumière de la loi sur le droit international privé et de la Convention de La Haye sur les conflits de lois en matière de forme des dispositions testamentaires, *Polish Ybk. Int'l L.* 85 (1992); S. Menglidou, *Problèmes des conflits de lois selon la Convention de La Haye en matière de forme des dispositions testamentaires* (1974); J. Muraoka, Japan's participation in the Hague Convention relating to the form of testamentary dispositions, 8 *Japan. Ann. Int'l L.* 60 (1964); K.H. Nadelmann, Formal Validity of Wills and the Washington Convention 1973 Providing the Form of an International Will, 22 *Am. J. Comp. L.* 365 (1974); L. Scheucher, Das Haager Testamentsabkommen, *Zeitschrift für Rechtsvergleichung* 216 (1964), 85 (1965); R. Van Der Elst, La Convention de La Haye du 5 octobre 1961 sur les conflits de lois en matière de forme des dispositions testamentaires, 98 *Rev. du Notariat belge* 115 (1972); A.E. von Overbeck, *L'unification des règles de conflits de lois en matière de forme des testaments* (1961); A.E. von Overbeck, Divers aspects de l'unification du droit international privé, spécialement en matière de successions, 104-III *Recueil des Cours* 529 (1961); W. von Schach, Das Haager Übereinkommmen über das auf die Form letztwilliger Verfügungen anzuwendende Recht, *Deutsche Notarzeitschrift* 131 (1966); W. von Steiger, La Neuvième session de la Conférence de La Haye, Testamentsformen, 17 *Ann. suisse dr. int'l* 25 (1960).

TRAFFIC ACCIDENTS: Hague Convention of 4 May 1971 on the Law Applicable to Traffic Accidents.

Hague Conference on Private International Law, *Actes et documents de la Onzième session (1968)—Accidents de la circulation routière* (1970); E. Essén, *Explanatory Report on the 1971 Hague Traffic Accidents Convention* (1970).

SECONDARY SOURCES: M. Aguilar Navarro, La Convención sobre la ley aplicable en materia de accidentes en la circulación por carretera, *Rev. Esp. Der. Int'l* 522 (1969); C.S. Armstrong, The Hague Convention on the Law Applicable to Traffic Accidents: Search for Uniformity Amidst Doctrinal Diversity, 11 *Col. J. Transn'l L.* 74 (1972); T.H. Badreddine, *La Convention de La Haye du 4 mai 1971 sur la loi applicable en matière d'accidents de la circulation routière: Son application par le juge français* (1993); G. Beitzke, Die 11. Haager Konferenz und das Kollisionsrecht der Strassenverkehrsunfälle, *RabelsZ* 204 (1969); M.T.W. Bourke, Birth of an International Convention—Hague Conference on Private International Law, Special Commission on Torts, *Harv. Int'l L.J.* 277 (1968); J-G. Castel & P.A. Crépeau, International developments in choice of law governing torts. Views from Canada, 19 *Am. J. Com. L.* 17 (1971); D.F. Cavers, Legislative Choice of Law: Some European Examples, *So. Cal. L. Rev.* 340 (1971); R. De Nova, La Convenzione dell'Aja sulla legge applicabile agli incidenti tradali, 13 *Dir. int'le* (1969); B. Dutoit, La *lex loci delicti* à travers le prisme des deux Conventions de La Haye sur les accidents de la circulation routière et la responsabilité du fait des products, *L'unificazione del diritto internazionale privato e processuale—Studi in memoria di Mario Giuliano* 417 (1989); A. Espiniella Menéndez, Accidentes de circulación por carretera: Del Convenio de La Haya de 4 de mayo de 1971 al Reglamento (CE) n1 864/2007 ("Roma II"), 7 *Ann. Esp. DIP* 505 (2007); H. Fischer, The Convention on the Law Applicable to Traffic Accidents, 19 *Can. Ybk. Int'l L.* 189 (1971); L. Forget, Les conflits de lois en matière d'accidents de la circulation routière, *Dalloz, Bibliothèque de DIP* 58 (1973); H. Hoyer, Haager Straßenverkehrsübereinkommen und Rechtswahl der Parteien, *ZfRV* 341 (1991); T. Kadner Graziano, *La responsabilité délictuelle en droit international privé européen* (2004); T. Kadner Graziano, La coordination des règlements européens et des conventions internationales en matière de droit international privé, *Rev. suisse dr. int'l & eur.* 279 (2006); E. Kounougeri-Manoledaki, *La responsabilité délictuelle en matière d'accidents d'automobiles dans le cadre des tendances contemporaines du droit international privé* (1974); Y. Loussouarn, La Convention de La Haye sur la loi applicable en matière d'accidents de la circulation routière, *Clunet* 5 (1969); Y. Loussouarn, Entrée en vigueur de la Convention de La Haye du 4 mai 1971 sur la loi applicable en matière d'accidents de la circulation routière, 28 *Rev. trim. dr. commercial* 680 (1975); N. Lépine, Examen critique du système de la loi applicable en matière d'accidents de la circulation routière selon la Convention de La Haye de droit international privé, 1968 *Can. Bar Rev.* 509 (1969); K.M.H. Newman, The Law Applicable to Traffic Accidents, *Int'l & Comp. L, Q* 643 (1969); W.L.M. Reese, Introductory Note on the Draft Convention on the Law Applicable to Traffic Accidents, 16 *Am. J. Comp. L.* 588 (1968); W. Reishofer, Das Haager Strassenverkehrsübereinkommen. Entstehung, Inhalt, Bedeutung, 22 *ZVR* 33 (1977); L. Schuermans & P. Lavrysen-Van Eupen, Les accidents de la circulation en droit international privé belge, 51 *Rev. dr. int'l & dr. comp.* 7 (1974); M. Schwiemann, Probleme des Haager Strassenverkehrsabkommens, 23 *ZVR* 161 (1978); F. Schwind, Die Haager Konvention über das auf Verkehrsunfälle anwendbare Recht, *ZVR* 326 (1973); A. Staudinger, Das Konkurrenzverhältnis zwischen dem Haager Strassenverkehrsübereinkommen und der Rom II-VO, *Die richtige Ordnung, Festschrift für Jan Kropholler zum 70. Geburtstag* 691 (2008); H. Stoll, Anknüpfungsgrundsätze bei der Haftung für Strassenverkehrsunfälle und der Produkthaftung nach der neueren Entwicklung des internationalen Deliktsrechts, *Mélanges Kegel* 113 (1977).

TRUSTS: Hague Convention of 1 July 1985 on the Law Applicable to Trusts and on their Recognition.

Hague Conference on Private International Law, *Proceedings of the Fifteenth Session (1984)—Trusts, Applicable Law and Recognition* (1985); Alfred E. von Overbeck, *Explanatory Report on the 1985 Hague Trusts Convention* (1985).

SECONDARY SOURCES: M. Arai, Legal Problems on the Internationalization of Trusts and the Hague Convention on Trusts—The Hague Convention on Trusts from the Standpoint of Comparative Law, 12 *Study of the Law of Trust (Shintaku-ho Kenkyu)* 97 (1988); J-P. Beraudo, La Convention de La Haye du 1er juillet 1985 relative à la loi applicable au trust et à sa reconnaissance, *Trav. Com. français d.i.p.* 21 (1986); M. Dogauchi, Legal Problems on the Internationalization of Trusts and the Hague Convention on Trusts—Convention on the Law Applicable to Trusts and on Their Recognition, 12 *Study of the Law of Trust (Shintakuho Kenkyu)* 65 (1988); A. Dyer, International Recognition and Adaptation of Trusts: The Influence of the Hague Convention, *Vand. J. Transn'l L.* 989 (1999); S. Ferrero, The Scope and the Effects of Mandatory Rules and Public Policy under the 1985 Hague Convention of the Law Applicable to Trusts and on Their Recognition, 11 *Il Nuovo Dir. Soc.* 35 (2013); E. Gaillard, Les enseignements de la Convention de La Haye du 1er juillet 1985 relative à la loi applicable au trust et à sa reconnaissance, *Rev. Jur. & Pol.* 304 (1990); E. Gaillard & D. Trautman, La Convention de La Haye du 1er juillet 1985 sur la loi applicable au trust et à sa reconnaissance, *Rev. critique DIP* 1 (1986); E. Gaillard & D. Trautman, Trusts in Non-trust Countries: Conflict of Laws and the Hague Convention on Trusts, 35 *Am. J. Comp. L.* 304 (1987); J. Harris, *The Hague Trusts Convention: Scope, Application and Preliminary Issues* (2002); J. Harris, The Trust in Private International Law, in James Fawcett (ed.), *Reform and Development of Private International Law—Essays in Honour of Sir Peter North* 187 (2002); D.J. Hayton, The Hague Convention on the Law Applicable to Trusts and on Their Recognition, *Int'l & Comp. L.Q.* 260 (1987); D.J. Hayton, The Hague Convention on Trusts: A Little Is Better than Nothing but Why so Little?, *J. Int'l Trust & Corp. Planning* (1994); Jauffret-Spinosi, C., La Convention de La Haye relative à la loi applicable au trust et à sa reconnaissance (1er juillet 1985), *Clunet* 23 (1987); F-E. Klein, A propos de la Convention de La Haye du 1er juillet 1985 relative à la loi applicable au trust et à sa reconnaissance, *Mélanges Paul Piotet* 467 (1990); P. Nygh & M. Pryles, The Hague Convention on the Law Applicable to Trusts and on Their Recognition, *Thirteenth International Trade Law Conference* 199 (1986); A.G. Paton & R. Grosso, The Hague Convention on the Law Applicable to Trusts and on Their Recognition: Implementation in Italy, *Int'l & Comp. L.Q.* 654 (1994); C. Reymond, Réflexions de droit comparé sur la Convention de La Haye sur le trust, *Rev. dr. int'l & dr. comp.* 7 (1991); J. Schoenblum, The Hague Convention on Trusts—Much Ado about Very Little, *J. Int'l Trust & Corp. Planning* 5 (1994); H. van Loon, L'actualité de la convention de La Haye relative à la loi applicable au trust et à sa reconnaissance, *Mélanges en l'honneur de Mariel Revillard* 323 (2007); A.E. von Overbeck, La Convention de La Haye du premier juillet 1985 relative à la loi applicable au trust et à sa reconnaissance, *Schweiz. J. für Int'les R.* 30 (1985).

IV. INTER-AMERICAN CONVENTIONS

CONTRACTS CONVENTION (MEXICO CITY): Inter-American Convention on the Law Applicable to International Contracts, Signed at Mexico, D.F., Mexico, on 17 March 1994, at the Fifth Inter-American Specialized Conference on Private International Law (CIDIP-V).

Acta Final. Quinta Conferencia Especializada Interamericana sobre Derecho Internacional Privado (CIDIP-V). Ciudad de México, Estados Unidos Mexicanos, 14 al 18 de marzo de 1994.

SECONDARY SOURCES: M.M. Albornoz, *La détermination de la loi applicable aux contrats internationaux dans les pays du Mercosur* (2006); M.M. Albornoz, Choice of Law in International Contracts in Latin American Legal Systems, 6 *J. Priv. Int'l L.* 23 (2010); M.M. Albornoz, El derecho aplicable a los contratos internacionales en los Estados del Mercosur, 125 *Bol. Mex. Der. Comp.* 631 (2009); M.M. Albornoz, El derecho aplicable a los contratos internacionales en el sistema Interamericana, 16 *Iustitia, Rev. Dept. Der.* 71 (2007); M.M. Albornoz, Une relecture de la Convention interaméricaine sur la loi applicable aux contrats internationaux à la lumière du règlement "Rome I," *Clunet* 1 (2012); J. Basedow, J.A. Moreno Rodriguez & D. Fernandez Arroyo (eds.), *¿Cómo se codifica hoy el derecho comercial internacional?* (2010); A. Boggiano, La Convention interaméricaine sur la loi applicable aux contrats internationaux et les Principes d'UNIDROIT, 2 *Unif. L. Rev.* 220 (1996); A. Boggiano, *Contratos Internacionales—Introducción al estudio de la Convención Interamericana sobre Derecho Aplicable a los Contratos Internacionales* (2d ed. 1995); A. Boggiano, *Curso de Derecho Internacional Privado. Derecho de las relaciones privadas internacionales* (2d ed. 2000); H.S. Burman, International Conflict of Laws, the 1994 Inter-American Convention on the Law Applicable to International Contracts, and Trends for the 1990s, 28 *Vand. J. Transn'l L.* 367 (1995); V. Djurovic, *La loi applicable aux contrats internationaux dans les Etats d'Amérique Latine. La CIDIP V: Convention interaméricaine sur la loi applicable aux contrats internationaux* (1996); A. Dreyzin de Klor & T. Saracho Cornet, La Convención Interamericana sobre Derecho Aplicable a los Contratos Internacionales, *Rev. Jur. Arg. La Ley* 1040 (1995); A. Dreyzin De Klor & D. Fernández Arroyo (eds.), *Contratos internacionales* (2008); D. Fernández Arroyo, *Derecho internacional privado de los Estados del Mercosur* (2003); D. Fernández Arroyo, *Derecho internacional privado interamericano: Evolución y perspectivas* (2d ed. 2003); D. Fernández Arroyo, *La codificación del Derecho internacional privado en América Latina* (1994); D. Fernández Arroyo, Proyecto de convenio sobre ley aplicable a los contratos internacionales en el ámbito de la CIDIP, 45 *Rev. Esp. Der. Int'l* 629 (1993); D. Fernández Arroyo, What's New in Latin American Private International Law?, 7 *Ybk. Priv. Int'l L.* 85, (2005); D. Fernández Arroyo & J. A. Moreno Rodríguez (eds.) *¿Cómo se codifica hoy el derecho comercial internacional?* (2010); D. Fernández Arroyo & N. González Martín (eds.), *Tendencias y Relaciones Derecho Internacional Privado Americano Actual* (2010); D. Fernández Arroyo, La Convención Interamericana sobre derecho aplicable a los contratos internacionales aprobada por a CIDIP-V, 5933 *Rev. Jur. Arg.* 820 (1995); D. Fernández Arroyo, La Convention Interaméricaine sur la loi applicable aux contrats internationaux: Certains chemins conduisent au-delà de Rome, 84 *Rev. critique DIP* 178 (1995); F. González de Cossío, Convención Interamericana y los contratos internacionales, 27 *Jur. An. Der. Univ. Iberoam.* 150 (1997); R. Herbert, La Convención Interamericana sobre Derecho Aplicable a los Contratos Internacionales, 1 *Rev. Urug. Der. Int'l Priv.* 49 (1994); E. Hernández-Bretón, La Convención de México (CIDIP V, 1994) Cómo modelo para la actualización de los sistemas nacionales de contratación internacional en América Latina, 9 *DeCITA* 167 (2008); F. Juenger, Contract

Choice of Law in the Americas, 45 *Am. J. Comp. L.* 204 (1997); F. Juenger, The Inter-American Convention on the Law Applicable to International Contracts: Some Highlights and Comparisons, 42 *Am. J. Comp. L.* 388 (1994); S.A. Malloy, The Inter-American Convention on the Law Applicable to International Contracts: Another Piece of the Puzzle of the Law Applicable to International Contracts, 19 *Fordham Int'l L.J.* 662 (1995); F. Mastrangelo & D. Fernández Arroyo, D. (eds.), *El futuro de la codificación del derecho internacional privado en America. De la CIDIP VI a la CIDIP VII* (2005); J.A. Moreno Rodríguez, La Convención de México sobre el derecho aplicable a la contratación internacional, in J.A. Moreno Rodríguez, *Temas de contratación internacional, inversiones y arbitraje* 113 (2006); J.A. Moreno Rodriguez & M.M. Albornoz, Reflections on the Mexico Convention in the Context of the Preparation of the Future Hague Instrument on International Contracts, 7 *J. Priv. Int'l L.* 491 (2011); J.A. Moreno Rodríguez, Los contratos y La Haya ¿ancla al pasado o puente al futuro? in J. Basedow, D. Fernández Arroyo & J.A. Moreno Rodríguez (eds.), *Cómo se codifica hoy el derecho comercial internacional* 245 (2010); M.B. Noodt Taquela, Convención interamericana sobre Derecho aplicable a los contratos internacionales, in *El Derecho internacional privado interamericano en el umbral del siglo XXI*, 89 (1997); D. Opertti Badán & C. Fresnedo de Aguirre, *Contratos Comerciales Internacionales. Últimos desarrollos teórico-positivos en el ámbito internacional* (1997); G. Parra-Aranguren, The Fifth Inter-American Specialized Conference on Private International Law, in *E Pluribus Unum—Liber Amicorum Georges A.L. Droz—On the Progressive Unification of Private International Law/Sur l'unification progressive du droit international privé* 299 (1996); L. Pereznieto Castro, Introducción a la Convención Interamericana sobre derecho aplicable a los contratos internacionales, *Riv. dir. int'le priv. & proc.* 765 (1994); L. Perret, La convention interaméricaine sur la loi applicable aux contrats internationaux adoptée par la C.I.D.I.P.-V avec des notes explicatives, 25 *Rev. Gen. Dr.* 625 (1994); J. Samtleben, Los principios generales del derecho comercial internacional y la lex mercatoria en la Convención Interamericana sobre Derecho Aplicable a los Contratos Internacionales, in D. Fernández Arroyo & N. González Martín (eds.), *Tendencias y Relaciones Derecho Internacional Privado Americano Actual* 15 (2010); M. Vargas Gómez-Urrutia, *Contratación internacional en el sistema interamericano* (2000); H. Veytia Palomino, La convención interamericana sobre derecho aplicable a los contratos internacionales, 25 *Jur. An. Der. Univ. Iberoam.* 387 (1995); A.M. Villela, L'unification du droit international privé en Amérique Latin, *Rev. critique DIP* 233 (1984).

CONVENTION ON GENERAL RULES OF PIL: Inter-American Convention on General Rules of Private International Law, Done at Montevideo, Uruguay, on 8 May 1979.
TEXT: http://www.oas.org/juridico/english/treaties/b-45.html

SECONDARY SOURCES: T. de Maekelt, *Normas Generales de Derecho Internacional Privado en América* (1984); T. de Maekelt, *Conferencia especializada de derecho internacional privado* (1979); T. de Maekelt, Resultados de la Segunda Conferencia Especializada Interamericana sobre Derecho Internacional Privado (CIDIP-II), in Organización de los Estados Americanos, *Cursos de Derecho Internacional*, v. I, part I: *El Derecho Internacional Privado en las Américas (1974–2000)*, 310 (2002); G. Parra-Aranguren, La Convención Interamericana de Normas Generales de Derecho Internacional Privado, *Ann. Jur. Interam.* 157 (1979); G. Parra-Aranguren, La institución desconocida en la Convención Interamericana sobre Normas Generales de Derecho Internacional Privado, *Rev. Der./Trib. Sup. de Just.* 313 (2002); G. Parra-Aranguren, La excepción de fraude a la ley en la Convención Interamericana sobre normas generales de

Derecho Internacional Privado, *Rev. Der./Trib. Sup. de Just.* 5 (2002); J. Samtleben, Die Interamerikanaischen Specialkonferenz für internationales Privatrecht, 44 *RabelsZ* 44 (1980); J.L. Siqueiros, Resumen de los resultados obtenidos en la Conferencia Interamericana de Derecho Internacional Privado (CIDIP-II) celebrada en Montevideo, Uruguay, del 23 de abril al 8 de mayo de 1979, in *Cooperacion Interamericana En Los Procedimientos Civiles Y Mercantiles* 683 (1982).

Index